AMAZON ALL STARS

13

THIRTEEN LESBIAN PLAYS

WITH ESSAYS AND INTERVIEWS

EDITED BY

ROSEMARY KEEFE CURB

APPLAUSE
NEW YORK • LONDON

An Applause Original
Amazon All Stars
edited by Rosemary Keefe Curb
Copyright © 1996 Rosemary Keefe Curb
ALL RIGHTS RESERVED.

Library of Congress Cataloging-in-Publication Data

Amazon all stars : thirteen lesbian plays, with essays and interview /
  edited by Rosemary Keefe Curb
    p.   cm.
    ISBN 1-55783-220-X
    1. Lesbians--Drama. 2. Lesbians' writings, American. 3. American
drama--Women authors. 4. American drama--20th century.   I. Curb
Rosemary, 1940-
PS648.L48A43   1996
812'.540809206643--dc20   96-1835
                                                            CIP

British Cataloging-in-Publication Data

A catalogue copy of this book is available from the British Library.

APPLAUSE BOOKS   Distributed in the UK by **A&C BLACK**
211 West 71st Street   35 Bedford Row
New York, NY 10023   London WC 1R 4JH
Phone (212) 496-7511   Phone 0171 242-0946
Fax: (212) 721-2856   Fax 0171 831-8478

Printed in Canada

TABLE OF CONTENTS

ACKNOWLEDGMENTS

Thank you to Glenn Young, Publisher of Applause Books, for readily recognizing the need for this collection and collaborating in the selection of plays.

Thank you to the playwrights who sent me plays, including those finalists whose work could not fit in this volume but may be published in later collections: Claudia Allen, Terry Baum, Martha Boesing, Sarah Brown, Caitlain C. Cain, Mary Casey and Pamela Gray, Heidi Carla, Leigh Curran, Nancy Dean, Jill Dearman, Sandra deHelen, Patricia Donegan, Sara Felder, Michelle Gabow, Jyl Lynn Felman, Mary Gail, Layce Gardner, Libbe HaLevy, Wendy Hammond, Barbara Kahn, Melinda Kay, Marty Kingsbury, Margery Kreitman, Susan Lersch, Harriet Malinowitz, Karen Malpede, Jesse Mavro, Rosemary McLaughlin, Bonnie Morris, Leslea Newman, Elizabeth Page, Adele Prandini, Marsha Lee Sheiness, Hilary Sloin, Sharon Wachsler, Julia Willis, Shay Youngblood. Some scripts are available in lesbian archives.

I am grateful to academic institutions that supported this project: Rollins College for a sabbatical (1992–1993); the Women's Studies program at Northeastern University, Boston, for an international scholar residency in Fall 1992; and the Institute for Research on Women, Douglass College, Rutgers University, for my residency in Spring 1993. Thank you to colleagues in the College of Arts and Letters at Southwest Missouri State University and especially to my secretary, Sharon Dingman.

Thank you to friends and colleagues with whom I have shared stages of this project for eighteen years. In 1991, Nancy Hellner solicited my help on her lesbian plays project. Although we have met only once in person, her scholarship and initiative set this book in motion. Nancy withdrew from co-editing the collection when finishing her doctoral dissertation on lesbian comedy took priority. Victoria Rue also worked with me, collecting and selecting scripts, while finishing her doctoral thesis in theology and theatre. Although I finished the book on my own, the wisdom and vigor of Nancy and Victoria were central to moving this project to completion, and I give them special thanks.

Thank you to friends who hosted readings of plays in Florida, California, Massachusetts, New York, and Missouri. Through readings, the language, emotions, and ideas of the scripts became embodied in the readers, whose hundreds of voices echo in my head. Thank you to friends wrote detailed evaluations of plays: Bobbi Ausubel, Terry Baum, Peg Cruikshank, Carolyn Gage, Marty Kingsbury, Nancy Manahan, Patricia Montley, Sandra Shotlander, Denise Walen. Thank you to readers of my introduction who offered substantive suggestions: Doris Burkemper, Carolyn Gage, Gloria Joyce Dickler, Jill Dolan, Sharon Harper, Shirlene Holmes, Jane Hoogestraat, Martin Jones, Madonne Miner, Catherine Nicholson, Joan Schenkar, Ralph Smith. Finally, I thank my supportive partner who notes that our twin cats, Tiger and Foxer, put their paws of applause on every page.

Rosemary Keefe Curb
Springfield, Missouri

INTRODUCTION

Rosemary Keefe Curb*

Amazon All Stars enters the political marketplace at a moment in American history when right-wing politicians are denouncing artists and public funding for the arts as immoral. Artists who do not reflect the heterosexist, racist, boringly conformist culture of the ruling class risk being shoved to the margins and closets of invisibility as the USA puffs itself into the last presidential election of the twentieth century. We can hardly overstate how precarious these times are for artists with challenging aesthetics or subversive politics. Simply putting lesbian characters on stage is a radical political action. Theatre daring to call itself lesbian dances to its own playful, spirited drummer. Although the title of this book comes from a play by Carolyn Gage, it actually encompasses all the plays, playwrights, and introductory essayists with a spunky "pride equals power" attitude that pays no tribute to the boys of whatever partisan stripe who think they rule the world.

Earlier in this last decade of the twentieth century, "lesbian chic" flashed a seductive, air-brushed "come hither" nonchalance from covers of glossy magazines. Such a phenomenon exploits, commodifies, and depoliticizes real lesbian concerns. A British collection of essays titled *The Good, The Bad and the Gorgeous: Popular Culture's Romance with Lesbianism* (1994) analyzes popular white North American lesbian icons as the heartthrobs of lesbian lust. North American lesbians are more likely, however, to idolize foremothers such as Sappho and Gertrude Stein and to refer to the serious writers and artists who have created lesbian culture such as Audre Lorde, Judy Grahn, Adrienne Rich, Pat Parker, Gloria Anzaldua, Paula Gunn Allen, etc. Popular American culture has provided a few mainstream films that most lesbians can count on one hand and recent "lesbian moments" on TV—a kiss, a look, a dance—to titillate the puritan public yearning to be bad. In a right-wing backlash, the so-called "bad girls"—especially lesbians—increase in erotic desirability. Meanwhile, serious avant garde theatre, including lesbian theatre, by artists whose private erotic lives may not necessarily be exhibited in their art, continues to create with or without popular notice.

Those of us who have lived and created lesbian nation for a generation or more know that lesbians also experience generation gap *angst*. Queer girls, sex radicals, lipstick lesbians in dress-for-success designer suits, neo-butches and femmes may assert their power by pushing against seventies' and eighties' radical lesbian feminists in what daughters of the lesbian revolution may view as the mothers' rumpled flannel of downward mobility. This collection spans the lesbian generation gap.

Theorists of lesbian representation and performance may seem to older radical lesbians and younger sex radicals to enjoy ivory tower luxury to interrogate multiple meanings of visibility and spectatorship without getting dirty in the street—seventies', eighties', or nineties' streets. In reality, theorists as well as artists may be activists taking back the night wherever they live, womanning the phone lines to rally votes for a local hate crimes ordinance, building grassroots rainbow coalitions to resist local bigots, and speaking out at rallies for a battered women's shelter or AIDS funding or a myriad of local causes. In their writing, however, they seem to breathe a rarefied air of pure thought. Nevertheless, even the tilted lesbian theory ivory tower can be rocked by storms of right-wing big-ots who find they can score political points better by attacking art they don't understand than theory they can't read. Ideas of the poststructuralist theorists appear in this book along with those who defend realism, neo-essentialism, and a never completely extinguished radical feminism.

More than half of the plays in this book are experimental or non-realistic, aes-thetically and intellectually complex. Even those who follow the Ibsen-Shaw-Hellman-Miller tradition of modern realism do so with a twist. At least they deviate dramatically from reinscribing the white, racist, middle-class, heterosexist, wife-bat-tering, patriarchal family of their ancestral theatrical models. About half of the plays in this book are full-length; others require less than half an hour for performance. Many plays focus on controversy sparked by race, ethnicity, class, and/or religion. Plays which do not specify race or ethnicity should not be assumed to be monocul-tural. On the contrary, diversity in casting by race, age, size, (dis)ability, etc. would enhance multiple meanings and textures of plays—especially those with large casts.

Rather than grouping plays by style, form, theme, chronology, geography, politics, or length, I present them alphabetically by playwright. Readers can make their own connections. This arrangement opens the anthology with the last play of Jane Chambers (1937–1983), the best known lesbian playwright in the heyday of lesbian feminism in the 1970s and early 1980s, and closes with a sassy, mid-1990s swat at the bard by playwright and teacher Paula Vogel. The book, there-fore, opens with a lesbian pioneer and closes with a revisioning of the western canon. In this introduction, I offer a quick glance at plays under thematic head-ings such as Lesbian Activist Heroes and Lesbian Relationships.

Each play and playwright is introduced at greater length by a different schol-ar. I invited playwrights to suggest scholars to introduce them. Other scholars I invited because I thought they would enjoy a particular play or playwright. Some scholars are well known for significant theoretical books and articles; others deny that they are scholars. No essay gives the only or correct reading of a particular play but a point of entry, a perspective to read with or against. For playwrights with a large body of work, the introduction can only provide a glimpse of the playwright's place in American or avant-garde theatre and ways that the selected play fits or departs from the playwright's characteristic style or themes.

All of the plays are lesbian in their portrayal of lesbian passion—erotic or polit-ical. Plays may narrate or dramatize the story of a woman's desire for another woman or show lesbian desire as a passion for social justice or a quest for spiritu-al wholeness. These thirteen plays feature lesbian activist heroes and communi-ties, lesbian relationships and families, and lesbian modes of canonical subversion.

Lesbian Activist Heroes

In *The Quintessential Image* by Jane Chambers, a famous, award-winning photog-rapher, Lacey Lanier, "comes out" in a TV interview with the closeted Margaret Foy. The play uses cameras, video monitors, enormous photo enlargements, and, in general, the apparatus of photography as a symbolic mirror for lesbian (in)visi-bility. The central joke of the short play reveals that what the famous Lacey was seeing through her pinbox camera—and throughout her career—was not what the photojournalist judges were seeing when they gave her prizes and scholarships. She was not trying to capture great freeze-frames of American history but only her girlhood "crush," Belinda, who never quite made it into the frame of Lacey's pictures or her life until much later, when Lacey could finally see Belinda without the romantic filter of lesbian lust and at last in the sharp focus of Belinda's meanness and family history of white Southern racist politics. Lacey is heroic in speaking the truth of her vision, although some readers may question the ethics of her "outing" the self-hating Margaret, whose glibness trips her and unmasks her homophobia.

In the award-winning *Sisters*, first produced in the 1980s, Patricia Montley features a lesbian nun as a political hero. At a crisis point in her life, Sister Joanna renews contact with five women from her novitiate group who have left religious life and who she thinks have a lesbian orientation which they are hiding or denying. Perhaps she hopes to form the lesbian community of her dreams, a perfect sisterhood of loving women committed to social justice. She hopes that her "sisters" will defend her against a mandate from her bishop to discontinue her public gay ministry or leave the order. One by one her sisters refuse to come out and then desert her. In her moment of classic recognition, Sister Joanna sees her true solitary status as well as the false pride of her coercion of her former sisters. Lesbian readers can bemoan the all too familiar spectacle of "sisters" deserting the "out" activist while enjoying memories of seventies' and eighties' communal struggles and sisterhood, as well as the Chambers-style snappy comic dialogue.

The Dissident by Canyon Sam presents the playwright/performer dramatizing a story from her life, her journey from San Francisco to China and Tibet. Because the solo performance piece has only been performed by the writer, who is known to be lesbian, the piece becomes lesbian theatre, even though the narrator never speaks about lesbianism. What the storyteller dramatizes as self and others is not individual desire but rather universal love and compassion for humanity based on Buddhist beliefs. In a performance of less than half an hour, the Chinese-American narrator plays out her spiritual and geographic journey in search of identity, her disillusionment with the uncompassionate Chinese, and her love of the land and people of Tibet, where she finds spiritual and political affinity with the Dalai Lama and his followers.

Lesbian Relationships

Many US lesbian plays dramatize coming out, falling in love, breaking up, and moving on in the repeated cycle of lesbian serial monogamy. Four plays in this collection focus on relationships. *A Lady and a Woman* by Shirlene Holmes portrays two African-American women falling in love in small town USA in 1890. Miss Flora, the middle-class lady, owns her own business, a hotel. Biddie, the working-class woman, works as a butcher. In almost a parody of the romanticized western, the transient Biddie blows into town looking for work and a place to stay. Finding much more than she dared hope for, Biddie ends up "marrying" Miss Flora and raising her baby. The baby is not the biological child of Miss Flora, but a baby she birthed as midwife, a baby rejected by her child-mother. Biddie and Flora approach their mutual desire with a tentativeness recognizable to most lesbians—first stirrings of desire, hope, casual touching, leaps of faith, consummation of passion, fears and jealousies, and finally commitment. The curtain drops on realism's portrait of an unconventional happy family, which challenges butch-femme stereotypes.

Small Domestic Acts by Joan Lipkin presents another unconventional happy lesbian family, set now—in the 1990s—a century later than *A Lady and a Woman*. The play shatters the realist conventions of closure in time and space. The fourth wall is immediately dissolved by direct address to the audience and by positioning the audience as a silent fifth character, whose response and judgments are anticipated. The drama presents a conflict of narratives, each character trying to claim ownership of the story they share—the story about the friendship of a butch-femme lesbian couple, Frankie and Sheila, with a straight couple, Frank and Sheila. Frank and Frankie, who work together as auto mechanics and who enjoy playing cards on breaks at work, decide to get together one evening for a foursome card game. Although both Sheilas initially fear the encounter, they end up as friends and finally lovers. How this happened is the story all four try to tell from their perspective. The play raises questions about gender and sexual identity.

Both *Springtime* by Maria Irene Fornes and *The Postcard* by Gloria Joyce Dickler portray love among the ruins and a search for private healing amidst public chaos. *Springtime* is the second one-act play in a cycle of four plays, titled *What of the Night?*, documenting the grinding effects of poverty and homelessness from the Great Depression into a twenty-first century ruled by greedy powers fattening themselves at the expense of the downtrodden. In the first play, *Nadine*, set in the dust bowl 1930s, Rainbow, a main character in *Springtime*, is a baby. In *Springtime*, set in 1958, Rainbow's German lover Greta falls ill with tuberculosis. In order to buy medicine, Rainbow prostitutes herself to the sadistic Ray, her half-brother, just as her mother had sold her body in order to feed her children. Not content with incestuously abusing Rainbow, Ray finally seduces Greta and destroys what at the outset had been an idyllic bond between the two women.

The Postcard portrays a Jewish lesbian couple in New York City in the 1990s being visited by a shadow pair of children from the Warsaw ghetto during the Holocaust. As the women, a therapist and a novelist, struggle in their relationship with contradictory fears of intimacy and abandonment, Shell, the novelist, attempts to create their future by rewriting the story of two Holocaust children who seek liberation, not only from the obvious threat of annihilation as individuals and as a people, but also from incestuously possessive mothers. By reaching back through time to free the children, the present-day lovers free themselves from personal histories of abuse. *The Postcard* symbolically links the individual liberation of all four characters with all historic liberations of Jews, including the historic freedom from Egyptian bondage commemorated at Passover.

Lesbian Families

Parents, children, blood relatives, ex-lovers, and multitudes of friends of lesbians constitute rippling concentric circles of present-day extended lesbian families. These are the people who attend deaths and births and all the emotion-laden ritual "family moments" in between. Such a group gathers at the hospital bed of the comatose Raleigh in *Nasty Rumors and Final Remarks* by Susan Miller. Raleigh is portrayed as talented, beautiful, and charismatic, but also as narcissistic, alcoholic, and negligent. The four people who love her most attend her dying: her present live-in, long-suffering, female lover Max; a male former lover to whom she is still emotionally bonded; her best female friend; and her teenage son, who has an ambivalent Oedipal obsession with her. Raleigh rises out of her body to replay scenes from her life with each. Through these time-travel scenes, an individual and extended family portrait which invites multiple readings sharpens into focus.

I'll Be Home Para la Navidad by Janis Astor del Valle presents a "guess who's coming to dinner" Puerto Rican daughter coming-out-to-mother drama in one act. The conflict centers on Cookie, the daughter in her mid-twenties, trying to persuade her mother, a fifty-something matriarch of a large extended family, to let her lover come to Christmas dinner. The short drama presents lively, sensual action. Mother and daughter argue, not only about the daughter's sexuality, but about race and color, when Cookie announces that her lover is African-American. Throughout the rapid volley of Spanglish, mother and daughter never stop chopping garlic, slicing onions, and pounding out the dinner, while arguing about cultural variations in seasoning, cooking, and preparing various Caribbean dishes.

Lesbian Communities

Both *The Amazon All-Stars* by Carolyn Gage and *Willa Willie Bill's Dope Garden* by Megan Terry conjure a golden age of lesbian separatist loving—an endless summer of Michigan Womyn's Music Festivals. Even though the plays make passing reference to the heteropatriarchy beyond the closed space of Amazon Nation, it does not intrude in the plays written for lesbians familiar with seventies' lesbian cultures and communities. The title play of this collection presents a well-made musical comedy version of lesbian pulp fiction or "Dykes to Watch Out For." The softball team called the Desert Hearts is fraught with girl problems. The arrival of Jan, a single, hot, new shortstop, sets the Hearts aflutter with fear and desire. She accepts a not very sisterly bet with Slide, the team's sleazy girl-chaser, that she can make it with Kelly, a desirable but spacy teammate, before the week is out or she'll lose her mitt (her symbolic ticket into this particular dyke jock community). Leona, who has a crush on team captain Hitch, is trying to shove Hitch's older, slower, and alcoholic ex-lover Ruth off the team. Hitch remains loyal to Ruth, who wryly comments that she's not the only Desert Heart with personal problems. Finger-snapping songs bounce this musical from locker room to bedroom to the Rubyfruit Bar and Grill, while the narrator, Leather-woman, vamps seductively for a presumably cheering lesbian audience.

Megan Terry has said that she wrote *Willa Willie Bill's Dope Garden* as a love song to the women's movement, and it truly captures a blissful lesbian garden of Eden. Four city dykes trek to the Nebraska countryside to climb Willa Cather's hill and have a love-in at the very spot where Willa composed love lyrics to her girl-friends. They come armed, if not literally, with Adrienne Rich's "book of myths" for a seventies' orgy with camera, sketch pad, wine, and weed to celebrate themselves and their foremother. This "Edenic moment" allows each of the four lesbians to pause for a ritual playful picnic before continuing a career climb through graduate school or into professional life as an artist.

Canonical Subversion

Two plays featuring serious intellectual engagement with ideas and classic forms leap to a world beyond Amazon USA—back to a time that probably never was, except in a wild and wicked lesbian imagination. The plays are reminiscent of Monique Wittig's classic lesbian novel *Les Guerilleres*, which invites would-be Amazons to imagine a time before sexual slavery, or failing that, to invent it.

Paula Vogel's *Desdemona: a play about a handkerchief* reinvents a backstage version of *Othello* with the three female characters. In contrast to Shakespeare's servile, simpering females, Vogel's Desdemona, Emilia, and especially Bianca, are rowdy and rebellious. Emilia's motives for concealing "the crappy little snot rag" from her mistress have less to do with fulfilling Iago's wishes than her own plots. Despite her uppercrust upbringing—or perhaps because of it—Desdemona finds lady life boring and Bianca's brothel escapades thrilling. Bianca's brashness excites Desdemona's lust for a free life of her own and for Bianca. *Desdemona* reads the bard against the grain.

Mythical Amazons, April and May, in *The Lodger* by Joan Schenkar, appear in a fantasy aftermath to the battle that killed their leader Iris. In revenge, April and May are holding captive in a Pinteresque lower depths a remnant of the enemy camp, a man. Although he never appears or speaks, the male presence provokes or stifles action between the women, who may have been lovers in a faintly remembered past time. Like Beckett's Didi and Gogo, April and May retell private and communal tales of a past that may have happened. Using classic stichomythia, the ritual exposition builds banteringly toward sudden revelations, such as the casual mention that Iris and April were lovers before May lured Iris away. At other moments the dialogue lunges hungrily toward violence—telling how the men cut Iris, how April cut the prisoner, how April and May plan to torture and kill him. In this endgame, as in classic drama, the theatrical action is linguistic rather than physical, as the women banter, spar, and sing toward an endlessly deferred anticlimax.

Significance of Collection

This book joins other recent provocative drama collections by women—especially by African-American, Hispanic, and Asian-American women—and by gay and lesbian playwrights which have enriched American theatre in the past decade or so. In gay collections, usually no more than one-third are lesbian plays. Women's collections often have only a single token lesbian play. *Places, Please! The First Anthology of Lesbian Plays* (1985), edited by Kate McDermott, was published by a small women's press more than a decade ago. Only a few plays in these collections have hit even Off-Broadway stardom.

Playwrights such as Maria Irene Fornes, Megan Terry, Joan Schenkar, Susan Miller, and Paula Vogel are known to any student of American avant-garde theatre. Jane Chambers and Carolyn Gage are favorites of devoted lesbian readers and festival goers. Patricia Montley teaches and directs theatre. Some playwrights are well known in particular cities: Shirlene Holmes in Atlanta, Joan Lipkin in St. Louis, Janis Astor del Valle in New York, Gloria Joyce Dickler in Woodstock, and Canyon Sam in San Francisco. Most plays are published for the first time in this collection.

Probably no festival will mount all thirteen plays published here in one space or at one time, although I'd love to be proven wrong. Meanwhile, I invite readers like myself, who live far from the centers of avant garde and queer culture, to a festival of imagination from the works of American playwrights and scholars, who most certainly do not agree with one another. Here are lesbian separatists and materialist feminists, liberals and revolutionaries, deconstructionists and modernists, realists and anti-realists, those who would wear the label "lesbian" as a badge of honor and those who eschew all labels beyond "artist."

As a teacher, I hope these plays will be studied in theatre, literature, and women's studies courses. Questions and controversies raised by the plays and essays will stimulate articles and theses, impassioned class discussion, and alternate critical and staged readings of plays "against the text." I trust that college and community theatre directors will find some selections from this smorgasbord tantalizing enough to give full productions.

* A personal note from the editor

Since 1976, when I completed my doctoral thesis on 1960s African-American drama and began searching for feminist/lesbian theatre, collecting lesbian plays has been my passion. I wanted to see the lesbian life I loved reflected on stage. In 1978, writing my first (and last) lesbian story got me fired from my first tenure track position. Being terrorized by the xenophobic heteropatriarchy ignited my fury and passion for justice for the rest of my life. Now in my mid-fifties, I celebrate the influence of lesbian culture on the scholarship, art, and literature many of us teach; and I am determined that right-wing bigots will not silence or harm new and old lesbian artists.

Since 1980, I've enjoyed feminist theatre festivals celebrating lesbian creations in Boston, New York, Santa Cruz, Toronto, Amsterdam, and Adelaide, Australia. I love the diversity of lesbian languages, erotic imagination, and spiritual vision. My introduction places this book in its political context because my seeking, selecting, and editing the plays and essays has been a labor of love and political passion—now more than ever. Difficult, atonal, eccentric, over-the-edge lesbian theatre can best awaken, alarm, call us to action, and effect social change. Lightness and making light that comes from lesbian/outsider vision and laughing at ourselves in the face of grief, fury, and despair invigorates our activism. In this playful spirit, I offer this collection to readers.

Rosemary Keefe Curb

Jane Chambers

Photo by Beth Allen

INTRODUCING *THE QUINTESSENTIAL IMAGE* BY JANE CHAMBERS

Nancy Dean

Before Jane Chambers wrote her twelve works for the stage, she wrote for television, and before that she wrote for radio. Her childhood theatre pieces are lost to us, ad-libbed for the cutouts of famous people she made from the pictures in *Life* magazine. She would draw new bodies for the celebrity heads, perch them on the wicker furniture on her porch, and let them talk. Young Jane wrote to the local radio station in central Florida where she lived with her mother and grandmother and asked for parts. She wrote for radio: "Girl Scout Time" and "Hi Time." At eight she was the child host of a children's program on radio called "Let's Listen." "Youth Pops a Question" was a Sunday afternoon TV show that she wrote, produced, and moderated [Glines 6]. In 1963, she became staff writer for WMTW-TV in Poland Springs, Maine, and wrote and produced "Merry Witch," a children's show in which she played the witch. She presented teen-age features and women's news [Glines 11]. In range and talent she far out-distanced Margaret Foy of *Quintessential Image*.

In 1971, Chambers' play *Christ in a Treehouse* won the award for Best Religious Drama on Connecticut Educational TV; and *Here Comes the Iceman*, the first sitcom featuring African-Americans, was optioned for TV, although it was never produced. Both of those works grew out of her activities in Corpswoman Theatre, a theatre group that she founded, which played mainly to African-American audiences. In 1972, she received a Eugene O'Neill Fellowship for *Tales of the Revolution and other American Fables*. She won the National Writers Guild Award of 1972–73 for writing for the popular TV daytime show "Search for Tomorrow." In that year, she founded, with Margot Lewiton, the Women's Interart Theatre where *Random Violence*, *Mine*, and *The Wife* were presented.

Although it wasn't known for twenty years, Chambers wrote her first lesbian-centered play in 1971—*Eye of the Gull*. In that play, revised by Vita Dennis

Note: I want to thank Beth Allen for her generosity and care in providing interviews and written materials about Jane Chambers.

under Beth Allen's supervision and first produced in 1991 by Footsteps Theatre in Chicago, Chambers departs from virtually every playwright portraying lesbians before her. Her crucial perspective is that lesbianism is not pathological. She sees homophobia as the sickness rather than homosexuality.

In *We Can Always Call Them Bulgarians*, Kaier Curtin observes the homophobia behind most portraits of gays and lesbians on the Broadway stage: "During the first half-century, gay men and lesbians were most often portrayed as suicides, seducers, murderers, drug addicts, traitors, transvestites, and bizarre grotesques... yet most were authored by straight writers." [Curtin 327].

In Chambers' view, homosexuality is merely one of the ways to be human. In *My Blue Heaven* (1981), for example, Chambers has fun with Molly's ingenuity in writing columns much beloved by America's heartland as she describes her wonderful life in a cabin in the woods with Joe. But Joe is really Josie, and a publisher who comes by with a lucrative offer is horrified at the revelation. That is, Chambers mocks the homophobe; she is not intimidated by him (or her). In 1974, as she considered whether to let *A Late Snow* be produced, Chambers knew she risked her career to some extent. *A Late Snow* was optioned for an Off-Broadway production, but it encountered the familiar homophobic resistance. As the producer put it, "I can't get backers interested in a play about lesbians" [Glines 18].

Considering theatrical history, the producer's reaction should not be surprising. There were a fair number of plays concerned with homosexuality before Chambers' very successful *Last Summer at Bluefish Cove* was presented at the Shandol Theatre in New York in February 1980. Some were very well produced and acted, but all assumed that homosexuality was a lurid, forbidden subject about sick people who corrupted or poisoned the lives of others, if they did not simply murder them or drive them to suicide, an attitude not unlike that shown in *The Killing of Sister George* by Frank Marcus.

Writing in the period under the Penal Code, which prohibited the portrayal of gays and lesbians on stage [Curtin 211], could not be expected to develop plays in which truths were plumbed on subjects threatened with censorship. Playwrights had to depend on suggestion and innuendo; producers were wary of productions that had homosexual themes and could cause their theatres to be closed. But when the code was changed, and in 1968 *The Boys in the Band*, written by Mart Crowley, appeared, with all its negativism, self-mockery, and self-hate, it was welcomed as telling the truth about the homosexual life. Plays which depicted healthy, self-accepting attitudes would not have been perceived as accurate portrayals, presumably. From the start, then, from *Eye of the Gull* (1971) and *A Late Snow* (1974), Chambers followed her own vision, unintimidated. In a sense, *Last Summer at Bluefish Cove* was her answer to *Boys in the Band*. Her subject, ultimately in that play, is the preciousness of life and loving under the threat of mortality. As Lil, a cancer patient, falls in love with Eva, who has just left her husband, she tries to protect Eva against loss, but then is drawn back by Eva who challenges Lil to live fully in the time they have. After her death, Lil's legacy of independence and courage is seen to survive. The play can be viewed as Chambers' loving praise for the women's community of friends and lovers, their courage and loyalty. There is humor but none of the self-lacerating wit of *Boys in the Band. Bluefish Cove* barely regards the outer world and its judgment, whereas the mordant wit of the Crowley play is virtually shaped by it.

Chambers' last two plays satirize society's homophobia more fully than do the earlier four plays. In *Kudzu*, Chambers displays impressive linguistic gifts as she renders southern speech in an exuberant and moving play in which Martha and Katy (lovers assumed by town folk to be sisters) make a home for Martha's Momma, Ginger, and Martha's bigoted cousin, P.T. The play was revised by Marsha Sheiness with Beth Allen's approval before its production at Theatre Rhinoceros in 1988.

Brief as *Quintessential Image* is, Jane Chambers' last play shows her signature on every page. Its wry humor, its mockery of pretensions, the solid support for the "simple" person who says the truth and shatters icons, the surprise truths at the heart of the story—these are her signature. In *Quintessential Image*, successful talk show host Margaret Foy interviews Lacey Lanier, Nobel laureate and six-time winner of the Pulitzer Prize for photography. In a gossipy interview format, private truths are revealed and set against public images.

In the play, Margaret Foy incessantly imposes lofty motives on her, but Lacey always answers simply, with a child's truthfulness: "I learned early the last thing any Mama wants from you is honesty." She focuses intently on everything, singly, while poor Margaret tries to engage her attention by every means, but mainly by flattery. Margaret gushes, "Even as a child, you sensed a momentous moment in history and seized that instant to take a photograph which has come to represent patriotism to most Americans." But Lacey was not trying to catch a returning soldier in her pin box camera; she was trying to catch a candid shot of Belinda Adams, and so begins the joke that runs through the play. While trying to photograph the girl she had a crush on, Lacey photographed important moments in history, and so built a public career and won prizes and recognition. The satire strikes at the hypocrisy of Margaret Foy, but also suggests the emptiness of awards themselves.

The picture that got Lacey a job on *The Tribune*, one showing a "colored janitor" mopping up the blood on the floor after Huey Long was shot, was taken to finish up a roll of film: "Belinda's daddy just loved Senator Long." Lacey herself didn't know the social importance of the picture she took.

Margaret asks her about her affairs and Lacey responds with accounts of women. When Margaret wants talk of "romance," Lacey talks further about women. Margaret tries to deflect her, "Guadalcanal. You were at Guadalcanal," indicating a photo. Lacey responds, "That picture there? The one with the soldier holding the bloody bayonet over his head? I took that in Los Angeles."

Chambers suggests that the violence in US cities makes them war zones. The unpretentious Lacey points out all the racism and cruelty without judgment: "See, those Mexican boys had come downtown in those zoot suits, and our boys in uniforms didn't like it. The streets of Los Angeles got so bloody, lord, the fire department had to hose 'em down." Everybody thinks the picture depicts Guadalcanal, and Lacey says, "Could have been. I was there, too. Looks just like the zoot suit riots."

That the great photographer was always looking at something else, winning awards for pictures aimed at something else, is acknowledged at the end as Lacey admits, "I could have spent all these years taking pictures of things that interested me." She tried to please Belinda, who never saw her, and a mother who always wished she was different. "I'm just not what either of them had in mind," she says in the rueful understatement that is both funny and desperate. But she decides to tell Rachel her story, Rachel who we learn is Margaret Foy's "roommate." At the end of the TV show, Margaret speaks of having a date with "the most exciting man," but she stays in the studio with the sound turned off just looking at her own image, while Lacey takes a taxi to her apartment to see Rachel—and surely to play a part in the further education of Margaret Foy.

In many ways this short play is very bitter. The successful Margaret Foy is afraid to acknowledge her own long standing relationship with Rachel. Rachel suffers from her partner's homophobia. Lacey, who has been open about her life, is rejected by her own mother and ignored by Belinda. She realizes her life has been spent pursuing what can't be won, instead of focusing on what she valued. The awards feel pointless in that they were never given for what she valued. When the interview on her life takes place, the interviewer wants to clip out the truth. Lacey objects: "All my life, I been clipping out moments to protect Mama's sensibilities. I got through clipping, waddn't much left. If you're going to do the same thing to me here, I might as well go home. I can sit with Mama and be somebody that I'm not." With all the bitterness in this amusing play, Lacey's firm self-acceptance comes through at the end: "You got to take a picture of yourself and get to love it, nobody else is going to do it for you."

Jane Chambers' death of a brain tumor in 1983 cut short a career that had just begun to bring her the rewards and recognition she had earned. Among the many awards in her honor she would surely be touched by the Jane Chambers Playwriting Award given by the Women in Theatre Program "to encourage the writing of new plays that address women's experiences and that have a majority of principal roles for women" [Dean, 115]. All women playwrights owe her respect and gratitude for writing honestly, when the primary reward was the applause of a grateful audience.

WORKS CITED

Curtin, Kaier. *"We Can Always Call Them Bulgarians": The Emergence of Lesbians and Gay Men on the American Stage*. Boston: Alyson Publications, 1987.

Dean, Nancy. "Jane Chambers." *Contemporary Lesbian Writers of the United States: A Bio-Bibliographical Critical Sourcebook*. Ed. Sandra Pollack and Denise D. Knight. Westport, Conn.: Greenwood Press, 1993, 111–117.

Glines, John. "In Her Own Words." Program produced at Zebra Crossing Theatre, Chicago, 1989; Courtyard Theatre, New York, 1989.

PRODUCTIONS OF *THE QUINTESSENTIAL IMAGE*

1985, Theatre Rhinoceros, San Francisco (Betty Award)
1987, Zebra Crossing Theatre, Chicago
1989, Courtyard Theatre, New York (John Glines, producer)
1995, Tribad Productions, Guerneville, California

CHARACTERS:

MARGARET FOY

LACEY LANIER

*The set for a TV interview show ("THE MARGARET FOY SHOW"). On a plat-
form are two upholstered swivel chairs, separated by a small table on which sits a
pitcher and glasses.*

On the walls are enormous enlargements of LACEY LANIER *photographs, all of
which depict momentous moments in the twentieth century. Studio lights stand
around the stage and cast a bright glare across the playing area. Downstage are three
TV monitors, their backs to us. We can see flickering light through the back of their
casings, and we know they are live.*

*At rise, members of the video crew are onstage adjusting cameras, getting audio
levels, etc.* MARGARET FOY *enters. She is about 30, lean and nervously vivacious.
She tries hard to please. Even so, she has a girlish charm as she darts to the edge of
the stage and addresses us as though sharing a wonderful secret:*

MARGARET: [*To audience.*] Welcome! She's back there, REALLY back there! Can
you BELIEVE it: I was scared she'd change her mind. You know, she just
doesn't do interviews, never has! Look at these photographs! [*She indicates
set.*] I used to have prints of some of these historic pictures on my bedroom
walls when I was a teenager. My mother—by the way, Mom used to ask me
why on earth I wanted to sleep under an enlargement of World War II and
wake up looking at the Great Depression. I told her, this photographer speaks
to me, speaks FOR me; it's as though this is the way I would have seen these
events if I had been there, you know what I mean? Now, she's never con-
sented to be interviewed anywhere before, and I know you're anxious as I am
to meet her, so let me explain quickly about this taping. Tape, you see, can
be cut and edited, so we won't stop unless the lens falls off the camera or a
monitor blows up—and that's not likely. It's never happened. Oh God,
wouldn't it be just like life? I don't want to think about it.

This is Camera 1. This one's Camera 2. This monitor shows what's being
recorded on tape. You'll see me looking at *this* monitor from time to time to
check my cowlick. Now, is everybody ready? [*She goes to her chair and sits.*]

Where are my notes? Jack, WHERE ARE MY NOTES? I'm sitting on
them, sitting on them! [*She recovers notes.*]

[*Embarrassed.*] Mom always said I'd lose my head if it wasn't attached. [*To
booth.*] Okay, all right, let's do it.

FROM MONITORS, THEME AND RECORDED V/O: LIVE ON TAPE FROM
PHILADELPHIA, THE MARGARET FOY SHOW...

[*Meanwhile,* MARGARET *is memorizing her notes.*]

RECORDED V/O: [*Cont'd.*] BROUGHT TO YOU BY FUNDING FROM THE
NATIONAL ARTS COUNCIL, THE PENNSYLVANIA CULTURAL
COMMISSION, THE MODESS FOUNDATION...

MARGARET: [*To booth, tapping mike.*] You checked the levels?

RECORDED V/O: ....AND A SPECIAL GRANT FROM THE HARRIET TUBMAN FUND OF THE NATIONAL ASSOCIATION OF RAIL-ROADS....

MARGARET: [*To floor manager.*] There's fresh water in the pitcher? You're sure?

RECORDED V/O: ...AND NOW, MARGARET FOY!

MARGARET: Thank you, thank you. [*Baby kiss to Mom.*] What an exciting evening we have ahead of us tonight! When people think about the First World War, and some people do, this is the image that comes to their minds. And this is, to most Americans, the essence of the Great Depression. World War II, Korea, Saigon—these photographs brought the 20th Century into American living rooms. We have perceived much of our history and our cultural heritage through the eyes of tonight's guest: six-time winner of the Pulitzer, Nobel Laureate, well, I could go on and on, but whatever I could say wouldn't be enough, so join me now in welcoming LACEY LANIER! [*She gestures to SR but no one appears.*]...LACEY LANIER! [*She moves toward the entrance. To booth.*] Lacey?

LACEY: [*Peeks awkwardly around one of the photographs.*] Now?

MARGARET: [*Turning, seeing her.*] There she is! Come right on out, Miss Lanier!

LACEY: [*Edging closer.*] Now?

[LACEY *is in her 60s, eccentric by the standards of our society, that is to say, her hair is wild from running her fingers through it, her dress is comfortable but without style, her shoes, worn and sensible. She has an earthy, no-nonsense appearance and a great deal of magnetism. She is at once tough and vulnerable. She is unfamiliar with the TV set-up and blinks against the lights, then squints at the camera.*]

MARGARET: Right over here.

[MARGARET *beckons* LACEY, *but* LACEY *spies the audience and freezes.*]

LACEY: Oh, Lord.

[MARGARET *is awkwardly embarrassed by all this. She shrugs cutely at the camera. The actress playing* MARGARET *should always be aware* MOM *is watching.*]

MARGARET: Come on, they're harmless. [*She moves to lead* LACEY *into set.*] I think so, anyway, they haven't attacked yet.

LACEY: [*At audience.*] So many of em. I believe I've changed my mind. [*She turns to go.*]

[MARGARET *grips her arm to stop her.*]

MARGARET: [*To audience.*] I told you, she's never been interviewed before. [*To* LACEY.] Now, you wouldn't leave me standing out here alone, would you? You promised. My mother's watching. [*Step by step, she has convinced* LACEY *into the set.*]

LACEY: [*Seeing photos on wall.*] They're too big.

MARGARET: Your photographs? Bet you never saw such enlargements of them before, huh? May I call you Lacey? It seems strange to call an institution by her first name, but then of course I don't suppose you think of yourself as an institution, I mean, does anybody? I wouldn't know, not being one myself.

[MARGARET *has lost hold of* LACEY *who moves toward photos on wall.*]

LACEY: I never meant those pictures to get so big.

MARGARET: [*Attempting to guide her to seat.*] Well, you just sit down...

LACEY: Too big.

MARGARET: [*Trying to herd* LACEY *to correct chair.*] Isn't that just like an artist?

LACEY: Bigger'n I am.

MARGARET: I mean, here are these GREAT photographs and...

[LACEY *sits in* MARGARET's *chair.*]

MARGARET: [*Cont'd.*] No, that's my chair. You sit over here. Well, I don't guess it matters. It's just that's where I usually... [*To booth.*] Does it matter? [*To* LACEY.] It matters. Right over here. [*Pats correct seat.*] It's exactly the same kind of chair.

[*She gets* LACEY *seated correctly.*]

MARGARET: [*Cont'd.*] Is this your good side? [*Pats her own cheek.*] Is that why you wanted to sit over here? Some people care about that, you know, I didn't think to ask you. Are you comfortable there?

[LACEY *has discovered the monitor and is peering at it.*]

MARGARET: [*Cont'd.*] Would you like some water? That pitcher's full.

LACEY: [*About monitor.*] Is that me?

MARGARET: That's you.

LACEY: [*At her own image.*] Well, I'll be goddamned.

MARGARET: [*Wagging finger, quickly.*] This is television, Lacey. We have to watch our language.

LACEY: I can't say goddam?

MARGARET: Don't worry, we can cut it. [*To booth.*] We'll cut it.

LACEY: Is that what people are seeing on their TV sets?

MARGARET: Now, we know historically that first famous photograph of yours was taken with a homemade pinbox, and by guessing at your age—and subtracting it from the date of the photograph—I know you were very young at the time you took it. Therefore, it must have been your mother who encouraged you.

LACEY: [*Having discovered the other monitor.*] Oh, look at you.

MARGARET: [*Looks.*] Yes. Who encouraged you, Lacey? I bet it was your mother!

LACEY: I think it's amazing how you can be sitting here and be in there at the same time.

MARGARET: What made you decide to come on my show?

LACEY: Did the image in the box ever start doing something different than you're doing?

MARGARET: Of course not.

LACEY: Now, that's what would make it interesting.

MARGARET: [*Checks her notes, befuddled.*] Let's start at the beginning, you were born in Louisiana? I got that out of *Who's Who*.

LACEY: Mama's eighty-eight and still keeps house.

[MARGARET *looks baffled.*]

LACEY: [*Cont'd.*] You asked about Mama.

MARGARET: Do you live with your mother?

LACEY: I stayed some other places most of my life but I always lived with Mama.

MARGARET: Mine lives in Detroit. What made you choose to come on MY show?

LACEY: The other day Mama went to church and she overheard the preacher talking about her, came home and told me that the preacher said she was getting senile, said it to somebody else, thought Mama didn't hear him. Well, Mama's not senile, but since she heard the preacher say she was, she believes it. So now I can talk.

MARGARET: [*Bewildered.*] You mean you never granted an interview in your whole career because you were protecting your mother's privacy?

LACEY: No, I was protecting me from Mama. I learned early the last thing any Mama wants from you is honesty.

MARGARET: You're kidding. She's kidding.

LACEY: No, I'm not. I never did a thing in my life pleased Mama. I was born too big for one thing. She was looking for a baby doll, and I was a big long thing with skinny legs and bald till I was three. I never was exactly what my mother had in mind.

MARGARET: But you started taking pictures at such an early age . . .

LACEY: You're talking about that one over there, the one I took with my pinbox?

MARGARET: You couldn't have been more than a toddler.

LACEY: Oh, I was walking by then, I had those big long legs. I saw a drawing in the newspaper of how to make that pinbox camera. There was something I needed to get a picture of, so I took a cardboard box out of Mrs. Wilson's next door garbage and found me a piece of mirror . . .

MARGARET: You NEEDED to take a picture. Needed. [*To camera.*] See, the creative instinct is inborn.

LACEY: I can't remember where it was I found that piece of mirror. Do you need to know that? Mama might recall, she remembers what she wants to.

[*The pinbox photograph on the wall depicts a World War I soldier stepping off a train, grinning broadly as he waves with one hand to the welcoming crowd. With the other hand, he holds a piece of homemade pie to his mouth.* MARGARET *indicates this photo.*]

MARGARET: Even a child, you sensed a momentous moment in history and seized that instant to take a photograph which has come to represent patriotism to most Americans.

[LACEY *rises and goes to picture as though drawn to it.*]

LACEY: I was trying to take a picture of Belinda Adams. That's her over in the corner, in the crowd. The little blonde girl, see she had those finger curls... [*She points out a blurred image in the corner of the photograph.*] Everybody in town said Belinda had a maid do those curls for her every morning. Every one of em perfect. There she is. Can you see her? Well, it was hard to aim right with that pinbox, and this was the first picture I ever took with it. See how everybody back there's blurred? That's cause they moved while I was taking it. You had to hold the lens full open and keep real still with a pinbox. This soldier here, he saw me aiming and he posed. That's how come he came out clear. After I took that picture, he ran off the train steps and asked me did my camera work. I said I hoped so because I was thinking, you know, I'd taken a picture of Belinda. Well, that soldier took my film right out and put a quarter in my hand, said he wanted a picture of himself coming home from war. I guess that soldier liked his picture because he sent it to the newspaper, and they printed it and gave it a prize. Then the newspaperman came looking, but Mama wouldn't let the newspaperman come in the door, Mama was always ashamed of how we lived back then. Mama had aspirations.

MARGARET: So this prize-winning photograph was, in fact, a happy childhood accident! [*To audience.*] Isn't life amazing?

LACEY: They gave me ten dollars for it, and Mama let me keep the money, wanted me to get a Sunday outfit, but I bought myself a Kodak so I could get a picture of Belinda.

MARGARET: [*To audience.*] A quirk of fate launched this magnificent career, do you believe it? [*To* LACEY.] The success of this photograph, of course, inspired you to keep on taking pictures.

LACEY: It was Belinda inspired me to keep on taking pictures because I couldn't ever get a good one of her.

MARGARET: So your little girlfriend was your earliest inspiration.

LACEY: She waddn't my girlfriend. Belinda didn't even know my name. She was the Mayor's daughter. We didn't even go to school together; mill folks had our own school. One time, Belinda was on a church committee that brought a turkey to our house for Christmas, but Mama was so mortified at being on the church poor list, she wouldn't let em in. I looked out at Belinda through the screen door, it was the closest I'd got to her back then. Lord, how bad I wanted a picture of her. I must have taken fifty pictures of her while we were coming up, but I never could get a good one because Mama would have been mortified, if Belinda'd known I was tailing her around snapping photos, so I had to hide behind something and take it while she was passing by, and they didn't have those high-speed films in those days.

MARGARET: Belinda was rich, you were poor. And that's how you developed your social conscience.

LACEY: It is?

MARGARET: Well, you were still a teenager when you took this remarkable photograph of a millworkers' strike during the depression.

LACEY: This picture here? I took that the day Mr. Hoover declared "The Star Spangled Banner" the national anthem. Mama said he did it because learning to sing that song would take our minds off the depression. The Mayor set up this big rally to happen during lunch-time outside the mill, see, and Belinda, she was supposed to have the prettiest singing voice. Well, she was set up on a platform, ready to lead us all in singing during lunch-time. Well, the workers at the mill hadn't gotten but half pay the week before, and they weren't much in the mood to be learning the national anthem. So when Belinda got up into place by the piano, and the mayor got the flag raised up high. And just about the time I got my camera aimed right, all of a sudden, hell broke loose...

MARGARET: [*To booth.*] We can bleep it.

LACEY: ...and there was shouting and yelling and waving of signs, and men were hitting each other. [*She peers at photograph.*] Belinda'd be right about here if there hadn't been such a hullabaloo. They knocked down the newspaperman and stepped all over his camera. That's how come the paper asked to print the picture I took.

MARGARET: That photograph hangs in the National Archives today.

LACEY: It's an ugly picture. It's a man punching another man right in the jaw. But it was that picture won me a scholarship to college, and Mama always said don't look a gift horse in the mouth. I studied to be a teacher.

MARGARET: A teacher?

LACEY: Well, they said I could be a teacher or a secretary or a bookkeeper. I didn't much care, and Mama thought if I was a teacher I might get to be a principal. I thought I might get to teach Belinda's children when she had some.

MARGARET: You didn't believe you could be a professional photographer?

LACEY: I never saw a woman doing that for pay. And I didn't believe I was too good at it. I never could get a decent picture of Belinda. If I'd been born a boy, I'd've gone into politics and been the Mayor like her daddy and I could've married her.

MARGARET: [*To audience.*] See the creative mind at work? She's using a metaphor here, stretching the truth of a childhood fantasy to illustrate a social point. [*To* LACEY.] That was a metaphor, wasn't it?

LACEY: No, it's the God's truth. Mama was always saying how Belinda was just the perfect little girl, tried to finger curl my hair to look like her. I couldn't be like Belinda no matter how Mama wished it, so instead I took to the idea of marrying Belinda, instead.

MARGARET: [*Laughs uneasily.*] The fantasy of a rejected child. [*To camera.*] I find it interesting that the seed of creativity is so often planted in the soil of rejection.

LACEY: When I told Mama it was my ambition to marry Belinda Adams, she knocked me clear across the room.

MARGARET: Your mother misinterpreted, of course, taking your metaphor at face value.

LACEY: I told my Mama the truth and she hit me. It was the last time I did that, I can tell you.

MARGARET: But with all the adolescent pain and suffering, creativity was flowering inside you by the time you left for college.

LACEY: I was at college when I took that picture there. That's the hallway of the Louisiana State House. Somebody's just shot Huey Long, and that's his blood there on the floor that fellow's mopping up. Belinda's daddy got himself elected to the legislature, see, and Belinda went to the State House every day to watch her daddy politicking. Belinda's daddy just loved Senator Long. Anyway, my college class went on a tour of the State House, and I brought my Kodak hoping to get a picture of Belinda in the gallery. Well, I took eleven of the pictures, but it was dark in there. Then there was some gunfire in the hallway and the police made us leave the building. This picture here was the only one on the roll came out. Mama said to me, now, why on earth would you waste good film taking a picture of a colored janitor? I told her, Mama, I was trying to finish up the roll. It was that picture got me a job on *The Tribune*.

MARGARET: [*Relieved.*] And that's when you went to New York City and began your remarkable career.

LACEY: Well, I came to work for *The Tribune*, but they didn't let me stay in New York City much. They kept sending me different places to take pictures. I never did keep an apartment in New York City. I could always find somebody to stay with.

MARGARET: I bet you had a lot of exciting affairs, travelling with all those famous people. Was there a great romance?

LACEY: Oh, I hooked up with this one and that one from time to time, and sometimes I thought I liked one better than the others, but time would pass, you know. I never met a woman could live up to Belinda.

MARGARET: I'm talking about the *men* in your life, of course. Did you ever get married?

LACEY: Mama doesn't have too much use for men. My daddy drank too much, I guess. Mama ran him off when I waddn't but a baby.

MARGARET: [*Quickly.*] Well, so much for romance.

LACEY: Oh, I had lots of romance. There was this one time, I was staying with somebody at the Barbizon in the 1940s—that was an all-woman's hotel, you know—

MARGARET: [*Quickly.*] It must have been very exciting, being assigned to cover action in World War II.

LACEY: . . . we got to making so much noise all night, they kicked us out. We had to sit up in a coffee shop until morning, when we could find some place else to go to. I tried to keep away from the Barbizon Plaza after that. Those women's hotels were real strict. When I met somebody, and she said she was living at the Barbizon, well, I just kept moseying on my way.

MARGARET: [*Interrupting.*] Guadalcanal. You were at Guadalcanal. [*She indicates photo.*]

LACEY: That picture there? The one with the soldier holding the bloody bayonet over his head? I took that in Los Angeles.

MARGARET: Los Angeles?

LACEY: That was the zoot suit riots. Belinda's first husband was stationed in Los Angeles then, and the *Tribune* had paid for me to go out to take some pictures of the servicemen shipping out to the Pacific. I figured to get a nice portrait of Belinda's husband and send it to her as a present, so I got her address out the phone book. I followed her husband downtown in Los Angeles—you can't hardly tell it's him in the picture—his face all mad and screwed up. See, those Mexican boys had come downtown in those zoot suits, and our boys in uniforms didn't like it. The streets of Los Angeles got so bloody, lord, the fire department had to hose em down. I never did send that picture to Belinda, it waddn't good of him.

MARGARET: Everybody thinks that's Guadalcanal.

LACEY: Could have been. I was there, too. Look just like the zoot suit riots. [*At next picture.*] Now, this next picture here I took in my old grade school yard when I was visiting Mama. It's the first grade class setting fire to a tepee. That was after the school board announced Hiawatha was a communist. That's Belinda's youngest boy. I sent that picture to her, but I didn't sign my name to it.

MARGARET: Now that was the McCarthy era, right? You were called before the committee yourself, weren't you?

LACEY: I went to Washington because Belinda's daddy was sitting on the McCarthy committee. I tried to get a portrait of him to send to her, but he'd got so old, you know, looked mean all the time. She wouldn't've liked the pictures I took of him.

MARGARET: Neither did the committee. Didn't they accuse you of making pro-communist statements with your harsh photographs?

LACEY: I don't believe that's why they called me up to that committee. I don't have a thimbleful of politics, never did. They called me up because when I got to Washington, I was looking for some place to stay for free, and I went to this little ol' bar and met up with a secretary, and she took a liking to me and let me stay at her place...

MARGARET: [*Interrupting.*] This is a picture of Korea, isn't it?

LACEY: [*Continuing her story.*] Turned out she was a girlfriend of one of those committee members, least he thought she was his girlfriend. She didn't want to give that man the time of day, but she was working for him, you know...

MARGARET: [*Interrupting.*] You won a Pulitzer for this. This is Korea, isn't it? This picture? Korea?

LACEY: It is. It's a graveyard over there—crosses go on as far as you can see. Belinda's husband was reported missing the first year of that war. I never sent that picture to Belinda, didn't want to make her cry. Belinda got married three times, but I always believe that was the only one of her husbands she gave a fig about.

MARGARET: Let's talk about the Nobel Prize.

LACEY: [*Continuing.*] Belinda was always marrying, seemed like she just had to have a husband. Course us southern girls were all raised to think like that, you know. Reason I never did marry a man was that I never came across one I could make sense out of. Men and TV sets are a mystery to me.

MARGARET: How did you feel when you won the Nobel Prize?

LACEY: I believe I might've married a woman, if they'd've let me.

MARGARET: [*To booth.*] We can cut that. We'll cut that. [*To* LACEY.] The Nobel Prize.

LACEY: You telling him to change what I'm doing here?

MARGARET: It's just editing, Lacey, we just clip a little moment out.

LACEY: I don't want you clipping moments out!

MARGARET: I have a responsibility to protect the viewer's sensibilities.

LACEY: All my life, I been clipping out moments to protect Mama's sensibilities. I got through clipping, waddn't much left. If you're going to do the same thing to me here, I might as well go home. I can sit with Mama and be somebody that I'm not.

MARGARET: Wait, don't leave! We're in the middle of taping a program. There's an audience out there!

LACEY: I came on this show because your friend Rachel asked me to.

MARGARET: Rachel did?

LACEY: [*To audience.*] Her friend Rachel came down south to visit me, said she writes books about people's lives and wanted to write the true story of mine. Said she'd gotten interested in me because of some tales she'd heard in the places where she and this one here hang out.

MARGARET: [*Panicked.*] It really doesn't matter why you came. You're here now. Let's talk about the Nobel Prize.

LACEY: [*Continuing, to* MARGARET.] Well, some of those tales weren't true, couldn't any one person have done all that carrying on. Lots of it was true, but I told your friend Rachel she couldn't print it in a book because of Mama. See, Rachel came to visit me, before Mama heard the preacher call her senile.

MARGARET: [*To audience.*] It does happen that I have a roommate named Rachel. I suppose she is a writer. You know we come and go. You know how roommates are—here today, gone tomorrow . . .

LACEY: [*Continuing.*] Rachel said it was too bad I couldn't let her write about the truth of my life. She said all the years she's been living with you, you been going on and on about how much you admired me, said if I could tell the truth in print, it might make you feel some better about yourself. [LACEY *is getting herself together to leave.*]

MARGARET: [*To booth.*] Don't worry. Sit down, Lacey, and tell me about this photograph. [*Leading her back to her seat.*] This is the shot that won the Nobel Prize for you, isn't it?

LACEY: I'm not talking any more if I can't say the truth.

MARGARET: Of course, we want to hear the truth—about this photograph. A beautiful, young Vietnamese girl, abandoned in poverty in a rice paddy, tenderly holding her half-caucasian baby.

LACEY: Belinda's grandchild. Belinda's youngest boy, the one by her third marriage, he went to Viet Nam and married that girl, and Belinda's husband wouldn't let him come home and bring her, so he stayed over there. I took this picture and sent it to Belinda, and that's when she wrote me a letter for the first time.

MARGARET: And you won the Nobel Prize.

LACEY: Well, first let me tell you, Belinda wrote me this little letter, peach colored paper folded in two, about this big, edges of it cut to like little scallops. Mama thought the paper was so pretty, wanted me to get some like it for myself. I told her I wrote too big for that kind of little paper. Mama said you can just look at that writing and tell Belinda is a real lady.

MARGARET: The Nobel Prize.

LACEY: Well, I'd already got that when Belinda wrote to me. She thanked me for sending her that photograph there of her grandchild which she had to hide in her bureau drawer so her husband wouldn't know she had it. But in appreciation, she said, she got her husband to organize a special celebration in honor of my getting the Nobel Prize. Belinda's husband was the Mayor, see, and he was going to give me the key to the City.

MARGARET: [*Pompously.*] And the cycle came full circle—it was Belinda who originally inspired your creativity, and it was Belinda who was responsible for your moment of triumph. I'd like to thank you for coming...

LACEY: Well, I got to shake her hand, if that's what you mean. Her fingers were as bony as a bird. I reminded her how she'd brought a turkey to our house one Christmas. Belinda said she guessed she must have delivered a thousand turkeys in her day and though she didn't recall that specific occasion when she came to our little house, she was filled with admiration that I'd risen to such heights of accomplishment from the depths of poverty. Mama stopped speaking to me when Belinda said that, didn't say another word to me until after the ceremonial dinner. I had Belinda sitting on one side of me and Mama on the other. I cleaned my plate and leaned back and was watching the two of them taking those tiny little bites and chewing with their mouths pursed, you know, and I saw how much they had in common: the way they sat with their backs so straight, the way they smiled when their eyes were just as cold, the way they complained about their food but wouldn't send it back. Then they called on Mama to make a speech and she stood up and said how proud she was of me and how she did always admire my spunky nature. Then he called on Belinda and she got up and said how she was in pure awe of my courage and achievements, and she believed I was the bravest woman she'd ever come across. Everybody clapped their hands and Belinda and Mama turned to look at me, smiling at me with those cold eyes, and that's when I saw how much they hated me for being all those things they just said they admired.

MARGARET: You mean, of course, they envied your success.

LACEY: You think so?

MARGARET: I'm asking you.

LACEY: I spent my whole life taking pictures of Belinda, trying to hold her still, to make her look back at me and see me. I always believed if she'd just really look at me, she'd be bound to love me back. Well, she looked at me a lot that night at dinner, just the same way Mama always has. I'm just not what either of them had in mind.

MARGARET: You are a great artist. You have documented our lives and times.

LACEY: It was like somebody cut my arm off with a buzzsaw.

MARGARET: As an artist you must take comfort in the knowledge that your work will touch the lives of thousands and outlive your generation.

LACEY: I could have spent all these years taking pictures of things that interested me.

MARGARET: We're nearly out of time. [*To audience.*] It goes so quickly, doesn't it?

LACEY: I could have moved in permanent with one of those women I stayed with in New York City, always having to pack up my underwear, hunt down my toothbrush, wonder where it was I left my overcoat. I could've stayed with one woman and built myself a darkroom. I could've kept a cat.

MARGARET: I do appreciate your dropping by today.

LACEY: I could've found somebody that cared about me. But I always turned my nose up, waiting for Belinda.

MARGARET: [*To audience.*] I want to thank you all for joining us . . .

LACEY: That's how come I'm going to call up your friend Rachel while I'm here in Philadelphia.

MARGARET: [*To camera.*] I hope you'll keep tuning into the show and tell your friends they can get tickets to see the taping by . . .

LACEY: [*To audience.*] If Rachel still wants to write a book about me, I believe I'll let her.

MARGARET: Tomorrow night, my guest will be that zany comic, commentator on our troubled times . . .

LACEY: [*To* MARGARET.] Rachel said I could stay with you two and save my hotel bill.

MARGARET: [*To booth.*] Are we still taping?

LACEY: I can get somebody from the church to look out for Mama. Telling the whole true story of my life might take a month or two.

MARGARET: [*To audience.*] Join me now in thanking Lacey Lanier! [*Applause sign on. To* LACEY.] That's it. We're through.

LACEY: Rachel said if I would tell the truth about my life, it might make you feel some better.

MARGARET: The show is over. [*To booth.*] Jack, get a taxi to take Lacey to the airport.

LACEY: And I believe your friend Rachel is right about that. I know you can't go chasing all your life after somebody else's image. You got to take a picture of yourself and get to love it, nobody else is going to do it for you. [*Suddenly sees monitor.*] Look there, the picture is doing something all by itself.

MARGARET: They're checking the tape, Lacey. Come on, you'll miss your plane. There'll be a taxi waiting for you right outside.

LACEY: [*About monitor.*] I don't care what Mama says, my hair looks fine to me.

MARGARET: [*To offstage.*] Tell him she's coming!

LACEY: Rachel gave me your home address. I wrote it on a slip of paper . . .

MARGARET: [*Shakes her hand.*] Nice meeting you. Lots of luck in the future.

[MARGARET *ushers* LACEY *out.*]

LACEY: [*As she goes.*] I'll just give it to the taxi driver. [LACEY *exits.*]

MARGARET: [*To audience.*] Well, one never knows what to expect when meeting genius. Now, I know you're eager to get up and stretch your legs, and I've got to dash, have a date with the most exciting man. Boy, roommates can get you into a lot of trouble, can't they? She's just a roommate . . . [MARGARET *tapers off, sits in her chair.*] Herbie, run the top part of the show for me, will you? The intro. Without sound. Run it several times. I want to watch myself.

[*And she is doing so as the lights narrow down to her and TV monitor, then to TV monitor alone.*]

I'LL BE HOME PARA LA NAVIDAD

excerpt from a Puerto Rican work-in-progress in Spanglish

Janis Astor del Valle

This play has been inspired by my own Mami
and by Carmen Kelly.

JANIS ASTOR DEL VALLE: SHE LIKES IT LIKE THAT

Dolores Prida

Janis Astor del Valle is a courageous and talented Latina lesbian playwright whose commitment and energy is a much-needed shot in the arm for the American theater scene in general, and the Latino artistic community in particular. She was born in the Bronx, but her family moved to Milford, Connecticut, when she was seven. On weekends, when she and her parents visited their extended family in the Bronx, Janis often wrote and directed scenes in which she and her cousins performed at their grandmother's house in Castle Hill. Her first play, *Jackie, Lee and Chicky*, about a trio of drug addicts struggling to survive in the South Bronx, was written at the age of nine. Three years later she scripted *The Family*, which focused on the comings and goings of a dysfunctional, matriarchal family. Janis was sixteen before she completed her next play, *Child of Vision*, which dealt with teenage alcohol and substance abuse in suburbia.

During her college years she was a radio announcer for various stations throughout Fairfield County, Connecticut, and Putnam County, New York. In 1986, she returned to her native New York City where she received a B.A. in Theater Arts from Marymount Manhattan College. Since then she has performed her plays and poetry at such New York City theatrical venues as W.O.W., the Duplex, Duality Playhouse, Madison Avenue Theater, and The Center. Janis is a founding member of She Saw Rep, a lesbian feminist troupe which made its debut at the National Lesbian Conference in April 1991.

In 1994 she was a member of the Latino Writer's Lab at Joseph Papp Public Theater, which I co-directed with George Emilio Sánchez that year, and a 1993–94 Van Lier Playwright Fellow at the Mabou Mines. Her full length play *Where the Señoritas Are* premiered at the Nuyorican Poets' Cafe in September 1994, and had a full-fledged production at the Perry Street Theater shortly thereafter. The play won the 11th Annual Mixed Blood Versus America Playwriting Competition, and has been performed in Washington, D.C., as a benefit for the Whitman Walker Clinic, at Mabou Mines, and the Women's Playwright Collective in New York.

She is also co-founder of Sister on Stage (S.O.S.), a multi-cultural trio of lesbian theater professionals dedicated to fostering the development of aspiring lesbian playwrights. In Spring 1995, she participated as a guest panelist of notable gay and lesbian playwrights at the Queer Theater Conference presented by The Center for Lesbian and Gay Studies of the CUNY Graduate School (CLAGS).

Latinos in general, and playwrights in particular, have fought long and hard against being categorized. For many, the label "Latina playwright" seems to imply that you cannot write about anything else but who you are. But for Janis Astor del Valle, a Bronx-born, second generation Puerto Rican writer, actor, and director, to be called a lesbian playwright is, in her own words, "an honor." And a commitment. Most of her recent work portrays the experiences of being a lesbian and a Latina. "It isn't that I can't write about other subjects," she says. "I just don't want to. Nobody asks heterosexuals why they only write about heterosexuals."

The subject of homosexuality in Latino theater is just beginning to come into its own. Until recently it had only been dealt with in an indirect manner. And even so, regular, staid, Latino theatergoers didn't take it lightly. A few years ago, a performance of Manuel Martin, Jr.'s *Union City Thanksgiving*, a play about a Cuban family in which a lesbian appears as a secondary character, provoked the ire of a member of the audience (a male), who got up in the middle of the performance, exclaiming loudly, "Such things don't happen in Cuban families!" then proceeded to leave the theater in quite a state of "his-teria."

Well, of course, such things do happen in Cuban, Puerto Rican, and all other varieties of Latino families. And I take my hat off to the new generation of playwrights who are up front and out there on the issue of their sexuality. They feel they have the responsibility to inform and educate the public—especially their own people—and in doing so commit acts of transgression against deeply rooted cultural canons in the Latino community. As Janis Astor del Valle puts it, "We are living, breathing, thinking people. We have the right to have our stories told—not misrepresented." The refusal to hide and keep silent on this subject is a subversion of culturally assigned roles, and as with all such subversions, not everyone will applaud.

But the resolve with which this new generation of dramatists plunges ahead is nothing short of admirable for those of us who have—pardon the pun—"skirted" around the issue for a long time. More rewarding yet is the warm reception that openly lesbian and gay works are having among an increasing number of Latino theatergoers. When Janis' full-length play, the charming *Where the Señoritas Are*, opened at the Nuyorican Poets Cafe—a venue originally perceived by many as a bastion of male wordbeaters—it was extremely well-received by the regulars.

In *I'll be Home Para la Navidad*, a short excerpt from what we hope will soon be a longer piece, Janis Astor del Valle shows great subtlety, humor, and respect for familial sensitivities. Among the fragrance of crushed garlic and chopped cilantro, in the altar room of every Latino home—the kitchen—mother and daughter share a special moment in a scene that has to be a first in Latino theater. Cookie has invited her lover Magdalena for Christmas dinner at her parents' home in Connecticut without first asking them. The traditional pernil is about to go in the oven, Magdalena is about to board a train in New York, and Mami and Papi don't yet know who's coming to dinner. Punctuated by the staccato of garlic being crushed in a pestle, with quick, lean dialogue, peppered with the right amount of laugh lines, Cookie makes a quite successful pitch for her mother's help in overcoming the biggest obstacle of all—her father. The scene ends with Mami promising she'll handle Papi's reservations. We have an inkling that she will do so as deftly as we've seen her peel, chop, and mix the sofrito ingredients, and also because Cookie has sworn that Magdalena can play the timbales almost as well as Tito Puente, her father's favorite musician.

This "happy ending" may seem facile to some, but in Janis's case—she likes it like that. Happy endings are entirely premeditated. It's not, however, a perfectly happy ending, since Mami imposes conditions: Cookie must not tell Papi the nature of her relationship with Magdalena. That is, she must stay in the closet. As Janis has stated: "In the old stories, homosexuals always either ended up dead or lived unhappily ever after. So, I write happy endings most of the time. In real life there are a lot of happy endings too, you know."

Yes, I know. And in avoiding the typical melodramatic outbursts that one would come to expect from a Latino mother facing her daughter's lesbianism, the play sets a lighter, refreshing tone in contemporary Latino drama dealing with gender issues.

This excerpt had a staged reading in the New Voices Festival at the Joseph Papp Public Theater in May of 1994 and was warmly received by the audience. It was first produced Off-Broadway professionally by Do Gooder Productions (Mark Robert Gordon, artistic director and general manager) at Theatre on Three, 8–26 November, 1995.

PRODUCTIONS OF *I'LL BE HOME PARA LA NAVIDAD*

Terri Vargas as "Mami" and Janis Astor del Valle as "Cookie," directed by Allison Astor, except where otherwise noted

Madison Avenue Theatre, produced by Village Playwrights (Directed by Kevin Brofsky), March 30–April 4, 1993

The Lesbian and Gay Community Services Center, produced by Crystal Quilt, November 1993

Nat Horne Theatre, produced by Mabou Mines for the Samuel French/Love Creek One-Act Play Festival (play—semi-finalist), April 1994

Joseph Papp Public Theater, produced by Papp/Latino Writers' Lab (part of the New Works Now Festival), May 1994

42ND ST. Collective (formerly Playwrights Horizons Theatre School), produced by Elgin Gordon (in celebration of Black History Month), February 1995

Nuyorican Poets' Cafe, produced by Miguel Algarin, April 1995, Samuel Beckett, produced by 42ND ST. Collective (as part of their Summerfest), July 1995

One Dream Theatre, produced by INTAR Latino Actors' Base (LAB), Directed by Bri MJS-Held, January 1994 (Gina Colon as "Mami" and Lisa Tamplenizza as "Cookie")

Janis Astor del Valle as "Cookie" and Terri Vargas as "Mami"

CHARACTERS

MAMI: Puerto Rican matriarch of Mendoza family, firm but lovable; wants to be bound by Latino/a traditions, but occasionally dons the armor of a liberated woman; claims her husband runs the show, when in reality she more often than not wears his as well as her pants; 50-something.

COOKIE: Mami's oldest daughter, "middle" and most outspoken child, first generation—and proud—Puerto Rican lesbian, lives in New York City, studies Modern Dance, waits tables part-time; very much in love with Magdalena; mid-20s.

SETTING: *8:00 A.M., Christmas in Mami's kitchen, Redding Ridge, Connecticut.*

SYNOPSIS (FOR EXCERPT/ONE-ACT VERSION)

While chopping garlic and slicing onions, Cookie, a Puerto Rican lesbian, asks Mami, "Guess who's coming to Christmas dinner?"

SCENE 1

MAMI *and* COOKIE *are preparing dinner.* MAMI *is marinating a roast pork and chopping garlic to mix with salt, pepper, and oregano in a pilon—mortar and pestle.* COOKIE *is peeling and slicing onions, green and red peppers.*

COOKIE: My friend and I went—

MAMI: [*Cutting her off.*] Did you wash your hands?

COOKIE: Claro que si! Anyway, my friend and I went to El Fundador the other night, and, what a meal! She had the arroz con pollo and they served it in this huge, cast iron pot—I mean, this thing was overflowing with mussels, shrimp, chicken and rice—but, you know, no beans.

MAMI: That's Spanish style—sin habicuelas. Dame la sal.

COOKIE: How come you always make it with beans?

MAMI: Because that's Puerto Rican style. Find a better knife, that one stinks.

COOKIE: It's not that bad.

MAMI: But it's taking you so long. At this rate, we'll be eating Christmas dinner on Easter. Tu sabes, I want this in the oven by 8:30 so we can start eating by 3.

COOKIE: I just have to break every once in a while for my eyes.

MAMI: Here, let me do it! You do the pilon.

COOKIE: No, it's okay.

MAMI: Ay, pero look at your eyes! C'mon, get away from there, I don't want tears in my sofrito.

[*They switch places.*]

COOKIE: Tu sabes, I had the pernil—

MAMI: Why did you have the pernil when I'm making it today?

COOKIE: This was last week. And, it was good, but not as tender as yours.

MAMI: Did they marinate it?

COOKIE: I didn't ask.

MAMI: It has to soak, like we did, overnight, in vinegar and a little bit of water. Then, we cook it all day today. They probably didn't let it soak and they probably didn't cook it long enough. You have to be very careful with pork. Especially if it's big—like this one—at least five to six hours. And for the first hour or hour and a half, at 325. Then, you can lower it to 300.

COOKIE: Well, my friend tried their flan—

MAMI: Which friend is this? The one you met at school?

COOKIE: Lena. We met in dance class. Neither of us had ever—

MAMI: How do you spell it?

COOKIE: L—e—n—a!

MAMI: Oh, like Lena Horne.

COOKIE: Yes, except—

MAMI: That's a black name.

COOKIE: Ma! Anyhow, it's pronounced Ley-nuh! Short for Magdalena.

MAMI: Oh. She's Spanish?

COOKIE: Half—her mother's Dominicana, her father's black.

MAMI: He's a black Dominicano?

COOKIE: No, he's black—African American.

MAMI: What is your friend?

COOKIE: I just told you!

MAMI: No, I mean, is she . . . tu sabes?

COOKIE: What?

MAMI: Morena o negra?

COOKIE: She's about as dark as Titi Luisa.

MAMI: Your father's sister?

COOKIE: No, your sister.

MAMI: That's dark.

COOKIE: Mira, Mami, don't start—

MAMI: Who's starting what? I'm not starting nothing! Where did you put the green peppers? All I said was she must be pretty dark.

COOKIE: I can't believe you! [*Motioning.*] In the fridge, by the carrots. Who were you engaged to before Daddy?

MAMI: Miguel Gonzalez.

COOKIE: And he passed for black.

MAMI: But he wasn't black. His mother was Puertorriqueña and his father was Dominicano—or was it the other way around? Anyway, he was dark, but he wasn't black.

COOKIE: What's the difference? We've got black blood in us—all Puerto Ricans do!

MAMI: We got a lot of things. My mother was part Indian, too.

COOKIE: Native American.

MAMI: Whatever. My grandfather used to call her Negrita.

COOKIE: Anyway . . . what was I saying?

MAMI: I don't know. Something about your black friend.

COOKIE: No! The flan!

MAMI: I never liked flan; I don't like anything that watery, makes me sick to my stomach.

COOKIE: Well, Lena and I split the flan. We were so stuffed by then. Lena said it was almost as good as her father's.

MAMI: Her father knows how to make flan?

COOKIE: Yeah.

MAMI: Her mother must have taught him.

COOKIE: No, actually he taught her. He was a cook in the Navy and stationed in Cuba before they got married.

MAMI: Oh, well, Cuban flan is different. Get me another green pepper.

COOKIE: Well, it tasted just like Tita's to me, and better than El Fundador's. [*Searching the fridge.*] Where is it?

MAMI: The bottom drawer—left side, near the ajo. You tasted his flan?

COOKIE: Yes.

MAMI: When?

COOKIE: Thanksgiving.

MAMI: They invited you?

COOKIE: Yes. I told you before . . .

MAMI: You never said it was them. You said a friend's.

COOKIE: Anyway, Lena's parents are in Santo Domingo for the holidays.

MAMI: That's nice. It's beautiful this time of year.

COOKIE: Yeah. She has no family in New York, not even the tri-state area. Her nearest relative is in Texas.

MAMI: Ay, bendito, so far.

COOKIE: So, it's okay if she comes for dinner, verdad?

MAMI: Ay, Cookie, I don't think your father will go for that.

COOKIE: Not to stay over, just for the day!

MAMI: He's never spoken to you about this—and he never will—but I know how he feels! It's tearing him up!

COOKIE: How do you feel?

MAMI: Well, I have to agree with him.

COOKIE: Why?

MAMI: All your life you like boys, and now, suddenly, a month ago, you tell us you're liking women?

COOKIE: There's nothing sudden about it. I told you—

MAMI: I know what you told us. I also know that just five years ago you were ready to marry Jose!

COOKIE: Yeah, and marrying him or any other man would have been a joke. Mami, I've always been attracted to women—I just couldn't face it then—

MAMI: Please! I don't want to talk about your problem!

COOKIE: Problem?

MAMI: Yes, that's what it is, a problem.

COOKIE: Why does it have to be a "problem"? Why can't you just accept the fact—

MAMI: I don't have to accept anything! You're my daughter and I will always love you, but I don't have to accept your lifestyle.

COOKIE: It's not a lifestyle, either! You think I woke up one morning and said, 'Oh, lemme try a woman today!'

MAMI: You could've married Jose or all the other men who chased you. But you ignored them. That was your choice.

COOKIE: Yes, that was my choice, because I didn't love them. But feelings, Mami . . . that's just natural—

MAMI: It's not natural! A man and a woman together—that's natural!

COOKIE: Says who?

MAMI: La Biblia.

COOKIE: La Biblia? When was the last time you went to church? 1951, your wedding day, so don't give me that crap!

MAMI: Don't you curse at me! I never let my sons swear in this house; I will certainly not let my daughter!

COOKIE: Crap isn't a swear word.

MAMI: The way you said it, it is. And I don't like the tone of voice you're using with me.

COOKIE: I'm sorry, but, Mami, it hurts when you say I've got a problem.

MAMI: I'm not trying to hurt you, I'm just telling you how I feel. Homosexuality is not normal.

COOKIE: Well, I know a lot of heterosexuals who aren't so normal.

MAMI: God made Adam and Eve—not Adam and Esteban!

COOKIE: You've been watching Geraldo again, haven't you?

MAMI: It has nothing to do with him! That's the way it's always been and the way it should be.

COOKIE: Sounds like a Carly Simon song.

MAMI: What?

COOKIE: Nothing. Mami . . . mira, Lena is very special to me. It's pretty serious—

MAMI: Yeah, they all were! Special friends!

COOKIE: Ma! That's not fair!

MAMI: Well, it's true! All those women you brought here, over the years, making us believe they were just your friends—and your father and me took each one into our house like they were familia—

COOKIE: They were!

MAMI: They were not! Cookie, you lied to us!

COOKIE: I had to!

MAMI: You didn't have to do anything but tell us the truth. At least then, maybe something could have been done...

COOKIE: Like what? [*Mocking* MAMI's *accent.*] Electric chock treatments?

MAMI: I don't know...something! We could have taken you to a doctor—

COOKIE: A doctor? I'm not sick!

MAMI: Or a priest—

COOKIE: Most priests are gay themselves!

MAMI: Don't you speak about priests that way!

COOKIE: You want the truth? I'll give you the truth: I love Lena!

MAMI: And you loved the others and where did it get you?

COOKIE: This is different! We've been together almost a year and—

MAMI: Almost a year! Big deal!

COOKIE: It is a big deal! I'm in love with her! We've talked about a future! We're living—

MAMI: I don't want to discuss this! Dame el pique!

COOKIE: Is that a "no" already or are you going to talk to Daddy?

MAMI: I will ask him, but I know my husband.

COOKIE: When are you going to talk to him?

MAMI: Don't push me, Cookie! I said I will talk to him! I have to do it in my own time.

COOKIE: I know, but...Lena was going to catch the 9:45 out of Grand Central this morning...

MAMI: The 9:45? To where?

COOKIE: Redding Ridge...

MAMI: Cookie, how could you? How could you have invited her without asking first?

COOKIE: I never had to ask for Brian McAllister! You went right up to him at Yolanda's wedding—never met him before that day—and invited him to spend the weekend with me in your home for Chrissakes! [*Imitating* MAMI.] "Oh, Brian, have you ever been to Connecticut? Especially in the summer, with all the trees so green? And we live right near the lake, and Cookie can take you out on her little rowboat, and she can fix you a nice lunch and yous can have a picnic right there in the boat!" Without bothering to ask me, you asked him!

MAMI: Because I thought he was your boyfriend! And he was a very nice boy. And certainly the most handsome—

COOKIE: Well, he wasn't my boyfriend!

MAMI: But you brought him to the wedding!

COOKIE: It was a cover! He was just a fuckin' cover date!

MAMI: Ay, Dios mio! What did I tell you about cursing! I have never heard the "f" word in this house and I'm not going to start now! Not even your father has said that word to me!

COOKIE: I'm sorry for swearing.

MAMI: Who do you think you are that you can come into my house and use that kind of street language? You may talk like that to your friends, but not to me and not in my house! I will not stand for it!

COOKIE: I said I was sorry.

MAMI: Put more ajo in there!

COOKIE: I'm finished

MAMI: Did you put more ajo? [*Looking over* COOKIE.] I don't think you put enough.

COOKIE: It's more than enough, believe me.

MAMI: What time were you planning to go to the store?

COOKIE: I don't know...

MAMI: You better get a move on because they closing early today. Necesito mas platanos, y the store is not gonna' stay open one minute past five just because Cookie Mendoza is a last minute shopper.

COOKIE: It depends...

MAMI: On what?

COOKIE: How soon I get done here—

MAMI: Don't worry about that, I can finish by myself. [*Drying* COOKIE's *hands with a towel and pushing her away.*] Vete! Y take your sister —

COOKIE: It also depends on what Daddy says about Lena...

MAMI: What do you mean?

COOKIE: I mean, I'm going to spend Christmas with her. Whether it's here or New York.

MAMI: You're saying if Daddy says no Lena, you're going back to the City instead of spending Christmas Day con tu familia?

COOKIE: She is my familia!

MAMI: I'm talking about your real familia, your brother and sister, your niece and nephew—your mother and father, who only brought you into this world—

COOKIE: Mami, why do you do this to me?

MAMI: You're the one who's giving us an ultimatum!

COOKIE: You don't understand!

MAMI: No, you don't understand that your father and me don't like ultimatums!

COOKIE: Well, I'm sorry you're looking at it that way...

MAMI: Friends come and go, pero tu familia will be there for you—always.

COOKIE: I know that. But I'm telling you, Lena is more than my friend. She's my wife!

MAMI: Wife? Ay, no! What are you telling me now? That you're gonna be a man?

COOKIE: Mami, no! I love being a woman. Mira, we moved in together and filed for a domestic partnership. They passed this law in New York—

MAMI: I always knew that city was crazy!

COOKIE: Maybe you think it's crazy, but the mayor and thousands of others didn't think so!

MAMI: Well, the mayor and thousands of others are not your parents.

COOKIE: Mira, Hector's girlfriend's coming over tomorrow, verdad?

MAMI: Kathleen? Of course, she'll be here. A donde esta el cilantro?

COOKIE: Yo no se. Pues, Hector didn't have to ask Daddy's permission!

MAMI: He's been going out with her for a while!

COOKIE: All of three weeks!

MAMI: He knew her from school!

COOKIE: I've known Lena a lot longer! Mami, if you just give it a chance...

MAMI: It's not only me, it's your father, too!

COOKIE: You would all get along so well! She's down to earth, very friendly, smart, warm, creative, a great dancer—she speaks Spanish fluently—

MAMI: Oye! Are you telling your friends we only speak Spanish? Just because I wasn't born in this country doesn't mean I can't speak English! I can't spell too good, but I can speak perfect English when I have to!

COOKIE: I know—she knows...mira, Mami, she's a good person...I know Daddy would love her...she's a Yankee fan—

MAMI: Oh, that, he'll love—

COOKIE: And she plays the timbales—almost as good as Tito Puente!

MAMI: No one can play as good as Tito!

COOKIE: She's pretty close...

MAMI: Ay, Cookie...

COOKIE: Ay, Mami...remember when I was five and first started taking ballet?

MAMI: Yes...you used to cry everyday before it was time to go, you hated it so much!

COOKIE: I would get so tired holding onto that bar and listening to that boring music...I would do it because I kept thinking how much you wanted me to be the first Puerto Rican in the *Nutcracker*...but, tu sabes, Mami, it wasn't in my heart...

MAMI: I know, mija...

COOKIE: But here I am, years later, all grown up now, and what am I doing? I'm dancing.

MAMI: And starving.

COOKIE: I get by all right. It's not ballet, but I'm still a dancer. I've still had to work and train hard...but it's worth it to me, because I'm finally dancing all the dances I ever wanted to—merengue, jazz, salsa, mambo—all the dances that have always lived in my heart...remember when I finally told you I wanted to quit ballet and start taking modern?

MAMI: I cried.

COOKIE: At first...but, after the tears, came the love. And the next day, you brought me to Miss Wilson's and signed me up for Modern Dance 101. You let me follow my heart, Mami. That's all I'm asking for now...

MAMI: Ay, mija...I don't wanna cry...

COOKIE: I know, but just remember what comes after the tears...

[MAMI *embraces* COOKIE.]

MAMI: Did I ever tell you you're a great dancer?

COOKIE: Great? I don't think you ever used the word, great...good, maybe, but not great...

MAMI: Well, I think you're a great dancer! Better than Chita Rivera!

COOKIE: Better than Chita?

MAMI: Yes.

COOKIE: How about Rita Moreno?

MAMI: Oh, si. And you got better hair then both of them! Oye, Cookie...tu sabes, we never had a gay person in this house...

COOKIE: What, I don't count?

MAMI: I mean, your father...to think about...the thoughts...you...and another woman...in our house...it's a lot...

COOKIE: We're not gonna do anything but eat! Dinner!

[*Pause.*]

MAMI: So, does your friend like pernil?

COOKIE: She loves it.

MAMI: You made it for her?

COOKIE: Once—a very long time ago.

MAMI: Did you marinate it?

COOKIE: Si.

MAMI: With the vinegar?

COOKIE: Claro que si! We took turns basting—it was a lot of fun!

MAMI: Oye, what you do in your own home is your business, pero in my house, no holding hands, no kissing, no sitting alone in la familia room with the door closed! And when Luisa Blanca y Luisa Vasquez get here, not a word to them—estas dos bochinchosas! They don't need to know nothing except that Lena is your friend.

COOKIE: What are you saying?

MAMI: I'm saying . . . can your friend bring the timbales? Your father would love that . . .

COOKIE: Mami, she's coming by train . . . Do you think I should . . . talk to him?

MAMI: Don't worry, you let me handle your father.

COOKIE: Thank you, Mami.

MAMI: Look at the time. You better hurry, or they gonna lock yous in the store. You laugh, but I heard that happened to someone last week. Did you put more ajo?

COOKIE: Si.

MAMI: Put a little more. A little ajo never hurt nobody.

COOKIE: Yeah, but we ain't got a little, we got a lot! We gonna have ajo comin' through our pores!

MAMI: That's all right; it's good for the soul.

END SCENE

THE POSTCARD

Gloria Joyce Dickler

I'd like to thank Marita Giovanni for looking into my heart and working with me psychically and dramatically to bring forth these stories. I'd also like to thank Marjorie Bair, Davida Bloom, Rosemary Keefe Curb, River Lightwomoon, and the Norns for their care, criticism and support; and last but hardly least, I'd like to thank the love that blessed and inspired this play.

Gloria Joyce Dickler

GLORIA JOYCE DICKLER, HEALING HISTORIC WOUNDS
Bobbi Ausubel

Gloria Joyce Dickler left her home in Florida after high school to study writing at different colleges in the USA and Canada. She quit graduate school at the University of Chicago when she decided that she didn't belong in academia and that she could learn the craft of playwriting on her own. After two years of trial and error in New York, Playwrights' Horizon gave a backers' audition to one of her plays. Although her need to write continued, it was overshadowed by the need to support herself. After seven years developing a lucrative career in broadcast advertising, she was able to return to writing full time.

Dickler began writing *The Postcard* in 1991, roughly two years after she founded Common Stage Theatre in Woodstock, New York. The company's mission was to produce and develop plays by women that showed transformation. Under Dickler's direction the company produced six east coast premieres—two of her own plays and two one-woman shows which went on to larger venues. *Two-Faced*, written and performed by Lynne Adams, enjoyed a long run in Los Angeles; and *Full Gallop*, a play about Diana Vreeland written and performed by Mary Louise Wilson, had a successful tour. From 1989 to 1994, Common Stage produced the work of thirty playwrights in full productions and staged readings, culminating with Dickler's direction of Victoria Rue's *Cancerbodies: Women Speaking the Unspeakable* (1995 title: *Ruffled Irises: Women Struggling with Cancer*). The play chronicles one lesbian's living with and dying of cancer, as she and her lover passionately experience their love through personal and cultural transformation, a theme Dickler had been developing in *The Postcard*. In 1994 Dickler left Common Stage to write screenplays in Los Angeles.

Through manipulation of time modalities, Dickler's plays show women healing from past wounds in order to emerge whole and empowered to act by their own agency in a world that offers little support for or understanding of the inner journey. An earlier play, *Moonflowers*, a comedy, follows the lives of the Manfrieds, especially Lily, the youngest daughter, who grows from childhood to adulthood.

When a witch-like grandmother, Zinnia, transports the family to a life after death, characters heal childhood wounds. *No Roses* moves back and forth in time as Gayle, a mother, is forced to face the lies she has created to mask her feelings of inadequacy when her son learns from his assumed grandmother the truth of his conception and Gayle's past. *Community* is a precursor to *The Postcard*. Like ghosts, the parents of two lesbians in a relationship fade in and out of present scenes in the women's lives, creating obstacles to their intimacy, but ultimately enabling them to face their demons, such as incest, and to emerge with their own agency. *The Postcard* goes further—from personal transformation to the beginnings of historical reconstruction.

The Postcard features two New York Jewish women, lovers, in the 1990s, who gain insight into their personal struggles when they buy a postcard showing two children in the Warsaw ghetto in the 1940s. Shell, a writer, and Ruth, a psychotherapist, love and fight, plan vacations, argue with the super of the apartment building, and celebrate holidays together. They also mysteriously journey into a "fold" in time where they meet the twelve-year-old boy and girl of the postcard. Their times, their worlds, collide and interweave. During the play, we come to understand why the children have come from the past, what they need, and how they can help Ruth and Shell.

One evening, after a Passover seder, the women, cuddling comfortably on the couch, study the postcard of the ghetto children and watch as the children come alive before their eyes. They witness the drama of the twelve-year-old Sheldon and Helen Elaina falling in love on the dangerous ghetto streets. A montage of ghetto sounds melds into present Manhattan street noises until time boundaries break and the four characters interact directly in each other's lives. The children reflect qualities in Ruth and Shell that are making their relationship difficult. Ruth and Helen Elaina can both be fearful and clingy. Shell and Sheldon can both be relentless and overpowering. The women argue about whether Shell should publish the novel she is writing about the children's story. Ruth feels that it is their private world. During a subsequent anguished period of separation, they learn from and help the children as all four characters progress toward healing.

Toward the end of the first scene, Shell poses the ritual Passover question: "What makes tonight different from all other nights?" and later answers "Tonight we were given the sign to go into the wilderness and in our wanderings we will find God's commandments." The play thus links the liberation of slaves from Egypt commemorated at Passover and their subsequent wandering in the desert with the individual journeys and liberation of the four characters.

Whereas other plays in the Western canon, such as Sophocles' *Oedipus Rex*, Ibsen's *Ghosts*, and Miller's *Death of a Salesman*, show present ills rooted in past evils, *The Postcard* is both post-Freud and post-Alice Miller. Miller, a pioneering psychologist, wrote *The Drama of the Gifted Child* and other books about adult healing from childhood wounds, in which she theorizes that adults are prisoners of their own wounded children. Through psychotherapy the adult experiences the child's early needs, emotions, and wounds in order to embrace the child-self with love. Dickler depicts character change through layering the action of the women with each other and with the ghetto children. Ruth and Shell fear that if they help the children they will lose what they hold most dear. Shell believes that she will lose Ruth, and Ruth believes that she will lose her mind. In accord with Miller's theories, the women choose to embrace and support the ghetto children, who reflect their own child-selves, ultimately allowing them to free themselves and the children from the past.

One liberation Dickler's characters seek is freedom from their mothers. Dickler bravely explores sexual molestation by mothers, a topic rarely discussed. The women's movement has revealed substantial evidence of sexual abuse of girls and women by men, but Dickler is willing to show mothers as perpetrators. The mothers of Sheldon and Helen Elaina both seek sexual comfort from their children as a way of managing or escaping terror. When no one else is around, the boy's mother visits him at night seductively. In turn, the girl's mother treats her daughter strangely and forces her to sleep each night under her mother's body while they are in hiding. This suffocating protection is excessive to hide from the German police. Helen Elaina calls on Ruth to help her fight off this "crazy" mother. Ruth refuses out of her own fear. Only later does Ruth tell Shell that her own mother was like the girl's mother.

For readers and spectators trying to understand mothers who seek sexual comfort from their children, Dickler shows the mothers' as well as the children's terror. Sheldon's mother says: "Do you know what I do all day to keep body and soul together? I wash the undergarments of the filthy pigs who are destroying our lives." Later we learn that she sleeps with a Nazi soldier for seven nights so that her family might get passage to Denmark. Helen Elaina's mother is forced to wait outside the temple with the other women as Nazis murder their husbands. "They have my husband in a cart…no burial. No washing. There will be no marker. No sign of his living." In present time scenes, Diana, one of Ruth's therapy clients, remembers her mother terrified for her life at the hands of a drunken, abusive husband. Diana's mother and the ghetto mothers betray the trust and innocence of their small children by seeking inappropriate comfort from them. By illuminating causes for the mothers' desperation and selfish brutality, Dickler permits the audience to feel compassion as well as outrage toward these women.

The play takes spectators beyond the immediate entangled lives of the mothers and daughters portrayed. It introduces a larger spiritual and historic perspective via the sound of an unseen woman crying and grieving. "Someone's crying," says Ruth. "It's the girl's mother," responds Shell. As the play unfolds, it is apparent, especially in the scene in which Ruth and Helen Elaina talk about God, that the grief portrayed is a universal condition. When Ruth asks who the woman crying is, Helen Elaina says, "Sometimes I think she's God's mother and other times I think she's his wife and they're having a fight. All I know is God's very unhappy about things because he can't do anything." When Helen Elaina begs Ruth to help her find her mother, Ruth tries to block her out, blocking out her own needs and the call of responsibility. The woman crying—God's wife, God's mother, trembling Mother Nature, or all the mothers fearful for their lives—is a prayer for healing.

The play depicts transformations into a more positive future. Shell initially writes a novel in which Helen Elaina dies and Sheldon becomes an American businessman. Sheldon, however, pleads for a happy ending in which he is reunited with Helen Elaina in Venice after the war. He reaches out of the death-drenched ghetto into Shell's era, asking her to rewrite history (which she does), so that he and others can find peace and happiness in a different future: "People need to know there's happiness even with all this mess." The playwright proposes that we can heal historic wounds by bonding empathetically with sufferers of the past. The play thus suggests that present recognition can free one from the recurring nightmares of private and public histories.

How can a play about incest and the holocaust have a "happy" ending? Those of us who pioneered in feminist theatre frequently argued about "happy" endings. We wondered whether it is more effective to dramatize the enormous obstacles facing women by having them lose or die, or whether it is better to depict characters who are free enough to make creative, positive choices and allow for a happy ending. All social protest theatre faces this dilemma.

Classic theater allowed only tragedy or comedy. But serious modern drama allows a happy ending to emerge out of a difficult struggle. Feminist drama can effect healing and changing so that, as characters gain strength enough to overcome obstacles, spectators experience renewed determination to continue personal healing and collective struggles for social justice. In Ntosake Shange's *For Colored Girls Who Have Considered Suicide When the Rainbow Is Enuf*, for example, the women's shared story telling and laying on of hands creates the healing. In *The Postcard* the victory of love in the face of difficult challenges is honestly earned through struggle with the past. The play's happy ending works because the characters have recreated themselves and thereby rewritten a piece of history. The play offers a vision of personal and even historic healing.

PLAY PRODUCTION HISTORY FOR GLORIA JOYCE DICKLER

1978: DESCRIPTIONS LTD. (staged reading); Playwright's Horizons, NYC.

1989: COMMUNITY; Common Stage Theatre at State University of NY, New Paltz, NY.

1990: NO ROSES; (staged reading), Cast Theater, Los Angeles, CA.

1991: MOONFLOWERS; WomanKraft and the Temple of Music and Art, Tucson, AZ.

1991: MOONFLOWERS; Common Stage Theatre, Woodstock, NY.

1992: PSYCHE'S WALTZ; Common Stage Theatre, Woodstock, NY

1994: THE POSTCARD (staged reading); FIRSTSTAGE, Hollywood, CA.

CHARACTERS:

RUTH: Early forties, therapist, private, shy, analytic, nurturing

SHELLEY: Early forties, writer, dreamer, eager, funny, devoted

DIANA: Thirties, forties, Ruth's client.

BOY: Polish Jew, 1939, resourceful, quick, twelve

GIRL: Polish Jew, 1939, twelve, introspective, intelligent.

BOY'S MOTHER: Polish Jew, 1939, late thirties/early forties, boisterous, self-promoting

GIRL'S MOTHER: Polish Jew, 1939, middle forties, lives in a state of fear

SETTING: *Time—The Present and 1939*
Place—New York City and the Warsaw Ghetto, Poland.

The Postcard was produced as a staged reading at FIRSTSTAGE, Hollywood, CA, February, 1994, and was directed by Marita Giovanni.

THE SET

The play is split between the past, which takes place in the Warsaw Ghetto and environs in 1939, and the present, which takes place in NYC. There are two settings in the present and various settings in the past. The present day NYC settings are realistic and if possible modular. Ideally they should be able to be moved off stage when not in use. The settings which evoke the past should be minimally drawn and easily assembled/disassembled.

THE PRESENT: In the present we have Ruth's and Shell's apartment and Ruth's office. The apartment, originally Ruth's until Shell moved in three years ago, reveals their living area and Shell's writing area. The sofa should be down-filled, enveloping, soft; the coffee table should be a light oak and glass. The lighting is soft, cosy and warm. Shell's writing area is functional: a small desk with file cabinet, a lap top, small book case or shelves, and a comfortable desk chair... arms, high back, swivel, etc. The chair is a mark of Shell's character: mobil, open, easy. The couch is Ruth's reflection: soft, fragile, nurturing. There's a small home entertainment center complete with remote and a small, round oak dining table. Next to Shell's desk is the living room window. This window shatters at the end of Act I, Scene 1, and in subsequent scenes should be boarded up against the cold. The window and its shattering is essential. The one other essential item in their space is the front door complete with the New York City armory of locks including one which only locks from the inside.

Ruth's office is distinctly more formal than their home. The sofa is stiffer than the one at home and Ruth's chair does not swivel, it is designed for a bad back and gives support to correct posture. The floor-to-ceiling bookcases would inspire awe in even the well-read. The carpeting is a practical sturdy weave but in a light color. The office gives an illusory feeling of light; it can become very dark there.

FLOWERS—Ruth loves flowers. At the start of the play there are fresh flowers in both spaces. In Act II, fresh flowers are in the apartment only at the top of Scene 5. These flowers should appear dead by Scene 8 when Ruth enters with fresh flowers, eventually replacing the old with the new. There are no fresh flowers in her office in Act II.

Both present day sets need to accommodate the arrival and departure of the past.

THE PAST: The settings suggestive of 1939 Warsaw Ghetto and environs are a ghetto street before and after a bombing, the sitting room of the Girl's Mother's house where the body of the Girl is laid out, a ghetto street with garbage, a small window in the Boy's Mother's house looking out onto the street, a barn complete with hayloft and ladder, the doorway of a building in an alley, the gray and meager living room of the Boy's house where the Boy sleeps in the corner, the dock at Stettin.

Depending upon the occurrence of these different scenes, some will be parallel either to Ruth's and Shell's living room or Ruth's office; others could be on scaffolding that surround or encompass the realistic settings. The idea is to have the space above and around the living room and office easily become 1939 when it is called for.

The script is marked when the characters of the past actually enter the present dimension and vice-versa. It is essential, therefore, that the settings be distinct yet open to each other.

ACT I
SCENE 1

Sirens from police and ambulance vehicles sound on an empty stage. These sounds are mixed with car alarms, cars backfiring and gun shots. Keys open several locks.

RUTH and SHELLEY enter from the outside into the living room of their home. They are grateful to be home. They are wearing heavy coats. SHELLEY has a broken umbrella. There are the sounds of SHELLEY flipping the standard locks.

In a ritual action, albeit hurriedly, SHELLEY helps RUTH off with her coat, and then hangs it on a coat tree as RUTH helps SHELLEY take off her coat.

RUTH takes a key from around her neck and locks the door from the inside and puts the key away.

SHELL: I can't believe how windy it is out there. We could have been blown apart.

RUTH: At least it's warm in here . . . and dry. I wish those sirens would stop.

SHELL: I wish wishing would make a difference.

RUTH: I don't remember it ever being this cold on Passover.

SHELL: It's too cold.

[*Again, as a ritual, they hurriedly huddle on the couch and rub each other's arms and backs to get the chill out.*]

RUTH: Your hands are like ice cubes. [*Warms them up.*]

SHELL: My circulation is getting worse. Your nose is dripping. [*Gives her a tissue.*]

RUTH: [*Blows her nose.*] My nose is numb. I hate the weather.

SHELL: [*Still warming her up.*] I'm so tired of talking about the weather. That's all anyone talks about anymore. Better?

RUTH: Um hm. You?

SHELL: Yeah.

[*They sit side by side.*]

RUTH: It's exhausting being outside.

[*RUTH puts her head on SHELLEY's shoulder. SHELLEY puts her arm around her.*]

SHELL: Happy Passover.

[*They both sigh in relief. Sirens, etc., fade out.*]

RUTH: Is this our third Passover together?

SHELL: [*Nods, "yes."*] I like having it here better.

RUTH: Next year it'll be our turn again.

SHELL: You're more relaxed here. You got drunk last year.

RUTH: I did not!

SHELL: You were so funny.

RUTH: Shh. Listen.

SHELL: What?

RUTH: It's so quiet...

[*They look at each other.* SHELL *strokes the space around* RUTH's *face, then touches her face.* RUTH *kisses her.*]

RUTH: [*Licks her cheek.*] Hm. You taste good.

SHELL: I can't believe you just licked my face! Sometimes I think you just can't handle intimate moments.

RUTH: Me! [*Beat. Goes to window.*] It's so quiet. Do you think something's wrong?

SHELL: Maybe the angel of death is passing through Manhattan. You think it'll come up to the twelfth floor?

RUTH: Do you think a lot of people will be dying soon like they say?

SHELL: [*With a Jewish intonation.*] We should put blood on the door?

RUTH: I don't think that will do it.

[*Pause.*]

SHELL: Tonight we celebrate our liberation from bondage. Tonight—

RUTH: Maybe we should be getting ready to leave.

SHELL: To go where?

RUTH: Somewhere safe.

SHELL: No matter where we go, we have to create the safe place.

RUTH: I want to go somewhere where it'll be easy.

SHELL: [*Laughs at* RUTH's *wishful thinking.*] You'd leave your clients?

RUTH: No.

[SHELLEY *thinks about getting postcard from* RUTH's *bag but instead picks out a CD. She puts on music: Glick's Hebraic Suite #1, Part II.*]

RUTH: I get so scared sometimes. Everything feels so crazy. Do you ever feel that way? How fast everything is? How busy we are?

SHELL: Would you like to dance with me? Slowly.

RUTH: I should stop.

SHELL: Yes.

RUTH: I make myself more neurotic than I already am.

SHELL: No comment.

[*They dance. Lights rise behind a scrim or on another level. The silhouettes of a* BOY *and* GIRL *on a street in a ghetto dance to the same music as* SHELL *and* RUTH.]

RUTH: Do you hear something?

SHELL: No, but I smell your hair.

RUTH: Like an echo? [*Moments pass.*] The boy and girl in the postcard.

SHELL: The one we found? [*Beat.*] What, Ruth?

RUTH: I get the feeling that they're dancing. [*Gives her the chills.*] Feels like someone is walking over my grave.

[*They have stopped dancing. The* BOY *and* GIRL *continue until the end of the song and then they sit together, holding hands, talking silently to each other. The* BOY *and* GIRL *should seem as shadows until they begin speaking.*]

RUTH: What are you thinking?

SHELL: How we've never gone into that card shop.

RUTH: It was so cold. Your hands were starting to hurt.

SHELL: And then we found it. Or it found us. And time stopped. Just like when we first got together. You felt it too.

[RUTH *nods fearfully.* SHELL *goes to get the postcard from* RUTH's *bag.* RUTH *stops her.*]

RUTH: Maybe we weren't supposed to find it.

SHELL: But we did. [*Takes out postcard.*]

RUTH: [*Looks at postcard.*] They look just like us.

SHELL: I'm the boy. [*Laughs.*]

RUTH: Something awful's going to happen.

SHELL: Ruth, it's okay. [*Holds her.*] Maybe I'll write a story about them.

RUTH: He's going to leave her.

SHELL: He's just about to touch her cheek.

RUTH: We found it because you're going to leave me.

SHELL: Ruth, please, I haven't had to leave in over a year.

RUTH: Then why am I so scared you will? [*Beat. Hands back postcard.*] I don't want to do this. [*Beat. Takes in* SHELLEY.] Tell me a story. One with a happy ending.

SHELL: [*Thinks, but is also still in the previous moment.*] You know my leavings have had everything to do with how you treated me.

RUTH: [*Almost angry.*] And you still make the choice to leave.

[*Pause.* SHELLEY *doesn't want to argue.*]

RUTH: [*Cont'd.*] Please tell me a story.

[SHELLEY *starts thinking of a story.*]

RUTH: [*Cont'd.*] I love your stories.

[*Beat.*]

RUTH: [*Cont'd.*] Do you want some tea?

[SHELL *shakes her head "no" and pats sofa to get* RUTH *to sit by her.* RUTH *sits and gets cozy.*]

SHELL: The boy's just about to touch the girl's cheek.

RUTH: [*Realizes it's the postcard, then.*] Only if it has a happy ending.

SHELL: It's gray on the street of the ghetto, a permanent haze in the air from the bombing.

RUTH: [*With Jewish intonation.*] They're in a ghetto and it's going to be happy?

SHELL: [*Lightly.*] You have to trust!

> [RUTH *obviously doesn't put much stock in trust.*
>
>   *As* SHELL *speaks, the lighting changes or the scrim rises. The* BOY *and* GIRL *on a ghetto street come parallel to* RUTH's *and* SHELL's *living room. The two areas, however, remain separate.*]

SHELL: The boy's small hand is gently about to touch the girl's cheek. They're fearful and he's comforting her. They've already been together an hour. He has helped her do her chores. He doesn't want to leave her. He doesn't want to ever leave her. The girl's alone. The boy knows her pain. He knows it deep in his chest. He wants to take her with him but he has so much to do. First, he must race across town to the butcher to have him hold a chicken, then he must run back to the ghetto to Weissman's who will buy his mother's gold wedding ring, then he must race back across town with the money to buy the medicine for his dying grandmother, then pick up the chicken, not get caught with the chicken, and be home before his mother gets back from the Commandant's. If he takes the girl with him, he knows it'll take too long and he'll be too worried to enjoy her company.

    Why can't his mother just let the old grandmother die? The sound of her constant coughing has kept him awake nights for as long as he can remember.

GIRL: What are you doing? Put your mitten back on, Sheldon Steinloff. It's too cold.

BOY: I want to feel your face. It's so soft. I love to touch your face.

GIRL: Your hand will freeze.

BOY: What if I don't see you again? What if they come for you in the night?

GIRL: We have to be brave. I will see you again and that's all we need to say.

BOY: But everything is getting worse. Has your father talked to the Rebbeh? [*Pronounced "reb be."*] What does he say to do? They are shooting Jews for no reason. Do you want some chocolate? I got it from one of the soldiers.

GIRL: You were outside?

BOY: Everyday now. I run errands for them. They like me.

GIRL: But you can't trust them.

BOY: I know.

GIRL: They shot the Rebbeh.

BOY: Oh no.

GIRL: They shot my father, too.

BOY: When?

GIRL: Yesterday. They lined them up in Shul. My mother was there. They made the women go outside.

BOY: Why didn't I hear? Why didn't anyone say?

GIRL: It's all happening too fast.

BOY: You shouldn't be out. You should be home.

GIRL: I had to get cheese for mother and I wanted to see you. No one is coming to see us. There are too many dead.

BOY: But you're not crying. You don't even look sad.

GIRL: Mother said not to look sad. She said to look as if nothing has happened. I shouldn't attract any attention to myself. If no one sees me, I won't be hurt.

BOY: I love you.

GIRL: Don't say that. I'll cry and that'll make mother mad.

BOY: I'll hold you.

GIRL: No, that isn't good, either. I can't be weak.

BOY: It's good to have someone hold you.

GIRL: Shh. I hear someone.

[*Lights up on* BOY'S MOTHER *looking out from the small window in her meager flat.*]

BOY'S MOTHER: Where is he? He should be home by now. I send him to buy the medicine and come back and he is gone too long. But he's too clever to be shot. He'll survive if no one else does. And he wouldn't run off to leave his mother and grandmother to die. So he must be with that sheyneh girl who thinks she's better than all of us because her father reads Torah every Sabbath.

GIRL: What is it?

BOY: A ghost.

GIRL: You believe in ghosts?

BOY: I believe I'll love you forever.

[*They kiss and cuddle.*]

BOY'S MOTHER: I'll kill him when he gets home. Making me worry as if I don't have enough to worry about. I look up to the sky and can see nothing. It is darkness. Not like before when I could see the stars and the moon promised I would be happy one day. But there are no more promises left for me. If I had married Alexander and moved to Odessa none of this—What if they have caught Sheldon? Oh God in heaven, what is going to happen to me?

SHELL: [*To* RUTH.] They don't so much talk as feel the fear of losing each other move through each of them. He's late and still he can't leave her. He wants to take her with him and something inside him says he can't. It's not just that he will have to hurry and she will slow him down. What is it?

RUTH: If no one sees me, I won't be hurt. That's what the girl said. I hide from you, Shelley.

[SHELL *kisses* RUTH'*s hand comfortingly.*]

RUTH: [*Cont'd.*] And you leave me.

GIRL: You go. I'll wait for you here. After you give the medicine to your mother say the butcher is making you take a delivery for him. Hurry. I'll wait for you here. Go, Sheldon Steinloff, and come back quickly.

[*Sounds of rifle shots.*]

BOY'S MOTHER: They are shooting by the pharmacy. [*Makes her way out of her "flat" and into the street.*]

BOY: I'll be back as soon as I can. [*Starts to go.*]

SHELL: He believes it would be his fault if a catastrophe happened and upset his mother.

GIRL: I don't want you to go. I'm scared.

[BOY *stops, returns to her.*]

SHELL: His mother is a woman of disaster and she feeds on him; the boy is her savior.

GIRL: Go, I'll wait for you. I will study. I can be brave and not worry. You will be back. I know you will.

SHELL: He turns from the girl and begins walking away. Something inside of him starts unraveling. He feels a breaking in his chest.

[BOY'S MOTHER *crosses upstage of her son and exits.* BOY *travels in the opposite direction.*]

SHELL: The girl does not move. She watches his back become smaller. She does not want to go home. She feels danger at home and in the streets. Her mother berates her and beats her for being clumsy and too tall and taking up too much space in their already too crowded lodging. She sleeps with her mother and hates it. Nothing is safe unless the boy is with her. She watches his back disappear. Her heart splinters into a thousand—

RUTH: [*Overlapping.*] NO!

GIRL: [*Screams.*] SHELDON!

[RUTH *is visibly upset.* SHELL *strokes her hand. Lights flicker on* GIRL, *her area blacks out. Sounds of bombing and sirens. The* BOY *doesn't hear her scream his name and continues on his journey.*]

SHELL: The boy hears the sirens and immediately thinks of her. She will have time to get indoors. She will have time, he tells himself. But he doesn't believe the words. He starts running back to where he left her. He runs faster than he's ever run in his life. He turns the corner.

[*Lights fade up on* GIRL, *curled in a ball on the street.*]

SHELL: [*Cont'd.*] There are people running in all directions. There is something in the middle of the street. He needs glasses but there's been no money. He can't make out the gray bundle lying ahead. He knows it's her. He knows. She's lying there. He left her and now she's lying there. Her eyes are open, looking at him, but her life is gone. He knew this would happen. He never loved anyone the way he loved her and he left.

[BOY *cradles* GIRL *in his arms, removes his mittens, strokes her face, hair. He weeps.*]

RUTH: This isn't happy, Shelley.

[*As* RUTH *and* SHELL *continue, the* BOY *lies down beside the* GIRL *and puts one hand under her head, the other around her chest. He pulls her close to him arranging her head on his shoulder.*]

SHELL: This is not the first time she's been left.

RUTH: You are going to leave.

SHELL: [*Trying to communicate to* RUTH.] Her soul knows this, knew this even as her mother was led away from her needing three-month-old body. So many times she's been left. Her soul does not count the times but remembers every one. Her soul does not count the times but remembers—

RUTH: I have to go to bed.

SHELL: Ruth, I'm not going to leave you.

[*Lights fade to ghosts on* BOY *and* GIRL.]

RUTH: That's not the story I wanted to hear.

SHELL: I can't control what comes out.

RUTH: Why not? You do in those romances you write.

SHELL: This is not a gothic romance.

RUTH: I know.

SHELL: Ruth, we're in this together.

RUTH: How can we be in this together if the girl dies?

SHELL: Maybe you have to write your own story.

RUTH: I'm not a writer.

SHELL: We both found the postcard. I think it's our way out.

RUTH: Our way out of what?

[*Police sirens blare. They both find the sirens amusing.*]

SHELL: Our way out of fear. You said we have to create a safe place.

RUTH: What I said was, I want to go somewhere where it will be easy. Shell, you're telling a story of a boy and girl destroyed by the Holocaust.

SHELL: Maybe it's about finding what can't be destroyed.

RUTH: You're always so optimistic.

[*Sirens slowly fade.*]

SHELL: That's why you love me.

RUTH: [*Beat.*] That's not the only reason.

SHELL: Tell me more.

RUTH: I do love you. [*Sits with her, affectionate.*] You love the quiet. You love sitting in it . . . being in it . . . you love to just stare out the window at the sky . . .

SHELL: Ruth, I'm not going to leave you.

RUTH: Don't you ever get scared? I know you do. I know just how you do.

SHELL: You should. You're the shrink.

RUTH: What is it, this thing?

[SHELL *signals she doesn't know.*]

RUTH: But you want to find out.

[SHELL *nods, "yes."*]

RUTH: I don't, Shelley.

SHELL: You know what makes tonight different from all other nights?

RUTH: It's Passover.

SHELL: Tonight we were given the sign to go into the wilderness and in our wanderings we will find God's commandments.

[SHELL *holds* RUTH. *They kiss and cuddle. There is the sound of a* WOMAN *crying and grieving. Lights up on* BOY *carrying* GIRL *to the* GIRL'S MOTHER'*s sitting room. The* GIRL'S MOTHER *sits, holds herself and rocks back and forth. The* BOY *lays the girl down with feet pointing downstage, lights candles and places candles at her head and feet. All this as . . .*]

RUTH: Someone's crying.

SHELL: It's the girl's mother.

RUTH: Maybe this is a dream.

SHELL: If it is, who's the dreamer?

RUTH: You're going to write, aren't you?

SHELL: Yes, I am.

RUTH: Well, I'm going to put my ear plugs in so I don't have to hear anything, not even the quiet.

SHELL: I wish you'd stay with me.

RUTH: I can't. I'm sorry. Did I lock the door?

SHELL: Yes, dear, I'm locked in.

[RUTH *exits.* SHELL *writes.*]

SHELL: The boy helps the girl's mother with the funeral arrangements. He pays for the wood in her grave with money he stole off a rich dead man in the street.

BOY: I'd like to say Kaddish for Helen Elaina at the service.

GIRL'S MOTHER: [*Wails.*] How can we have a service when the cemetery is not even ours anymore? They have my husband in a cart with others. No burial. No washing. There will be no marker. No sign of his living. Now my daughter. What am I going to do?

BOY: You could come and stay with us, Mrs. Klein.

SHELL: He knows she'll say no because of their class differences.

GIRL'S MOTHER: No.

BOY: [*Relieved.*] Thank you, God.

GIRL'S MOTHER: Say Kaddish for her now. Say it now while she and I can hear you. It will be our last blessing.

[*The* BOY *recites Kaddish through to the end of the scene as the* GIRL'S MOTHER *wails in grief and rocks back and forth.*]

SHELL: He remembers his beloved rocking that way. They had been kissing. Deeply. He had touched her small, just barely forming breast. She had offered her body willingly. Moving to his touch. Moving into his touch. He had gotten on top of her. Their boundaries had been melting, their bodies becoming one even with their clothes on. Suddenly she had started crying. He rolled onto his side and held her. Her head lay on his shoulder just as it had on the day of her death. Then she moved away. She could not allow herself to be touched. She sat and rocked to a rhythm he could not hear. She rocked the same as her mother now rocked next to him. She rocked and grieved over a death more ancient than memory.

GIRL'S MOTHER: [*As she speaks she beats the* BOY's *chest with her fists. He allows it at first then holds her wrists. She stops resisting and collapses into him. He holds her and continues reciting Kaddish as lights fade to black.*] You killed my baby. If she hadn't gone out to see you, she'd be alive. I knew she was going to see you. You destroyed her . . . dirty prost ways. She never stood in the streets until she met you. Never. She was home. Home. She was always home.

SHELL: Over time the pain of his leaving her becomes greater than the pain of her death.

Deep inside he always knew he would have to go.

He knew from a long time ago that his leaving was so he could return but only if he agreed to leave again.

It was his sacred covenant. It was the only way he thought he could love.

[BOY *enters the blank space outside the apartment and moves toward* SHELL.]

SHELL: [*Cont'd.*] He left to do the chores for his mother, that way he could return to the girl, whole, able to love again. He believed he had to go so he could return.

[*Unseen by* SHELL, *the* BOY *enters her space.*]

SHELL: [*Cont'd.*] But he died when he turned his back on love.

BOY: I never left.

[SHELL *turns around and sees the* BOY. *She moves toward him. At the same instant, the window near her desk shatters. When* SHELL *turns toward the window, the* BOY *exits.* RUTH *enters from the bedroom.*]

RUTH: What was that?

SHELL: [*To* RUTH.] The window shattered.

[*Blackout.*]

SCENE 2

RUTH's *office is distinguished by floor-to-ceiling, filled-to-the-brim bookcases.* DIANA, *sitting on the couch, is whistling.* RUTH *is in her chair. There are fresh flowers in a decorative vase on a pedestal.*

DIANA: What are you smiling at?

RUTH: You look very sweet when you don't want to tell me something.

DIANA: You really read all those books?

RUTH: Yes.

DIANA: I know, why'd the Santa Fean cross the street? [*Beat.*] Because he was channeling a chicken. [*Beat*]

Okay, okay, you want the good stuff. You want to know what happened last weekend. [*Whistles.*] I'm going to tell you, Ruth. I am. I want to. [*Takes a deep breath.*]

Robert and I made love Saturday night and I flipped out. I've never flipped out before. It started out I was relaxed, open, like always and then all of a sudden, out of the blue, everything got very dark and I felt like I had this infection running all over me, like there was something...I don't know. I had to stop. It was crazy. I felt like I could be really violent, like I could smash his face.

RUTH: Did you feel alone?

DIANA: I felt awful.

RUTH: Like you were locked up and no one could hear you?

[DIANA *is shocked that* RUTH *has identified her feeling.*]

RUTH: [*Cont'd.*] It's a very difficult feeling.

DIANA: I can't believe you know what I'm talking about. You do, don't you?

RUTH: Yes.

DIANA: I was so afraid if I didn't go on, he'd never want to make love with me again, so...

RUTH: That doesn't sound like Robert.

DIANA: Yeah, but that's what I was thinking.

RUTH: Maybe that's your mother's voice.

DIANA: I couldn't even let him comfort me.

RUTH: What were you afraid of?

DIANA: If I knew would I be paying you a hundred dollars an hour? [*Beat.*] Shit, I'm sorry.

RUTH: This is very important, Diana.

DIANA: I know. I've been waiting all week to talk to you about it and now that I'm here, I don't want to say a fucking thing.

RUTH: You're saying a lot.

DIANA: It's a fucking nightmare. Something's going on, and I don't know what to do. What are you looking at?

RUTH: I'm sad to see you in so much pain.

DIANA: Well, I'm scared to death to make love again. And it's not like I don't want to. Believe me.

RUTH: I believe you.

[DIANA *starts crying.*]

RUTH: [*Cont'd.*] What is it?

DIANA: It sounds so stupid.

RUTH: I don't think you could sound stupid.

DIANA: You said you believed me. No one has ever believed a god damn word I said.

RUTH: I know.

DIANA: Don't say that. I won't be able to stop.

RUTH: You don't have to.

DIANA: Yes I do.

RUTH: I'll hold you if you'd like.

[DIANA *hesitates then goes to her and puts her head in* RUTH's *lap and sobs.* RUTH *strokes her hair as . . .*
Making sure the coast is clear, the BOY *enters an alley in the ghetto. He motions to the* GIRL *that it's okay to join him. They sit in the doorway of building.*
RUTH *senses/hears the* BOY *and* GIRL *as if they were voices in her own mind. She does not see them, yet.*]

BOY: It's okay. We'll be safe here. No one will see us.

GIRL: It's not safe anywhere.

BOY: I bought you a present. Guess what it is? [*Gives her a package wrapped in news-paper.*]

GIRL: It's another book. Why are you so good to me? I don't give you anything.

BOY: You give me a reason to live.

GIRL: *The History of Civilization.* Sheldon, this is wonderful.

BOY: Open it.

GIRL: Gold!

BOY: It'll help you if you get in trouble.

GIRL: But what about you?

BOY: I can get more. [*Kisses her.*] I'm going to take care of you forever.

[*The* GIRL *kisses him deeply and then starts crying. He holds her, helps her sit, gives her his handkerchief, etc. as . . .*
DIANA *looks up at* RUTH, *feeling embarrassed, and goes back to her seat.*]

DIANA: What?

RUTH: I was wondering if anyone ever just held you and let you cry.

DIANA: You mean, like my mother? I held her is more like it.

RUTH: Because she was afraid?

DIANA: I guess so.

RUTH: What was she afraid of?

DIANA: Being alone. She could never be alone. She always had to be on top of everything I did. Everything. What? Your eyes are getting all teary again.

RUTH: Can you remember a time when you felt safe? When you felt cared for?

DIANA: [*Laughs.*] Me? [*Imitating DeNiro's* Taxi Driver.] You talking about me?

[*Sounds of soldiers talking and walking.* GIRL *and* BOY *leave the alley and hide among a pile of rubble and discarded household items.*]

RUTH: Do you believe that you deserved to have that?

DIANA: Deserve to feel safe? That's like asking if I deserve to win the lottery. Kind of doesn't matter, you know.

RUTH: It does matter.

DIANA: My father was a drunk, and my mother was either hysterical or being dragged off to the loony bin. Very caring. [*Beat.*] I know, I know, you want me to feel like I deserved it, but I can't. How am I going to fix things with Robert? I'm afraid I won't be able to.

RUTH: Talk to him.

DIANA: I do, but it's not enough. He wants me and I don't know where I am half the time and I can't fake it.

RUTH: We can try and feel some of your pain now if you want.

DIANA: Whatever gave you the idea that I was in pain?

RUTH: [*Smile.*] Why don't you close your eyes and try to go back and see yourself as a little girl.

[*Moments pass.* BOY *and* GIRL *come out of hiding and return to the doorway in the alley.*]

DIANA: Okay, I'm little.

RUTH: What do you see?

GIRL: I'm scared, Sheldon.

BOY: I know. So am I.

DIANA: I'm in the barn. I'm hiding. I've got my Raggedy-Anne doll. Mom and Dad were fighting and he left.

BOY: They lie to us.

GIRL: Everyone's afraid.

DIANA: I can see her through the slats. She's so beautiful in the moonlight. She calls my name. Diana Emily.

[GIRL'S MOTHER *enters a ghetto street nearby.*]

GIRL'S MOTHER: [*Harsh, loud whisper.*] Helen Elaina.

[*The* BOY *and* GIRL *hear her but do not see her. The* GIRL *gets up and looks for her. He tries to comfort her but she doesn't let him.*]

DIANA: "Where are you, Diana?" My doll says to run and never look back.

GIRL'S MOTHER: Where are you, Helen Elaina?

BOY: She won't find us.

[BOY, *again, tries to comfort* GIRL. *She won't let him.*]

DIANA: Mother comes into the barn. "Do you want me to hold you, Mother?"

GIRL'S MOTHER: Where are you? We must go.

DIANA: She sees me and starts yelling at me for leaving her alone with him.

[*The two units below happen simultaneously.*]

DIANA: . . . and I tell her I was scared and she sits next to me and starts crying and I want to run but I hold her.

GIRL: I must go to her.

BOY: No, please. [*He holds her. She struggles against him and then finally lets him hold her as . . .*]

DIANA: [*Continues.*] We sit there for hours and every time I try to get up she won't let me go. She won't let me go. I don't know what to do. I want to get away from her. [*Gets caught in the memory and can't continue.*]

GIRL'S MOTHER: I know you're with that boy. I'll find you. [*Exits.*]

GIRL: Let me go now. She needs me.

BOY: I want to be with you. I'd rather be dead than not be with you.

GIRL: If she finds me with you— [*Realizes she's never going to see him again.*]

DIANA: My father comes home. He's drunk and starts screaming at her.

GIRL: I'm never going to see you again, Sheldon. I know it. [*To* RUTH.] Please, help me.

[RUTH *looks at* GIRL, *then quickly back at* DIANA.]

DIANA: She picks up the pitch fork and throws it at him and it hits him in the leg. It bleeds and she runs to him and begs his forgiveness and then he says he's taking her somewhere where she can't hurt anyone and she starts screaming no.

GIRL: She's coming.

DIANA: He drags her off. I'm screaming for her not to go, for him not to take her away. I'm screaming no. [*Screams.*] NO!!!

[MOTHER *enters their space.* BOY *and* GIRL *freeze.*]

RUTH: Louder, Diana. Make them hear you.

[MOTHER *grabs* GIRL.]

DIANA: NO, GOD DAMN IT!!! LEAVE HER ALONE!!! LEAVE HER ALONE!!! LEAVE ME ALONE!!

[BOY *runs off as* DIANA *starts to cry.* MOTHER *sits in the alley doorway and makes* GIRL *sit in front of her on the sidewalk.*]

RUTH: That's good, Diana. You're not responsible for her. Not anymore.

[*Goes to her, kneels and holds her. Lights shift.* DIANA *exits as* RUTH *moves to her desk and begins reading from a log.*]

RUTH: [*Cont'd. Reading.*] Clients suffering from trauma are extremely defended against intimacy.

GIRL: I'm sorry, Mother.

GIRL'S MOTHER: What good is sorry if you get us killed!

[RUTH *hears the* GIRL, *sees her and her* MOTHER. *She is stunned by their emergence and tries to disperse them through her work.*]

RUTH: Clients will open fire if necessary to protect themselves.

GIRL'S MOTHER: Do you know how long I've been looking for you. [*Raps her on the head.*] Do you know? Do you?

RUTH: What will trigger development...

GIRL: Please, Mother.

RUTH: ...will also expose the wound.

GIRL'S MOTHER: They're coming for everyone. Everyone. Do you hear? You come to see him, and you get us all killed. We must go.

[MOTHER *gets up and pulls her by the hair toward the exit.*]

GIRL: Seeing Sheldon cannot hurt anyone.

GIRL'S MOTHER: You have nothing to say. Remember that.

GIRL: No.

[*Fire alarms go off.* RUTH, *the* GIRL, *and* MOTHER *are all startled.* RUTH *stands. For a few moments,* RUTH *is not sure where she is. Sounds near of a crowd on cobblestones marching and shuffling.* RUTH *at her desk is the crowd to the* GIRL *and her* MOTHER.]

GIRL'S MOTHER: Don't look at them, look straight ahead.

GIRL: Mother, they are Jews.

[GIRL *breaks free and runs toward* RUTH. GIRL'S MOTHER *runs after her and catches her by the hair. They have penetrated* RUTH'S *space.* RUTH *sees the* GIRL *but tries to continue her work.* RUTH *unconsciously strokes her hair, unconsciously feeling the pain of it being pulled.*]

RUTH: Gaining Diana's trust is essential.

GIRL'S MOTHER: [*Pulls her by the hair in the direction opposite of* RUTH'S *office.*] I should kill you and make my life easier. No one would be the wiser. Stand up straight and keep your head down. Don't speak. You hunch like that and everyone will know you're afraid of them.

GIRL: [*Overlapping.*] Please, mother, you're hurting me. Please...it hurts.

GIRL'S MOTHER: I am helping you live. Remember that. Walk.

[*They exit.*]

RUTH: [*Still touching her hair but hard-focused on her work.*] We must open the door to the self which cannot be victimized.

[*Blackout.*]

SCENE 3

The window that shattered is now covered by plywood.
    SHELL *is writing. There is the sound of keys opening locks.* RUTH *enters.* SHELL *gets up to help* RUTH *with her coat.*
    RUTH *locks the inside lock.*

SHELL: You're home early.

RUTH: I had a cancellation. She drives in from Great Neck. We're supposed to get six inches tonight.

SHELL: The news is calling it the longest winter on record.

RUTH: Why hasn't my window been fixed?

SHELL: Excuse me?

RUTH: If the super was going to put up plywood, he just as easily could have fixed it.

SHELL: [*Realizing* RUTH *is not in the best of moods.*] I went out for a run and came back and the super was boarding it up. He just left a bit ago. It's the third window in the building it's happened to this week so we shouldn't feel special.

RUTH: He said that?

SHELL: Not the special part. [*Trying for sympathy.*] You know, I'm lucky. I could have been sitting there when it happened.

[*Sounds of a jet overhead.* RUTH *tries to see through cracks in the plywood.*]

RUTH: But you weren't.

SHELL: Thanks for the concern.

[*Beat.* RUTH *looks at her.*]

SHELL: [*Cont'd.*] He's ordered the glass. It'll be fixed in a day or two. How was your day?

RUTH: I'm going to have a drink. You want one?

SHELL: No. I'm going to work some more.

RUTH: Go ahead, I won't bother you.

SHELL: Good, don't.

[RUTH *exits and* SHELL *goes back to work.* SHELL's *upset.* RUTH *returns with a drink.*]

RUTH: I'm sorry. I was selfish. It's your window too. You could have been hurt.

SHELL: I look out that window all the time. I get ideas looking out that window.

RUTH: Well, maybe we have enough ideas right now. [*Beat.*] I saw the woman who reminds me of me.

SHELL: Woman who reminds you of you. With a name like that she could be Native American. Ruth, you're shaking.

RUTH: Maybe I'm still cold.

[SHELL *rubs her back to get her circulation going.*]

RUTH: [*Cont'd.*] I want to blame all this on you. I do. I saw the girl and her mother and the boy. I sensed them the whole session and I don't like it. [*Pause.*] Is that what it's like when you write? You just see and hear these people?

SHELL: That's pretty much what it is, but these people are different.

RUTH: How?

SHELL: They're alive.

[RUTH *finishes her drink in one swallow.*]

SHELL: [*Cont'd.*] That scares you?

[RUTH *chooses not to respond to the obvious.*]

SHELL: [*Cont'd.*] Well, I know your mother was in and out of the loony bin for her paranoia.

RUTH: [*Cruelly.*] Sometimes you can be so stupid. [*Pause.*] I'm sorry.

SHELL: Me too. What happened?

RUTH: Did you miss me today?

SHELL: As a matter of fact, I did. I couldn't write.

RUTH: You only miss me when you're stuck! How comforting!

SHELL: No. I don't know why the boy leaves her.

RUTH: Ask him.

SHELL: He said he never left.

[*Car alarm goes off.* RUTH *jumps.*]

RUTH: Maybe it is time to move.

SHELL: You haven't told me what happened with you.

RUTH: [*Sarcastic.*] Nothing much. The girl and her mother had to leave the ghetto. The girl had to say good-bye to the boy. Nothing much.

SHELL: Ruth, talk to me.

RUTH: She leaves him. Does that mean I'm going to leave you? I don't want to. I've never loved anyone the way I love you.

SHELL: Maybe that's why this is happening.

RUTH: Because I have to leave you?

SHELL: Because we love each other so deeply.

RUTH: I don't follow.

SHELL: All I know is I have to stay with this and I think you do, too.

[*Lights fade up on the* GIRL *and her* MOTHER *approaching a pile of garbage in a ghetto street. There are sounds of people walking, gun shots.*]

RUTH: Do you hear them?

[SHELLEY *nods and leads* RUTH *to the couch as . . .*]

GIRL'S MOTHER: Get in there.

GIRL: It's garbage, Mother. It's awful.

GIRL'S MOTHER: Get in there. Hurry. Quietly. And leave room for me.

GIRL: It smells.

GIRL'S MOTHER: And you think you smell sweet. [*Climbing in.*]

GIRL: Mother, please, I can't move.

GIRL'S MOTHER: Good. Don't. Sssh. Someone's coming. Don't move.

GIRL: I can't breathe. I have no room. You're too heavy. You're crushing me.

GIRL'S MOTHER: You would rather be dead than bear my weight? Fool. I am saving us. Sssh. Someone is coming.

[*The* BOY *enters and searches the area.*]

BOY: Helen Elaina, are you there? Helen Elaina? I have food. I have found a way out for us. I miss you so much. Oh God, let me find her. If her mother's taken her away, I'll die. Helen Elaina, I've found a place for us to hide. We'll be safe until we can get out. I want to take care of you. Oh where are you? God, please let me find her.

[BOY *races off.* MOTHER *rolls out of the hiding place with the* GIRL. *She brushes the garbage off the* GIRL *and herself.*]

GIRL'S MOTHER: He is not the right kind of boy for you. He doesn't study Torah. And his father before him didn't study Torah. Dirty ways.

GIRL: He is good. Ouch!

GIRL'S MOTHER: I know what is best for you. Don't talk. Your voice will get us killed, it's so shrill. Come here. You must eat.

[MOTHER *gives* GIRL *bread and cheese, takes none for herself.* GIRL *offers her some.* MOTHER *declines.*]

GIRL'S MOTHER: [*Cont'd.*] You need the food. I don't. This food is my sacrifice to your greatness. You will grow up and I will be proud of you. You will be great. It's in your eyes. You have the brains of greatness. Amen. Eat. We'll sleep in there tonight and tomorrow we'll go to Uncle Issac's farm in Lvov.

GIRL: I don't want to sleep in garbage.

GIRL'S MOTHER: What was that? Did you hear something?

GIRL: No, mother.

GIRL'S MOTHER: Eat. Don't look at me. Keep your head down.

[*Lights fade to black on* GIRL *and* MOTHER.]

RUTH: You saw all that.

[SHELL *nods "yes."*]

RUTH: [*Cont'd.*] I'm afraid it'll get so I can't concenetrate in my sessions. If I had made a mistake with Diana today, she was in such a fragile place . . .

SHELL: I'll pretend I didn't hear that.

RUTH: What? Oh God, I said her name. I did, didn't I? I never do that.

SHELL: You didn't say her last name.

[*Pause.* RUTH *gets up.*]

RUTH: I'll leave you alone so you can work.

SHELL: I can work with you here.

[*Sirens. Sounds of gun shots.*]

RUTH: I can't even look out the window to see what's going on.

SHELL: We could never see anything, anyway.

RUTH: The angel of death.

SHELL: Of liberation.

RUTH: I think I'll take a shower and read in bed.

SHELL: I love you, Ruth. It's going to be okay.

[RUTH *goes to* SHELL *and kisses her gently on the lips. After a moment, they share a long passionate kiss that expresses their fear. They slowly part.* RUTH *exits.* SHELL *paces and tries to look through the cracks in the plywood-covered window.*]

SHELL: The boy wants to hold himself and cry over his lost love but there is no time. She is dead. The girl is never coming back. He is exploding inside and there is no time to grieve.

[*Sound of a woman crying, grieving.*]

SHELL: [*To the unseen, crying woman.*] Who are you?

[*Lights up slowly on the* BOY'S MOTHER *as she looks out her window and sees the* BOY *approaching their humble, and in her eyes distasteful, home.*]

SHELL: When the boy gets home, he presents his mother with the medicine for the grandmother, and his mother slaps him across the face.

[*The* BOY *enters.* MOTHER *slaps him and takes the medicine.*]

BOY'S MOTHER: I have been worried sick.

SHELL: The boy runs to his corner of the living room.

[MOTHER *slowly follows after the* BOY. SHELL *follows their movements.*]

SHELL: He wants his own room. The grandmother is coughing her lungs out in the room he wishes was his. In his mind he sees her endless spitting of blood into the three handkerchiefs his mother washes out every night and hangs to dry so they'll be ready in the morning to again receive the old woman's blood. He wants her to die.

His mother's shadow looms over him as he squats in the corner holding himself.

MOTHER: I want to know how you could do such a thing to me. Is it you think I don't deserve any better? Your own mother?

BOY: I got everything you wanted. And the chicken is big.

MOTHER: You were with that girl. She does awful things to you. Makes you not want to be my son.

BOY: I want to be your son. I am your son. And I love you with all my heart and I would do anything for you.

MOTHER: You're such a good boy when you want to be but you'd rather be with that girl.

BOY: No, mother—

MOTHER: And for that I can't forgive you.

BOY: She's good.

MOTHER: Do you know what I do all day to keep body and soul together? I wash the undergarments of the filthy pigs who are destroying our lives.

BOY: Oh mother, don't cry.

MOTHER: I'm not crying.

BOY: Yes, you are. I'm sorry I hurt you. I swear I never will again. I'll always be here for you.

MOTHER: What's going to happen to me?

BOY: I'll take care of you.

MOTHER: I hear your father. Go see if it's him.

BOY: [*Looks, sees* SHELL.] Yes.

MOTHER: Tell him to come up.

BOY: [*To* SHELL.] Father, come up. Mother wants you.

[SHELL *realizes the* BOY *is talking to her. She panics.*]

BOY: [*Cont'd.*] I think it's important. You better come. She's not in the best mood.

[SHELL *leaves her space and joins them.*]

BOY: [*Cont'd.*] He's coming.

MOTHER: It's about time. He must think he's the only one who's life is unbearable. [*To* SHELL.] Father, take off your belt. You heard me, take off your belt and beat your son. He was late and made me worry and someone has to teach him to obey his mother and father. Don't look at me like that.

BOY: No, Father, I promise, I'll never do it again.

SHELL: [*Surprised at her perplexing situation.*] What?

BOY: Helen Elaina. I was with her and it made me late. She was killed, Father.

MOTHER: Then she is lucky to be taken from this nightmare. Beat your son, father. You want him to be a mench?

SHELL: He already is a mench.

[*As* MOTHER *lays into* SHELL, BOY *creeps back to his corner, holds himself and cries over his lost love.*]

MOTHER: What kind of a father are you? What are you doing to get us out of here? What kind of life can we expect to have? You think the Germans won't get tired of ordering you around and shoot you and then what? And then your son won't come home either. One day neither one of you will come home and where will I be? He'll run off with that girl.

SHELL: No, he won't.

MOTHER: What do you know?

SHELL: He won't, I tell you!

BOY: Please, Mother, please, I'll do whatever you want. I want you to be happy again like before.

MOTHER: When was I ever happy? You think your father makes me happy. If you don't beat your son, Mikhail Steinloff, I swear to you I'll tell all the women in the square tomorrow how you are not a man, how... [*Sees she's getting her way.*]

[SHELL *takes off her belt.*]

MOTHER: [*Cont'd.*] how there is to be no reason left in this family of ours.

BOY: Father, please.

[*Rifle shots.*]

MOTHER: Use it! Go ahead. What are you waiting for?

[SHELL *is ready.*]

MOTHER: [*Cont'd.*] Sheldon, take your punishment. You will learn to honor your father and mother.

[*The* BOY *stands and lowers his pants and bends slightly from the waist. More rifle shots as* SHELL *whips the* BOY.]

BOY: I will make it up to you. I will not feel the sting of his belt on my thighs. I will get out of here. I will not feel the sting of his belt on my thighs. I will live. I will live for you.

[*Rifle shots cease.* SHELL *stops.*]

MOTHER: Now let's get you cleaned up. You look like a beggar.

[*The* BOY *and* MOTHER *exit. The set remains.*
    SHELL *is left holding her belt. She doesn't know what to do with it. She slowly moves back to her desk.*]

SHELL: I could feel his flesh move... her fear, like salt, tightening my skin, her sweat. [*Wipes her sweat from her arm.*]

[RUTH *enters in a nightgown.*]

SHELL: [*Cont'd.*] I will live for you. He would do anything for her. I beat him.

RUTH: Shell, what happened?

SHELL: Oh my God, you scared me.

RUTH: What happened?

SHELL: Oh God.

RUTH: Talk to me.

SHELL: I beat the boy.

RUTH: What?

SHELL: I did. I beat him.

RUTH: No, you didn't. You just imagined you did.

SHELL: I did, god damn it. They were right there.

[*The* BOY *re-enters, goes to his corner and gets in the bedroll.* RUTH *and* SHELL *both see him.*]

RUTH: [*Protesting the whole thing.*] No.

SHELL: What do you want? I'm working.

RUTH: Don't yell at me.

SHELL: I'm sorry.

RUTH: What's going on?

SHELL: I don't know.

RUTH: You have to know.

SHELL: Why do I fucking have to know?

RUTH: Because you started this.

SHELL: I didn't start anything.

RUTH: Are you going to get consumed by this? Is that how you're going to leave me?

SHELL: Can't you think of someone besides yourself?

[RUTH *starts off.*]

SHELL: [*Cont'd.*] Fuck. Ruth, come back. Please. Ruth, please.

[RUTH *stops.*]

SHELL: We have to have faith.

RUTH: Are you through working?

[SHELL *shakes her head "no."* RUTH *exits.* SHELL *looks at the* BOY. *The* MOTHER *enters and moves toward the* BOY. *She does not reach him before the end of the scene.*]

BOY: I lie in my bedroll by the wall. I cry so no one will hear. My mother comes out from the bedroom in her nightgown. She sits on the floor next to my head. She strokes my hair.

SHELL: NO MORE!

[*Blackout on* MOTHER *and* BOY. SHELL *collapses into her chair. Blackout.*]

SCENE 4

RUTH *is setting the table for dinner: place mats, ceramic dishes, flowers.* SHELLY *brings out the salad and a bottle of wine. She opens the wine.*

SHELL: I got us a Nouveau Beaujolais.

RUTH: Good. Dinner will be ready soon.

SHELL: Roast lamb and wild rice is my most favorite smell in the whole world outside of you.

RUTH: Did you see the super today?

SHELL: He's sick. He said he'd try and fix the window tomorrow.

RUTH: Did you write today?

SHELL: No. I was afraid to. [*Beat.*] Anything?

RUTH: No, thankfully.

SHELL: I think it'll stop if we want it to. I think we can have some control.

RUTH: But you don't want it to stop.

SHELL: I don't know.

RUTH: I heard a woman crying again.

SHELL: The girl's mother?

RUTH: I don't know who it was. I cleaned my office while I waited for my next client. I listened to music. I'm afraid of what I might do if I can't . . .

SHELL: If you can't what?

RUTH: It feels like I could lose control, Shell.

SHELL: I feel that way too.

RUTH: Don't say that. You're supposed to say we will be able to control what we need to.

SHELL: I know that's what I always say but I don't think we can this time.

RUTH: Can't you just take care of it?

[SHELL *is despondent.*]

RUTH: [*Cont'd.*] It's not fair that I've given you all this responsibility . . .

[*Beat. They exchange loving glances.*]

RUTH: [*Cont'd.*] How come you knew before it was going to be okay and you don't know now?

SHELL: It's gotten bigger than I am. It's not just about my writing. They are alive and they need things from us.

RUTH: Well, we'll just have to put our foot down and stop it.

SHELL: [*Lightly.*] I'm with you. Cheers.

RUTH: We won't think about it.

SHELL: To not thinking about it.

[*They clink glasses.*]

SHELL: [*Cont'd.*] We don't have a choice.

RUTH: We always have a choice.

SHELL: We chose the postcard.

RUTH: So we'll unchoose it.

SHELL: Can't.

RUTH: See. You want it to continue.

SHELL: Not tonight.

RUTH: I'll get the roast.

[RUTH *goes off.* SHELL *gets two candle holders and puts in two candles.* RUTH *reenters.*]

SHELL: It's kind of like our second date, except you made chicken.

RUTH: And I was lighting the candles when you knocked.

SHELL: In that case, I'll leave.

RUTH: Don't go.

SHELL: I'm not going anywhere. [SHELL *gives her the matches and tries to go out but the door is locked.*] I need the key.

[RUTH *unlocks the door with the key that's around her neck, then comes back and lights the candles, smiling hopefully.* SHELL *knocks.*]

RUTH: [*Goes to door and lets her in.*] Hi. Come in.

SHELL: Hi. Nice place.

RUTH: Thanks. It's small, but—

SHELL: But it's yours. You own it?

RUTH: Yes.

SHELL: Mazel tov!

RUTH: [*Breaking the spell.*] Shelley . . .

SHELL: Shh. [*Kisses her lightly then back into the past.*] So, you got all this at the deli?

RUTH: [*Shy, embarrassed.*] No. I decided I felt like cooking.

SHELL: So, you're a cook, too. Martha didn't mention that when she was singing your praises.

RUTH: Speaking of Martha, there's been a change in plans for tonight. I debated whether to call you.

SHELL: So this meal isn't for me? You're canceling and I'm going to eat deli food? I hate—

RUTH: [*Overlapping.*] Martha is not going to the benefit tonight and I know you weren't crazy about going so I wanted to give you the choice or rather I thought [*Shyly says "we."*] we could talk about a Plan B.

SHELL: [*Touched by her shyness, then playful.*] Well, seeing as it's a benefit for an AIDS group I've never heard of and it's a play by Susan Sontag . . . just one of those would be enough for me to pass—

RUTH: Martha said you liked plays.

SHELL: I do. But a Susan Sontag play would be like watching paint dry.

RUTH: You're very funny.

SHELL: Did Martha tell you that too? Why do you think we're doing this? I mean I know this isn't a date, because God knows neither of us wants to go out on a date with each other because like all good lesbians we'd move in with each other on the second one.

RUTH: We did. [*Laughs shyly.*]

SHELL: We did not. It was the fifth one. Shh.

[*Back to the past.*]

SHELL: [*Cont'd.*] So this is casual, what we're doing. Some easy, no preparation food—how long did it take for you to make all this?

[RUTH *is too embarrassed to answer.*]

SHELL: [*Cont'd.*] And later, we'll nap, sitting up, while the enlightened of the earth discuss the meaning of life and death in the age of AIDS.

RUTH: Were you asking me a question?

SHELL: Why are we doing this if we don't like each other? After our first date, we both told Martha we wouldn't waste our time.

RUTH: Are you hungry?

SHELL: [*Shyly.*] Yes. These plates yours too?

RUTH: [*Surprised by question.*] Yes.

SHELL: Mazel tov.

RUTH: Would you like me to serve you?

SHELL: [*Suddenly filled with a rush of sexual excitement.*] Yes, I would.

[RUTH *serves her.* SHELL *can't take her eyes off her.* RUTH *becomes self-conscious, looks at her.*]

SHELL: [*Cont'd.*] You changed your mind about me. Why?

RUTH: Martha said you were funny and kind. I thought my perception of you might be wrong. Happens sometimes.

SHELL: Only sometimes? [*Beat.*] I was too nervous before to be funny. I've thought of going out with you for the past four years, but either I was with someone or you were sending out not interested signals.

RUTH: I haven't been interested in seeing anyone.

SHELL: And that's changed?

RUTH: I guess. You're not eating.

SHELL: You do Jewish mothers too? [*Resumes eating, then stops again and stares at* RUTH.]

[RUTH *sees* SHELL *staring at her.*]

SHELL: [*Cont'd.*] I can't help looking at you. You're very beautiful.

RUTH: I don't know what to say.

SHELL: You could say thank you.

RUTH: Thank you.

SHELL: You're welcome.

RUTH: Well, I've been aware of you too since I first met you. Is it four years already? And I've always thought you were attractive. Is it warm in here?

SHELL: Yes.

RUTH: Must be the . . . broiled chicken.

[*They both laugh; then the following silence becomes charged.*]

RUTH: [*Cont'd.*] Shall we go?

SHELL: To watch paint dry?

RUTH: We could do something else.

SHELL: I don't know what to say.

RUTH: About what?

SHELL: About being here with you. It feels very good. [*Beat.*] I'll help you put the food away. Maybe we'll be hungry after— [*Realizes she shouldn't say "we".*] I mean you'll have food for the week.

RUTH: Maybe *we* will . . . be hungry after.

[*As she gets up,* RUTH *puts her hand on* SHELL*'s shoulder. The contact is electric for both of them.* RUTH *then slowly clears the table.*]

SHELL: Watching you move that night was like watching a ballet, except I was on stage too. You leaned over the table, self conscious of my looking at you and enjoying it. You had opened your shirt an extra button, enough for me to see the swellings of your breasts. Your movements were slow, precise. Your eyes shyly brushed over mine. I grew to twice my size in your gaze.

[RUTH *exits with dishes.*]

SHELL: [*Stands to continue to reach out to* RUTH] The room became very animated. The table was aglow with colors I'd never seen before, colors I could feel on my skin. The air was a warm gel . . .

[RUTH *reenters. They connect again and become completely still.*]

SHELL: [*Cont'd.*] ferrying us to another dimension. We were meeting again. Our bodies merging without even touching. We had known each other before this moment. Known each others' souls. We knew this. We knew we had to be together.

[SHELL *slowly moves toward* RUTH.]

RUTH: Popcorn. [*Beat.*] I think we should eat popcorn and watch TV. I'll get it. [*Goes off.*]

[SHELL *is hurt, crushed.* RUTH *reenters with popcorn.*]

RUTH: Want some?

SHELL: No.

RUTH: Don't be mad.

[SHELL *sits in her desk chair, tears falling from her eyes.* RUTH *joins her, kneels.*]

RUTH: I hurt you just now.

SHELL: They need our help. There's no accident we found the card. They knew we could help them. They knew we knew.

[RUTH *walks away from her.*]

SHELL: Ruth, we have to give them a home. We won't be able to rest unless we do. They are us.

RUTH: Be careful, Shelley.

SHELL: What?

RUTH: Just be careful.

SHELL: I don't understand.

RUTH: Don't tell me what I have to do.

SHELL: You know as well as I do—

RUTH: Please, it's been a nice evening, let's not spoil it. I'm going to read. [*Goes to re-lock front door from the inside.*]

SHELL: Don't lock the door. I'm not going to leave you, and if I was, that stupid game you play with the key wouldn't stop me.

[RUTH *locks door with her key.* SHELL *goes to her.*]

SHELL: Give me the key, Ruth. Give it to me.

[RUTH, *afraid of what she'll do if she stays, starts to leave the room.*]

SHELL: [*Cont'd.*] You fucking leave but you expect me to stay. How long will you be gone this time?

RUTH: You have no idea who I am or what I need.

SHELL: Poor martyr. I'm so sick of bending over backwards to make sure you're okay. You're not that fragile. You don't need the key. WE don't need it.

[RUTH *continues to go off.* SHELL *grabs her arm.*]

SHELL: [*Cont'd.*] Give me the key.

RUTH: Take your hand off me.

SHELL: [*Let's go.*] Give it to me.

RUTH: I hate you for doing this.

SHELL: I'd rather have you hate me than we both pretend you're some kind of emotional invalid.

[RUTH *throws the key at* SHELL *which hits her in the head and causes bleeding.*]

RUTH: You've destroyed everything You should have just left. It would have been kinder. Don't bother to come back this time.

SHELL: I'M NOT THE ONE WHO'S LEAVING!!

[RUTH *exits.* SHELL *goes to her desk and begins packing up her laptop, her notes, pads, etc., as the* BOY *enters through blank space and goes to* SHELL. *He takes the laptop and holds it to his chest.*]

SHELL: [*Cont'd.*] What do you want? [*Beat.*] WHAT DO YOU WANT?

[*Blackout.*]

ACT II
SCENE 1

RUTH's *office. It is dark. We can barely see* RUTH *asleep on the couch. We only hear the voice of the* GIRL. *There are no flowers in the vase.*

GIRL: [*Offstage.*] Where are you? Mother, please, tell me where you are. I've looked everywhere.

[*Lights up on an area that looks like a barn complete with hayloft.* GIRL *enters the area with a candle.*]

GIRL: [*Cont'd.*] If you went to town, you should have told me. I don't want to wake up Uncle Issac. I'd have to leave the barn, and you told me not to, so I won't, but you should have told me, Mother. Why did you leave me?

[*Lights up on* RUTH *as she bolts awake.* GIRL *leaves the barn and goes into* RUTH's *office.*]

GIRL: [*Cont'd.*] Have you seen my mother? She left me. Have you seen her?

RUTH: No. Go away. Please.

GIRL: Will you help me find her?

RUTH: What are you doing here?

GIRL: My Uncle Issac is hiding us in the barn. I was asleep, but a bad dream woke me up and Mother was gone. Did she tell you where she was going? Please help me. Please. I'm afraid something awful has happened. She always pins a note to my panties if she leaves. Not always. Sometimes she forgets. She's sick. [*Points to her head.*]

RUTH: You're not happy she's gone? She doesn't let you breathe without her.

GIRL: That's because she's afraid of what might happen to me.

RUTH: Of what might happen to her.

GIRL: Can you help me? Can you?

RUTH: Why would she leave and not tell you?

GIRL: To test me. To see how strong I am. To see if I really love her.

RUTH: To see if you'll wait for her.

GIRL: I always do. I work. I study. I'm going to be a great doctor one day. I will have read every book in the world.

[RUTH *regards her own bookcases. Sound of the woman crying/grieving. They both hear her.* GIRL *becomes frantic.*]

GIRL: [*Cont'd.*] Make her stop crying. I know you hear her. It's why you hear me. Please, make her stop. You must. You must.

RUTH: [*Overlapping, comforting her.*] Shh. Quiet. It's okay. I don't know who she is or why she's crying. I don't even know why you're here.

GIRL: Because you asked me.

RUTH: I did not. I'm sorry, but I wouldn't do this. I have clients and a practice—

GIRL: [*Overlapping.*] I'm reading Freud. *Civilization and Its Dicontents.* My aunt at the farm brings me books. I've already learned German, to read it, not to speak it. I don't like Freud. He's like you. He doesn't know how to believe in God, not really. God doesn't make him feel good about people.

[RUTH *is frustrated, not wanting to participate.*]

GIRL: [*Cont'd.*] I talk to God but it's gotten hard to hear anything back. I just hear the woman crying.

RUTH: [*Barks at her.*] Who is she?

[GIRL *is shocked by* RUTH'*s bark.*]

RUTH: [*Cont'd.*] Who's crying?

GIRL: Sometime's I think she's God's mother and other times I think she's his wife and they're having a fight. All I know is God's very unhappy about things because he can't do anything.

RUTH: Then why do you believe in him?

GIRL: I love him. He told me he doesn't have anymore words left.

RUTH: [*Looking at her watch, realizing she must get ready for her first client of the day.*] Well, neither do I.

GIRL: But if she keeps crying there will be great floods and if she can't stop after that, there will be earthquakes from her shaking inside and then tornadoes... you have to stop her.

RUTH: You have to go now.

GIRL: No, you have to help me find my mother.

RUTH: I can't.

GIRL: You don't know that.

RUTH: I know it's easier to be alone and not need anyone. That's what I know. That's all I can teach you.

GIRL: She left because she knows I hate her.

[*Beat.* RUTH *decides to ignore her and goes about tidying her office.*]

GIRL: [*Cont'd.*] I already know how to be alone. You have something else to give me.

[*They have eye contact, then the* GIRL *slowly goes back to the barn as lights fade along with the sound of the woman crying.*]

SCENE 2

SHELL *is at her desk trying to work on one of her gothic romances, not the story of the postcard. The* BOY *is pacing in her area. She finds his presence very distracting.*

SHELL: Look, I'm not working on your story right now, okay? Ruth hasn't been home in a week.

BOY: And you haven't worked on the story in a week.

SHELL: Be grateful I'm not blaming you for her leaving. I'd rather write a gothic romance right now, for obvious reasons.

BOY: I want you to send it out.

SHELL: Send what out?

BOY: The story of me and Helen Elaina.

SHELL: I'd rather have hemorrhoids!

BOY: You have to send it out.

SHELL: I'll lose Ruth if I send it out.

BOY: If you don't send it out, I'll leave.

SHELL: You forgot to strike a pose. [*Feigns melodrama.*] I can't believe you're serious. What if I send it out and it gets published?

BOY: It will.

SHELL: Great. I finally write something that can be called art and I can't do anything with it.

BOY: You want me to leave?

SHELL: You're issuing an ultimatum? You or Ruth?

BOY: You don't know you'll lose her.

SHELL: That's what you think. [*Beat.*] Why should I send it out?

BOY: Because people need to know there's happiness even with all this mess. They need to know it can't be destroyed. Let's go to work.

[*Lights begin to change as the* BOY's *living room set comes on stage. The sounds of a woman crying come up faintly. The* BOY *makes his way to his corner and his bedroll as . . .*]

BOY: [*Cont'd.*] Trust me. I have your best interests in mind.

[BOY *gets into his bedroll. His* MOTHER, *in a nightgown, slowly approaches him. The scene becomes a continuation of the end of Act I, Scene 3.*]

SHELL: The boy lies in his bedroll by the wall. He cries so no one will hear. The noise of his father's snoring helps to drown out the sounds he has been hearing since before his memory. Sounds he thinks are his grandmother's coughing but when she is quiet they are still there. The sound is of a woman crying. He must find the girl.

The other family that was in the three small rooms with them have been taken away. He is happy there is less noise in the house, but also he is frightened. His mother has come out of the bedroom and has sat down on the floor next to his head. She strokes his hair.

BOY'S MOTHER: You must learn to obey your parents. When you're grown, you'll know about discipline and you'll thank us.

SHELL: The boy reaches out and pulls himself into his mother's lap and buries his sobs in the folds of her nightgown.

BOY: The girl died.

MOTHER: What did you say, son?

BOY: [*Choking on his sobs.*] The girl died and it's my fault.

MOTHER: How could it be your fault? Everywhere people like her are dying. She's better off dead, she's a Jew. They would be coming for her any day.

BOY: But we're Jews, mother.

MOTHER: We're different. We look Polish. We'll survive. They're better off dead. Nothing but misery. Nothing to live for. [*Strokes his head.*] You will have everything to live for.

SHELL: He knows his mother is wrong. She always thinks she is special. She can't see that they too will disappear or be shot like what is happening everyday all around them.

MOTHER: Would you massage my neck for me, Sheldon? It is very sore.

[BOY *massages her neck.*]

MOTHER: [*Cont'd.*] You have the best hands.

SHELL: It is that night that the boy begins to plot their escape. He will provide for his parents until they are safe, then he will set off on his own and become a different person. He has to. He knows if he stays he will become just like his mother, bending people to his will without regard for their needs.

[*As lights fade on* MOTHER *and* BOY, MOTHER *gets into the bedroll with the* BOY. *The sound of the woman's crying gets louder.* SHELL *is mesmerized by what she sees and hears.*]

SHELL: [*Cont'd.*] The boy doesn't know the seeds from his mother and father have already sprouted, that he has been watering them for centuries.

[*Faint sound of woman crying fades out.*]

SCENE 3

DIANA has arrived and a session with RUTH *is in progress. The* GIRL *is in the hayloft reading by candlelight.*

DIANA: Is it a crime to not want to talk about my mother? I am so sick of talking about my mother.

RUTH: You know your unresolved issues with your mother are affecting your life today.

[DIANA *whistles.*]

RUTH: [*Cont'd.*] I'm going to call you my whistler.

DIANA: Nobody else you see uses this tactic to avoid the you know what?

RUTH: No. You're unique.

DIANA: I knew it. I always knew it. Well, that's taken care of. I can stop therapy now. Thank you, Ruth.

RUTH: Do you want to stop?

DIANA: I don't want to stop seeing you.

RUTH: But?

DIANA: I'm so scared. It's getting worse instead of better. Maybe we're doing something wrong.

RUTH: I saved this article for you. [*Hands her a copy of a magazine article.*]

DIANA: Pain is the soul's signal that it needs healing. Oh great!

RUTH: I think you'll enjoy it.

DIANA: The healing? Not so far. Especially since I keep feeling like I'm dying. I know, I know, I'll arise from the ashes of the phoenix. Sometimes I wish I was like Robert. When he wants to be close to me, he just tells me. It's not complicated. His erections aren't complicated. His orgasms aren't complicated. I'm a fucking basket case.

RUTH: What's happening in your body, Diana?

DIANA: Body? Do I have a body?

RUTH: Go inside your body, Diana. Close your eyes if you want. Try and see if anything comes up. Any image.

DIANA: [*Closes her eyes, sees something, becomes very scared.*] I'm back in the barn. I'm hiding. In the hayloft.

GIRL: Her mother turns on her.

DIANA: My mother comes into the barn. I don't see her. I smell her. I know that smell. It's so sweet... but I'm afraid... no... [*Starts crying.*]

RUTH: Stay with it, Diana. What do you see?

GIRL: She can't. Her mother's smell is her perfume.

[RUTH *looks at girl as . . .*]

DIANA: [*Opens her eyes.*] I can't.

RUTH: I'd like to hold your hands, Diana, so I can stay attuned to you better.

[DIANA *gives her her hands.*]

GIRL: I wish you'd hold my hands. Oh, no, I think she's coming.

RUTH: What happened in the barn?

DIANA: I can't do it, Ruth.

RUTH: What was the smell?

GIRL: It's dry and brittle like it could crack your skin.

DIANA: It was very hard.

RUTH: You said it was sweet.

DIANA: I don't want to go back there. Something happened in that barn and I don't want to know what it is. Don't make me go there, Ruth.

RUTH: I won't make you go there. I won't make you go anywhere you don't want to go.

[*Faint sound of the woman crying returns. Only* RUTH *and* GIRL *hear it.*]

GIRL: I need your help. She's coming. She's going to kill me. Please.

DIANA: I hate being this damaged woman who can't let a man touch her. I hate it. I want to be free. I want it to be easy.

RUTH: Then you'll have to love the child who's been so hurt.

GIRL: Why should she if you can't?

DIANA: I don't know how. [*Cries.*]

GIRL: Please, I'm afraid.

RUTH: We can make that the focus of our work together.

DIANA: Our time's up, isn't it?

GIRL: Yes, it is.

DIANA: Well, I'll just whistle until I see you again. Just whistle a happy tune and no one will know I'm afraid. [*As she gets up to leave, she tries to whistle and can't.*]

RUTH: You can take a few moments. I don't have another client.

DIANA: I love you, Ruth. I really do.

RUTH: I love you, too.

[DIANA *exits exactly as* GIRL'S MOTHER *enters into the barn area. Sound of woman crying stops.* MOTHER *sees the lit candle and goes into a rage. The* GIRL *blows out the candle as* MOTHER *climbs the ladder into the hayloft.*]

MOTHER: What kind of fool are you? Are you insane? Do you know what that little light will do? It will destroy us. Fool. [*Slaps the* GIRL.]

[RUTH *feels the pain of the slap.*]

MOTHER: [*Cont'd.*] You did this just to see what I'd do? Am I right? Why must you always provoke me and make everyone think I'm a bad mother to you?

GIRL: There's no one to see us, mother.

MOTHER: Everyone sees us. Don't talk back. Get into bed. You cannot read at night. How many times do I have to tell you the light will kill us. In the morning you can read. You can read all day. Not at night.

GIRL: I was afraid you had left me. I woke up and there was no note. Where did you go?

MOTHER: [*Overlapping.*] Shh. I hear something. Get into bed.

GIRL: Mother, please talk to me. I was so afraid. I studied like I always do but—

[MOTHER *throws* GIRL *into bed of hay on her stomach and gets on top of her.*]

GIRL: [*Cont'd.*] No, please, I don't have to sleep under you. Not anymore. We're safe here. Someone help me.

[MOTHER *boxes her ears.*]

RUTH: She doesn't have to sleep with you.

MOTHER: If they come in the night and shoot me, they will not see you and you can escape after they are gone.

GIRL: They won't come, Mother, please—

MOTHER: Lower your voice. [*Puts her hand over the* GIRL's *mouth.*] If you cry out you'll get us both killed.

RUTH: Leave her alone.

MOTHER: Tuck your feet under my legs. Bring your arms in.

RUTH: [*Still remaining in her space.*] I said, leave her alone. Can't you hear me? She can't breathe. You're choking her.

[SHELL *knocks, then enters.*]

SHELL: Ruth? . . . Hello?

[RUTH *is stunned, unable to speak.*]

SHELL: [*Cont'd.*] What is it? Are you all right?

RUTH: What do you want? What are you doing here?

SHELL: I'm sorry I surprised you. There's a message from me on your machine. I know your last client leaves at seven or so. I—. . .

[*Overlapping* SHELL, *the* MOTHER *moves adjusting herself on the* GIRL *and the* GIRL *manages some freedom for a moment.*]

GIRL: Please, mother.

[MOTHER *again reclamps* GIRL's *mouth.*]

RUTH: [*Cutting* SHELL *off, hardly able to hear her, focused on* GIRL *and* MOTHER.] I'm working. You shouldn't be here.

SHELL: You have another client coming?

RUTH: No, but . . .

SHELL: You haven't been home in a week. Things have happened. I miss you. I want to talk to you.

[RUTH *has made a fist and is hitting her open hand. She's aware of the movements in the hay as the* MOTHER *increasingly takes total control of the* GIRL. *Sounds of men's voices outside the barn rise in volume as the tension mounts between* SHELL & RUTH.]

SHELL: I know you don't have an early day tomorrow. Have dinner with me.

GIRL'S MOTHER: Shhh, someone's coming. Be still. Be still and we'll be okay.

SHELL: What is it, Ruth? Talk to me.

RUTH: You have to go before I do something . . .

SHELL: Ruth, I'm getting clearer about why the boy left.

RUTH: You can't come in on me when I'm working. You can't. We've discussed it. You can't. You can't be here.

SHELL: I need your help. I can't do this alone.

RUTH: You need what?

SHELL: I need your help. We have to talk. You haven't been home—

RUTH: [*Overlapping.*] Now you want me to be your shrink! I'm not your god damn shrink. I can't help you. I have no desire to help you. When do you ever think of helping me? When? Coming in here? Do you think that is a help? Do you think you're helping me by destroying my day, invading the only space I have that's mine? Do you? Do you? Answer me! You don't know anything about me? If you did you wouldn't be here! Would you? Don't you even know? Do you know anything about me?

SHELL: You're seeing the girl, aren't you? Ruth, it's okay.

RUTH: DON'T TOUCH ME. GO.

SHELL: You're running away—

RUTH: DON'T YOU DARE TELL ME WHAT I'M DOING! GET OUT! GET OUT!

[*Beat.* SHELL *doesn't move.*]

RUTH: [*In a total rage, vicious.*] Do I have to physically hurt you? Is that what you want? Evidence that I abused you? Is that it? I can't talk about this now, I can't listen to you. I'm not available. Go tell your story to someone else.

SHELL: Go fuck yourself.

[SHELL *exits.* RUTH *paces.* RUTH *realizes all that's gone down. Lights fade on* MOTHER *and* GIRL. *The voices outside the barn fade out.* RUTH *starts to cry. Lights fade to black.*]

SCENE 4

SHELL *and* RUTH's *apartment.* SHELL *is alone, writing. The* BOY *enters and walks the streets of the ghetto and plays to the fourth wall.*

SHELL: The soldiers like the boy. He makes them smile, he makes them laugh. He gets them things other Jewish boys can't. Times are very hard for everyone except the soldiers. The boy knows their loneliness and he knows they secretly hate him. He never forgets that.

BOY: You want female companionship? I can get it for you. Very discrete Polish girls, if the money is right. [*Beat.*] In advance. [*Beat.*]

I split the money in half with the girls. It is only fair. I am amazed at how often the soldiers need to be with the girls. I am grateful they are such pigs. [*Counts money.*] I save enough money to get false identification for my father and mother and myself and to buy tickets for the train to Stettin. It is good my grandmother died. She looked too Jewish and would have gotten everyone shot. [*Goes to a dock opposite* SHELL'*s desk*.] When we arrived in Stettin I arranged for us to be driven to Swinemunde where I booked passage to Sweden. From Sweden we will go to Copenhagen, and then I will leave Mother and Father to start my own life. I am twelve. I will have plenty of time to be happy. [*Stands resolved, arms folded, then to* SHELL.] You haven't sent out the manuscript yet.

[RUTH *enters unseen by* SHELL.]

SHELL: No, I haven't. And Ruth hasn't been home in two weeks and I'm not sure what I'm going to do. I'm not sure I'm willing to risk it all for you.

RUTH: Hi.

[*Fear, love and anger rip through* SHELL. *She can't move.* BOY *exits as does the dock setting.* SHELL *thinks she might be losing the* BOY.]

RUTH: Looks like it was my turn to interrupt you.

SHELL: Are you coming home?

RUTH: Yes. [*Beat.*] I'm sorry for what happened at my office last week. I was awful to you. I was so afraid. I never want to be that way again. [*Pause.*] The window's still not fixed?

SHELL: The super's in the hospital. He's very sick. We're supposed to have a meeting of the co-op committee to see about hiring someone. There's a lot of problems in the building because of the weather.

RUTH: I finally had to cancel all my appointments and sleep. I've been exhausted. I've slept for the last two days.

SHELL: It is very tiring.

RUTH: You really trust what's happening. I don't know how you do it.

SHELL: I guess I love the boy.

RUTH: The girl is being molested by her mother. I don't know for sure but she sleeps with her, sleeps under her and she doesn't want to. It's so awful, Shelley. She's more and more desparate...she hates her and loves her...she can't leave and I hate her for not being able to leave. When you walked in, it was all happening at once. And the woman was crying. God, I know I hurt you. I didn't want to. I don't have any control anymore...

[*Pause.* SHELL *wants to go to her but she's also afraid of* RUTH.]

RUTH: I was so afraid you weren't going to be here.

SHELL: [*Tearful.*] This is my home.

RUTH: It's my home too.

SHELL: Yes. [*Holds back the tears.*] I wrote something for you. [SHELL *hands it to her.*]

RUTH: It's nice to see you. I forgot how pretty you are.

SHELL: I didn't forget how beautiful you are. Not for a moment. Don't touch me, I'll cry.

[*They hug and kiss tearfully. Finally, they get tissues and* RUTH *looks at the paper* SHELL *had handed to her.*]

RUTH: [*Reads.*] After the boy leaves, the girl goes to the book store owned by Rebbeh Jacob's brother, Richard. [*To* SHELL.] Like my Uncle Saul?

[SHELL *nods.*]

RUTH: [*Cont'd.*] She has told Richard that when she grows up she's going to be a doctor of the mind. What she doesn't tell him is that she's studying so she can cure her mother who she's sure is paranoid. That afternoon she reads Freud's *Civilization and its Discontents.* One sentence stays with her as she walks home. "Man's judgments of value are an attempt to support his illusions with arguments." She hears the words in her mind for years afterwards.

   That night, the girl lies in bed dreading her mother's coming in. The girl and her mother have slept together always.

SHELL: There's more.

RUTH: [*Hands it back to her, trying not to react negatively.*] It's very nice.

SHELL: I looked through your old books. You'd underlined that quote three times.

RUTH: Value judgments are arguments to support illusions.

SHELL: Who would have thought Freud was a latent Buddhist?

RUTH: Or that I was. The girl was reading the same book. What's going on? I can't do this. I'm losing my mind.

SHELL: This wouldn't be happening if we didn't have what we have together. We're being given something extraordinary.

RUTH: But why? I don't know what to do anymore.

SHELL: We could pray.

RUTH: I don't know what to pray for. I don't even know what to pray to.

[SHELL *gets a candle and lights it.*]

RUTH: [*Cont'd.*] I don't want the pain, Shelley. [*Laughs.*] I can't believe I said that. People pay me thousands of dollars because they hope I'm going to help them get through their pain. And I'd do anything to get through this another way. The girl's mother is my mother.

SHELL: I know. She's mine and the boy's.

RUTH: And she's crying.

SHELL: Over her sons and daughters.

RUTH: But they're brutal. They're not crying for anyone but themselves.

SHELL: It's never just one thing.

[*Beat.*]

RUTH: You've always left before when I left you. How'd you do it? How'd you stay?

SHELL: The boy wouldn't let me.

[*Beat.* RUTH *doesn't know how to respond.*]

RUTH: How's the writing going?

SHELL: I'm just working on the story of the postcard.

RUTH: No more gothic novels?

SHELL: I have two months before the next one is due.

RUTH: You mean you're not turning this into a gothic romance!

SHELL: Don't be disrepectful.

RUTH: I was only teasing. I know how important this is. [*Ready to pray, she takes* SHELLEY's *hands in hers.*] How should we do this?

SHELL: We could put our heads together.

RUTH: Two heads are better than one.

[*They put their heads together, forehead to forehead. Their lips slightly touch.*]

SHELL: Dear God, please help us understand what you want from us

RUTH: Dear God, please help us understand what you want from us

SHELL: So that we may serve you and help all those in need.

RUTH: So that we may serve you and help all those in need.

SHELL: Please help us love each other.

RUTH: Please help us to love each other. [*Starts crying.*]

SHELL: It's okay, Ruth.

[SHELL *holds her.* RUTH *burrows into her.* SHELL *rocks her as the* BOY *did the* GIRL *in Act I, Scene 1. The sound of the woman crying comes up very softly. Lights slowly change.* RUTH *is curled up on the couch.* SHELL *puts a blanket over her.* SHELL *writes. The* BOY *and* BOY'S MOTHER *enter on the dock at Stettin. They are huddled together under one blanket.*]

SHELL: [*Cont'd.*] The Steinloff family now known as Feudakowski sleep huddled together under one blanket near the dock.

[BOY *mimes the actions.*]

SHELL: [*Cont'd.*] The boy is fearless. Each day he trades cigarettes for their bread. The mother complains but the boy convinces her they have to be quiet. Their papers could be traced.

On the third day of waiting for passage across the Baltic Sea, the boy falls ill with a fever. The next day the father is overtaken with chills. The mother leaves them to find help.

MOTHER: A dry place to sleep for my husband and son and some broth. They have fever. They must have help.

SHELL: Everywhere she goes, the answer is the same.

MOTHER: Please, Officer, I am a poor Polish woman who is trying to reach her sister in Copenhagen.

SHELL: The Nazi soldier tells her he will give her what she needs, but she must spend her nights with him until her family can get passage.

MOTHER: Never. [*Spits. She walks away. Stops. Comes back and begins to disrobe as . . .*]

SHELL: For seven nights she lies with the soldier and each night she prays she will say or do nothing to signal she is a Jew. She is so terrified something awful will happen to her and her family that she does not feel the violations inflicted on her body by the German soldier. For seven nights she does not sleep. For seven nights she remembers nothing but to remain silent. She never speaks to anyone of the German soldier. Never.

[MOTHER *wraps her shawl about her and stares as one suffering from shock.*]

SHELL: [*Cont'd.*] The boy goes to America and becomes a successful businessman. He has mistresses and a good wife. He never knows his mother saved his life and asked nothing from him in return.

[MOTHER *exits with the dock. The* BOY *remains in the blank space and confronts* SHELL.]

BOY: I knew what she had done. She had the smell of sex on her same as the Polish girls after they'd been with the Nazi soldiers. I knew she didn't want me to know. [*Beat.*]
 You must send out the manuscript.

SHELL: I'll destroy everything.

BOY: You don't know what everything is. And I didn't go to America.

[*Exits. Blackout.*]

SCENE 5

SHELL *and* RUTH *are comfortable in their enveloping sofa looking through travel brochures. There are fresh flowers on the coffee table.* SHELL *is not happy but she is trying to act as if everything is fine. Two weeks have passed.*

RUTH: Look at this. Waterfalls and miles of hiking. "Lose yourself in the splendor." That's what I want to do. Lose myself.

SHELL: Well, I don't want you to lose yourself. Who would be my partner?

RUTH: Let's do it. Let's go to Hawaii.

SHELL: I've always wanted to go to Hawaii. Three weeks in August?

RUTH: Let's go for four weeks.

SHELL: There was one about a private cottage with ocean views. Where is it? It looked great. It had a terrace.

RUTH: It'll be our best vacation yet. God, it's May and there's still snow in New York. It's not right.

SHELL: I heard if you can find a good guide, you can go to places tourists never get to. Sacred burial grounds, energy centers.

RUTH: I'll stay with the tourists. [*Beat.*] Is that okay, Shell?

[SHELL *winces, frowns.*]

RUTH: [*Cont'd.*] You're not happy with me.

[SHELL *gets up, paces.*]

RUTH: [*Cont'd.*] Say something.

SHELL: How long's it been now?

RUTH: How long has what been?

SHELL: Since you've seen them.

RUTH: Two blissful weeks. You think I've blocked them out. Well, you're right. That's exactly what I've done. I'd much rather curl up in your arms than be on a stretcher heading for a psych ward.

SHELL: It's a journey, Ruth. It's as glorious as going to any tropical island.

RUTH: For you, it's glorious. For me, it's terrorizing. You're a writer. You like going into the darkness.

SHELL: Don't tell me you don't get into some weird places with your clients?

RUTH: I do my best to keep my darkness out of it.

SHELL: How can you?

RUTH: Let's change the subject. So, shall we do this?

SHELL: Sure.

[RUTH *goes to her.*]

RUTH: Maybe I just need some time to get used to this sort of thing. I'm from Queens. I've never been outside this country. I have limited vision.

SHELL: No, you don't.

RUTH: Well, I'm scared of heights.

[*Beat. Puts her arms around* SHELL.]

RUTH: [*Cont'd.*] Please, just let me be with this. I don't want to feel judged. Your disappointment feels very much like something tight around my throat and you know how I hate turtlenecks. Please.

SHELL: I'm sorry. I just keep thinking it's our story.

RUTH [*Teasing.*] It is. But I'm writing my part and you're not! You killed the girl off in the first scene. Remember? [*Kisses her.*] Just have some patience.

[*As* RUTH *starts to walk off,* SHELL, *with pent-up passion, grabs* RUTH *from behind and kisses her forcefully. Moments pass between them. They both soften.*]

RUTH: You're scared. [*Hugs her.*] I'm sorry, Shelley. I didn't realize . . . [*Kisses* SHELL *on the lips, cheek, forehead, holds her.*]

[*The phone rings. They both laugh.*]

SHELL: The machine's not on.

RUTH: I'll get it.

SHELL: Don't. Let's make love.

RUTH: We just made love this morning.

SHELL: We have months to make up for.

RUTH: I'll just get it . . . go light some candles . . . [*Answers the phone.*] Hello. [*Put off by the agressive voice on the other end.*] No, just a minute. Who should I say is—? [*Handing phone to* SHELL.] Cynthia Rodman from Simon & Schuster. [*Covering receiver.*] She sounds like she just had a quart of caffeine. [*Beat. Not giving up the receiver yet.*]
   Isn't that the editor we met at the Seder?

SHELL: [*Nods "yes."*] Hello . . . Yes, hello. You did? That's good. . . . Tomorrow? I guess. I don't have—. . . No, the afternoons are better, I work in—. Yes . . . Three is good . . . Right, well, I'm glad you liked it . . . I didn't even know about that part, it just came out and took me . . . Real life is a different story? I don't know. It's pretty much full of surprises too . . . The ending? . . . No, I'm not committed to that . . . Okay, I'll see you then. Bye.

[*Beat.* SHELL *is excited but scared to tell* RUTH.]

RUTH: Don't tell me. If it's what I think it is, I don't want to know. [*Beat.*] What is it?

SHELL: Simon & Schuster is buying my story. They want me to finish it, they want to give me an advance.

RUTH: This is a novel? As in art? Not formula?

SHELL: As in art, yes.

RUTH: That's wonderful, Shelley. It's the story of the postcard, isn't it?

SHELL: Yes.

RUTH: [*Sarcastic.*] I must be psychic.

SHELL: I proposed it as a novel. I sent her the first seven chapters. Up to the point where the boy gets to Denmark. I sent a proposal for the rest.

[*Knows the axe is going to fall.*]

RUTH: Who is Cynthia Rodman?

SHELL: An editor.

RUTH: I know what she is. I want to know who she is.

SHELL: I'm not seeing her.

RUTH: Yet! She's interested in the story of the postcard. Perhaps she'd like to share it with you...go into her deepest recesses...since I don't seem to be able to do that. Perhaps she'd like to share it with you in bed...with a name like Rodman she's right up your alley. [*Hating her own pun. Beat.*]

So you're turning our story into mass market fiction! No wonder you didn't have the guts to tell me. Are they going to put it on the checkout lines with the rest of your gothic junk?

SHELL: [*Explodes.*] IT'S NOT JUNK!!

[*Pause.*]

RUTH: Couldn't you have given me some time?

SHELL: [*Fighting off overwhelming desire to walk out, then finally.*] It's not like you've made this easy for me.

RUTH: Don't blame me for this one. You do, don't you? You think it's my fault I feel betrayed. My fault you sent it out.

SHELL: Don't be so fucking paranoid.

RUTH: I can't believe you just said that. I can't believe—! Is it my paranoia that makes me think I'm losing the most important person in my life or is it my common sense? [*Storms off.*]

SHELL: [*Finds her leaving perversely humorous.*] You're going to leave again?

RUTH: I have to go to work.

SHELL: Your first client's not for hours!

RUTH: [*Comes back in to yell at her.*] That's right and if I walked in like this, I'd have to pay them.

SHELL: Maybe I'll have to leave this time, Ruth. I can't stand your leaving me anymore. I can't stand it!

RUTH: Don't forget your manuscript and if you make love to that woman I'll never ever talk to you again.

[RUTH *goes off.* SHELL *starts to pace. Police sirens go off.*]

SHELL: Fuck. [*Beat.*]

The boy dies when he leaves. He dies when he turns his back on love. The girl doesn't die. He does. How am I turning my back on love? When he leaves the mother, he dies. [*Repeating what she had heard before.*] He never leaves. What does that mean, he never leaves? It's got nothing to do with the girl... The boy's panic has nothing to do with the girl. Nothing to do with Ruth.

[RUTH *enters with a packed suitcase. Sirens fade.*]

RUTH: How could you, Shelley? I trusted you.

SHELL: I sent the story out because you had walked out on me. No, that's a lie. I sent it out because it was the only way I could stay. I had to have something that was mine.

RUTH: Why couldn't you have just given me some time? [*Beat.*] You can't sell our story.

SHELL: I'm a writer.

RUTH: I know you are and I love your stories and I've always thought they should be published but not this one. This was our way home. You made me believe that. You made me trust you. I thought it could help and now you've taken that away.

SHELL: You stopped.

RUTH: You've destroyed everything.

SHELL: No, I haven't. That's not possible. Don't make me feel guilty for your fucking quitting.

RUTH: Is the story of the little girl in there too?

SHELL: Ruth . . . please try and understand—

RUTH: Is it?

SHELL: That's Part Two.

RUTH: Well, I guess we won't be going to Hawaii.

[*Beat. Silence as they stare at each other.*]

SHELL: I won't sell it. I'll see Cynthia tomorrow—

RUTH: Cynthia!

SHELL: I'll call her and tell her it's off. You don't have to be the postcard anymore, neither do I.

[RUTH *exits, slamming door.*]

SHELL: Ruth . . . [*Goes to her desk, throws something across the room then looks around for the* BOY.] Where are you, you little bastard? I told you this would happen. I told you. [*Beat.*] Ruth . . . don't go.

[*Blackout.*]

SCENE 6

Lights rise on MOTHER *asleep in the hayloft and the* GIRL *reading by candlelight below in the barn.*

   RUTH *is in session with* DIANA *and is determined to stay focused on* DIANA.

DIANA: So, what do you think? Are you angry? Do you think I'm crazy? What?

RUTH: Is this why I haven't see you in a month?

DIANA: Is it a month? You missed a week and I missed two. A month. Damn. Think how much money I saved.

RUTH: Why, Diana?

DIANA: Because I can't go on like this.

RUTH: Something has happened at home?

DIANA: No, everything's fine now. No problem. I've turned off my brain and Robert and I are very happy. We're fucking like bunnies! [*Beat.*]

   I wasn't even going to come back but I had to say good-bye. It's a pretty expensive good-bye, but—. Oh, shit, what?

RUTH: I'm going to miss you. I've grown to love you, Diana.

DIANA: Don't say that.

RUTH: You've opened some dangerous doors for yourself and I admire your courage.

DIANA: Great!

RUTH: What?

DIANA: Shit. I'm going to miss you, too. I don't know what to do. He said he'd leave if I didn't stop coming to see you. I almost walked out right then. But I haven't wanted to make love with him, I haven't even wanted to be around him and he's been so patient. So, I found this cure. If you don't think about stuff, it goes away.

RUTH: Not completely.

[*The* MOTHER *stirs, the* GIRL *registers her breath, as does* RUTH, *even from the distance.* RUTH *reacts physically.*]

RUTH: [*As much to herself as to* DIANA.] But you're right. You do have to want to take the journey.

DIANA: You think I'm crazy for doing this, don't you?

RUTH: No, I understand.

DIANA: You do?

RUTH: I've walked out on a few opportunities myself.

DIANA: You have?

RUTH: Yes.

[MOTHER *rouses, unconsciously feels for the little* GIRL *under her.* GIRL *quickly blows out the candle.*]

GIRL: Will you help me this time, please?

[RUTH *doesn't respond.*]

DIANA: Looks like you're sorry you did.

RUTH: [*To* DIANA *and* GIRL.] We don't always know what to do, so we have to wait.

DIANA: What to do about what?

RUTH: The journey inside. What you've begun. There are times when we have to wait before we know what to do next. Sometimes that's the hardest part.

DIANA: I'm going to miss you so much.

[GIRL *enters* RUTH's *area to hide.* RUTH *does her best to ignore her.*]

RUTH: [*To* DIANA.] My door's open. You can come back whenever you want.

DIANA: I might. But everything would have to be so different.

GIRL'S MOTHER: [*Hushed.*] Where are you? Where are you?

RUTH: It's not easy.

DIANA: But you've done it, huh?

RUTH: Sometimes only in very small degrees. And sometimes I've run away.

[MOTHER *gets up, brushes dirt and straw from her skirt, and descends the ladder to look for the* GIRL.]

GIRL: Will you protect me? Will you? Please.

GIRL'S MOTHER: Where are you?

DIANA: If I stay here any longer I'm going to want to have a regular session because I'm starting to feel stuff and I don't want that so I'm going to split now. [*Whistles.*]

RUTH: I just want you to know I'm really going to miss your whistling. I never learned how to whistle.

DIANA: I could have taught you. We could have traded. Whistling lessons for therapy.

[DIANA *stands, as does* RUTH. *They hug.*]

GIRL'S MOTHER: You make me look for you. You make me sick with worry.

GIRL: Please.

RUTH: [*To* DIANA.] We can talk about how you're feeling now.

DIANA: No.

GIRL'S MOTHER: I would kill myself before I would let anything happen to you. And you run off!

DIANA: I've had fantasies of killing you. Did you know that?

RUTH: Because I remind you of your mother?

DIANA: I guess.

GIRL'S MOTHER: [*Overlapping.*] If you leave me you can never come back. It is the law.

RUTH: That's normal for the work we do. But I'm not your mother. And you can come back.

GIRL'S MOTHER: You can't leave me. I can't allow that.

DIANA: I don't want to go. I have to. Good-bye.

[DIANA *exits.* RUTH *sighs, she wants to go to sleep.*]

GIRL: She's coming. She's coming. What are you going to do?

RUTH: I don't want you here. This is where I work. Please, I've told you—

GIRL: You help everybody but me. [*Beat.*] You couldn't help anyway. You're a coward.

[*This hurts* RUTH *but she won't let the* GIRL *in.*]

RUTH: You don't really want to leave her so there's nothing I can do.

GIRL: It's you who won't leave her. [*Walks off toward where* MOTHER *is.*]

RUTH: [*Follows* GIRL *into barn area.*] What do you mean?

GIRL: I'm over here. I didn't leave you, mother.

GIRL'S MOTHER: Where are you? Come where I can see you.

GIRL: I'm not going to sleep with you anymore, mother. I won't leave you but I won't sleep with you.

GIRL'S MOTHER: What are you saying? All I do for you is to protect you. I see you. Come over here.

GIRL: Only if you promise.

GIRL'S MOTHER: I do my job as my mother did hers. Come. I have food and fresh milk and my bones are aching especially this morning.

RUTH: What do you mean, I can't leave her?

GIRL [*To* RUTH.] I came because we could help each other. You won't help me because you won't take my help.

GIRL'S MOTHER: [*As much to herself as to the* GIRL.] It is the books you read. They make you think bigger than you are. Give you ideas you shouldn't have.

RUTH: How can you help me?

GIRL: You're very stupid.

RUTH: Please, tell me.

GIRL'S MOTHER: You are a child. You can do nothing for yourself. Now come over here and eat some bread. Don't make me come over there.

GIRL: What you do is wrong, mother. I know what's right and what you do is wrong.

GIRL'S MOTHER: These are not good times. You cannot be the child you'd like to be or me the mother.

GIRL: No. You touch me and it's wrong.

GIRL'S MOTHER: We know that and we go on as best we can.

GIRL: [*To* RUTH.] Help me.

RUTH: I don't know what you want.

[GIRL *sits by her* MOTHER.]

GIRL'S MOTHER: You had me very scared. And I am already very scared. It is not good.

RUTH: Stop looking at me like that.

GIRL'S MOTHER: Go ahead and eat.

RUTH: No one is going to help you. You're just going to have to live with it like everyone else. [*Starts to go back to her space.*]

GIRL'S MOTHER: I'll just get my gloves. There's a chill.

GIRL: [*To* RUTH.] I hate you.

[MOTHER *goes to the bedding and gets rope and tucks it under her skirt.* RUTH *sees this and is horrified.* MOTHER *rummages to find her gloves.* RUTH *stays in the barn area.*]

RUTH: She's going to tie you up.

GIRL: And I will feel her weight on me through the night.

RUTH: I can't take you with me.

GIRL: I will study. I will study in my sleep and I will not feel her. I'll become a great doctor and nothing anyone can do will hurt me. I'll live with it.

[MOTHER *returns*. RUTH *moves out of the way*. MOTHER *sits next to* GIRL *and watches her eat. She doesn't see* RUTH. RUTH *paces*.]

GIRL'S MOTHER: Pass your cup, we have fresh milk.

[GIRL *passes her cup*, MOTHER *fills it from a pitcher. As* GIRL *drinks*, MOTHER *takes the rope from under her skirt*. RUTH *sees*.]

GIRL'S MOTHER: [*Cont'd.*] Put down your cup now and face me. Hold your hands out.

[GIRL *obeys*. MOTHER *begins tying her hands*.]

RUTH: Don't give her your hands. Fight her.

GIRL: I can't.

RUTH: Then it's your own fault. You're causing this. Don't look at me like that. Do something for yourself. Do something!

GIRL: [*Yells*.] I CAN'T.

RUTH: [*Pushes* MOTHER *away from* GIRL *and puts herself between them*.] Leave her alone.

GIRL'S MOTHER: Who are you?

RUTH: I am Ruth.

GIRL'S MOTHER: You can't tell me what I can and can't do with my child. I'll do as needs fit.

RUTH: You don't own her. You have no right to tie her up. She is human. She is not—

GIRL'S MOTHER: Get out of my way. [*Forcefully pushes* RUTH *out of her way*.]

[RUTH *grabs hold of the* MOTHER. *They struggle*. RUTH *tears at her, then feeling overpowered by the woman*, RUTH *picks up the pitcher of milk and smashes her in the side of the head as the* GIRL'S MOTHER *falls*. RUTH *drops the pitcher. Milk spills. The sound of the woman crying fades up slowly*.]

GIRL: Did you kill her?

RUTH: [*To* GIRL.] No. Let's go. You can't stay here.

GIRL: She's crying again. She's crying because of you.

RUTH: She's crying because she never meant for any of this to happen. She never meant for your mother to be with you that way. She never meant for her to be so scared that she would hurt you the way she did.

GIRL: Mommy...I'm sorry. What am I going to do without her?

RUTH: You'll have me.

GIRL: But you hate me.

RUTH: I'm afraid to love you. There's a difference. Can you understand that?

[GIRL *is not sure*.]

RUTH: [*Cont'd.*] I will learn to love you. I want to. I do. Please trust me.

[GIRL *gives her a sign she's willing...a little*.]

RUTH: Let's go. She'll wake up soon.

GIRL: But she needs me. She'll die if I leave her.

RUTH: She won't die and you won't have to be alone. I'll take care of you.

GIRL: You promise?

[GIRL'S MOTHER *stirs, groans.*]

RUTH: I promise.

GIRL: You really want me?

RUTH: I really want you.

[*They go off. The sound of the woman crying fades as do lights.*]

SCENE 7

Lights rise on the BOY, *scared, in the bedroll in the corner of his living room as before.* SHELL *is in the blank space between his area and her desk/living area.*

SHELL: [*To* BOY.] We've done that part. You're a man now. It's 1962, you're thirty-three, married, in America, you have an Oldsmobile car dealership, and you're miserable, but Cynthia doesn't want you to commit suicide. So we have to come up with something different. [*Gives in.*] Jesus, what is wrong with you? You look like you are going to die. All right, we'll do that part again. [*Trying to nail down the scene once and for all.*] After the beating, after he had taken the girl's body to her mother's, the boy lies in his bedroll by the wall. The grandmother is coughing louder and more furious than before. The boy hears his mother get up. At first he thinks she will go to the grandmother. But then his breathing stops. Time stops. His body remembers. [SHELL *registers a change in the story.*] He hears his mother's footsteps softly gliding without weight or thought over the stone floors. [*Surprised by the change in the story.*]

[MOTHER *enters and slowly makes her way to the* BOY.]

SHELL: [*Cont'd.*] His body remembers the gentleness of her movements as she came into his room. All those years of her coming into his room before they had moved to the ghetto. She had only come into him once that way since they had moved. For so long, there had been the other family. But now they were gone. It is the same sound, her footsteps defying gravity. He knows it is her because he cannot hear the grandmother's coughing anymore. It has become masked by that steady pounding in his chest, that rhythm. What is that rhythm? He feels the familiar hollowness spreading out from his stomach, down his legs, through his arms, to his fingers, throughout his chest. The rhythm of his life.

[MOTHER *has sat down next to the* BOY. *She strokes his hair while looking off into the distance.*]

BOY: Mother, I've been thinking, we must leave soon.

MOTHER: Yes. Soon.

[*Brings his head to her lap.*]

MOTHER: [*Cont'd.*] I forgive you for not coming straight home. What's important is you are here now, in my arms, and I have nothing to worry about.

SHELL: She is gentle and delicate with him. She kisses the top of his head, deeply inhaling his fine silken hair. She kisses his cheek with its soft down covering. She kisses his neck. Her hand travels down his side, over his narrow hip, to the inside of his thigh. She lies back bringing his body on top of hers. There are no sounds in the streets as she guides him into her. No sounds but the rhythm of her need filling his body and soul. The rhythm of her need.

She has held him inside her for centuries.

[SHELL *is speechless.* BOY *gets up, leaving the* MOTHER *and goes to* SHELL. *Lights fade to black on* MOTHER.]

BOY: What are you looking at?

SHELL: I don't know.

BOY: It's not my fault. It's not.

[SHELL *is dazed.*]

BOY: [*Cont'd.*] When she touches me, I forget everything.

SHELL: I know.

BOY: Everything!!

SHELL: Okay!!

BOY: You should know that.

SHELL: I know that, already!

BOY: Are you okay?

SHELL: No, because I didn't know.

BOY: Timelessness. Time stopping. When she touches me, time opens to timelessness, just like you said. Everything becomes one and you forget the pain.

SHELL: I never knew where it came from. I thought that feeling was holy. I worshipped that feeling.

BOY: It's why you beat me. You couldn't walk away from her. She feeds on our love just like you said in the story. [*Pause.*]
I forgive you for beating me.

SHELL: I'm so sorry. I had no power to deny her. I was proud of you and I beat you.

BOY: Will you be able to now?

SHELL: What do you mean?

BOY: Have your own voice. Your publisher. She wants me in America. I don't belong there. That's not where I go.

SHELL: Where do you go?

BOY: I meet Helen Elaina again in Venice and we marry. We planned it that way. I'm a painter. She's my model. She's my life. It's a happy ending.

SHELL: I thought she died.

[*Lights rise on* RUTH *and* GIRL *embracing and saying good-bye.*]

BOY: Exactly. You thought she died.

[*She embraces him, cries . . . pulls herself together.*]

SHELL: Can you go to Venice by way of some unhappiness in America? Just a minor compromise. It has to sell books.

[*He agrees. She holds him to her as* GIRL *slowly walks away from* RUTH *and says good-bye.*]

BOY: Thank you for finding me and giving me back my Helen Elaina.

[*Lights fade to black on* BOY *and* SHELL, RUTH *and the* GIRL.]

SCENE 8

SHELLEY *is finishing repairing the window and cleaning up the mess. As she exits with the tools, she takes the dead, almost petrified flowers from the vase on the coffee table.* RUTH *enters with her bag and fresh flowers, sees the window and goes to it.* SHELL *reenters. They both stop.*

SHELL: Is that you?

[RUTH *nods.*]

SHELL: [*Cont'd.*] I've been spending so much time with the boy, I thought for a second you were in the same dimension as he is.

RUTH: No. It's Saturday afternoon, in the last decade of the twentieth century, and I've been away a long time.

SHELL: What's it been? Two weeks or three. I lost count.

RUTH: Almost three. You fixed the window.

SHELL: I got tired of waiting.

RUTH: Did you get tired of waiting for me?

SHELL: I stopped. I went on with my life.

RUTH: So did I.

SHELL: Are you coming home or just picking up stuff or maybe you think it's time I left since this really is your place?

RUTH: I'm home. I want to apologize. [*Beat.*] I don't have anymore words than that.

SHELL: You want to sit down? You want something to drink?

[RUTH *sits. Long pause.*]

RUTH: I don't think I'll ever be that desperate again.

[SHELL *goes to the window and stares out.*]

SHELL: What's happening with the girl?

RUTH: She's safe. She's with me.

SHELL: Well, I hope not literally.

RUTH: I was able to help her. We've been spending a lot of time together too.

SHELL: According to the boy, they meet up again in Venice and get married.

RUTH: I was able to help her.

SHELL: He's a painter. She's his model. She's the joy of his life. [*Beat.*] I heard you.

RUTH: I don't expect you to forgive me all at once or trust me right away. [*Pause.*] What's happening with Simon and Schuster?

SHELL: I got an advance. The book will be out next year.

RUTH: What about the girl's story?

SHELL: I'm not sorry I sent out the manuscript, Ruth. I'm sorry for some of the things I said to you, I could have been gentler, but I couldn't stop living because of your fear.

RUTH: What about the girl's story?

SHELL: You changed her story. She doesn't die.

RUTH: But are you still writing her story?

SHELL: No. It's yours.

[RUTH *cries.*]

SHELL: So what do we do now? Buy another postcard?

RUTH: You're not serious.

SHELL: Why not? What else is there to do!

RUTH: [*Takes plane tickets out of her bag.*] I didn't know if it would be okay but I got us tickets to Hawaii . . . I thought maybe we could go where there aren't any tourists. [*Police sirens come and go quickly.* RUTH *jumps.*]

RUTH: Why can't I get used to that?

SHELL: Maybe we're not supposed to. Maybe it's time to leave.

RUTH: I just got here.

SHELL: You think the girl really meets him in Venice?

RUTH: I think so.

SHELL: Maybe we should go to Venice.

RUTH: No, they have what they need.

[*As they wonder if they have what they need and accept each other, lights fade to black.*]

THE END

© Kim Zumwalt

Maria Irene Fornes

INTRODUCING *SPRINGTIME* BY MARIA IRENE FORNES

Assunta Kent

In the early 1960s, Cuban emigrée Maria Irene Fornes, a novice playwright, burst onto the Off-Off-Broadway scene with a series of successful experimental plays. Since that time, Fornes has devoted her life to writing plays, teaching playwrighting, and directing, designing, and producing her own and others' new works. By 1990, Fornes was acclaimed as a major voice in American theatre for her foundational contributions to US traditions in experimental, women's, and Latina/o theatre. She has garnered eight Obie awards including, in 1982, a "sustained achievement" award "for the wit, imagination, and social outrage she has brought to Off-Broadway for twenty years." Early broad satires include *Tango Palace* (1963), *The Successful Life of 3* (1965), *Promenade* (1965), *Dr. Kheal* (1967), and *Molly's Dream* (1968); her later more realistic plays include *Fefu and Her Friends* (1977), *The Danube* (1982), *Mud* (1983), *Sarita* (1984), *Abingdon Square* (1984), and *The Conduct of Life* (1984).

From her first plays, Fornes' irreverent, charming, visceral, and often enigmatic productions have intrigued audiences and critics—particularly those interested in avant-garde and feminist theatre. In her later work, Fornes plays the wise fool, using identification and revelation to remind us that life is more complex than any single theory can grasp, and that our experiences exceed our ability to express them with language. But Fornes' "feminist strategy" is not so much *gestic*, characterizing the entire structure of society, as *jestic*: questioning assumptions, overturning social hierarchies, and making visible the inherent oppositions elided by our pictures of reality. Not surprisingly, Fornes does not exempt theoretical and critical assumptions from this treatment. Fornes' evasion of critical categorization and the perspicacity of her dramatized social visions question current theoretical assumptions, necessitating more practicable and practice-based methods for evaluating feminist theatre.

Fornes' conscious blurring of the aesthetic/political dichotomy so prevalent in drama criticism has often confused critics, who have yet to fully analyze the complex relationships between Fornes' aesthetic innovations and unconventional social politics. Beneath the witty surface of her early satires, Fornes lampooned the unequal relations more clearly exposed in her later plays. She directs her social critique to the predominately white, educated, middle-income or "privileged poor" patrons of U.S. avant-garde theatre, who she believes "have the knowledge, the intelligence, the perspective" to bring about social change.

In *What of the Night?* (1989–90), a cycle of four one-act plays meant to be performed sequentially in one evening, Fornes traces the increasingly deleterious effects of poverty and greed in America from the Great Depression to the next millennium, a time after nationwide economic collapse. Through terse scenes of daily interaction (typical of her later plays), Fornes conveys her perception that poverty and homelessness at the end of the century differ fundamentally from the "hard times" of the 1930s. In the first play (*Nadine*), about a single mother struggling to raise "good" children without house or husband, Fornes dramatizes her sense that "during the Depression, people were homeless and living in the streets, but there was a sense of family, there was hope." In the next two plays (*Springtime* and *Lust*), Fornes contrasts the petty crimes that poor people commit in order to survive with the pervasive social damage caused by the acquisitive empty lives of the wealthy. By the fourth play (*Hunger*), most people are scavenging through rubble in crime-ridden streets, gravitating every evening to vast bureaucratized homeless shelters, outside the armed enclaves of a rich minority. In Fornes' epic, "night" comes for all characters rich and poor; even the most privileged lose their souls, their children, their self-respect, and their peace of mind.

What of the Night?, Fornes' most historically-based and overtly political work to date, is structured by Fornes' perception that there has been a dramatic lessening in compassion for others in the US since the Depression. Fornes draws an important (and often overlooked) distinction between the needs, motivations, and social effects of the petty crimes of the poor and the overwhelming structural and spiritual damage wrought by corporate executives and politicians, without flattening characters or resorting to simplistic analyses. By comparing and contrasting the strong family ties among a single mother's destitute family with the cold, gender-divided, and monetary-based interactions of a wealthy family, Fornes overturns the commonly-held assumption that the "lower classes" are necessarily the spawning ground for the breakdown of the "American family."

In *Springtime* (set in 1958), Fornes focuses on the intersection of poverty with sexism and homophobia in the sad tale of Rainbow's love affair with Greta, a German lab technician. In her own productions, Fornes began *Springtime* with the German/English love scene (now Scene 5) set in the courtyard of a medical school. As the strains of "Bei Mir Bist Du Schoen" [You Are Beautiful to Me] fade, Rainbow, now working as a janitor, transforms Greta's critical comment into a playfully intimate encounter. After Rainbow cajoles Greta into translating some of their conversations into German, Rainbow declares dreamily, "I love German!" and swoons to the floor. Although the current placement of the scene simplifies the setting and allows the women's relationship to begin *in medias res*, the previous version underscored Greta's higher status (at the low end) of a work place hierarchy as well as the precariousness of status based on employment.

When Greta contracts tuberculosis, Rainbow immediately turns her tiny room into an infirmary and resorts, almost automatically, to petty thievery in order to pay for Greta's treatments. However, as Greta had feared, Rainbow is soon caught—by Ray, a "nasty" man who makes her agree "to do something for him" in order to avoid being sent to jail. Nonetheless, for a while, things go better for the lovers: Greta seems to be getting stronger, Rainbow has settled into working for Ray, and the women reaffirm their love for each other, pushing aside Ray's growing influence on their lives. In Scene 4, Rainbow laughs away Greta's fear that if she dies, Ray would replace her in Rainbow's heart. In Scene 6, Rainbow recounts for Greta Ray's "brotherly" advice that she should "choose to love a man," and her logical defense of her sexual orientation: "It doesn't make a difference to anyone else, but of course, it makes a difference to me."

Employing what I term "familiarization," Fornes successfully mainstreams the lesbian couple. Only after these characters are firmly established does she introduce a dissenting (and discredited and disembodied) homophobic voice. By then we are already accustomed to Rainbow and Greta as lovers and interested in their individual situation—their tenderness, Greta's illness, the illegal work that Rainbow performs to support her—so the questioning of Rainbow's sexual preference by a disturbed, if not totally evil, character garners little audience sympathy. Fornes ably treads the dangerous line between reinscribing or subverting dominant representations of these tabooed subjects.

Fornes ends the central section of the play with a charming reprise of the earlier German wordplay:

> GRETA: Your life was peccable when you were working for him. But now that you've paid your debt to him and you don't work for him anymore your life is impeccable. It was he who made your life peccable. [RAINBOW *laughs*.] Why do you laugh?
>
> RAINBOW: How do you say peccable in German?

However, an uneasiness lies beneath the gentle humor, for Greta re-emphasizes that she does not condone Rainbow's illegal and dangerous activities on her behalf. In contrast, Rainbow, buoyed by her active love for Greta and proud of her ability to provide, has become more assertive, while once dominant Greta has been forced into relative passivity and helplessness. And even though Rainbow has repaid her debt, Ray continues to dominate first Rainbow's and then Greta's thoughts and conversation.

Their relationship begins to unravel after Greta discovers photos of Rainbow's continuing work for Ray—the seduction of powerful men for blackmail purposes—and Greta is not consoled by Rainbow's heartfelt explanation that she does "that . . . because you [Greta] must have treatment. I don't mind. It's for you." The final blow comes when Rainbow's feeling that Greta is keeping things from her and no longer "adores" her is confirmed—when she discovers that Ray, who had argued against her lesbianism, has been seducing Greta. The audiences' knowledge that Ray is actually Rainbow's half-brother only adds a further twist to this man's rapacious need to insert himself into Rainbow's home life and destroy the women's relationship.

Like her mother and brother before her, Rainbow has no ambitions to advance in the criminal world or to make money for herself. In these first two plays, Fornes overturns the popular presumption that people most often turn to crimes such as prostitution and thievery in order to obtain illicit drugs to please or perhaps to numb themselves; instead Fornes depicts petty crimes as a desperate tactic that out-of-power nurturers may employ in order to secure legal but prohibitively expensive prescription drugs (and other treatments) for loved ones. Along with poverty, tenderhearted Rainbow "inherited" from Nadine a commitment to others and an ability to endure personal danger and humiliation for them. It is tempting to fault Rainbow for her devotion to love and mutual "adoration," but such judgments are mitigated by Fornes' spare yet inescapable rendering of the multiple pressures that force her characters to endure abuse and to perform onerous tasks in order to survive emotionally and physically. However, such dedication loses its value when she dies or is destroyed. Since she cannot love "only halfway," in the penultimate scene Rainbow leaves Greta to the strains of "Melancholy Baby." In the final scene, Rainbow's untimely death is foreshadowed in a love letter that Greta discovers after she has gone. The lights fade on the set, leaving a spot on the compassionate singer who, with sad irony, repeats, "Smile, my honey dear, as I kiss away each tear. Or else I shall be melancholy too."

As a jestic dramatist, Fornes militates against merely psychological readings of her characters' actions and motivations, encouraging audiences to see the systemic problems that condition and delimit her characters' choices. At the same time, she creates unique individuals acting and reacting in particular situations to present her "history" of US poverty and her prophecies and warnings for the future. To accomplish this jestic overturning of cultural truisms, Fornes "familiarizes" the daily lives, choices, and feelings of the poor, hoping to inspire the audience with empathy and understanding. And on a more deeply political level, she works to "defamiliarize" privileged possessions and points of view too easily taken for granted, such as access to nourishing food and medical treatment or the belief that one's opinions express universally accepted "truths."

SELECTED LIST OF PLAYS BY MARIA IRENE FORNES

Tango Palace (1963)
The Successful Life of 3 (1965)
Promenade (1965)
Dr. Kheal (1967)
Vietnamese Wedding (1967)
Molly's Dream (1968)
Fefu and Her Friends (1977)
The Danube (1982)
Mud (1983)
Sarita (1984)
Abingdon Square (1984)
The Conduct of Life (1984)
And What of the Night (1989–1990)

CHARACTERS

RAINBOW: 29 years old, slim and spirited

GRETA:　　26 years old, slim, handsome, and shy

RAY:　　　27 years old, high strung and handsome; he wears a dark suit

SETTING: *A small Eastern city, 1958.*

SCENE 1: GRETA IS ILL

RAINBOW's *bedroom. A small room. On the left wall there is, upstage, a small door; downstage of the door there is a small window. Downstage of the window there is a chair. In the up-right hand corner of the room there is a small bed with metal foot and headboard. On top of the bed there is a nightgown. To the left of the bed there is a night table. On the night table there is a book, a pitcher of water, and a glass. On the back wall there hangs a painting of a landscape.* RAINBOW *and* GRETA *have just entered.* GRETA *takes off her dress, sits on the bed, and starts to put on the nightgown.*

RAINBOW: Don't worry, Greta. I know what to do.

GRETA: What, Rainbow? What can you do?

RAINBOW: I'll find some money. Don't worry.

GRETA: How?

RAINBOW: I'll find money, Greta. I can't tell you how.

GRETA: Why not?

RAINBOW: You won't love me anymore if I tell you how.

GRETA: Tell me.

RAINBOW: Please don't make me tell you.

GRETA: I don't want you to do anything that would make you ashamed.

RAINBOW: I've been in jail.

GRETA: Why? What did you do?

[RAINBOW *helps* GRETA *lie down. She covers her with the sheet.*]

GRETA: [*Cont'd.*] Tell me.

RAINBOW: I've been in jail for stealing.

GRETA: Stealing?

RAINBOW: Yes. I haven't done it since I know you. But now I must do it again. You're ill and we must take care of you.

GRETA: No! I don't want you to steal for me. You'll be arrested. You'll go to jail. You mustn't.

RAINBOW: I must, my darling.

[*There is a silence.* GRETA *puts her face on the pillow and sobs.*]

SCENE 2: STEALING FOR GRETA

GRETA *is lying in bed.* RAINBOW *sits on the chair.*

RAINBOW: I got it off his pocket. He came out of the store and put it in his pocket. I grabbed it and ran. He ran after me and grabbed me. He tripped. I yanked my arm off and I threw him. Look. He tore my sleeve. [*Putting a wristwatch on* GRETA'*s hand.*] He ran after me but I was gone. Went in a building and hid. Saw him pass. Went to the back of the building and got out through the yard. I was afraid to go in the street. I was afraid he may have gone around the block. There's no one there. I walk to the corner and grab a bus. I didn't look like a thief. Would anyone think I'm a thief? Wasn't out of breath. Sat calmly— [*Getting the watch from* GRETA.] It's a good watch.

GRETA: Get rid of it.

RAINBOW: I'll sell it.

GRETA: To whom?

RAINBOW: I'll find a buyer.

GRETA: I'm afraid.

RAINBOW: Don't be.

GRETA: Just get rid of it.

RAINBOW: We need the money. For you. To make you well.

SCENE 3: RAINBOW IS CAUGHT

RAINBOW *sits turned away from* GRETA. *Her hand covers her cheek.* GRETA *lies on the bed.*

GRETA: Look at me! Who hurt you like that?

[RAINBOW *turns to face* GRETA.]

GRETA: [*Cont'd.*] Who did that to you?

RAINBOW: The man whose watch I took.

GRETA: I knew you'd get hurt. I knew you couldn't do what you were doing and not get hurt.

RAINBOW: I got careless. I went back where I got the watch.

GRETA: Why?

RAINBOW: He came from behind. He grabbed me and made me go with him.

GRETA: Where?

RAINBOW: To his place.

GRETA: Oh!

RAINBOW: I tried to get away. He forced me. I resisted and he pushed me in. He said he'd put me in jail.

GRETA: What did he do to you!

RAINBOW: I had to agree.

GRETA: To what?

RAINBOW: To do something for him.

GRETA: What!

RAINBOW: Meet someone.

GRETA: Who!

RAINBOW: He didn't say.

GRETA: What for?

RAINBOW: He's nasty.

GRETA: Are you afraid?

RAINBOW: Yes.

SCENE 4: GRETA WONDERS IF RAINBOW LOVES RAY

GRETA *lies in bed.* RAINBOW *stands left.*

RAINBOW: He's like a snake.

GRETA: Do you love him?

RAINBOW: Love him? I hate him. He hates me. He hates me for no reason. Not because of the watch. He never cared about the watch. Just for no reason. He never cared about the watch. That was nothing for him. He hates me. Just because he wants to. —I hate him but I have a reason. [*She goes to the chair.*] I understand him though.

GRETA: You do?

RAINBOW: Yes.

GRETA: How can you?

RAINBOW: I think in his heart of hearts he's not the way he appears to be.

GRETA: What is he like? He couldn't be good and do what he does.

RAINBOW: Well, he's not what he appears to be.

[*Pause.*]

GRETA: ... Could I have some water?

[RAINBOW *pours water. She lifts* GRETA'S *head up and holds the glass to* GRETA'S *lips. When* GRETA *drinks,* RAINBOW *puts the glass down and sits.*]

GRETA: [*Cont'd.*] Didn't you already do what you had to do for him? Didn't you already pay—for the watch? Why do you still have to work for him?

RAINBOW: He's a friend.

GRETA: If I die . . . Will you love him then?

RAINBOW: . . . If you die?. [*She goes to the side of the bed and kneels.*] If you die I'll love you—whether you live or die it's you I love. And if I ever loved anyone else, it would not be Ray. Not Ray. Never Ray.

[GRETA *laughs.*]

SCENE 5: HEUTE SIND KLEIDER ENG

RAINBOW *sweeps the floor.*

GRETA: You never wear clothes that fit.

RAINBOW: This?

GRETA: That's a size too small.

RAINBOW: It's my size.

GRETA: Clothes should be looser.

RAINBOW: Not any more, madam. Now clothes are tight—how do you say that in German?

GRETA: What.

RAINBOW: What I just said.

GRETA: What?

RAINBOW Now clothes are tight.

GRETA: *Heute sind Kleider eng.*

RAINBOW: [*Mispronouncing.*] *Heute sind Kleider eng.*

GRETA: [*Impatiently.*] *Heute sind Kleider eng.*

RAINBOW: How do you say, "You lose your temper too easily"?

GRETA: Who?

RAINBOW: You.

GRETA: I lose my temper?

RAINBOW: Yes.

GRETA: I don't.

RAINBOW: How do you say it?

GRETA: That I lose my temper?

RAINBOW: Yes.

GRETA: I don't lose my temper.

RAINBOW: How do you say it?

GRETA: *Ich werde niemals hefiig.*

RAINBOW: *Ich werde niemnals hefig* . . . I love German. [*She swoons to the floor.*] . . . I love German.

GRETA: That means "I don't lose my temper." Ha!

SCENE 6: RAY GIVES ADVICE TO RAINBOW

RAINBOW *stands right fluffing the pillow.* GRETA *sits up against the headboard.*

RAINBOW: Can you imagine?—And I said to him, "It's you who places too much importance on whether I like men or I like women. For me it's not important. What's important is that since I met Greta it's only she I love. [*Placing the pillow behind* GRETA.] That's what's important. [*Taking the bedspread off the bed.*] Why should it be important whether I like men or women? Does it make any difference to anyone? — [*Taking the bedspread out the door to shake it.*] If it doesn't make any difference to anyone, why should anyone care?" [*Turning to* GRETA.] He said, "If it doesn't make any difference why don't you choose to love a man?" And I said, "It doesn't make a difference to anyone else, but of course, it makes a difference to me." [*Placing the cover over* GRETA.] If I don't like men why should I pretend that I do? Why should I try to love someone I don't love when I already love someone I love? And besides, do you think it makes a difference to anyone?

GRETA: I suppose it doesn't make any difference to anyone.

RAINBOW: That's right. Why should I force myself. [*Sitting next to* GRETA.] And he said, "What difference does anything make? Live, die, it doesn't make any difference." And I said, "Live or die makes a difference. I want to live and I want to be happy but I don't care about the things you care about." And he said, "What things?" And I said, [*Walking to the chair.*] "The way you see things." And I said that I'm not going to pretend to see life the way he does. And he said, "Why not?" that he thought I should. And he said that I should care about those things and if I don't I should pretend that I do. And I said, [*Sitting.*] "Why?" And he said that he talks to me as a brother would, for my own good. And I said I thought he had some nerve because I thought his life was far from impeccable—far from it—And I told him that.

GRETA: His life is far from impeccable.

RAINBOW: I told him he had some nerve.

GRETA: Your life is impeccable now.—I don't see anything wrong with it.

RAINBOW: . . . Neither do I.

GRETA: Your life was peccable when you were working for him. But now that you've paid your debt to him and you don't work for him anymore your life is impeccable. It was he who made your life peccable.

[RAINBOW *laughs.*]

GRETA: [*Cont'd.*] Why do you laugh?

RAINBOW: How do you say peccable in German?

GRETA: Why?

SCENE 7: GRETA WONDERS HOW RAINBOW SEES THINGS

GRETA *lies in bed.* RAINBOW *sits by the window looking out into the yard.*

RAINBOW: With time and money they look better and better.

GRETA: What, honey?

RAINBOW: The flowers.

GRETA: How could that be?

RAINBOW: Maybe it's the fertilizer I put on the soil.

GRETA: What looks better?

RAINBOW: The colors. They look healthier.

GRETA: How do you see things? Do you see things different from the way I see them?

RAINBOW: Why do you ask?

GRETA: [*Smiling.*] I just wondered.

RAINBOW: Why?

GRETA: I worried...

RAINBOW: That we see things differently...?

GRETA: Yes.

RAINBOW: We don't.

SCENE 8: GRETA DISCOVERS WHAT RAINBOW DOES FOR RAY

GRETA *is standing on the chair. She is opening an envelope. She takes out some pictures and looks through them with alarm. She throws them on the floor and stares into space.* RAINBOW *enters. She looks at the pictures on the floor. Then, she looks at* GRETA.

GRETA: Is that what you do for him!

[RAINBOW *kneels down to get the pictures.* GRETA *tries to reach for the pictures.*]

GRETA: [*Cont'd.*] Why! Why!

[GRETA *starts pounding on* RAINBOW. RAINBOW *tries to hold her down.*]

GRETA: [*Cont'd.*] Why! Why are you doing that when I asked you not to! Why do you do that! —Why do you do that! —Why do you do that! You're lying naked with that man! Who is that man! What is he doing to you! Why do you do that! Why do you take your clothes off? Why do you take such pictures.

RAINBOW: I'm sorry! I'm sorry!

GRETA: Why do you do that!

RAINBOW: I have to.

GRETA: Why!

RAINBOW: Because you must have treatment.

[GRETA *cries.*]

RAINBOW: [*Cont'd.*] I don't mind. It's for you.

[GRETA *sobs.*]

RAINBOW: [*Cont'd.*] It's for you.

SCENE 9: GRETA ADMIRES THE SUNLIGHT

The shutter is closed. GRETA *sits upstage of the window. The chair faces front.* RAIN-BOW *stands next to her.*

GRETA: Could you open the window?

[RAINBOW *opens the window.*]

GRETA: [*Cont'd.*] I like to sit here and see the sun coming in. I like to let it come in through the open window. The sun is brighter that way—or so it seems to me. There are times when I feel disturbed. I feel restless. I feel nasty. And looking at the sun coming in makes me feel calm.

SCENE 10: GRETA THINKS THAT RAY IS IN LOVE

GRETA *stands left of the bed straightening the bed.* RAINBOW *sits on the chair.*

GRETA: Ray was here this afternoon.

RAINBOW: What did he want?

GRETA: He didn't say— He waited for you and then he left. [*She starts moving down as she straightens the side of the bed.*] Does he sound to you like he's in love?

RAINBOW: No.

GRETA: He sounds to me like he's in love.

RAINBOW: Who with?

GRETA: I don't know, but he sounds to me like he's in love.

RAINBOW: How does a person in love sound?

[GRETA *sits on the right side of the bed.*]

GRETA: A person in love holds his breath a little after inhaling or while they inhale. They inhale, stop for a moment and inhale a little more.

RAINBOW: I haven't seen him do that. [*She lies on the bed.*]

GRETA: I have.

RAINBOW: He seems preoccupied to me.

GRETA: Yes, I think he sounds preoccupied. Maybe he's lost money in the Market.

RAINBOW: Maybe he has. Why are you concerned about him?

GRETA: I'm not.

RAINBOW: You sound concerned.

GRETA: He's preoccupied.

SCENE 11: RAINBOW DOESN'T FEEL LOVED ANYMORE

GRETA *lies in bed.* RAINBOW *stands by the door facing her.*

RAINBOW: Something's wrong. Something's wrong because you're not happy, because you have to keep things from me. I know you don't tell me what you think—not everything. Did you ever keep things from me before? Is this something new or have you always kept things from me? [*Pause.*] Is it that you don't love me anymore?

GRETA: [*Shaking her head.*] No.

RAINBOW: For me to love is adoring. And to be loved is to be adored. So I never felt I was loved before. Till I met you. But I don't feel loved anymore.

SCENE 12: RAY WANTS SOMETHING FROM GRETA

GRETA *lies in bed.* RAY *stands to the left of the bed by her feet, facing her. She is frightened like a trapped cat.*

GRETA: I lash out at you because I can't deal with you. I can't even understand what you are.

[*In the course of the speech* RAY *moves closer and closer to her and starts to lean towards her, she recoils.*]

GRETA: [*Cont'd.*] You're like some kind of animal who comes to me with strange problems, to make strange demands on me.

[*She pushes him off. He persists.*]

GRETA: [*Cont'd.*] You come in all sweaty and hungry and you say you want this and you want that. Take your hands away from me! Not again! Not again! Never again. Don't touch me! Leave me be! I have nothing to give you. Don't tell me that you want these things. Talk about something else. What else can you talk about?

[RAINBOW *enters. She is obviously alarmed. She looks at* GRETA, *then at* RAY; *then at* GRETA *again.* GRETA *turns her head away and sobs.* RAINBOW *and* RAY *look at each other.*]

SCENE 13: RAINBOW LEAVES GRETA

RAINBOW *stands at the door looking out.* GRETA *sits on the bed looking at her.* "Melancholy Baby" *is heard:*

Come to me, my melancholy baby.
Just cuddle up and don't be blue.
All your fears are foolish fancy, baby.
You know, honey, I'm in love with you.

[GRETA *moves to the chair. She sits facing* RAINBOW. *She looks down.*]

Every cloud must have a silver lining.

[GRETA *looks at* RAINBOW.]

So wait until the sun shines through.
Smile, my honey, dear,
While I kiss away each tear.
Or else I shall be melancholy too.

[GRETA *reaches out and takes* RAINBOW's *hand.* RAINBOW *allows her to hold her hand, but does not respond.*]

Come sweetheart mine
Don't sit and pine.
Tell me all the cares
That made you feel so blue.
I'm sorry, hon.

[RAINBOW *faces* GRETA.]

What have I done.
Have I ever said
An unkind word to you.
My love is true.

[RAINBOW *leans over and puts her head next to* GRETA's.]

And just for you.
I'll do almost anything
At any time.
Hear when you sigh
Or when you cry.
Something seems to grieve
This very heart of mine.
Come to me my melancholy baby.
Just cuddle up and don't be blue.

[RAINBOW *walks to the door and stands there looking out for a while. Then she exits while the song plays to the end.* GRETA *lowers her head. Then, she looks to the back. As the song is coming to an end, she looks down again.*]

SCENE 14: GRETA READS RAINBOW'S LETTER

GRETA *walks to the chair holding a book. She sits down and opens the book. An envelope falls from it. She opens the envelope, takes out a letter and reads it.*

GRETA: "My beloved, —I'm sometimes obliged to do things that are dangerous,

—and to do things that I hate. To befriend people and then betray them. Someday I may be hurt. If this happens, and I'm not able to tell you this, I hope one day you'll open this book and find this note. I love you more than anything in the world and it is to you that I owe my happiness. I always felt that I didn't want to love only halfway, that I wanted to love with all my heart or not at all and that I wanted to be loved the same way or not at all. With you, I had this and if anything happens to me I wanted you to remember this: that you are my angel and I will always love you. Even after death. Forever yours, —Rainbow."

Carolyn Gage

CAROLYN GAGE: AN AMAZON ALL-STAR

Bonnie J. Morris

Carolyn Gage's catalogue of plays includes four one-woman shows, five full-book musicals, seven full-length dramas and comedies, and twelve one-act plays. Her work has been produced extensively at theatres, conferences, and festivals throughout the United States and Canada. Her collection of radical feminist historical dramas, *The Second Coming of Joan of Arc and Other Plays* (HerBooks, Santa Cruz), was named a National Finalist for the Lambda Literary Award in drama.

In addition to being a full-time lesbian playwright, Gage has also toured nationally as a solo performer and served as artistic director for three different theatre companies. Between 1989 and 1991, she ran a radical women's theatre in Southern Oregon, where she directed and produced nineteen plays, thirteen of which were her own. For this work, she received the Oregon Arts Commission fellowship. She has written the first manual on lesbian theatre production and direction, titled *Take Stage!*, and she continues to challenge and appropriate the conventions of traditional theatre.

Regional work of Gage's quickly moved beyond the Pacific Northwest, and two of her one-act plays were brought to the East Coast Lesbian Festival in 1993. This crossover by Gage and other playwrights into festival staging, another primary venue for the presentation of recent texts in lesbian drama and comedy, is significant. For twenty years, women's festivals in the United States—the Michigan Womyn's Music Festival, the National Women's Music Festival in Indiana, the East Coast Lesbian Festival, and a dozen others—have offered the best in women-identified entertainment: musical performance, comedy, one-woman shows. Assuming the lesbian sensibility of the audience present, festivals are able to introduce performance art which expands an awareness of lesbian identity in other cultures—deaf, Jewish, Asian, Latina, African-American. This multi-cultural lesbian intensity, humor, and wordplay of the festival stage sheds light on what lesbian audiences crave: lesbian realities without apology. It was at just such a festival that I, along with hundreds of other women, first encountered Carolyn Gage's notorious one-acts: *Louisa May Incest* and *The Second Coming of Joan of Arc*.

Gage's particular brilliance lies in her skill at juxtaposing lesbian reality with our collective herstoric imagination as a people. Her signature one-act works, *Louisa* and *Joan*, compel us to view heroism and martyrdom in lesbian context and to re-examine the lives of actual women whose probable lesbianism was written out of history by scholarly or religious curators.

In Gage's *Louisa May Incest*, the author Louisa May Alcott is confronted by her own "boyish" creation, Jo March, just at the moment when the author has decided to marry off the character to Mr. Bhaer, a moral father-figure, at the end of *Little Women*. Horrified, the character Jo, who appears here as lover, muse, alter ego, and dependent invention, insists that Louisa herself is lesbian and that Jo must live out that reality on the printed page, rather than reproduce the hinted incestuous relations between the child Louisa and her eccentric father Bronson Alcott. The play is a phenomenal tribute to the real-life Louisa May Alcott's compromises in supporting herself as a writer in the moralistic nineteenth century. Moreover, it feeds a very real desire in an audience of literate American women for more rebellion from the beloved character Jo March. In reconstructing both Jo and Louisa as lesbians, Gage acknowledges lesbian readers' early identification with Jo.

For Gage, both *Louisa May Incest* and the even more radical *Second Coming of Joan of Arc* pose risks as herstory and psychodrama. Posthumously attributed lesbianism remains one of feminist theory's great conflicts. In *Feminist Theory: A Critique of Ideology*, Ann Ferguson refutes Adrienne Rich's popular essay "Compulsory Heterosexuality and Lesbian Existence" by asserting the following:

> First, and tautologically, a person cannot be said to have a sexual identity that is not self-conscious, that is, it is not meaningful to conjecture that someone is lesbian who refuses to acknowledge herself as such. Taking on a lesbian identity is a self-conscious commitment or decision...A second condition for self-conscious lesbian identity is that one live in a culture where the concept has relevance...Thus, in a period of human history where the distinctions between heterosexual, bisexual and homosexual identity are not present as human categories (namely, until the twentieth century), people cannot correctly be said to have been lesbian or bisexual. [Ferguson, 154–155][1]

While numerous theorists have debated Ferguson, other critics also warn against any posthumous conjectural identification of public figures as lesbians. One misplaced motive for such reticence is homophobic "respect" for families of the deceased, as in the speculation about Eleanor Roosevelt's lesbianism. In resurrecting Joan of Arc, Gage asks her audiences to question the hegemonic bogeyman of historical accuracy. Are Church interpretations of Joan the only truth? Why is Alcott's family-values literature promoted as such without the context of

1. Ferguson, Ann. "Patriarchy, Sexual Identity, and the Sexual Revolution." *Feminist Theory: A Critique of Ideology*, ed. Nannerl O. Keohane, Michelle Z. Rosaldo, and Barbara C. Gelpi (Chicago: University of Chicago Press, 1982), 154-155.

her father's experimentation on his children? Who decides how defiant women's lives are represented, posthumously?

When I saw Gage's *Joan* and *Louisa* at the East Coast Lesbian Festival in 1993, the festival audience of present-day Amazons, fresh and fierce from several days of lesbian political networking, were ready to question any authority or orthodoxy. Watching Jo confront Louisa, the audience's collective belief marked a new point in taking ourselves seriously as people with a herstory; as creators and receivers of lesbian mysticism and art. Lesbian writers, theorists, and professors—in large numbers at ECLF—were absolutely transported by the academic significance of Gage's work. Lesbian cultural institutions, such as festivals, conferences, and retreats, must do more to promote the work of playwrights such as Gage.

The title of Gage's musical *Amazon All-Stars* comes from the fantasy life of one character in the play, who, like many lesbians, prefers the symbolism of sisterly utopia to the reality of personal and team relationships. And that's a fitting introduction to the play text itself. This two-act softball musical was successfully produced in both California and Oregon in 1990–91. Sue Carney, who composed the music, lost a teaching job as the result of her association with the lesbian revue. Unlike *Louisa* and *Joan*, *Amazon All-Stars* utilizes a contemporary setting, with fictive but eminently recognizable characters whose very disharmony and interdependence as a softball team is a microcosm of the lesbian community.

Among the team characters are the persons we have been, are afraid of becoming, or would secretly like to be: Ursula, the baby dyke no one takes seriously; Slide, the confident stud; K.C., her frantic and clinging partner; Ruth, the stubborn alcoholic; Jan, the new player in town with an eye for some action. As nearly all scenes move between locker room, bedroom, and bar room, we recognize three archetypal dyke environments invoked as backgrounds for relationship staging. Themes of longing, confrontation, forgiveness, and loss are the four bases of this softball diamond, but even more aptly, Gage exposes the lesbian community's most frustrating soul-search: Do we want to play hard, play hard to win like the boys, or do we have the feminist responsibility to cooperate, to be kindly rather than competitive, to take care of our own? These are not just athletic concerns. While players may argue the rules of softball, the play subtly suggests, at least rules are written and confirmed by coaches, umpires, and clearly declared winners. Lesbian relationships operate without such clearly posted guidelines.

In Gage's musical, the arrival of new player Jan is the catalyst for upheaval on the "Desert Hearts" team, named for the 1986 lesbian film based on Jane Rule's novel *Desert of the Heart*. Gage uses this convention of the newcomer to reveal an array of familiar human weaknesses in the team personalities. Jan is a skilled shortstop, but unfortunately that team position has always been held by Ruth, an alcoholic haunted by the loss of her lover of eight years. Ruth's ex-lover happens to be the team's inconsistent manager, Hitch, who collapses into fresh ambivalence over the challenge of whether the new and better shortstop should replace Ruth. To whom is loyalty due? Should Hitch promote the more reliable Jan or reward Ruth's contributions to the early days of the team by granting her tenure at shortstop? Jan impatiently waits for a decision while setting her cap for Kelly, the remote fielder consumed by fantasies of glory and recognition.

These dramatic tensions are interrupted by humorous and hard-hitting musical numbers, which pay homage to contemporary lesbian culture in their stream of references to Joann Loulan, *On Our Backs*, the Michigan Womyn's Music Festival, and closeted women's studies professors. In one song, "When Women Do It To Each Other," Ruth laments the lingering breakup process between women, pointing out that when men dump women, "...it's nasty, it's mean; it's over, it's finished, but dammit, it's clean!" Jan, in attempting to seduce the other-worldly Kelly, experiences the ghosts of all her ex-lovers rising up to taunt her in a hilarious musical dream sequence. Again, these songs reveal a popular subject in lesbian culture: the ranking of relationships, the struggle of finding, keeping, or simply defining a primary lover in a world which seldom acknowledges our romantic commitments.

Gage deftly portrays such lesbian contradictions. When Leona, who secretly covets Hitch, urges her to replace the troubled Ruth altogether, Hitch objects:

HITCH: I don't know, Leona. It just seems like lesbians have it hard enough everywhere else. When we get together to play softball, maybe it's more important to let people do what they want.

LEONA: And have a shitty team that nobody takes seriously. I don't want to come out and practice unless I know we're doing our damndest to win.

HITCH: But that's what the whole straight world is about—winning. Isn't there a place where people can just do what they do and enjoy it, without always getting criticized and judged about it?

LEONA: You tell me when you find that place.

Gage's Desert Hearts act out the no-win dilemma many women face. Competitive hardness in women is the quality least forgiven by male society; and niceness has been pathologized as codependent behavior. Bar culture remains vulnerable to the charge of fostering decades of lesbian alcoholism, and sex in the age of AIDS kills. Only the playing field seems safely apolitical. We know from Martina Navratilova's experience that lesbian girljocks don't win endorsements. We play well for the thrill of it, often without witnesses, a style than informs our "action" off the field as well.

Gage's play offers forgiveness as well as loss. Ruth gets her say in a powerful scene at the play's end, where she indicates that her struggle with alcohol is not necessarily more of an escape than Slide's manipulative seductions or Kelly and Hitch's different fantasies of the perfect sisterhood nation. Each player is forced to confront her personal demons and to compromise. Gage asks us to consider how well-conditioned we are, as a community, for batting and fielding one another's awkward truths.

CHARACTERS

LEATHER WOMAN: The Emcee. Also plays the Sportscaster, the Bartender, the Pageant Emcee, the Dark Alley Dyke, the Starship Captain, and the Doctor.

URSULA: First base, baby dyke. Seventeen. Also plays a Butchette, Bass Player for the Electric Clits, and the Ex-Best Friend.

SLIDE: Second base, record for stealing bases, third base's lover. Early twenties.

GLORIA: Center field, peacemaker, passes for straight. Thirty. Also plays a Butchette, the Bossy Femme, and the Third Grade Teacher.

LEONA: Catcher, in love with the pitcher. Forties. Also plays a Butchette, the Women's Studies Professor, and the Little League Coach.

HITCH: Pitcher/manager for the Desert Hearts. Late thirties or early forties.

RUTH: Short stop, former lover of the pitcher, an alcoholic. Late thirties.

K.C.: Third base, second base's lover. Early twenties.

JAN: New member of the team, always gets on base. Mid-twenties.

KELLY: Left field, prefers to live in her fantasy world most of the time, survivor. Mid-twenties.

PHOTOGRAPHER: Also plays Rubyfruit Dancer, Swedish Weightlifter, Last Girlfriend, Starship Crew Member.

REPORTER: Also plays Rubyfruit Dancer, Australian Weightlifter, Starship Navigator, Kelly's Mom.

SYNOPSIS OF SCENES

ACT I

Scene 1: The interior of a women's locker room located in the town where the show is being produced.
Scene 2: The press box of the World Series of Women's Softball.
Scene 3: The locker room.
Scene 4: The sidewalk outside the Rubyfruit Bar and Grill.
Scene 5: The interior of the Rubyfruit.
Scene 6: The stage of the Miss Butch Universe Pageant.
Scene 7: The Rubyfruit Bar and Grill.
Scene 8: The porch of Kelly's house.
Scene 9: The interior of Jan's bedroom.

ACT II

Scene 1: The theatre.
Scene 2: The interior of the locker room.
Scene 3: The bridge of the Starship Intercourse.
Scene 4: The locker room.

Scene 5: The ball field.
Scene 6: The interior of the Rubyfruit Bar and Grill.
Scene 7: A bench outside the Rubyfruit.
Scene 8: The interior of the Rubyfruit.
Scene 9: The locker room.

SYNOPSIS OF MUSIC

ACT I

"Cruisin'" ....LEATHER WOMAN

Scene 1:
"Come Out For The Team" ....URSULA, LEONA, GLORIA,
SLIDE, K.C., HITCH, JAN
"She Doesn't Even See Me" ....JAN

Scene 3:
"When Women Do It To Each Other" ....RUTH

Scene 5:
"The Rubyfruit Bar and Grill" ....LEATHER WOMAN, RUBYFRUIT DANCERS

Scene 6:
"The Ballad Of The Butch" ....LEATHER WOMAN, BUTCHETTES

Scene 9:
"Is She A Butch Or A Femme?" ....JAN
"Hex of the Ex's" ....LEATHER WOMAN, EX-LOVERS

ACT II

Scene 1:
"Cruisin'" (reprise)..LEATHER WOMAN

Scene 3:
"Sisterspace"................LEATHER WOMAN, NAVIGATOR, CREW MEMBER, THE BAND

Scene 4:
"Pour Me" ....RUTH

Scene 5:
"You Gotta Get Under The Glove"..................LEATHER WOMAN, SLIDE, HITCH,
LEONA, K.C., GLORIA, URSULA
"She Doesn't Even See Me" (reprise) ....JAN

Scene 9:
"The Wrong Song" ....THIRD-GRADE TEACHER, LITTLE LEAGUE
COACH, EX-BEST FRIEND, KELLY'S MOM
"Cruisin'" (reprise)..LEATHER WOMAN

Finale
"Come Out For The Team" (reprise) ....FULL CAST

ACT I

PROLOGUE

The curtain is drawn, or the stage is completely dark.

The overture ends, and drum roll is heard. Cymbals crash as a spotlight comes up on a woman dressed in leather, standing in front of the curtain, or in the area of the stage where the fantasy scenes will be played.

LEATHER WOMAN is our surrealistic Mistress of Ceremonies for the evening. She is part of the show, but she maintains an identity apart from the action.

LEATHER WOMAN: Welcome to *The Amazon All-Stars*! I know you're all here tonight to meet the members of [*name of town where the theatre is located*]'s hottest lesbian softball team, the Desert Hearts! The girls with the spikes... [*Cymbals crash.*]... the girls with the gloves... [*Cymbals crash.*]... and they can't wait to meet you... but before they do their little show for you, the Desert Hearts wanted me to come out... [*Drums.*]... and tell you how happy they were to hear you were here. Tonight we are going to take you on a journey to the center of lesbian culture to witness the secret rituals and ancient rites of a tribe which is as old as history, as universal as sex, as primitive as lust, and as juicy as they come. Tonight you will see lesbian life as it has never been shown before on any stage. You will see acts which will amaze you, which will outrage you, which will leave you helpless in the aisles, begging for more. Everything you've heard about lesbians... It's all true, and tonight you're going to see it and more, live and on stage. So, sit back, relax, enjoy the show! And, girls—please, let's not be formal... Come as you are! [*She sings "Cruisin'" while she cruises through the house, the spotlight tracking her.*]

I see you lookin'—
You like what you see?
Yeah, I'm lookin' at you,
And you're lookin' at me!
Because we're cruisin'—

Cruisin' tonight—
Cruisin' kinda heavy,
Cruisin' kinda light—
But we're cruisin' the girls—
You all look so fine—
Cruisin' tonight—
I'm losin' my mind!

You're lookin' good,
You're lookin' fine—
I'm lookin', you're lookin'—
Hope you don't mind,
'Cause I'm on a mission,
I'm on a roll.
I sing while I do it—
It's called cruise control!

That's what we do
On the girls' night out—
We cruise.
Yeah, cruise—
'Til they turn the lights out.
Cruise the girls
Cruisin', cruisin'—
Oh, baby, we're cruisin' tonight.

That's what we're here for
Just so you know
The cast and the crew—
We're doin' the show
So you can all go
Cruisin', cruisin' tonight
Cruisin' kinda heavy,
Cruisin' kinda light—
Cruisin',
Cruisin',
Cruisin' tonight!

[*At the end of the song, the* LEATHER WOMAN *takes a bow and her spotlight disappears. Blackout.*]

SCENE 1

Lights come up on the interior of a women's locker room, with a locker unit, benches, and a garbage can. There is a team tournament chart on the wall.
    URSULA *enters, followed by* GLORIA *and* LEONA.
    URSULA *is a baby dyke, the youngest member of the team. She's still in high school, and the others tease her about this. She plays first base, and she's very serious about her game.*
    GLORIA *is the center fielder. She is a femme, passing on the job. She is the team diplomat.*
    LEONA *is the catcher. Like a good catcher,* LEONA *sees it all. She is impatient with human weaknesses, and her crush on the pitcher is causing her a lot of problems.*
    The women are busy dressing down for practice.

URSULA: Hey, where is everybody? I thought I was going to be the last one here today.

GLORIA: They're all late.

LEONA: They're all lesbians.

URSULA: Yeah, but we're lesbians too, and we're not late.

LEONA: That's because you're too young to know better, Gloria's in the closet, and I'm so deviant I don't even make a good dyke.

[SLIDE *enters, singing* "What's Love Got To Do With It." SLIDE *is second base.*

She thinks about sex most of the time, except when she's asleep, and then she dreams about it. SLIDE *holds the league record for stealing bases.*]

URSULA: Hey, Slide! I saw you last night at the bar. Who was that beautiful woman you were dancing with?

SLIDE: We didn't just dance, and wouldn't you like to know?

URSULA: Hey, come on . . . What's her name?

SLIDE: No way, baby dyke! Get your own girlfriends.

GLORIA: Did you and K.C. break up or something, Slide?

SLIDE: Where'd you get that idea?

GLORIA: Well, if you're out dancing with somebody else last night . . .

SLIDE: So—I'm out dancing with somebody else . . . That doesn't mean I'm breaking up with K.C. What she doesn't know isn't going to hurt her.

[*No one says anything.*]

SLIDE: [*Cont'd.*] Come on . . . Do you think I could stand living with K.C. for three years if I didn't go out with other women? How else am I going to stay faithful to her?

LEONA: Oh, yeah. What you say, Slide.

SLIDE: Get real, Leona. Stealing's just part of the game.

LEONA: Just wait till you get caught. You'll be singing out of the other side of your face.

SLIDE: Who's gonna catch me?

GLORIA: K.C.

SLIDE: K.C? She'd be the last one to catch me.

URSULA: How you figure that?—

SLIDE: Because K.C. isn't gonna see what she doesn't want to see . . . Just like most people . . . even you, Leona.

LEONA: Me?

SLIDE: Yeah, you. Everybody knows who you've got a crush on, except you.

[*Just then* HITCH *enters.* HITCH *is the pitcher/manager of the Desert Hearts.* HITCH *wants everyone to like her, which seriously impairs her ability to manage the team effectively.*]

HITCH: Hi, guys!

SLIDE: Speak of the devil.

LEONA: [*Brightening up at the sight of* HITCH.] Hey, it's Hitch!

SLIDE: Hey, Hitch, when do we get to meet the new player?

HITCH: She's supposed to be here today for the practice.

SLIDE: Yeah? What's she look like?

GLORIA: The point is what does she play like?

URSULA: Yeah, Hitch... What position is she gonna play?

[RUTH *appears in the doorway. She is the team's current short stop. At one time she was a powerful player, but her alcoholism has begun to impair her judgment and her ability. She is the pitcher's former lover, and she is in denial about both her drinking and the reality of that relationship.*]

RUTH: She's going to play right field.

[*There is silence from the rest of the players.*]

URSULA: How you feeling Ruth?

RUTH: Fine. I feel fine.

[*Silence.*]

RUTH: Is there something wrong with that?

HITCH: We just didn't expect to see you back so soon.

RUTH: It was just lousy flu, that's all... What'd you think? I'd be gone for three weeks or something?

URSULA: Last time it was a month.

RUTH: Last time it wasn't flu. But this time it was. Okay?

[*Silence.*]

RUTH: Well, isn't anybody glad to see their short stop?

HITCH: Yeah, okay, Ruth... Everybody's glad to see you.

RUTH: And that new girl is going to play right field.

LEONA: I'm glad you're back, Ruth, but it's not up to you where she plays.

RUTH: It's obvious, isn't it? Joanne is gone. We need a right fielder. A new player shows up. She plays right field... What's the problem?

URSULA: Maybe the new player's better at something else. I mean, anybody can play right field. That's where you want to put your weakest player. Maybe she's too good for right field. It wouldn't make sense to put her there just because she's new.

LEONA: Ursula, honey, even for a baby dyke you still got a lot to learn.

URSULA: [*Crossing to* LEONA, *in front of* SLIDE.] Well, I mean, I know we all like the positions we play, but if somebody came along who was better, wouldn't we all want to see the best person in the best position?

SLIDE: [*Grabbing* URSULA.] Yeah!

URSULA: [*Disentangling herself from* SLIDE.] Slide! I mean, that's the whole point— what's best for the team.

LEONA: Like I say, a lot to learn.

RUTH: She's playing right field.

LEONA: Ruth, we all elected Hitch to be our manager, and it's her job to make decisions like this. She's the only one who says what position the new girl plays.

RUTH: Right field, isn't it Hitch?

HITCH: [*Avoiding the conflict.*] Hey, gimme a break. She hasn't even gotten here yet.

[HITCH *crosses upstage to the tournament chart with her clipboard. Just then* K.C. *walks in. She is looking for* SLIDE. *She is in love with* SLIDE *and jealous about her, but she is even more afraid of losing her.*]

URSULA: K.C! Guess what? We're getting a new player today!

K.C.: [*Only aware of* SLIDE.] Where were you?

SLIDE: [*All innocence.*] What do you mean, where was I?

K.C.: I mean, where were you? I went by to pick you up at work and the guys at the warehouse told me you never showed up today. They said you called in sick.

SLIDE: Oh, yeah. Well, a friend was moving and I had to help her.

[URSULA *and* GLORIA *exchange a look.*]

K.C.: Who?

SLIDE: [*Pulling at* K.C.'s *sweatshirt provocatively.*] Someone from work. [*Nestling against her.*] Look, I've already forgotten her name.

K.C.: Why didn't you say something about it this morning? You could have taken me to work and had the truck.

SLIDE: I forgot.

[*A tense silence.*]

SLIDE: [*Cont'd.*] Hey, if you don't want to believe me . . .

K.C.: [*Giving in to* SLIDE's *attentions.*] I didn't say I didn't believe you.

GLORIA: So, Hitch . . . Tell us what you know about the new player.

HITCH: Well, her name is Jan and she's new in town. She says she's been playing fast pitch for ten years.

URSULA: Is she a dyke?

LEONA: Ursula, use your head.

SLIDE: Better technique.

[*The team responds to* SLIDE's *innuendo with a groan.*]

URSULA: [*Protesting.*] What? I mean, she could be a straight woman and she signed up by accident.

LEONA: If she's signed up for the Lavender League to play softball with the Desert Hearts, and she hasn't figured out we're all lesbians, then I'll eat my hat.

SLIDE: Why don't you eat mine?

[*Another team groan.*]

LEONA: [*Referring to* SLIDE.] Would somebody spay her?

HITCH: Don't worry . . . Jan's a lesbian. One of the reasons why she wants to join the team is so she can meet other lesbians.

SLIDE: Why else does anybody play softball? That's how we met, me and K.C. [*She sings the opening verse of "Come Out For The Team."*.]

> I met her at the park one day
> When I was playin' ball.
> She was standin' by the bleachers.
> She was leanin' on a wall.
>
> I said:
>
> You're lookin' kinda lonely, girl—
> You know what I mean.
> You can get to play with me,
> If you come out for the team.

CHORUS: Come out for the team—
You know what I mean!
You can't do it by yourself alone!
Come out for the team!
Out for the, out for the team!

URSULA: I was walkin' home from school one day—
I was feelin' kinda blue
I passed a field of rowdy girls
Who told me what to do.

> They said:
>
> Don't waste your time just watchin', girl—
> Find out what we mean:
> You learn the game by playin' it—
> So come out for the team!

CHORUS: Come out for the team—
You know what I mean!
You can't do it by yourself alone!
Come out for the team!
Out for the, out for the team!

GLORIA: I was sittin' in the church one day.
I was kneelin' in the stall.
I closed my eyes and said a prayer—
The answer came, "play ball!"

> I didn't know a single girl—
> If you know what I mean,
> But in my heart I knew that day
> I'd come out for the team!

CHORUS: Come out for the team—
You know what I mean!

You can't do it by yourself alone!
Come out for the team!
Out for the, out for the team!

[*The Desert Hearts break out into dancing during the instrumental bridge. Suddenly the door slams open. The women freeze, and all of the music and singing stops.* JAN *enters, holding a glove and a ball.*]

JAN: Hi, I've come out for the team!

[*She pitches the ball to* LEONA *and breaks into song.*]

When I was just a baby girl,
Before I learned to walk—
I pitched my bottle 'cross the room,
'Cause I was born a jock!

I was born to play with girls—
If you know what I mean—
So every time I get the chance,
I come out for the team!

CHORUS: Come out for the team—
You know what I mean!
You can't do it by yourself alone!
Come out for the team!
Out for the, out for the team!

[*At the end of the song, the players return to their benches, lacing up shoes and getting equipment out of their bags.*]

HITCH: You must be Jan, the new player.

JAN: Yep.

HITCH: Welcome. I'm Laura. We spoke on the phone.

URSULA: Laura? Hey, that's not her name. It's Hitch.

JAN: Hitch?

HITCH: Yeah. Hitch. As in "pitch," as in "bitch" . . .

RUTH: As in "ditch."

LEONA: [*Intercepting.*] We call her Hitch, because right before she throws the pitch she always does this thing with her sleeves. [*She demonstrates the way* HITCH *hitches up her sleeves.*]

GLORIA: She's also our manager.

RUTH: She likes being the one on top.

HITCH: [*Cutting* RUTH *off.*] This is Ruth.

RUTH: Short stop.

JAN: Yeah? That's what I used to play on my old team.

[*She extends a hand to* RUTH, *who ignores it.*]

RUTH: You're going to play right field for us.

[RUTH *exits the locker room, and* LEONA *starts to go after her.*]

HITCH: [*Quickly, to stop* LEONA.] Jan, this is Leona. She's our catcher. She never misses anything.

LEONA: [*Glaring after* RUTH.] Almost never. [*She lightens up as she turns to* JAN.] Welcome to the team, Jan. We're glad to have you.

HITCH: And Slide... our second base. She holds the league record for stealing bases.

SLIDE: You single?

K.C.: [*Jumping up to intercept.*] She always makes jokes like that. Don't take her seriously. I'm K.C. Third base. Slide and I live together. We've been together almost three years.

JAN: Nice to meet you both.

HITCH: And this is Gloria, center fielder.

JAN: Gloria...

SLIDE: [*Cutting in.*] Gloria's really a football player.

GLORIA: Slide, what are you talking about?

SLIDE: Oh, come on, Gloria... Don't be so modest. She's famous for passing.

JAN: Oh, yeah?

SLIDE: [*Laughing at her own joke.*] Yeah. You can't even tell she's a dyke!

[*The team groans as* K.C. *pulls* SLIDE *back to the bench.*]

GLORIA: [*Ignoring the remark.*] Jan... welcome to the team. You can see what we're up against.

SLIDE: [*Pulling away from* K.C.] You all wish!

[*More groans.*]

HITCH: And Ursula, our baby dyke. She's still in high school.

URSULA: I'm older than I look.

JAN: [*Smiling.*] In that case, I'm younger than I look.

HITCH: She's our first base. The best one we've ever had.

URSULA: Hey, thanks Hitch.

JAN: So... someone's missing. Where's your left fielder?

SLIDE: Where else? Out in left field!

GLORIA: That's not funny.

SLIDE: What? She is! Kelly's always out in left field.

HITCH: Kelly plays left field. She's usually a little late, but she'll be here.

SLIDE: She may be present, but whether or not she's really here—well, that's another story.

GLORIA: Come on, Slide. Lay off.

SLIDE: Hey, look, I like Kelly as much as anybody, but let's face it—the girl's got a definite problem.

[*Silence.*]

SLIDE: [*Cont'd.*] What? Is somebody going to tell Jan about it, or do we all just stand around and pretend Kelly's normal?

GLORIA: She is normal!

SLIDE: Oh, right!

HITCH: Different. Kelly's different...in a...a...different way. You see, she... well, Kelly...

URSULA: If you just yell her name when the ball's heading her way, she's great. She hardly ever misses. You just have to remember to yell at her, that's all.

GLORIA: Yeah. It's no big deal.

SLIDE: See? Normal. Perfectly normal.

HITCH: Kelly has a habit of...well, she...She kind of goes off into her own world.

SLIDE: Try "outer space."

HITCH: And when she does that, she doesn't see or hear anything that's going on around her.

JAN: Is she brain damaged or something?

HITCH: No, she just...Well, she got hurt a lot as a kid, and I think she just finds it safer to stay in her fantasy world. That way no one can hurt her. But she's a real sweet girl, and we all love her. She's just...different.

[HITCH *retreats to her locker.*]

SLIDE: [*Sizing up the new player.*] So...Jan, what's your story?

JAN: Me? Well, I've been playing short stop ever since high school, for ten years now.

SLIDE: Ten years as short stop? Pretty tough position.

JAN: [*Sizing up the competition.*] I'm a pretty tough girl.

SLIDE: Yeah, but how are you as a hitter?

JAN: Put it this way—I always get on base.

SLIDE: As a runner?

JAN: [*Smiling.*] I don't stay too long in one place.

SLIDE: Sound pretty sure of yourself.

JAN: Yeah.

HITCH: [*Cutting in.*] Welcome to the Desert Hearts, Jan. Take any locker you want. Here's Joanne's old uniform. See you on the field. Let's go girls...Hustle!

[SLIDE *lingers to talk to* JAN *after the others have left, but* K.C. *knows what she's up to.*]

K.C.: Come on, honey!

[K.C. *pulls her lover out to the field. The locker room is empty, and* JAN *begins to dress down. Slowly the door to the locker room swings open, and* KELLY *wanders in. She walks as if she is in some kind of trance. The onset of* KELLY's *trances is always accompanied by the sound of fantasy music. Crossing to her locker, she takes off her shirt, which is over a tee shirt, and changes her shoes absent-mindedly.* JAN, *attracted to her, makes a bid for her attention.*]

JAN: Hi.

[KELLY *does not notice her.*]

JAN: [*Cont'd.*] I'm the new right fielder.

[KELLY *still doesn't hear her.*]

JAN: [*Cont'd.*] The rest of the team's already out on field . . . I'm a little late.

[*No response.*]

JAN: [*Cont'd.*] Say, you must be the one who's in left field . . . I mean . . . You must be Kelly. [*Suddenly* JAN *remembers* URSULA's *advice.*] That's it! Yell at her . . . [*Yelling.*] Kelly! Kelly!

KELLY: [*Turning suddenly in the direction of the voice, and extending her glove as if to catch a fly.*] What? Oh . . .

JAN: [*Extending her hand.*] Hi, I'm Jan. I'm new on the team. This is my first day.

KELLY: Oh, hi. I'm Kelly. Glad to meet you. [*She goes back into her trance-like state, finishes dressing, and heads out to the field.*]

JAN: [*Unaware that she is alone.*] Yeah, well, I just moved to town, and I haven't really met anybody yet . . . you know . . . so I'm really happy to connect with a lesbian softball league. Back home, I used to play short stop for a team and I had a pretty good batting average, too. In fact, last year I had a reputation for . . . [*Turning around, she realizes that* KELLY *has left. She finishes her remark talking to herself.*] . . . always getting on base. [*She laughs ruefully and sings "She Doesn't Even See Me" as she finishes changing.*]

She doesn't even see me.
Well, what a big surprise . . .
I want her to believe me—
I don't want her to leave—
Even though I know it's a lie.

She doesn't even know who I am.
I told her I could be someone to hold her—
But could I?

[JAN *picks up* KELLY's *shirt reflectively.*]

She doesn't even see me.
I can't imagine why—
Why did I tell her those lies?

[*At the end of the song,* SLIDE *appears in the doorway.*]

SLIDE: Forget it.

JAN: [*Startled, she drops the shirt and moves away from it.*] Oh! You surprised me.

SLIDE: If you're thinking about Kelly, forget it.

JAN: Who says I'm thinking about anyone?

SLIDE: [*Picking up the discarded shirt.*] Well, you're singing about somebody.

JAN: Maybe I am, and maybe I'm not.

SLIDE: Nobody gets anywhere with Kelly. Believe me . . . nobody.

JAN: Does that mean you tried?

[JAN *stands tossing a ball.*]

SLIDE: Yeah, sure I tried. I'm not blind.

[*She intercepts the ball, and then pitches it back to* JAN.]

SLIDE: [*Cont'd.*] But she is. Never mind what the others say . . . There is something wrong with that girl. Not playing with a full deck, you know? Doesn't have both oars in the water . . . The elevator doesn't go to the top floor . . . [*Crossing so close to* JAN, *she is touching her.*] Know what I mean?

JAN: [*Appraising* SLIDE.] Maybe.

SLIDE: [*Pulling away, irritated.*] Maybe nothing. I been playing with the Desert Hearts for five years, and I've known Kelly all that time, and . . .

JAN: And if you couldn't make it with her, nobody can.

SLIDE: [*Eyeing her competitively.*] Yeah. Yeah, you might say that.

JAN: [*She laughs.*] You might say it . . . I wouldn't.

SLIDE: [*Riled.*] I've got a hundred dollars says you're not going to get to first base with Kelly.

JAN: I don't have a hundred dollars.

SLIDE: How about your mitt?

JAN: Against your hundred dollars?

SLIDE: Yeah.

JAN: Your loss.

SLIDE: Maybe.

JAN: What's the time limit?

SLIDE: [*She laughs.*] It isn't going to matter.

JAN: One week.

SLIDE: One week? You must be pretty sure of yourself.

JAN: Like I told you, I always get on base. [JAN *crosses towards the door.*]

SLIDE: Well, don't wear your glove out in the meantime.

JAN: [*Turning around, she throws the ball to* SLIDE.] Let's play ball!

[JAN *exits and* SLIDE *follows after her, tossing the ball up and talking to herself.*]

SLIDE: One week . . . in your dreams!

[SLIDE *exits onto the field as* HITCH *ushers* RUTH *into the locker room.*]

RUTH: All right, all right, all right! Here we are in the locker room. Now what is it you want to tell me that you can't say in front of the rest of the team?

HITCH: Ruth, it isn't something I couldn't say in front of the team. It just seemed better if we had some privacy.

RUTH: And since when do you and I have anything to be private about?

HITCH: Please, Ruth . . . don't . . .

RUTH: [*Cutting her off.*] Right—don't bring up the past. We lived together for eight years, but one day you just decide it's over and I have to move out, and now nobody's allowed to mention the subject. Right.

HITCH: [*Determined not to get hooked.*] That isn't what I wanted to talk about.

RUTH: I know what you want to talk about. You want to talk about where I was last week. You and the rest of the team think I was out on a binge like last time. Well, I wasn't. I had the flu. But there's no use in telling you, because I know you won't believe me.

HITCH: I believe you. That's not what I wanted to talk about.

RUTH: [*Surprised and not a little hurt.*] Good, because I don't want to talk about it either.

HITCH: It's about Jan . . . the new player.

RUTH: [*Giving her a warning look.*] You mean the new right fielder.

HITCH: That's what I want to talk about, Ruth. I want her to play short stop.

[RUTH *responds to this with a long silence.*]

RUTH: [*Finally.*] Well, go ahead, Laura—drop the other shoe. I can't stand the suspense.

HITCH: I want you to take right field.

[RUTH *begins to laugh.*]

HITCH: [*Cont'd.*] What are you laughing at?

[*No answer, as* RUTH *continues to laugh.*]

HITCH: [*Cont'd.*] Ruth! What's so funny?

RUTH: You, Laura. You're funny.

HITCH: What do you mean?

RUTH: Because you're so transparent.

HITCH: What do you mean?

RUTH: Why don't you just come out and ask me to quit the Desert Hearts? It's obvious to me that's what this is about.

HITCH: No, it isn't. The new player has a lot more experience as short stop, and I think it's the best thing for the team.

RUTH: Oh, sure . . . the perfect cover. Laura, you are such a coward. You always were and you always will be. You never could just come out and say what you meant.

HITCH: [*Frustrated.*] Stop trying to make this personal! It's a professional decision.

RUTH: Oh, sure. Sure. That's why you had to bring me into the locker room to do it. I guess the principal's office wasn't available.

HITCH: Dammit, Ruth! Everything doesn't have to be so hard! Why do you always have to make it that way?

RUTH: Me? I didn't kick myself out of your bed after eight years. I didn't kick myself out into right field. I am not the one making things hard, Laura. Let's get that straight. You're the one who has decided that I'm not good enough for the positions anymore. I didn't decide that. I still think I'm a damned good short stop, and I have never stopped being your lover and I never will, whether or not you want me.

HITCH: [*She sighs.*] Okay, Ruth . . . How about this—Would you just try right field, so we can see how Jan looks as a short stop?

[RUTH *doesn't say anything.*]

HITCH: [*Cont'd.*] Just for a while.

[RUTH *still doesn't say anything.*]

HITCH: [*Cont'd.*] If you don't like it, you can go back to being short stop.

RUTH: How long?

HITCH: Well, I don't know . . .

RUTH: One week. But that's all.

HITCH: Thanks, Ruth.

RUTH: No problem.

[RUTH *exits.* HITCH *stays behind to recover from the encounter.* LEONA *enters.*]

LEONA: Hitch?

HITCH: Yeah?

LEONA: Just wondering where you went.

HITCH: I'll be out in a minute.

LEONA: You told Ruth, didn't you?

HITCH: Yeah.

LEONA: She doesn't look too happy about it.

HITCH: Well, who would be? It's tough to play right field when you want to be short stop.

LEONA: Yeah, but that's part of the game. You gotta go with what's best for the team.

HITCH: Not everyone's a team player.

LEONA: [*Picking up on* HITCH's *attitude.*] Hey, you didn't back down, did you?

[HITCH *looks at her hands.*]

LEONA: [*Cont'd.*] Aw, Hitch—how long are you gonna let that woman make you feel guilty?

[HITCH *doesn't answer.*]

LEONA: [*Cont'd.*] So she's not gonna take right field?

HITCH: She'll try it for a week.

LEONA: A week? Dammit, Hitch, you gotta get that woman to understand what is going on. She's an alcoholic. We never know if she's even going to show up for a game. And even when she's stone sober, she's still a half-assed short stop. She hasn't got the hustle.

HITCH: Leona, you don't understand Ruth. She's scared of a lot of things. You can't just lay all that on her at once.

LEONA: The hell you can't! Look at the shit she lays on us—on you! It's time you told her off. She's lazy and self-indulgent, and . . .

HITCH: . . . and she' been hurt a lot. You don't know what her life has been like.

LEONA: Yeah, and she doesn't know what mine has been like, but I don't go around making her pick up my dirty socks. You gotta do it, Hitch.

HITCH: [*Considering.*] How come you're so interested in seeing me tell Ruth off?

LEONA: [*Trying to cover her confusion.*] I'm not! I mean, I just think . . . Well . . . It's for the sake of the team.

HITCH: Are you sure that's all?

LEONA: Yeah, I'm sure. Why else would I care? I mean . . . Hey, it's getting late! We gotta get back to practice.

[LEONA *exits quickly.* HITCH *watches her exit.*]

HITCH: Hmmm . . . [HITCH *exits.*]

[*Blackout.*]

SCENE 2

The fantasy scenes are played either in front of the curtain or in a special area of the stage, above or to the side of the main set.

    KELLY's *fantasy music is heard, followed by the sound of crowds cheering. A spotlight comes up on the fantasy area.* KELLY *is standing in the center of the light. A* PHOTOGRAPHER *and a* REPORTER *are off to the side.*

REPORTER: Hey, there she is! There's Kelly!

PHOTOGRAPHER: There's the gal who made the quadruple play from out in left field!

REPORTER: She just won the World Series of Softball!

[LEATHER WOMAN *rushes up with a microphone.*]

LEATHER WOMAN: Kelly, this must be tremendously exciting for you. Could you tell the fans how it was that you got four runners out in one play?

KELLY: [*Modest, but glowing.*] I just saw what had to be done, and I did it.

[*A burst of cheering, as* KELLY *begins to strike jock poses for the* PHOTOGRAPHER.]

LEATHER WOMAN: Do you realize that today you have made softball history? Do you realize that your name will go down in the Sports Hall of Fame for being the first athlete to make a quadruple play? Do you know what you've done for women's softball?

KELLY: Yes.

[*More cheering.*]

LEATHER WOMAN: Ladies and gentlemen—Here we have it—the little girl who single-handedly rescued her team from obscurity and brought women's softball into the national spotlight, edging out men's baseball for the title of "national pastime." Who is this mysterious woman in left field? Where does she come from? And how did she do it?

KELLY: [*Talking into the microphone.*] Well, I just always knew that someday I would be great . . . [*Making sure the* REPORTER *is getting this all.*] . . . you know, famous. I always just felt that I had something special in here . . . [*She points to her heart.*] . . . and that some day I would have the opportunity to show the world who I really was . . . And I guess today was the day . . .

[*Deafening cheering, as the fans begin chanting her name. Blackout.*]

SCENE 3

The locker room.
    KELLY *is sitting on a bench in a trance. The voice of* JAN *is heard offstage.*

JAN: [*Offstage.*] Kelly! Kelly! [JAN *enters.*] Kelly!

KELLY: [*Jumping up to catch a fly ball.*] What? Did you say something?

[SLIDE *enters the locker room unobserved by the two women.*]

JAN: Yeah . . . I was wondering if you'd like to go to the bar with me later tonight.

KELLY: Oh, thanks, but I have to go home and feed my cat.

[*She stares out into space, and fantasy music is heard.* JAN *tries to see what* KELLY *is looking at.*]

KELLY: [*Cont'd.*] See you guys later.

[*She turns and exits, and* JAN *continues to stare into space.*]

SLIDE: [*Stepping forward.*] Three strikes and you're out. [*She picks up* JAN's *mitt and tries it on.*] What do you know? Fits like a glove.

JAN: I've still got a week.

SLIDE: Oh, yeah, sure. Hey look, Jan, why don't you come to the bar with me? We'll call a truce.

JAN: I'm busy.

SLIDE: Kelly might show up later.

[JAN *looks at her.*]

SLIDE: [*Cont'd.*] Sometimes she does...

JAN: Yeah, okay. Where is it?

SLIDE: I'll give you a ride.

JAN: I've got my own car.

SLIDE: Then you can follow me.

JAN: [*Pulling her glove off* SLIDE's *hand.*] I'll wait for you outside.

[JAN *exits and* K.C. *enters, eyeing the new player uncomfortably as she passes her.*]

K.C.: [*To* SLIDE.] Good practice, honey. Lookin' good. You want to go to the bar with me tonight?

SLIDE: [*Crossing to her locker and getting out her leather jacket.*] Sorry, but I can't. I'm gonna work out at the gym. Look, K.C., can you get a ride home with somebody? I need the truck.

K.C.: I'll give you a ride to the gym.

SLIDE: [*Arranging her scarf and jacket, her back to* K.C.] Hon, I don't want you to have to come pick me up. It would be easier for both of us if you can get a ride with somebody at practice. Okay? [*She finally turns to look at* K.C.] Hey— what are you looking at me like that for?

K.C.: Like what?

SLIDE: Like you don't trust me or something.

K.C.: I didn't look at you like that! I trust you!

SLIDE: Well, I don't know...

K.C.: [*Fishing for the keys to the truck.*] Here, take the keys. I'll get a ride. Don't worry about me.

SLIDE: You sure?

K.C.: Yeah. I'll have some enchiladas when you get home.

SLIDE: Don't wait dinner. I'm gonna be late.

K.C.: Okay, honey. They'll be there when you want them. I love you.

[SLIDE *has begun to exit, but she turns back as an afterthought and gives* K.C. *a perfunctory kiss. She exits.* GLORIA, URSULA, HITCH, *and* LEONA *enter.*]

URSULA: That was a great practice game! Next week when we play the Leather and Laces, we're gonna kick some ass!

GLORIA: Jan was a great short stop!

URSULA: I'll say! I think we could even have a shot at the pennant with her playing short stop. Hey, Hitch... You gonna let Jan keep that position?

HITCH: Maybe.

URSULA: Hey, K.C... What'd you think of Jan?

K.C.: [*Uncomfortable.*] She's pretty good.

URSULA: Good? I mean, did you see the way she could field the ball?

[RUTH *enters.*]

URSULA: [*Cont'd.*] Hey, Ruth, did you get a load of how Jan could field the ball?

RUTH: [*Glaring at* HITCH.] I got a load all right.

[LEONA *slams her locker in response to* RUTH, *and* RUTH *begins to cross towards her menacingly.*]

GLORIA: [*Creating a diversion.*] Ruth, you did a great job in right field.

[RUTH *glares at her.*]

URSULA: [*Realizing that she has been insensitive.*] Yeah, Ruth—you were real good in right field!

HITCH: [*Stepping between* RUTH *and* LEONA.] Thanks for switching with Jan. You both did a great job today.

RUTH: [*Crossing away from them all.*] Shit.

URSULA: [*Sensing a storm brewing.*] Well... see you guys at practice tomorrow— or maybe tonight at the bar.

K.C.: Oh, Ursula... Can I talk to you a minute? [*She crosses up to her, not wanting the others to hear.*] Can I catch a ride home with you?

URSULA: I thought you had the truck?

K.C.: Slide had to go somewhere.

URSULA: [*Embarrassed.*] Oh... sure. Sure, I'll give you a ride.

GLORIA: Hey, wait up! I'm leaving too. [*She looks at* RUTH *who is glowering in a corner.*] You coming, Leona?

LEONA: Me? [*She gets the hint.*] Oh, right.

[GLORIA, URSULA, K.C., *and* LEONA *leave.* RUTH *crosses in silence to her locker, as* HITCH *watches her.* LEONA *stands in the doorway.*]

HITCH: Say, Ruth... Would you like to go out to dinner with me? I'm buying.

RUTH: [*Turning her back.*] I'm not for sale.

HITCH: I just meant... you know, if you felt like...

RUTH: [*Spinning around to face her.*] Oh, Laura... FUCK OFF.

LEONA: [*From the door.*] Come on, Hitch. You can have dinner with me. I'll buy.

[HITCH *looks at* RUTH,, *and then exits with* LEONA. RUTH *slams her locker door hard enough to be heard in hell. She begins to sing. She performs a parody of flamenco dancing and bull-fighting, using a towel for a cape.*]

RUTH: [*She sings "When Women Do It To Each Other."*.]
When a man says it's over, he means that he's through:
Don't call us, honey—we will call you.
Don't leave the light on. Don't hold your breath.
When the horse has just died, you don't flog it to death!
When men do it to women, it's nasty, it's mean—
It's over, it's finished, but dammit it's clean!

When women do it to each other, they do it.
They do it good.
When women do it to each other—yeah—
They do it real good.

They do it so softly,
You can't feel the punch.
You won't know what hit you—
"Say, Ruth, let's do lunch!"

They do it much nicer.
It's oh so much sweeter.
They do it much kinder—
"I want you to meet her."

[*She throws the towel down and grinds her heel into it. She dances the instrumental bridge aggressively on the towel.*]

When women do it to each other, they do it.
They do it good.
When women do it to each other—yeah—
They do it real good.

They do it with care,
With lots of respect.
Nothing has changed—
"We just won't have sex!"

They feel awful about it.
They hope you're okay.
They hope you forget them—
"I'll call every day."

When women do it to each other, they do it.
They do it good.
When women do it to each other,
Lots of luck—
When women do it to each other—
You really get fucked!

[RUTH *raises her arm in a flamenco pose. Her third finger is raised. Blackout.*]

SCENE 4

Area in front of the curtain or to the side of the stage.
Spotlight comes up on HITCH *and* LEONA, *who are on their way to the bar.*

HITCH: Maybe I shouldn't try to manage the Desert Hearts anymore. No matter what I do, somebody's going to hate me.

LEONA: Nobody likes hearing they're not the best, but somebody's got to say it.

HITCH: I don't know, Leona. It just seems like lesbians have it hard enough every- where else. When we get together to play softball, maybe it's more impor- tant to let people do what they want.

LEONA: And have a shitty team that nobody takes seriously. I don't want to come out and practice unless I know we're doing our damnedest to win.

HITCH: But that's what the whole straight world is about—winning. Isn't there a place where people can just do what they do and enjoy it, without always get- ting criticized and judged about it?

LEONA: You tell me when you find that place.

[HITCH *and* LEONA *exit. Blackout.*]

SCENE 5

The Rubyfruit Bar and Grill, the local women's bar. There is a bar along the upstage wall, with stools. There is also a table with four chairs downstage right. The Ruby- fruit Dancers are seated at the bar.
Spotlight comes up on LEATHER WOMAN, *at the back of the theatre. Working her way to the front of the house, she sings "Rubyfruit Bar and Grill," snapping her fin- gers and vamping the audience.*

LEATHER WOMAN: Doo-doo-doo-doo-do-doo
Doo-doo-doo-doo-do-doo
Doo-doo-doo-doo-do-doo
Doo-doo-doo-doo-do-doo

When it's five, five o'clock,
Then it's time, time to stop.
She takes off her sweater.
She puts on the leather—

[*At the end of this verse,* LEATHER WOMAN *reaches the stage, and the lights come up full on the main playing area, as the onstage dancers and the backstage actors blast into the chorus. The Rubyfruit Dancers swivel on their bar stools to face the audience.*]

CHORUS: For the Rubyfruit!
Rubyfruit Bar and Grill!

LEATHER WOMAN: [*Working her way behind the bar.*]
When it's five, five o'clock.

Time to close, close the shop.
She takes off her linen suit
She puts on the cowboy boots—

CHORUS: For the Rubyfruit!
Rubyfruit Bar and Grill!

LEATHER WOMAN: When it's five, five o'clock
Straight world gets, gets a shock.
She writes him a note good-bye—
Walks out with his coat and tie

CHORUS: For the Rubyfruit!
Rubyfruit Bar and Grill!

[*The Rubyfruit Dancers slide off their stools and do a sleazy apache dance during the instrumental bridge. At the end of their dance, they make their way back to the bar.*]

LEATHER WOMAN: When it's five, five o'clock
The world blows, blows its top
Girls slam out the door—
They come lookin' for

CHORUS: The Rubyfruit!
Rubyfruit Bar and Grill!

[*At the end of the song, the Rubyfruit Dancers exit the bar, passing* SLIDE *and* JAN *on the way out.* LEATHER WOMAN *stays unobtrusively behind the bar as bartender.*]

SLIDE: Well, here we are. This is the women's bar for this town—Rubyfruit Bar and Grill, better known as Rubyfruit Bar and Girl.

[JAN *groans and moves away from her.*]

SLIDE: [*Cont'd.*] Hey, what are you doing?

JAN: Looking for Kelly. You said she might be here.

SLIDE: Yeah, but she might not be. Come on—Here's a table. Let's sit down and relax.

[*She steers* JAN *to a table.*]

SLIDE: [*Cont'd.*] What do you drink?

JAN: Nothing. I don't drink.

SLIDE: You what?

JAN: I don't drink.

SLIDE: Oh, come on. How about a beer?

JAN: You get one. [*She is still looking around.*]

SLIDE: Hey, like I told you, she's not here. So ... Why don't we dance?

[*Just then,* KELLY *enters the bar. She is in a trance state, and her theme music is heard.*]

JAN: Kelly! Kelly!

KELLY: [*Coming out of her trance.*] What? Me?

JAN: We've got a table over here! Come on and join us!

KELLY: Okay.

SLIDE: [*Irritated by* KELLY'S *arrival.*] So, Kelly—Pull up a chair. Don't forget to sit in it.

JAN: I wanted to tell you how much I enjoyed playing with the team today.

[SLIDE *sniggers.* KELLY *is off in space again.*]

JAN: [*Cont'd.*] With you in left field, Slide on second, and me as short stop, I don't think they're gonna be able to hit anything on our side of the field.

SLIDE: Why don't you try it in sign language?

JAN: [*Determined to ignore* SLIDE.] So, Kelly . . . When did you start playing softball?

SLIDE: [*Doing an imitation of* KELLY.] About the same time "Star Trek" went into reruns.

JAN: [*Ignoring* SLIDE.] How long have you been with the Desert Hearts?

SLIDE: [*Still imitating* KELLY.] Say, you must want to sleep with me pretty bad . . .

[JAN *reaches across the table and grabs at* SLIDE. *The actors freeze and* KELLY'S *theme is heard. Blackout.*]

SCENE 6

An area in front of the curtain or to the side of the stage: the scene of the Miss Butch Universe Pageant.

The spotlight comes up on LEATHER WOMAN, *who is holding a microphone and standing in front of an enormous styrofoam barbell. She is emceeing the Miss Butch Universe Pageant.*

LEATHER WOMAN: Welcome to Atlantic City and to the [*current year*] Miss Butch Universe Pageant!

[*Cheering is heard backstage, similar to the sounds of an all-star wrestling crowd.*]

LEATHER WOMAN: Tonight we are proud to present the three international finalists. Only one of these will win the title, and tonight we're here to find out who that girl will be. Mirror, mirror on the wall—Who's the dykiest diesel of them all? Tonight some lucky little butch is going to walk away with a free year of parts and labor for a Harley Davidson . . .

[*Fanfare and drums.*]

LEATHER WOMAN: [*Cont'd.*] . . . a year's supply of Budweiser . . .

[*Fanfare and drums.*]

LEATHER WOMAN: [*Cont'd.*] . . . a case of Bull Durham chewing tobacco . . .

[*Fanfare and drums.*]

LEATHER WOMAN: [*Cont'd.*] . . . and a copy of the Sports Illustrated annual swimsuit edition!

[*Fanfare and drums.*]

LEATHER WOMAN: [*Cont'd.*] The winner will also embark on a year-long, round-the-world goodwill tour, where she will make public appearances in forty-two countries and fifty-two states. Representing the gay community as Miss Butch Universe, she will help tear down the prejudice of old stereotypes and build new bridges of understanding to the lesbian community. So, let's give these gals a big hand, and give it to them where it counts . . . the [*current year*] Miss Butch Universe Pageant!

[*Wild cheering from backstage.*]

LEATHER WOMAN: [*Cont'd.*] Our first contestant is Eva from Australia!

[*Wild cheering as* EVA *enters. There is a drum roll while she gets into position in front of the weights. She takes a series of exaggerated breaths, grimaces, and lifts the weight to her knees. She drops the weights and moves to the side amid wild cheering.*]

LEATHER WOMAN: And our second contestant, Ingrid from Sweden!

[INGRID *enters with attitude, crosses to the weights, snarls at the crowds, and begins her lift to the sound of a drum roll. She drops the weight. There is booing and cat-calling from backstage, which only makes her angrier. She attempts a second lift, this time bringing the weights all the way to her chest. She drops the weights amid mixed cheers and boos.* INGRID *moves to the side and turns her back on* EVA.]

LEATHER WOMAN: And our third and final contestant, from Fort Wayne, Indiana— Kelly!

[*Wild applause as* KELLY *runs on and trips. She lifts the weight over her head with one hand and tosses to the other. She does this back and forth, accompanied by drum roll and cymbals. At the end, she drops the weights. Delirious applause.*]

LEATHER WOMAN: The envelope, please!

[*Someone in the band hands her an envelope. She tears it open.*]

LEATHER WOMAN: [*Cont'd.*] And the winner of the [*current year*] Miss Butch Universe Pageant is . . .

KELLY: Kelly?

LEATHER WOMAN: KELLY!

[*There is a fanfare and wild cheering.* KELLY *tosses the weight to* INGRID *and* EVA, *who stagger offstage with it.*]

LEATHER WOMAN: [*Cont'd.*] And now for a little entertainment from the Butchettes!

[*She escorts* KELLY *to the side, as the* BUTCHETTES *run onstage. The entrance of the* BUTCHETTES *is accompanied by the sound of girls screaming.*

The BUTCHETTES *are* URSULA, GLORIA, *and* LEONA. *They are dressed in metallic sheath dresses, which go to the floor and are slit up the side to the waist. They wear high heels, lipstick, and enormous hair.*

LEATHER WOMAN *grabs the mike stand and sings "The Ballad of the Butch," imitating fifties' male rock-and-roll singers. The* BUTCHETTES *accompany all the singing with elaborate synchronized hand gestures and body movements.*]

LEATHER WOMAN: I listen to my radio—
I hear songs to Mary Jo,
To Peggy Sue and Mary Lou—
I hear songs to Harry, too...

There's tears on my pillow
As I cry all night long,
'Cause I never, never, never
Hear them playing my song...

'Cause I'm a butch, I'm a butch,
I'm a big, bad butch,
And I'm never gonna find
Another word that's gonna rhyme
With butch...

I'm a butch, I'm a butch,
I'm a big, bad butch,
And I'm never gonna find
Another word that's gonna rhyme
With butch!

I go to the corner store
To buy a card for the dyke next door.
I see cards for everyone—
For mother, father, brother, and son.

There's cards with a verse
For the whole family tree
But where in the world
Is the card just for me?

BUTCHETTES: You're a butch, you're a butch... etc.

LEATHER WOMAN: I taught myself to play guitar.
I was gonna be a star.
I would wear the skin-tight jeans,
I would make the young girls scream.

But they turned me away,
And it made my eyes sting—
They said, "We want the girls
Who wear dresses and sing."

BUTCHETTES: Lipstick, makeup, hairspray, tease—
Come on, baby, come on, baby, fuck me, baby, please!
Lipstick, makeup, hairspray, tease—
Come on, baby, come on, baby, fuck me, baby, please!

LEATHER WOMAN: So I lie in my bed

And I play with myself
But I dream that I'm playing
With somebody else...

LEATHER WOMAN:
  'Cause I'm a butch, etc.

BUTCHETTES:
       Baby, you're a bu-bu-butch
       Baby, baby, baby,
       You're a bu-bu-bu-butch

[*The final chorus repeats itself four times as the lights fade. As the song ends, the sound of someone calling* KELLY's *name is heard. Blackout.*]

SCENE 7

The Rubyfruit Bar and Grill.
      Lights come up on JAN *and* SLIDE, *who are still frozen in the positions they held at the end of Scene 5.* KELLY *is back in her chair, still in a trance.*

JAN: Kelly! Kelly!

KELLY: What? Me? Did you say something?

JAN: Do you want to dance?

KELLY: No thanks. I don't drink.

      [SLIDE *makes a rude noise, and* KELLY *goes back into her trance. Just then* K.C. *enters.*]

JAN: Hey, Slide—It's K.C. [*Before* SLIDE *can say anything, she calls her over.*] K.C.! Come on over!

K.C.: [*Eyes only for* SLIDE.] I thought you were going to work out at the gym tonight.

SLIDE: Sprained my knee. I was just telling Jan about it. [*She turns to* JAN.] It's an old softball injury. [*She eases her leg up onto the table.*]

JAN: [*Shoving the leg off.*] One of the hazards of stealing.

SLIDE: [*To* K.C.] I tried to call you to see if I could pick you up, but you weren't home, so I figured I'd see you here.

K.C.: I was home.

SLIDE: Maybe I dialed the wrong number. [K.C. *looks skeptical.*] Well, anyway, what's the problem? You're here—I'm here. Pull up a chair.

K.C.: [*Suspicious of* JAN.] Did you come here by yourself?

SLIDE: [*Angry.*] What the hell kind of question is that?

K.C.: [*Scared.*] Sorry, honey.

SLIDE: Yeah, hey...It's okay. Sit down.

      [HITCH *and* LEONA *enter the bar. Looking for a diversion,* SLIDE *hails them.*]

SLIDE: [*Cont'd.*] Hey, look! It's Hitch and Leona. Come on over and join us!

LEONA: [*Wanting to be private.*] There's more room at the bar.

[*She and* HITCH *cross to the bar.*]

SLIDE: Oh, sure.

[*Suddenly the door crashes open and* RUTH *enters. She is very drunk and acting out.* HITCH *and* LEONA *are engrossed in conversation. They don't see her.*]

SLIDE: Hey, Ruth! Come on over!

RUTH: [*Reeling over to the table.*] Well, if it isn't the *temporary* short stop.

JAN: Hi, Ruth.

RUTH: I'm sorry, but I don't remember your name.

JAN: Jan.

RUTH: Oh, yes. Jan. Well, Jan... How do you like the Desert Hearts?

JAN: Fine, so far.

RUTH: Good... Good... Just let me give you a little piece of advice. [*Her arm around* JAN.] You do want a little piece of advice, don't you?

JAN: Sure.

RUTH: Don't mix softball and sex.

[JAN *is uncomfortable.*]

RUTH: [*Cont'd.*] Because when you do—things get messy. [*She looks at* SLIDE *and* K.C.] They get real messy. [*Suddenly she spots* HITCH *and* LEONA *at the bar. She stands up and begins to speak louder.*] REAL MESSY. And it gets real hard to concentrate on the game anymore, and the next thing you know—just when you figure you've got it made—you get thrown out at home.

[*Her voice has gotten louder and louder. The bar is very quiet.* HITCH *and* LEONA *are the last people to notice her. There is a moment of tense silence as* HITCH *and* RUTH *look at each other. Finally,* RUTH *speaks.*]

RUTH: [*Cont'd.*] Isn't that right, Laura?

HITCH: I didn't hear what you said, Ruth.

RUTH: I said, if you mix softball and sex, you get thrown out at home.

HITCH: Why don't you come over and join us, Ruth?

RUTH: [*Not moving.*] Isn't that right?

HITCH: Come on, Ruth. There's a place here...

RUTH: Isn't that right, you shouldn't mix softball and sex?

LEONA: [*Seated with her back to* RUTH.] You shouldn't mix softball and alcohol.

[*Everyone holds her breath.* SLIDE *lets out a whistle.* RUTH, *livid, takes a step towards* LEONA.]

RUTH: I'm sorry, Leona. I didn't quite catch that.

LEONA: There's a lot of things you don't quite catch these days.

RUTH: [*Enraged.*] Oh, yeah? Well, you catch this!

[*She goes to throw a punch at* LEONA, *but trips over the back of* KELLY'S *chair.* KELLY *rises and the chair goes over.* RUTH *falls to the floor on her face and passes out.*]

HITCH: [*Rising with concern.*] Ruth!

SLIDE: [*Rushing over.*] She's out cold!

K.C.: Get some water! [*To the bartender.*] Somebody bring some water!

HITCH: Is she all right?

JAN: [*To* KELLY.] Let's get out of here!

[*No response.*]

JAN: [*Cont'd.*] Kelly!

KELLY: [*Coming out of the trance.*] What? Did you say something?

JAN: Let's get out of here!

[*She grabs* KELLY *and pulls her towards the door. They exit.* KELLY'S *keys are on the table. Blackout.*]

SCENE 8

An area in front of the curtain or to the side of the stage: KELLY'S *front porch.*
    Lights come up on KELLY *and* JAN, *who are standing on* KELLY'S *front porch.* KELLY *is absent-mindedly feeling around in her pockets for her keys, while* JAN *tries to come on to her.*

JAN: So this is where you live . . . Looks nice. I bet it's even nicer inside.

[KELLY *is feeling inside her front pants pockets.*]

JAN: [*Cont'd.*] I mean, it's still pretty early . . . So if you'd like to go somewhere else . . . You know . . . see a movie, or something . . .

[KELLY *is feeling in the right breast pocket of her shirt. This activity is distracting to* JAN.]

JAN: [*Cont'd.*] Or . . . I've got some videos at my house. We could make some popcorn and sit around . . .

[KELLY *feels inside the left breast pocket.* JAN *begins to squirm.*]

JAN: [*Cont'd.*] Or we could go to a drive-in movie . . . if there's something you'd like to see . . . Or maybe just take a drive somewhere . . .

[KELLY *is now feeling back in her pants pockets, and* JAN *is nearing the end of her self-control.*]

JAN: [*Cont'd.*] Look, let's just rent a hot tub . . . Kelly! WHAT IS YOUR PROBLEM?

KELLY: [*Startled by the yelling.*] What? Oh . . . I'm looking for my house key. I must have left it in the bar.

JAN: Don't you keep a spare?

KELLY: It's in the house.

[JAN *turns away in exasperation.*]

KELLY: [*Cont'd.*] Hey!

JAN: What?

KELLY: I just got an idea! Why don't I spend the night at your house?

[JAN *does a slow take to the audience, a mixture of shock and wonder. Blackout.*]

SCENE 9

JAN's *bedroom, a disaster area. The bedroom is hung with posters of k.d. lang and Martina. Clothes are strewn all over the floor, and a large pizza box lies open at the foot of the bed. The double bed is center stage, and it looks like a tornado has hit it.*

Lights come up dramatically, as an orchestral version of "Tonight We Love" thunders through the theatre. The music fades, and JAN *rushes in. She surveys the wreckage, and begins frantic efforts to clean the room.*

She steps in the pizza and takes her shoe off, shoving the whole mess under the bed. She pitches the other clothes under the bed. She begins to straighten the covers, discovers her teddy bear, hugs it for a second, and then pitches it under the bed also.

JAN: [*Yelling towards the wings.*] Which side? [*No answer, and then she remembers.*] Kelly! KELLY!

KELLY: [*From offstage.*] What? Did you say something?

JAN: Kelly, which side of the bed do you want?

KELLY: The one by the wall.

JAN: [*Upset.*] There isn't any.

KELLY: [*Offstage.*] Then it doesn't matter.

JAN: I could move it against a wall...

[*She begins to shove the bed.* KELLY *appears at the door.* JAN *rushes over to block the view of the room.*]

KELLY: No, don't do that. It's just that sometimes I roll out. But that doesn't happen often, only every once in a while. And I don't wake up anyway.

[KELLY *leaves, and* JAN *closes the door.*]

JAN: [*To herself.*] Oh, jeez... She rolls out... [*She walks around the bed.*] Why am I so nervous? Come on, champ... This is your own home stadium you're playing in. [*She takes off her other shoe and takes her pants down. She is wearing jockey shorts.*] So she doesn't care which side. She doesn't care. It's no big deal. Either side. [*She yells at* KELLY *again.*] Is the left side okay? [*She trips over her pants, which are around her ankles.*] KELLY!

KELLY: [*Offstage.*] What?

JAN: [*From the floor.*] Is the left side okay?

KELLY: Sure, that's fine.

JAN: So the left side is okay. [*Having taken the pants off, she gets into the bed on the right side. She unbuttons the top button of her shirt and strikes a butch pose.*] Wait a minute... Maybe she likes femmes. [JAN *strikes a playgirl femme pose.*] What if I'm wrong? How am I gonna know? [*She sings "Is She A Butch Or A Femme?".*]

> Is she a butch or a femme?
> Is she an "s" or an "m?"
> Does she like leather,
> Or maybe a feather?
> Is she a butch or a femme?
>
> Is she a bottom or top?
> Does it mean "go" to say "stop?"
> Should I restrain her?
> Is she a complainer?
> Is she vanilla or not?

KELLY! What the hell are you?!

[*Just as she yells this,* KELLY *enters wearing a short tank top and underpants.*]

KELLY: [*Puzzled by the question.*] Left field... Why?

JAN: [*Completely embarrassed.*] Oh... nothing.

[KELLY *turns her back on* JAN *and plumps the pillow and turns back the covers.* JAN, *watching her from behind, bites her knuckles.*]

KELLY: [*Crossing to* JAN.] This is so sweet of you. [KELLY *crosses back to the bed and gets under the covers.*]

JAN: [*Crossing to close the door.*] Kelly, can I ask you something?

KELLY: [*Sitting up.*] Sure.

JAN: [*Nervous laughter.*] Are you a lesbian?

KELLY: [*Laughing.*] Of course, silly. How else do you think I'd be playing for the Desert Hearts?

JAN: [*Laughing with her.*] Yeah... The Desert Hearts... [*She crosses over to* KELLY *and leans close to her.*] I mean, Kelly, why are you lesbian?

KELLY: [*Surprised, she turns over to look at* JAN.] Because I like women better. Don't you? [*She gives* JAN *a friendly punch on the arm.*]

JAN: [*At a loss.*] Yeah...

[KELLY *turns back over.*]

JAN: [*Cont'd.*] I mean... what I wanted to ask was...

KELLY: Good night.

JAN: Kelly...?

[KELLY *doesn't respond.* JAN *hesitates for a moment. Then she decides to make her move. She starts to get in bed. A shrill laugh is heard.* JAN *jumps out of bed and looks around the room. She decides it must have been her imagination. She tries to get into bed again, but this time the laugh is very deep and raucous.* JAN *springs out of bed again. Again, convinced it is her imagination, she takes a running leap back into the bed. This time, she hears a whole chorus of women laughing.* JAN *springs out of bed, crosses her arms this time, and addresses the voices.*]

JAN: All right, you guys! I know you're here.

[*Collective laughter.*]

JAN: [*Cont.*] I know who you are.

[*More laughter.*]

JAN: [*Cont'd.*] You're the ghosts of my ex-lovers . . . You might as well come out.

[*Fantasy lighting comes up, and one by one, the ghosts of* JAN's *former lovers crawl out from under the bed. This is a nightmarish crew of exaggerated lesbian types. They wear ghostly make-up. As each one emerges, they greet* JAN.
  The BOSSY FEMME *has big hair and wears stiletto sling heels and a ridiculously small dress. She carries a tiny little purse. She is played by* GLORIA.]

BOSSY FEMME: [*Kissing her finger and then putting it on* JAN's *lips.*] Hi, Jan, honey—remember me? The women's bar in Chicago? I broke my heel and you helped me fix it . . . and you said you had some hot glue back in your hotel room . . .

[*Just then the* WOMYN'S MUSICIAN *emerges. She is a very young woman with a shaved head. She wears a tutu and army boots, and carries a bass guitar shaped like a woman's torso, with two knobs where the nipples would be and a triangular metal plate where the strings are attached. She is played by* URSULA.]

WOMYN'S MUSICIAN: Hey . . . "Joan," wasn't it?

JAN: Jan.

WOMYN'S MUSICIAN: Oh, yeah . . . Jan! Second night at the Michigan Womyn's Music Festival last year . . . right? Yeah! I remember you. Joan was the first night. Or maybe that was Rose. Anyway, I was the bass player for the Electric Clits. Remember?

[*She plays a riff.* JAN *is in shock.*
  The LAST GIRLFRIEND *emerges. She is the least outrageous of all. She's butch and wears the uniform of* JAN's *old team.*]

LAST GIRLFRIEND: [*Slapping her on the back.*] Jan . . .

JAN: [*Completely terrified.*] Brenda!

LAST GIRLFRIEND: Yeah . . . Who's your new squeeze? [*She walks over to look at* KELLY.] Sweet . . . She looks real sweet. You must be doing all right for yourself, Jan.

JAN: Well, she's not really my girlfriend, you know. We're just sleeping together.

LAST GIRLFRIEND: [*An awkward laugh.*] Come on, Jan. I understand. [*She puts her arm around* JAN.] I got me somebody else too. Not much good having a lover in another city, you know. I understand. We had some good times.

JAN: Yeah. We did.

LAST GIRLFRIEND: Can't ask for more than that, can you?

[JAN *looks sad. She starts to say something, but just then the* WOMEN'S STUDIES PROFESSOR *crawls out. She wears fashionably ethnic clothes with a large fringed scarf and Birkenstocks. Her hair is politically-correct gray, but permed. She carries her roll book. She is played by* LEONA.]

PROFESSOR: [*The first thing she does is pull the pizza box with the tennis shoe stuck to it out from under the bed. She holds it under* JAN's *nose.*] Hello, Janice. I'm sure you haven't forgotten your women's studies professor. I think we should talk about your incompletes in Woman's Sexuality. [*She flips open the roll book.*] Perhaps you'd like to schedule another appointment with me to see what you can do to make up the work?

[JAN *pulls the sheet over her head. One last woman emerges: the worst. This is the* LEATHER WOMAN *disguised as the* DARK ALLEY DYKE. *She has a nightstick strapped to her belt, along with a pair of handcuffs. She carries a whip, and her head is shaved and tattooed.*]

DARK ALLEY DYKE: Hey, Jan, baby...I got some new toys! Hey, bitch, you're gonna love these! [*She cracks the whip.*]

JAN: [*Shaking her head.*] Oh, no...Wait a minute! This is too much! I don't remember you. You don't belong here!

DARK ALLEY DYKE: Oh, I don't?

JAN: No! Absolutely not. Now, the rest of you guys... [*She turns towards them.*] Okay...I can take some responsibility for you...Some. But you... [*She turns back to the* DARK ALLEY DYKE.] No way! You must have wandered in from someone else's nightmare. I know I never slept with you!

DARK ALLEY DYKE: That's right, bitch. Nobody sleeps when I'm working on them...unless they're dead. [*She cracks the whip again.*]

JAN: No! Absolutely not! I would remember.

DARK ALLEY DYKE: [*Leaning across the bed.*] Times Square...New Years Eve...1986?

JAN: [*In horror.*] That was you?

[*The* DARK ALLEY DYKE *just laughs and cracks the whip.* JAN *retreats under the blankets, peering out while the women perform the rap number,* "You'll Never Live Us Down."]

BOSSY FEMME: I am what you call a femme, I do the "S," but not the "M"—
I'm on top—bossy femme!

I am sweet and I'm petite—they say I'm good enough to eat
And when I get between the sheets, there is no one to compete
With the femme—bossy femme
I'm on top!

I'm a sexual ath-e-lete, I've got the style, I've got technique:
The others may be Maybelline, but, baby, I am pure Clinique.

I'm unique! Bossy femme—
I secrete!
Yeah, watch me come—

[*She simulates an orgasm, which terminates abruptly.*]

I am always in control—baby, I can rock your soul.
I never play my hand until the ace is in the hole.
I got control!
Take a poll!
The prisoners of desire, they don't ever get parole
Once they've had a little taste of my sweet jellyroll!
I'm in control!

[*She runs her tongue over her lips.*]

I am firmly in the saddle with the women that I straddle,
From Topeka and Topanga and Durango and Seattle!
Bossy femme—
I'm on top!

And if you think I'm foolin' you can go ask Joanne Loulan
Where the baby dykes all go when it's time to get their schoolin'?
To the femme—bossy femme—
She's on top!
Who's on top?
Bossy femme—
I'm on top!

CHORUS: She is a bossy femme, she does the "S" but not the "M."

BOSSY FEMME: I'm on top!

CHORUS: Bossy femme!

BOSSY FEMME: I wear designer gowns, I'm indisputably uptown,
And, girlfriend, let me tell you—you will never live me down!

CHORUS: We may look like we're clones, or we may look like we're clowns,
Or we may look more like something that you picked up from the pound—
Should have thought of that before, 'cause you'll never live us down!

WOMYN'S MUSICIAN: I am punk and I am young—you give me lip, I'll give you
tongue,
'Cause I got no time for lectures—I'm too busy havin' fun!
I'm young!

I met you up at Michigan and it was quite a scene:
Thirty women in a line to use the next latrine,
And you were soaking wet, from standing in the rain
And I had just come out—of the porta-jane.
The second time I saw you at the workshop for karate—
I said, "Remember me? I was at the porta-potty?"
You said you couldn't tell from looking at my face,

But the fact that I was naked made me easier to place—

On your face . . .
On your back . . .
In your face . . .
Back-to-back!

Eeeeeow—
I'm eighteen!
I'm a rock and roll queen, I play the bass guitar and I beat the tambourine.
I do original routines—I can spread like margarine.
I can slide like vasoline, I can lube like valvoline.
I am gourmet cuisine, I go down like a submarine.
I can rush you like caffeine, addict like nicotine.
I get down and in between, I will ravish your ravine.
I am the kind of girlfriend that you wish for in your dreams.
I do the kind of sexy things you read in magazines—
On our backs!
I make the scene!
If sex is fantasy, then baby—I am halloween!
Eeeeow—
I'm eighteen!

CHORUS: She is punk and she is young—give her lip, she'll give you tongue,
'Cause she's got no time for lectures—she's too busy having fun!
She is young!

WOMYN'S MUSICIAN: You know I've got the rhymes, and you know I've got the
sound,
And you know it for a fact, that you will never live me down!

CHORUS: We may look like we're clones, or we may look like we're clowns,
Or we may look more like something that you picked up from the pound—
Should have thought of that before, 'cause you'll never live us down!

PROFESSOR: I work in women's studies, but I ain't no fuddy-duddy—
I just want to be your buddy—
Study buddy.

I know the ancient matriarchs from Boadicea to Joan of Arc.
My grading may be very hard, but I'm an easy mark.
I know more words for my clitoris than are in Roget's *Thesaurus*,
And just in case you're wondering, my rising sign is Taurus.
I read the works of Mary Daly, Dworkin, and bell hooks
But if you want to know a secret—I prefer the Naiad books.
I'm pro-choice and feminist, anti-porn and—nuke
Right-wing fundamentalists, they make me want to puke.
In other words, in all respects, I am "PC"—politically correct!

CHORUS: She's "PC" in all respects except for when it comes to sex!

[PROFESSOR *glares at them.*]

PROFESSOR: Although a lesbian inside, I say "woman-identified."
In my heart I have gay pride—I don't need to march outside.
I'm not ashamed, and I won't hide—that would be undignified,
But I don't think I should decide on academic suicide—

CHORUS: Come on out!

PROFESSOR: I don't have to.

CHORUS: Come on out!

PROFESSOR: I don't want to.

CHORUS: Come on out!

PROFESSOR: I'm not going to.

CHORUS: Come on out!

PROFESSOR: Don't shout!

CHORUS: She works in Women's Studies, but she ain't no fuddy-duddy
If things get homophobic, she can always be your buddy—
Study buddy!

PROFESSOR: You're never going to catch me playing out-of-bounds,
Which is probably the reason you will never live me down!

CHORUS: We may look like we're clones, or we may look like we're clowns,
Or we may look more like something that you picked up from the pound—
Should have thought of that before, 'cause you'll never live us down!

DARK ALLEY DYKE: I am dangerous. I'm a dyke, so take it any way you like—
I do!
I'm a dyke—
Righteous dyke!

I am a contradiction, I'm your sexual addiction—
I operate outside of all your social jurisdictions!
I'm the part you can't control, I'm the dark side of your soul—
I'm the aspect of your psyche that you can't pigeonhole!
Rock-and-roll!

I will tie you to the bed, I will chain you to the wall,
I will make you kneel before me, I will teach you how to crawl—
I'm dangerous!
Ask your mother!

CHORUS: She is dangerous, she's a dyke. She takes it any way she likes—
She's a dyke!

DARK ALLEY DYKE: Get behind it!
I'm a dyke!
Let me be your tour guide to the underground—
Baby, I will make damn sure you never live me down!

CHORUS: We may look like we're clones, or we may look like we're clowns,

Or we may look more like something that you picked up from the pound—
Should have thought of that before, 'cause you'll never live us down!

[*At the end of the song, they all turn and point at* JAN, *who is frozen in horror. With the drum machine still going, the women take their leave one by one.*]

BOSSY FEMME: If you're ever in Chicago, honey...I'm in the book. [*She blows her a kiss. Before she exits, she turns for a last reminder.*] But remember, I'm not really lesbian. I'm *bi-sexual*. [*She says "sexual" with all three syllables.*]

WOMYN'S MUSICIAN: Michigan...next August. You can't miss my tent. The flaps look like labia. [*She exits with another bass riff.*]

LAST GIRLFRIEND: Well, Jan. I was really sorry when you left town.

[JAN *looks down.*]

LAST GIRLFRIEND: [*Cont'd.*] Hope your new lover makes you happy. She's real cute. [*She looks at* KELLY *again.*] Yep. Well...[*She punches* JAN's *arm.*] We had some real good times. [*She exits awkwardly.*]

PROFESSOR: That incomplete is going to stay on your record permanently, Janice. I'm afraid it's going to follow you through life.

[*She hovers near* JAN, *but* JAN *turns away.*]

PROFESSOR: [*Cont'd.*] Well...it's up to you. [*She exits.*]

DARK ALLEY DYKE: Whaddaya say, Sweet Meat?

[*She grabs* JAN's *nipple and twists it.* JAN *slugs her. The* DARK ALLEY DYKE *grabs her own crotch and moans.*]

DARK ALLEY DYKE: [*Cont'd.*] Hurt me! Hurt me!

JAN: You get out of here! Now!

DARK ALLEY DYKE: Okay, okay...I'm going.

[*She executes a series of cracks with the whip, which send* JAN *for cover under the blankets. She turns towards the audience and throws a handful of confetti.*]

DARK ALLEY DYKE: [*Cont'd.*] Happy New Year! [*She exits with a final crack of the whip and a burst of demoniacal laughter.*]

[JAN *remains with her head under the covers for a few seconds. The music of "Auld Lang Syne" is heard. Slowly she peers out, to make sure the coast is clear. She looks ruefully at* KELLY, *who has slept through all of this.* JAN *pulls the blankets up snug around* KELLY, *takes her own pillow, and climbs out of bed. She puts the pillow on the floor and curls up in a miserable heap as the last strains of "Auld Lang Syne" fade out. Blackout.*]

ACT II
SCENE 1

The curtain is drawn, or the stage is completely dark.

A drum roll, and the spotlight comes up on an area in front of the curtain or to the side of the stage. LEATHER WOMAN *appears.*

LEATHER WOMAN: Welcome back. I hope you all had enough time to exchange phone numbers. If you need a little more time, we could always take another intermission...It's up to you. This is your night! No? Well, if you're all set, let's see if the girls are ready. [*She begins to cross towards the dressing room.*] You know, I have to tell you about the working conditions in this theatre...Twelve women all squeezed into a hot, tiny dressing room. Twelve women all trying to take off their clothes at the same time, practically on top of each other... [*She exits towards dressing room and calls from offstage.*] Are you ready, girls?

[*Noisy sounds of delight from many women offstage.* LEATHER WOMAN *enters slightly disheveled.*]

LEATHER WOMAN: [*Cont'd.*] Well, I guess they're ready. Band, are you ready?

[*Drums.*]

LEATHER WOMAN: [*Cont'd.*] Well, then let's go! [*She sings a reprise of "Cruisin'."*]

I see you lookin'—
Lookin' at me.
I'm thinkin' the same thing
You're thinkin' about me!
'Cause we're
Cruisin'—
Cruisin' tonight—
Cruisin' kinda heavy,
Cruisin' kinda light
But we're cruisin' the girls—
You all look so fine—
Cruisin' tonight—
I'm losing my mind!

You're lookin' good,
You're lookin' fine—
That should explain why
I'm taking my time
If we're cruisin' together
At the end of the night,
Cruisin' like this,
Who knows what we might—

That's what we do
On the girls' night out—
We cruise.

Yeah,
Cruise
'Til they turn the lights out.
Cruise the girls
Cruisin', cruisin'—
Oh, baby, we're cruisin' tonight!

[*Blackout.*]

SCENE 2

The locker room.

The Desert Hearts are having a collective meeting. They are all wearing lavender tee shirts with "Desert Hearts" on them. URSULA's *is fringed at the sleeves and the bottom.* SLIDE's *has the neck ripped out. Everyone is there except* JAN, KELLY, *and* RUTH.

HITCH *is upstage, copying something from the tournament chart onto her clipboard, trying to ignore the proceedings. Everyone else is shouting at once.*

SLIDE: Hey, there isn't anything to argue about! After last night, Ruth ought to be suspended. That's all there is to it.

GLORIA: It's not fair! You can't just tell her she can't play anymore!

URSULA: But we've got somebody who can really play short stop now...

K.C.: You can't just dump a player because you get tired of her!

LEONA: [*Rising and shouting.*] Quiet! Quiet!

[*Everyone becomes quiet.*]

LEONA: [*Cont'd.*] Well, Hitch ... You're the manager. What do you say?

HITCH: [*Miserable.*] I think Ruth should be here if we're all going to talk about her. She's still part of the team.

SLIDE: [*Jumping up.*] Hey, this is a scheduled practice—She should be here anyway. If she showed up on time—which she never does—she'd be here for the meeting. But, as usual, she's sleeping it off...

GLORIA: [*Interrupting.*] She was hurt last night! Maybe she's too injured to play. But if she knew there was a meeting, she might have come.

HITCH: I don't like talking behind her back.

LEONA: Hitch—come on. This woman has not been willing to play where the team wants her, she misses half the practices, she disappears for weeks at a time. I don't think we need Robert's Rules of Order to get rid of her.

SLIDE: [*Still standing.*] She's right, Hitch. Something's gotta be done, and done fast. With Jan, we've got a shot at the league pennant this year.

HITCH: What do you want me to do?

SLIDE: Can her ass! There's still time to find a right fielder.

GLORIA: That's not fair!

SLIDE: Why not? She asked for it!

GLORIA: She can't help herself!

LEONA: Hold it! Hold it! Let's all take turns, and that way everybody will get a chance to be heard.

[*She stares at* SLIDE, *who eventually gets the hint and sits.*]

LEONA: [*Cont'd.*] Slide . . .

SLIDE: She's too old to run, too uncoordinated to catch, too lazy to practice, and too selfish to quit.

GLORIA: That's not fair!

LEONA: Gloria! It's K.C.'s turn.

K.C.: [*Uncomfortable with displeasing* SLIDE.] She's been playing with the Desert Hearts for a long time. It was Ruth and Hitch who started the team. We can't just dump her now because somebody younger and better looking comes along.

SLIDE: Looks have nothing to do with it!

LEONA: Slide! Let her finish!

K.C.: I think she should stay.

SLIDE: Yeah, great. There goes the pennant.

LEONA: Ursula . . .

URSULA: Well, I don't know Ruth as well as the rest of you, because this is my first year with the team, but it does seem she's been gone a lot . . . at least this year.

SLIDE: *And* last year. *And* the year before.

LEONA: Slide!

URSULA: I guess I feel like we should get the best people to play the best positions.

HITCH: She's playing right field now.

URSULA: But she doesn't seem to like it. I think she'd be happier off the team than in right field.

SLIDE: Exactly! It's for her own good.

LEONA: Gloria . . .

GLORIA: I agree with Hitch. I think Ruth should be here.

SLIDE: Well, she's not.

GLORIA: And I think we're not being straight about this.

SLIDE: We're lesbians, Gloria.

GLORIA: I mean I think we're not being honest about our motives.

URSULA: Like what?

GLORIA: I think that several people here have personal reasons for getting rid of Ruth that have nothing to do with how she plays.

SLIDE: Like what?

GLORIA: I don't want to say.

SLIDE: Oh...you "don't want to say." Don't make an accusation unless you can back it up.

GLORIA: I think you want to meet a new player.

SLIDE: Oh, yeah, sure. That's really my whole reason for living. [*She looks at* K.C.]

K.C.: That's pretty low.

SLIDE: What about Leona? She wants to get rid of her. Does she want to meet a new player?

GLORIA: I think Leona has her reasons.

[LEONA *looks uncomfortable.*]

SLIDE: What? Well...Come on, tell us!

GLORIA: [*Looking down.*] Because Ruth used to be Hitch's lover.

[*There is a silence.* HITCH *jumps in.*]

HITCH: Okay. I think everybody has said what they want to say.

SLIDE: Wait a minute. Leona didn't. Come on, Leona.

LEONA: Yeah, okay. Yeah, I want Ruth to leave the team. Sure. She's got this chip on her shoulder. She always pulls some power play when Hitch tries to make a decision. It's disruptive. That's the only reason I want to see her out. She's bad for the team morale.

GLORIA: I don't think people are being honest with themselves.

URSULA: What about you, Hitch?

HITCH: I want what's best for the team. I'll go with whatever you decide.

SLIDE: [*Calling it like an umpire.*] Ursula, Leona, and me—three strikes, she's out!

GLORIA: Not so fast. Kelly has to vote.

URSULA: And Jan.

GLORIA: No. Jan's only been with the team a day. Right, Hitch?

HITCH: Jan shouldn't vote because she's replacing Ruth as short stop.

[*Just then* JAN *and* KELLY *enter.* KELLY *carries a big box of doughnuts. They are also wearing team tee shirts.* JAN *hawks the doughnuts as if she were selling concessions in the bleachers.*]

JAN: Hey, guys! Doughnuts! Get your doughnuts! We got glaze, cake, sprinkle, chocolate...[*She notices the somber atmosphere.*] Hey, what's going on?

GLORIA: We're having a meeting about what to do with Ruth. You can sit in, but you can't vote. But Kelly has to vote.

HITCH: [*She crosses down to* KELLY.] We need your vote. [*She reaches out to touch* KELLY's *arm.*] KELLY!

[KELLY *drops the doughnuts and goes into a trance. Her theme music is heard, and the actors freeze. Blackout.*]

SCENE 3

Area in front of the curtain or to the side of the stage: the control room of the Starship Intercourse.

The "Star Trek" theme music is heard, and a spotlight comes up on the STARSHIP NAVIGATOR, *who sits in a chair monitoring a computer screen. A* STARSHIP CREW MEMBER *looks over her shoulder.* LEATHER WOMAN, *the Captain of the* S.S. Intercourse, *stands downstage of them, gazing out over the audience with an air of concern. The* NAVIGATOR *and the* CREW MEMBER *wear polyester stretch jumpsuits, or tunics and tights.*

NAVIGATOR: Captain! Captain!

LEATHER WOMAN: Yes, what is it?

NAVIGATOR: There is some kind of alien life form attempting to communicate with the *Starship Intercourse.*

LEATHER WOMAN: Can you make out the language?

CREW MEMBER: It appears to be using our language, but it isn't making any sense.

LEATHER WOMAN: Ahh ...

NAVIGATOR: [*Reading her screen, puzzled.*] "Surrender yourselves." "You are completely under my power." "You must give yourselves up." "It is useless to resist." "You must obey my commands."

CREW MEMBER: Is this some kind of code?

LEATHER WOMAN: No, girls, it's no code.

NAVIGATOR: What is it?

LEATHER WOMAN: What we have encountered is a rare specimen left over from the Gender Wars five hundred years ago.

NAVIGATOR: [*Alarmed.*] You don't mean ...

CREW MEMBER: It can't be ...

LEATHER WOMAN: It is. It's a man.

[*Both women gasp in horror and make the sign of the vulva, holding their hands up, thumbs and forefingers together.*]

LEATHER WOMAN: [*Cont'd.*] You don't need to be alarmed. They are utterly impotent.

NAVIGATOR: But what about their nuclear experiments?

CREW MEMBER: That's right! Weren't they willing to destroy the whole planet rather than surrender to the women and children?

LEATHER WOMAN: Well, these are obviously renegades. It's doubtful they would have escaped with nuclear weapons, but we'll need to be sure. Better call Dr. Kellinka.

NAVIGATOR: [*Speaking nasally into an imaginary intercom.*] Dr. Kellinka! Dr. Kellinka to the bridge!

[KELLY *runs onto the set and trips. She is wearing her clothes from the last scene.* KELLY *is never in costume for her fantasies.*]

LEATHER WOMAN: Kellinka—Does the alien life form threatening the Intercourse have nuclear weapons?

KELLY: [*Delighted to be helpful . . . after all, this is her fantasy.*] Yes, Captain. Their spaceship is equipped with nuclear missiles.

NAVIGATOR: Oh, no!

CREW MEMBER: What can we do?

NAVIGATOR: Look! Another message! [*Reading the screen.*] "You have thirty seconds to surrender unconditionally, or your ship will be destroyed."

CREW MEMBER: Thirty seconds! Captain, what can we do?

KELLY: I have an idea!

LEATHER WOMAN: What is it?

KELLY: We can use our superior imaginative force to put ourselves in Sisterspace where they'll never find us.

CREW MEMBER: That's right, Captain. The men have never been able to penetrate Sisterspace. Even in primitive times, women used it for sanctuary.

LEATHER WOMAN: You're right, Kellinka. We'll do it.

NAVIGATOR: [*Looking at the screen.*] They've begun a count-down! "Ten—nine . . ."

LEATHER WOMAN: There's no time to lose. [*To the audience.*] We need your help. Close your eyes. Now—everyone, quickly—to Sisterspace!

[*There are prolonged sounds of a crash. The women jolt back and forth as if the starship was tilting. Suddenly they all fall to the ground and there is a blackout. The spotlight comes up with a deep purple gel. The women move tentatively, seeing if they have survived the crash.*]

NAVIGATOR: What happened?

LEATHER WOMAN: Read your screen. What does it say?

NAVIGATOR: [*Rising.*] It says, "Make yourselves at home. There's pie in the fridge. And don't forget to wipe your shoes."

CREW MEMBER: It's Sisterspace! We made it! We made it!

NAVIGATOR: The aliens are gone!

LEATHER WOMAN: Thanks to Dr. Kellinka, our *Intercourse* has been saved!

KELLY: It was nothing.

LEATHER WOMAN: Nothing? You call this nothing? [*She motions to the members of the band.*] Sisters, come join us here in Sisterspace and let's really feel the energy flow!

[*The members of the band join them on the circle with conga drums and tambourines.*

They wear headbands, feathers and other Goddess gear. LEATHER WOMAN *sings "Sisterspace." The women all dance with ecstatic swaying motions and willowy arm movements. The* NAVIGATOR *and* CREW MEMBER *come in with a repeating chorus halfway through and make it a round. They sway and do hand gestures as they sing.*]

We are women,
We are beautiful—
Women strong and free!
We are women,
We are wonderful—
Wonderful you and wonderful me!

We are women
In the sunrise
We hold hands and sway
Side to side,
Back and forth,
This is what we say:

<table>
<tr><td>

LEATHER WOMAN:
Sisterspace, Sisterspace
How grand it will be
When the men are all gone
And the world will be free!

</td><td>

NAVIGATOR & CREW:
Side to side
And back and forth,
Wonderful you
And wonderful me!
[*Repeat as a round.*]

</td></tr>
</table>

Sisterspace, Sisterspace—
Peace in the land!
When the men are all gone
We'll stand hand in hand
And sway!

ALL: [*Raising their arms together and shouting.*] Blessed be!

[*Blackout.*]

SCENE 4

The locker room.
    The Desert Hearts are in the same positions they were in at the end of Scene 2. KELLY *is back in position in front of the spilled box of doughnuts.*

HITCH: Kelly! Kelly!

KELLY: [*Coming to.*] What? Did somebody want a doughnut?

GLORIA: We want your vote.

KELLY: About what?

SLIDE: About kicking Ruth off the team.

GLORIA: Wait a minute, Slide. There are some of us who think Ruth should stay. That's why we need your vote.

SLIDE: [*Eating a doughnut off the floor and talking with her mouth full.*] She's got a bad attitude, and she never shows up...

GLORIA: Let Kelly make up her own mind. What do you think?

[*The team waits for* KELLY's *decision.*]

KELLY: I like Ruth. I think she should stay.

[*The locker room erupts into a heated argument, everyone shouting at once. This scene is in blatant contrast to the vision of sisterhood just presented in the song. The following dialogue is simultaneous.*]

GLORIA: She stays! She stays!

URSULA: Does this mean she plays short stop? What about Jan?

SLIDE: [*To* K.C.] See what you've done?

K.C.: I wasn't the only one who voted for her!

SLIDE: Yeah, but it wouldn't have been a tie.

LEONA: [*Rising.*] Hold it! Hold it! Ladies! It's a tie vote. Hitch, you'll have to vote to break the tie.

[*There is a silence. The players all turn to* HITCH.]

HITCH: I can't.

LEONA: You have to.

HITCH: [*After a tense silence.*] I can't vote against Ruth.

LEONA: Then I guess she stays.

HITCH: I guess she does. [*Nobody says anything.*] Come on, team. We have a practice today, remember?

[GLORIA *picks up the doughnuts and exits with* URSULA, HITCH, LEONA, *and* K.C. KELLY *stands looking spaced out.* JAN *appraises her, and* SLIDE *is watching the interaction with an eye to her investment.*]

SLIDE: [*To* JAN.] So... You and Kelly brought the donuts.

JAN: Yeah.

SLIDE: Does this mean you had breakfast together?

JAN: Ask Kelly.

SLIDE: Kelly!

KELLY: What?

SLIDE: Did you and Jan have breakfast together?

KELLY: Yeah.

SLIDE: So you two had a date?

KELLY: No. I just had breakfast with her, because I slept with her.

[*She exits onto the field.* SLIDE *does a long take on her exit.*]

SLIDE: [*Turning to* JAN.] You just met her yesterday.

JAN: Yeah, well, it wouldn't have taken me so long, except I'm new in town.

[SLIDE *takes out her money and begins to count out bills.*]

JAN: [*Cont'd.*] Naw . . . save your money.

SLIDE: [*Still counting.*] A bet's a bet.

JAN: No, really—forget it.

SLIDE: Hey, I always pay on my bets.

JAN: [*Uncomfortable.*] Well, look, Slide. Actually, we slept together, but nothing happened.

SLIDE: You're kidding.

JAN: No, I'm not.

SLIDE: You and Kelly slept together last night and nothing happened?

JAN: [*Looking down.*] That's right.

SLIDE: Oh, kid, you're dead meat now! Ha ha! [*She stuffs the money back in her pocket and dances around.*] That mitt is as good as mine.

[SLIDE *exits laughing and gloating.* JAN *picks up her glove and looks at it.* RUTH *enters looking like hell and terribly hung over. She has a large bruise on her cheek from where she landed on the floor.*]

JAN: Ruth! What are you doing here?

RUTH: [*Growling.*] It's on the schedule isn't it?

JAN: Well, yeah, but we thought . . .

RUTH: And why the hell aren't you out on the field, "Short Stop"?

JAN: I was feeling kind of blue.

RUTH: Oh, tell me about it!

[*She starts to dress down.*]

JAN: I can't seem to get Kelly's attention.

RUTH: Try yelling her name.

JAN: Not that kind of attention.

RUTH: Yeah. I know what you mean. It's easy to get people's attention, but it's always the wrong kind.

JAN: She doesn't seem to know I'm here.

RUTH: That's because she's got it all figured out in her head how it ought to be, and you don't fit the fantasy.

JAN: Yeah, I guess.

RUTH: Now, maybe if real life would just come a little bit more in line with what we think it *should* be, maybe then people like Kelly would sit up and take notice. Personally, I think she's got the right idea. Why the hell shouldn't we all live in La-la Land? Who the hell wants to be underpaid, overworked, and starved for affection?

[*She sings the cynical number, "Pour Me".*]

Peelin' plaster ceilin',
Paint flakin' off the walls,
The sound of someone screamin'
'Round the corner down the hall—

The bathroom pipes are broken
For the fourteen thousandth time,
But the landlord's gonna tell you
That your rent's a week behind.

And the dishes in the sink,
They never go away—
Get up, get movin', honey—
It's a brand new, stinkin' day—

So pour me something magic,
Liquid gold that makes me feel—
Pour me something burnin' down
And show me something real.

Pour me out a fantasy,
And let me dream a dream—
Pour me out my own sweet self,
My liquid self-esteem.

I'm somebody special!
I'm somebody grand!
Pour me out that girl who died,
'Cause no one gave a damn!

Pour me out some lovin'—
I'll take it in a cup.
Pour me liquid lovin'
And watch me lap it up.

[JAN *has been thinking about something during the song. Suddenly at the end, she jumps up.*]

JAN: The fantasy... Yeah! The fantasy! Why didn't I think of that? [*She runs towards the door.*] Thanks, Ruth! Yeah, the fantasy! [*She exits.*]

RUTH: Hey! Where are you going? Hey! [*To the audience.*] What did I say?

[*Blackout.*]

SCENE 5

The area in front of the curtain or to the side of the stage: a ball field.
Lights come up on SLIDE, *who is standing far stage left, on second base, and* K.C.,

who is far stage right. URSULA *is running back and forth between them, trying to avoid being tagged.* SLIDE *catches the ball and tags her out just as she touches the base.* LEATHER WOMAN, *wearing an umpire shirt, has been standing behind them, watching the play.*

LEATHER WOMAN: [SLIDE *has just tagged* URSULA *out.*] She's out!

URSULA: Aw, darn! [*She throws her hat down.*] I never get on base! Guess I'm just not fast enough.

LEATHER WOMAN: Speed's got nothing to do with it, girlfriend. It's your elevation.

URSULA: What do you mean?

LEATHER WOMAN: Listen, I'll tell you.

[*She rips off her umpire shirt, revealing a shredded leather top underneath, and grabs the microphone.* SLIDE *whistles for the rest of the team, and* GLORIA, HITCH, *and* LEONA *run on.* LEATHER WOMAN *sings the rock and roll number "Under The Glove.".*]

I never used to get on base,
I never used to score—
Until the coach said, "Listen, girl—
That's what your knees are for!"

CHORUS: She said
You gotta get dirty—
You gotta get down!
You gotta play ball
The way you make love—
You gotta get under the glove!
Under the glove,
Yeah,
Under the glove,
You gotta get under the glove!

SLIDE: [*Stepping out of the chorus and up to the mike.*] The bases are all loaded...

LEATHER WOMAN: The score says you are tied...

SLIDE: This ain't no time to be polite—

SLIDE AND LEATHER WOMAN: Get in there girl, and slide!

CHORUS: You gotta get dirty, etc.

LEATHER WOMAN: You know you gotta get on base
In order to survive—
You can't just pussyfoot around
Get on it, girl, and dive!

CHORUS: You gotta get dirty, etc.

[*There is a blackout, and when the lights come up,* LEATHER WOMAN *and her microphone have disappeared.*

HITCH *and* K.C. *are in a conversation, and* GLORIA, LEONA, *and* URSULA *are talking in another group.* SLIDE *is still on second base.*]

SLIDE: [*Looking at her watch.*] Well, kids, gotta go. Working swing shift at the warehouse.

URSULA: [*An aside.*] Hope she's cute.

SLIDE: [*Cutting her off.*] Get outta here. [*To the others.*] See you later.

[*She exits and the teams begins to disperse.*]

K.C.: Wait, wait, wait! Before everybody goes—I have an announcement to make! [*She calls them into a huddle.*] Hey, where's Kelly? [*She calls her.*] KELLY!

[KELLY *comes running, glove up as if to catch a ball.*]

K.C.: [*Cont'd.*] Now, listen . . . Tonight is Slide and my third anniversary of living together, and I'm having a surprise party for her at the Rubyfruit. I want everybody to come and help celebrate.

GLORIA: If it's a surprise party, how do you know Slide will be there?

K.C.: Oh, I know. She's working the late shift. She always stops by the bar before she comes home. She'll be there.

HITCH: What time, K.C?

K.C.: Nine. Are you coming?

HITCH: Wouldn't miss it.

K.C.: You'll tell Ruth?

HITCH: Yeah, sure.

GLORIA: We'll be there.

K.C.: Kelly? Kelly!

KELLY: What?

K.C.: I'm having a surprise party for Slide tonight at the bar. Nine o'clock. You gonna be there?

KELLY: Oh, yeah, sure. [*Suddenly looking around.*] Hey, where's Jan?

GLORIA: I don't know.

URSULA: She left before practice started.

K.C.: I'll tell her about the party if I see her.

[K.C. *and the rest of the team exit.* KELLY *wanders around the field, with an eye out for* JAN.
Suddenly JAN *enters. She is wearing a disguise: a trench coat, sunglasses, and a hat. She talks with a different voice. She looks around to be sure that she and* KELLY *are alone before she speaks.*]

JAN: Hey! Hey, you! Yo—Left field!

KELLY: Me? Are you talking to me?

JAN: Yeah, you. There isn't anybody else out here is there?

KELLY: [*Looking around.*] No...

JAN: Then I'm talking to you. I've had my eye on you.

KELLY: [*Checking her clothes.*] You have?

JAN: Oh, yeah. I've been watching you play for weeks.

KELLY: Really? I've never seen you here before.

JAN: That's because you concentrate so hard on the game.

KELLY: I do?

JAN: Sure—That's why you cover left field so well.

KELLY: [*Brightening.*] I do?

JAN: [*An arm around her shoulders.*] You've got talent, kid, real talent. But you've got more than that. You've got attitude. Kid, you've got what it takes to be great.

KELLY: [*Really coming alive.*] I do?

JAN: Oh, yeah, sure. Don't tell me you didn't know.

KELLY: [*Taking her aside, very animated.*] Well, you know something—and I've never told this to anybody before—but I always had the feeling there was something different about me.

[JAN *nods.*]

KELLY: [*Cont'd.*] I was never really like the other girls.

[JAN *nods again, trying to keep her face away from* KELLY *who is peering into it.*]

KELLY: [*Cont'd.*] I always felt there was something kind of special about me.

JAN: Special—hell, kid—You're one in a million!

KELLY: You don't know what a relief it is to hear somebody else actually say that. I feel like I'm not crazy after all!

JAN: Crazy, hell! You're just the best lesbian left fielder in the whole United States, that's all!

KELLY: You really think so?

JAN: Think so? I *know* so. That's my job. You see, I'm putting together the hottest women's softball team this country's ever seen—the Amazon All-Stars.

KELLY: The Amazon All-Stars?

[*Sound of her theme music is heard.*]

JAN: Kind of catchy, isn't it? Yep. And these Amazon All-Stars are going to tour the country playing exhibition games and holding sports camps for women.

KELLY: [*Tremendously excited.*] Really?

JAN: Really. [*She walks away, fiddling with her watch.*] I've been traveling all over, looking at lesbian softball teams and recruiting players. And I think I'm not bragging when I say I've got the best... except for a left fielder. Haven't got a left fielder yet...

[*She turns to look at Kelly who is so excited she is about to wet her pants.*]

JAN: [*Cont'd.*] So, how about it, Kelly? Want to be an All-Star?

KELLY: Me? You want me to play on a national team? Me?

JAN: That's right. You're the best.

KELLY: The best!

JAN: The best.

KELLY: [*Trying it on.*] I'm the best. I'm the best. I'm the best!

JAN: Well, look—you think it over. I'll be in town until morning. If you decide you want to join, come by the Overnighter Motel tonight, and we'll go over the contracts. Room 14.

KELLY: [*To herself.*] I'm the best.

JAN: Room 14, the Overnighter. I'll have a bottle of champagne. [*She starts to leave.*]

KELLY: Oh, wait! I don't even know your name.

JAN: [*Having to think about it.*] Dusty.

KELLY: Room 14.

JAN: Room 14. [*She starts to exit again.*]

KELLY: Oh, wait! I just remembered! I have to go to a party tonight. It's at nine.

JAN: So do I. Meet me at midnight.

KELLY: You sure?

JAN: It isn't every day I get a chance to sign someone as special as you.

KELLY: [*Suddenly overcome with shyness.*] Well, uh . . . yeah. Well . . . guess I better go. Gotta feed my cat. [*She begins to back away.*] See you later . . . uh . . .

JAN: Dusty.

KELLY: Dusty.

[KELLY *waves awkwardly, turns, and runs off.*
   JAN *waits for a minute after* KELLY *has exited. Apparently* KELLY *is still waving at her.* JAN *waves back. Then, when* KELLY *is finally out of sight, she turns away. She takes the sunglasses and the hat off and speaks in her normal voice.*]

JAN: [*A little stunned by her success.*] Well, that was easy. Like falling off a log. [*She crosses over to a base.*] The Amazon All-Stars. [*She scuffs the base with her shoe and throws a practice pitch.* JAN *sings a reprise of "She Doesn't Even See Me.".*]

She doesn't even see me.
Well, what a big surprise . . .
I want her to believe me—
I don't want her to leave,
Even though I know it's a lie.

She doesn't even know who I am.
I told her I could be someone to hold her—

But could I?

She doesn't even see me.
I can't imagine why—
Why did I tell her those lies?

[*Blackout.*]

SCENE 6

The Rubyfruit Bar and Grill. It has been decorated for a party.
  K.C. *is addressing the team, who are gathered at her table. Everyone is there except* KELLY. JAN *sits at the far end of the bar, her trench coat draped over the stool. She looks miserable.*

K.C.: So you all know what to do when Slide shows up?

GLORIA: Right.

URSULA: Got it.

K.C.: I'll give the signal, like this. [*She raises her arm and brings it down.*]

HITCH: How will you know when Slide's coming?

URSULA: She starts moaning a lot.

  [*A collective groan.*]

LEONA: Not another one!

K.C.: If I stand here, I'll be able to see when her truck goes by. That'll give us enough time to get into position.

GLORIA: Hey, look! Kelly made it!

[KELLY *bursts through the door with uncharacteristic energy.*]

KELLY: Hey, you guys! You guys!

GLORIA: What happened Kelly? What's the matter?

URSULA: She's been attacked.

HITCH: Here, just sit down, Kelly. Take your time. What happened?

LEONA: Did someone attack you?

KELLY: [*Laughing.*] No, nobody attacked me. It's good news. You'll never believe what happened to me. Guess!

[*There is stunned silence. They have never seen their teammate outgoing like this.*]

KELLY: [*Cont'd.*] Well, come on everybody—guess.

HITCH: Kelly, have you been in some kind of accident?

LEONA: Hit your head on something?

URSULA: Maybe it's drugs.

GLORIA: Can you remember anything?

KELLY: Listen you guys! It's nothing like that. It's the most wonderful thing in the world. It's a dream come true! And it happened to me, Kelly!

LEONA: Feel that child's head. She's got a fever.

KELLY: No, I don't, Leona! Guess! Come on guess! It's too good to be true, except it is! Jan, guess!

JAN: [*Shrinking into the bar.*] I don't know, Kelly.

KELLY: You guys! Come on! Use your imagination!

URSULA: You're in love?

KELLY: Better than that!

K.C.: What's better than that?

RUTH: [*An aside.*] You ought to find out.

GLORIA: What is it?

KELLY: You give up?

HITCH: Yeah, we give up.

KELLY: [*Bursting out.*] I'm going to be a star!

LEONA: A fever for sure.

HITCH: Kelly, why don't you sit down and have some water?

KELLY: [*Ignoring* HITCH, *she crosses to* RUTH.] I'm going to be a star. I'm going to be famous and popular and important. I'm going to be a star.

LEONA: Unh-hunh.

KELLY: And if it weren't for all of you, this wouldn't have happened.

HITCH: Kelly—*What* wouldn't have happened? [HITCH *finally gets her on a bar stool, the one next to* JAN.]

KELLY: I've been recruited to play on a national lesbian softball team—the Amazon All-Stars.

LEONA: A national *lesbian* softball team? [*She yells towards the bar.*] Could we have some ice over here?

KELLY: No, Leona, it's for real this time. It's not a fantasy. It's finally real.

[JAN *sinks lower in her chair.*]

KELLY: [*Cont'd.*] I'm signing the contract tonight.

HITCH: Kelly, I think someone's pulling your leg.

KELLY: Aw, Hitch, aren't you glad for me? I've been waiting all my life for someone to recognize who I am, and now it's finally happened.

HITCH: Sure. Sure, I'm happy for you. We all are. You are a star.

RUTH: Shit.

KELLY: I always felt like I was one deep in here . . . [*Pointing to her heart.*] . . . but people would just laugh at me if I told them. And now they're going to have to take me seriously.

URSULA: I always took you seriously.

KELLY: Well, I mean, I'm just another player to you, but now I'll be a national star. I'll *really* be somebody. You can all be proud to know me.

[*Nobody says anything.*]

HITCH: [*Breaking the silence.*] Well, this really has turned into a surprise party, hasn't it? How about a toast?

URSULA: [*Rising and lifting her glass.*] To the Amazon All-Stars!

GLORIA: [*Rising and lifting hers.*] And to K.C. and Slide's third anniversary!

RUTH: [*Rising and lifting hers.*] And to Peter . . . and Wendy . . . [*She toasts the audience.*] . . . and all the folks out there in Never-Never Land.

HITCH: Ruth? Would you care to dance?

RUTH: Moi? What is this? Be-Good-To-Your-Ex-Lover Week? No thanks, I don't need a foster partner.

HITCH: I'm just asking you to dance.

RUTH: [*Hesitating to save face.*] Sure. [*She gets up, and she and* HITCH *exit.*]

GLORIA: K.C.? Want to dance?

K.C.: Love to, but I've got to check with the kitchen about the cake. [*She exits.*]

GLORIA: Ursula?

URSULA: Yeah, sure. [URSULA *and* GLORIA *exit.*]

KELLY: [*Turning suddenly to* JAN.] Jan—You want to dance?

JAN: [*Lost in her own misery.*] What? You talking to me?

KELLY: You sound like I used to! You know I never asked anyone to dance before. I never felt like I was good enough. You're the first person I ever asked! You want to dance?

JAN: [*Rising.*] Kelly, I have to talk to you. Could we go outside for a minute?

KELLY: And then we'll dance?

JAN: Yeah, sure.

[JAN *exits, but* KELLY *lingers to talk to* LEONA, *who is the only one left.*]

KELLY: Excuse us, Leona. My partner wants to step outside for a minute. Why don't you ask someone to dance? It's really not as scary as it looks. All you do is just go up to somebody and say, "Want to dance?" That's really all you have to do. [*She crosses to the door, and turns again to* LEONA.] That's all there is to it. [*She rushes out after* JAN.]

LEONA: [*To herself.*] Yeah, Leona. Why don't you just go up to somebody and ask them to dance? Good question. [*She raises her glass to toast the dancers, and drinks the rest of the beer. The lights fade on the bar. Blackout.*]

SCENE 7

An area in front of the curtain or to the side of the stage: a bench outside the Rubyfruit.
  Lights come up on JAN, *hunched miserably while she waits for* KELLY. KELLY *rushes on and trips in her excitement. She sits very close to* JAN *on the bench. Neither woman says anything for a moment,* JAN *lost in her misery, and* KELLY *bursting with anticipation.*

KELLY: [*Enjoying her new identity, she nudges* JAN.] Hey, this is kind of romantic, isn't it? You and me, sitting here and it's night and all?

JAN: [*Moving away from her.*] Kelly, we slept together last night.

KELLY: But that wasn't romantic. I wasn't really there.

JAN: I noticed.

KELLY: I just felt like I was nobody. But tonight, I'm all here, because I'm somebody. Tonight is romantic.

JAN: [*Rising.*] Kelly, I have to tell you something about the All-Stars...

KELLY: You know about them? You know somebody who's playing on the team?

JAN: I know they don't exist.

KELLY: Yeah, they do. I met the recruiter. I mean, they haven't started their tour yet, so of course there hasn't been any publicity, but it's a real team. I know, because I met the recruiter. Her name is Dusty, and I'm meeting her tonight at her motel so we can sign the papers.

JAN: [*She sits again.*] What if I told you that Dusty was a fraud.

KELLY: Why would she be a fraud? Why would she have been watching me play for weeks if she wasn't a recruiter?

JAN: Maybe she was coming on to you.

KELLY: Oh, that's silly. Who would want to do that—well, I mean, before I *was* somebody?

JAN: [*Taking a deep breath.*] Me.

KELLY: [*Surprised.*] You? You're kidding?

JAN: No, I'm not.

KELLY: *You* wanted to come on to *me*?

JAN: Yeah.

KELLY: [*Rejecting the thought.*] That's so silly.

JAN: Yeah, it was, wasn't it?

KELLY: I mean *then*. But now everything's different.

JAN: [*Looking down.*] Sure is.

KELLY: Before I couldn't even be friends with people, but *now* ...

JAN: [*Rising.*] Kelly!

KELLY: What?

JAN: I have to tell you something.

KELLY: What, Jan?

JAN: Wait a minute. Close your eyes. It's easier if I just show you.

KELLY: [*Tremendously excited, anticipating a kiss.*] This is *really* a night for first times! [*She closes her eyes.*]

JAN: [*She takes out the hat and dark glasses that she wore as the recruiter.*] This is going to be a first all right...for both of us.

KELLY: [*Eyes closed.*] You too? Really?

JAN: [*Putting on the disguise.*] Really.

KELLY: [*Eyes still closed.*] I can't wait!

JAN: Open your eyes.

KELLY: [*Eyes closed.*] But you haven't kissed me yet...

JAN: Kelly, OPEN YOUR EYES!

[KELLY *opens her eyes and stares uncomprehending for a moment at* JAN. JAN *can't bear it.*]

JAN: Yeah, it's me. I was the recruiter. Get it, Kelly?

[KELLY *doesn't move.* JAN *takes off the disguise.*]

JAN: [*Cont'd.*] It was a joke, a trick. There aren't any Amazon All-Stars and there never have been and there never will be. You can just go back to left field and all your fantasies, because life's never going to be like that. It's just a raw deal with sleazy characters like me trying to hustle you all the time. That's all there is.

[*She thrusts the hat and glasses into* KELLY'*s hands and exits.* KELLY, *numb, turns the glasses over and over in her hands as the lights fade. Blackout.*]

SCENE 8

The Rubyfruit Bar and Grill.
    GLORIA *and* URSULA *are sitting at* LEONA'*s table, and* RUTH *and* HITCH *are standing by the bar, talking.*
    JAN *enters with her glove. She throws it on the table.*

JAN: Here—Here's a present for Slide. I can't stay.

URSULA: But it's your glove.

JAN: Yeah, well, she had her eye on it.

URSULA: But aren't you going to need it?

JAN: I'm quitting the team.

[*This catches* HITCH'*s attention.*]

URSULA: Quitting? You can't quit now! We're going to win the pennant!

HITCH: Jan, let's talk about this.

RUTH: [*Intercepting* HITCH's *cross.*] What's to talk about? The girl wants to quit. It's none of your business why.

LEONA: You keep out of this, Ruth. This is between the manager and a player.

RUTH: *You* keep out of this! Who do you think you are? Laura's bodyguard?

HITCH: Ruth, please!

RUTH: What's this "Ruth, please" stuff? You two are the ones interfering with somebody, prying into her affairs and trying to change her mind about what she's doing.

JAN: She's right. Thanks, Ruth.

RUTH: You bet.

JAN: You ought to take people on their word. [*She crosses to the bar stool to retrieve her trench coat.*] Leave people the way you find them. Leave them and their little fantasies alone. [*She rushes out.*]

URSULA: What was that all about?

LEONA: We just lost our short stop.

RUTH: I beg your pardon?

LEONA: [*Exploding.*] Shit, Ruth—Why don't you wake up and smell the coffee?

RUTH: [*To* HITCH.] What does she mean by that?

HITCH: I don't know, Ruth.

RUTH: Does she mean that I don't know I'm not the world's greatest short stop? Since when did the Desert Hearts turn professional?

GLORIA: Come on, Ruth... Let's not spoil K.C.'s party.

RUTH: K.C.'s party? Why doesn't somebody tell K.C. the truth about herself? Why is it you all want to tell me I'm an old alcoholic who can't play ball, but nobody wants to tell K.C. that her partner sleeps around on her every chance she gets? That her anniversary is just a farce? That the only thing she has to celebrate tonight is three years of being made a fool of?

HITCH: Ruth...

[K.C. *comes running out of the kitchen.*]

K.C.: Here she comes! I just saw her truck pull in! Places! Everybody get in your places! Here she comes!

[*The women move more or less quickly against the wall with the door.* RUTH *is the last one in place.*]

K.C.: [*Cont'd.*] Okay, everybody...

[*The door begins to open slowly.* K.C. *gives the signal.*]

EVERYBODY: SURPRISE!

[SLIDE *enters with a beautiful dyke on her arm. Everybody freezes. Blackout.*]

SCENE 9

The locker room. It's the morning after.

URSULA *creeps in and opens her locker. She begins to take out her uniform and put it in a bag.* GLORIA *sneaks in and starts to head for her locker. The two women don't see each other at first, and when* GLORIA *slams the locker door,* URSULA *screams in surprise, and then* GLORIA *screams.*

GLORIA: Oh! Ursula! You scared me to death!

URSULA: Me too.

[Neither women say anything for a moment, and then they both speak at once.]

URSULA:	GLORIA:
I was here because I . . .	I was just going to . . .

[Embarrassed, they both stop, and then try again.]

URSULA:	GLORIA:
I was going to tell you . . .	I was here because I . . .

[They stop again. This time GLORIA *speaks.]*

GLORIA: Practice isn't until noon.

URSULA: I know. I . . . uh . . . I thought I'd wash my uniform. Yeah . . . you know, for the big game next week.

GLORIA: *[Embarrassed.]* Oh, right.

URSULA: What are you doing here?

GLORIA: Uh . . . I . . . thought I'd get my shoes and put new laces in them. You know, for the big game next week.

[Just then K.C. *enters. She is annoyed that the others are here.]*

URSULA: Hi, K.C.

K.C.: I didn't know anyone was here.

URSULA: Yeah. Me and Gloria.

K.C.: *[Crossing to her locker.]* I . . . uh . . . thought I'd get my stuff. Got a hole in the knee.

GLORIA: Mend it for the big game?

K.C.: Yeah.

[At this moment SLIDE *starts backing in the door. She backs all the way into the room before she turns around and sees them.]*

SLIDE: *[Covering her shock.]* Well, hi, guys . . . Well, I see we're all set to practice.

URSULA: Slide, it's nine o'clock in the morning.

SLIDE: No, really? My watch must be fast. I thought it was noon.

K.C.: *[Very cool.]* Let me see your watch. Maybe I can fix it.

SLIDE: No, that's okay. Probably just needs a battery.

K.C.: I want to see your watch.

[*This is a new tone of voice from* K.C., *and* SLIDE *doesn't like it.* SLIDE *crosses to her, with an attitude of a juvenile delinquent sent to the principal's office. She shoves her arm out.*]

K.C.: [*Cont'd.*] It says nine. [*She looks at* SLIDE.]

SLIDE: Yeah? Well, it must have slowed down again . . . or maybe I read it wrong. So, what do you think I am, a liar?

K.C.: [*A long moment.*] Yes.

SLIDE: [*Uncomfortable.*] So . . . what are the rest of you doing here so early? [*She looks at* URSULA.]

URSULA: [*Looking at her feet.*] Just . . . checking up on our equipment.

SLIDE: Is it still here?

URSULA: Yeah.

[*Just then* LEONA *shows up. She stops at the door when she sees them all.*]

LEONA: What's going on? Why's everybody here so early?

SLIDE: [*Looking at* K.C.] Got the time wrong. [*To* LEONA.] What about you?

LEONA: I . . . uh . . . thought I'd come out and run some laps before practice.

GLORIA: In your sandals?

LEONA: [*Looking at her feet.*] Well, how about that . . .

GLORIA: Come on, everybody. I think we can all tell the truth. We're all here to clean out our lockers, because we're all quitting the team. Right?

[*They all answer at once:.*]

SLIDE: No . . . It's my watch!

URSULA: My uniform's really dirty!

K.C.: I can show you the holes.

LEONA: Just felt like running.

[*There's a moment of silence, and then they all answer together:.*]

SLIDE, K.C., URSULA, LEONA: Yeah.

GLORIA: Maybe we ought to call Hitch and tell her.

[*Just then* HITCH *appears in the doorway.*]

HITCH: Tell her what?

GLORIA: Hitch!

HITCH: Well, what are you going to tell me?

[*Nobody says anything.*]

HITCH: [*Cont'd.*] Never mind. I think I know, because it's the same reason I'm here. You're quitting.

[*Nobody says anything. They look at their shoes. Just then* RUTH *shows up.*]

RUTH: Well, isn't this cozy? I go out for a little breakfast, and what do I see? The whole parking lot at the ball field is just full of cars. And I think, "Wonder who's playing this early in the morning... They must be crazy." And then I look again, and I say to myself, "You know, that looks like Slide's truck... and Leona's motorcycle... and Gloria's Datsun..." And then I say to myself, "I wonder why they're having practice so early... and I wonder why they didn't tell me."

HITCH: It's not a practice.

RUTH: I know what it is. I wasn't born yesterday. It's some kind of sorority meeting to blackball me, isn't it? Well, let me just tell you all something right now: I started this team, and I don't care what kind of nasty little collective vote you take—I'm not leaving.

[*Nobody says anything. The women all look at each other.*]

RUTH: [*Cont'd.*] You heard me. I'm not quitting.

GLORIA: Ruth, everyone else is.

RUTH: Everyone else is what?

URSULA: Quitting.

RUTH: You can't do that! Laura, tell them they can't do that.

HITCH: I'm quitting too.

RUTH: Great. May I ask whose idea this was?

GLORIA: It wasn't anyone's idea. We all had it at the same time.

URSULA: Too much fighting.

SLIDE: [*To* RUTH.] Yeah, *too much fighting*.

RUTH: [*Crossing to her.*] Don't look at me! Who ruined the little party last night? You did that all by yourself. You and whoever your latest little...

LEONA: [*Cutting her off.*] Look who's talking!

RUTH: I'm not speaking to you.

GLORIA: This is what I can't stand—all this fighting! We're breaking up the team, now—let's at least be civilized about it!

URSULA: What about Jan and Kelly?

HITCH: Jan quit last night and Kelly's going to be an all-star, remember?

RUTH: So I'm the only one left, is that right? I'm the whole team?

HITCH: Looks that way.

RUTH: I know what you're all thinking... Good luck, right? Yeah, I'm not as fast as I used to be, and, yeah, I've got a problem with alcohol—but I'm not quitting yet. And I'm in love with somebody who doesn't want me anymore. And I'm fighting that, too. So if you think that having a lousy softball team walk out is going to be any worse than that, you better think again. [RUTH *begins to get very angry, confronting the women individually.*] Let me tell you something. I'm a lesbian and I've been a lesbian since before most of you were born, and I've been disinherited, and I've been dishonorably discharged, and I've been fired, and I've been beat up, and I can't say I enjoyed it, but I can say they haven't got me on the mat yet.

[HITCH *starts towards her, but* RUTH *stops her.*]

RUTH: [*Cont'd.*] No! So you all just go on looking for that perfect team, for those lesbian all-stars or that amazon nation, or whatever the hell your fantasy is where everybody loves everybody and sisterhood is beautiful and nobody's got any human weaknesses!

[*Nobody says anything for a moment, and then* GLORIA *reaches out and touches her.* RUTH *turns towards her with rage, and then breaks down in tears in* GLORIA's *arms. There is an awkward moment, and then* HITCH *crosses to* RUTH.]

HITCH: [*Touching her shoulder.*] Ruth, I'm sorry. I'll stay . . .

[RUTH *turns to embrace her, but* HITCH *holds her off.*]

HITCH: [*Cont'd.*] . . . IF you'll take right field.

[RUTH *begins to react with childish rage. She turns to* GLORIA, *who looks at her steadily.* RUTH, *after a long moment of wrestling with herself, suddenly lets go of her sense of betrayal and takes her first step towards sobriety.*]

RUTH: Yeah. Okay. I'll play right field.

GLORIA: [*Acknowledging* RUTH's *gesture.*] I'll be center.

URSULA: First base.

SLIDE: Need a good base runner?

HITCH: Sure.

SLIDE: [*Turning to* K.C.] How about it, K.C?

K.C.: I don't know, Slide. Things can't be the same between us.

SLIDE: Hey, we can still play ball together, can't we? Just like it was before, in the beginning, before we got so serious . . .

K.C.: [*She makes up her mind.*] No, we can't Slide. *I* can't. I'm sorry. [*To the team.*] I can't stay. [*She turns and leaves. Nobody says anything.*]

URSULA: [*Quietly.*] What about you, Leona?

LEONA: I have to think about it.

RUTH: I don't know about the rest of you, but I'm going across the street for breakfast. [*She heads for the door.*]

SLIDE: [*Tentatively.*] Ruth . . . ? Want some company?

RUTH: Yeah, sure, Slide. [*She puts her arm around her and crosses to the door.*]

GLORIA: Ursula? I'll buy.

URSULA: Sure.

RUTH: [*Turning back.*] Laura? Coffee?

HITCH: In a minute.

[*They all exit.* HITCH *sits.*]

HITCH: [*Cont'd.*] Sure hate to lose a catcher like you.

LEONA: [*Crossing to her locker.*] There's better catchers.

HITCH: That's not what I meant.

[LEONA *looks at* HITCH, *but* HITCH *says nothing.* LEONA *opens her locker. Alarmed,* HITCH *crosses to her.*]

HITCH: [*Cont'd.*] It's Ruth, isn't it? You're worried she's not going to be responsible.

LEONA: It's me I'm worried about.

HITCH: What do you mean?

LEONA: [*She changes her mind, closes the locker, and faces* HITCH.] At least Ruth is honest about herself.

HITCH: I don't understand.

LEONA: [*As much honesty as she can handle in one day.*] Maybe someday I'll tell you. Come on. Let's join the rest of the team.

[LEONA *puts her arm across* HITCH'S *shoulders, and they exit. After a moment,* KELLY *enters. She is completely dejected. She goes to her locker and begins to empty everything out of it. She takes it over to the trash can and dumps it in. Then she sits on a bench and begins to go into a trance. Her theme music is heard, and the lights go out.*
When the lights come up, KELLY *is lying on the bench, holding her head.* LEATHER WOMAN, *wearing a lab coat and a stethoscope is at the door, talking to a noisy crowd and trying to keep them out.*]

LEATHER WOMAN: No, go away! No, you can't come in! She's been hurt! She's been hit on the head with the ball! No, you can't come in! No, no pictures! [*She slams the door, crosses down to* KELLY, *and examines her head with the stethoscope. She speaks to the audience.*] I'm afraid this is serious. In fact, she only has a few more minutes to live. Kelly . . . Can you hear me?

[*Sentimental violin music comes up.*]

KELLY: [*Faint.*] Yes, I think so.

LEATHER WOMAN: I said you're going to die.

KELLY: That's not important . . . Who won the game?

LEATHER WOMAN: We did, Kelly . . . Right after the ball landed on your head, you caught it.

KELLY: Then it's been worth it.

LEATHER WOMAN: Before you die, there are some people here who want to talk to you. Do you want to see them?

KELLY: I can't. I'm blind.

[*Just then a woman rushes into the locker room.* LEATHER WOMAN *exits. The woman is* KELLY'S THIRD GRADE TEACHER, *played by* GLORIA. *She is dressed severely and carries a ruler.*]

THIRD GRADE TEACHER: Kelly! Kelly! Remember me?

KELLY: Not really.

THIRD GRADE TEACHER: It's your third grade teacher. You must remember me... I have been carrying around this terrible secret for all these years, and I was so afraid you would die before I could confess. Kelly, can you hear me?

KELLY: Barely.

THIRD GRADE TEACHER: I hated you. I hated you for no reason at all. You were just a sweet, innocent little seven-year old girl, and I was a sick... [*She hits her wrist with the ruler on every adjective.*]...twisted...evil... malicious... egomaniac! I made you look stupid in front of the class. I did it on purpose. [*Another whack.*] I confess it. When I leave here, I'm going to get the professional help I should have had twenty years ago.

[*She crosses to stand in the corner. Suddenly another woman rushes in. She is* KELLY'S *old* LITTLE LEAGUE COACH, *played by* LEONA.]

LITTLE LEAGUE COACH: Kelly! Hey, it's me! Sandy...

[*She accidentally knocks* KELLY *off the bench.*]

LITTLE LEAGUE COACH: [*Cont'd.*] Hey! Where'd you go? Come back here...I gotta talk to you.

[*She helps her back up.*]

LITTLE LEAGUE COACH: [*Cont'd.*] It's your old coach from Little League. Remember that season when I never let you play in any of the big games?

KELLY: I'll never forget.

LITTLE LEAGUE COACH: That was the worst mistake of my life. I lie awake at night and think of how everything in my life would have been different if I'd only seen your potential. The thought tortures me. [*She breaks into a frenzy of beating her head.*] Many a time I've considered just killing myself. If only I could go back to that summer.

KELLY: We can never go back.

LITTLE LEAGUE COACH: [*Crossing to the lockers.*] I know! I know! And now it's too late...too late! [*She bangs her head repeatedly against the locker until she knocks herself out—an illusion which can be created by kicking the locker.*]

[*A young woman tiptoes up to the bench. She is expensively and conservatively dressed, carrying a large, but tasteful purse. It's the* EX-BEST FRIEND, *played by* URSULA.]

EX-BEST FRIEND: Kelly, do you know who this is?

KELLY: No.

EX-BEST FRIEND: It's Mary Richland. Your best friend in high school, remember...I used to be your next door neighbor?

KELLY: I remember a girl named Mary Richland, but after she started dating boys, she didn't have time for me anymore.

EX-BEST FRIEND: What a fool I was! [*She opens her purse and takes a pill. She reconsiders and takes a whole handful.*] Being your friend was the only bright spot in a life which has been a weary trail of broken promises, betrayed hopes, and blighted prospects. O Kelly! The cruelty, the abuse! But I will spare you my troubles. You have enough of your own. But when you die, you go to your grave with a pure heart and the knowledge that you were a true friend to one who abandoned you in your youth. O Kelly! You've been a better friend to me than any boy could ever be. I'm so sorry, I didn't see that then. If it's any comfort, my entire life is ruined.

KELLY: [*Nodding thoughtfully.*] Some comfort.

[*The* EX-BEST FRIEND *retreats to a bench, sobbing, as* KELLY's MOTHER *comes in. She wears an apron and a house dress.*]

MOTHER: Kelly! My baby! My little girl! What's wrong, honey? [*Noticing her clothes.*] Uhhh ... where'd you get that shirt? My baby, what's happened to you?

KELLY: Mother, I'm dying.

MOTHER: Don't die before I tell you how proud I am of you. I always secretly wanted a daughter who could play left field.

KELLY: I thought you always wanted grandchildren.

MOTHER: I lied. All I ever dreamed of was having you grow up to be strong and athletic, and wear very, very short hair and date other nice girls. I never told you! I'm sorry! I'm so sorry.

KELLY: You mean you don't mind that I'm a lesbian?

MOTHER: Mind? Me mind that you're a lesbian? It's the answer to my prayers!

[*There is a chord from the piano, and the women all kneel and sing "The Wrong Song" in the best barbershop quartet style.*]

MOTHER, EX-FRIEND, COACH, TEACHER: We've come here today
To sing you this song:
You've always been right,
We've always been wrong.

You've been a true friend.
You've always had class.
We, on the other hand,
Were a pain in the ass.

We've been tacky and selfish
And petty and vain.
We're going to lie down now
In front of a train.

You were so brilliant
It made us look dumb.

We fed ourselves steak
And left you the crumbs.

We envied your talents,
We envied your gifts.
We're going to hold hands now
And jump off a cliff.

We just couldn't stand you,
Or anyone else.
And that is because
We can't stand ourselves.

This is a boring,
Monotonous song—
Just like our lives
It's gone on too long.

Let's get out our razors,
Let's get out our wrists.
Let's all count to three
And cease to exist...

COACH: One, two...

KELLY: [*Rising heroically on an elbow.*] Wait! I forgive you. I forgive you all! I forgive you...I forgive you...

MOTHER, EX-FRIEND, TEACHER, COACH: [*The women retreat, calling her name as the lights fade.*] Kelly! Kelly! Kelly...!

[*In the blackout, the voices segue into* JAN's *voice. When the lights come up,* JAN *has entered the locker room.* KELLY *is still lying on the bench, in the fantasy.*]

JAN: [*Standing over her.*] Kelly! Kelly!

KELLY: [*Eyes still closed.*] I forgive you...I forgive you...

JAN: KELLY!

KELLY: [*Waking up.*] Oh!

JAN: Are you okay?

KELLY: [*Rising from the bench to avoid* JAN.] Oh...yeah, sure. [*She starts to leave.*]

JAN: Wait...I wanted to tell you I'm sorry about the mean trick I pulled on you, about the All-Stars and everything.

[KELLY *doesn't say anything.*]

JAN: [*Cont'd.*] And I'm quitting the team, so you won't have to see me anymore.

KELLY: [*Angry with* JAN.] You don't have to do that. I already quit.

JAN: Why?

KELLY: Because you made me realize I've just been fooling myself about how I play. I'm never going to be a great softball player.

JAN: Maybe not great, but you're better than a lot of players.

KELLY: What's the point? You know—hit the ball, run around in a circle. It's not getting me anywhere.

JAN: But it makes you happy.

KELLY: Not anymore.

JAN: Kelly, I feel awful! I didn't know this was going to happen. I feel like I could just die. [*This is a realization.*] I'm the one who's going in circles. I'm the one who's not going anywhere. You have your dreams and fantasies, but at least you keep them separate. I'm *living* in mine. I've been using people to make mine come true. Kelly, I'm the one who should quit, not you. [*She crosses to the bench where* KELLY *is standing.*] Please don't leave the Desert Hearts!

KELLY: But I told everybody I was going to be an all-star. They're all going to laugh at me.

JAN: Nobody's going to do that. They couldn't love you better if you were an All-Star. Don't you know that? Don't you know your friends love you?

KELLY: No.

JAN: They do. [JAN *holds out her hand to* KELLY.]

KELLY: Is this another joke?

JAN: It's no joke. I'm shaking inside.

KELLY: [*Very slowly, and in incremental movements,* KELLY *puts her hand in* JAN's. *After a pause, she speaks.*] It feels like another fantasy.

JAN: It's real.

[*The two women freeze, their arms outstretched and their hands touching.* LEATHER WOMAN *appears. Very softly and tenderly, she sings "Cruisin'.".*]

LEATHER WOMAN: I see you lookin'—
You like what you see?
Yeah, I'm lookin' at you,
And you're lookin' at me—
Because we're cruisin'-
Cruisin' tonight—
Cruisin' kinda heavy,
Cruisin' kinda light—
Baby, oh, baby, oh baby—
We're cruisin' tonight!

[*As the piano trails off, the lights fade on* LEATHER WOMAN *and the two lovers. Blackout.*]

FINALE

The locker room.
  Lights come up on an empty set. The actors come on for their curtain call. When

all of the actors are on stage, including LEATHER WOMAN, *they join hands and sing a reprise of "Come Out For the Team."*

ALL: Come out for the team!
      You know what I mean—
      You can't do it by yourself alone!
      Come out for the team—
      Out for the, out for the team!

[*Blackout.*]

THE END

A LADY AND A WOMAN

Shirlene Holmes

For S. Faybell Ma-Hee
and all the lovers that have to hide.
Rebecca Ransom: Thank you for "Secrets"
With courage and pride,
Shirlene Holmes
Atlanta, GA
Oct. 31, 1990

Shirlene Holmes

INTRODUCTION TO *A LADY AND A WOMAN* BY SHIRLENE HOLMES

Willa J. Taylor

"Oppression is having other people tell your story." That is why Shirlene Holmes' play, *A Lady and a Woman*, is so important. It is very rare to find a play about being Black and lesbian. The two sides of myself—blackness and gayness—always exist in distinct dramatic universes on stage and screen. That's not to say there haven't been Black characters in gay plays, and sometimes—albeit rarely—gay characters in black plays, but often these are caricatures, one-dimensional exotics peripheral to the story. They are, however, almost always gay men. Film has grudgingly admitted the existence of Black lesbians in the past several years. Spike Lee's first commercial success, *She's Gotta Have It*, has a Black lesbian character, and Whoopi Goldberg's portrayal in *Boys On The Side* has forced my African-American and gay communities to entertain the notion of my existence. Around the country, millions (well, maybe only hundreds) of Americans now know that there are indeed Black lesbians thanks to the producer-writers of television's *Courthouse*. But Spike's lesbian is the stereotypic predator, perpetuating that old myth; Whoopi's a lesbian because of a smart casting director and not the character breakdown; and *Courthouse*'s Black lesbian judge—the script's delineation—has so much internalized homophobia that she has denied her girlfriend of eleven years to every one of her colleagues.

While television and film are both mediums with tremendous reach and greatly influence our perceptions of what is reality, they have always been about the "hook," the gimmick that will get you to tune-in or come in. Audience interaction is not required, only the purchase of a ticket or the switch of a channel. Theater, however, demands participation, for in the specificity of the drama, we find the universality of human experience. Audience and actors join in creating—for each performance—a singular community with a common language and shared sense of humor and pathos. Theater is the keeper of our culture, the record of our struggles and triumphs.

Queer theater and Black theater both grew out of our communities' separate struggles against oppression and the fight to tell our own stories. In the early part of this century, Black theater was a direct contradiction to the minstrel show. Performed mostly in church basements, schoolhouses, and social clubs, the plays presented for the first time images other than shuffling, shiftless Negroes that dominated white-authored entertainment. Black women playwrights and their male counterparts used drama as education and protests in a society where lynchings were commonplace and Jim Crow was the law of the land.

In 1916, the NAACP's Drama Committee produced the first recorded play written and performed by Blacks in this century, Angelina Grimke's *Rachel*. The program for the production, performed in New York City and Cambridge, Massachusetts, noted the importance of the occasion: "This is the first attempt to use the stage for race propaganda in order to enlighten the American people relative to the lamentable condition of ten millions of Colored citizens in this free republic." Plays drawn from the folklore of southern Blacks, like Zora Neale Hurston and Langston Hughes' collaboration, *Mulebone*, showcased Black folk culture, increasing the diversity of images of Blacks that both white and Black audiences were exposed to.

As sit-ins and demonstrations escalated the struggle for civil rights, Black theater reflected and fueled this new aggressiveness, paving the way for more realistic images of Negroes on stage. With the burgeoning Off-Broadway movement's commitment to incorporating voices of disenfranchised communities, Black playwrights began making significant inroads into commercial theater. In 1955, Alice Childress became the first Black woman to have a play produced Off-Broadway when her Obie-winning *Trouble in Mind* opened, and in 1959, Lorraine Hansberry's *A Raisin in the Sun* broke the color line of Broadway theater. The success of the play—and of Hansberry—acted as a catalyst for a new generation of writers who would continue the traditions of using theater for social change.

Queer theater as we know it today began with the 1968 production of Mart Crowley's *The Boys in the Band* and coincided with the Stonewall riots in New York. Before that, the existence of gay characters was rare. Alphonse Daudet's *Sappho*, a play about the lesbian poet, was performed in the US in 1895, but its revival was banned in 1900. As late as 1944, theaters in New York City refused to rent to producers of The Baker's *Trio* because the play dealt with an older woman's "unnatural" feelings for a girl. When there were gay and lesbian characters in plays, they were always portrayed as unhappy, pathetic or psychotic. As Blacks had been stereotypically depicted as shiftless, lazy and comic, so gays and lesbians were shown as sick, flaming and suicidal. By the late 1950's, more sympathetic characters began to appear but gay context was still mostly between the lines. New York state law officially prohibited depictions of homosexuality onstage until 1967.

The Stonewall riots galvanized the lesbian and gay community as the sit-ins and boycotts had done for the Black community a few years earlier. The community demanded more realistic and diverse portrayals of gay characters, formed theatrical performance troupes like the Ridiculous Theater Company, and gave birth to a cultural movement that has helped change the face of theater today. Where would Broadway be today without Tony Kushner, Terence McNally, Harry Kondolian, Holly Hughes, Larry Kramer, and Harvey Fierstein?

The world of theater is our society in microcosm, and as such is not exempt from the -*isms* that plague our daily lives. The reality of professional theater—where commerce and subscribers often drive the "art"—is that women's work gets produced sometimes, but never proportional to the number of actresses working in the field (and often not to the number of women in the audiences). Black playwrights often only have February, and Black women writers struggle to get produced at all (though smart theaters try for two-for-one and include *A Raisin in the Sun* in their seasons). Community theater—not the type found in the malls of America, but the space where a specific community reaffirms its existence—is never inclusive of the whole of its constituency. As produced in this country, queer/gay theater is really the canon of gay white males. Black theater continues to see women in the classic images: long-suffering straight mammy/wife, aggressive seductive straight vixen, tragic straight womanchild. Lesbian theater, though certainly more conscious of diversity than queer theater, still most often addresses this diversity in the casting, and not in the writing or direction. Holmes' play fills the void that forces Black lesbians to choose between our sexual and ethnic identities. In its presentation of two strong absolutely Black women steeped in their love for each other and love for themselves, we see true images: our grandmothers and sisters, our neighbors and aunts, ourselves then and now. We hear our stories told in a language at once familiar and true.

Although lesbianism was sketchily implied in Lorraine Hansberry's *Toussaint* as early as 1961, it wasn't until the 1980s that Black women playwrights began to seriously look at it as a part of women's sexuality. Black women's reality. With plays like *No* and *A Season to Unravel*, Alexis DeVeaux dealt explicitly with love between two women. And P. J. Gibson's 1985 piece, *Long Time Since Yesterday*, about the friendships between black women, features a lesbian relationship as a central plot point. It went on to win five AUDELCO awards, including Best Dramatic Production.

A Lady and a Woman continues where those plays left off. Focusing on the blossoming relationship between a butch and femme, Holmes' play melds the southern folklore of early Black theater with the exploration of sexual roles, desires and discovery that so often informs queer and lesbian theater. For a new generation of Black lesbians whose only media images are straight actors playing gay, this is a piece to be admired for its honesty. For an older generation accustomed to looking ourselves in the images of others, it is a play to be cherished. For anyone interested in good drama, it is a play to be treasured and performed.

Holmes, an associate professor of communication at Georgia State University and an expert in solo drama and storytelling, captures the essence of what it means to be a Black woman-loving woman, not only through plot and setting, but through the intimacies of touch and look, the everyday ways of relating unique to a culture used to hardship and filled with hope. It is a voice whose authenticity breaks the silence of oppression and gives color to often invisible lives.

Brenda Porter as "Biddie Higgins" and Sondra Barrie as "Miss Flora"

ACT I
SCENE 1

The time is about the 1890s. It is morning at FLORA'S INN.

At the front desk is MISS FLORA DEVINE, *a 6 foot, buxom, 40-ish divorcee. She has a long keloid scar on the right side of her face and is wearing a rather low cut dark purple cotton handmade dress.* MISS FLORA *is busy tending to her paperwork when in walks* BIDDIE, *a mannish 4 foot 8 inch butcher wearing a leather hat, vest and pants. She is in her mid-thirties.* BIDDIE *puts down her luggage and wipes her sweating brow; she checks her underarms for an odor. While looking around her eyes fall upon* MISS FLORA; *she is immediately enraptured.*

BIDDIE: Umm. Excuse me. I'm looking for Miss Flora Devine. I'm told she's the owner of this place.

MISS FLORA: Are you all right?

BIDDIE: [*Removing her hat.*] Just fine, ma'am. Little worn, traveling all night, you know.

MISS FLORA: Who wants Miss Flora Devine?

BIDDIE: I do.

MISS FLORA: Who are you and what's your business?

BIDDIE: I'm a stranger in town in need of a place to stay, and I was wondering if Miss Devine can help me.

MISS FLORA: She's me and the cost is $2.00 a night. Does that suit you?

BIDDIE: Suits me fine. Sure got a nice place here. Yes, a fine place. How long you been in business?

MISS FLORA: I've been running this inn for five years and been owning it for ten. If you want "business," you have to go down the street near the tavern. This ain't that kind of place.

BIDDIE: Let me catch my tongue. You know flapping this piece of red flannel will get you in a lot of trouble sometimes. I didn't mean no harm. I'd like to have a room. Not near a lot of people, though, 'cause that gives me headaches. I'd like something on the first floor, basement if you got it.

MISS FLORA: How long you need the room for?

BIDDIE: Can we just say "until"; I'll be needing the room until.

MISS FLORA: Until when?

BIDDIE: Until I don't need it no more.

MISS FLORA: Now, this ain't no boarding house; I'm running an inn. A respectable place where strangers and locals can come rest their heads if they want to.

BIDDIE: That's fine. Just charge me till the end of the week. Then we'll see. This is a nice place. Who did you say helps you run this inn?

MISS FLORA: I didn't say nobody helps me. I run it myself.

BIDDIE: [*Moving closer to* MISS FLORA.] By yourself?

MISS FLORA: Course I got a couple of hired men and a cleaner who come in and give me a hand, but this is my inn, and I have all the say so here.

BIDDIE: And your husband?

MISS FLORA: I think that's the worst subject this early in the morning.

BIDDIE: That good to you, huh?

MISS FLORA: A friend once told me that "marriage is one of them institutions for the insane."

BIDDIE: I ain't never been married so I ain't qualified to say. So it's safe to say you don't have no husband?

MISS FLORA: Don't got one and don't want one. The one I had been tossed out about five years ago now. How about room 1-B. It's off to the back where no one can bother you.

BIDDIE: He left you with this inn to run?

MISS FLORA: We had a parting of the ways or in other words I throw him out.

BIDDIE: You look like the type.

MISS FLORA: What type?

BIDDIE: The type to put a train back on track if it get off, that's all.

MISS FLORA: Well that's one train been derailed and won't be coming this way no more. My used-to-be is a blessed man.

BIDDIE: You got to be the only woman I ever heard bless her gone husband.

MISS FLORA: I didn't say I blessed him; God blessed him. If it was up to me, he'd be eating ribs with the devil right now.

BIDDIE: What did he do 'cause I sure don't want to follow in his footsteps.

MISS FLORA: When we got married my granddaddy say to me, "Flora, if he raise his hand up make sure he go to jail, but if he bring that hand down, make sure you go to jail." That's what happened the night he hit me in my face and I went back into the wall mirror. The doctor wanted to stitch up my face, but I wouldn't have it. When I got my mind back, I was sitting in jail and he was gone; ain't seen him since.

BIDDIE: So that's how you got that long scar on your face?

MISS FLORA: Doctor say I'm lucky I got sight; I said he lucky he still got a behind. We both ate a lot of glass that night.

BIDDIE: It's a beautiful scar. I think it adds something to you. It's just like a medal or something. Says you been in the war of life and made it back from the last battle. Hell, I got some on me, too. You know, Miss Flora, I like looking up at you. From where I'm standing, you look just like a statue or something.

MISS FLORA: I don't know about all that. I ain't no piece of stone. I'm flesh and blood.

BIDDIE: Oh, I see that quite well.

MISS FLORA: [*Facing* BIDDIE *again.*] That'll be $14.00. I'm gonna need $4.00 today just to keep us honest. Business don't have no friends.

BIDDIE: [*Puts hat back on and takes out a wad of money and passes some to* MISS FLORA.] That's fine, but I want you to know you can trust me.

MISS FLORA: [*Smelling the money.*] I don't trust nobody on first glance; not even myself. You say you're a stranger. Where you from?

BIDDIE: Out of Virginia. I travel a lot, especially during this season.

MISS FLORA: What's your work?

BIDDIE: I cut hogs. Really, I cut everything there is. I get plenty of work during this time of year and that tides me over during winter months when I just do some house repair for folks.

MISS FLORA: That's men's work.

BIDDIE: Not if I get to it first. I'm good. Just have to be. When you're dark and knee high to a duck's ass, everything you do better be worth paying for. God's been good to me; I don't want for nothing except a friend to talk to every now and then.

MISS FLORA: I never heard of no woman cutting hogs. Where'd you pick that up?

BIDDIE: I was the only girl in a house of ten brothers. And the oldest, too, so I spent lots of time doing hard work. Every time I tell my daddy that my back was hurting from lifting and picking and carrying three and five times my weight, he'd spit and say, "Gal, you ain't got no back. All you got is gristle."

MISS FLORA: [*Laughing.*] Well, I done heard it all. A woman cutting hogs.

BIDDIE: I cut anything: cows, rabbits, goats. I know just how to half 'em. All the parts be perfect. My daddy made me do it till I did it right.

MISS FLORA: It paid off; you'll find plenty of work here. Folks ready for a cutter. You kill, too?

BIDDIE: I can, but I ask people to kill the meat first then bring it to me. It keeps the blood off my hands.

MISS FLORA: I know what you mean. That animal spirit be all over you. I wrung a chicken's neck once and every night for thirty-seven days it seem like I was spinning. I know that chicken was riding me 'cause I can't as much as eat an egg now. Give me your name for the register.

BIDDIE: Mary Higgins, but folks call me Biddie.

MISS FLORA: Biddie Higgins. Where does Biddie come from?

BIDDIE: Well, my mother always called me Iddie Biddie and I got teased for it, being I'm short and all, but Biddie stuck. Back home, I don't think half my brothers know my real name is Mary.

MISS FLORA: Mary, that's sweet. You'll be in room 1-B, Miss Higgins, and...

BIDDIE: Just call me Biddie. I reserve "Miss" for ladies.

MISS FLORA: Ain't you a lady?

BIDDIE: You're the lady, Miss Flora, I'm a woman.

MISS FLORA: I don't know if I understand you, Biddie.

BIDDIE: You're the flower. I'm the blade. You seal up and I open up. You the kind that carries and I'm the kind that hauls.

MISS FLORA: I think I understand, but stick around till I'm real clear about it.

BIDDIE: I will, Miss Flora.

[*Pause.*]

MISS FLORA: That's a nice hat; you didn't get it here.

BIDDIE: [*Smiling broadly.*] No ma'am! I knew this hat maker once when I was passing through Frankfort, Kentucky. I cut her meat, and she made me this hat from the skin.

MISS FLORA: It was born for you; fit like a saddle on a horse. You need help with that heavy satchel?

BIDDIE: Not me. These my tools; I only trust me with them.

MISS FLORA: Supper's at four o'clock.

BIDDIE: I'll bring my hungry belly.

MISS FLORA: And I'll feed it.

BIDDIE: I'm already much obliged.

[BIDDIE *picks up the key, satchel, and suitcase and exits, leaving* MISS FLORA *watching in awe.*]

SCENE 2

Several days later: Enter BIDDIE *carrying her work satchel.* MISS FLORA *looks up from her needlework.*

BIDDIE: You're a good sight to come home to. I'm bone tired. I cut two hogs, today, seven possums and ten coons for the Kimbles. Made a good piece of money.

MISS FLORA: [*Rising to greet her.*] You smell like fresh blood.

BIDDIE: That'll wash away.

MISS FLORA: Three more folks done come in today looking for you to cut their meat.

BIDDIE: It's a good time.

MISS FLORA: The word's getting 'round that you in town; there's plenty of work. It pays to do everything in season. You plan on staying on?

BIDDIE: For awhile. You really good to me, Miss Flora. If I didn't have all this blood smell on me, I'd kiss you. [*She kisses* MISS FLORA'S *hand.*] You'd make a man a good wife. I think you could make a monument out of any man that could love you right.

MISS FLORA: I don't think I want no man.

BIDDIE: Not now, but you will, just wait. I want one myself sometimes, but it's just a thought that goes by.

MISS FLORA: I think people got you all wrong. You ain't no man inside.

BIDDIE: Oh I'm mannish all right.

MISS FLORA: Don't live beneath your privilege trying to be no man. That crust you got is so folks won't rub up against you without being scratched. I know you gentle inside.

BIDDIE: I always had to protect myself. [*Pause.*] Today, I was cutting up one of them 'coons and found there was a baby inside. That's mighty strange 'cause there's always more than one chile. But this morning there was only one. I opened the sack and it was a boy 'coon. I started ringing inside, just ringing and shaking. The biggest tears run down my face and I was trying to rub them out of the creases of my neck with my free hand. The blood mix with the tears. All I know was that I was so grateful that it wasn't me that killed that mother and her baby.

MISS FLORA: That's really something.

[MISS FLORA *embraces* BIDDIE *and walks her to sit down.*]

BIDDIE: You know, Miss Flora, I never told nobody this, but I always wanted me a son. My mother had ten brothers for me, that I even helped raise, but that wasn't enough. I want my own. I don't even know why, I just do.

MISS FLORA: It ain't over yet. You still seeing your flow; why don't you go on and have a baby. You do everything else you want to whether God like it or not; you can do that, too.

BIDDIE: I ain't fit for birthing. You're the one ought to be having the children. You're the lady.

MISS FLORA: I declare I don't understand you sometimes. Anyways, I have been down that dead end street and ain't going back. These stretch marks are crawling on me like worms.

BIDDIE: Someone should kiss every one of 'em. Those marks are a woman's honor.

MISS FLORA: I ain't never heard that said before. Not many people know I'm a childless mother. I keeps my body hid; I had that child when I was eleven. Midwife say the cord rang his neck 'cause I was young and the moon was over full. See I got mad and cut off my hair that day; I didn't know the baby was coming. Never cut your hair when you know the moon is full.

BIDDIE: Who fathered that chile?

[*Pause.*]

MISS FLORA: My father.

BIDDIE: Your father or your mother's husband?

MISS FLORA: My mother's third husband. They locked me away in my auntie's house for almost a year.

BIDDIE: [*Holding and rocking* MISS FLORA.] It's all right, Miss Flora. I'm here now. No more pain.

MISS FLORA: I never know to this day why momma believe him over me; I was telling the truth.

BIDDIE: Mommas can scar more than just your body; they can cut your soul where no needle made will stitch you up again.

MISS FLORA: I was talking truth, but she beat me and sent me away. That baby boy was cursed with his daddy's face; they buried him out back at my auntie's. I ain't been back to her house since. I don't want to hold no more dead babies.

BIDDIE: I don't want to see no more.

MISS FLORA: I need you.

[BIDDIE *proceeds to kiss* MISS FLORA *but she draws back.*]

MISS FLORA: [*Cont'd.*] You smell like fresh blood.

BIDDIE: That's a woman's right. It'll wash away.

[*Lights fade.*]

SCENE 3

The next day: BIDDIE *and* MISS FLORA *are sitting down to tea.* MISS FLORA *is serving.*

MISS FLORA: This ease-your-belly tea is gonna make you feel real good, Biddie.

It's got eucalyptus, peppermint and a secret I learned from a woman in it.

BIDDIE: What woman?

MISS FLORA: A spirit woman that comes to visit me from time to time in the night. She told me where to find the herb, and I went and pulled it and boiled it in this tea.

BIDDIE: It smells good. My belly sure can use some easing. I believe that was the sweetest cobbler I had in years.

MISS FLORA: I could tell you like peaches.

BIDDIE: How?

MISS FLORA: I can just tell.

BIDDIE: You right. My mother say she marked me when she was carrying me 'cause it was winter and she couldn't get no peaches when she was craving them.

MISS FLORA: That will mark a chile for sure.

BIDDIE: I got a dark spot the shape of a peach about seven inches above my belly button.

MISS FLORA: [*Avoiding* BIDDIE's *innuendo.*] Mine's here on my ankle; it's shaped like a pineapple slice. My mother say she got the pineapple, but it was the next day, so I got this light mark on my leg. You know your mother had it bad when the mark is dark.

BIDDIE: Mine is dark black.

MISS FLORA: It's a shame a woman got to suffer so when she's carrying a chile.

[*Pause.*]

BIDDIE: You sure have touched me.

MISS FLORA: I'm glad you stayed on.

BIDDIE: You ever go to town, Miss Flora?

MISS FLORA: Not me.

BIDDIE: Never?

MISS FLORA: Wouldn't go by myself and never took no one up on the offer.

BIDDIE: Why not?

MISS FLORA: I think that may be what causes trouble and spread disease, going to town.

BIDDIE: [*Chuckling.*] Oh, I don't think so. I go to town every time I get a chance.

MISS FLORA: That don't sound good for me, that going to town.

BIDDIE: How do you know. Miss Flora, would... would you go to town with me?

MISS FLORA: It's too soon to tell.

BIDDIE: Sounds like you're thinking on it. What you afraid of?

MISS FLORA: No telling what might happen.

BIDDIE: You might find out you like it.

MISS FLORA: I think I better stay home and not go looking for trouble.

BIDDIE: [*Tries to corner* MISS FLORA.] I find that going to town can ease your mind, Miss Flora.

MISS FLORA: I appreciate your telling me about it, but I don't know what I'd go to town for.

BIDDIE: To see if you like it. To make somebody happy or just to . . . eat.

MISS FLORA: [*Escaping.*] Now, Mary Higgins, would you like some more tea.

BIDDIE: I do believe my cup don't need no more filling.

MISS FLORA: I got plenty dishes and kitchen to clean waiting for me. Seems to me that tea would work better on you if you go lay down.

BIDDIE: I'd much rather help you with that kitchen.

MISS FLORA: You done help me enough. I'll see you in the morning.

BIDDIE: [*Surrendering and crossing to exit.*] Goodnight, Miss Flora. Hope you go to town with me.

MISS FLORA: Goodnight, Biddie.

SCENE 4

A week later: The scene begins with uproarious laughter. They are in BIDDIE'*s room. She is semi reclined and* MISS FLORA *is sitting at her feet. It is near midnight.*

MISS FLORA: Lord have mercy, Biddie, if you tell me another tale like that, I'ma bust my side wide open here.

BIDDIE: Sure is good to laugh with you, Miss Flora. Makes me feel so much better.

MISS FLORA: Laughter is medicine; make you well.

BIDDIE: I been here two months and I can't leave. It's time for me to move on and I can't.

MISS FLORA: I ain't ready for you to go nowhere. Losing friends is hard.

BIDDIE: My heart tells me to stay.

MISS FLORA: Well, you do just that.

BIDDIE: I listen to the head more than the heart.

MISS FLORA: You can get something if that head ache you, but when that heart get to aching, ain't much you can do.

BIDDIE: I guess you right.

MISS FLORA: I know I'm right. Looka here, I'ma show you how glad I am you staying. [*She pulls a small bottle out of her pocket, spills some of its contents in her hands and then begins rubbing* BIDDIE'*s feet.*]

BIDDIE: [*Humbled and aroused.*] Thank you, Miss Flora. Now, I know how Jesus felt when he got his feet washed in oil by that woman.

MISS FLORA: Ain't too many people I'd be rubbing feet for. Or using my blessed oil. I had it prayed over when the woman evangelist come to town. It heals. I had a nasty mole under my breast; I anointed it and the next morning, that black thing fell right off in my hand.

BIDDIE: You musta known my dogs were barking.

MISS FLORA: I seen you hobbling in this evening; but you gonna be better now.

BIDDIE: You just a blessing, Miss Flora. What can I do to pay you?

MISS FLORA: You can't pay me, but I wish you'd tell me more about you. I realize today when I was ironing your work shirt and pants, I hardly know you.

BIDDIE: Let's see. I was born in a crowded house: fourteen people, including me. My daddy was a hard worker and a drinker. My momma raised me at a distance; I don't know today if she loved me or not. That's the good part of my life.

MISS FLORA: You go to school?

BIDDIE: All I know, I taught myself. I had to work with Daddy, no time for school.

MISS FLORA: I went long enough to learn reading and writing. Everything else I know, I learn from the heavens and the earth.

BIDDIE: I left home at fifteen; sure glad you didn't know me then. I was full of the Devil.

MISS FLORA: A little love'll put the Devil on the run. Anything I ever touched prospered. I done helped the best and the worse of people. It's just a gift God give me. I can make a crop come up outta the dust.

BIDDIE: I think you done pulled me up outta the dust. You're so beautiful.

MISS FLORA: Just hush.

BIDDIE: I wish I could teach folks how to look at you, the way you deserve to be looked at. I love that scar on your face.

MISS FLORA: It's ugly, but I got to live with it. Sometimes it itches and burns so bad, it feels like fire crawling around in my face and can't get out. If I rub it, it burns worse than hell. All I can do is make a poultice, as hot as I can stand it, and that cool the fire down.

BIDDIE: It's just a part of you and that's all right with me.

MISS FLORA: It's been a burden to me. When mama saw my face for the first time with this scar, she shook her head and told me I was ruined. She never put no pictures up of me since my face was cut.

BIDDIE: Mothers don't know everything. There was this woman on the land two roads down from us. I mean she was burned in a fire so bad that wasn't nothing much left of her original face. Momma called her pitiful and said she "oughta drink a cup a poison and die; ain't no man gonna want her." She didn't have to worry about being alone, I saw to that. Miss Sophia Elouise Gent taught me lessons so deep, I don't need another teacher. I ain't never been scared of no woman's scars, and don't you be.

MISS FLORA: Did your momma know you was up there loving on Miss Sophia?

BIDDIE: I never hid nothing from my mother and nobody else either. If anyone deserve the respect of keeping myself secret, it was her, but I never could live a lie. It's easier to live a hard life than a lie. So I been living hard a long time. Just rambling. Doing my work in the day and finding someone to spend the night with.

MISS FLORA: Than ain't no kind of life.

BIDDIE: I know, Miss Flora. I never believed anything good could happen to me. I just told myself that if I could keep going, it wouldn't be so bad. I'd find another job, another room and a few more good looking gals to make me sleep better. Then I checked in this inn. And met you. I'm kinda scared, Miss Flora. Here I am talking about staying. It's always been so easy to pack my bags and head to the next town, but you ain't gonna be in the next town. If I go, I got to say goodbye, and I can't. [*She cries.*] If you'll have me, Miss Flora, I want to stay.

MISS FLORA: [*Crossing over to hold* BIDDIE.] You don't never have to go. The only thing you gotta say goodbye to is that hard life. I got you, now.

BIDDIE: You make me feel safe, Miss Flora. Nobody's ever done that for me.

MISS FLORA: If you stay here, nothing's gonna hurt you no more, just believe.

BIDDIE: I believe.

[*Lights fade slowly on them.*]

SCENE 5

Three weeks later: Lights up. MISS FLORA *is at the door and* BIDDIE *is in bed sleeping.*

MISS FLORA: Biddie! Biddie!

BIDDIE: [*Stirring.*] Damn! Who is it?

MISS FLORA: Biddie, it's Flora.

BIDDIE: [*Jumping up and rushing to door.*] Miss Flora. Is something wrong?

MISS FLORA: No. I didn't mean to wake you. I hadn't seen you this evening and was wondering if you was well.

BIDDIE: I musta dozed off when I come in from work. Pardon me for not being dressed.

MISS FLORA: Oh that's all right; I sleep in the raw sometimes, but it takes me longer to get to sleep when I do. Ain't nothing wrong with it; that's how we come into the world with not a stitch on. Only thing, you got to watch the seasons when you sleep raw 'cause the elements will get you.

BIDDIE: The elements don't worry me.

MISS FLORA: They should worry you. Don't ever forget that water puts out fire and wind blows the earth away. If I were you, I wouldn't want the elements working against me.

BIDDIE: I'm gonna remember that. Miss Flora I was wondering, since you're here, if it isn't no trouble, could you take up my new work coat? [*Crosses to get her work coat.*] Just need a little off the sleeves and the bottom. I always have trouble with clothes; nothing much fits me well.

MISS FLORA: I bet I could get that coat to fitting well. Let me measure you; I got my tape right here in my pocket. [MISS FLORA *measures* BIDDIE'S *arm length and measures for her hem.*]

BIDDIE: You sew and cook like nobody's business. Your soup today, I don't think I ate nothing that good.

MISS FLORA: It was the bone you give me that made the tomato eye soup so good.

BIDDIE: Why you call it tomato eye?

MISS FLORA: It's according to how you cut those tomatoes. If you see them 'fore they go in the pot, they sliced just like eyes. The pupil part.

BIDDIE: I was so busy filling my belly, I didn't see nothing. You sure put your foot down on that pot of soup. I had two helpings and woulda had three if I wasn't so ashamed.

MISS FLORA: No need to feel shamed. I always cook enough. You never know when you have to entertain an angel, so you better make extra. That's what my mother said.

BIDDIE: You talk a lot about your Momma; she still living?

MISS FLORA: No, she's gone on home. Disease ate her; I nursed her till the end. It was a blessing for me, 'cause now I ain't scared of nothing. I used to be scared to be left alone, but not no more. I been alone since mama died two years ago now, and I'm fine.

BIDDIE: I'm sorry about your Momma; that's a hard thing to face.

MISS FLORA: Your mama gone, too?

BIDDIE: Ten years now. Vein busted in her head. Pressure the doctor said.

MISS FLORA: I wish I could have got to her. A little ginger root, garlic and gin flower, and she would still be here looking at you. No use in sorrowing for the dead; they resting now. There, I think I got the measurements I need.

BIDDIE: I sure appreciate you working on this coat for me; I got a big job to do at the end of the week and I'll be needing it then.

MISS FLORA: I'll have it ready. It won't take me long. I'm good with a needle and thread.

BIDDIE: I got to say how much I admire that dress. Did you make it?

MISS FLORA: Yes I did, from an old curtain I found in the basement of the church.

BIDDIE: It's mighty holy.

MISS FLORA: Folks laughed when I told them I was gonna make a pretty dress. See, I can look at something and tell that what it is, ain't what it's gonna be.

BIDDIE: All I do know is that's a good color for you.

MISS FLORA: Purple makes my glory stand out.

BIDDIE: [*Embracing her.*] You smell good, Miss Flora.

MISS FLORA: [*Nervously stepping away.*] I call that Lavender wash. I can tell you how to make it if you like.

BIDDIE: Oh, I'm satisfied just smelling it on you. [BIDDIE *crosses and touches* MISS FLORA's *hair.*]

MISS FLORA: You lost something, Biddie?

BIDDIE: I just been wondering what your hair feels like, that's all.

MISS FLORA: Feels like a wool throw blanket.

BIDDIE: [*Rubbing* MISS FLORA's *hair.*] It's like a cotton comforter to me.

MISS FLORA: You making me nervous, here.

BIDDIE: [*Kisses her neck.*] There ain't nothing to worry about. One thing I ain't gonna do is hurt you.

MISS FLORA: If I didn't know better, I'd think you're trying to wake up the dead.

BIDDIE: You ain't dead, Miss Flora, you just resting.

MISS FLORA: Seem like one of us is gonna get in trouble.

[BIDDIE *wraps her arms around* MISS FLORA *and kisses her cleavage. Pause.*]

BIDDIE: Say something, Miss Flora.

MISS FLORA: You worrying me.

BIDDIE: Worrying you?

MISS FLORA: Since you been here, I been, been enjoying your company and . . .

BIDDIE: What you trying to say, Miss Flora?

MISS FLORA: I think I'm starting to . . . love you.

BIDDIE: I feel love for you, too, Miss Flora.

MISS FLORA: I don't think you're hearing me.

BIDDIE: I know what you're saying.

MISS FLORA: I don't know where these feelings to touch you is coming from, but they here and they so real. This seem like a funny way to be talking to a woman. I don't know if I'm saying the right things.

[*Pause.*]

BIDDIE: Stay with me tonight, Miss Flora?

[*Lights begin to soften as* MISS FLORA *crosses to the bed, but stops.*]

MISS FLORA: Biddie, I don't know where the parts go. I ain't never read no book about this.

BIDDIE: There ain't no book, Miss Flora. The parts go just where you want them to. Trust me, you'll know. [*In the soft light, the two get in the bed.*]

MISS FLORA: Lord.

BIDDIE: Trust me.

[*They kiss and begin... as the lights fade.*]

SCENE 6

Next morning: Just before sunrise and MISS FLORA *pulls the covers over* BIDDIE, *tucking her in and then pours water from a pitcher into a basin. She takes a white cloth and washes up. After a moment* BIDDIE *stirs. Pause.*

BIDDIE: You haven't said nothing.

MISS FLORA: I thought you were sleep.

BIDDIE: You doing okay, Miss Flora?

MISS FLORA: I'm fine.

BIDDIE: Was this too fast for you, Miss Flora?

MISS FLORA: No.

BIDDIE: I know something's wrong. I felt your mood change. You got so cold and blue. [*Pause.*] You worry me.

MISS FLORA: I don't mean no harm; I just got to think. You know this ain't something that happens everyday.

BIDDIE: Do you wish it could?

MISS FLORA: I can't say. Part of me is grateful and the other part is just...

BIDDIE: [*Sitting up.*] Just what?

MISS FLORA: Numb. Like I can't wake my old self up. My new self is wake, but my old self is slumbering. I don't want her to die.

BIDDIE: You saying I killed you, Miss Flora?

MISS FLORA: No. I'm wondering about myself, my spirit. Mrs. Porter one time told me that the flesh and the spirit don't mix. "It's like a spoon full of oil in an ocean of water, you gonna see it." I'm just worried about my spirit.

BIDDIE: You think we wrong with God, don't you? I used to believe that years ago when I was wasting myself, hopping around like a rabbit. But not with you, Miss Flora. It just don't feel the same. Last night you made me feel like it was my first time, too.

MISS FLORA: I never felt nothing like this in my life; you so soft and gentle. [*Pause.*] I've had women friends for as long as I been in this world and never once laid hands on them. I always knew that wasn't right. But here you come and it seem like I'm supposed to. I keep searching myself. Looking up under all my feelings. Moving aside what I think people gonna say.

BIDDIE: You sorry, Miss Flora?

MISS FLORA: No, but I'm numb. I want to feel again, just so I know my spirit ain't been damaged.

BIDDIE: [*Smiling.*] I can feel your spirit; it's fine.

MISS FLORA: Your feeling it ain't got nothing to do with it. I got to feel my own spirit for myself.

BIDDIE: You can keep trying to feel for that old self if you want, but she's changed. You can't never go back to who you were after you been with another woman.

MISS FLORA: I'm scared. [*Pause.*] Sometimes I think God is up there playing tricks, but I ain't foolish enough to tell Him so.

BIDDIE: It took me a long time to like God because of His reputation. That's 'cause I was only going on hearsay, back then.

MISS FLORA: You got to know God for yourself. That's what my momma always told me.

BIDDIE: You the only God I need to know.

MISS FLORA: Now you talking crazy.

BIDDIE: Seem to me I can touch you a lot better than I can touch Him.

MISS FLORA: This is serious, Biddie. I been trying to stay away from you 'cause you bring out my carnal nature.

BIDDIE: You wasn't trying to stay away too hard. [*Softens.*] I only brought out what was already there.

MISS FLORA: I'm an upstanding woman in this town.

BIDDIE: That ain't changed. Ain't nobody challenged your dignity and better not while I'm around.

MISS FLORA: They whispering. Talking 'bout you all the time. How you think you're strong as a man.

BIDDIE: I am. Stronger than many I know 'cause I can show my feelings. It's a waste of time measuring a woman to a man, ain't no comparison.

MISS FLORA: They call you a BULLDAGGER WOMAN.

BIDDIE: That's all right, I'd rather they call me a bulldagger than a nigger. Nothing hurts worse than that.

MISS FLORA: I never thought I grow up and be no bulldagger.

BIDDIE: Who said you're one? You're what you are; Miss Flora Devine and that's all you got to claim. Send the rest to me.

[MISS FLORA *ties her head and gets ready for work.*]

MISS FLORA: I can't live without God.

BIDDIE: Don't have to. As long as we live, God'll be in the midst.

MISS FLORA: Blessing or cussing. I done had my fair share of sorrow and don't need no more.

BIDDIE: You blessing me; I'm gonna bless you back.

MISS FLORA: [*Kissing her.*] You trying to be God, now, Biddie? Come on. We done burned up enough daylight. I got an inn to run.

BIDDIE: It's the best inn in town where a stranger can come lay her head and get some . . .

MISS FLORA: Rest!

BIDDIE: That's just what I was thinking. And get some rest.

[*They share a laugh.* MISS FLORA *exits. Lights go down.*]

SCENE 7

A month later: MISS FLORA *is patch quilting with* BIDDIE *who pricks her finger.*

BIDDIE: [*Puts bleeding finger in her mouth.*] Great God from Zion!

MISS FLORA: Now, you know your finger was under there.

BIDDIE: That hurt.

MISS FLORA: [*Tickled.*] It should. Mean to tell me, you can handle a knife, but you can't handle a needle.

BIDDIE: Don't be picking on me.

MISS FLORA: Bet I'll never trust you with my finger. If you do that to yours, what will you do with mine.

BIDDIE: Just hush, woman. This gonna be a wonderful quilt.

MISS FLORA: Quit your praise.

BIDDIE: One day you gonna learn how to take a compliment. It ain't no sin accepting your due praise.

MISS FLORA: It'll make your head swell, and God's gonna have to slap you down.

BIDDIE: You thinking like an old woman; God don't slap nobody down. But I might as well be talking to this thread I'm pulling here. Colored women sure are something.

MISS FLORA: They sure are. Let me see that finger. [*She kisses* BIDDIE'*s hurt finger.*]

BIDDIE: It's better already. You looking brighter; your spirit numbness is gone ain't it?

MISS FLORA: I believe so. I been feeling more good each day and I ain't doubting my power like I was. I knew I was all right when I brought the breath back in Nellie Small's baby boy.

BIDDIE: I didn't even know that baby was in trouble.

MISS FLORA: I was out front of the inn dropping off the mail when Nellie come a-running. "Miss Flora! Miss Flora!! Save my baby!!" I looked down in her arms and there was the chile, blue as the covers he was wrapped in. I touched his neck and it was soft, then I touch his little chest and it was thick as beef meat. That was the sign that the lungs had give way. So I lift him to my face and when I couldn't get his wind, I rolled him over in my hand. He ain't but two months old. And I heard the spirit say, "Put a cross in the center of his back and flat hand slap him three times." After that I turned to his face, opened his little mouth, cleaned it out, and puffed some breath in it. He didn't do nothing for ten minutes or more. Nellie eyes was a big as white saucers. Then I felt them little legs jump and a life quiver went through him and I knew he'd be all right.

BIDDIE: What was wrong with him?

MISS FLORA: Suffering from ungodly medicine. Nellie done give him some of that doctor medicine and it quench his life force. You got to watch what them doctors give you. Half time it ain't got no anointing. It just ain't natural for life to leave a baby and turn him blue like that. Man's medicine do that; a little woman's medicine cure anytime.

BIDDIE: I know that's true.

MISS FLORA: This gonna be his little quilt. I told Nellie to keep him outta blue for 30 days till his breath get strong. This cover will give some strength.

BIDDIE: It's a honor to be with you, Miss Flora.

MISS FLORA: You sure it ain't no accident.

BIDDIE: I don't believe in accidents; God gave you to me.

MISS FLORA: [*Avoiding the compliment.*] Watch what you doing before you stick one of them fingers again.

SCENE 8

Later that same day: Lights up on BIDDIE *sitting in a chair and* MISS FLORA *braiding her hair. It is in the wee hours of the morning.*

BIDDIE: Holy Jesus, Miss Flora, can't you be gentle?

MISS FLORA: I'm doing my best, but you need to talk to your momma and daddy about this hard hair you got. I put some nettle on it, that ought to make it a little softer.

BIDDIE: Put some more on it. As long as I been living, I ain't never liked my head combed. I'd sooner leave it and just see what happens.

MISS FLORA: It'll mat all up. [*She lays hands on her head as if she's a preacher trying to heal* BIDDIE'*s hair problem.*] Then nothing short of a miracle from Jesus would untangle it.

BIDDIE: Think I care? I'd put a hat on and dare somebody to say something.

MISS FLORA: Thank God I'm here to make sure you don't have to die with a hat on.

BIDDIE: Sweetie.

MISS FLORA: Yeah.

BIDDIE: I needed that bath. When I was pouring that water out, it was like throwing away all my trouble. And I feel so good from that lotion you rubbed me with. What you put in that?

MISS FLORA: That's my love liniment. I made it and let it sit just for you.

BIDDIE: I appreciate it. How you know to do things so far ahead. I think about what's in front of me; you think about what's in front of you and everybody else.

MISS FLORA: Not everybody else, just you. [MISS FLORA *takes the comb and rakes the nape of* BIDDIE's *neck*.]

BIDDIE: Oh savior!!!!!!!!

MISS FLORA: Now stop whining; I got to get this kitchen. [BIDDIE *reaches up to touch her hair*, MISS FLORA *pops her hand with the comb*.]

BIDDIE: Ouch! Miss Flora, are you my woman or my mother? Sometimes I think Hattie Higgins done jumped up from her grave and moved into you.

MISS FLORA: I'm Flora Devine and when I say keep still, I mean just that. Now sit still 'fore I wear you out.

BIDDIE: [*Smiling*.] Yes, momma.

MISS FLORA: You so hard-headed. If you keep still and stop whining, this wouldn't be so bad. You know what a hard head makes?

BIDDIE: A soft behind?

MISS FLORA: That's right, sister.

[MISS FLORA *finishes her braiding and kisses* BIDDIE *on the forehead*. BIDDIE *grabs her and wrestles her to the floor where she begins tickling her and planting kisses all over her face*.]

BIDDIE: I know that's right!

MISS FLORA: [*With uncontrollable laughter*.] I mean, you bettah stop while you have a chance. When I get up from here . . .

BIDDIE: I ain't scared of you, Hattie Higgins!

MISS FLORA: That's Miss Flora Devine to you! [MISS FLORA *overpowers* BIDDIE *and rolls her on her back. She tickles her mercilessly then kisses her passionately*.] Now, get up off this floor; I just bathed you.

BIDDIE: You think you are my mother.

MISS FLORA: [*Folding towels*.] I oughta be somebody's mother the way I'm not appreciated.

BIDDIE: [*Seriously*.] Don't ever say you ain't appreciated. What do you want? Just ask it and I'll make it with my bare hands.

MISS FLORA: [*Touched*.] Look over there and bring me that jar of peach wine and two drinking cups.

BIDDIE: [*Crossing excitedly*.] Now you talking! I love peach wine. [*Noticing something in the jar*.] Why you got this rock in the bottom.

MISS FLORA: [*Taking the jar and holding it close to her breasts*.] That's a smooth stone. You always put one in peach wine to keep in the smooth.

BIDDIE: Let me pour. [*Handing a cup to* MISS FLORA *and keeping one for herself. She raises her cup for a toast*.] To the most beautiful woman in the world.

MISS FLORA: You ain't been all over the world, how you know if I'm the most beautiful?

BIDDIE: Clamp your lips and take the compliment. Drink up. [*They click their cups.*] Damn good wine.

MISS FLORA: That's better than they make in the store.

BIDDIE: I appreciate you. [*Pauses.*] I would give you a baby if I could, but God didn't fix it that way.

MISS FLORA: This wine got you talking foolish.

BIDDIE: I know how bad you want a chile. I feel you, you know.

MISS FLORA: I had my one; he died and that's the end of it, I guess.

BIDDIE: Your body had that baby, you didn't.

MISS FLORA: I must have had something. I bore all the pains. I got the marks.

BIDDIE: You still bearing them. [*She takes* MISS FLORA's *glass, sets it down and holds her for the remainder of the scene.*] If I could give you a baby what would you want to have?

MISS FLORA: A girl and depending on how the light hit her, she could look like me or she could look like you.

BIDDIE: And what would you name her?

MISS FLORA: Jesus.

BIDDIE: Jesus?

MISS FLORA: It's the sweetest name I know.

BIDDIE: And what you gonna say when people start talking, saying you blaspheming?

MISS FLORA: If you give me a baby, they gonna be talking anyway. I don't care what they say. Jesus means Savior and that's what we need in our life.

BIDDIE: Jesus is a man's name.

MISS FLORA: No it ain't. It's an anointed name. Our daughter's gonna be able to do miracles, help people just like we do.

BIDDIE: If we have her, she's gonna be a miracle.

MISS FLORA: But you said you wanted a son.

BIDDIE: I always have.

MISS FLORA: If we have a son, what you gonna name him?

BIDDIE: Euphrates.

MISS FLORA: U who?

BIDDIE: It's the name of a great river; I seen it in the bible, that's all I know.

MISS FLORA: Euphrates. Sounds nice and strong. You need a strong name so folks will leave you alone.

BIDDIE: Maybe they'll think our son is some kind of royalty...

MISS FLORA: From African, maybe. You think Euphrates is an African name?

BIDDIE: I got it from the bible.

MISS FLORA: The African part?

BIDDIE: I don't know.

MISS FLORA: I'm sure gonna ask the preacher come Sunday. Pharaoh Euphrates. But I don't think I know how to raise no boy.

BIDDIE: You'll know what to do. They nurse at the breast like girls do; you just have to mold and make them before they start smelling themselves.

MISS FLORA: I think it's something in the seed that make them so contrary and contradicting.

BIDDIE: Won't matter. A woman done bore every boy and man that's come into the world; they ain't nothing to be afraid of. They got to come through us just to get into this world.

MISS FLORA: I ain't never thought about it that way. We're the gate keepers to the world.

[*They stop, look at each other, and click their glasses in celebration and affirmation.*]

BIDDIE: If we have us a girl, I'll teach her everything I know, and that's something I wouldn't do with a boy.

MISS FLORA: I couldn't either. I love you, Biddie.

BIDDIE: I love you, too. [*Pause. Putting down her cup.*] Miss Flora, I want to talk to you about something.

MISS FLORA: What on earth is it?

BIDDIE: You sure you want to talk?

MISS FLORA: Come on, what is it?

BIDDIE: I was wondering what a hard head make?

MISS FLORA: You know what it make. A soft behind.

BIDDIE: [*Rubbing against* MISS FLORA.] That's just what I want to talk to you about.

MISS FLORA: You a mess, Biddie.

[*Lights fade.*]

SCENE 9

A month later: MISS FLORA *is scrubbing the floor on her hands and knees. She is concentrating on scouring a very serious stain.*

MISS FLORA: [*Singing the "Wash Floor Blues."*] This floor of mine
needs some scrubbing, baby
This floor of mine needs a sheen

If you love me right
with soap and water
I know that, baby, you'll get me clean.

[*Laughing at herself.*]

Get a rag and water
and come down on your knees
I said get a rag and water, baby
and get way down on your knees
If you scrub me the right way, baby
I'll do just what you please.

[BIDDIE *comes in; she is very anxious.*]

BIDDIE: Miss Flora, can I speak to you a minute?

MISS FLORA: Now, what on earth can you want while I'm scrubbing this floor?

BIDDIE: I got a question for you, and I just need a short answer; then I'll leave you alone.

MISS FLORA: It bettah be a short one; I'm gonna get you if my soap and water cool off.

[*Crossing over to* MISS FLORA, BIDDIE *makes the mistake of stepping on the wet portion of the floor.*]

BIDDIE: Miss Flora, would you...

MISS FLORA: [*Hitting* BIDDIE's *feet with wet rag.*] If you don't get your hoofs off my wet floor I'll...

BIDDIE: I'm sorry, Sweetie.

MISS FLORA: Sweetie, nothing. It took me twenty minutes to get that molasses up off that spot. If folks around here didn't have holes in their lips, I wouldn't be scrubbing floors on my knees.

BIDDIE: Woman, you act like scrubbing a floor is a work of art.

MISS FLORA: I sure would like to see what you could do with a rag and some soapy water.

BIDDIE: Give it here.

[BIDDIE *gets the pail from* MISS FLORA *and proceeds to scrub.* MISS FLORA *grabs another rag, wets it and joins her in scrubbing the floor.*]

BIDDIE: [*Cont'd.*] You got to be the evilest woman I know.

MISS FLORA: I ain't evil, I'm mean. Evil women sweat on they lip. I sweat on my brow.

BIDDIE: Well, I come in here to ask you a question and you took me off track.

MISS FLORA: Scrub that spot harder; it's still gray.

BIDDIE: I was in my room thinking to myself how I would ask you this.

MISS FLORA: The best way to take medicine is SCRAIGHT; that's what my grand daddy say.

BIDDIE: Here it is: [*She stops scrubbing, dries her hands on her pants and lifts* MISS FLORA's *face towards her.*] Miss Flora, will you marry me?

[*Pause.*]

MISS FLORA: You say some of the craziest things.

BIDDIE: Will you marry me?

MISS FLORA: For how long?

BIDDIE: Until.

MISS FLORA: Until when?

BIDDIE: Come on, woman. I need an answer.

[*Pause.*]

MISS FLORA: Awright. Yes, I'll marry you.

BIDDIE: [*Excitedly.*] You want a wedding?

MISS FLORA: No. I done had one of them. Let's just keep this between you and me.

BIDDIE: Why?

MISS FLORA: You need to be put right in a crazy house.

BIDDIE: When you happy, you want every one to know.

MISS FLORA: They know already. Marriage happens before people propose to one another.

BIDDIE: Let's go somewhere and celebrate.

MISS FLORA: Somewhere where? Celebrate? I got this floor to finish.

BIDDIE: This dirty floor is gonna be here when we get back.

MISS FLORA: I ain't even dressed.

BIDDIE: Woman, don't kill my joy. Go get ready. We'll go out and when we get back we'll ...

MISS FLORA: And no we won't. The moon is full tonight and that's no time to be in a crowd. Besides, these are my holy days, and I don't want nobody touching me.

BIDDIE: I won't touch you if you don't want.

MISS FLORA: It's not that I don't want, but when I see my blood, for seven days I'm sanctified and you mess with my power. But I'll marry you and fix you a big dinner.

BIDDIE: Can I hold you hand?

MISS FLORA: I guess you can if you get outta here and let me clean my floor.

BIDDIE: [*Taking a cloth from her pocket.*] Since you are the bride ...

MISS FLORA: And what are you?

BIDDIE: I'm still the woman.

MISS FLORA: Who's the husband?

BIDDIE: He's the one you threw out the door.

[*They both laugh.*]

BIDDIE: [*Cont'd.*] Now, I made this ring outta a wish bone I come across a while back. It oughta fit. I whittled it the best I could.

[BIDDIE *puts the ring on her finger.*]

MISS FLORA: This gonna do awright in water?

BIDDIE: I took it outta blood; I don't think water is gonna hurt it. Blood's thicker, you know. I'm gonna go get ready for my dinner.

MISS FLORA: [*Marveling at the ring on her finger.*] Don't rush me; I got to take my time.

BIDDIE: That's fine, Mrs. Higgins.

MISS FLORA: [*Adamantly.*] Oh, no. There won't be no name changing around here. You call me Flora Devine.

BIDDIE: Mrs. Flora Devine?

MISS FLORA: That'll be all right. I didn't know your daddy and your daddy didn't know me, so it don't make no sense for me to die with his name. I'll keep my own, thank you.

BIDDIE: [*Checking* MISS FLORA'*s top lip.*] You sure you don't sweat on your lip. [BIDDIE *steals a kiss.*]

MISS FLORA: [*Laughing.*] Get outta here and let me scrub!

BIDDIE: I'll be waiting, Miss Flora.

MISS FLORA: [*Waving her left hand.*] That's Mrs. Flora to you.

[BIDDIE *smiles widely and the lights fade as* MISS FLORA *is holding her left hand close to her and beaming with joy.*]

ACT II
SCENE 1

A month later: BIDDIE *finds* MISS FLORA *in her room sitting weeping and cracking pecans. She looks very weary.* MISS FLORA *is wearing a darker home made purple dress with a contrasting light purple apron.*

BIDDIE: Sweetie, what's wrong? [*Pause.*] Come on, honey, answer me.

MISS FLORA: I can't talk about it.

BIDDIE: You worrying me.

MISS FLORA: Don't mind me; I can't talk just now.

BIDDIE: People been talking again?

MISS FLORA: Nobody's talking.

BIDDIE: Then what is it?

MISS FLORA: I did something shameful today. It happened before I could catch myself.

BIDDIE: You didn't follow the spirit?

MISS FLORA: Almost that bad. I don't know how to say this to you.

BIDDIE: Scraight. Ain't that what your granddaddy say.

MISS FLORA: I don't want you turning away from me.

BIDDIE: I won't never do that.

MISS FLORA: I don't want you to get mad at me.

BIDDIE: I won't get mad.

MISS FLORA: Yes you will. I know it.

BIDDIE: [*Standing.*] Miss Flora Devine, tell me right now 'cause I can't stand it.

MISS FLORA: I knew it. When you stand up, you're mad.

BIDDIE: I'm not mad about nothing except you holding back on me.

MISS FLORA: I ain't holding back. I'm just trying to think of how to put it.

BIDDIE: Dry your eyes and tell me. We ain't got no secrets between us.

[*Pause.*]

MISS FLORA: I denied you today.

BIDDIE: What you say?

MISS FLORA: [*Crying.*] I done cried enough tears to fill this bowl because of it.

BIDDIE: Hush now and explain.

MISS FLORA: This morning when I was gathering dew water to make skin wash, I run into Cornelia Hooks and she see my finger and ask "When you get married, Flora?" I keep gathering cause I didn't like how she sound talking to me like that. Then she say, "Flora Devine, are you married?" Then she turns her wide backside round and says, "What you wearing that ring for?" "I married myself, is that all right with you?" That's what I say back to her, and soon as the words left my mouth, I feel this sharp pain dead in the center of my chest. That's the conviction pain you get when you lying and you know you lying and God knows you lying. It's still hurting.

[BIDDIE *rubs the center of* MISS FLORA'S *chest.*]

BIDDIE: I don't appreciate that woman calling you out of your title. You're MISS Flora Devine. And she ain't got no business harassing you. I got a mind to go over there and answer all her questions.

MISS FLORA: Now don't you go raising sand. She just need something to put her big nose in.

BIDDIE: Nobody should be harassing my wife. One of these days I'm gonna lock the door on this place and we ain't never leaving.

MISS FLORA: [*Moving* BIDDIE'S *hand.*] Help me shell these pecans 'cause you losing your mind. What we gonna live on if we don't go outside?

BIDDIE: We'll eat love and drink prayer just like we been doing.

MISS FLORA: I didn't mean to deny you. When I said I'd marry you, my word was good. I sat here crying so long 'cause I was scared. When you can't speak your heart, you need to be scared.

BIDDIE: I know you married to me, and it don't matter who else knows or not.

MISS FLORA: Yes it do. The Bible say "if you deny me, I'll deny you." God is all I got and you are all I got.

BIDDIE: That's all you need.

MISS FLORA: Why people and what they think mean so much, I don't know. I want people to think the best of us. We're good, me and you.

BIDDIE: Forget about people. If Jesus worried about what people think, he'd never got one of those miracles done.

MISS FLORA: Why people hate you when you true to yourself? All I wanna do is love you.

BIDDIE: Miss Flora, if you asking people if it's all right for you to love me, you'll be crying a long time 'cause they don't know. The answer ain't in them; it's in you. You only love when God let you; you been free to love me a long time; you just ain't grabbed that freedom yet.

MISS FLORA: I don't know. I believe in people. They ain't going no where. Much as you fuss, Biddie, you gonna need some people.

BIDDIE: I may need them, but I ain't gonna let them control when I love and who I love. I'll tell wide behind Cornelia Hooks that you my wife and I'm your wife and that we are happy, and until she respect that don't speak to either one of us again.

MISS FLORA: You got such a mean streak.

BIDDIE: When people look at me and you, they just don't know what they see.

Mattie Macuchin come babbling the other day, "you need to move outta that inn, 'cause folks talking 'bout you and Flora."

MISS FLORA: I went to school with Mattie Macuchin, and she ain't said doodlely squat to me.

BIDDIE: Just a babbling brook, I told you. So I say back to her, "Me and Miss Flora doing wonderful up there in that inn and we don't have no shame about it." Love takes away shame, Miss Flora. If you love me, all you sins are washed away. All those people scratching and itching about me and you just scared of themselves and what they liable to do if folks didn't talk. A whole lot of people would live their lives freer if they wasn't so scared of what would be said about it. I learned that a long time ago.

MISS FLORA: I don't want you to leave me for a woman that got her heart fixed and her mind made up.

BIDDIE: If I walk out, I got to leave myself. I have to leave my soul; woman, you got my soul.

MISS FLORA: That sound like a piece of a song they play down there in that tavern.

BIDDIE: You can't love nobody and not give them a piece of you.

MISS FLORA: Give me more time to understand things.

BIDDIE: Suppose you don't never understand things.

MISS FLORA: What you mean?

BIDDIE: You thinking on this too hard with your head; this is a heart matter.

MISS FLORA: You gonna wait on me?

BIDDIE: Forever.

MISS FLORA: You ain't got no forever.

BIDDIE: Well, just as close as I can get to it, then.

MISS FLORA: I lit me a candle in the bathroom and burn me some sage, so I'm gonna let it rest. The answers be in the wax or the ashes tonight.

BIDDIE: And you gonna pick this same burden up until you look in you 'steada in your signs and wonders.

MISS FLORA: The wax may fool you, but the ashes never lie.

BIDDIE: I ain't worried about the ashes; I'm worried about you. That's why you need to just go on and marry me.

MISS FLORA: I did marry you.

BIDDIE: I mean, we need to have a ceremony. That'll help you believe in us more.

MISS FLORA: No. This is something I don't want nobody seeing but God.

BIDDIE: Why?

MISS FLORA: 'Cause my last wedding was full of folks and look what happened. Besides, who we know gonna come see two women hitch up?

BIDDIE: You ain't gonna vex me, woman. I don't care if ain't nobody here but you, me, God and a couple of flies, I want to get married. Let's do it now.

MISS FLORA: Now! I ain't dressed. The dust need to be cleaned off the floor. You never get married without cleaning the dust; it's bad luck. And we got to boil some water.

BIDDIE: We getting married, not having no baby.

MISS FLORA: But it's a beginning; we got to drink sterile water; then what about a preacher?

BIDDIE: We don't need no preacher for God to be in the midst.

MISS FLORA: You blaspheming, so nuff.

BIDDIE: The preacher just represent God. Ain't that what you do?

MISS FLORA: Yes, but . . .

BIDDIE: But nothing. If you can heal and bring babies into the world, you can marry us. Stop stalling.

MISS FLORA: Let's wait til sunrise, I . . .

BIDDIE: Come on here, woman.

MISS FLORA: [*Kneels and quickly dusts floor. She then takes her apron off and spreads it on the floor.*] Awright, but we got to have some purple for under our feet. Let's lift our hands up. Now, face south, north, then west and east. Let's pray.

[*The lights should dim, and then highlight the two standing on the apron.*]

MISS FLORA: [*Cont'd.*] God we coming right now and this minute
first to praise you
we only got these many hands to lift up;
accept these now.
Second, Mother, Father, God
we asking you to marry us
before You and the angels.
You ain't a money God
can't be bought or sold
make our love and faith the power
and turn that into something
for us to live on
and we'll do the best we can
for as long as we live.

[*Pause.*]

MISS FLORA: [*Cont'd.*] Lord, now Biddie need to talk.

BIDDIE: [*Surprised, very hesitant at first.*]
Lord, make this a day that never has no ending.
Let us be good to one another.
And I thank you.

[*Pause. Lights brighten.*]

MISS FLORA: Well, we married now. Get off my apron. [*She picks up apron and puts it back on.*]

BIDDIE: Not yet. We ain't vowed forever and kissed.

MISS FLORA: We ain't got no forever.

BIDDIE: Married people talk about forever.

MISS FLORA: So do divorced. Forever is God's alone. All we got is now.

BIDDIE: All I want to say is "I do" and kiss you like everybody else.

MISS FLORA: We ain't like everybody else.

BIDDIE: You ain't gonna steal my joy, woman. Could you grant me a wedding kiss, then?

MISS FLORA: You gonna get that and then don't mess with me, Biddie Higgins.

[MISS FLORA *gives* BIDDIE *a peck on the lips.* BIDDIE *tenderly embraces her and kisses her passionately. Lights fade.*]

SCENE 2

A week later: BIDDIE *enters her room in a huff;* MISS FLORA *follows calmly.*

MISS FLORA: I mean you acting just like a chile.

BIDDIE: I got a right.

MISS FLORA: You gonna get your stomach upset with all that jealousy.

BIDDIE: I ain't jealous. I just don't like nobody 'round you, not that close anyway.

MISS FLORA: That's plumb crazy. People got to be around me; I'm a healer.

BIDDIE: I know, but she was way outta line.

MISS FLORA: All she done was touch my hair and tell me she like my dress.

BIDDIE: You as green as a blade of grass, woman.

MISS FLORA: She was trying to be nice. You the one acting colored.

BIDDIE: She was trying to get your attention, and it's already taken.

MISS FLORA: All I did was go in the store and say "Linda Ruby, how you and what's the cost of this material?"

BIDDIE: And she say, wit her fast self, "Low enough for you to get and take home." She wasn't talking about no material.

MISS FLORA: You making too much of her. Linda Ruby just think a lot of me.

BIDDIE: I know, and I don't want you going in there no more without me.

MISS FLORA: Now, you making a suggestion and not telling me what to do, right? 'Cause I know you know bettah that that.

BIDDIE: I just want to protect you.

MISS FLORA: From what, Biddie?

BIDDIE: From anybody that wants to take you away from me.

MISS FLORA: Can't nobody take me away from you; I'll have to go. Nobody takes me no where without my permission.

BIDDIE: So you saying you gonna leave me if the right one come along?

MISS FLORA: Nobody wants me. Not with this mark on my face.

BIDDIE: You just don't see how folks be looking at you. Men and women.

MISS FLORA: You reading too much in people. What they looking at is the light I got around me; they ain't looking at me.

BIDDIE: Now, I'm short, but I ain't stupid. I know when folks looking at light and when they just looking.

MISS FLORA: I don't know Linda Ruby real well, but I can tell you she don't want no woman.

BIDDIE: You don't know. You didn't want no woman, remember? Just stay far from her. She ain't got no respect.

MISS FLORA: She didn't do nothing wrong to us.

BIDDIE: Anybody but the blind can see that I'm with you when we out. She just took it upon herself to look right over it.

MISS FLORA: Better watch all that jealousy; it'll put knots in your back. My daddy was so jealous he went to his grave with humps in his back the size of garden rocks. They didn't hurt him none, but they was there.

BIDDIE: I can't lose you, Miss Flora.

MISS FLORA: And where am I going?

BIDDIE: You act like you don't understand. Ain't you ever had something so precious you didn't want nothing to touch it, nothing to take it away? I don't want nothing spoiling you but me. Is something wrong with that?

MISS FLORA: It is when you put that precious thing in a box and don't trust it to live on its own. You can't cage me, Biddie.

BIDDIE: I trust you; I just don't trust other folks. You supposed to protect what is yours.

MISS FLORA: I ain't yours.

BIDDIE: [*Hurt.*] Then whose are you?

MISS FLORA: I'm my own, but you welcome to share.

BIDDIE: But we belong to each other.

MISS FLORA: We belong with each other.

BIDDIE: When we got married, I left everything behind and cleaved to you.

MISS FLORA: I love you for it; but I can never give my power up. It's a spiritual matter.

BIDDIE: Linda Ruby don't understand that.

MISS FLORA: I don't think you have to worry about Linda Ruby. You stared her down so hard that if she see me coming down on one side of the street, she'll cross over to the other side.

BIDDIE: Good. That's my blessed assurance.

MISS FLORA: She's a nice woman. I healed her insides once.

BIDDIE: Which insides?

MISS FLORA: Her woman insides. She had a ball of tissue in her the size of a grapefruit, and I melted it with a turpentine rag. That musta been three or four years ago.

BIDDIE: How come that don't sound good to me.

MISS FLORA: I drew that ball down till it was the size of a pea, and I cut it from her wall with my sharp knife. That's why when she sees me she want to get close.

BIDDIE: [Sarcastically.] I'm glad she's better, but she don't have to get no closer.

MISS FLORA: [Salutes.] You acting like a little soldier; you can't be standing guard over me.

BIDDIE: You ain't understanding me. I don't share you 'cause I want to, it's 'cause I got to and you ain't helping none.

MISS FLORA: What you want me to do? I ain't thinking about nobody else and if they thinking about me that's a problem they got to sleep with.

BIDDIE: [Surrendering.] I'm gonna stop while I'm ahead.

MISS FLORA: I believe you bettah before you back gets a hump.

BIDDIE: Woman, come here.

[BIDDIE *pulls* MISS FLORA *to her and embraces her, staring up lovingly.*]

SCENE 3

Six months later: It's Friday night and MISS FLORA *is in the kitchen about to peel vegetables. Enter* BIDDIE *who sneaks up and hugs her.*

BIDDIE: What you cooking for supper?

MISS FLORA: Sunday soup. You know I don't cook on the Sabbath. This pot is gonna be GOOD. I put some clover leaf in it; that eases your belly on the way down. All I got to do is peel 5 onions.

BIDDIE: Why so many?

MISS FLORA: I cook by numbers. You don't put even numbers in soup; make it so thin it don't have no flavor. Sunday soup call for 3 carrots, 15 tomatos, 9 potatos, 5 onions, 1 celery and a half pepper.

BIDDIE: I'll get outta your way.

MISS FLORA: [*Grabbing her by the arm.*] You just in time to help me.

BIDDIE: No ma'am! I can't stand no onion peeling, puts my eyes right out. Momma made me peel onions so long and hard one day, I smelled onions for six months.

MISS FLORA: [*Passing her a knife and onion.*] You suffer 'cause you don't know what you doing.

BIDDIE: Wait a minute. I'll eat onions all day for you, but don't wait on me to peel none.

MISS FLORA: I'm gonna teach you how to peel so your eyes won't hurt no more.

BIDDIE: [*Protesting.*] Miss Flora . . .

MISS FLORA: Miss Flora, nothing. The first thing you do is rise up and step back from the onion. Show it some respect. Then you turn it on its head so the juice point down. Let the knife bite the end off and skin it down, all the same direction. REMEMBER: DOWN not up, 'cause if you go north 'steada south, you'll be singing the blues with a lot of tears in your eyes.

BIDDIE: I'm only doing this for you, woman.

MISS FLORA: Do it for yourself. You gonna need a peeled onion one of these old days.

[BIDDIE *carefully peels the onion under* MISS FLORA's *watchful eyes.*]

BIDDIE: Who taught you this? Mama?

MISS FLORA: Naw. I did all the cooking in the house. When Mama cooked, the dogs missed supper. Aunt Gwen, Mama's close friend, she showed me. She had sugar, so I sat with her a lot. This just one of the things she taught me.

BIDDIE: [*Sarcastically.*] God Bless Aunt Gwen.

MISS FLORA: Yes Lord. When she died I was fourteen and a half. She taught me so many things: how to massage with witch hazel, make onion syrup for a cough and how to wash myself with vinegar and water.

BIDDIE: This onion lesson was okay. Any pie left?

MISS FLORA: Apple or sweet potato?

BIDDIE: Sweet potato.

MISS FLORA: Just two slices and one belongs to me.

BIDDIE: Awright mama. Did I tell you while I was working on the Townsend's roof they asked me to tell you they need you to come and catch their grand daughter's baby.

MISS FLORA: Cora?

BIDDIE: Yeah.

MISS FLORA: She ain't but eleven or twelve.

BIDDIE: Neither was you.

MISS FLORA: I ain't seen her in so long. I just kept asking for her in church and Mrs. Townsend steady covering it. When she need me?

BIDDIE: Anytime now. She's ripe; I saw her when I had to go up to the attic.

MISS FLORA: I'll get my bag fixed. I ain't delivered in 3 months. Cora's a baby; who did it?

BIDDIE: Mr. Townsend was grumbling and cussing Brown, the one with the crippled hand that used to do some yard work for them.

MISS FLORA: Brown! I thought he was a good man; he even worked for me a little while.

BIDDIE: All I know is the chile look bad. She's about to bust and don't lift her head to look at nobody.

MISS FLORA: They done blamed her like they done me.

BIDDIE: Her grandmother say she stop talking months ago. Don't open her mouth to say nothing to nobody. I try to talk to her, but she just stare.

MISS FLORA: She'll open her mouth soon enough. When those pains hit, everything be open; eyes, mouth, legs, everything. It feel like everything's trying to come out of one spot at the same time.

BIDDIE: Go try to help, Miss Flora.

MISS FLORA: I'll take my bag and see what I can do, but she got to travail.

BIDDIE: What you need me to do?

MISS FLORA: Light the fire to sterile the water and help me get the pig grease smooth.

BIDDIE: Pig grease. What you gonna cook?

MISS FLORA: You make as much sense as that onion you just peeled.

BIDDIE: Look, I don't know nothing about birthing matters.

MISS FLORA: The grease is for stretching her so she don't tear. I tore and you ain't right after that. We got to whip that grease so it don't lump. Let's get things ready.

BIDDIE: Awright.

[*Lights fade as they exit.*]

SCENE 4

Daybreak the next morning: MISS FLORA *comes in the door with her birthing bag. She is visibly exhausted; she almost collapses.* BIDDIE *catches her and helps her to lie down.*

BIDDIE: [*Earnestly.*] Baby? Sweetie? What do you need me to do?

MISS FLORA: Nothing you can do. Just sit here with me; I'll be all right in a minute.

BIDDIE: What Cora have?

MISS FLORA: A little girl. She just as sweet and black. I mean the chile so black she blue. Seem like when you hold her, it's like having a piece of coal in your hand. You think some the black gonna come off on you when you put her down.

BIDDIE: How the baby get so black. Cora's dark, but she ain't black and Brown is medium black. I don't see how the baby get black black.

MISS FLORA: She ain't black black; she's blue black with a shine to her. I'll tell you what cause it. Coffee.

BIDDIE: Drank too much?

MISS FLORA: Mrs. Townsend say that's all she craved. Drinked it night and day. Strong too, with lots of sugar and no cream.

BIDDIE: It's a wonder the baby ain't soot. What she name it?

MISS FLORA: Little thing ain't got no name. Cora won't look at her, and her grandparents saw that black skin and couldn't do nothing but act foolish. I had to get outta the room for I picked one up and beat the other with him.

BIDDIE: Ain't nothing wrong with being black; I'm dark.

MISS FLORA: I know it and I love it. Tell you the truth, I wouldn't have no light chile no way; the skin ain't rich enough to take the sun.

BIDDIE: I bet you like that good hair them light children got?

MISS FLORA: Good hair is one thing, and light skin is another. Give me a dark berry any day; it's sweeter.

BIDDIE: Did Cora make it through the birth okay?

MISS FLORA: Naw. Lord, it was terrible. She travailed. She scream til the veins broke in her face. I was sitting with her and I kepa saying, "Cora, don't hollah, honey, you drawing the baby up." But she couldn't hear me. I touched her once on her belly; it was harder than rock. Every muscle she had was drawed up. I put the ax under the bed with the blade up to cut the pain, but that only last a minute. Three hours pass and the pain got more violent. All I could do was walk around the bed. I walked 7 times around and then I turned east and clapped my hands 5 times. That relieve her. She didn't scream no more. Just moan. And she moan. Lord, I kepa praying that the pain would hit me so she could just sleep, but it wasn't my pain to have. When that last hour come, she and me both was sweating. Before I could wipe her, she was drenched again. She got to shaking, and I was riding her moans. That's what you have to do, ride the mother's moans. It come time to grease her down. I took two hook fingers full with my right hand and put the pig grease in my left hand and I worked it between my palms till it got hot and loose and then I went to stretching her. She was so young that I had to work against her, pulling, pulling, pulling. And she moaned. I was stretching when the tongues took over me. My tongues came forth and then "Jesus." I could hear me saying "Jesus, Jesus." And Cora repeated me, "Jesus, Jesus," but it was in a whisper. I thought it was her last breath. That last time we say the name of the Lord together, the blood came forth. Flowing everywhere. My God, my God. A fountain in that chile opened up, and her life was going everywhere. All on the sheets and the floor and on me. I had to wash the blood off my face and arms 'fore I could come home. There wasn't a sound after that 'cept the sucking and popping of that baby crowning. She had a head full of hair. She slide into my hands and when

I looked into that face, it was covered in a mucous veil. My God. I didn't want to take it off right away because that mess with her power, so I laid that baby on Cora's bloody stomach and just waited on the spirit to tell me what to do. The after birth come, and I just cut the cord. I didn't take that veil off for half hour. Mrs. Townsend screaming then, "You want a doctor? We need a doctor?" I hit my knees and started praying right in the pool of that chile's blood. And I was thanking the Lord for letting us both live through the storm.

BIDDIE: What happen to the baby?

MISS FLORA: They called her ugly and put her in the corner. Cora wouldn't give her the breast or nothing. I put her on mine, even though they ain't nothing in it. Mrs. Townsend made some bottles, and I'll be going back over there later to see what they gonna do.

BIDDIE: They gonna keep the baby?

MISS FLORA: I don't know.

[Pause.]

BIDDIE: You think they'll give her to you?

MISS FLORA: I was thinking to ask, but I didn't know how you'd feel. We could raise her. Give her a good family, right?

BIDDIE: Sure we could, baby. You can name her.

MISS FLORA: Jesus. [Fighting back tears.] And we can bring her home and take care of her 'cause she's special. The mucous veil mean she's a seer.

BIDDIE: I don't have no problem getting work. You can stay home for as long as you need. I'll take care of both of you.

MISS FLORA: No you won't either. I can stay home for as long as you need. I'll take care of both of you.

BIDDIE: Woman! Won't you let me do anything for you?

MISS FLORA: You do what I need you to do; you don't have to answer my wants.

BIDDIE: But that's the best part.

MISS FLORA: I'll think about it.

BIDDIE: Whatever you say about this baby, I'll follow.

MISS FLORA: I want her. She's gonna need a lot of love 'cause she dark and this world hate dark skinned people.

BIDDIE: I'll make sure she understands that. We can love that away.

MISS FLORA: I'll take care of her hair. Never have my baby with a matted head from not combing it.

BIDDIE: It wouldn't matter to me if you cut if off.

MISS FLORA: Never mind. I'll make sure she's a lady.

BIDDIE: And I'll make sure she's a woman.

MISS FLORA: I'm going over there later this morning and ask them for her.

BIDDIE: Suppose they say no?

MISS FLORA: It'll be the right answer no matter what. God's yes and God's no mean the same thing. It's best for you.

BIDDIE: It be nice to have a little girl around; I think I'm ready for a real family. I know enough to make me worthy. Long as Jesus knows not to call me daddy, it's fine.

[*During* BIDDIE's *talking,* MISS FLORA *has gone to sleep and snores lightly.* BIDDIE *crosses over to her, covers her with a quilt and kisses her goodnight.*]

SCENE 5

The next morning: MISS FLORA *is busy fixing a dresser drawer for the baby.* BIDDIE *enters holding a small ball.*

BIDDIE: Mrs. Flora, we can afford to get the chile a baby bed.

MISS FLORA: That's not what she need right now. All she got to have is somewhere to lay down.

BIDDIE: But this is a dresser drawer that you took clothes out.

MISS FLORA: If you put babies in those high and fancy things, once they get the smell, you won't be able to satisfy them. I'm not gonna have a daughter that don't know how to want for nothing.

BIDDIE: Why we gonna raise a daughter full of want? Let her have something and not suffer like you and me did.

MISS FLORA: I can tell you ain't gonna be no good at this. You need some backbone if you call yourself raising a girl. Now, boys less developed and you can close both eyes, but girl, you bettah sleep with one eye open. We gonna go get Jesus and put her in this drawer and that's it.

BIDDIE: All right, Momma. You tell them you gonna name this baby Jesus?

MISS FLORA: Sure did. Mrs. Townsend frown up her face, but I don't care.

BIDDIE: Me neither, and it ain't gonna matter what people say or think about us raising our little girl.

MISS FLORA: Mrs. Townsend say she know about me and you, but she sure we ain't gonna hurt the baby none. It seem like since this baby been born I ain't been worried about nothing. For the first time, I ain't thinking about people. I got my mind on Jesus.

BIDDIE: As long as we got our mind on Jesus, we'll be all right.

MISS FLORA: [*Holding up a purple baby dress that matches her own outfit.*] Look at this little dress I made her.

BIDDIE: It's sweet. Purple, too. I bought her this ball. I know she ain't able to run yet, but...

MISS FLORA: [*Grabbing the ball from* BIDDIE.] She'll be able to run soon enough. I can't wait. Biddie, I love you for standing with me. This is my dream.

BIDDIE: I don't believe in dreams; this is a vision and I seen it all along.

MISS FLORA: This is my vision. Thank you.

BIDDIE: Don't thank me. I'm supposed to stand with you. You're my wife.

MISS FLORA: And you're my wife.

BIDDIE: Forever?

MISS FLORA: As close as we can come to it.

BIDDIE: I want Jesus to come, and we ain't half ready.

MISS FLORA: I'm ready. Come and go with me.

BIDDIE: [*Grabbing her hand.*] Come on.

MISS FLORA: [*Pauses.*] Lord.

BIDDIE: Trust me.

[*They embrace, then grab hands and exit.*]

[*CURTAIN.*]

[*Amen.*]

[*Awoman!*]

Photo by Suzy Gorman

Joan Lipkin

PLAYING WITH GENDER:
LESBIAN IDENTITIES, THEATRICALITY, AND THE SOCIAL IN JOAN LIPKIN'S *SMALL DOMESTIC ACTS*

Stacy Wolf

"It's hard to stay in the present, instead of the past," Straight Sheila tells the audience in Joan Lipkin's *Small Domestic Acts*. While Sheila as character refers to the play's project of telling the story of the characters' relationships, Sheila as actor reminds the audience of the very presentness of theatre. As Lipkin herself says, "I view the theatre as one of the few places where ideas are still discussed; I see a play as a public conversation that can go out into the world" [Branham].

The "public conversation" of *Small Domestic Acts* focuses on the friendship between two couples, one heterosexual (Sheila and Frank) and one lesbian (Sheila and Frankie), the difficulties in each relationship, and the ensuing romance between the straight woman and the femme lesbian (both Sheilas). The play both draws on and diverges from Lipkin's earlier work. Always a political, feminist playwright, as well as the founding artistic director of That Uppity Theatre Company in St. Louis, Lipkin boldly represents issues which other playwrights soften or avoid. Compared to Lipkin's earlier plays, the comedy in *Small Domestic Acts* may be less broadly played, its characters more realistically drawn, but its politics remain unflinching and uncompromising, and humor remains a driving force. The play forces the audience to be aware of our complicity, not only in how stories are told and what they mean, but also in the formation and rigid expectations of gendered and sexual roles.

Rather than using the overt social satire of her earlier plays, though, in this self-reflexive comic drama, Lipkin portrays what one reviewer described as "emotion recollected in terrible lack of tranquility" [Weber]. Lipkin's earlier plays frequently engage directly with legislation, urging spectators, in a fast-paced, gender-bending, musical format, to practice progressive, feminist politics. In 1989, upon the twentieth anniversary of the Stonewall riots, she wrote *Some of My Best*

Friends Are...A Gay and Lesbian Revue for People of All Preferences to protest Missouri's sexual misconduct law. A year later, in response to the Supreme Court ruling in *Webster v. Reproductive Health Services*, the decision against a St. Louis abortion clinic which began the derailment of *Roe v. Wade*, Lipkin created *He's Having Her Baby*, a gender-reversed, pro-choice musical comedy.

Small Domestic Acts addresses feminism from another perspective—that of the domestic, the private, the family. Here Lipkin follows in the footsteps of other women writers, from Austen to Glaspell, who represent the quotidian details of daily life both to revalue "*small domestic acts*" and to show the ways in which these small acts become the building blocks of larger social gestures and contain the potential for larger social change. As she explains, "In some ways the work is no less political because it seeks to get beneath the surface of legislation or social structures to expose the biases embedded in language and culture" [Pesner, 21].

In a review in the regional lesbian/gay newspaper, Lipkin describes *Small Domestic Acts* as "a cross between Brecht meets Pirandello meets 'As the World Turns'" ("Play Breaks"). Much of the dialogue is quite realistic. In the characters' awareness of their situation as characters, the play is reminiscent of Pirandello's *Six Characters in Search of an Author*. In its effort to encourage the audience to think about how the story is constructed and to imagine the other ways in which it might be told, the play is solidly Brechtian, foregrounding the "not, but," the representational and historical choices that might have been made differently. The characters interact with the stage manager, delighting in a correct sound cue, as the very constructedness of theatre's apparatus is constantly noted. They observe the audience and comment on their behavior, locating the audience as the play's fifth character, always aware that the telling of the story has implications outside the theatre. The characters also make the audience aware that our reactions matter. Frankie, for example, argues that the audience will see them merely as a "freak show," as token lesbians. By articulating what some audience members may be thinking, Frankie asks spectators to reconsider their assumptions. Making the audience's activity explicit refuses a masculinist binary of the public and the private: the characters' private lives are made public as the audience observes them, not voyeuristically, but as active collaborators of meaning.

While some lesbian theatre focuses on coming out stories or the difficult place of lesbians in mainstream society, or celebrates a separate sphere for lesbians, *Small Domestic Acts* both accepts lesbian identity as a real, material, and sexual position while simultaneously emphasizing the fluidity of sexuality itself. Three "performances" of lesbian sexuality appear—the butch, the femme, and the heterosexual. Straight Sheila's decision to have a lesbian relationship is not questioned in the play, and Lipkin avoids a teleological narrative that would suggest that Straight Sheila was "really" a lesbian all along. In this way, *Small Domestic Acts* asserts an anti-essentialist perspective without privileging any single lesbian position or relationship; the difficulties of each are recognized, and all are significantly sexual relationships.

Although the play traces parallels between the two couples, it does not equate the butch-femme relationship with the heterosexual one, as some lesbian-feminists have argued is the case. To revalue the significance of the butch's dilemma in mainstream society, Lesbian Sheila explains how she and Straight Sheila can "pass," while Frankie, as the butch, is always marked as lesbian. Interestingly, Frankie describes how she once passed as Lesbian Sheila's brother to get into her hospital room. The play employs both meanings of passing, again resisting a privileging of one lesbian identity over another. *Small Domestic Acts* sustains a tension between the ways in which the two couples are similar (repeated dialogue, character names) and different. Thus the play treads a fine line between the general and the particular. Straight Sheila insists that the audience sees "four different people. Four different points of view."

The play also foregrounds the constructedness of gender. Performances of gender, like those of sexuality, shift in the course of the play. From the beginning, Frank and Frankie are good friends. Although one is (biologically) a man and the other a woman, they are gendered as stereotypically masculine. As Frankie says, despondently, near the end of the play, "I wasn't enough of a woman for her," meaning that she lacks typically feminine ways of interacting.

Despite their initial suspicion and jealousy of each other, the two Sheilas become friends. Drawn together because of similar problems in their relationships, they unexpectedly find themselves falling in love. Their growing affection and desire for each other connects to a mutual desire for self-empowerment and change—both in their jobs and in their relationships. They both want to go to school, to have a child; they both have middle-class, perhaps even feminist aspirations. Much of their attraction also derives from the connection that intimate conversation can bring. Telling and retelling their stories transforms their frequent telephone conversations into erotic play. As if caught unaware by the power of language and shared experience, Lesbian Sheila asks, "When did the talking become sex?" Frank and Frankie, on the other hand, are happy in their jobs as mechanics and want to play cards, drink beer, and talk only about tangible realities. The two Sheilas' transformation from friends into lovers demonstrates, as Lipkin says, "how intimacy can become reconfigured as desire" [Lipkin, 120]. Still, the play insists that in the context of a lesbian relationship, what "family" means is anything but obvious, and that the baby of Sheila and Sheila's future does not represent a traditional or easy choice.

Unlike much traditional theatre which features a male protagonist flanked by women as others, *Small Domestic Acts* eschews the individual (typically male) protagonist. All four characters must participate in the telling of the story that belongs to all of them; they all struggle to gain centrality, and the stakes are high. When Frank opens the play, "In the beginning," evoking the Bible, his masculine bravado is immediately undercut by Straight Sheila's refusal to let her story be told by him. Frankie must also participate so that Lesbian Sheila can tell her version. Thus Lipkin raises the question of the story's boundaries and its ownership: whose story is it? When does the story begin? And why do such issues matter, in this play, in theatre, and in life?

All of the characters at various points in the play express anxiety about how they are being represented, about how their story is being told: "I get to play the jerk." "I get to play the bitch." Lipkin writes the audience's interpretive activity into the very lines of the play. We are aware, particularly in these moments, of the closed space of theatre's apparatus, of the labor of the playwright, the director, and the actors. The play continues past the end of the "story," with Frank still insisting that it would have been different if he (the straight male; the teller of most stories, the single protagonist of most plays) had told it. Although there is a "story" that takes place over time, the play comments doubly on traditional theatre; first, by allowing numerous women to tell their own stories, and second, by constantly interrupting the action and replaying its scenes.

Small Domestic Acts also marks a place outside the world of the play that is about history and individuals' place in it and of it. The characters agree to tell their stories by reenacting them, but they are still uncertain about the meaning of their stories. We find out near the end, for example, that Frankie has come to tell the story in hopes that she will win Lesbian Sheila back. There are several scenes in which the characters diverge from the (true?) story in the past. What is real? the play asks. Lipkin makes it clear that history is always about the present; that the present gives history its meanings; that history is the stories that those who can speak tell about the past.

Not only do all four stories carry equal weight in the narrative, all four characters are crafted sympathetically and revealed intimately. Frank, for example, is surprisingly sensitive (if guileless); his behavior is marked against other typically homophobic or intolerant men. Friendships matter in Lipkin's play as well as romance. In group scenes and monologues directed to the audience, each character occupies a legitimate, clearly socially-constructed position, one of particular power, status, and desire. By refusing to authorize one perspective over another, Lipkin exposes the falseness of the assumption of objectivity in traditional epistemologies.

The final moment and its chilling ambiguity also requires the audience's active emotional and intellectual involvement. Interestingly, in early workshops and productions of the play, audiences were frequently divided in their response to the characters, some arguing that Frank and Frankie were unfairly "jilted," with others asserting that butch-femme relationships no longer exist and are "an outdated style of relationship." That the audience discussion generally functions as the final action of the play, even after the lights have come up, underlines Lipkin's feminist belief that "the audience should feel challenged to accept their responsibility for pursuing truth, particularly those truths which we rarely hear, at the conclusion of the show." Unlike much theatre which positions the spectator with the active, straight, white male protagonist/hero, Lipkin's play, in its complex ambiguity, implicates each spectator directly, and asks each spectator to figure out where she is in this landscape of small domestic acts.

WORKS CITED

Branham, Joe. 1993. "Playwright/Director Joan Lipkin Tackles Diverse Roles." *Outlines*, Vol. 7, No. 2 (July).

Lipkin, Joan. 1995. "Identity, Sexuality, and the Female Body in Small Domestic Acts." *Australian Feminist Studies Journal*, No. 21 (Autumn), 119-125.

Pesner, Ben. 1994. "Trouble in the Heartland: An Interview with Joan Lipkin." *Dramatists Guild Quarterly*, Vol. 31, No. 2, 15-21.

"Play Breaks Political and Theatrical Ground." 1992. *The Lesbian and Gay News-Telegraph*, Vol. 12, No. 2 (November).

Weber, Harry. 1992. "Theater: Domestic Bliss." *The Riverfront Times* (9 December).

PLAYS BY JOAN LIPKIN

Will The Real Foster Parent Please Stand Up? 1988. Performed in shopping centers, Union Station, and the Cervantes Convention Center.

Some of My Best Friends Are...A Gay and Lesbian Revue for People of All Preferences (music and lyrics by Tom Clear) 1989. St. Marcus Theatre, St. Louis.

He's Having Her Baby (co-written with Tom Clear) 1990. St. Marcus Theatre.

Love and Work and Other Four-Letter Words 1991. St. Marcus Theatre. Forthcoming in *Fallow Fields: A Collection of Drama from the American Midwest*.

One Sunday Morning 1993. The New Theatre at the Missouri Historical Society. An adapted version will appear as *Making a Community in Mythic Women/Real Women: Plays and Performance Pieces*, ed. Lizbeth Goodman. Faber & Faber, 1996.

Stories from Generation X (Y, Z...) Studio Theatre, Washington University, 1995.

The Pornography Letters, 1995.

ARTICLES ABOUT JOAN LIPKIN'S WORK

Goodman, Lizbeth. "Death and Dancing in the Live Arts: Performance, Politics, and Sexuality in the Age of AIDS." *Critical Quarterly* 35.2 (Summer 1993).
____ "Theatre of Choice and the Case of 'He's Having Her Baby.'" *New Theatre Quarterly* 9.36 (November 1993): 357-366.
Watson, Van. "A Review of Small Domestic Acts." *Theatre Journal* 45.4 (1993): 543-545.

INTERVIEWS WITH JOAN LIPKIN

Goodman, Lizbeth. "Rabble-Rousing in St. Louis with That Uppity Theatre Company: An Interview with the Playwright-Founder of a Distinctive Company." *New Theatre Quarterly* 9.36 (1993): 367-378.
Smith, Iris. "'Who Speaks and Who Is Spoken For?,' Playwright, Director, and Producer Joan Lipkin." *TDR* 38.3 (1994): 96-126.

ARTICLES BY JOAN LIPKIN

"A Fairy Tale About A Queer Play, Not for Fairies Only." *Feminist Theatres for Social Change*. Eds. Susan Bennett, Tracy C. Davis, and Kathleen Foreman. (forthcoming).
"Aftermath: Surviving the Reviews." *Upstaging Big Daddy: Directing Theater as if Gender and Race Matter*. Eds. Ellen Donkin and Susan Clement. Ann Arbor: University of Michigan Press, 1993. 317-24.

L. to R: Larry Dell as "Frank," Pook Pfaffe as "Frankie," Carolyne
Hood as "Lesbian Shelia," and Debbie Dawson as "Straight Sheila"

Photo by Suzy Gorman

NOTES FROM THE AUTHOR

This is a challenging play to do, both thematically and structurally. Not because of demanding technical requirements or expensive production values, but because the characters must, in effect, become time travellers as they move in and out of enacting scenes from their past, trying to negotiate their present day differences and charting their individual and collective futures.

Simultaneously, the play also critiques the potential and problems of theatrical illusionism. The nature of this play necessarily requires that it challenge the linearity of traditional realism to more fully make it possible to tell the stories of people whose stories don't usually get told. Perhaps as much at issue as sexual identity here is the question of narrative voice, and the relationship between the two.

The characters speak both in past and present tense in and of their relationships because of their uncertainty of where they stand. Like memory and history, where they stand continually shifts, depending upon who is doing the telling. In some ways, the action of the play is the narration of the story. But this is no small thing. There is something very much at stake for who tells the story and how it gets told. We, like the characters, do not know how things will end, only that nothing can be settled until we work our way through a maze of personal and shared histories. There is true urgency for everyone involved; things simply cannot remain in limbo.

And unlike in many contemporary plays, the audience isn't let off the hook very easily. It's not enough that they have come to the theatre as spectators. While they are never called upon to participate in a literal sense, they should feel their role quite actively as the fifth character in this play. Sometimes, they function as a confessor, at other times, as a voyeur, and still at others, as a conduit for the characters who speak through them in order to say things they can't say to each other. Ultimately, the audience should feel challenged to accept their responsibility for pursuing truth, particularly those truths which we rarely hear, at the conclusion of the show.

The play asks some difficult and often troubling questions. What happens when one part of a couple changes? What is the basis of sexual identity? Of sexual attraction? Is there anything to be gained from the roles that people play? Why can't people understand the people they love? Why can't they change? And finally, what can we, as an audience, learn from watching these stories and grappling with these questions?

I believe that the theatre is a place where we can go to envision our future while we excavate our past. Unconventional as this play may be, it is my hope that it helps us to do that.

CHARACTERS

Note to the actors: When the play opens, the original couples, Frank and Straight Sheila and Frankie and Lesbian Sheila, are having problems. They have now come together, after being separated for an indeterminate period of time to see what's up and possibly resolve their differences. The stated fact here of this separation is only for the sake of the actors so they can more fully inhabit their parts. From the audience's point of view, however, the status of these relationships should be deliberately ambiguous in order to heighten the dramatic tension. What eventually happens is something we all discover together.

FRANK: Frank is in his early thirties or older. He works at the machine shop with Frankie and lives with Straight Sheila. He drinks a little too much sometimes. He is not a bad guy and shouldn't be played as such. He has come to tell his story because it's important to him to set the record straight so that he doesn't look like a jerk.

STRAIGHT SHEILA: Straight Sheila is in her early thirties or older. She has a good sexual relationship with Frank, with whom she lives, but finds him increasingly difficult to talk with. She is curious and feisty. She has come to tell her story because she wants the audience to know why what happened, happened.

FRANKIE: Frankie is in her mid to late thirties or older. She works at the machine shop with Frank and lives with Lesbian Sheila. She is a lesbian butch of the old school, slightly cocky, ironic and courtly. She has come to tell her story to try to win Lesbian Sheila back.

LESBIAN SHEILA: Lesbian Sheila is in her early thirties or older. She does clerical work and lives with Frankie. She is a lesbian femme. Although she should be feminine in appearance and dress, that does not need to be overplayed nor should she be caricatured. She is a peacemaker, has a soft, yielding quality and is endearing and frequently comical in her sometimes anxious attempts to please. She has come to tell her story because she wants to be heard.

THE AUDIENCE: The audience is, without question, the crucial fifth character, sometimes seen as confessor, at other times as arbitrator or voyeur. The other characters vie for the approval of the audience or may feel embarrassed by their presence when the material gets particularly personal. They also use the audience as a conduit to say things that they can't say to each other. The audience has come to hear the story because they are curious or want to hear the kind of story that rarely gets told in the theatre or maybe because they thought they might see their friends there.

SETTING: *The play takes place in both the present and the past. The setting could be any theatre or space in which the play is being performed. The characters have come together to tell their stories to the audience. The set can be fairly makeshift since the literal theatricality of the setting should be heightened, rather than downplayed. Rehearsal cubes and sundry pieces of furniture will do just fine. There should, however, be several separate playing areas, indicated both by set pieces, as well as by lighting, to demarcate private and shared domains. Lighting, at least as much as the set, is key in establishing various playing areas, shifts in time, and mood. A card table with four chairs should be center stage. On either side, either on wings, or slightly upstage, should be playing areas to indicate each couple's bedroom. The actors carry on pieces of the set and move chairs, as they begin to do the play, as if they are arriving and setting up the performance. A prop box which contains such items as a TV dinner carton and a cooler containing beer should be visible.*

STYLE: The actors should employ a variety of acting styles, depending upon whether they are deeply engrossed in the moment and interacting among themselves, or perhaps, self-consciously suddenly aware of playing to an audience. The clarity of these different levels of experience, to give but a few examples, will do much to add both humor and depth to the performance.

And humor is very important to this piece. The issues that the play raises and the pain that the characters frequently experience would be far too intense without comic relief. Besides, even in the midst of the most awful circumstances, things often are funny.

Much of the meaning of the play is contained within the transitions between the scenes as the characters try to understand how they feel and what to do next. Although most of this is nonverbal, it is crucial to the unfolding of the play, which has a distinct progression, albeit nonlinear. The actors should take as much time as necessary to explore these moments which point up contrast to their more stylized play acting on stage. And as they take turns watching each other enact various scenes, they should also be aware of what it means to watch and to be watched.

Throughout the script, places for specific audience address have been indicated. Although these work well, the director and actors should feel free to make alternative or additional choices based on their own explorations in rehearsal. They should also feel free to experiment with the rhythm of various lines, overlapping at times, where it might seem appropriate.

All of the actors come on stage, or through the house, carrying props, things to drink, etc. The house lights are up and the dialogue should begin while the audience is still being seated. The effect should be one of spontaneity and the audience should be unsure of whether or not this opening scene is actually part of the play.

LESBIAN SHEILA: [*To* FRANKIE.] Hi.

FRANKIE: [*To* LESBIAN SHEILA.] Hi. [FRANK *walks to center stage, finds and toes an imaginary mark and says his first line with an unnatural theatricality.*]

FRANK: In the beginning . . . [*Beat. Trying to get the audience's attention.*] Excuse me. We're going to go ahead and get started here. [*To the actors.*] I'd like to know why everyone is always late to the theatre.

STRAIGHT SHEILA: [*Coming downstage to correct him.*] Not *everyone*, Frank.

LESBIAN SHEILA: [*Joining her on his other side, creating a bookend effect.*] Not *always*.

STRAIGHT SHEILA: [*To* LESBIAN SHEILA.] Besides things happen. People have car trouble.

LESBIAN SHEILA: [*Speaking across* FRANK, *intimately continuing the conversation.*] Or the baby-sitter calls in sick.

FRANK: [*He wants to break this female web.*] We should have just started without them.

STRAIGHT SHEILA: We couldn't. There is no story without them to tell it to.

FRANK: Well, they're not doing their part. They wouldn't be late to a movie.

FRANKIE: Why don't we just get started.

FRANK: Fine by me. The sooner we get started, the sooner we can set the record straight, and go home. I'm dying for a beer. [*He begins. The house lights come down. Again, theatrically, and then unsure, he looks for confirmation from the others. He has never done this before.*] In the beginning . . . isn't that how things always begin? You know, in the beginning?

[FRANKIE *encourages him. A bit more surely, he continues.*]

FRANK: [*Cont'd.*] So, in the beginning, everything was fine. We had our friends. We all played cards. It was nice. Real regular like until one day when—

STRAIGHT SHEILA: [*Interrupting.*] Wait a minute. Why are *you* telling this story?

FRANK: What do you mean, why am *I* telling it? I'm telling it because it happened to me.

STRAIGHT SHEILA: Am I in it?

FRANK: Of course you're in it. You're here, aren't you?

STRAIGHT SHEILA: Then it didn't just happen to you. It happened to me, too. [*To the audience.*] Excuse me. I'm Sheila.

FRANK: Oh, sorry. That's Sheila.

STRAIGHT SHEILA: I can introduce myself. They know who I am. They don't know who you are.

FRANK: [*He realizes that she's right. Then, to the audience, introducing himself.*] Frank.

Hi. Hi. Oh, and these are our friends. [*He gestures to* LESBIAN SHEILA *and* FRANKIE *who wave.*]

LESBIAN SHEILA: Sheila.

FRANKIE: Frankie.

FRANK: [*By way of summary and acknowledging the coincidence of the similarities in their names.*] Sheila. Sheila. [*Re-introducing himself.*] Frank.

FRANKIE: Frank-ie.

FRANK: [*To the audience.*] Don't read too much into it, folks. It happens. [*Beat.*] Anyway, it all started when we were—

STRAIGHT SHEILA: [*Interrupting.*] Frank, you're telling the story.

FRANK: [*To* STRAIGHT SHEILA, *flirting with her to get his way.*] Look, babe, let me tell the story and I'll make it up to you.

STRAIGHT SHEILA: [*Flirting back.*] No.

FRANK: No?

STRAIGHT SHEILA: [*She zings him.*] No, you won't. Besides, then it'll be some other story. It won't be this one. I want this one. This is my story.

FRANKIE: Whoa, this is *her* story?

LESBIAN SHEILA: Frankie, stay out of this.

FRANKIE: Well, it's my story, too. Why should she get to tell it when it's my story, too?

LESBIAN SHEILA: Why should he? Besides, you don't even like to talk. I can hardly get you to say two words half the time. So why should you care who tells it?

FRANKIE: Yeah? Well, just because I don't talk a lot doesn't mean I want someone talking for me.

LESBIAN SHEILA: I give up.

STRAIGHT SHEILA: Let's just start over.

FRANK: [*Noticing the audience.*] Sheila, this is embarrassing. We can't just start over. We're in the middle of something here.

STRAIGHT SHEILA: So?

FRANK: So once you get started, you have to finish something. You have to go through with it.

STRAIGHT SHEILA: What if you change your mind?

FRANK: But if you changed your mind every time something got started, nothing would ever get finished.

STRAIGHT SHEILA: Like war.

FRANKIE: What?

STRAIGHT SHEILA: Like if you started to fight but changed your mind and felt okay about changing, you could stop. [*Scoring a point with the audience.*] Maybe there wouldn't be any more war.

LESBIAN SHEILA: [*Seriously considering this idea.*] No, there'd still be war. But there would be less killing.

FRANK: [*To* STRAIGHT SHEILA.] Oh, Sheila, let's not talk about the war thing again. [*To the audience.*] Ever since that whatchamacallit, Middle East thing, she talks about war all the time.

STRAIGHT SHEILA: This is getting us nowhere. I'm making a decision. We're starting over.

FRANK: Just like that?

STRAIGHT SHEILA: Just like that. [*To some unseen, imaginary stage manager at the back of the house.*] Would you bring up the house lights, please? Hi, I'm... [*The lights come up.*] Thank you. Hi, I'm Sheila.

FRANK: I'm Frank.

FRANKIE: Frank-ie.

LESBIAN SHEILA: [*Mortified.*] Sheila. [*The lights come back down again.*]

FRANK: [*Beat.*] So. Who's going to tell the story?

[*Beat. They all look around awkwardly.*]

FRANK: [*Cont'd.*] Well, this is the problem, Sheila. *Somebody* has got to be in charge.

STRAIGHT SHEILA: Why? Couldn't we just take turns?

FRANKIE: Too confusing.

FRANK: Let's be logical. The one who gets to tell the story is the one who was affected the most.

STRAIGHT SHEILA: You mean the one with the loudest voice?

FRANK: [*Suddenly, he can barely contain his rage.*] Look, it's my story because I'm the one who suffered.

STRAIGHT SHEILA: And *I* didn't?

LESBIAN SHEILA: [*Trying to diffuse this potential time bomb She pulls* STRAIGHT SHEILA *off to the side to talk with her privately.*] Let it go. Let him tell it.

STRAIGHT SHEILA: What?!

LESBIAN SHEILA: You think just because he tells it—

STRAIGHT SHEILA: [*Interrupting.*] Because he starts out telling it...

LESBIAN SHEILA: [*Continuing.*] Because he *starts out* telling it, it's his story? You think *they* can't tell whose story it is?

FRANKIE: [*Feeling left out.*] Hey!

LESBIAN SHEILA: [*Discovering what she means as she says it, in a comic yet profound logic that picks up speed until she reaches her triumphant conclusion.*] Sometimes, it's the ones who don't talk whose story is the loudest. Sometimes, you start to tune out the ones who usually talk because you're so used to them talking, what you really hear is the ones that don't say anything.

STRAIGHT SHEILA: You think so?

LESBIAN SHEILA: [*To the audience with the pride of discovery.*] Oh, yeah.

[*Beat. Confidentially to* STRAIGHT SHEILA.]

LESBIAN SHEILA: [*Cont'd.*] Besides, he's only going to start out telling it.

STRAIGHT SHEILA: And I can come in whenever I want?

LESBIAN SHEILA: [*As they exit.*] Whenever you want. [*To* FRANK.] Things change. I don't see where it's set in stone.

STRAIGHT SHEILA: All right.

[*They exit.*]

FRANK: All right! [*He shoots* FRANKIE *the high five. Beat. They both notice the audience, look awkwardly around and then decide to resume the story.*]

FRANKIE: Well, now that you won, Frank, what are you going to tell them?

FRANK: Gee, I don't know. [*Beat.*] I could just tell them what happened. How we met.

FRANKIE: That's good. Tell them how we met. [*She moves stage left to get ready to play her part.*]

FRANK: [*Coming downstage.*] Well, I'm working at this machine shop, see? The guys I work with are decent enough but I can't take all the pissing and moaning. All Al can talk about is the job he used to have. How much it paid. How great the benefits were. But he got laid off so now he's here. And Chico, he's pissed because he's got himself a college degree and this is all he can find. Like life turned out for any of us the way we pictured it. Hell, with the way things are going, I'm just grateful to be having a job. And all this talk upsets my stomach. I guess that's why I started talking to Frankie, even if she was [*Beat.*] a lesbo.

[*He is half needling* FRANKIE *and half affectionate with this last remark.* FRANKIE *shoots him a look. He laughs.*]

FRANK: [*Cont'd.*] The guys thought I was cracked. But let me tell you. She was a lot easier to deal with than them sometimes. So she likes girls. [*Joking.*] Who doesn't? She was a good worker. Always steady and quiet. Kept to herself mostly. And she never bothered anybody. Brought her lunch every day.

[FRANKIE *goes over to the cooler, takes out a sandwich and checks her watch.*]

FRANK: [*Cont'd.*] Ate it lickety split so she could play a hand of cards before the boss got back.

[FRANKIE *starts to play cards.*]

FRANK: [*Cont'd.*] One day we were going to get a game going on account of the boss being sick. But we needed a fourth. I wanted to ask Frankie. Al said he wouldn't sit at the same table as that she-he. Chico said he didn't care as long as she played a decent hand. I went over to see. [*He walks over to the card table.*] Hey.

[FRANKIE *looks up. Takes a drag from her cigarette.*]

FRANK: [*Cont'd.*] What you doing all alone?

FRANKIE: [*Sarcastically.*] I'm playing with myself.

FRANK: [*He laughs and then looks and gestures towards an imaginary* AL *and* CHICO *offstage.*] Al and Chico got a big kick out of that one. Al says, what do you expect from a big queer? But Frankie, she don't bat an eye. She keeps dealing her hand, nice and cool like. [*To* FRANKIE.] You want to play cards?

FRANKIE: [*Blowing smoke in his face.*] I am playing cards.

[*They both move into different areas, to indicate that they are now in their respective homes.* FRANK *moves stage right and* FRANKIE *moves stage left.* STRAIGHT SHEILA *joins* FRANK *stage right and* LESBIAN SHEILA *joins* FRANKIE *stage left. At some point in the scene, all four should indicate that they are perhaps changing clothes, getting ready to go out and that they are within the intimate setting of the bedroom that they each share as a couple.*]

FRANKIE: [*Cont'd.*] But when he asked us to come over to his house, I figured, what the hell. I've got to work with the man.

[*Beat. With a heightened and self-conscious theatricality of performing in front of an audience, she repeats her line for* LESBIAN SHEILA *who has obviously missed her cue.*]

FRANKIE: [*Cont'd.*] I said, what the hell, I've got to work with the man. [*Beat.*] Sheila. Sheila? Are you there?

[*They all wonder where* LESBIAN SHEILA *is.*]

LESBIAN SHEILA: [*Rushing in unexpectedly.*] I'm here. Sorry. I guess I'm a little nervous. I was backstage practicing my line. I'm sorry I missed my cue. I hope I haven't ruined everything.

FRANKIE: Of course not, baby.

STRAIGHT SHEILA: We understand that you're nervous, Sheila. I think we're all a little nervous. [*To the audience.*] Maybe even *them.*

FRANK: There's nothing to be nervous about, babe. Just tell it like it happened. We all know how it comes out.

FRANKIE: Don't be so sure.

[*This is true. They all exchange glances.*]

FRANK: [*Back pedalling.*] What I *meant* was that we mostly know how it—

FRANKIE: [*Overlapping and interrupting him because of her concern for* LESBIAN SHEILA *who is flustered.*] Are you okay?

LESBIAN SHEILA: [*Sitting down.*] It's just nerves.

STRAIGHT SHEILA: [*To the audience.*] Stage fright.

LESBIAN SHEILA: Exactly. I don't know these people. They don't know me.

STRAIGHT SHEILA: We don't have to do this if you're not ready. No matter what we said. We could do it tomorrow or next week instead.

[FRANK *and* FRANKIE *do not appreciate the possibility of postponement.*]

FRANK: [*Expressing disbelief.*] What the hell . . .

FRANKIE: [*Overlapping.*] No way.

LESBIAN SHEILA: I know. But we're all here now and I want them to know what happened.

STRAIGHT SHEILA: [*To the audience.*] And *why* it happened.

LESBIAN SHEILA: Yes. And I want to tell my story. But considering everything that's gone on, I guess I feel a little silly about this part.

FRANKIE: We have to begin somewhere, baby. And the way it started is the first time we were going to go over to their house. Don't you remember?

LESBIAN SHEILA: Well, that's the first time we met them. But I'm not sure that it didn't start before that and that we shouldn't start further back. Like telling what we wanted when we first started—

FRANK: [*Interrupting.*] Are we doing this thing or *talking* about it?!

STRAIGHT SHEILA: [*Startling.*] We're doing it. We're doing it.

FRANK: Because we can't tell every little thing that happened or we'll never get out of here.

LESBIAN SHEILA: That's true. But what we tell or don't tell is really important. It affects the way they see it.

STRAIGHT SHEILA: We can't have it letter perfect, Sheila. Life isn't like that. You might leave out this or that. Maybe even drop a line or two but it'll all come out in the end. Besides, we have to give them [*Meaning the audience.*] some credit for being able to figure it out.

LESBIAN SHEILA: You're sure? Because I want to get it right.

FRANK: Hey, we *all* want to get it right.

STRAIGHT SHEILA: Only refrigerators come with guarantees, Sheila. You've got to take a chance here. Okay?

LESBIAN SHEILA: Okay.

STRAIGHT SHEILA: [*Reassuringly to her.*] Okay.

FRANK: [*Irritably, wanting to get the show on the road.*] *Okay*!

STRAIGHT SHEILA: Go ahead, Frankie. Give her her line again. [*To the audience.*] Sorry. [*Beat.*] Stage fright.

[STRAIGHT SHEILA *and* FRANK *return to their bedroom stage right and* FRANKIE *to her bedroom stage left.* LESBIAN SHEILA *remains downstage, confused about where to go.*]

FRANKIE: [*Gesturing.*] Sheila, over *here*.

[LESBIAN SHEILA *exits upstage and then re-emerges briefly, having forgotten a prop. They continue.*
  We are now back in the past.]

FRANKIE: [*Cont'd. Beat.*] But when he asked us to come over to this house, I said to Sheila, what the hell. I've got to work with the man. And he's not like the others.

LESBIAN SHEILA: [*Entering.*] Where have I heard that before?

STRAIGHT SHEILA: [*To* FRANK, *who is now stage right in their apartment.*] And I said, they're what?!

FRANK: [*Addressing* FRANKIE *across the stage in the present.*] To tell you the truth—

STRAIGHT SHEILA: They're coming *where*?!

FRANK: Sheila wasn't exactly wild about getting together.

FRANKIE: [*Addressing* FRANK *across the stage from her apartment in the present.*] My Sheila, neither. Even though she's always ragging about how we should get out of the house more often. Make some new friends.

LESBIAN SHEILA: *Breeders*?!

FRANKIE: [*To the audience, ironically.*] Guess that's not the kind of friends she had in mind.

FRANK: Honestly, hon. You'll like them. They're...

LESBIAN SHEILA AND STRAIGHT SHEILA: [*Simultaneously.*] Different.

STRAIGHT SHEILA: I hate games. Someone always has to win.

FRANK: It isn't like that. You play cards. Have a few beers.

STRAIGHT SHEILA: A few, huh?

FRANK: [*Defensively.*] Just to be social.

STRAIGHT SHEILA: A bunch of men sitting around seeing who can be the best. A bunch of boys.

FRANK: I told you, babe. It's two *women*.

LESBIAN SHEILA: [*To* FRANKIE *in their apartment, sputtering.*] She'll probably make me look at baby pictures or something.

FRANKIE: Oh, hon, let's not start that business again.

LESBIAN SHEILA: That doesn't mean that I don't have feelings, Frankie. I have my feelings.

FRANKIE: Come on, baby. It'll be fun. We need someone to play with.

LESBIAN SHEILA: Oh, I don't... know.

STRAIGHT SHEILA: [*Simultaneously.*] No.

[FRANKIE *and* LESBIAN SHEILA *cross stage right to* FRANK *and* STRAIGHT SHEILA's *doorstep which is imagined, rather than literal space. They straighten each other's hair and clothes in nervous anticipation and possibly mime knocking on the door. We do, however, hear the actual sound of a doorbell ringing. The actors could conceivably respond to the sound effect with surprise and pleasure that the stage manager has things under control and that the theatre is running smoothly.* STRAIGHT SHEILA *walks reluctantly to the door, then puts on a social face.*]

STRAIGHT SHEILA: Hi. I'm Sheila.

LESBIAN SHEILA: [*Surprised.*] So am I.

[*Nervous laughter all around. A long collective sigh.*]

STRAIGHT SHEILA: [*Beat.*] Well, I like your *name.*

FRANK: Shy little thing, isn't she?

STRAIGHT SHEILA: Don't mind him. He comes with the house. Come on in. [*She shoots him a look and rolls her eyes.*]

[*We are now in the present. Everyone but Frank sits at the card table and begins to play cards.*]

FRANK: [*To the audience, standing*] That first meeting, I thought they were nice. What's her name ... Sheila, *Frankie's* Sheila, wasn't too swift with the cards but we decided to play again the following week. She had a sweet way about her. I guess I was hoping that Sheila, *my* Sheila, might learn something from her. I never wanted a bimbo. I get bored too quick. I like 'em feisty. But Sheila is a handful. Sometimes, she did everything but go straight for my balls.

LESBIAN SHEILA: *From where she is seated at the card table.*] Frank. *Please.*

FRANK: Sorry. Anyway, we played a few hands. Drank a few beers. It wasn't like any bells and whistles went off or anything. [*He joins the others at the card table.*] What's to say? We were seeing if we could be friends.

[*They all exchange glances at the irony of his statement. There is an awkward silence and then both couples stand and return to their respective apartments, getting ready for bed. Lights up on* STRAIGHT SHEILA *and* FRANK *who are in an affectionate mood. We are now back in the past.*]

STRAIGHT SHEILA: I don't know. It just seems unnatural. Don't you think it's unnatural?

FRANK: I never really thought about it.

STRAIGHT SHEILA: Well, think about it.

FRANK: I don't know. Frankie's good people and they're doing it. So if they're doing it, it must be natural, huh?

STRAIGHT SHEILA: But two women?

[*Lights down on* STRAIGHT SHEILA *and* FRANK. *Lights up on* LESBIAN SHEILA *and* FRANKIE.]

LESBIAN SHEILA: She's not so bad.

FRANKIE: [*Amused.*] Well, what did you think, I'd make you spend the night with a monster?

LESBIAN SHEILA: I mean for a *straight* woman.

FRANKIE: I like Frank.

LESBIAN SHEILA: Do you think she's pretty?

FRANKIE: It's kind of nice to have someone to talk to at work for a change.

LESBIAN SHEILA: *Frankie.*

FRANKIE: What, baby?

LESBIAN SHEILA: Do. You. Think. She's. Pretty?

[*Lights down on* LESBIAN SHEILA *and* FRANKIE. *Lights up on* STRAIGHT SHEILA *and* FRANK *cuddling in bed.*]

FRANK: To tell you the truth, it's kind of a turn on. Thinking about two women going at it.

STRAIGHT SHEILA: [*Teasing*] You pervert. You just wish you were in the middle of it.

FRANK: Why not? I can handle it.

STRAIGHT SHEILA: You think so, huh?

FRANK: You know it.

STRAIGHT SHEILA: I know you've got a pretty big impression of yourself.

FRANK: Tell me that I'm wrong.

STRAIGHT SHEILA: [*Carefully.*] When you haven't been drinking.

FRANK: [*Suddenly turned off and turning away from her.*] It's getting late.

STRAIGHT SHEILA: Still. [*Beat. Elbowing him.*] Frank?

FRANK: *What?*

STRAIGHT SHEILA: Don't you think it's a bit queer?

FRANK: That's what they call it.

STRAIGHT SHEILA: No, silly, I mean odd...unnatural.

FRANK: What's unnatural, girl, is this need of yours to keep me up all night gabbing.

STRAIGHT SHEILA: Be serious.

FRANK: We had a nice time. Played a few cards. Drank a few beers. Jesus Christ, Sheila. Give it a rest.

[*He turns over to go to sleep. Lights down on* STRAIGHT SHEILA *and* FRANK. *Lights up on* LESBIAN SHEILA *and* FRANKIE.]

FRANKIE: I don't know. I hadn't really thought about it.

LESBIAN SHEILA: I do.

FRANKIE: You do what?

LESBIAN SHEILA: Think she's pretty. Don't you?

FRANKIE: She's okay. [*Beat. Finally getting the idea and trying it out.*] She's not as good looking as you.

LESBIAN SHEILA: Lord give me strength, I do believe you're learning.

FRANKIE: Actually, she's pretty butch.

LESBIAN SHEILA: [*Excited.*] You think so?

FRANKIE: Oh, yeah. She's so butch, if she wasn't straight, I'd think she was...you know.

LESBIAN SHEILA: Get out of here.

FRANKIE: Swear to God.

LESBIAN SHEILA: Oh, Frankie. You think *every* woman's a lesbian.

FRANKIE: Well, aren't they?

LESBIAN SHEILA: No.

FRANKIE: Sure they are. They just don't know it.

LESBIAN SHEILA: [*Laughing.*] Stop. You are so bad.

FRANKIE: I'm so bad, I'm good. [*They kiss.*]

LESBIAN SHEILA: Do you like her?

FRANKIE: [*Looking at* LESBIAN SHEILA's *chest and pretending to compare the two.*] Nah. Her tits aren't big enough.

LESBIAN SHEILA: Frankie!

FRANKIE: I'm just joking, baby. You know anything more than a handful is a waste.

LESBIAN SHEILA: You think they're talking about us like we're talking about them?

FRANKIE: Beats me. Whatever they're doing, I hope it's *not* talking.

[*She reaches to embrace* LESBIAN SHEILA. *Lights out on their part of the stage. Lights up on* FRANK *and* STRAIGHT SHEILA. *He leaves their bedroom and comes downstage.* FRANKIE *and* LESBIAN SHEILA *break their embrace, awkward and confused by the feelings that touching creates, under the present circumstances, especially in front of* FRANK *and* STRAIGHT SHEILA *and the audience. The others move again towards the enactment of a card game. We are now in the present.*]

FRANK: Soon we were making it a regular thing. I used to play with Al and Chico Friday nights.

STRAIGHT SHEILA: [*Leaving the bedroom.*] Which suited me just fine. Games!

FRANK: But they had other things in mind. How's it go? Oh, yes. Friday night is for girlfriends and Saturday night is for wives? The guys weren't always available on Friday night. I like to think I can count on something. Look forward to it. I could count on a game with Frankie and Sheila.

FRANKIE: [*Coming downstage.*] I like the routine myself. Besides, Sheila and me, we pretty much kept to ourselves. Sometimes we would go to the bar but there's too much mixing and matching. You can get into trouble that way. [*To* LESBIAN SHEILA *who is playing cards.*] Right, Sheila? But . . . [*Beat.*] there was no fear of that around Frank and Sheila.

[*With a burst of laughter, we are back in the past, playing cards. The scene is very playful.* LESBIAN SHEILA *flirts with* FRANK. STRAIGHT SHEILA *flirts with* FRANKIE. *High spirits all the way around.*]

LESBIAN SHEILA: I wouldn't be too sure of that, Frankie. He's not so bad . . .

STRAIGHT SHEILA: For a *man*!

[*They all laugh.*]

FRANK: [*To* STRAIGHT SHEILA.] Listen to you. You like it all right. Else you wouldn't stick around. What's your bet?

STRAIGHT SHEILA: That doesn't mean I'm not curious. [*Batting her eyes.*] Eh, Frankie?

FRANK: It's your bet, Sheila.

STRAIGHT SHEILA: I'm feeling lucky. I'll bet a dime.

FRANKIE: Whoa! Lord save me from beautiful women and high rollers. I'll see your dime and raise you a nickel. [*To the audience, in the present.*] It kind of went on like that. Fun. Harmless. My favorite kind of flirting. The kind that doesn't get . . .

LESBIAN SHEILA: [*Playing cards, in the past.*] Full house!

FRANKIE: Serious. [*Back in the past, to* LESBIAN SHEILA.] That's good, babe. That's real good. [*To the audience, speaking in the present.*] See it wouldn't necessarily be this way with women. I mean, with gay women. All relaxed and easy. Sheila's a looker and unless they were a married couple, some butch on the loose might see Sheila and before you know it, there'd be trouble.

[*We are back in the present and the mood suddenly shifts.*]

STRAIGHT SHEILA: [*Shaking her head disapprovingly at Frankie's choice of words.*] Butch.

FRANKIE: Hey, if the shoe fits.

FRANK: Or the leather jacket.

[*The two of them laugh together.*]

LESBIAN SHEILA: The fights we used to have.

FRANKIE: [*Suddenly switching gears.*] Like you're not worth fighting over?

LESBIAN SHEILA: Frankie, if I've told you once, I've told you a thousand times, there are other ways to settle an argument. [*She throws down her cards in frustration.*]

FRANKIE: Hey, I know how to defend what's mine and I'm not ashamed who knows it. [*She throws down her cards.*]

STRAIGHT SHEILA: You mean your property? [*She throws down her cards. Beat.*]

FRANK: I think we're getting a little off the track here.

FRANKIE: Right. Sorry. [*Beat.*] Man, this is harder than I thought.

FRANK: No kidding.

LESBIAN SHEILA: [*Beat.*] Go on.

FRANKIE: What?

LESBIAN SHEILA: It's okay, Frankie. Just go on with your line.

STRAIGHT SHEILA: It's your line.

FRANKIE: Oh. Right. [*Beat. With deliberate but half-hearted vigor.*] This way I didn't have to worry.

FRANK: [*Trying to encourage her.*] I was surprised how well we all got along. I mean, Frankie and me, working together, we got all kinds of things in common. Engines.

FRANKIE: [*Brightening.*] And carburetors.

FRANK: Pistons.

FRANKIE: Pistons.

STRAIGHT SHEILA: [*Sarcastically.*] *Real* things.

FRANK: [*Defensively.*] Things like that. But the girls, they really seemed to take to each other. And what did they have in common?

FRANKIE: Except being girls.

FRANK: They sure like to talk, though. Maybe being girls gave them a lot to talk about. First it was just when we played poker. Then it was lunches. And then it was—

[*The phone rings.* STRAIGHT SHEILA *runs to answer it.*]

STRAIGHT SHEILA: I'll get it!

FRANK: —on the phone. I was glad. Glad Sheila had someone to talk to.

STRAIGHT SHEILA: [*From offstage.*] Glad to have the pressure off *you.*

FRANK: Hey, I talk when I have something to say.

FRANKIE: Exactly. There's nothing I can't stand more than someone flapping their jaws over nothing.

LESBIAN SHEILA: Is that how you still see it, Frankie, as *nothing*?

FRANKIE: [*To the audience.*] Is it any wonder I don't open my mouth? [*To* STRAIGHT SHEILA.] She didn't used to be like this, you know.

STRAIGHT SHEILA: Don't look at me. It's not my fault that you all don't get along.

FRANKIE: Who says we don't get along? [*To* LESBIAN SHEILA.] What have you been saying to her?

LESBIAN SHEILA: Nothing.

FRANKIE: I'll bet. You know that if there's one thing I can't stand, it's airing dirty laundry in public. [*Beat.*] Besides, you only make it worse by saying it out loud.

STRAIGHT SHEILA: I think you make it worse by keeping it bottled up.

FRANK: Does anyone want to play cards?

LESBIAN SHEILA: [*To* FRANKIE.] I wish you would have talked to me more.

FRANKIE: I will, baby. I promise.

LESBIAN SHEILA: When?

FRANKIE: What do you mean, *when*? Later. When we get out of here.

LESBIAN SHEILA: What's the matter with now?

FRANKIE: Now? In front of all these...? What do you need, *witnesses*?

STRAIGHT SHEILA: There's no time like the present.

FRANK: Or the past, if you ask me.

LESBIAN SHEILA: Tell me now. What you wanted to tell me then. Tell me what's in your heart, Frankie.

FRANK: [*Embarrassed by this display of emotion.*] Oh jeez.

STRAIGHT SHEILA: [*Pulling him off to the side.*] Frank, this is *real*.

FRANK: No, it's not. Real is when we're at *home*, playing cards or playing around. This is something else. It's got [*Beat.*] them. [*Indicating the audience.*]

STRAIGHT SHEILA: That doesn't make it any less . . . real.

FRANK: [*Overlapping.*] Like you're not cleaning this whole thing up for company?

STRAIGHT SHEILA: Sssshh.

FRANKIE: Please, Sheila. You know how I . . . that there's never been anyone else who, who . . .

LESBIAN SHEILA: Yes?

FRANKIE: Aw, Christ. Why do I have to put it in words?

STRAIGHT SHEILA: Because that's what she needed to hear.

FRANKIE: It's just that . . . when I try to . . . [*To the audience.*] I couldn't. I don't know why. [*To* LESBIAN SHEILA.] And the more you want me to, the less I can. [*To the audience.*] You know, it's funny. I have so many conversations in my head but when it's time to open my mouth, the words just leave me. I love Sheila. I love coming home, making love to her, fixing things around the house. But that's not enough. [*To* LESBIAN SHEILA.] You want more. You want me to talk all the time and I just don't know what to say. [*To the audience.*] Maybe it's because *she* talks. Maybe I want her to talk for me. Maybe it's because I live in my head. But Sheila doesn't get that, see? And I don't know how to tell her. Maybe I don't want to tell her. Maybe she's right and I do want something that's just my own. I don't really think anybody can understand another person, anyway. At least, not the way it is for me. I don't know. See, this is exactly what I don't like. All this deep talk and thinking. It leads nowhere. I get so frustrated. But Sheila. [*To* LESBIAN SHEILA.] You want words. Spoken *out loud* words. And no matter what else I give you or do for you, it isn't enough. [*To the audience.*] She thinks I'm holding back. [*Beat.*] Maybe I am. Sometimes, when we're lying in bed at night and I hear the sound of her breathing, I start to choke. I look at her lying there next to me. I see the curve of her breast. This need rises up in me so deep, I can't think where she begins and I leave off. And then when she looks at me with those big eyes, I can't say anything. The air feels so heavy and moist with the scent of her body and the smell of our sex. Sometimes, I envy Frank and Sheila asleep in their house, where the air is cool and thin. Each in their own separate world. Everything neat and clear.

LESBIAN SHEILA: Why didn't you tell me?

FRANKIE: Wouldn't have changed anything. You think I could have acted different?

LESBIAN SHEILA: You could have tried.

[*They are both enlightened and disappointed by this exchange.*]

FRANK: [*To the audience, changing the subject to his life.*] Sheila didn't want to change anything. She just wants to bellyache.

STRAIGHT SHEILA: Talking about my feelings is not bellyaching, Frank. It's communicating.

FRANK: [*Sarcastically.*] Please. What did you do, get that out of one of your damn college classes? I believe in action. [*To the audience.*] If she comes to me with a problem, I want to try to find a solution.

STRAIGHT SHEILA: [*To the audience.*] All I wanted to do was tell him about it.

FRANK: [*To the audience.*] But *I* want to find a solution. I can't stand to just sit and listen.

STRAIGHT SHEILA: Because it bores him.

FRANK: [*Beat.*] Because it makes me feel helpless. [*To STRAIGHT SHEILA.*] If you've got a problem and you're upset, I feel like I'm supposed to do something. Or else why would you tell me? [*To the audience.*] But a lot of the things that she tells me, I couldn't do anything about. I can't do anything about her damn boss. I couldn't do anything about the fact that she and her sister don't speak. So what's the point?

STRAIGHT SHEILA: I tell you to share, Frank. I know that's a little hard for you to understand but isn't that what being together is supposed to be about? *Sharing?*

FRANK: Spare me the sarcasm, will you, Sheila? I've had a rotten day. Al got laid off.

LESBIAN SHEILA: Gee, Frank, that's too bad.

FRANK: And they moved Chico to nights.

LESBIAN SHEILA: [*Sympathizing with* FRANK *and gesturing to* STRAIGHT SHEILA *to try to get her to appreciate his dilemma.*] Guess you're kind of worried about your job, huh?

FRANK: [*Referring to* FRANKIE.] And I don't have a friend left in the place. But I don't suppose Miss Night School here wants to hear about that.

STRAIGHT SHEILA: And you think *I'm* sarcastic?

FRANK: [*Escalating.*] You know something, Sheila? Sarcastic would be too nice a word for what you—

LESBIAN SHEILA: [*Interrupting.*] Hello? Excuse me? I think we're getting a little out of hand here. I thought we agreed that we would try to say what was on our minds without getting nasty about it.

STRAIGHT SHEILA: You're right. I'm sorry. [*To the audience.*] It's just that it's hard not to get caught up in all of this. You know what I mean? It's hard to stay in the present, instead of the past.

LESBIAN SHEILA: [*Looking at the audience.*] I'm sure they understand. They seem like very nice people.

FRANKIE: [*Looking at the audience and sizing them up.*] I wouldn't go that far.

LESBIAN SHEILA: Well, they came here, didn't they?

FRANKIE: Yeah. To see the *freak* show.

STRAIGHT SHEILA: Oh, honestly, Frankie. You don't know that. [*Still, she is suddenly thrown off guard by the reality of this possibility. Trying to recover, she addresses* LESBIAN SHEILA.] Where was I?

LESBIAN SHEILA: [*So seriously, she has a comic effect.*] I think you were talking about what you talk about.

STRAIGHT SHEILA: Right. [*Beat.*] I don't just talk about my sister or my boss, Frank. I talk about us. Only you don't hear.

FRANK: What do you mean I don't hear? I hear everything you say. Go on. Ask me.

STRAIGHT SHEILA: What?!

FRANK: Ask me what you just said.

STRAIGHT SHEILA: What I just said is beside the point, Frank.

FRANK: [*To the audience.*] So who's not listening? Who's not talking now?

STRAIGHT SHEILA: I don't believe this.

FRANK: Then just what is the point, Sheila? What is the bloody point?

STRAIGHT SHEILA: [*Losing her cool.*] It's *all* the point, Frank. It's the accumulation of all of the points.

FRANK: [*To the audience.*] Don't you just love these generalities?

STRAIGHT SHEILA: Okay. Okay. You want specifics? It was dinner that night.

FRANK: I don't remember.

LESBIAN SHEILA: [*Needling him gently.*] Frank.

STRAIGHT SHEILA: When I came home late from class...

FRANK: Well, gee, *that* narrows it down.

LESBIAN SHEILA: You don't remember? It was *this* dinner. [*She places a TV dinner with distaste on the table, which sets the scene in motion for re-enactment.*]

FRANK: Oh. [*He remembers.*]

[*We are now back in the past.* STRAIGHT SHEILA *enters the scene.* FRANK *is already seated.*]

STRAIGHT SHEILA: What's this?

FRANK: It's a TV dinner. What does it look like?

STRAIGHT SHEILA: I know what it is. What *is* it?

FRANK: What do you mean, what is it? It's dinner. What do you think it is?

STRAIGHT SHEILA: Where's the vegetables?

FRANK: There. See? Meatloaf. Brownie. *Macaroni.*

STRAIGHT SHEILA: Macaroni is not a vegetable, Frank. Vegetables are green.

FRANK: Potatoes are a vegetable and they're not green.

STRAIGHT SHEILA: All right. So potatoes are a vegetable. So where are they?

FRANK: They don't come with the meatloaf dinner.

[*Beat.*]

STRAIGHT SHEILA: [*Tearing up.*] Where's the salad?

FRANK: [*Bewildered.*] It's my night. You said I could make whatever I want on my night. I wanted to make TV dinners.

STRAIGHT SHEILA: I didn't say you could make garbage. *This* is garbage.

FRANK: Look, it's my night. Didn't you say?

STRAIGHT SHEILA: On my night, we had Beef Stroganoff. You make TV dinners.

FRANK: I got tired of hot dogs.

STRAIGHT SHEILA: On my night, we used place mats. And candles. I know what you're doing, Frank, and it's not going to work.

FRANK: I don't know what you mean. [*Beat.*] Are you going to eat this?

STRAIGHT SHEILA: No.

FRANK: [*Eating it and then speaking conversationally, trying to be friends again.*] You know, this is not too bad. The only problem with TV dinners is that they don't give you enough. You have to eat at least two or three of them to get enough.

STRAIGHT SHEILA: And what am *I* supposed to eat?

FRANK: [*Trying to make a joke and yet his underlying message is still clear.*] You could make dinner.

STRAIGHT SHEILA: Fuck you, Frank. *Fuck* you.

[*We are now back in the present.*]

LESBIAN SHEILA: [*To* STRAIGHT SHEILA.] Easy, Sheila, easy. [*To* FRANK, *as she removes the dinner with distaste and puts it back in the cooler or prop box.*] Remember now?

FRANK: [*Beat. To* FRANKIE.] She's always angry these days. I didn't know it when we were first together. Because she was sweet then. I guess we were both on good behavior. You know, polite. Asking which movie the other one wanted to see. And now, there is all this anger. I feel a little cheated. Like she is not the girl she made herself out to be. [*To the audience.*] Sometimes, it scares the hell out of me. And the littlest things set her off. Things I don't even care about. She didn't used to be like this. Or maybe I just didn't know. She says she's been changing. And the older she gets, [*Mimicking* STRAIGHT SHEILA.] the less bull- shit she wants to put up with. And moody. God, is she moody. Now, me? I'm just regular all the time. The same. What you see is what you get. [*Beat.*] For a while I thought, this is for the birds. Who needs this? I can find myself some- one else. Somebody nice and sweet and uncomplicated. And then I thought, how? And where? And I didn't want to have to get comfortable with someone else again. [*Beat.*] Most of the time, it's pretty good. I love sleeping with her and she does nice things for me sometimes. She'll pick up a movie I want to see or make something special for dinner. She won't pick up my shirts from the cleaners, though, and she gets mad if I ask her. I don't get it. I mean, what's the difference between picking up my shirts or picking up a movie? But I'll tell you something. Maureen, my last girlfriend? She never got angry. And she was pretty. I was never as hot for her like I am for Sheila, but it was okay. It was comfortable. We had the house and we had our friends and in the beginning, she used to bake all the time. Just like my mom. I'd come home and the house would smell like chocolate. But one day, she came home and said she wanted out. Just like that. I wanted to work it out. I even said I'd go see someone and I don't go in for that kind of bullshit. But she said it was too far gone. Too much had happened that she couldn't live with. So now, even though I don't understand it and it sometimes makes me crazy, I'll take Sheila's anger any day. Besides, with someone else, if it wasn't this, it would be something else. [*To* STRAIGHT SHEILA.] Okay, so maybe I should have made something else for dinner. Next time, I'll bake a ham. Or roast a friggin' turkey with all the trimmings. [*To the audience.*] She can pretend that it's Thanksgiving.

STRAIGHT SHEILA: Oh please.

FRANK: [*To the audience.*] This is the kind of piddly ass shit that drives me crazy. [*To* LESBIAN SHEILA *who has been conveying disbelief.*] What? You don't think this is piddly?

LESBIAN SHEILA: [*Bringing* STRAIGHT SHEILA *downstage next to* FRANK, *trying to facilitate communication.*] Not to her, it isn't. That's the thing, Frank. How does it feel to *her.*

FRANK: [*To* STRAIGHT SHEILA.] I didn't know you were so upset.

LESBIAN SHEILA: She's been telling you.

FRANKIE: [*Beat.*] Well, go on. Aren't you going to finish it?

FRANK: What?

FRANKIE: Kiss her. I want to see this.

LESBIAN SHEILA: Frankie! [*She ushers* FRANKIE *off to the side.*]

FRANKIE: Well, if that's what happened. Are we telling the story or not?

FRANK: Okay by me.

STRAIGHT SHEILA: [*Reluctantly.*] Great.

[*We are now back in the past.*]

FRANK: I'm sorry, baby. Come here.

[*He begins to kiss her. She kisses him back but their kissing is punctuated by her commentary. She is both aroused and troubled.* FRANKIE *and* LESBIAN SHEILA *both watch this scene with differing responses.*]

STRAIGHT SHEILA: This doesn't solve anything, Frank.

FRANK: *Sure it does.* [*To the audience, joking.*] We can't fight when we're fucking.

STRAIGHT SHEILA: [*She mock hits him with her fist.*] Why does it turn you on when we fight?

FRANK: You turn me on. [*He walks expectantly toward their bedroom.*]

STRAIGHT SHEILA: [*Remaining center stage, distressed.*] But you wear me out. [*She comes downstage center and addresses the audience. We are now back in the present. She tells the story of their courtship as if it is the first time she has ever said it aloud. She is alternately embarrassed, defiant, explanatory, distressed, and confused, and only realizes the significance of what she is saying as she comes towards the end of her speech.*]

It is a mutual discovery for both her and the audience.] The sex was the easy part. Once you get past doing it the first time. Well, the first *few* times. The first time I slept with Frank, I was scared to death. Scared he wouldn't like what he saw. I'd be too ripe. My breasts would jiggle. Turns out that's what he likes. But I didn't know that at the time. I wanted to say, wait. But I was scared I'd lose him. He'd find some other girl that would and he wouldn't even know the difference. [*Beat.*] I was okay on my own. I had a job and a regular bank account. It wasn't much, what with the rent and the utilities and my car payment. It was the first time I had something that was all mine. But damn if my friends didn't make me feel like I was doing something all wrong. There we'd be, having a pizza, or a few drinks, and it would be men. And if they weren't talking about men, they'd be working real hard *not* to talk about them. Laughing too loud, tossing their hair back at the bar. I figured the only way to get away from this man thing...was to get one. So when I met Frank and liked him okay, I thought this is it. You've got to make a decision sometimes. So this thing with Frank happened pretty quickly. Before I know it, we're living together. One day, I wake up and say, who is this man I sleep next to every night? Who is he really? Who am I? [*Beat.*] When I think back on how nervous I was. Would he like me? And would it be okay in bed? Shoot, that's the easy part. Talking and getting along day to day is what's hard. All I could think about was would he like me. I was so busy thinking about would he like me, I never stopped to think...did I like him? [*Disturbed by this realization, she moves towards the table to play cards, resolved to be cheerful and to make things work, at least at this point in the story.*] Thank God for poker. Yeah, I know I didn't like it at first. But I was actually getting pretty good at it. Besides, everything was easier when there were other people around. [*Beat.*] Until that night.... [*Beat.*]

[*We are now back in the past.*]

STRAIGHT SHEILA: [*Cont'd. To* LESBIAN SHEILA.] So I'm thinking about taking this class.

LESBIAN SHEILA: Great.

FRANK: [*To* FRANKIE.] *Another* class.

LESBIAN SHEILA: What in?

FRANK: Monday. Wednesday. Friday.

STRAIGHT SHEILA: [*To* LESBIAN SHEILA.] Accounting.

FRANK: Ante up.

FRANKIE: *Three* nights a week?

LESBIAN SHEILA: Aren't you something. I could never do that.

STRAIGHT SHEILA: Why not?

LESBIAN SHEILA: I'm too busy.

FRANKIE: [*To* FRANK.] Yeah. Taking care of me.

STRAIGHT SHEILA: [*To* FRANK.] It's only one semester. [*To* LESBIAN SHEILA.] It's concentrated.

LESBIAN SHEILA: I don't know. I'm not smart like you.

STRAIGHT SHEILA: Sheila, you're plenty smart. You run your whole damn office.

FRANK: [*Interrupting.*] Are you girls in or out?

STRAIGHT SHEILA: In.

LESBIAN SHEILA: [*Imitating her.*] In. I don't know. I don't know how you do it.

STRAIGHT SHEILA: [*To* LESBIAN SHEILA.] Well, it's not easy, after working all day. And it takes a little getting used to. But if you want something badly enough. And I just thought, with the economy being the way it is and all. If I had a real skill.

FRANK: You do have a real skill. Sit on my lap. Maybe it'll improve my hand.

[*He and* FRANKIE *laugh.*]

STRAIGHT SHEILA: [*Blowing it off lightly and turning back to* LESBIAN SHEILA *as if to continue.*] I will not.

FRANK: You're right. [*Beat.*] Sit on my face instead.

STRAIGHT SHEILA: What?!

FRANK: You heard me.

LESBIAN SHEILA: We all heard you, Frank.

[*Beat. Awkward silence all around.*]

FRANK: It's a little joke, that's all. Can't a man make a little joke in his own house?

FRANKIE: [*Lightly.*] Forget it, Frank. I'll take three.

FRANK: [*To* LESBIAN SHEILA.] How many cards do you want?

LESBIAN SHEILA: *Frankie.*

FRANKIE: [*Oblivious.*] What? How many cards? Remember, baby, when you play Five Card Draw, you can ask for up to . . . [*She trails off, cut short by the power of* LESBIAN SHEILA*'s silence.*]

LESBIAN SHEILA: Never mind. I fold.

FRANKIE: Let me see your hand. You've got three of a kind! That's a great hand, baby. Why'd you want to fold?

FRANK: [*To* STRAIGHT SHEILA, *who doesn't answer. Beat.*] How many cards do *you* want, Sheila? Sheila? How many cards? [*Beat.*] Aw, forget it. I need another beer, anyway. You want one, Frankie?

FRANKIE: Sure, I'll take another.

STRAIGHT SHEILA: No more beer, Frank. Please.

LESBIAN SHEILA: I think we better be going.

STRAIGHT SHEILA: Oh no, don't go. I made a cake.

LESBIAN SHEILA: It's late.

STRAIGHT SHEILA: It's chocolate.

FRANKIE: [*Confused by this exchange.*] No, it's not. It's early.

STRAIGHT SHEILA: I could put on a fresh pot of coffee.

FRANK: And there's plenty of beer.

LESBIAN SHEILA: [*Returning to their bedroom.*] I *said*, it's late, Frankie.

[*We are now back in the present.* FRANKIE *moves downstage center to address the audience.*]

FRANKIE: First she couldn't wait to get there and then she can't wait to leave.

FRANK: [*Joining her.*] You're telling me. So maybe things *were* a little rocky but give me a break.

FRANKIE: Everyone has their ups...

FRANK: Their downs.

FRANKIE: Their downs.

FRANK: But suddenly, I'm living with Emily friggin' Post.

FRANKIE: And I don't know who *I'm* living with anymore.

[*Lights up on* FRANKIE *and* LESBIAN SHEILA'*s bedroom.* FRANKIE *sneaks into bed, pretending to be asleep so that she will not be noticed by* LESBIAN SHEILA, *who is clearly agitated.* FRANKIE'*s entrance could be exaggerated to point up the comedy of one who is trying to avoid being in the dog house as well as to show her heightened awareness that this is an instance where she is performing in front of an audience.*]

LESBIAN SHEILA: I can't believe he talked to her that way. [*Beat.*] *Frankie!*

FRANKIE: [*Startling.*] What, baby?

LESBIAN SHEILA: I *said*, I can't believe the way he talked to her. I don't know what I'd do if you talked to me that way.

FRANKIE: What? Sit on my face? [*Beat. Making a joke.*] It's not such a bad idea.

LESBIAN SHEILA: Frankie!

FRANKIE: Look, baby. It's none of our business.

LESBIAN SHEILA: But he embarrassed her in front of us. She's my friend.

FRANKIE: And I have to work with the guy. So they have a few problems. It has nothing to do with us.

[*Lights down on* LESBIAN SHEILA *and* FRANKIE. *Lights up on* STRAIGHT SHEILA *and* FRANK. *He is eating cake.*]

FRANK: [*Trying to make amends.*] The cake is great, babe.

STRAIGHT SHEILA: It was supposed to be for company.

FRANK: So this is the way it's going to be for the rest of the night? Look, babe. It was a joke.

STRAIGHT SHEILA: I have never been so humiliated in my life.

FRANK: Oh for Christ's sake, Sheila. What do you think *they* do, anyway?

[*Lights down on* STRAIGHT SHEILA *and* FRANK. *Lights up on* LESBIAN SHEILA *and* FRANKIE..]

LESBIAN SHEILA: You ever think about going back to school?

FRANKIE: What for? I like what I do. Except for Chico and Al ragging me. But I'm used to that.

LESBIAN SHEILA: I hate it.

FRANKIE: You hate what I do?

LESBIAN SHEILA: Yes. No. I mean, I hate what *I* do. What do I have to look forward to?

[*Lights down on* FRANKIE *and* LESBIAN SHEILA. *Lights up on* FRANK *and* STRAIGHT SHEILA *in their bedroom.*]

FRANK: Come on, Sheila. You gonna stay mad at me the whole night? I said I was sorry. [*Beat.*] What do you have to take another class for, anyway?

STRAIGHT SHEILA: Is that what this is about? You encouraged me to go to school. You said you liked the fact that I was smart.

FRANK: I do. But how many friggin' classes do you need? Last semester, it was Art Appreciation. This time, it's Accounting.

STRAIGHT SHEILA: I like Art Appreciation.

FRANK: That's not even what you do. So what's the point, except you're gone all the time?

[STRAIGHT SHEILA *breaks the scene to be in the present as she suddenly has a revelation. Beat.*]

STRAIGHT SHEILA: Wait a minute. Oh, I get it. I get it *now*. Why couldn't you just have told me that you missed me?

[*They all notice that she is breaking the scene.* LESBIAN SHEILA *and* FRANKIE *watch nervously from their area, unsure about what will come next.*]

FRANK: [*Responding in the present and snapping.*] I *did*. I *was*.

STRAIGHT SHEILA: If I was a *mindreader*. Why couldn't you just have *said* it? [*Beat.*] Frank? *Frank?* [*He doesn't respond. Beat.*] Oh I see. We're just going to do the scene. The one where I get to play the bitch.

FRANK: Yeah, well I get to play the jerk so I guess we're even.

STRAIGHT SHEILA: If you had just said that you... Look, do you want to talk about this? Frank? *Frank?* [*Beat. With quiet anger.*] Okay. Fine. [*Beat. Trying to recall.*] What did I say? Oh, yeah.

[*Beat. They resume the scene and are back in the past.* STRAIGHT SHEILA's *anger from the preceding interlude carries over.*]

STRAIGHT SHEILA: [*Cont'd.*] I'm planning for the future, Frank. I like to plan ahead.

FRANK: And what am I supposed to do while you're off planning for the friggin' future? Sit here and play with myself?

[*Lights down on* STRAIGHT SHEILA *and* FRANK. *Lights up on* LESBIAN SHEILA *and on* FRANKIE *who is trying valiantly to stay awake.*]

LESBIAN SHEILA: [*Said somewhat rapidly, as if in a stream of consciousness aloud to herself.*] So they make me office manager. So what? My boss still comes on to me. I get a raise of a 75 cents an hour *which* I have to pay taxes on. Only now I'm responsible for everyone else's shit, instead of my own.

FRANKIE: [*Fully awake now and up to the challenge, she punches her palm with her fist.*] I told you, baby. Just say the word and I'll bust his face.

LESBIAN SHEILA: That is no solution. But just once I'd like to be able to tell him where to stick it. And I'd like to get paid decent. We do all the work. He and the others do all the talking and get all the credit. And all the money. But that's the problem. When you work the kind of job I do, you can't say nothing.

FRANKIE: [*She leaves their bedroom and comes downstage to address the audience. We are now back in the present.*] And that is how it all started.

FRANK: You can say that again.

STRAIGHT SHEILA: *Frank.*

LESBIAN SHEILA: No, Frankie. That is not how it started.

STRAIGHT SHEILA: It's just what showed it.

LESBIAN SHEILA: Well, part of it, anyways.

FRANKIE: Baloney. Suddenly, being a secretary isn't good enough for her anymore. I'm not good enough.

LESBIAN SHEILA: [*Going to* FRANKIE.] I never said that.

FRANKIE: Like I can't take care of you.

LESBIAN SHEILA: That is not the issue here.

FRANKIE: I'll say it is. Because then it got completely out of hand. [*To the audience.*] Suddenly she's talking about going to night school.

LESBIAN SHEILA: What was the matter with wanting to go to night school?

FRANKIE: Wanting to better herself. [*To* LESBIAN SHEILA.] You quit fixing your hair. [*To the audience.*] Started wearing flats! Before you know it, she was in fantasy land about things she had no business even thinking about. Things we settled a long time ago.

STRAIGHT SHEILA: She had no business thinking about?! What do you do, control her thoughts? You are so selfish.

FRANKIE: This is none of your business.

STRAIGHT SHEILA: She was my friend.

FRANKIE: That didn't give you the right. Some things are private between Sheila and me.

STRAIGHT SHEILA: Oh, yeah, it's real private when she was moping around so bad, she could hardly bet her hand.

FRANKIE: It was not that bad. Women do go through these things, sometimes. [*Stage whispering.*] Especially around that time of the month.

[*Everyone reacts to this statement.*]

STRAIGHT SHEILA: [*Incredulously.*] Oh please.

FRANKIE: You know something? We should never have met you. If we had just kept to the way things were, we would have been okay. We were doing just fine.

STRAIGHT SHEILA: This is why you're losing her.

FRANKIE: You're the ones. *You are the ones.*

STRAIGHT SHEILA: Why don't you just do the scene, Frankie, and let them decide?

FRANKIE: [*Snapping.*] Which one?

STRAIGHT SHEILA: You know which one.

FRANKIE: [*Beat.*] That is personal.

STRAIGHT SHEILA: This whole thing is personal. What did you think? We were going to get up here and tell our stories and not get personal? You know what we agreed to do. Why'd you say you'd do it if you didn't want to tell the story?

FRANKIE: I don't know. I wanted to see Sheila. [*Panicking.*] Sheila, where are you?

LESBIAN SHEILA: [*Joining her.*] I'm right here, Frankie. I'm right here.

FRANKIE: [*Pulling her aside.*] Sheila, I don't like this. It's one thing to tell a few jokes or even to argue a little. But this is our life. This is my stuff they're hearing up here.

LESBIAN SHEILA: I know. But it's my life, too, Frankie. And I can't tell *my* story unless you do this scene.

FRANKIE: Why can't you do it without me?

LESBIAN SHEILA: Because you're in it.

FRANKIE: Well, then why can't you just do another scene?

LESBIAN SHEILA: Because this one is really important.

FRANKIE: Then do another important one. [*Beat.*] Like when I held you all night when your father died. Remember that?

LESBIAN SHEILA: You were really there for me that night, Frankie.

FRANKIE: [*Gaining ground. She puts her arm around* LESBIAN SHEILA *and slowly begins to walk her downstage, creating a private space for the two of them.* STRAIGHT SHEILA *watches, nervously.*] You know it. And when you lost your job and I was working swing shift?

LESBIAN SHEILA: Those were some hard times.

FRANKIE: Yeah. But it wasn't all hard. Even when it was. Remember when you burst your appendix?

LESBIAN SHEILA: Yeah. And we didn't have any health insurance.

FRANKIE: Hey, *I* paid it off, didn't I?

LESBIAN SHEILA: [*Chuckling at the memory.*] And you snuck into the hospital and told them you were my brother Johnny so they'd let you stay.

FRANKIE: And they did.

LESBIAN SHEILA: And we played pinochle when you got off work for hours until closing.

FRANKIE: Those were some good times. Just you and me.

FRANK: [*Wanting to encourage* FRANKIE *and to get the show back on the road.*] That sounds great. Do that one.

LESBIAN SHEILA: [*Beat.*] It's less personal.

FRANKIE: Baby, when it comes to you, it's all personal.

LESBIAN SHEILA: [*To* STRAIGHT SHEILA.] She's in so many scenes in my story. [*To* FRANKIE, *tenderly.*] There were a lot of scenes. Hundreds, really. It's hard to choose when you come down to it. [*Beat.*] But this one's really important. You know how some things just stick out more clearly in your mind?

FRANKIE: [*Ironically.*] Oh, I know.

LESBIAN SHEILA: And they're all important. And they're all personal. But maybe some are *more* important.

FRANKIE: I have a problem with this. I guess I don't understand why *your* need to tell the story is more important than *my* need for it *not* to be told. [*To the audience.*] Am I crazy here, or what?

LESBIAN SHEILA: [*Seriously considering, with new realization.*] You've got a point, Frankie. I never thought about it that way.

FRANKIE: This is an invasion of my privacy.

LESBIAN SHEILA: I'm invading your privacy? Oh god. I'm really sorry, Frankie. [*To* STRAIGHT SHEILA, *panicking.*] I don't know what to do.

STRAIGHT SHEILA: Well, if you don't do the scene, the story can't go forward.

FRANK: Sounds pretty cut and dried to me.

STRAIGHT SHEILA: You do want the story to go forward, don't you, Frankie?

FRANKIE: [*Resolutely, willing and needing to play this thing through.*] I'm here, aren't I?

LESBIAN SHEILA: Are you sure, Frankie? Because I don't want to be invading your *privacy.*

FRANKIE: I can handle it. [*To* LESBIAN SHEILA.] What's my line?

LESBIAN SHEILA: I think you said, what's the matter, baby. It was that day I came home from work.

FRANKIE: Right. [*Almost in spite of herself, affectionately at* LESBIAN SHEILA's *turn of phrase.*] What's the matter, baby.

[LESBIAN SHEILA *gives her the thumbs up sign of encouragement and then exits. We are now back in the past. To* LESBIAN SHEILA *who enters.*]

FRANKIE: [*Cont'd.*] What's the matter, baby? Did you have a bad day?

LESBIAN SHEILA: Lisa's pregnant. [*She sits slumped at the table with this news.*]

FRANKIE: [*Joking, trying to jolly her out of a bad mood.*] God, they pop 'em out at that office of yours faster than a Xerox machine.

LESBIAN SHEILA: We all chipped in for lunch today and they're gonna have a shower at Saralee's next month. Her colors are pink and blue. Since she doesn't know yet.

FRANKIE: I don't know why they don't just take it directly out of your paycheck. Every time you turn around, they're hitting you up for this one's birthday or that one's baby shower.

LESBIAN SHEILA: I like it. It's homey. Makes it feel more like family.

FRANKIE: Well, it's not.

LESBIAN SHEILA: [*Beat.*] I know it's not.

FRANKIE: Family is who will be there when you need them. When the chips are down.

LESBIAN SHEILA: I know.

FRANKIE: You think those people would be there if the chips were down?

LESBIAN SHEILA: I don't know. Maybe.

FRANKIE: Don't be naive, girl. They're all too busy with their husbands and their wives and all their damn babies to be there even if they wanted to. [*She begins to massage* LESBIAN SHEILA*'s neck.*] I'm here. I'm who is here. I'm the one you can count on. [*Beat.*] Let's go in the other room.

LESBIAN SHEILA: I've got my period.

FRANKIE: I know. You know I don't care about that. Just makes you feel more like a woman.

LESBIAN SHEILA: Lisa thinks it's gonna be twins.

FRANKIE: Come on, baby. I'll make you remember how much of a woman you are.

LESBIAN SHEILA: Maybe if she had two, she could give one to me.

FRANKIE: *Sheila.*

LESBIAN SHEILA: I'm just joking, Frankie.

FRANKIE: Are you? Because you know those women aren't half the woman you are. Any fool can have a baby. Any dumb teenage girl.

LESBIAN SHEILA: [*Trying to make a fresh case for what is clearly an old argument for them.*] It's not like we don't make enough money. And we've got the space.

FRANKIE: That is not who we are. Or what we do. We do *other* things. [*Kneeling and imploring her.*] Like I'm trying to show you, baby, if you'd just give me half a chance.

LESBIAN SHEILA: But why can't we do that, too? There *are* ways.

FRANKIE: [*She stands abruptly and walks away.*] Now that's some sick shit and I don't want to hear you talking like that.

LESBIAN SHEILA: It is not. It's just a way. What difference does the way make?

FRANKIE: We've been over this before, Sheila. I thought we had it settled.

LESBIAN SHEILA: I know, Frankie. But things change. People change.

FRANKIE: [*Beat.*] Is that why you never want me to touch you any more? You want a man? You want a fucking man? Is that what you want? You just see if he treats you as good as I do. You just see.

LESBIAN SHEILA: I didn't say that. You're not listening to me. I know you treat me good. [*Correcting herself.*] I mean, *well.* I just sometimes think that there could be more.

FRANKIE: It takes more than that to be a woman.

LESBIAN SHEILA: How would you know?

FRANKIE: What?!

LESBIAN SHEILA: Never mind.

FRANKIE: What's that supposed to mean?

LESBIAN SHEILA: I'm sorry. Forget it.

FRANKIE: No, Sheila. I want to know what you meant by that. [*Following her closely around the table, as the fight begins to escalate.*]

LESBIAN SHEILA: I can't talk to you, anymore, Frankie. Sometimes, I just can't talk to you.

FRANKIE: Not when you talk nonsense.

LESBIAN SHEILA: Yeah? Well, Sheila didn't think it was nonsense.

FRANKIE: Sheila?! Jesus H. Christ! Is nothing private around here? I cannot fucking believe that you told her that.

LESBIAN SHEILA: She is my friend. I can talk to her.

FRANKIE: And you can't talk to me? Since when can't you talk to me? Since when do you need to talk to someone else? What the hell is with all this talking, anyway? How much can there be to say? Lunches, dinners, phone calls. Suddenly, you're the poker queen. If I didn't know better, I'd think you were sleeping with her.

LESBIAN SHEILA: No!

FRANKIE: [*Beat.*] Oh my God, you are sleeping with her.

LESBIAN SHEILA: No, no, I haven't done anything. I haven't, Frankie. Honest.

[*Beat.*]

FRANKIE: No, of course you haven't. It's worse than that. [*Beat.*] You're not.

LESBIAN SHEILA: [*To the audience. We are now back in the present. Beat.*] When did the talking become sex? It wasn't. I mean, I hadn't done anything. But suddenly, I felt like I had. You know what I mean? A look feels like a touch. A whisper like a kiss. Or you're just sitting there talking. And suddenly you feel so close because they understand you and you understand them, that you feel naked. Like you're making love. And then maybe you want to make love because of the way you've been talking. Maybe it's not so sudden. Maybe it's been creeping up on you all this time and you suddenly notice it. [*To* FRANKIE.] But honestly, Frankie, I don't think I understood that at the time. And I hadn't done anything. Honest.

[*This next exchange by* STRAIGHT SHEILA *and* LESBIAN SHEILA *is said intermittently to the audience, and to each other. It is unabashedly intimate, filled with embarrassment and pleasure as they recall the unfolding of their relationship and the various points at which they understood its unfolding.*]

STRAIGHT SHEILA: I don't know what *I* understood. Since I'd never felt like that before. All I knew was that I started wanting her to call.

LESBIAN SHEILA: [*Chuckling at the memory.*] A lot. [*Beat. Miming being on the phone.*] Hi!

STRAIGHT SHEILA: [*Picking up an imaginary phone.*] Oh. [*Beat.*] Hi. How are you?

LESBIAN SHEILA: What's the matter? Did you have a fight with Frank again?

STRAIGHT SHEILA: Not exactly. It's just that . . . [*She walks over to* LESBIAN SHEILA, *as if they are no longer on the phone but now are in the same space. She is upset. Beat.*] It's nothing.

LESBIAN SHEILA: [*Putting her arms around* STRAIGHT SHEILA, *comforting her.*] Nothing can really be something, sometimes. Huh, sweetie? [*She laughs.*] That was really dumb, huh?

STRAIGHT SHEILA: No, that was really really smart. I love the way you say things sometimes. The way you make words your own. I love the way you . . .

[*She stops herself. They look at each other, move apart and resume telling the story to the audience. Beat.*]

STRAIGHT SHEILA: [*Cont'd.*] There were a lot of phone calls.

LESBIAN SHEILA: [*Half embarrassed.*] A lot.

STRAIGHT SHEILA: I'd play little games with myself. Willing her to call, tricking her into calling. I'd run a bath, thinking she might call as soon as I stepped in.

LESBIAN SHEILA: I'd eat ice cream. Chocolate. Actually, what I'd do is go to the freezer and get the ice cream out, thinking I shouldn't be eating this. She'll call just as I'm getting ready to—

[LESBIAN SHEILA *interrupts her story to mime suddenly answering the phone. It is* STRAIGHT SHEILA, *who also mimes using the phone.*]

STRAIGHT SHEILA: Hi Sheila.

LESBIAN SHEILA: [*Guiltily and suddenly caught off guard.*] Um, hi.

STRAIGHT SHEILA: What are you doing?

LESBIAN SHEILA: *Not* eating ice cream?

STRAIGHT SHEILA: [*She laughs.*] Sheila. [*Beat.*] Without *me*?

LESBIAN SHEILA: Oh, God. I left it dripping on the counter.

STRAIGHT SHEILA: [*Conscious of the sexual connotations and quietly aroused. Beat.*] Dripping.

LESBIAN SHEILA: [*Now, she, too, is conscious of the connotations.*] Dripping. Thinking she would save me from myself.

STRAIGHT SHEILA: [*Moved by the memory, and looking to be saved.*] Myself.

LESBIAN SHEILA: [*Trying to put their relationship in its rightful place.*] Just two friends, two friends who really . . .

STRAIGHT SHEILA: [*Emphatically.*] really . . .

LESBIAN SHEILA: like to talk to each other. [*Beat.*] That would have been fine for me—

STRAIGHT SHEILA: [*Interrupting.*] For a while.

LESBIAN SHEILA: You're pushing again, Sheila. Please don't push. Frankie and me, [*Correcting herself.*] Frankie and *I*, had been going through a rough time but when Sheila came into my life, it got easier. I could talk to her. And unlike Frankie, she talked *back* to me. It's like having her in my life made it possible to stay.

STRAIGHT SHEILA: I don't know how you can say that. Having her in my life made it necessary to go. [*To the audience.*] Because I *could* talk to her.

FRANK: I have had just about enough of this. Is this ridiculous or what? This is what I don't understand about women. All this yakety yak. And it's not like anything had even happened. I can't believe you make such a big deal over nothing.

STRAIGHT SHEILA: If it's not a big deal, Frank, then why do you care?

FRANK: [*Exploding.*] Because nobody told me! You came into *my* house and played *my* game and drank *my* beer and I knew nothing. [*He starts to leave.*]

LESBIAN SHEILA: [*Panicking.*] Where are you going?

FRANK: [*He leaves the stage, walking through the audience to make his exit.*] I've had enough. If you think that I'm going to hang around and watch you make me look like a jerk, you've got another thing coming.

FRANKIE: [*She needs him to stay, to continue the story and affect how it ends.*] We all agreed to do this thing. And you know why we came here tonight.

[*After pausing momentarily when* FRANKIE *addresses him,* FRANK *resumes walking away. In desperation, she throws him another road block. Beat.*]

FRANKIE: [*Cont'd.*] I don't know about you but where I come from, a deal's a deal.

FRANK: [*Defensive, he stops.*] Hey! My word is good.

FRANKIE: We all have our part to play, Frank. Aren't you supposed to deal?

[*Beat.* FRANK *returns to the stage. To* LESBIAN SHEILA *and the others who then move back to the card table to resume playing the game.*]

FRANKIE: [*Cont'd.*] Well?

[*Everyone is seated at the card table. They are also disconcerted by this latest exchange but shake it off to resume telling the story. Beat. We are now back in the past.*]

FRANK: [*He begins to deal cards. He is in a good mood. He knows nothing about what has gone on between* LESBIAN SHEILA *and* STRAIGHT SHEILA. FRANKIE, *however, has strong inklings. There are definitely two games going on in this scene.*] Okay, listen up, ladies. The game is Five Card Stud. You all still remember how?

FRANKIE: Some things you never forget. [*To* LESBIAN SHEILA.] Right, baby?

STRAIGHT SHEILA: Maybe you should go over the rules, Frank.

LESBIAN SHEILA: It's okay. I remember the rules.

STRAIGHT SHEILA: Different game. Different rules.

FRANKIE: She remembers.

FRANK: All right then. [*He cuts the deck.*] How the hell are you, anyway, Sheila? Is that a new dress?

STRAIGHT SHEILA: [*Too quickly.*] No.

LESBIAN SHEILA: [*Covering.*] No. Things have been really crazy at work.

STRAIGHT SHEILA: No kidding. I called three times. Didn't you get my messages?

FRANKIE: [*Sending her a message.*] Sheila and me have been really busy lately.

FRANK: [*To* LESBIAN SHEILA.] Ho, ho! King of Diamonds! Looking good, Sheila. The night looks good for you. What do you bet?

STRAIGHT SHEILA: How about lunch tomorrow?

LESBIAN SHEILA: I'll check.

FRANKIE: I thought we were supposed to go to my cousin's.

FRANK: You'll check? I thought you said you remembered how to play?

LESBIAN SHEILA: [*Becoming flustered from multiple conversations and multiple pressures.*] No, what I meant was . . . [*Correcting herself.*] What I mean is, is that I'll check about Saturday.

FRANK: Because when you say, I'll check, you delay the pot.

STRAIGHT SHEILA: Leave her alone, Frank.

FRANK: Hey, are we playing cards or filling out our dance cards, here?

FRANKIE: [*To* FRANK.] She remembers how to play the game, Frank. Look, we'll all check and get a free card.

FRANK: You'll all check?! Unfucking believable. You all are too dangerous for me tonight.

STRAIGHT SHEILA: Frank, watch the mouth, please.

FRANK: Sorry, babe. I'm going to get another beer. [*He rises.*]

STRAIGHT SHEILA: Oh great.

FRANK: Anybody want anything?

[FRANKIE *signals that she wants a beer as* FRANK *passes behind her chair.*]

STRAIGHT SHEILA: So what about lunch tomorrow?

LESBIAN SHEILA: [*Trying to put her off gently at the same time that she really wants to see her.*] I'm busy. This thing with Frankie's cousin.

STRAIGHT SHEILA: Oh right. Well, I understand. How about next week?

LESBIAN SHEILA: I don't know if I can make it

STRAIGHT SHEILA: Next week is a whole week, Sheila. Seven whole days.

LESBIAN SHEILA: [*Suddenly panicking.*] Bring me a beer, too. Would you, please, Frank?

FRANK: Ooh-ooh, Sheila's going to party tonight.

FRANKIE: You haven't finished the one you're drinking, baby.

LESBIAN SHEILA: [*Curtly.*] I'm thirsty.

FRANK: [*Re-entering.*] Here you go, Sheila, my pet. Now are we ready to put our money where our mouths are?

FRANKIE: I am.

STRAIGHT SHEILA: [*Matching her.*] So am I.

LESBIAN SHEILA: I think I'll wait this one out.

FRANK: [*To* LESBIAN SHEILA.] Holy Jesus. The cards are in your favor tonight, girl. You gotta bet now. What's your bet?

LESBIAN SHEILA: [*Drinking.*] How much do I have to put in?

FRANKIE: You know it's a nickel, baby. We've been through this before.

STRAIGHT SHEILA: I could just meet you for a drink. You know, after work.

LESBIAN SHEILA: [*In response to all the building pressure, both spoken and unspoken, she begins two-fisted drinking, drawing from both beer cans. Although the situation is not funny, it's a funny sight.*] It's not my game, Frankie. I don't like gambling. I'm doing the best I can.

STRAIGHT SHEILA: I think you're doing just fine.

FRANKIE: She's doing better than that. She's doing just great. Right where she is.

STRAIGHT SHEILA: Well, then why change anything, huh, Frankie? Why not just play the same damned cards over and over.

FRANK: [*Oblivious to what is going on and with simple logic.*] Because that's not the way the rules work. She knows that. [*To* LESBIAN SHEILA.] What do you say, babe? What do you want to do?

FRANKIE: [*To* STRAIGHT SHEILA.] Big talk from someone who just learned to play the game.

FRANK: [*Not understanding the subtext.*] All right! Maybe we're going to have a decent game tonight after all.

STRAIGHT SHEILA: Maybe I don't have your experience but I know how to play.

FRANKIE: You wouldn't know what to do.

STRAIGHT SHEILA: Try me. [*Beat.*]

FRANK: [*Confused.*] Are we talking or playing here?

FRANKIE: Oh, we're playing a game all right.

[*To* LESBIAN SHEILA, *putting her on the spot. Maybe she's being cruel; maybe her show of bravado is meant to intimidate or bluff* STRAIGHT SHEILA. *In any case,* LESBIAN SHEILA *is suddenly exhausted and overwhelmed by what has just transpired.*]

FRANKIE: [*Cont'd.*] Put the nickel in, baby. Place your bet.

LESBIAN SHEILA: [*Beat.*] I'm sorry. I don't think I'm feeling very well. I want to go home.

FRANKIE: That's okay, sweetheart. I'll get your coat.

STRAIGHT SHEILA: No, don't go. How about an aspirin? You want an aspirin? [*Trying to stop her from leaving.*] What do you need?

FRANKIE: What she needs isn't here.

FRANK: [*With genuine concern.*] Are you okay, babe? Because suddenly, you don't look so good. Do you want to lie down?

STRAIGHT SHEILA: Please don't go.

LESBIAN SHEILA: [*Responding to his kindness, uncomfortable that he doesn't know what is going on, and upset with both* FRANKIE *and* STRAIGHT SHEILA.] I'm really sorry, Frank. I was looking forward to this but I guess I just don't feel like playing tonight.

STRAIGHT SHEILA: We don't have to play. We could just talk.

FRANK: [*Confused and frustrated.*] Oh my God. What is it with you people? I've been looking forward to this game for three weeks and now you want to talk. [*Beat.*] *Again.* [*Beat.*] What the hell. I'm hitting the rack. It's been a hell of a week. [*To* FRANKIE.] Later, bud. [*He exits to bedroom.*]

FRANKIE: [*To* LESBIAN SHEILA.] Wait for me in the car.

LESBIAN SHEILA: Frankie.

FRANKIE: I *said*, in the car.

> [LESBIAN SHEILA *exits to their bedroom. Long beat.*
> STRAIGHT SHEILA *and* FRANKIE *size each other up and* FRANKIE *stares her down.* STRAIGHT SHEILA *doesn't quite know where this is leading and starts to clear the table out of awkwardness.*]

STRAIGHT SHEILA: I know you think all this talking is just a joke.

FRANKIE: Not when *I* have something to say. [*Beat.*] I know what you're doing here. What butch in her right mind wouldn't want Sheila?

STRAIGHT SHEILA: Oh please.

FRANKIE: Tell me you don't.

STRAIGHT SHEILA: This is not just about what I want. It's about what she wants, too.

FRANKIE: Sheila doesn't know what she wants. She gets confused sometimes, see? It's hard being in the life. You wouldn't understand. We'll get through it all right. But you don't care. You don't care who you hurt along the way. Her. Us.

FRANK: [*From the bedroom, oblivious to this discussion.*] Sheila? My back's bothering me again. Are you coming, babe?

STRAIGHT SHEILA: [*Nervously, wanting to prevent* FRANK *from overhearing this conversation.*] In a minute.

FRANKIE: [*Continuing.*] My buddy in the next room. You know, I thought about telling him but I'm waiting for this thing to blow over. And besides, after that business with Maureen, it'd like to have tore him up. He doesn't talk about it or anything but I know it hurt him bad.

STRAIGHT SHEILA: I have needs, too. Maybe if things could be different.

FRANKIE: So he's not perfect. Like you are? You don't even know who or what you are. He's a decent enough guy. And he's been real decent to me. Frankly, lady, I don't know how you can sleep at night. [*She exits to upstage.*]

STRAIGHT SHEILA: [*Beat. To the audience. Now she is in total crisis and we see a crack in her brisk facade.*] I can't. Just because I'm not in love with him doesn't mean I don't have feelings. *In love.* Whatever that means. That's the thing about talking, isn't it? You talk to be understood and yet the only words I know sometimes make it impossible. I have feelings for Frank. How could I not? We live in the same house. We sleep in the same bed. But lately, I feel like I've been living a half-life, like I'm sleepwalking my way through life. Is it my fault that I woke up? Or started having different dreams? Is that wrong? Life is so short. You've got to make a decision sometimes. But then, when I think about leaving, I get terrified. It's like stepping off a cliff. I don't know who or what is waiting for me on the other side. And will I fly or hit the ground with a sickening thud? [*Beat.*] It's never easy to leave someone if you care for them at all. But is it fair to him or me to stay, feeling like I do?

FRANK: Honey, it's getting late.

STRAIGHT SHEILA: Coming, sweetheart. I'm coming. [*Beat.*] So I knew I had to do something. What I had to do was to see Sheila. Even if it did mean going to her office.

[*A long beat. She walks over to where* LESBIAN SHEILA *is sitting, studying a file with papers in it, as if she is in her office.* LESBIAN SHEILA *startles upon seeing her.* LESBIAN SHEILA *is initially happy and then apprehensive to see her.* STRAIGHT SHEILA *is nervous but determined. She is filled with feeling. She has come there, in part, to see how she feels. She finds out.*]

STRAIGHT SHEILA: [*Cont'd.*] Hi, Sheila.

LESBIAN SHEILA: Oh. Hi. [*Beat.*]

STRAIGHT SHEILA: Hi. Why have you been avoiding me?

LESBIAN SHEILA: Sheila, please. Let's not do this here.

STRAIGHT SHEILA: Then where? When? We have to talk about what's happened.

LESBIAN SHEILA: [*Looking around, nervously. Smiling at imaginary passersby.*] Sheila, this is not the place. [*Half joking.*] What are you trying to do here? Get me fired?

STRAIGHT SHEILA: I'm not leaving until we talk.

LESBIAN SHEILA: You've just never had a good friend before.

STRAIGHT SHEILA: I've had a good friend.

LESBIAN SHEILA: Someone who listens. Someone who cares.

STRAIGHT SHEILA: I've never felt like this before. I didn't even know that this was possible.

LESBIAN SHEILA: [*Reaching out to her impulsively.*] Honey, please. You don't know what you're saying. [*And then checking herself and pulling back.*] Why can't we just keep things the way they are?

STRAIGHT SHEILA: Because that's *not* the way it is and you know it. Don't lie to me, Sheila. And don't lie to yourself. You know what's happened.

[FRANKIE *comes downstage, interrupting the scene. We are now in the present.*]

FRANKIE: Sheila, baby. You don't have to finish this scene. If you stop now, we can go back home and pretend this whole thing didn't happen.

FRANK: [*In distress.*] Oh Christ.

FRANKIE: I don't even care if you slept with the woman or not. Even though the thought of anybody even looking at you kills me. But we've been together a long time, baby. It happens. Please, baby. You don't want this. This isn't what you want. And we don't owe anybody [*Meaning* FRANK *and* STRAIGHT SHEILA *as well as the audience.*] anything. Come on, we're going home. [*She reaches for her hand.*]

STRAIGHT SHEILA: I don't believe you. You never learn. When are you going to stop telling her what to do?!

[FRANK *audibly crumbles his beer can.*]

LESBIAN SHEILA: Stop it, both of you.

[FRANK *tosses his beer can.*]

LESBIAN SHEILA: [*Cont'd. Crossing to* FRANK *who has retreated and is sitting dejectedly and drinking.*] Are you all right?

FRANK: Like you give a rat's ass.

LESBIAN SHEILA: I do. I really do.

FRANK: Little Miss Innocence.

LESBIAN SHEILA: Do you think this is easy for me? Do you think this is easy for any of us?

FRANK: [*First angrily, then imploring.*] Leave me the fuck alone. Please.

LESBIAN SHEILA: [*With genuine compassion and concern.*] Oh, Frank.

STRAIGHT SHEILA: Sheila. You have to decide. As if he's [*Meaning* FRANK.] not bad enough, you want this poor excuse for a man?

[*Beat.* LESBIAN SHEILA *and* FRANKIE *exchange looks and* FRANKIE *walks away upstage.*]

LESBIAN SHEILA: How dare you speak about her that way. What could you possibly understand? You know nothing about our lives. What she is. Who she is to me. She's a hero. It's easy for you or me. We can pass. But she walks down the street and doesn't apologize for who she is. I could have had a man. I've had a few. [*To* FRANK, *who has expressed disbelief.*] Well, what did you think? But all the men I knew were either like you or never had enough get up and go. [*Continuing to the others.*] And let me tell you something. Sometimes, I think it takes a woman ... to be a real man. You look at her and see one thing. I look at her and see something else. Someone who lets me know who she is and who we can be together. You can't understand that, Sheila. You can't know what it's like to live our lives. She left her home, her family, even her church to come here and search for me. Women like me and Frankie had to look for each other. But it was hard. And how could we find each other, if she couldn't show me who she was? [*Beat.*] The first time I saw Frankie, she was playing pool. I still remember the starch of her button-down shirt. The way she looked in her Levi's. I saw the way she circled the table. The way her eyes curled against the smoke. I saw the way she looked at me. And I knew in that instant, if I was with her, what I wanted, what I needed so desperately, would be okay. And all those desires that I was told I should forget, I could have. Maybe we paid the price. The way we've been has kept us from other people. Maybe it hardened her along the way. But she has been my home. My harbor. My family. She took such good care of me.

[FRANKIE *reaches out her hand to* LESBIAN SHEILA, *still not sure of the outcome of this speech.* LESBIAN SHEILA *is also not sure of the outcome until the final moments.*]

LESBIAN SHEILA: [*Cont'd.*] I loved you, Frankie. I'm sorry. [*She weeps.*]

STRAIGHT SHEILA: [*Quickly going to* LESBIAN SHEILA *and embracing her.*] We'll take care of each other.

FRANKIE: [*In a fit of rage, kicking the table or knocking a piece of furniture over.*] Goddamnit! [*She moves in a blind fury toward the others.*]

FRANK: Motherfucking queers!

LESBIAN SHEILA: Frankie, no!

FRANKIE: [*To* FRANK.] Why didn't you keep your fucking wife at home?!

[FRANK *and* FRANKIE *begin to fight physically.* LESBIAN SHEILA *tries to stop them.*]

LEASBIAN SHEILA: [*Screaming.*] No. No. No.

[*Beat. There is a long, awkward silence on stage as everyone struggles to deal with the aftermath of what has just taken place.* STRAIGHT SHEILA *rearranges the furniture and props that were knocked to the ground.* LESBIAN SHEILA *stands shell-shocked before finally moving to assist her.* FRANK *and* FRANKIE *move to opposite sides of the stage, each with a pack of playing cards. They fiddle with the cards as they speak. They primarily address the audience, rather than each other. Occasionally, however, they sneak a look at one another when they think the other one isn't looking, as if they are yearning for the friendship they had before all this happened.*]

FRANK: She wanted me to change. But if you ask me, there's too damn much change in the world these days.

FRANKIE: Suddenly, everything's an argument.

FRANK: Or a discussion.

FRANKIE: Used to be, you knew who was who.

FRANK: And what was what. Now I don't get it.

FRANKIE: There have got to be rules. Things were easy when she did her part and I did mine. Life's hard enough without mixing it all up like that. I can't do it. I just can't do it.

FRANK: She wanted to talk. If you ask me, we talked too much. I made her happy enough. Didn't screw around. I was home most every night. And we had *good* sex. Hey, it worked good enough for my folks. I just don't get it.

FRANKIE: They're making the rules up as they go along. Well, I'm just not made like that. I can't do it. I just can't do it. And to think that all this time, I used to worry that I wasn't enough of a man for her. Turns out, I wasn't enough of a *woman*. [*Beat.*] Ain't that a bitch?

FRANK: What the fuck. [*Pitching cards.*] Jack of Diamonds.

FRANKIE: [*Pitching cards.*] Six of Spades.

[*Lights up on* STRAIGHT SHEILA *and* LESBIAN SHEILA *who are upstage, center, making a grocery list, possibly miming looking in an imaginary refrigerator.*]

STRAIGHT SHEILA: Half gallon of milk.

LESBIAN SHEILA: A dozen eggs.

FRANK: Three of Hearts.

FRANKIE: Five of Clubs.

STRAIGHT SHEILA: Chocolate?

LESBIAN SHEILA: Chocolate. Chocolate chip.

[*We hear the sound of a baby crying offstage. Both* FRANK *and* FRANKIE *startle. This is new information.*]

LESBIAN SHEILA: [*Only mock aggravated.*] Not again. I'll go.

FRANK: What the fuck?!

STRAIGHT SHEILA: No, it's my turn.

FRANKIE: Wait a minute. [*The sound effect of a baby crying stops abruptly.*] That wasn't in the script.

STRAIGHT SHEILA: Well, [*Beat.*] not *yet*.

[FRANK *and* FRANKIE *try to take in this unexpected development. Beat. They all look at each other. This is uncharted territory.*]

LESBIAN SHEILA: [*Flustered.*] Where were we? [*Beat.*] Could you roll the tape again please?

[*We hear the sound of a baby crying again offstage.*]

LESBIAN SHEILA: [*Cont'd. Only mock aggravated.*] Not again. I'll go.

STRAIGHT SHEILA: No, it's my turn. [*She begins to exit.*]

LESBIAN SHEILA: Wait a minute.

STRAIGHT SHEILA: What?

LESBIAN SHEILA: Come here, you.

[*She reaches for* STRAIGHT SHEILA *and they kiss It is a deep, passionate kiss. Beat.*]

FRANKIE: Well, that just about does—

FRANK: [*Overlapping, abruptly.*] Could we have the house lights, *please*? [*The lights come up.*] Thank you.

LESBIAN SHEILA: [*Pleased with her performance.*] I think that went pretty well. What do you guys think?

STRAIGHT SHEILA: [*Aware of the others' feelings and trying to be considerate.*] I think it went fine, honey.

LESBIAN SHEILA: It did, didn't it?

FRANK: Well, one thing is obvious. *I* should have told the story. It would have been different if *I* had told the story.

STRAIGHT SHEILA: You think if you had, it would have come out differently?

FRANKIE: Well, it was a shot.

LESBIAN SHEILA: I'm sorry that you feel that way, Frank. But at least this way, everybody got their say. Don't you think everybody got, [*Correcting herself.*] I mean, had their say?

STRAIGHT SHEILA: Sheila, it was fair. If anything, it was more than fair.

FRANKIE: Easy for you to say. You got what you wanted.

LESBIAN SHEILA: It's not about who won or lost, Frankie. It's about why we came here tonight. We came here to tell our stories.

FRANKIE: That's not why I came here, Sheila and you know it. I thought maybe if I played your little game, it might have come out different.

LESBIAN SHEILA: [*With finality but real caring.*] Frankie, it's over. You know that. I'm sorry. [*Beat. To* STRAIGHT SHEILA.] Isn't there something you wanted to say?

STRAIGHT SHEILA: [*Sheepishly.*] Do I have to?

LESBIAN SHEILA: Of course not. But we did talk about it.

FRANK: Jesus Christ.

[*Beat.*]

STRAIGHT SHEILA: Frank.

FRANK: *What?*

LESBIAN SHEILA: Go on.

STRAIGHT SHEILA: I'm sorry, too.

FRANK: For what? For making me look like a jerk? These people think I'm a jerk.

STRAIGHT SHEILA: No. What I'm sorry about is that it didn't work out.

FRANK: You know, it really gets my goat that these people think I'm a jerk.

LESBIAN SHEILA: Nobody said you were a jerk, Frank.

FRANK: Bullshit. I think we should go back.

STRAIGHT SHEILA: What?!

[*They all react in disbelief.*]

FRANK: Like back to the dinner scene. I've got a few things to say there. You made me look like a moron just because I didn't feel like cooking some fancy five course meal. Well, I work hard. [*He has a new idea.*] If we go back, I could say that I'm tired when I come home. I didn't feel like cooking.

STRAIGHT SHEILA: [*Beginning to argue again.*] Well, I work hard, too. You're not the only one who works hard, Frank. I could have used a little help.

LESBIAN SHEILA: Honey, that's all in the past, now.

FRANKIE: Maybe telling these stories wasn't such a good idea, after all.

LESBIAN SHEILA: [*Exuberantly.*] I think telling these stories was great. I never got to tell my story before. [*To the audience as well as to* FRANKIE.] I'll admit it, I was a little nervous at first. But now that I did, I feel great. They know me.

FRANKIE: You think so? Look at them. What do you think they see?

STRAIGHT SHEILA: They see people, Frankie. Four different people. Four different points of view.

LESBIAN SHEILA: Yeah. That was the point of telling our stories. So they would hear what doesn't usually get said.

FRANKIE: Bullshit. We're just the token lesbians now. I'm the butch. You're the femme.

FRANK: Yeah. And I'm just a jerk.

STRAIGHT SHEILA: Come on, Frankie. I'm sorry that you were hurt. But don't take it out on us. Or on them. [*To the audience.*] Why can't you give them a little credit? They know that this is just one story. They know that we can't speak for all people. Why can't you just let people be people? [*Beat.*] You know something? It's a good thing that we're finished here because I am sick to death of you and your labels.

FRANKIE: Are you?

STRAIGHT SHEILA: Yeah.

FRANKIE: Are you now? You think they're just mine? [*Beat.*] Give it six months.

[*They all look nervously at each other and at the audience as the realization of these implications hit them. The lights slowly fade.*]

END PLAY

Susan Miller

THE ARCHITECTURE OF RELATIONSHIP

Tish Dace

Unlike her *Confessions of a Female Disorder*, Susan Miller's *Nasty Rumors and Final Remarks* does not dramatize a lesbian coming out or anybody dealing with her sexual orientation. Rather, Miller presents Max's lesbianism and Raleigh's bisexuality as givens, then writes about human relationships as well as the person serving as the fulcrum of those, a beautiful, witty, talented, lively woman who experiences a cerebral hemorrhage.

But first let's get our periods straight. This 1970s play reflects the ethos of the era termed "the sixties," because that freewheeling time really occurred in the seventies. Playwright Susan Miller figures "I probably wrote *Nasty Rumors and Final Remarks* in 1978, and the seventies were about breaking free of the fifties. It was an adventure—an ephemeral and dangerous one as it turns out—but one we had to pass through." For swinging urban dwellers, the seventies proved conducive to casual sex, multiple partners, even non-monogamous serious relationships. Quicksilver Raleigh, as free with her body as with her spirit, could suggest group sex and voyeurism and enjoy the love of both her live-in female lover and her more occasional male sweetheart because she lived and loved before AIDS, before rampant herpes, even before some of our more virulent sexually transmitted diseases had entered the consciousness of most people not employed in a medical profession.

Although such historical perspective provides a valuable entree to appreciating Raleigh's spirit and behavior, in another sense she and her experience prove timeless. Much as she brings herself and those around her to the edge, she also cherishes her relationships and therefore has attracted an extended family. "She counted on her primary relationships," Miller explains. Having eschewed conventional domestic arrangements and given birth to two children by two different men, Raleigh nevertheless has surrounded herself with people who love her. Max—a television producer but also a "traditional" woman—cherishes, nurtures, protects, and provides emotional support for her, but manages not to throw her out when Raleigh doesn't come home at night. "Max wants to take care of her and make a home for her, so Raleigh allows this and finds comfort in it," Miller confirms. Although Nicholas can't quite admit it, he'd also follow his impulse to keep his relationship with Raleigh monogamous. And Fran, conventional friend, married woman and mother, would never indulge in an affair.

Compared to these three, her chosen family, Raleigh's biological relatives seem remote from her daily concerns. Her mother clearly does not occupy even a peripheral place in her consciousness. Her daughter Cat we hear about briefly, but do not even meet, whereas we experience firsthand son T.K.'s bitterness and longing for connection with his mother. Asked why only the boy appears, Miller reflects "There's a sense in which Raleigh seems not a mother. There's a sense in which she's chosen another life. To have one child off somewhere reflects Raleigh's relationship with her children in that sometimes they seem to betray her. They would disappear or not show up or show up suddenly expecting the relationship to go back to a sort of normal mother/child relationship. It also puts the son in another context—that he has a sister somewhere with whom he can share something about their mother. I also wanted to show Raleigh has a difficult relationship with Cat. Raleigh chooses to remember her daughter as a child in her Brownie uniform. Those children have cost her so much pain she might not be there for them. She leads several different lives, as lots of us did in the seventies."

All Miller's plays concern complex human relationships, generally domestic relations, but in this one she began with the notion of the hospital waiting room and how "people are transformed in that space, the holiness of that space, the compression of that space. It resembles the magical space of the classroom in *Flux*. I was also struck by the fact some people can't just die and leave us." When the EEG shows flat brain activity, "it isn't over because the images, the sound of the voice, the effect on us remain. So I thought, if, in fact, somebody in a coma, as we've been given to understand might be the case, may be able to hear us, might even be able to see us, why not have that person interact with the people in the waiting room? And so I have Raleigh actually walk into the room and touch someone on the shoulder or say something, and then that person gets up and moves to another place on stage, which represents the past, and interacts with Raleigh. Also, I got a chance to get into the posture of someone in Raleigh's circumstances, to create what it might be like."

In addition to evoking the lingering presence of someone dying or recently deceased, Miller considered "what survivors need to deal with when they're suddenly left. Fran sees it as abandonment and complains 'You took all my stuff with you.' It's like, when we make ourselves known to other people, we're giving them parts of ourselves; we're giving them our history; we're saying words we're never going to say to someone else in exactly the same way—and that person is then in charge of it, becomes the storehouse of it. And when that person goes, dies, disappears, whatever, they've taken that with them. You can't get that back. You can't call up and say 'Hey, do you remember that conversation we had the other day? What did I say to you?'" Thus Miller observes the way in which a lover or friend or family member's death takes something of us, too.

Of course, the playwright also dramatizes how the bereaved grieve and the way in which communal grief bonds four people who previously may have resented each other for occupying Raleigh's time and affections. Even the bickering by her female partner, male partner, best friend, and son takes on a tone of domestic wrangling. Miller elaborates "I was really interested in the dynamic of how people in an extreme situation become a family. They all love this woman, but each has experienced her differently, so—who becomes the caretaker? Who gets the coffee? Who gets angry?"

Like all of us who have lived with others, Miller knows that territory. Married to a man as a young woman, the mother of a grown son, and the repository of wisdom derived from the bulk of her adult years spent with live-in or sleep-out female partners, Miller writes scenes recognizable, authentic. We see or read them and feel "Oh, yes. I experienced that betrayal. I said those words. I felt that embrace. I cried those tears. I burned with that resentment. I knew that elation."

Yet Raleigh does not come across as a generic Everywoman. Miller terms her "almost a creature of the night; her demons deny her much light heartedness." Her protagonist shares with the dramatist's own seventies' self an edginess, a wariness about opening her heart to others. Miller speculates that her early characters such as Raleigh and *Flux*'s Jess, resulted from "a message I got from the world, that if you do cross boundaries, if you get too close, if you are intimate, things will explode. Just as Jess tries to change the architecture of the classroom, Raleigh tries to change the architecture of relationships."

On the trajectory of Miller's life and work, however, intimacy and commitment have assumed a new primacy, as her second Obie-Award winning play, *My Left Breast*, makes clear. Bereft of a relationship, "Susan" recounts "I was sitting in a cafe, and a man with ordinary difficulties is complaining 'our water heater is on the fritz.' Just like that he says it. 'Our something isn't working, and *we* are worrying about it.' I want to say 'cherish the day your car broke down, the water pump soured, the new bed didn't arrive on time. Celebrate the time you got lost and maps failed. On your knees to this domestic snafu, you blessed *pair*!'" Miller adds, "The notion of every day with one other person, that coupling has taken on a richness and a magic for a lot of us."

Although Miller's work—particularly *Cross-Country* and *My Left Breast*—seems sprinkled with autobiographical elements, *Nasty Rumors and Final Remarks* does not specifically reflect Miller's own life. She wrote it when her son was still a baby, she had not herself experienced a coma or died, she had not lived through the seventies from the perspective of a teenager, and so on. The dramatist regards Raleigh as a character she had to create, observe, and, yes, inhabit, but in Raleigh's mode. "It's a Raleigh death. It's got to be her coma, in her way, with her style, and her humor. That was the challenge. I was much more aligned with the central characters in *Flux* and *Cross-Country*. Yet even in somewhat autobiographical plays, there's craft involved. You're making choices and creating a structure, but life doesn't happen that way. Even in *My Left Breast*."

This one-person show in which Miller creates herself as a character shows how Miller has evolved on the terminology of sexual orientation. Although once relatively private, until recently preferring the word "gay" to "lesbian," she refers to *My Left Breast*'s "Susan" as a "Jewish bisexual lesbian mom." She describes Raleigh, "if we must label her, as bisexual. I think these things are fluid, and if a person has once loved a man, that ought not to be negated by some term later on which says this cannot be the case. Look at filmmaker Maria Maggenti. She still calls herself a lesbian although now she's with a man. Max, on the other hand, does not have relationships with men. There! I've authenticated the play's presence in a lesbian anthology." The reader must remember Miller is not doctrinaire, and labels and sexual politics do not figure as issues in this play.

Rather than espousing some party line, the forthright Miller has always adhered to a searing honesty about human fears and failures. The characters may practice denial or they may speak the truth, but whatever *they* do it renders ineffectual our efforts to evade our own personal truths.

In order to receive this strategy's full impact, the reader must strive to see *Nasty Rumors and Final Remarks* in the theatre of her mind's eye. The playwright has written extensively for television and film and has served as story editor of others' screenplays. Her histrionic imagination crafts a quintessentially cinematic style, a structure of jump cuts, simultaneous segments, and time so fluid that "flashback" does not do it justice. Although Miller acknowledges a fondness for the novel as an art form and often asks her characters to narrate as well as enact, few of her plays progress in a directly linear fashion. For all these reasons, anyone who reads this play rather than watching it mounted must visualize the flow of life upon the stage. Robert Yodice's set for the Public Theater production by the New York Shakespeare Festival contained three hallways which served as corridors of the mind quite as effectively as places in which the characters might literally wander. That set especially helped spectators to appreciate the manner in which the woman who has brought these people into her orbit both moves among them and no longer inhabits their world.

Jean Paul Sartre based his *Being and Nothingness* on the premise "being precedes essence," for we cannot know anyone fully until her life has ended, thereby precluding her making any more character-revealing choices. Miller gives us the opportunity to know Raleigh fully because this charismatic actor by play's end has finished creating herself. Thus this play, like most of Miller's others, dramatizes endings—of relationships such as motherhood, friendship, and love affairs, of a career, of inhabiting her apartment, of anticipating the future, of the tumult she attracts, and of her life. That termination the playwright renders especially poignant by an understated and economical device which wrenches our hearts more than wailing would. But let the reader discover this for herself.

PRODUCTIONS OF PLAYS BY SUSAN MILLER

No One Is Exactly 23. In *Pyramid I*, 1968; produced University Park, Pennsylvania, 1968.

Daddy, and A Commotion of Zebras. Produced New York, Alice Theatre, 1970.

Confessions of a Female Disorder. In *Gay Plays*, Avon, 1979. Produced Los Angeles, Mark Taper Forum, 1973; Waterford, Conn., O'Neill National Playwrights Conference, 1973.

Flux. Unpublished. Produced New York, Phoenix Repertory Co., 1975; London, American Repertory Co., 1976; New York, N.Y. Shakespeare Festival, 1977; New York, Second Stage, 1982.

Cross Country. In *West Coast Plays*, I, 1977. Produced Los Angeles, Mark Taper Forum, March-June 1976; New York, Interart Theatre, 1977.

Nasty Rumors and Final Remarks. Produced New York, N. Y. Shakespeare Festival, 1979 (Obie Award; Finalist Susan Smith Blackburn Prize); Chicago, St. Nicholas Theatre, 1980.

Arts and Leisure. Unpublished. Produced Los Angeles, CAST Theatre, 1985.

Repairs. In *Facing Forward*, Broadway Play Publishing, 1995. Produced New York, Home for Contemporary Theatre and Art, 1989.

For Dear Life. Unpublished. Produced New York, N.Y. Shakespeare Festival, 1989 (Finalist Susan Smith Blackburn Prize).

It's Our Town, Too. In *The Best American Short Plays 1992-93*, Applause Books. Produced Los Angeles, Fountainhead Theatre Co, Nov.-Dec. 1992.

My Left Breast. In *Plays from the 1994 Humana Festival of New American Plays*, Smith and Krause, and *The Best American Short Plays of 1993-94*, Applause Books. Produced Louisville, Actors Theatre of Louisville Humana Festival of New Plays, 1994; New York, Watermark's Wordfire Festival at the Ohio Theatre, 1995; Austin, Frontera/Hyde Park Theatre, 1995; Philadelphia, Walnut Street Theatre, January 1996. Obie Award, shared Susan Smith Blackburn Prize, 1995.

Nasty Rumors and Final Remarks

CHARACTERS

RALEIGH: A charismatic woman in her late 30s, with ancient wounds and a history. She's an actress, a mother, and lover of Max and Nicholas.

MAX: A woman in her early 30s, who possesses a dry wit. She lives with Raleigh, and is a television news producer.

NICHOLAS: A man in his 40s—a writer. A wry observer with well maintained defenses. A boy again and swept away with Raleigh, her literary potential as well as her actual self.

FRAN: A woman in her late 30s or 40s. A worrier, an avid reader, bound to tradition. She is Raleigh's nurturing best freind.

T.K.: Raleigh's son—17 to 19. Lost.

DOCTOR: A man—any age.

WOMAN: In her early 60s. Appears only at the beginning of Act II.

ACT I

The major portion of the stage is dark, except for the house area, where RALEIGH *sits, smoking and holding a telephone. She is listening to* NICHOLAS, *who we see speaking to her from an area of the stage which represents his cabin. He is in mid-sentence, reading to her from the typewritten pages of his manuscript.*

NICHOLAS: [*Reading.*] " . . . and the burial place—one expected majesty. She preferred the Lexington Avenue entrance to Bloomingdales. That window. Cloaked in a trenchcoat, menacing the other statues. A fedora pulled over her eyes. She had the structure to carry it off. The cold beauty. The stone posture. The treacherous angles of her face. She could carry this off without a trace of life. Something to fire the spirit of a lonely window dresser. Only now and then, a passer-by, someone who'd never even shopped at Bloomingdales, would suspect a corpse. The Egyptians were on to something." [*He stops, waiting for* RALEIGH'S *response.*]

RALEIGH: [*After a beat.*] What color is the trenchcoat?

NICHOLAS: Tan. Were you laughing? I couldn't tell. What were you doing when I was reading it to you?

RALEIGH: [*Keeping him on edge a while longer.*] I was chewing on a fingernail. And I was wondering what shirt you were wearing.

NICHOLAS: The plaid flannel.

RALEIGH: You don't even own one. You should, but you don't. What do you look like when you're working?

NICHOLAS: Never mind that.

RALEIGH: Never mind that. "What do you think? Do you like it?"

NICHOLAS: The usual disclaimers first. It's only—

RALEIGH: [*Joining him, as they say in unison:*] —It's only a rough draft.

NICHOLAS: And I don't like the names of my characters. They all seem to end in EEEE. So don't even bother scolding me for that. But otherwise, what do you think? Do you like it?

RALEIGH: It's libelous for starters. There's a person in there who bears a striking resemblance to someone you promised you'd never write about.

NICHOLAS: I lied.

RALEIGH: Chapter Five was hard to understand. Chapter Seven was my most favorite. The first sentence I'll probably dream about. And I think you're a son of a bitch to steal my secrets and give them to some character I won't even get to play, but you're so fucking good, I forgive you. When are you coming back? And Nick, baby, I'm not sure about the title.

NICHOLAS: The title? That's the best part. I'm terrific with titles. It's endings. I can't get off the page worth shit.

RALEIGH: What are you wearing, really?

NICHOLAS: Corduroy.

RALEIGH: Perfect. [*Beat.*] I want you to say it over to me. Every word.

NICHOLAS: You liked it then.

RALEIGH: There's only one thing that worries me. The bleak part. There's a lot of bleak in this one.

NICHOLAS: Humorously bleak?

RALEIGH: No. [*Pause.*] I'm sorry. Don't ponder. I shouldn't have said anything. Every truly significant book should have its bleakness. I was just thinking about you, personally. That maybe you aren't as—happy as you used to be.

NICHOLAS: Who is?

RALEIGH: Well, yes. I know. But, it struck me in one of my own several, empty places and I got scared. It's such a beautiful book otherwise, Nicky. It's a splendid piece of work.

NICHOLAS: You know the page that comes after the title — the title you don't like that I think is one of the best I've ever come up with—well, the page that comes after it, where the author always puts something blatant and sappy like—*this book is dedicated to Marge and Bill and my children who were so patient*—well, right at the bottom of that page, sort of off center, it says: *for R.* I hope you don't mind. Especially since it follows a title you aren't sure about. I only used your initial, but it's still a dedication any way you look at it, even in lower case letters.

RALEIGH: [*Visibly moved, but trying not to cry.*] That's a terrible thing to do to me. What does a person say to something like that? Christ, Nicky.

NICHOLAS: It's nothing. It just gives you the right to criticize my titles.

RALEIGH: Is it for the whole book? The dedication—is it for the whole book?

NICHOLAS: Only Chapters 2 through 6. The rest go to my aunt in Cleveland.

RALEIGH: I don't want to hear from you again until you've finished it. And I think Gilda's a good name for one of those characters. Or if that reminds you of Rita Hayworth, just call her Rita. Is it cold there?

NICHOLAS: Raw. Now what about you? Have you heard anything about P's film yet?

RALEIGH: It's official. I will be doing an interesting, though thinly written part originally intended for P's wife, who declined because she's smarter than he is. They think I'm 29 or 30 and the character's name is *Britain*, if that gives you any idea. We start shooting next week.

NICHOLAS: For Christsakes, that's terrific, Raleigh. I hope you have a good attitude. Don't fuck it this time.

RALEIGH: You'd be proud of me. Anyway it's the best attitude I could muster up in December. You're missing the whole season, lucky man. The lights are up. People are killing turkeys.

NICHOLAS: What? You're not excited about the picture? C'mon. This is news, honey.

RALEIGH: I don't want to think about it. When it actually happens, then I'll let you buy me a very old wine and take me to one of your literary hangouts. [*Beat.*] It's cold here, too. Your kisses would be a relief.

NICHOLAS: The general store is running out of coffee. I'll be back soon.

RALEIGH: Nicholas— [*She stops, then almost too quietly, says:*] Thank you for the book.

[*They do not hang up immediately. For all their witty exchange, the moment is important, the relationship is fragile and perishable. They actually care more than they ever will admit. After a beat, they both hang up, stand for a moment. Then each goes back to the phone, picking it up as if to call one another again. But, simultaneously, they both put the phone handle down, off the hook.*

Lights up on Cafeteria. The DOCTOR *sits alone at a table. He picks at his food. There is a fatigue which he never quite gives in to. He directs himself to the audience.*]

DOCTOR: People die here. You can expect it. At least one in a batch. Whole families sometimes. The hospital has become—well, it's just preliminary, you know. The farewell. The shock of it. The fatigue. We've got death on our hands here and no one knows what the hell to do with it. [*Pause.*] These eggs are bloody cold. [*Shouts, as if to cafeteria personnel.*] EGGS ARE BLOODY COLD!

[*House Area.* RALEIGH *is off balance. Unsteady. Something is happening to her. She talks as if she were in shock, and there is a strange rhythm in the way she speaks. Perhaps she moves around her space, trying to find something to steady her.*]

RALEIGH: Suddenly. The whole thing. Stops. Suddenly. The whole thing...stops. Noise. Traffic. Groaning. Earwax. [*Pause.*] Suddenly the whole thing— [*Faster.*] Suddenly the whole thing— [*Beat.*] I have a terrible headache.

[*From the cafeteria. The* DOCTOR *speaks to himself, almost as if he were rehearsing.*]

DOCTOR: I'm sorry...to have to...tell you this.

[*Lights up on the corridor and lounge.* FRAN *has been waiting in the lounge as* MAX *enters.*]

FRAN: Where was he?

MAX: Hiding out. Some stupid little town. He's going to get the earliest flight.

FRAN: Is he ok?

MAX: I don't think Nicky believed me. He kept bitching about the weather and how nobody in the Midwest understands a word he says.

FRAN: You want a cup of coffee? Max?

MAX: I never wanted to go on this goddam vacation. I knew I should have stayed. But Raleigh said— [*She falls silent.*]

FRAN: She was fine. She was going to start work. How could you know?

MAX: God, how she must hate Christmas to do such a thing!

[*A beat.* MAX *starts to laugh, then begins to sob. In house area,* RALEIGH *pours herself a glass of wine and begins to observe the others. In the cafeteria, the* DOCTOR, *alone, still working on his speech.*]

DOCTOR: I'm sorry to have to tell you this.

[*In House.* RALEIGH *picks up phone and dials. She is still holding her wine glass, and talks as if she were ordering room service.*]

RALEIGH: I'd like an ambulance, please. My head hurts. Oh, and would you ask them not use the sirens. It would only disturb the neighbors, and I had hoped to avoid that, if you don't mind. [*She hangs up.*]

[*In Lounge.*]

FRAN: [*To* MAX.] You've got to eat.

MAX: Why? Why do I have to do anything I did before. If Raleigh can't eat, I don't want to eat. I don't want to *need* to goddam eat.

[*The* DOCTOR *enters Lounge.*]

DOCTOR: I'm sorry to have to tell you this. It's very grim, I'm afraid. She's had a massive cerebral hemorrhage. There isn't much of a chance ever with that kind of thing. We had to drill a hole and what's happening now is that the fluid is draining, so the pressure on her brain is being relieved. But she's in a fourth state coma. [*Pause.*] I'm sorry.

MAX: I should make phone calls, then. I better do that.

DOCTOR: We need to have a relative. Can you contact a relative?

MAX: She had sinus headaches.

[*From House.*]

RALEIGH: [*Speaking to audience.*] Her head was actually bleeding, but the paramedics suspected drugs and they were very rude. "You want us to call someone, you're gonna have to give us a number." *Assholes.* She never could remember anyone's number when she was healthy and sober; how in God's name did they expect her to do it with a coma coming on?

[*In Lounge.*]

DOCTOR: I'll leave you alone.

[*He exits, down Corridor. As the* DOCTOR *moves up one corridor,* RALEIGH *moves down another corridor. She is wandering now, trying to find her way in a new state of consciousness. She moves past a spot on stage, which may simply be a lighted area, or a door, representing the intensive care room.*]

RALEIGH: Looking down, that's how it seemed. She was maybe on the ceiling, looking down at herself, poor baby. And she had, for the first time, but just for a moment, genuine affection for her body. Strong fucker. Even when she tried to get out of her own accord, it had no mercy. It would continue. Her skin was—she usually looked pale, and now, wouldn't you know it, there was color in her cheeks. Perhaps someone—the nurse, probably—applied lotion. Knew how dry—how it hurt if she didn't use a lot of lotion.

[*In Lounge.*]

FRAN: She ought to get the first issue of the Italian *Vogue* sometime next week. That's when the subscription starts, I'm almost positive. I probably should've gotten her the French *Vogue*, I don't know. It's a gorgeous magazine. [*Pause.*] Well, this is charming. This is a lovely way to spend the last of days. [*Beat.*] I should call my children. [*Beat.*] No. They're fine. [*Beat.*] So. When it comes to her house now...what? [*Beat.*] Of course, it isn't the kind of magazine where—We would take these quizzes. Raleigh had to call me up with these magazine things, these questionnaires. We aren't going to have that kind of experience with the Italian *Vogue*, of course. I should call my children. Tell them something. [*Beat.*] *What kind of lover are you? Do you A: Make love with the lights on? B: Dim the lights? C: Let him undress you?*

[*Lights off Lounge, Up on Corridor.*]

RALEIGH: [*With a sense of discovery and recognition.*] *She . . . is . . . me.* [*Pause.*] This has to do with pronouns. Not with verbs. Someone can't *do* anything anymore. It has to do with that. Who can't *verb* anymore. [*Pause. She tries to talk and it comes out jumbled, inarticulate.*] Ainebtgubs— [*She tries again.*] Thirnlmedop— [*Surprised.*] *She* can't speak as well as I can. [*Tries determinedly again.*] Brrr— Brrnitol— [*Pause.*] Sounds like a Bergman film. [*Pause.*] If we can't say our words right, there's not much future in it. [*Pause.*] *She . . .* feels a lot like me. [*Raleigh continues walking. Singing.*] My body lies over the ocean. My body lies over the sea. My body likes over the ocean, oh bring back my—

[*She stops abruptly, then walks to Cafeteria, where the* DOCTOR *is sitting at his table.*]

RALEIGH: [*Cont'd.*] I wonder if I'm doing it right.

DOCTOR: I wouldn't worry.

RALEIGH: Gracefully.

DOCTOR: Well, one likes to think it can be done, but it's rather like the other end of the spectrum. Birth, I mean. Clumsy. We don't have much to go on either time.

RALEIGH: Was I crying or anything? When they brought me in. I don't remember. How did I act?

DOCTOR: You didn't appreciate our methods. We had to fight with you. One of the ambulance drivers got quite a nasty bruise. He said, "We're trying to save your life, lady." And you said, "Oh, please!" Just like that. "Oh, please!" as if you were bored by the whole idea.

RALEIGH: Maybe it should be big. Yes, to die big! And noisy. Make a real commotion out of it. [*She laughs.*] That's something. To think you'd have to worry about doing the last thing you ever do—*properly*. God. Well, I am a Southern girl, sweet Jesus. I might soil my dress. Oh lord, I might do a naughty thing. I might burp right out loud. Shame on me. [*Pause. Abruptly, she gets up from her seat.*] I don't like wanting it. How it sticks to you.

[*She walks away, but listens to* FRAN *and* MAX, *as the lights go up in Lounge.*]

MAX: There's no will.

FRAN: Of course not. No religion either. How do we get our comfort.

[RALEIGH *moving closer to Lounge, talks to her friends.*]

RALEIGH: About what's going on. The light— the amber gel is fine. But what if it doesn't last? And the demons—the way it was before—my own demons— follow me through to the death? [*Beat.*] Is that what this is? Am I having my death? One minute I'm sure and then . . . it's so familiar. [*Beat.*] Graves are next to other graves. It's like the suburbs. My friends know better.

FRAN: [*To* MAX.] So what happens? In case?

MAX: The kids get whatever there is.

FRAN: They'll kill each other. You better forge one.

MAX: I have a will. I left everything to Raleigh.

[*Light change. A kind of conversation begins between* RALEIGH *and* MAX, *though they are in different areas of the stage. We see* MAX *speak, as if she were remembering. They don't look at one another as they speak. And toward the end of this dialogue, the memory moves* MAX *up a Corridor, out of the Lounge.*]

RALEIGH: Don't depend on me.

MAX: So who'd be crazy enough to do that?

RALEIGH: Just checking. I mean, that's part of the premise, right?

MAX: And the other part is that you *can*... are allowed to depend on me, right?

RALEIGH: Wanna take it back?

MAX: Just checking.

RALEIGH: Just don't lose touch with your old friends, Max. Because when you've had enough of me, you'll want to ring them up.

MAX: [*To herself.*] Don't lose touch with your old friends, Max.

[*Lights change, as* MAX *disappears from Lounge, and walks down another Corridor, into House, where* RALEIGH *is now waiting.* MAX *enters, as if she has just come home from work.* RALEIGH *greets her.*]

RALEIGH: Two tickets to Chicago. Your treat.

MAX: How can I go? I can't go. I'm working.

RALEIGH: I'm unemployed. You have to go.

MAX: They're changing the whole format of the show. I have meetings every day. Honey—

RALEIGH: All the terrible things that go wrong with me are going to go wrong with you. Ulcers. Coronaries. Impotence. This trip might save your life.

MAX: You'll drag me to every bar in the city. We won't sleep for days. My life? My life won't be worth shit.

RALEIGH: I thought we'd take the train. Get a compartment.

MAX: Oh. Don't. Don't do this.

RALEIGH: I have to get away. I want you to come with me.

MAX: Why do I get the feeling your invitation will not pass this way again?

RALEIGH: Because you know me to be the vindictive slut that I am.

MAX: Why Chicago, anyway? Why not some place pretty?

RALEIGH: Don't look a gift horse in the mouth.

MAX: I thought you said I was paying.

RALEIGH: But I'm initiating.

MAX: How about the mountains?

RALEIGH: I can't breathe there. Besides, I like cities.

MAX: Then let's just go to a Holiday Inn. You can still smell the cars, and I can go to work in the morning.

RALEIGH: [*Beat.*] I don't want to be in town for my birthday.

MAX: Ah. [*Beat.*] Well, don't worry. No one's throwing a party. No one would dare to send a card. You won't even notice.

RALEIGH: It's not because I'm going to be 38. I never liked my birthday, even when I was going to be ten.

MAX: You have no customs, do you?

RALEIGH: I have circumstance.

MAX: What is it? The cake with the candles. The trains around the Christmas tree? I mean, what exactly bothers you about all of it?

RALEIGH: It tosses me. I lose description. So many reunions on so many specific days of so many years. But nobody looks familiar. I just...I have no prayer for these holidays

MAX: And I want all of it. I cook turkeys at Thanksgiving. Good ones. And I keep family albums. I need to know I have a connection to people. You won't acknowledge that you do.

RALEIGH: I was 8. I had a dog. It wasn't supposed to follow me on this particular path, which was dangerous, I guess. But he came along. And he was killed. The damn dog died on me. I hate dogs. If he had any kind of loyalty, he would have stayed at home. Animals don't like me anymore. They know I think they're crazy and dumb. Animals love you. Everything loves you. Garbage men. And moving men. Plumbers. I'll bet no dog ever died with you around. Waitresses. They love you. They always serve you first.

MAX: Why do you care if the garbage man likes me or not?

RALEIGH: What am I? Medusa? It's either "Hey Lady" or they don't look at me at all. For you they do favors.

MAX: I'm one of the guys. I give them beer. You have other things on your mind.

RALEIGH: I want to be liked. I really do.

MAX: [*Laughing.*] Save me.

RALEIGH: It's perfectly human.

MAX: But you're not. I mean, you don't exactly participate in the ordinary. It's either a grand passion or a vendetta. People don't know what to do with that.

RALEIGH: I go to restaurants. I have dealings with clerks in department stores. They never go well. I try. What's your secret? That smile? Those teeth you flash? What?

MAX: You want to fight with me. You're picking a fight with me. I'm not sure why, but I can tell. My jaw is beginning to lock.

RALEIGH: No, baby. I just want to know what I do wrong. Why do telephone operators hang up on me and never return my dimes?

MAX: All right. It's coming. I'm going to get it anyway. [*Beat.*] The other night, for instance. In the restaurant. You were very hungry and the waitress was hassled. I said thank you every time she moved a plate. You glared. Or you didn't look at her at all. She wasn't a person to you. She was a function. The food came and went and you didn't know how it got there or who took it away.

RALEIGH: You're telling me I'm rude.

MAX: No, you're too polite to be rude. You're just oblivious.

RALEIGH: See, that's why you need to go away with me. To be my interpreter.

MAX: The thing you're missing here is, I may get served on time and have my garbage removed neatly, but let's not weigh it against the occasional limousine that shows up at your door, or the genius or two who have sworn themselves—*pledged* themselves to your life. So what's *your* secret?

RALEIGH: That's not the same. It's not the real world. I don't trust any of it.

MAX: You opened your eyes and looked at somebody in a certain way and let yourself be known. A sorcerer. A hitch-hiker, maybe. And whoever saw this, you gave permission to see this. You trusted. You had to, Raleigh.

RALEIGH: I don't give you enough.

MAX: I used to think that.

RALEIGH: It's easier than it's ever been for me. You make it easy.

MAX: I try and keep it light.

RALEIGH: I would . . . give you something else . . . .

MAX: I've had a change of heart. Or maybe it's the change of life. I don't know. You're here. You could just as easily be somewhere else. And that's the only thing I worry about. Even if you don't show up for a couple of nights, your clothes are in the closet. And your skin cream is on the sink. So . . .

RALEIGH: I'll take care of you in your old age.

[MAX *laughs, amused by such a preposterous offer.*]

RALEIGH: [*Cont'd.*] Of course, I don't think any of us is going to have an old age. [*Pause.*] Maybe Nicholas. Yeah, Nicky will. He'll be stuck alone in a garret. Nicky's definitely gonna be old someday.

MAX: Fuck Nicky.

RALEIGH: Be nice.

MAX: He's a thorn in my heart. He's a clear and present danger.

RALEIGH: I think the three of us should go to bed together.

MAX: Have you fucked his wife yet?

RALEIGH: Oooh, that's my girl.

MAX: Why do you insist that your lovers be friends?

RALEIGH: Because you're all terrific people and fucking has nothing to do with it. Fucking doesn't last. It isn't there in the middle of a conversation when one person says something intelligent and someone else appreciates it. Fucking has nothing to do with it.

MAX: It has to do with where you put your hand on someone's body when you're having that conversation. Fucking is around. It's noticeable.

RALEIGH: It passes.

MAX: Nicholas and I try. We do our best.

RALEIGH: I know.

MAX: Other people don't behave so well. Other people think we're unholy.

RALEIGH: I love you. Does it matter who else I love? [*Beat. With tongue in cheek:*] I always introduce you. I always make sure you're introduced.

[*Light change* MAX *leaves House, and walks up Corridor, where she stops. From two different areas on stage,* MAX *and* RALEIGH *speak.*]

MAX: *A Sadomasochistic Dream:* I lay the equipment on the bed. There are handcuffs. Ties of leather. And a whip. She strokes the whip. And laughs.

RALEIGH: This is wicked, you know.

MAX: I am thrilled with her disapproval. "Don't you like my toys?"

RALEIGH: You were naughty to buy them without telling me. You'll have to be punished.

MAX: For every act of disloyalty. Every betrayal. Every success that isn't hers, I beg forgiveness.

RALEIGH: Very bad.

MAX: Above me, with a child's heart, she grows strict. "I am sorry, darling."

RALEIGH: How? How sorry?

MAX: "So very very—"

RALEIGH: What will you do to make it up to me?

MAX: "Anything. I'll do —"

RALEIGH: Anything.

MAX: Now the swift penance. Bringing us both to our consequence. There is trust in this arrangement. We are only having a game. Nobody's hurt. Nobody suffers. That happens outside the room. The secret marries us. When I wake, it's the hospital. And *she* is strapped to the bed.

[*Lights come up on Lounge.* T.K., RALEIGH's *son, stands at the entrance.*]

RALEIGH: [*To audience.*] She saw her child, shivering in his pea coat. Motherless. At twenty, one ought to be motherless. Their last meeting had not gone well.

[*Lights up on Lounge.* T.K. *is shivering, his hands deep into the pockets of his oversized coat.*]

FRAN: [*Going toward the boy.*] I'll take you to see her.

T.K.: She's done with me.

MAX: It's nothing personal, T.K.

FRAN: C'mon, I'll take you.

MAX: This isn't happening on account of you, T.K. Sorry to horn in on your guilt.

FRAN: Max! [*To* T.K.] Would you like some coffee or something?

[T.K. *shakes his head, meaning no.*]

FRAN: Sit down.

[*She leads him to a seat.*]

FRAN: [*Cont'd.*] I'll get you something.

[RALEIGH *comes over and sits on the arm of a chair or sofa, slightly behind her son. He doesn't see her. She touches his hair lightly.*]

RALEIGH: There's not much comfort in a room full of my friends, is there? What are you going to do now, poor darling? [*Pause.*] Never mind. I don't want to know.

FRAN: T.K., the Doctor's been waiting to talk to you. Do you think you can handle it now? Or should I tell him—

RALEIGH: [*Cont'd.*] I mean, that's the point, isn't it? Not to know. Whether you have one friend in the whole damn world. Or a place to sleep. Or scars on your wrist. This is my emergency, not yours. And frankly it's going a lot better than any of yours ever did. [*Pause.*] You might suffer less if you knew that.

[NICHOLAS *enters, stops at Lounge entrance.* RALEIGH *sees him and retreats to the House area.*]

NICHOLAS: So. [*Beat.*] You're all here. I guess it's no publicity stunt. Jesus. [*Pause.*] I'd like to see her.

FRAN: I'll walk with you.

NICHOLAS: This is crazy. I just talked to her. Well, Nicholas, that's classic. [*Pause.*] T.K.'s here, huh? Someone give that kid a drink. He looks terrible. [*He moves towards* MAX.] What can you tell me?

MAX: Just what I said on the phone. Nothing new.

NICHOLAS: But she's alive.

MAX: She's breathing. On a respirator.

FRAN: [*Trying to get him out of the room.*] We'll take a walk.

NICHOLAS: This place looks familiar. Weren't we here before?

MAX: The pills.

NICHOLAS: Which one of us? Never mind. I think it was a different floor. [*Pause.*] It's too quiet here. I think what I'll do is get us some champagne and we'll tell stories. How about that? You like that? I think that's what I'm gonna do.

[*Light change. From House Area.*]

RALEIGH: She loved writers.

[*From Lounge.*]

T.K.: She loves writers.

[*From House.*]

RALEIGH: When she was a child and held to the circumstance to which she was born, they gave her another place to go. For this she loved them. And when she grew to be a woman, took these authors to bed.

[*From Lounge.*]

T.K.: [*Directed toward* MAX.] At least Nick never took any shit.

[*From House.*]

RALEIGH: She wanted to see him make love to another man.

[NICHOLAS *joins her in House Area, where* RALEIGH *has setup a game of back-gammon.*]

NICHOLAS: I'm not attracted to men.

RALEIGH: But they are to you.

NICHOLAS: I can't.

RALEIGH: Would you like to watch me with someone else?

NICHOLAS: In my fantasies.

RALEIGH: I could arrange it.

NICHOLAS: Eventually, you'll give me a heart attack.

RALEIGH: Have you ever been with a whore? [*Beat.*] Could you get a woman for me? A prostitute?

NICHOLAS: Christ. It makes me want you.

RALEIGH: Say my name to me. Call me—

NICHOLAS: Lovely.

RALEIGH: Call me bitch.

NICHOLAS: [*As he moves out of the House back toward Lounge.*] Lovely bitch.

RALEIGH: [*To audience.*] She might end the affair. But she would never stop buying his books. Or recommending them to her friends.

[*Lounge.* NICHOLAS *has now joined the others.*]

T.K.: You all fucked her. I'm in a room with my mother's fuckers. We had only a hugging relationship, Raleigh and I. Did you ever meet my father? I'm supposed to look like him.

MAX: Is Cat coming?

T.K.: I couldn't get her on the phone. Out somewhere. She'll probably never come back. Cat and I almost made it once, but I was too passive. She could mess around for years thinking Mom's alive. [*Pause.*] If nobody wants to talk to me, that's all right. Just remember something. Her children. We're first. She always put us first.

MAX: *You* remember it.

T.K.: What do you tell her? I want to say it, too. I want her to smile like that to me. [*Pause. No one speaks.*] It's all right. You don't have to. [*Pause.*] I just want her books. That's the only thing. She said I could have the books.

[*From another area:*]

RALEIGH: [*To audience.*] You remember what it was like before you had sexual intercourse? The way it was to have something forbidden and terrible. All those years. And then to assign one Sunday for a wedding. And in a few hours, it just didn't matter anymore. [*Pause.*] Dying is like that, I think.

[*Corridor. MAX, FRAN, and NICHOLAS are gathered here. In different postures. Their conversation is almost choral.*]

MAX: She was alone. That's the way she knew it would be.

FRAN: No one was with her.

MAX: They took a gram of cocaine, but left her identification. They never went back to find out who she was. Although they will probably go back to arrest her.

FRAN: She was supposed to be at a rehearsal. She didn't show up. Someone called. We got worried. Not like her. Work is everything.

MAX: She's disappeared before, but not if there was work. Sometimes she didn't answer her phone, but there were signs. Of life. Of something living, even if it were hiding out.

NICHOLAS: This time? What? This time—

FRAN: Nobody knew.

NICHOLAS: Maybe she left the country, changed her name.

FRAN: I broke in. The apartment seemed at first to be in order. She wasn't there. That was good. I was relieved. She wasn't there. Then everything in the apartment started to look different. I saw things I didn't see at first. There was. First, her rings. Wallet. Purse. They were all on the dresser. She never went out without those things. Then I saw her bed. It scared me. I called the police. They checked their lists and called me back. And said she was in the hospital. That's all I knew. The hospital.

[*Light change.*]

RALEIGH: [*Wandering.*] Nobody would tell her where she was . . . *exactly*. This wasn't clear. She could not distinguish whether she was still one among them or one apart. Nicholas would, for instance, touch her hand. And this feeling would summon her. Nicholas would leave the room and she followed him down the hall, though he didn't show any sign of knowing. Perhaps he knew but couldn't make any sense of it. She had an urge on one of these expeditions to urinate and tried to find the Ladies' Room. But a fear came instead. That she wouldn't be able to do it the old way. She stopped thinking about it, and the urge passed.

[*Lights up on Cafeteria. NICHOLAS and the DOCTOR sit at table.*]

NICHOLAS: Doctor, tell me, when you're dealing with the brain—the functions and disorders of the brain, well, what can you do when it comes to that? I mean, on the outside, we hear a lot about right sidedness and left sidedness and I was wondering if it was her right side that caught this piece of bad luck, if you couldn't just pluck it out and let the other half take over? [*Pause.*] I mean I read *Psychology Today.*

[*The* DOCTOR *isn't amused.*]

NICHOLAS: [*Cont'd.*] Please. I'm just having my fun. I can't talk to anyone . . . connected. You seemed . . . well, go on, finish your coffee. [*Pause. He won't let up.*] Hemorrhage . . . sounds so bad. It's kind of the last straw, isn't it? Complete refusal to submit to any more pressure. Perfect for Raleigh.

DOCTOR: You shouldn't worry about the pain. Quite naturally, the consciousness succumbs and, well, the route to fear and suffering are quickly cut off.

NICHOLAS: How do you know? For sure?

DOCTOR: It's what I think. It seems.

NICHOLAS: Lousy coffee. [*Beat.*] Are you Australian?

DOCTOR: Afraid not.

NICHOLAS: I was married to an American.

DOCTOR: But, aren't you? American?

NICHOLAS: Yes, but she is really. Enjoys it.

DOCTOR: Have all of you stayed the night?

NICHOLAS: Oh yes. But we're old crisis buddies. Ready for emergency. Know which hospitals have 24 hr. service. When the phone rings at 5 a.m., you say "I'll be there. Which one?" You have the sweats for awhile and your teeth chatter, but you manage to get your clothes on and drive, all the time bargaining for recovery. Giving up property, pleasures, whatever it takes. Just cancel the tragedy. It's a real love story, if you're interested.

DOCTOR: That's a strong lady. Hasn't given it up, I don't think. I would. I fight bed. Always have. Since I was a small one. Might miss something. But give me the warm blanket, lift me up, put me on cool sheets and the sleep comes. You have to deliver some people.

NICHOLAS: Raleigh had insomnia.

DOCTOR: Yes, I expect so.

NICHOLAS: I don't trust you, Doctor. You've got a good face and sorrow in it, but you wouldn't tell me if somebody fucked up around here. Seventeen hours and nobody goes back to find out who the hell she is and who her friends are. Strange, you'll agree. Not your fault. This isn't blame. This is something else. But you'll never tell. A good man, I can see that, but the medical conspiracy has locked this one up tight. All we can do is speculate. Did she call someone's name? Did she panic?

DOCTOR: [*Getting up from seat.*] Excuse me.

NICHOLAS: Doctor, why do you look so sad?

DOCTOR: No. It's fatigue.

NICHOLAS: Will you come and have a drink with us later? We're having a party in the lounge. Quite a group you've got parading around here. You should see us in restaurants. Particularly if someone's singing. There's always a misunderstanding. Great swooping exits. No one's sure who paid the bill so everybody leaves money. Money all over the table. It continues in the street.

DOCTOR: [*As he leaves.*] Everybody's got a history. [DOCTOR *exits.*]

NICHOLAS: I keep mine in a desk drawer. But I can tell you things. About the dying woman and her friends, I mean. [*The* DOCTOR *is gone, but* NICK *keeps talking.*] My mother was a doctor. A shrink. [*Beat.*] That's not true. But she was Jewish. And she always knew when I had a fever. I thought she was a doctor for years. [*Beat.*] She had a sense of humor, though. Most real doctors don't.

[RALEIGH *walks over and sits with* NICHOLAS.]

RALEIGH: Darling, why do you do that?

NICHOLAS: What?

RALEIGH: The way you talk to people. It's so unattractive.

NICHOLAS: Once I start, I can't seem to stop.

RALEIGH: You know what you're doing. There's nothing innocent about it.

NICHOLAS: Well, I'm very unhappy. So I thought I'd have a conversation. I can't help it if my good friend,the doctor or the lawyer or the Indian chief won't be rotten back at me. It's better than throwing things. [*Pause.*] For some of us.

RALEIGH: Oh, baby, to think that you've never destroyed property in the name of rage.

NICHOLAS: You're barbaric. I don't approve of you at all. It's just that there's nothing better to do. [*Pause.*] Make me happy.

RALEIGH: There's only one thing for you. It's the same for me. Work is all.

NICHOLAS: I get depressed.

RALEIGH: I'll kiss you. Here. [*She kisses him lightly.*] Now. Will you still be bad?

NICHOLAS: Yes.

RALEIGH: If you were actually handsome, I wouldn't stay another minute. [*Pause.*] Sometimes I wish your name was Jake.

NICHOLAS: Impossible. My mother's name was Jake.

RALEIGH: Sometimes . . . now don't get mad . . . I think of you as someone else. Not Nicholas. When you're an old friend who wears sweaters, then it's Jake. But when you're reading the newspapers, it's Nicholas. If you're sprawled out on the couch, reading the newspaper—in your socks— then I'd call you Jake.

NICHOLAS: I'm hungry.

RALEIGH: Now, if you went to the refrigerator and made yourself a sandwich, I could not in good conscience address you as Nicholas. And in most restaurants I'd have to call you Nick.

NICHOLAS: I was thinking we could go out and get a couple of hot dogs. Of course, then I'd have to call you Rose.

RALEIGH: I'm on a diet.

NICHOLAS: Perfect. I've never known a Rose who wasn't.

RALEIGH: I love you. [*Beat.*] Quite, quite mad about the boy.

NICHOLAS: Which one?

RALEIGH: [*Kissing him.*] Oh, darling, darling Jake, how could you even ask.

[*Blackout. Lights up on Corridor.*]

MAX: Look, Doctor, I know about the rules. The rules here don't apply. Raleigh had a point of view her family isn't aware of. Would probably never share. She had confidences. You can't turn it over to her family. They don't know her.

DOCTOR: [*Weary.*] It comes down to signatures. [*He would like to be sympathetic, but can't afford to be.*] The name of a blood relative. The permission of a blood relative. Or a spouse.

MAX: Or a spouse. How about someone who holds her in the night when she's sweating from a bad time of it? How about someone who balances her checkbook from time to time and harbors her renegade children when they've come home from the wars.

DOCTOR: She has a son. And a mother.

MAX: And so at the end, she belongs to them . . . when in her whole life she didn't belong to anyone? By whose authority?

DOCTOR: It's . . . a regulation.

MAX: There are decisions to make. Her son can't do that even for himself. And her mother. Grace doesn't know. Grace . . . she's not prepared.

DOCTOR: Please. It's a legal problem. I can't. It's not . . . you should try and get some sleep.

MAX: Why do we have our babies here? I hate this place.

[*Lights up on House.*]

RALEIGH: [*Pouring herself glass of wine.*] This coma thing has its advantages. For one thing, it's got a certain color. Really. And a whirring sound. Not unpleasant. The only drawback is not knowing exactly whether you'll have it entirely or whether you'll have to come out of it. Because there is an adjustment. [*Pause.*] When I was twenty, it seemed clear one day that I should commit suicide. And I went through the afternoon and the evening with this in mind and the plans exact. But that night, when I went in to the children to kiss them goodnight, it fell apart. Thinking about how they would live without a mother, I cried myself to sleep in their room. And it was a wonderful surprise when they woke to see me there. I got their breakfast. One, a bottle, and postponed the event. Later, I read in the paper about a woman, 23, who threw her babies off a bridge and then jumped herself. All drowned. Nobody knew why, except she had said something about missing her husband who was in basic training. [*Pause.*] The coma has deep possibilities.

[*Sound of laughter. Lounge.*]

FRAN: [*Drinking.*] There's a man from Texas who calls to invite her to certain . . .

parties. She won't tell me who he is. "You don't want to know him," she says. He called once and I answered. He mentioned *God*. He called me, "Darlin'." [FRAN *starts to move out of Lounge.*] There's a sordid tale in it somewhere. [FRAN *exits with drink in hand.*]

T.K.: There were detectives once.

NICHOLAS: I'm more interested in the politician. The one with the private plane. A slightly bluish gentle-man.

T.K.: One of our fathers wanted one of us back. Or something like that. One of the families of one of our fathers wanted one of us back. To continue the line. They sent detectives.

MAX: [*To* NICK.] Remember the prop girl who followed her out from the coast? The last of Raleigh's virgins. What was her name?

NICHOLAS: Michele.

MAX: Andrea. Poor kid just couldn't be persuaded to go home. We had to put her on the train. She still sends letters doused with Jean Nate.

[*House Area.* FRAN *and* RALEIGH *are languishing on the sofa. They are drinking wine.*]

RALEIGH: Think about climates, Fran. We're on the wrong side of the equator. It gives you a false sense of things. It makes things seem to be what they are.

FRAN: That's fine with me.

RALEIGH: In the South, you get a little bit closer to the sweetness. The early decay. When I take you to Louisiana, you'll see what I mean.

FRAN: I thought you were talking about South America. Anyway, I have been to the tropics, in case you didn't know.

RALEIGH: I didn't.

FRAN: One of my honeymoons.

RALEIGH: Fran, you've always had the same husband.

FRAN: We try to break up the monotony. It was a terrible trip. Everything was so balmy.

RALEIGH: Did you dream any differently

FRAN: What do you mean? In South America?

RALEIGH: Uh huh. Were your dreams . . . strange?

FRAN: Mostly I was in a stupor. What are you talking about, anyway?

RALEIGH: When I'm in different places, the dreams change. The way they come. The dreaming of something in Connecticut is not like the dreaming of something in Brazil. [*Beat.*] When you come with me to Louisiana, we'll have to go off our diets.

FRAN: So when are we going? You've been threatening for years.

RALEIGH: Soon. One morning, I'll wake up—

FRAN: One *afternoon* you'll wake up—

RALEIGH: And it will be absolutely impossible to do anything else. And we'll go. I don't always sleep late.

FRAN: I know. Sometimes you don't sleep at all.

RALEIGH: When do your kids get back from school?

FRAN: How soon they forget.

RALEIGH: No. No. See, my children didn't always get back from school. If they went to school. But yours do, and I want to take them to a museum. Let's take them, Fran. Somewhere. I like your kids. They aren't quite as urban as you are.

FRAN: They are every bit as urban as I am.

RALEIGH: I love you, Fran. I love you, but your son's going to be an archaeologist someday and dig up the world with a spoon. And your daughter could easily become a psychoanalyst. She'll diagnose our city sleep and chew her fingernails the way her mother does.

FRAN: [*Purposely takes a beat.*] Sheila's got Yoga class and David's got basketball. They won't be home until six. [RALEIGH *starts to laugh.*]

FRAN: What?

RALEIGH: Nothing.

FRAN: That's what I thought.

RALEIGH: We are excellent friends. In case you hadn't noticed. [*Beat.*] I'm dying for something chocolate. What've we got?

FRAN: Sara Lee. Frozen.

RALEIGH: Shit. What'll we do?

FRAN: Crave something else. Shall we drink? [*She moves to get more wine.*]

RALEIGH: Do you have any Visine?

FRAN: This does not follow.

RALEIGH: Audition tomorrow. In the morning. If I drink, I will continue to drink all afternoon and into the dark. So . . . can you get the red out?

FRAN: I'll think of something. A nice home remedy in the *Joy of Cooking*, maybe.

RALEIGH: Good. Then I'm in your hands.

FRAN: [*Pouring wine.*] Pouilley Fuisse?

RALEIGH: When I die, you must sprinkle a bit of this over my body and then fill every cup as frequently as possible.

FRAN: When I die, you may not drink at all.

RALEIGH: That's boring.

FRAN: It'll give you something to look forward to. Speed up the grief.

RALEIGH: I like that. Now, defrost the Sara Lee.

FRAN: You are a terrible influence on my life.

[RALEIGH *dabs a bit of her drink behind her ears, then behind* FRAN's. *Lights off on House. Lights up on* NICHOLAS, *alone.*]

NICHOLAS: There was some talk of her night walks. She spelled poorly. Things were accomplished. She polished brass. Cleaned her bathroom floor with paper towels. There was bravery. She had recently purchased a new wind chime, for example, and would buy more even though Southern California was certain to have an earthquake and Manhattan was said to have a fault.

[*Corridor.*]

DOCTOR: She won't last the night.

MAX: Someone should be with her. Someone should be in there with her.

DOCTOR: There are things...the nurse has to do for her.

MAX: What things? Why is everything so damn mysterious.

T.K.: She doesn't even look sick.

MAX: What are we waiting for?

DOCTOR: Electroencephalogram.

MAX: Maybe we should call a specialist.

DOCTOR: She can't recover from this. You can call anyone. You can do that. I'll give you some names. But there is no activity in the brain. There is no life there. You can pray for it to be some other way. Sometimes people do that.

MAX: What is the nurse doing, then? What are we waiting for?

DOCTOR: To be sure. To be certain.

MAX: She doesn't want to be buried.

T.K.: She doesn't look sick.

MAX: She'd rather go up in flames.

T.K.: My grandmother won't like that. Grace won't let you do that.

MAX: I'm going to sit with her.

DOCTOR: In a few minutes.

[*He exits to the Cafeteria.*]

MAX: She doesn't want the ground. I know that. Raleigh said something once about...her eyes. And her heart. About giving them to someone else.

T.K.: I'll take them.

MAX: There's no will. She didn't write it down or anything, but she told me.

T..K: [*Hysterical.*] Shut up! Shut up about it! My mother doesn't even look sick!

[*Lights up on* DOCTOR, *alone in Cafeteria.*]

DOCTOR: [*Troubled. He speaks as if this were a litany, a chant, a question for him to resolved.*] Heart and mind. Heart and mind. The music of the mind is—beep beep beep. The waves must be the taste of dinner, the memory of unfortunate, as well as fortunate occasions. The waves recognize a sour wine. They undulate language. They wash over infancy. They collect edges of experience. They eat away the shore with opinion, battering other people's waves—mixing with idea and fact and lunacy.

[*Lights up on Lounge.*]

T.K.: Mom likes this one poem of mine. It made her cry.

NICHOLAS: Well, then—

T.K.: Would you read it?

NICHOLAS: No. A new one, maybe. Give me a new one. You shouldn't really fuck with poems, T.K. They're very dangerous. I never write them, myself. [*Pause.*] Do you know it by heart?

T.K.: What?

NICHOLAS: The poem you mentioned. Did you memorize it?

T.K.: I could probably—

NICHOLAS: Not to me. To her. Say it to your mother. Go on. Tell the nurse what you're going to do. She's very sweet. No problem.

T.K.: Raleigh can't hear a fucking thing. Her head's all bandaged.

NICHOLAS: If I had what you claim to have—if I were her son, if I were that child and managed out of it all to make a poem that touched her, I would beat a path directly to her door and tell her again.

[*After a hesitation,* T.K. *leaves the Lounge.*]

MAX: That was nice.

NICHOLAS: Why, don't you think I'm nice? We're all nice here. Wanna play some cards. Whaddya play? I'm a Rummy man, myself. Gin rummy. You got any cards? I got—[*Searches in his wallet.*]—Fifty bucks says you're nice and wanna beat the shit out of me. [*He heads out of lounge, stops, turns.*] I was just fooling. [*Pause.*] But I do have gambling instincts.

[*Corridor. Near the room or area representing Intensive Care,* RALEIGH *is watching an unseen nurse go through her routines with the body.*]

RALEIGH: Saint Nurse. Dear Nurse. You won't let anyone see this!

[*Lounge.*]

MAX: "If it happens to me ... " Don't you remember when she said that? All those articles in *Newsweek* and *Time.*

RALEIGH: [*Horror stricken at her body's state of helplessness, but still the observer.*] I'm an infant.

MAX: "If it happens to me, one of you better pull the plug."

[*Corridor.*]

RALEIGH: Your life won't be worth a piece of shit, believe me. Prison won't compare to what I'd do to you.

MAX: And I said—why think about the end? And Raleigh said, "Because I want to make sure there is one."

[*Lights up on House, we hear* RALEIGH *laughing.*]

RALEIGH: [*Sitting in a chair, she talks to the audience.*] I was—laughing about—an idea whose time had come. That phrase. It just struck me as pretty damned amusing. Pretty damned apt. I wonder where they put my diamond earrings? You know, I get the idea I'm being fed, somehow, but it's a bit too bland for me. Of course, nobody knows how to season properly. I could die for a pizza. [*Pause.*] Remember *Our Town*? I must've read it a couple of hundred times. They'd never cast me in it, though. I wasn't wholesome enough. I finally convinced someone once in summer stock to let me play a dead person. I was incredibly good. I practiced being a dead person in front of the mirror. Sometimes, in a restaurant I'd just go right into it and I'd be a dead person with a cheeseburger in a corner booth. I practiced staring ahead a lot because that's what the dead people in *Our Town* do. They stare ahead. I told the director that maybe dead people did other things, too, you know? That maybe they didn't just sit by their cemetery plots and stare ahead. But he was a very traditional man. So, we stared. [*Beat.*] It's easy to see why a person in that circumstance would lose interest.

[*Light change, as* T.K. *approaches the House Area.*]

T.K.: Mom?

RALEIGH: Yes.

T.K.: Can I come in? Your light was on.

RALEIGH: What is it, T.K.?

T.K.: Why do you always think it's something.

RALEIGH: Because it always is.

T.K.: I just wanted to talk.

RALEIGH: [*Guarded.*] All right.

T.K.: Nice place.

RALEIGH: [*Coolly.*] Glad you like it.

T.K.: Did I do terrible things to you? [RALEIGH *doesn't answer.*] That must be it. I don't remember. But, I must have done terrible things to you.

RALEIGH: Take off your coat. Stay awhile.

T.K.: You're pissed I didn't call first. Most people don't have to call their mothers. Most people can just drop in, hang out. Most mothers would be glad to have the visit. Most mothers would probably have a house with an extra room or two for their kids. Most people wouldn't believe that I can't just knock on your door without feeling guilty I did some terrible terrible thing.

RALEIGH: Yes. You've got something there. When you put it like that. But the thing you wouldn't guess is that I'm more shocked by the entire situation than you are. I mean, when you read off the list of sins like that, I can see how— we just aren't the mother and son I hoped we'd be. Actually that's the part you probably—well, how could you know? You were just a baby when you were born. [*Pause.*] Smile. Smile, goddamit. Don't get glum with me.

T.K.: You won't cop to it. You never take the blame for one piece of my shit.

RALEIGH: Oh, no sweetcheeks, I'm yours. Was. Was yours. Shit not withstanding. Shit, in fact, coming with the package. I'm just not accepting anymore at this time, that's all. Not to be confused, honey. I took as much blame as I could get. If my son is naughty, if my son is gloomy, if my son gets hepatitis from shooting up with a dirty needle, if my son runs naked in the respectable suburban streets, trashing his mother— then his mother must be trash.

T.K.: You changed. You took us everywhere and then you didn't anymore. You were something to a lot of other people. They did whatever you wanted them to do. [*Pause.*] I call you. The machine answers. I write you letters—

RALEIGH: Love letters, T.K., for god sakes, they're love letters!

T.K.: I want to be a part of your life.

RALEIGH: You want to play in it. Roll around in what you think is the exotic dirt of it. Listen to me, T.K., I'd love to have your affection, but we are not going to be lovers. My friends are not going to be your friends, and this romance you have with me on paper does not make up for the war that goes on whenever we actually come together.

T.K.: You're so cold. Why are you so cold? I'd like to take a razor blade and cut you. [*He turns from her and speak as if writing a letter.*] Dear Raleigh, if you were still my mother, I wouldn't do this, but now that you're someone else, I can tell you. How it makes me hard. How it makes me bonehard. Your men and your women and what you do with them. Somebody saw your picture, one of my friends, and said it was style. That's what she's got. Well, I just want to be a part of that, you know. It's a real kick thinking about how you've got a mother that guys jack off to. Listen, I dedicated my first real, recognizable erection to you. I had it in your name—quite a few years ago. But I always think of you whenever it comes up again. [*Pause.*] I just want to be a part of your life. [*Pause.*] Dear Mom, I'm in love with an older woman. [*Turning back to his mother again, he screams:*] You dyke! [*Beat.*] I just want to be in your life.

RALEIGH: [*After a moment.*] When I was your age, I had two babies. Did I ever tell you about how I was so afraid because the doctor said to sterilize everything that I boiled your diapers and the vaseline.

[*She moves to* T.K., *holds him and rocks him.*]

RALEIGH: [*Cont'd.*] I boiled the fucking vaseline because it didn't say sterile on it. [*Pause.*] You said something about a poem. You were going to read me a poem. I think it would be nice right now to hear a poem.

[*Lights dim on House, come up slowly on Lounge. It is night. All are asleep, except* NICHOLAS, *who talks to everybody as if they were still awake.*]

NICHOLAS: Dinosaurs...if you think about them. Those must've been some times, huh? The big, stupid creatures. They make me think about museums. The dinosaur, itself, was not a happy beast, but it was the precursor of a more evolved and happier species. They were so big. They were really too big. I mean, for anyone to know what to do with. Pre— hi—stor—ic. And unfulfilled. [*Beat.*] We are just beginning to understand dinosaurs.

[NICHOLAS *settles into sleep.* RALEIGH *drifts towards lounge. She approaches* FRAN, *who doesn't hear her, but stirs as* RALEIGH *speaks to her.*]

RALEIGH: Fran, were you sleeping? Listen to me, will you? I don't give a damn if you're tired. It's important. Fran? [*Pause.*] I want you to have my purses. [*Beat.*] Well, you know, I never could find the right one. They're on top of my closet. [*Pause.*] The other thing is—I was thinking what if you were the one who died, you know? What would I like of yours? And Fran, I think what I'd like is one of your coffee mugs. So since I can't have one of yours, would you take one of mine?

[RALEIGH *touches* FRAN's *arm, then moves out of the lounge and goes to the Cafeteria, where she joins the* DOCTOR.]

RALEIGH: I was dreaming about you.

DOCTOR: Yes?

RALEIGH: We were dancing. Are they going to give my parts away?

DOCTOR: Isn't that what you asked them to do?

RALEIGH: I'm wondering how it will affect my social standing. With the other recently departed. I don't like operations. A person could stop breathing.

DOCTOR: Well—

RALEIGH: Well, I am still breathing. I may not be thinking, but my chest is definitely going up and down. [*Beat.*] Who gets me?

DOCTOR: Different people.

RALEIGH: Same old story.

DOCTOR: It won't hurt.

RALEIGH: I'll bet you say that to all the girls.

DOCTOR: I hope it won't hurt.

RALEIGH: Thank you. For the margin of doubt. It gives me something to go on. [*Pause.*] Why don't you eat?

DOCTOR: Wasn't I? I thought I was. [*He takes a feeble bite from something on his plate.*]

RALEIGH: I like you. But you should have your uniform pressed.

DOCTOR: First chance I get.

RALEIGH: In the dream you looked quite elegant. [*Pause.*] If I don't die, what will it be like?

DOCTOR: Very unpleasant.

RALEIGH: Miracles happen.

DOCTOR: You don't strike me as someone who'd count on it.

RALEIGH: No. [*Pause.*] Except when I meet someone who changes my mind.

DOCTOR: You have devoted friends.

[*She is moved by this thought, but doesn't want to give in to it.*]

RALEIGH: Yeah. I'd be pretty pissed off if one of them did this to me. I mean, if one of them had a goddam cerebral accident right smack in the middle of— [*Beat.*] What would it be like if I didn't die?

DOCTOR: Paralysis. Blindness.

RALEIGH: Do you dream about your patients? [*Beat.*] I kind of wanted to make it to 40. Women are terrific at 40. Do you believe in life after death? [*Without waiting for an answer.*] A boy on the beach throwing a frisbee and a black dog shaking the water off. That's how they end the movie. It's an image of hope. [*Pause.*] I don't know if I'd come back or not. I mean, if I had the chance. You'd probably have to be a baby again and that's so inconvenient.

DOCTOR: Would you like a cigarette?

RALEIGH: I'd love one. Take this thing out of my mouth. [*Referring to unseen respirator.*]

DOCTOR: Sorry. Do you mind if I smoke? [*He takes out a pack of cigarettes.*]

RALEIGH: For a Hershey Bar, I'd come back. [*Pause.*] How old are you?

DOCTOR: Thirty-five.

RALEIGH: Do you deliver babies? Or just perform hopeless neurosurgery?

DOCTOR: Infants die, too. And quite a few are born without—one thing or another. And some are monsters.

RALEIGH: In the dream you were smiling. And I was smoking a pack of Galouise.

[*Lights dim on cafeteria, a* DOCTOR *moves to Lounge.*]

DOCTOR: Can I talk to you for a minute? [*Slowly, everyone begins to wake.*] There was slight flutter on the EEG. I'm sure it was mechanical, but you never know. So we'll have to do it again.

[DOCTOR *leaves the Lounge. Everyone is stunned.*]

FRAN: He said it was just mechanical.

MAX: But it could be something else.

NICHOLAS: She was probably having a bad dream.

[*From another area.*]

RALEIGH: It occurred to me, that's all. For a brief—just a flutter of a—I was thinking about dancing. And how I would probably miss that.

[*From the Lounge.*]

FRAN: Max, don't hope for it.

NICHOLAS: [*Begins to sing slowly, as if the song were being drawn out of him from some unexpected source.*]
"Hear the beat—of the dancing feet. It's
the duh duh duh—I'm taking you to—
[*Beat.*]
—42nd street."

[*Raleigh is clicking her fingers to the same rythym. Lights fade on all areas.*]

ACT II

[*Lights up on Lounge. There is a great deal of chaos as* FRAN *tries to pass out food. The voices overlap.*]

FRAN: Ham and Swiss?

[*Someone grabs it.*]

FRAN: [*Cont'd.*] Ham and Swiss, no mustard.

NICHOLAS: Mayonnaise. No mayonnaise.

FRAN: Ham and American.

NICHOLAS: I like mustard. You can't eat these without mustard.

FRAN: Tuna?

MAX: Egg salad.

FRAN: Then who's got the tuna? [*To* MAX.] They were out of egg salad.

NICHOLAS: [*To* T.K.] Did you get a pickle with yours?

[FRAN *starts passing out coffee.*]

T.K.: I'll take mine black.

MAX: Styrofoam.

FRAN: [*Pulling the real thing out of her bag.*] Cups!

[*During this madness, an older* WOMAN *has entered the Lounge. Bundled in a coat, holding some flowers. Out of place and perplexed by this gathering, she goes unnoticed until finally—*]

FRAN: Would you like something to drink? Sorry about the paper cups.

WOMAN: No...I couldn't.

FRAN: It's Scotch. You'll feel better. Really.

WOMAN: I don'...usually—

MAX: It's all right. Nobody's doing anything they usually do. Go ahead.

WOMAN: It's my daughter.

MAX: Yes.

WOMAN: You know her?

MAX: Your daughter? Never met. It's just that...we're all here for the same thing, aren't we?

WOMAN: A mother should die first. Are you here for somebody?

MAX: The one in 317.

WOMAN: Barbara's in 316.

NICHOLAS: [*Almost to himself.*] Small world.

WOMAN: Is he very sick, your friend?

MAX: She.

WOMAN: Oh.

MAX: No. She's not sick.

WOMAN: I don't know what to do. If I should—the Doctor seems so sure. He seems so sure. He's very young, though. Your friend, she's going to be all right, then?

MAX: We're not thinking about it.

WOMAN: Barbara's not going to be all right.

MAX: Don't think about it. That's what we're doing, not thinking about it. This is the room of drinking and forgetting.

WOMAN: Are you all together?

NICHOLAS: A tribe.

FRAN: Why don't you have something to eat? We can't possibly eat all of this.

WOMAN: First, I thought there was a party. I wasn't sure. It's nice that you all came together—to be here for someone.

FRAN: Please, you look tired. Take a sandwich.

WOMAN: I don't feel right about that . . . no. I'll just finish my drink and—

FRAN: I make a terrific tuna salad. With cottage cheese and a bit of lemon juice and green onions. Actually, I stole the recipe from the woman in 317. Please . . . try it.

WOMAN: You're very kind. Thank you. But I'm not very hungry.

FRAN: I'll wrap it up for you.

NICHOLAS: She's got this philosophy about food in a crisis. It's probably genetic.

FRAN: [*To* WOMAN.] Here. Save it for later. It'll keep.

[*The* WOMAN *searches through her purse, takes some money out of her wallet and lays it on the table.*]

WOMAN: The drink—it helped.

MAX: [*Trying to give back money.*] No—you don't understand.

WOMAN: I'd feel better.

MAX: We'd only gamble it away. Listen, anyone who comes in this room is entitled to drinks on the house.

FRAN: It's not necessary. A time like this.

WOMAN: I'd feel better.

[*She goes to Doorway. Everyone speaks at once.*]

WOMAN: I hope your friend—   OTHERS: I hope Barbara—

[WOMAN *exits. There is a beat. A silence that threatens to oppress them, until* NICHOLAS *speaks to fight it.*]

NICHOLAS: What do you think there is afterwards? No, just for the hell of it. C'mon.

T.K.: I don't know what there is now.

NICHOLAS: A rapier wit. Just like his mother. All right, *now* is one thing. But *after* . . .

like *dead*. I want to know what everyone thinks because I have a certain blank spot when it comes to all matters spiritual.

FRAN: It's nothing. We're something. And then we're not.

MAX: Not? No, maybe different. Maybe we *are* still—just different.

FRAN: The lights go out. Nobody home.

T.K.: What do you care?

NICHOLAS: See, if I thought I'd come back again, I might take up skiing. And smoke a lot more. Mainly, I could convince my publisher to extend his deadline.

MAX: Listen, if Raleigh goes, she'll fuck the first angel she sees and we'll never hear from her again.

FRAN: [*A bit drunk.*] You know, it's not the dying person whose life flashes in front of her. [*Starts moving out of Lounge.*] It's the poor suckers who are left behind. We're the ones who see it over and over again.

[*From House,* RALEIGH *watches* FRAN.]

RALEIGH: Fran?

[*Lounge.*]

T.K.: Do you think she knows what's going on? I mean, what's happening to her. Do you think she knows?

MAX: I hope to hell she knows. We're drinking twenty year old Scotch. I hope to hell she knows.

[*Fran enters House Area.*]

RALEIGH: Fran, you look depressed. We'll rent *Jaws*. You'll be so terrified, you won't be depressed anymore.

FRAN: Couldn't we see a love story?

RALEIGH: That's the worst thing you could do. There's always someone who doesn't love somebody else as much as. Or there's a terrible, hopeless disease. With sharks, at least you know where you stand.

FRAN: Anyway, I'm not depressed.

RALEIGH: What is it, then? You haven't fucked in a week?

FRAN: Weltschmerz.

RALEIGH: That bad. My god, we'll have to see *Earthquake*, too.

FRAN: World weary. Sadness for the world.

RALEIGH: I know what it means. I just don't want you to have it. We'll go to a dirty book store.

FRAN: I'll be all right.

RALEIGH: I'm worried about you.

FRAN: You're worried about me.

RALEIGH: You don't have an escape plan. Everybody needs one.

FRAN: I climbed out a bathroom window once.

RALEIGH: Under duress, as I recall.

FRAN: Oh—that's right. You were there.

RALEIGH: You know why you're sad? Because you're sane. You're too sane.

FRAN: What a terrible accusation.

RALEIGH: You are one of the few people I love but don't fuck. Do you know how much that means to me, Fran?

FRAN: Are you coming on to me? I can't tell.

RALEIGH: Fran, for Christ sake.

FRAN: Well, why not? Sometimes I wish you would.

RALEIGH: You're not as sane as I thought.

FRAN: Just for the hell of it. I'd never submit, of course.

RALEIGH: I think you're gorgeous, but I'd rather admire you from afar.

FRAN: You won't even pretend to try and seduce me?

RALEIGH: You know what it would be like for us? A pajama party. Two giggling girls at a pajama party.

FRAN: That only reminds me of my painful adolescence. Now I am depressed.

RALEIGH: Put on your coat.

FRAN: Where are we going?

RALEIGH: To a motel.

FRAN: Oh, you wouldn't!

RALEIGH: We'll have room service. We'll watch the soaps on their color TV.

FRAN: Is that what you do with all your cheap little numbers?

RALEIGH: This is not a sexual interlude. I do not watch television during sexual interludes.

FRAN: You won't mind if I take a nap, then?

RALEIGH: Sleep your weltschmerz away.

FRAN: I really don't know why you're worried about me. If anyone should be worried about anyone—it's well—it's the other way around. That's probably why I'm—the way I am. I'm probably worried about you.

RALEIGH: Don't. I have friends, offspring, credit cards. Life is full. [*Pause.*] Put on your coat.

[*Up on Lounge.*]

NICHOLAS: She is . . . traveling. She is . . . polite with the stewardess and asks for champagne. They have wine. But she wants champagne. The stewardess arranges it. Raleigh is sleepy but smiling. And in this case, the stewardess, who normally caters only to men will try to do everything she can for another woman.

T.K.: She is . . . on a huge featherbed. It floats. There aren't any more nightmares.

[RALEIGH *walks down Corridor.*]

RALEIGH: She is . . . I am . . . lost. I stop two people and ask for directions. They're sexless, these people. Forms. They promise to take me somewhere. I resist, of course. But they seem so—warm. They seem to know something. "We're your guides." I love it! *guides.* Terrific. I hope all the other people on the tour brought their Instamatics. Where are we going, anyway? See the *great void* in 21 days? [*Pause.*] If that's a laugh, I can't exactly tell. They don't speak. They sound. It reverberates. My own voice separates. [*Pause.*] Were you laughing? Do you have a sense of humor? If Max were here, she'd know what to do. She'd give you a six pack and you'd already be great pals.

[*Lounge.*]

MAX: She's sitting at a bar. She's burned her Driver's License. She always hated the picture, anyway. She's thinking . . . "I never have to do laundry again."

T.K.: She's nowhere. She's nothing. She's—

RALEIGH: —lost.

[*Fran returns to Lounge.*]

FRAN: I'm worried about Cat. Where the hell is she?

T.K.: I don't know.

MAX: Think about it.

T.K.: Nobody in my family believes much in forwarding addresses.

FRAN: T.K., get on the phone and make some calls. You know some of her friends.

MAX: [*With sarcasm.*] Isn't she still living with the cowboy?

FRAN: Max, for God sakes!

MAX: Rodeo rider. I'm sorry.

FRAN: [*To* T.K.] Call somebody.

T.K.: It'll be a mess. Suppose she's alone? It'll be a mess.

MAX: You better do something to find your sister, T.K. I'll talk to her if you can't. Just get her on the phone. Do that one thing.

[*Lights up on House.* RALEIGH *is on phone.*]

RALEIGH: Hello. I'd like to talk to Cat. Is she there? Well, when do you expect her back? That's amusing. Are you a friend of hers? Good. She may appear to be one thing, but trust me, she's really something else, and I'm glad to know you aren't her friend.

[*As* RALEIGH *hangs up and dials again, in another area,* T.K. *dials a phone, simultaneously.*]

RALEIGH: Catlin, please.

T.K.: Cat?

RALEIGH: Then wake her up.

T.K.: Listen to me. Wait a minute. Don't hang up. Jesus Christ.

RALEIGH: I don't care to leave a message. Wake the girl up and tell her to get her firm little ass to the phone.

T.K.: You have to come home, Cat. Right now. Mom's in the hospital. Raleigh's in the hospital.

RALEIGH: Baby—Catlin, honey, it's me. Look, whatever they tell you, don't panic. All is forgiven. I remember you only as the innocent in her Brownie uniform.

T.K.: She's unconscious. And the Doctor needs to tell you a couple of things. And you better come now because he doesn't think—[*Beat.*] Cat? who is this? Help her, then. Help her back to the goddam phone. Don't you have any respect for someone who's about to be a fuckin' orphan? Help her, man!

[*Light change.* NICHOLAS *begins to talk to himself, as if he were narrating. At the end of his speech,* RALEIGH *joins him and they are in a "scene" together.*]

NICHOLAS: In a conversation, he would prefer a cigar. She had qualifications. She remained alive to see the thing she remained alive for. He hated to be alone, nevertheless, he worked that way. She said your work has to be the most important thing. He remarked that the paint was peeling and certainly that came first. She ordered croissants and took the pewter coffee pot from the hotel. He said, "But, darling!" She walked into one of the shops in the lobby and bought him a hat.

RALEIGH: Don't you like the rain? I do. I require it.

NICHOLAS: He pulled up the collar on his coat. It was merely damp. She was already thinking about a hot tub.

RALEIGH: There's a chocolate shop!

NICHOLAS: And he bought her the most expensive candy. Deep dark chocolate. Semi-sweet. Truffles. Chunks of cocoa. She wiped the corner of his mouth with her hand. He had been so excited.

RALEIGH: He had been so excited.

NICHOLAS: And then she licked her fingers. [*Pause.*] Well? Well?

RALEIGH: Yes, it's wonderful—but, oh god, Nicky...

NICHOLAS: Don't say it.

RALEIGH: I'm sorry.

NICHOLAS: You'd give all this up for a fucking Hershey Bar.

RALEIGH: Worse. A Milky Way.

[*They join one another in House Area.*]

RALEIGH: Don't promise.

NICHOLAS: I'll put it in the contract.

RALEIGH: You're lucky your own name's in it.

NICHOLAS: It doesn't get done without you.

RALEIGH: Suddenly you have that kind of power?

NICHOLAS: Suddenly I have that kind of book. And they want it. I don't know anything about movies. I don't ever want to know. It just doesn't happen without you, that's all.

RALEIGH: Listen, you just . . . you . . . it doesn't work that way. [*Pause.*] Marty Feller doesn't know what to do with me. He was the first person to tell me something I've heard so many times since, it's my calling card. I read for him a few years ago. He had me come back. I even tested for the part. The designer was frothing over my classic lines, the chiseled look—which viewed in the wrong light can be very cold. But I was celebrating. It all looked real to me. And I was, I thought, perfect for the part. It's right. The timing, the vehicle. My kids were away at school. Just 30, looking 25. It's going to happen! But it didn't. Like so many times after that. Marty had his Jewish guilt, so he asked me out to dinner. And I had my Southern Pride, so I went. And he told me true, I've gotta say that about the man. He told me, "Look here," he said, "You may come from farming people but nobody's gonna believe you're a peasant. You've got big eyes and there's a child in there, but, honey, the bones—they make you hard, sometimes. And just too classy. Sounds ridiculous? Well, I'll tell you. The actor who's starring in this picture, he doesn't want you. Just between you and me, he thinks you're too intelligent. He's scared shitless, and if I pushed for you, there'd be goddawful fights. And then you'd give me a rough time, I can tell. Just the way you're looking at me. You'd argue if you didn't like what I told you to do and you'd give me an ulcer and it just isn't worth it. I think you'd be smashing on film—just the face, forget you got ability, just the style—but, honey, I swear to you, I don't know why . . . it's my gut feeling . . . but you're gonna have to do something nobody's ever thought of to make somebody take a chance on you. It's the terrible irony of this business. So, have another drink. And don't ask me why this is so." [RALEIGH *lights a cigarette.*]

NICHOLAS: I'll change it.

[RALEIGH *laughs.*]

NICHOLAS: She laughs. She doesn't believe me. I love her, even with her laughing. And I'll change it. See if I don't.

RALEIGH: You just don't know, do you? Really?

NICHOLAS: What do you mean?

RALEIGH: You can be so definite. Oh, god, it would be terrible to believe in someone again. But it's not going to happen . . . what you're offering me.

NICHOLAS: Here's a story. Boy has no dreams. He wakes in the morning. He falls asleep at night. In between— not a thing. Clear as a whistle, clean as a bell. People say, "Tell me what you dreamed last night." He's so embarrassed, the kid makes something up. I dreamed . . . there was a house with no windows. Or I dreamed . . . I was in the middle of a big city street and everyone was throwing ticker tape at me. Pretty soon, he gets very good at these little stories, and although he still can't remember having a real dream, he's got a whole lot of pretend. So when he gets to be a man and needs saving, days and nights he takes himself to his machine and tries the stories out. I'm telling you, Raleigh, now my life is dense with dreams, but people don't ask me anymore what I dreamed. They ask me what I'm doing. "What's your life *really* like." And it's so embarrassing. So the man makes up stories. About the day. [*Pause.*] You're my partner in this, Raleigh. Because you're the link between the dream and the day. So give me a little rope to hang myself by. Indulge this man's tiny power play with the big movie moguls. Tell me you believe I can do it.

RALEIGH: [*Moved.*] I believe . . . you want to do it. [*She moves toward him.*] I love your hands.

NICHOLAS: Even my knuckles.

RALEIGH: [*Kissing his hands.*] Especially your knuckles.

[*Lights dim on House. Lights up on Corridor.* MAX *stands alone, creating the impression that she is in the Intensive Care Room with* RALEIGH.]

MAX: The nurse said I could have a couple of words with you. I'll bet you just love that. Someone else giving me permission to come and go. Breaks every rule in the house, doesn't it? Listen, I can't find your Tiffany earrings anywhere. If I do, should I give them to Cat? Not that I've been very successful at finding Cat. But don't worry, she usually leaves some kind of trail. We're having a bitch of a time here with all your worldly goods, such as they are. I'm probably going to sell my car and buy yours from the kids. They could use the money. And besides, I like the way your car smells. As far as the taxes and bills and all that business shit, Nicky's got a good lawyer—except you did stuff the Sears bill between pages 104 and 105 of Tennessee Williams' Collected Plays, so God knows where the Department of Water and Power will show up. Now all of this is just in case. This does not mean you have to take it seriously. You can change your mind. I'll keep my crummy car. I'm only telling you these things so you won't be worried about details. But you can sit right up and shock the hell out of everyone, as far as I'm concerned. This place could use a little slap in the face, you know. Or, I mean, if that's too hard right now, just move your index finger. Curse. Whatever. All miracles accepted. Shit, I believe in miracles. Clap your hands if you believe—[*Pause.*] This is terrific. I could sit here all day and talk, repeat all my old stories and you can't even tell me to shut up. Except you aren't laughing and that's really what kept me talking all these years. [*Pause.*] Actually, I'd love to hear you say *shut up.* Go on, go ahead. Just for old times sake. Give it to me good. C'mon. *shut up, Max.* Huh? How about it—please. Please tell me to shut the fuck up! [*Pause.*] God, you're beautiful. You're not supposed to be that beautiful. This is intensive care, remember?

[*Cafeteria.*]

DOCTOR: I'm sorry to have to tell you this.

[*From another area,* RALEIGH *walks around and moves in a way that suggests a change in her perception.*]

RALEIGH: Something's wrong with my eyes. My eyes in my head don't work. I can see everything outside, but it's not happening in here. The place is hollow. I'm blind. I can't read my books. Oh shit. I'm losing it. Music. This is really bad. No music. I can't hear a damn thing. Don't want to stay here. I was in the middle of a very good book. Dear God, nothing works.

[*Lounge. The* DOCTOR *walks in, where everyone is gathered.*]

DOCTOR: It was flat.

RALEIGH: I'm 38. I'm 38. My names are... [*She can't remember.*] I have lived at these addresses... [*She struggles to remember, but fails.*] I drive a... [*Beat.*] I was in a play once with this line...

[*Lounge.*]

MAX: You took it again?

FRAN: Nothing? It was flat?

DOCTOR: Must have been what I thought... just mechanical. An error. It's not that I didn't tell you.

RALEIGH: [*Still struggling with her memory.*] I have a question.

DOCTOR: Well, that's the end of it, anyhow.

T.K.: What do we do now?

DOCTOR: You mean—

T.K.: I mean, what do we do now?

DOCTOR: There was something mentioned about—donating certain... [*He is having difficulty.*] We should talk about that as soon as you're able.

T.K.: Cat's not even here.

FRAN: [*To* DOCTOR.] If we could have some time.

[*Doctor nods, then leaves.*]

MAX: Her room smells like Chanel No. 5. When do you suppose that'll stop?

NICHOLAS: Shit. This is death here. We're talking about death, for God sakes!

MAX: I'll go to the apartment. When Grace comes... and Cat, they'll need a place to stay. It has to be cleaned up.

FRAN: Do you want some help?

MAX: No. It's ok, thanks. I'm the only one who knows where everything belongs. And if Raleigh came home and something was out of place, it would just be my fault. Believe me, you don't want to know the wrath of a woman who can't find her black turtleneck sweater.

FRAN: Don't go alone.

MAX: It's not for anyone else to see.

[MAX *leaves Lounge.*]

FRAN: Why isn't someone denying this!

[FRAN *leaves lounge.*]

T.K.: MAMA! Oh, Jesus, what do you do here? What do you do? I'm gonna fuckin faint, man. Oh, crap.

[*Corridor.*]

DOCTOR: Corridor. The angles of it are—no, it's the waiting. Postures of wait-ing. The air is heavy with it. That's been said. All right, the air is thin with it. Sorrowful hall.

[*House.* RALEIGH *watches* MAX *survey, straighten up.*]

RALEIGH: My dirt. My human filth. It all came out of me. It wouldn't stop. The bed is wet with it. The rug. [*To* MAX.] You'll clean this up for me? All the time we lived together, I always closed the bathroom door. And to every hotel room, my own disinfectant. Remember me scrubbing bathtubs? [*Pause.*] Don't stay here.

MAX: [*To herself.*] I'll take care of it. It doesn't matter.

RALEIGH: All my towels are white. You can't even buy white towels anymore.

[*Lounge.* FRAN *has returned, with candles, which she lights.*]

NICHOLAS: What the hell are you doing?

FRAN: I'm mourning. I don't care what the rest of you do. And I'm mourning in the Jewish tradition because it's handy. All I've got is a candle.

NICHOLAS: You'll have the place looking like a Shul in no time.

FRAN: Well, that's what this is, isn't it? A goddam Chapel. Don't let the uniforms fool you. Nurses, doctors, priests—it's all the same. You'd think they'd have a whole stockroom full of candles.

NICHOLAS: Blow them out, Fran. Put the fuckers out. They make me feel queasy.

FRAN: Why can't we have some death rites around here, anyway? A little chant-ing. A barge down the river, bearing it away. We're entitled. We're entitled to some sign of the passing.

T.K.: She's still here.

NICHOLAS: All that wax melting is giving me a terrible stomachache. Why are you doing this, Fran? Can't you grieve in the cafeteria?

FRAN: You know why her head went *boom*, Nicky? Because we gave her too much. She stored all our energy up there. We let her hold too much of it. And if you don't let it out pretty soon, Nicholas, something's gonna go boom in you, too. Maybe not your head. Maybe your delicate stomach. But I'm gonna have my grief wherever and whenever the hell it comes.

[RALEIGH *wanders nearby, observing them.*]

T.K.: [*Singing.*] "When I'm tired and I can't sleep, I count my blessings instead of sheep, and I fall asleep, counting my blessings."

FRAN: Damn mess. It's a shitload you dumped on us, Raleigh. What happened to our famous trip to Louisiana? It was always a lie. The big tease. Well, I don't have another friend who knows me like you do, so give me back my secrets. Give me every damn thing back before you desert me. I don't even remember what I told you. There are parts of me I can't remember anymore. Doesn't that make you feel bad? Why didn't you take better care of yourself? This wouldn't have happened if you'd have taken better care of yourself. Now I go, too. Up in smoke. You tangle me up in your life. You take a red pencil to mine. You fucking traitor. Jesus Christ, if I did this to you, you'd never speak to me again.

RALEIGH: Christmas list: Fran—one cheap lunch. No inspiration. Chalk off Christmas. Birthday list: Fran—one cheap lunch.

T.K.: I still have things to say.

NICHOLAS: Write them down.

RALEIGH: I could have loved it better. I could have loved the hours from 4 till 7 but they were always depressing to me. They would be still, I suppose.

T.K.: Once—she was going to punish me. I was maybe ten. And I took the belt off my pants and she thought it was so noble of me to offer her my belt, but instead I used it against her.

[MAX *returns during this.*]

T.K.: [*Cont'd.*] I fought her off. We ended up on the floor, fighting. She almost—she did win. She won.

MAX: She definitely won.

FRAN: Who's going to write the obituary?

NICHOLAS: Just list her favorite bathoils and take it from there.

T.K.: She isn't even dead. My mother's heart is going. They can't do anything without Cat, anyway.

MAX: How many days will that be?

T.K.: I don't care if it's never.

RALEIGH: [*To her friends.*] You heard the doctor. No pretty patterns on the paper anymore. Max? Max, I don't want to stay here. You do this for me, honey. Take care of this one, last detail. Soon. No shit, Max, I won't behave well. I'll go mad here. The machine's not bleeping. Now darlings, let me tell you, if I can't get a rise out of a machine, then I'm not much of my old self, am I?

[NICHOLAS *rises moves out of Lounge towards* RALEIGH.]

NICHOLAS: [*Angry.*] Why do you always run away from it?

RALEIGH: I'm simply going home.

NICHOLAS: Retreating.

RALEIGH: Whatever you'd like to call it.

NICHOLAS: Stay here. Fall asleep in my arms. Don't leave my house at 5 in the morning. There's a storm coming.

RALEIGH: I have to.

NICHOLAS: Your exits suck, mam. Forgive me, but it's a blight on your otherwise irrepressible style.

RALEIGH: Where are my goddam keys?

NICHOLAS: Is this a reason to walk out in the middle of the sacred night?

RALEIGH: I did not like those people. You apparently did. They're wretched and cruel and they turned your head. It makes me sick to remember.

NICHOLAS: Amused. Not enchanted. You sometimes get the signals confused.

RALEIGH: There was a look. Your cheeks were actually flushed. I can't get enough of it look.

NICHOLAS: Bitch.

RALEIGH: Don't . . . get me hot. Just say goodnight.

NICHOLAS: Look, give me the ground rules one more time. I'm slow but I pay attention to details.

RALEIGH: You hurt me.

NICHOLAS: Well, somebody did. That's clear.

RALEIGH: You took me on. Nobody asked you to. I said I was a bad risk.

NICHOLAS: It's almost day. I can see the sun. You don't have a prayer. Let's take a bath.

RALEIGH: Why do you want me to stay?

NICHOLAS: This will work out. You know? I have this crazy feeling in my tennis elbow it's gonna work out.

[RALEIGH *laughs*.]

NICHOLAS: What's so damn funny?

RALEIGH: That I'm here. With your fucking optimism.

NICHOLAS: It stinks, doesn't it? I'm lousy with it. But you could school me.

RALEIGH: Oh! You are more deeply rotten than I am. Which is the only reason we endure. [*Pause*.] God, the sun is coming up. I'll have to stay. I hate it.

NICHOLAS: I think we'd make fantastic adversaries, don't you? Imagine if we were both in love with the same woman? The contest! The duel! Sometimes, too, I see you as my mother walking in on me as I abuse myself.

RALEIGH: Why am I still here? You broke my stride. It's embarrassing. I'm not used to it.

NICHOLAS: No, it was you. You realized that you were treating me badly. You don't know how to handle guilt. Never will. So let's pull the shades. Your eyes are getting puffy. C'mon. Bed. Huh?

RALEIGH: Like regular people?

NICHOLAS: Think we can pull it off?

RALEIGH: How do regular people sleep?

NICHOLAS: Peacefully.

RALEIGH: You promise you'll never take me to another party like that again?

NICHOLAS: Can we just brush our teeth now and call it a night.

RALEIGH: Will you sing to me?

NICHOLAS: Torchy or lullaby?

RALEIGH: Musical comedy.

NICHOLAS: Sometimes I wish people still got engaged.

[*Cafeteria.*]

DOCTOR: A sudden rise in blood pressure, as with straining, coughing, sneezing, or sexual intercourse can sometimes be documented just prior to the cerebral accident itself. [*Pause.*] Cerebral hemorrhages occur with remarkable regularity deep in the hemisphere most commonly in the region of the internal capsule and basal ganglia and often extending into the subthalmus and tectum. They are frequently massive. The outlook in cases of massive cerebral hemorrhage is notably bad. [*Pause.*] TREATMENT: The treatment of intracerebral hemorrhage is almost entirely supportive. [*Pause.*] There's nothing I like better than a good detective story. In paperback. Coltrane's nice to listen to. But jazz doesn't always have a resolution. That's the thing about a good detective story. I have a pretty nice collection. Charlie Parker, Miles Davis. Sometimes I don't listen to my records for weeks. [*Pause.*] The onset in cerebral hemorrhage is abrupt and dramatic and almost always during waking hours. [*Pause.*] When I sleep with the light on, it's only because I've gotten accustomed to it and forget to turn it off. [*Pause.*] We don't have enough blankets here for the people who wait. It's a shame, really.

[*Corridor, or Cafeteria.* MAX *and* NICHOLAS *are alone.*]

MAX: Look, I went through her things and I thought you'd probably want all your letters back. They're in a bag.

NICHOLAS: How did you know they were mine? Sometimes I don't sign my name.

MAX: She had them in a special place. I just figured they were yours.

NICHOLAS: No. Tell me I had a style. And you recognized it.

MAX: Throw them away, then. It doesn't matter to me.

NICHOLAS: Good idea. Then I won't have to think of them as returned. Nobody likes to get his mail back. [*Pause.*] I'm sorry. Max...I'm sorry. It's your function. It's always been your function to—take care of things. Certain things. Matters of— it's not that I don't understand how hard— how hard it is now, but I don't want those letters, Max. I'd like to tuck one in Raleigh's pocket, though, give her something familiar to take along as a letter of introduction. But the important thing is I don't want to look into that bag you filled with all my apologies and pleas and affection. I know why you did it, Max. Look at me. I'm the widower. You're the widow. I know why you did it. But she should be surrounded by her loveletters and her books and bathsalts. We ignite all of it. We do not get our gifts back.

RALEIGH: [*Announcing:*] The OBITUARY. Can we get on with it?

[*Lounge.* MAX *and* NICHOLAS *return.*]

T.K.: She was 38.

FRAN: [*Writing on notepad.*] Let's compromise and say 30.

MAX: Hometown: Somewhere in Louisiana. Do we say when she escaped?

FRAN: Arithmetic. She was not very good at.

RALEIGH: And could not spell for shit.

NICHOLAS: Gershwin. Cole Porter.

MAX: Sometimes Barry White.

FRAN: You must be kidding.

MAX: In the aroused state. In the car. "Love Unlimited." Fuck music. She could be a peasant.

FRAN: Do you think the chronology matters?

MAX: Maybe we could just use her resume.

FRAN: Which name do we use?

MAX: Raleigh, a.k.a. Elizabeth, a.k.a. Anne—

FRAN: Did you know her when she was Annie?

NICHOLAS: Fortunately not.

T.K.: I knew her when she was Mommy.

MAX: You've known her the longest. You get to pick what name you'd like to use.

T.K.: I didn't know her at all.

NICHOLAS: Yes you did. Oh, yes you did, T.K. In a way some of us tried to duplicate, but it's only meant for mothers and sons.

MAX: She smelled good. I want the newspapers to say that.

RALEIGH: They don't remember the bad parts.

FRAN: *The Bad Parts!* [FRAN *laughs all of a sudden, as if this new idea, this new turn of purpose, is a great release.*]

MAX: Why are we doing this?

FRAN: Because.

MAX: Because?

FRAN: That's what my mother always said.

NICHOLAS: Yours, too? Ah, it's no wonder, then.

FRAN: *The Bad Parts.*

NICHOLAS: I believe in lists. It's a holy act to catalogue.

FRAN: She was a shit sometimes. And we'll all be better off if we remember it. All those times you thought, "I've had it with this crazy dame."

NICHOLAS: This loony tune.

T.K.: Yeah, I remember. I couldn't even bring any friends home. I remember.

MAX: That's all you do is remember. You couldn't make it through the day without having a little remember, could you, T.K.?

T.K.: She dumped out all the money in her purse. Right in the middle of the goddam floor and told us to get a motel room. They were my friends. We'd been on the road for three days. They thought she was some freaked out movie star. And I had to call her Raleigh, so nobody believed she was even my mother. Oh yeah, there were a lotta good bad parts.

FRAN: That's the spirit, boy.

MAX: I'm gonna weep for you. And those sweet young things you brought home to meet momma. It was also my house so I have a faint recollection of your companions, smelling bad, burning holes in the sofa with their cheap dope.

FRAN: No, honey. Your own bad parts, Max. Not his. And don't defend Raleigh. Think of all the times she hurt you or disappointed you.

NICHOLAS: This is fun.

MAX: I don't want to. What the hell do you want from me? She ate my popcorn at the movies, ok?

FRAN: Won't do.

MAX: She arrived late and left early. She kept me waiting. She kept me hoping. What's the difference, I'd do it again.

NICHOLAS: The kind of lady you turn into fiction. Maybe she lived just to give us . . . an idea.

FRAN: I knew her when she was Anne.

RALEIGH: Sweet Jesus, you could get me crazy with those faces. Don't get maudlin on me now. You were doing so well. [*She walks towards them, touches* MAX.] Oh, sweetheart, say something funny. C'mon, baby. It's really a funny situation, if you think about it. Now just give me— [*Starts to tickle* MAX.] — a— [*Continues tickling.*] —nice—

[MAX *starts to smile, as if she has just remembered something.*]

MAX: That time in the movies. We did it with our hands.

RALEIGH: Yes, that's it.

MAX: Under the coats. She made me do it.

RALEIGH: [*To* MAX.] You beautiful teeth, you!

[RALEIGH *leaves Lounge, joins* DOCTOR *in Cafeteria.*]

RALEIGH: There's something on my mind. Or, since I don't have a mind anymore, there's something disturbing me.

DOCTOR: Let's hear it.

RALEIGH: If you're going to transfer me to someone else . . . to various others . . . when exactly do I die? When is the precise moment of death? Total death, I mean.

DOCTOR: That's hard to say.

RALEIGH: Well, you better damn well say it. Or find me a book on the subject.

DOCTOR: You are dead. Already. According to the law and medical theory. Your brain is dead.

RALEIGH: But there's still something going on. And whatever it is, I want to know when it's going to stop.

DOCTOR: Separation isn't so easy. It doesn't happen all at once.

RALEIGH: But my friends are getting tired. I don't want them to be bored with me. And I thought, being unconscious, I'd finally get a good night's sleep. But it's the same as ever. I keep getting interrupted. I keep remembering things. I'm still having conversations.

DOCTOR: Soon.

RALEIGH: They come to the bed and talk to her. The shell of me. They want to know that I've heard them. They want a sign. [*She shouts to Lounge area.*] You want a sign? I'll give you a sign. When I'm a full fledged ghost, I'll give you a goddam sign. When I'm all dead, I'll come and whisper in your ear, walk in your sleep, move things around the room. Whatever the fuck spirits do, I'll do. Just, finish me off. [*Pause.*] Doctor? [*Pause, then quietly.*] Finish me off.

[*The* DOCTOR *takes a moment, then walks to the Lounge. He addresses everyone, after he enters.*]

DOCTOR: If you want to say goodbye, this would be . . . this would be the best time.

[*A moment of stillness.*]

MAX: Goodbye? As in . . . *goodbye?*

DOCTOR: Things will move along pretty fast now.

MAX: You mean, go in there and say goodbye.

NICHOLAS: We don't believe in that sort of thing, Doctor. Raleigh won't have any part of it. We're your basic catch as catch can group.

FRAN: I'd like to see her. Close the book on it.

NICHOLAS: She didn't say goodbye to us.

MAX: Yes, she did. From the start. In the first words. [*Beat.*] T.K. are you going to make this? Do you want someone to walk with you?

FRAN: I'll take him.

NICHOLAS: Give her my best.

[FRAN *and* T.K. *leave lounge.*]

NICHOLAS: [*To* MAX.] Did she ever rock you? Feed you and rock you?

MAX: Didn't she give you all the graphic details?

NICHOLAS: Not about you. She wouldn't talk about you.

MAX: An honorable woman. A decadent whore of an honorable woman.

NICHOLAS: Ain't it the truth. [*Beat.*] I hate sudden death.

MAX: It certainly puts a damper on things.

NICHOLAS: Shoots your plans all to hell.

MAX: There's something to be said for terminal illness. [*Beat.*] I didn't mean that. I didn't mean that about terminal illness. It's just that there's something to be said for giving people a little time to get used to the idea.

NICHOLAS: There goes our *menage à trois.*

MAX: Where will I kiss her? There's no place to kiss her.

[*Area representing Intensive Care.*]

T.K.: I wish I knew you when you were a little girl. A badass kid. I'll bet you had crazy eyes. I've got a bad feeling in my hands. The man who was my father, he must've been just a kid, too. If I ever run into him, I'll just beat the shit out of the guy. Or nothing. Mom...I've got a bad feeling.

[T.K. *moves off.* FRAN *comes to same spot.*]

FRAN: I like things to be...I like coats, buttoned. I'll read a novel straight through not to have markers in it. You know that. You've got the picture. So. Goodbye. That's all. Not that I feel this is actually happening. If I could go with you to the incinerator, maybe then. But let me tell you, I am not satisfied. This is no way to die. Turn blue. Rot. Do something to convince me. Shit. Shit, it was a good thing we had.

[FRAN *moves off.*]

RALEIGH: [*Who has been listening and watching.*] Christ, they're so devastating. The face. Regard the terrible, beautiful human face.

[T.K. *and* FRAN *enter lounge.*]

T.K.: In the morning. That's when the Doctor said.

[*The lights begin to dim, indicating night.* NICHOLAS *begins to talk and by the time he is done, everyone is asleep.*]

NICHOLAS: It's the phone calls in the middle of the night. "Nicholas, baby, I was at a party. And I spread your name all over the room. Tuesday Weld was there. I told her you loved her work. You do, don't you? I was very bad. I tried to get her to go with me to some motel, but she had her little boy with her. Anyway, everybody knows who you are now. Goodnight.

[*He falls asleep.* RALEIGH *walks into Lounge, and among them.*]

RALEIGH: I know these people. I know about them. Kiss me, Nicky, before I forget what it is. [*She kisses him in his sleep.*] I don't want Fran to get a face lift. I don't want her children to leave the country. Fran, who worships *The New York Times.* Dear Editor, this is your archive. I don't want her to get cancer.

[RALEIGH *moves to* MAX, *kisses her fingers. Takes the gold ring from her own hand and puts it on* MAX'S.]

RALEIGH: [*Cont'd.*] MEMO: Regarding Max's news special next Tuesday night. Everyone will watch it, of course, and then everyone will call the network several times and say, in cleverly disguised voices, how brilliant and daring it was and how you'd like to see more programs by this Max person.

[*She crosses to* T.K.]

RALEIGH: [*Cont'd.*] Who's the sad boy? Whose child is this? I don't live to see you make a tragedy out of it. And I don't live to see you prove me wrong. Dear boy, complete something. Feel the way it is to call it done. Do you want to be my baby again? We'll love that way just once before I take away another parent.

[*She pulls* T.K. *to her breast.*]

RALEIGH: [*Cont'd.*] Drink, baby. Drink and grow. Grow into someone. All gone. Too soon. So big. [*Singing, she lets go of him gently.*]

"When I'm tired and I can't sleep,
I count my blessings instead of sheep...
and I fall asleep, counting my—"

[*Beat.*] And don't you dare do anything stupid like killing yourself, you son of a bitch and make my death as miserable as you made my life. Grow old. Have children. See how they run. [*Pause.*] Mother loves you. Mother really does.

[RALEIGH *slowly retreats from Lounge to the Corridor. Her movements and attitude are now of someone fading.*
Lights come up slowly, to indicate DAWN. *The* DOCTOR *has been sleeping in the Cafeteria.* NICHOLAS *is the first to rise in Lounge. He gets up, looks around.*]

NICHOLAS: [*Softly.*] The sun came up. [*Then in a loud voice, announcing to the others.*] I said the sun came up!

[*The others start to wake.*]

NICHOLAS: [*Cont'd.*] Do you believe it? This calls for darkness. Don't you understand? Darkness.

[*There is movement. A slow, awkward effort toward leave-taking. Nobody can bring himself to go.* RALEIGH *sees the difficulty her friends are having.*]

RALEIGH: BEAT IT! SCRAM!

[NICHOLAS *finally makes a move towards exit.*]

NICHOLAS: Remember when Doctors used to give out lollipops? [*He exits.*]

FRAN: [*To* MAX.] I'll call you. We'll have lunch. I'll make a quiche. [FRAN *exits.*]

T.K.: I'll take her to the ocean. I'll carry her to the water.

MAX: Should we rent a boat? Have caviar?

T.K.: I guess after this I won't see you anymore?

MAX: I don't know, T.K. I don't know about anything yet.

[*She touches him, as* T.K. *leaves.* MAX *is alone, the last one left in the waiting room.*]

MAX: The least it could do is rain!

[*Lights fade on* MAX, *as she exits.*
Lights up on DOCTOR *in Cafeteria.*]

DOCTOR: THE FAIRY TALE. She was frightened by a hideous thing. With a horrible shape. It came out of the closet and she was terrified by the form of it, but too scared to move or call for help, so she screamed from the outside in and it hurt her ears from the inside out, and the monstrous thing, the deep unknowing of it, grew closer. When she was four years old, it was a witch. When she was eight years old, it was a werewolf. When she was ten, it was a man with a sack who stole children. But now it wasn't anything. And she couldn't remember a story to go with it. And so, without a frame of reference, her head began to hurt. And her brain worked itself into a state. And the beautiful, adult, Caucasian female...lapsed. [*Pause.*] If the poison is administered by an envious old crone, or the bite of a vampire, we can kiss the victims back to life. There is a precedent. But this most fair, most lovely damsel, cannot receive the kiss; her lips, fastened around the modern savior—the cold pump of his love. A machine, not a prince. [*Pause.*] It is too real. She'll perish. They'll never marry.

[*Lights fade on* DOCTOR.

Lights up on NICHOLAS, *who is sitting in area representing his Cabin.*]

NICHOLAS: I can't get it out, you know? It's necessary to put on a sad song. Really. Can you beat that? I find a record and as soon as it starts, I just fall flat on the floor and sob. As soon as it stops, I've done, too. I'll tell you what else. It's the monumental ego. It's a laugh—but I think she died because I let her down. Classic. Now, if there's a success, something going well, I can't celebrate. It's off. [*Pause.*] Your last exit was the best of all, baby. I'll give you that. You did yourself proud. And nobody's trying to rob you of a fitting end, so don't misinterpret this, Raleigh, but there was a thing left to do. There was something maybe left to have. Still to come. [*Pause.*] Just a little heartbreak, dedicated to R. In memory of R. [*Beat.*] I want to make amends. I want . . . just for good measure . . . to say it again. Just to make sure I'm covered. Represented in heaven. And you're going to let me say it. And then you're going to say it back to me.

[*Corridor.*]

RALEIGH: [*Speaks, knowing it is her last connection with anyone.*] Nicky . . . that moment of falling to the knees. Oh, darling, that act of falling to the knees. Love pushing you to the floor in one arc. One arc of surrender. Of falling to the knees.

[*She stops abruptly, turns her back to him and to audience.*]

NICHOLAS: You're gonna say it back to me. Sealed with a kiss. Forever. All gone. Absolved. I love you. My best. YOU BITCH. YOU BEAUTIFUL, BEAUTIFUL THIEF. [*He picks up telephone. Dials.*] Goddammit, you tell me. You tell me!

[RALEIGH *turns slowly and moves up corridor . . . moves up corridor . . . away . . . as if she is pulled away . . . finally, as we hear the taped message from the telephone.*]

V.O.: The number you have reached is not in service at this time, and there is no new number. Please be sure you have checked the telephone directory for the right number and dailing correctly. This is a recording.

[*Lights fade.*]

SISTERS

Patricia Montley

For Jeannine
with admiration, gratitude, and affection

Patricia Montley

INTRODUCTION TO PAT MONTLEY'S *SISTERS*

Madonne Miner

Neither race nor gender nor homosexual difference alone can constitute individual identity or the basis for a theory and politics of social change. de Lauretis 26

Throughout the 1970s and 1980s, lesbian and feminist critics interested in theatre and performance studies debated definitions: what makes a play "lesbian"? what dramatic forms qualify as "feminist"? should we consider the sexual/political orientation of playwrights? what about the "vision" expressed by the play? With respect to feminist theatre, Susan M. Steadman, in an overview of criticism and theory, cites Janet Brown's early claim that a play is feminist "when its central rhetorical motive is woman's struggle for autonomy within an unjust sociosexual hierarchy" [23], only to contrast that claim to Rosemary Curb's more encompassing definition of feminist drama as "'all drama by and about women characterized by multiple interior reflections of women's lives and perceptions'" [Curb 302, qtd. in Steadman 23]. Ultimately, Steadman insists "there is no *one* feminist criticism of drama/performance/theatre, no discrete ideology that places its stamp of approval on this body of writing" [14].

We see similar patterns of discussion taking place with respect to lesbian theatre. Jill Dolan and Sue-Ellen Case, for example, insist that lesbian theatre can occur only in modes that challenge realism, since realism is inherently heterosexist and conservative. Dolan proposes that lesbian theatre/performance occurs in postmodernist styles, styles that work at "constructing what has been called a 'collective subject,'" ["Lesbian" 172] as opposed to the isolated and marginalized lesbian subject of realistic drama. Case urges us to identify lesbian theatre as "butch/femme" or camp, as these forms may articulate "the lives of homosexuals through the obtuse tone or irony and inscribe their oppression with the same device" ["Butch" 287].

Less restrictive than Dolan and Case is Nina Rapi, who lists several features that she sees as characterizing lesbian theatre (role-playing, flexibility with respect to gender identification, intersubjective reciprocity, shifts in 'the axis of categorization' [147-58]) and concludes that "lesbians can create radical theatre choosing whichever form and structure they like, provided that these are informed by a lesbian perspective" [153]. Opening up the definition of lesbian drama even further are Jill Davis and Teresa de Lauretis. The former, writing in defense of Sandra Freeman's play, *Supporting Roles*, which has been criticized for portraying lesbians who seem to mimic heterosexual roles, observes: "lesbians do live those lives, and lesbian theatre, lesbian culture needs to hear as wide a range of lesbian voices and experiences as possible. It would be absurd, given the long silence imposed on lesbians by the heterosexual world, if we imposed our own form of censorship, screening out from public utterance all but one agreed definition of lesbian experience" [x]. De Lauretis, I believe, would agree; she asserts that the project of lesbian performance is to "alter the standard of vision, the frame of reference of visibility, of *what can be seen*" [33]. Such an alteration cannot occur if we require that lesbian theatre be only camp, only non-realistic, only experimental. To alter "what can be seen" requires a range of forms, styles, and content.

I introduce Pat Montley's 1981 play, *Sisters*, with this debate for two reasons: first, understanding the terms of the debate may help readers understand Jill Dolan's banishment of *Sisters* from the lesbian agenda (Dolan maintains that *Sisters* is a play "that defies lesbian feminist identification" ["Women's" 11]); and second, within its realistic frame, *Sisters* surveys precisely those issues that lesbian and feminist communities have been debating. It asks readers to consider and reconsider questions about identity (what makes one a feminist? a lesbian? a heterosexual?); about identity politics (what do "individuals" gain by aligning themselves with families/groups/institutions? what do they lose?); and about patterns within our culture that encourage even those in positions of very minimal power to impose bi-polar, "either-or" thinking on others.

Given Dolan's suspicion of realism as a mode appropriate for the lesbian experience (a suspicion shared by Elin Diamond, Jeanie Forte, Janelle Reinelt and others), her criticism of Montley's well-made *Sisters*—as performed at the ATA Women's Theatre Program, August 7–10, 1983—comes as no surprise. What is surprising is Dolan's unwillingness to approach the play on its own terms; that is, to appreciate it as a play about seven women, women whose identities cannot be reduced to single elements (Sister Joanna is not simply a lesbian; rather, she is a lesbian, Catholic, celibate nun, "daughter" to Mother Superior Naomi, "sister" to the five ex-nuns she invites for a weekend reunion, citizen, activist, and so on). Dolan complains that *Sisters* is not "an expression of lesbian existence in the 1980s" ["Women's" 12], but no play can express "lesbian existence in the 1980s." What *Sisters* can do, however, is represent some of the joys and tensions experienced by a particular subset of women as one of them, Sister Joanna, urges the others to accept "lesbian" as a term appropriately descriptive of their own identities. Granted, Joanna's "sisters" refuse to embrace the term as Joanna desires; but their refusal is not an indictment of lesbianism. Instead, it functions first as a reminder of how powerful heterosexist imperatives can be, and second, as a critique of the reductive approach ("either/or," "all or nothing") that Joanna falls into here.

In one of *Sisters'* early scenes, Joanna explains that she has invited Carol, Leslie, Maria, Rosalie and Helene (now all "lay persons") to join her for a twenty-year reunion of select members from their novitiate class because "there was something special about each of you that I . . .admired" [1.2.19]. Act I provides evidence of how these women *are* special; they tease one another, care for one another, show us their talents. This opening act is upbeat, warm, and comic; we laugh as these ex-nuns and Sister Joanna re-enact the Chapter of Faults ("I Sister Leslie humbly acknowledge that I broke *our* racket when I lost *our* temper" [1.2.15]), attempt to sing "Jubilate Deo" but stumble after the first few lines, and share a meal of spaghetti and memories.

But for Joanna, the five women she's invited are "special" in yet another way.

Joanna believes that she and they share a sisterhood not only as nuns (or former nuns), but also as lesbians. This latter bond/identity is especially important to Joanna, as she recently has been censured by her Bishop for her work in gay ministry. While it's true that a minority of the Catholic clergy pursued such work in the 1970s and 1980s, the official party line of the Church condemns homosexuality and condemns homosexuality in its clergy with a special vehemence. Joanna, through Mother Superior Naomi, receives word that the Bishop expects her to toe this line. Through Naomi, the Bishop presents Joanna with a choice: "if you decide to continue in this work, you will have to do so as a lay person" [2.3.16].

This institutional ultimatum ("be fully one of us—or no longer one of us") functions as an example of patriarchal, heterosexist, bi-polar ("either/or") thinking at its worst. It requires that Joanna sacrifice various parts of her identity (her lesbianism, her activism) so as to retain other parts (her status as a Catholic clergyperson, her sense of herself as a sister among sisters, as a daughter to Mother Naomi). Delivered from above, the ultimatum both demands allegiance and articulates the costs of non-allegiance: a wayward daughter may be disowned.

Sisters encourages its lesbian and feminist readers/viewers to sympathize with Joanna as she struggles to retain all of the various, perhaps contrary features of her identity, at the same time she attempts to remain a member of the family/the institution to which she has pledged herself. Further, the play enjoins us to question the institutional sadism of an entity (here, the Catholic Church) that insists upon writing one plotline for all, thereby denying the complexity of individual subjects who comprise this "all."

Where *Sisters* goes further than many other early feminist and lesbian critiques of bi-polar thinking, however, is in its recognition that even the most politically marginalized may engage in practices that reduce others to "either/or," practices that demand a narrow allegiance to party lines, thereby robbing members of complexities of identity. *Sisters* asks lesbian and feminist readers to question not only demands made by the Bishop, but also—and here's the rub—those made by Joanna. The Bishop has a plotline for Joanna; Joanna has a plotline for Carol, Leslie, Rosalie, Helene and Maria. The Bishop's plotline is reductive; so too is Joanna's. Neither can allow for the radical complexity of the characters involved. Further, both imply punishment for non-compliance—the Bishop, overtly: you will no longer be a sister; Joanna, covertly: you will no longer be my sisters.

Certainly, Joanna's attempt to sign-up her sisters as lesbians differs from the Bishop's attempt to sign her up as an "obedient daughter" in that the Bishop acts with the full force of tradition and heterosexual culture on his side. While some might argue that Joanna correctly pushes her "sisters" to walk out of their closets, to stand beside her and be counted, *Sisters* does not allow for such an easy answer with respect to questions of identity and identity politics. The play repeatedly articulates characters' desires to pledge themselves to larger parties/institutions but also reveals the way such desires may restrict characters' breadth and growth. One of the most interesting of these articulations arises out of Helene's request that together they sing "Salve Regina"; in response, Carol observes, "[t]he beauty of the chant is the unity of many voices in the single melody" [1.4.36]. In consideration of what can be achieved by a choir instead of a soloist, many voices come together in a single voice; together, they produce the chant. Only in unison, only as a group, can these women effectively sing "Salve Regina"; but singing in unison, each one sacrifices something of her own voice. So too, *Sisters* suggests, do the politics of identity function. Only by aligning ourselves as lesbians or feminists or women of color or working-class women can we hope to produce change; when making such alignments, however, we need to be aware of those parts of ourselves that we sacrifice, of the voices that we silence.

Sisters asks us to consider the demands we—those of us willing to assume politically-motivated labels—impose on our sisters. How productive are those demands? How reductive? How much "play" do they allow? How much do they concede to varieties of experience? In *Sisters'* Prologue, Mother Naomi counsels her fifty new novitiates to "love one another always in the bonds of true sisterhood" [Prologue]. Montley's play struggles with questions of what "true sisterhood" might be—and asks us to do the same, as activists and critics, as readers and audience members, as lesbians and feminists.

WORKS CITED

Case, Sue-Ellen. "Toward a Butch-Femme Aesthetic." *Making a Spectacle: Feminist Essays on Contemporary Women's Theatre*. Ed. Lynda Hart. Ann Arbor: U. of Michigan P, 1989. 282-99.

Curb, Rosemary K. "Re/cognition, Re/presentation, Re/creation in Woman-Conscious Drama: The Seer, The Seen, The Scene, The Obscene." *Theatre Journal* 37 (1985): 302-15.

de Lauretis, Teresa. "Sexual Indifference and Lesbian Representation." *Performing Feminisms: Feminist Critical Theory and Theatre*. Ed. Sue-Ellen Case. Baltimore: Johns Hopkins UP, 1990. 17-39.

Davis, Jill. Introduction. *Lesbian Plays: Two*. London: Methuen, 1989. i-x.

Diamond, Elin. "Mimesis, Mimicry, and the 'True-Real.'" *Modern Drama* 32 (1989): 58-72.

Dolan, Jill. "'Lesbian' Subjectivity in Realism: Dragging at the Margins of Structure and Ideology." *Presence and Desire: Essays on Gender, Sexuality, Performance*. Ann Arbor: U of Michigan P, 1993. 159-77.

_____. "Women's Theatre Program ATA: Creating a Feminist Forum." *Women and Performance: A Journal of Feminist Theory* 1.2 (1984): 5-13.

Forte, Jeanie. "Realism, Narrative, and the Feminist Playwright—A Problem of Reception." *Modern Drama* 32 (1989): 115-27.

Freeman, Sandra. "Supporting Roles." *Lesbian Plays: Two*. Ed. Jill Davis. London: Methuen, 1989. 47-90.

Rapi, Nina. "'Hide and Seek': The Search for a Lesbian Theatre Aesthetic." *New Theatre Quarterly* 9:24 (1993): 147-58.

Reinelt, Janelle. "Feminist Theory and the Problem of Performance." *Modern Drama* 32 (1989): 48-57.

Steadman, Susan M. *Dramatic Re-visions: An Annotated Bibliography of Feminism and Theatre 1972–1988*. Chicago: American Library Assn, 1991.

CHARACTERS

MOTHER NAOMI: 55–60. Once Mistress of Novices, now Provincial Superior of the Sisters of Our Lady of Good Hope. A committed, pragmatic leader, but genuinely warm and sympathetic. (Wears a full-length traditional habit and veil in the Prologue; thereafter, a modified habit—dark suit with white blouse, short veil, pumps.)

SISTER JOANNA: 38–40. An activist. Intelligent but vulnerable, dedicated and sometimes intense, but charming and playful. Planner of the reunion. (Wears denim suit with print blouse, and flat canvas shoes [no veil] in I-1; same costume without jacket for rest of play.) The others are all her former classmates—now ex-nuns.

ROSIE: 38–40. An artist. Good-natured, excitable, up-beat, sloppy, enjoys life. Her speech rides a roller-coaster, with excessive vocal variation and undue emphasis. (Wears colorful, outrageous, artistic get-ups.)

CAROL: 38–40. A music therapist. Fine singing voice; conventional Catholic; wholesome-looking, but somewhat overweight; lives with Leslie. (Hair and clothing are conservative, modest, tasteful.)

LESLIE: 38–40. A high school physical education teacher. Still an athlete but out of condition; not butch. Conservative; straightforward; lives with Carol. (Hair and clothing are casual, clean, neat, but without concern for fashion.)

HELENE: 38–40. A writer. Attractive, sophisticated, theatrical, keyed-up; sense of humor; parodies her own pretentiousness. (Dresses fashionably, expensively.)

MARIA: 38–40. A nurse. Traditional wife-and-mother. Sensitive, nurturing; more reserved than others. (Hair and clothing are conventional, unobtrusive, soft.)

SETTING: *Prologue: convent motherhouse chapel, early 1960s. The rest of the action takes place in the early 1980s, alternating between a beach house (and beach) and the motherhouse (a garden or an office). The scenes at the beach house are in chronological order and take place over a summer weekend. Some of the scenes at the motherhouse between* JOANNA *and* NAOMI *are in this chronology, others are reenacted from* JOANNA's *memory.*

MUSIC NOTES: *The* Posit Signum *(Gregorian Chant) is from the ceremony for the Profession of Vows. The* Dies Irae *(Gregorian Chant) from the Requiem Mass, and the* Salve Regina *(Gregorian Chant) from Compline can be found in most books of plainchant. The* Jubilate Deo *is a motet in two-part harmony, with music by Mozart. One version can be found in* The Gregory Hymnal and Catholic Choir Book *edited and arranged by Nicola A. Montani and published by the St. Gregory Guild, Philadelphia, © 1947.*

PROLOGUE

Motherhouse chapel. Sound of women signing Gregorian chant: Posuit Signam. *A tight circle of light comes up on* MOTHER NAOMI, *in a traditional habit, at the edge of stage, facing out. As singing crescendos, she seems to be watching a procession approach. The singing stops.*

NAOMI: In the name of Jesus Christ, of our Holy Father the Pope, of His Excellency our Bishop, and of our Reverend Mother General of the Sisters of Our Lady of Good Hope, I accept your Holy Vows of Poverty, Chastity, and Obedience. [*Becoming more personal.*] You sixty have been especially dear to me, my Daughters, in the two years you have been my novices. And as you are sent forth to do the Lord's work, I ask you to keep these two things in mind: Remember from whom you come; and remember to whom you go. It is from God you come and to God you belong. Be ever mindful of the words you have just sung: "He has placed his seal upon you that you may admit no other lover." And it is to God you go—to find Him in the poorest of his creatures. For those with the greatest need have the first right to help. [*Formal again.*] May the blessing of God go with you. Pray for me, Sisters, as I will for you. [*Personal again.*] And let us love one another always in the bonds of true sisterhood.

[*Chant is resumed and sung softly as the light on* NAOMI *dims. As if performing a ritual, she takes off her traditional wimple, coif, and veil. She lets the long habit drop from her, revealing a short blue suit and white blouse underneath. She puts on a short veil to complete her modernized habit.*]

ACT I
SCENE 1

Motherhouse (garden or office). Crossfade as NAOMI *crosses to this area and is joined by* SISTER JOANNA. *Though they are in the middle of a confrontation, they are genuinely fond of each other and never lose sight of that.*

NAOMI: Is it possible you *like* . . . being controversial?

JOANNA: You mean the publicity?

NAOMI: Dramatizing the situation, providing copy for sympathetic reporters, confronting bishops.

JOANNA: [*Matter-of-factly.*] I'm not the first to confront a bishop.

NAOMI: You may be the first to enjoy it so much!

JOANNA: You think it's fun to be chastised like a school girl by the bishop?! You think I relish getting anonymous hate mail from my own sisters?! You think I enjoy . . . [*Beat. Softer.*] *this.*

NAOMI: This?

JOANNA: [*Painfully.*] Your . . . disapproval.

NAOMI: I've always acknowledged your talents, Sister Joanna, and tried to give you enough ... freedom to use them.

JOANNA: But now the tether's being shortened?

NAOMI: It doesn't have to be. Just take up a different cause.

JOANNA: [*Pleading.*] Mother Naomi, I need to do this work.

NAOMI: Need?

JOANNA: I feel called to it—to speak out, to lay the groundwork for change.

NAOMI: To be the Voice in the Wilderness preparing the way? Why must you be the one?

JOANNA: Because no one else is doing it.

NAOMI: Do you have some special investment in this...because...you yourself are...?

JOANNA: That's not the reason.

NAOMI: Then what makes you so convinced of this calling?

JOANNA: My faith.

NAOMI: Are you sure it's not your pride?

JOANNA: Don't worry—I haven't seen any visions. But I have seen people in pain. And I've listened. And I know I have to help. That's all. You said not to expect fireworks. That God's will is revealed in simple ways.

NAOMI: Beware, Joanna. That's the ultimate temptation: seeing yourself as sole interpreter of God's will.

JOANNA: I'll just have to take that risk.

NOAMI: That always has been your specialty, hasn't it? [*Beat. Partly teasing.*] You should have joined the circus.

JOANNA: [*Matching her tone.*] I thought I did.

NAOMI: The daring young nun on the flying trapeze.

JOANNA: Now who's dramatizing?

NAOMI: Listen to me—I can't be your safety net any longer.

JOANNA: Can't or won't?

NAOMI: [*Softening.*] Joanna, I'm afraid for you.

JOANNA: Are you sure it's for me?

[*Pause.*]

NAOMI: The Provincial Council meetings start Friday.

JOANNA: Will you let me know?

NAOMI: Of course, Love.

JOANNA: I'm going to the beach house for the weekend.

NAOMI: Retreat?

JOANNA: Reunion.

NAOMI: Your class?

JOANNA: A few of them. [*Beat.*] It's been twenty years.

NAOMI: [*Nostalgic.*] My first novices.

JOANNA: Want to come? You'd have a better time.

NAOMI: I'll know their decision by Saturday afternoon.

JOANNA: I'll come back then.

[NAOMI *exits.* JOANNA *crosses to beach house. Crossfade with her.*]

SCENE 2

Friday evening. A simple beach house with a sitting area (sofa, chairs, stereo) and a kitchen area. Stairs lead to a second floor. A door leads to a porch.
There is a small beach area on another part of the stage.
JOANNA *is cooking.* ROSIE *is on the floor, working on a large pastel drawing. Gregorian chant—women's voices as in the Prologue—is coming from the stereo.*

HELENE: [*Calling from upstairs.*] Joanna! Give the Singing Nuns a break! You're going to wear that record out!

JOANNA: [*Calling up to her.*] I'm tripping out on nostalgia.

HELENE: [*From upstairs.*] How can anyone who reads *Psychology Today* be so medieval?

JOANNA: [*Calling up to her, crossing to stereo.*] Listen, Helene—Gregorian Chant is probably the only thing that got those poor nuns through the Middle Ages. [*Wistfully, to* ROSIE.] It reminds me how simple it used to be. When we sang like that, only the music mattered. Sometimes I miss it. [*Turns music off.*]

ROSIE: Me too! This was a great idea, Jo. What made you think of it?

JOANNA: I guess I just wanted to be with you all again. I miss you.

ROSIE: Aw . . . isn't that sweet!

JOANNA: How's the mistresspiece coming?

ROSIE: Chalk's not really my medium.

JOANNA: [*Looking at drawing.*] I like it. It's very . . . colorful.

ROSIE: Gaudy. That's what the critics say. The three "g's"—glaring, garish, gaudy.

JOANNA: Just like God.

ROSIE: What?

JOANNA: Haven't they ever seen a jungle? Rosie, you're just divinely inspired!

ROSIE: Now I remember why I liked you, Joanna. How'd you like to be my agent?

JOANNA: [*Crossing to kitchen.*] What do you think, Rosie—sit-down or buffet?

ROSIE: [*Counting chairs.*] There's you and me and Helene. That's three. Carol and Leslie make five.

JOANNA: Six if Maria comes.

ROSIE: You think she'll show up?

JOANNA: She never actually said no. Just all this stuff about hospital duty and the kids' summer camp.

ROSIE: Maybe she's nervous.

JOANNA: She wouldn't be the only one.

ROSIE: You worry too much, Joanna. You ought to go into therapy. My therapist is wonderful. I'm just crazy about her. But it's all right—you're supposed to be in love with your therapist. It's called "crossference' or something. Anyway, what's there to worry about?

JOANNA: What if somebody's become a Republican? Or a Total Woman?

ROSIE: What if somebody still goes to church?

JOANNA: I still go to church.

ROSIE: It's good for your credibility.

JOANNA: It's just that I want us to still have something in common .... I guess I want us to still be ... sisters.

ROSIE: Relax, Joanna. Nobody's going to make a scene.

JOANNA: Maybe that's what I'm afraid of—it'll be so boring!

ROSIE: So run a psychodrama session.

JOANNA: Better yet-Chapter of Faults!

ROSIE: Wouldn't that be a gas! I vote buffet. It's more ... dynamic.

JOANNA: Did you tell Carol and Leslie salad dressing?

ROSIE: And napkins. Isn't Leslie a great swimmer?.

JOANNA: Leslie's great at everything athletic. Don't you remember?

ROSIE: I never saw her swim: In the old days we weren't allowed.

JOANNA: What do you think about those two?

ROSIE: What do you mean?

JOANNA: How long have they been living together?

ROSIE: Since they left. Why?

JOANNA: Just wondering. How can you tell if spaghetti's done?

ROSIE:Throw a piece against the wall; if it sticks, it's done.

JOANNA: Are you sure?

ROSIE: Is the Pope Italian?

JOANNA: No.

ROSIE: Well I am! Take it from Mamma Rosa.

JOANNA: Does it matter which wall? Painted, paneled, papered, brick—they all work?

[LESLIE *and* CAROL *enter onto porch.* LESLIE *carries a case of beer which she starts to unload into a cooler on the porch.* CAROL *comes into the house with a bag of groceries.*]

CAROL: Smells great in here—who's on cooking?

JOANNA: [*Raising her hand.*] We're having off-the-wall spaghetti.

ROSIE: Drum roll, everybody—here it is. Da-da-da, dat, da-da! [*She holds up the drawing. It is the motherhouse, with a domed tower, flanked by wings, enclosing courtyards. Off to one side is an apple orchard.*] So what do you think?

JOANNA: Makes me homesick.

CAROL: It's beautiful! I mean it's so realistic. Did you do it from memory?

ROSIE: No, Carol, I copied from a postcard! Of course, I remember every inch of the motherhouse! Don't you? Come on—help me hang it.

[ROSIE *and* CAROL *hang the drawing.*]

JOANNA: Hey, Rosie—do me a favor and put blossom on the apple trees, would you? Lots of little pink blossom.

ROSIE: Aren't apple blossom white?

JOANNA: Biology was never my forte.

ROSIE: Is that why you're still celibate?

JOANNA: Someone has to atone for all that S.E.X. out there.

ROSIE: You're a regular saint. You and Agnes.

CAROL: And Lucy!

ROSIE: And Maria Goretti!

CAROL: [*Chanting with quick pace and mock seriousness.*] Sancta Joanna

CAROL AND ROSIE: [*Chanting quickly.*] Ora pro nobis.

CAROL: [*Chanting quickly.*] Omnes sanctae Virgines.

CAROL AND ROSIE: [*Chanting quickly.*] Orate pro nobis.

JOANNA: [*Mock pronouncement.*] The virgin martyrs are the jewels in the crown of the Church.

ROSIE: Translation: Better a dead woman than a sexy one.

JOANNA: Now that you two are warmed up, let's celebrate the "unveiling" with a song! How about it, Carol?

CAROL: The Choir Director is taking requests.

ROSIE: How about *Laetentur Coeli*?

CAROL: That's Christmas. What we need is . . . a motet for festivals. How about *Jubilate Deo*?

JOANNA: Hit it, Sister!

[CAROL *hums the starting note. They break into harmony,* CAROL *conducting with exaggeration.*]

ALL: [*Singing.*] Jubilate Deo omnis terra,
Servite Domino

in laetitia
in laetitia . . .

[*They all take a deep breath, get ready to start the next part, but all have forgotten what comes next. They break into laughter* ROSIE *throws an arm around* CAROL.]

ROSIE: We were counting on *you*, Choir Director.

CAROL: I thought *you* all would remember!

JOANNA: It's been so long!

CAROL: All right, Sisters—rehearsal before morning prayer!

JOANNA: Where's Leslie?

CAROL: Icing down the beer.

LESLIE: [*From porch.*] Don't talk about me—I can hear you!

CAROL: [*Calling out to her.*] We're not that desperate!

JOANNA: How about a drink before dinner? White wine or red?

CAROL: White, thanks.

ROSIE: I'll take red.

JOANNA: What about Leslie?

CAROL: She'll drink beer.

LESLIE: [*From porch, simultaneously with* CAROL's *line.*] I'll drink beer. [LESLIE *enters, drinking beer, sees the drawing, moves around the room pretending to be criticizing it from different angles.*] Perfect. But you forgot the tennis courts, Rosie. How come you didn't get her on that, Carol?

ROSIE: Do you suppose Artemesia Gentileschi had to deal with this?

LESLIE AND CAROL: Who?

ROSIE: [*Exiting, disgusted.*] I'll get the chalks.

JOANNA: [*Unpacking groceries.*] Salad dressing . . . napkins . . . what's this starch for?

LESLIE: Helene.

JOANNA: What are you up to, Leslie?

LESLIE: Don't you remember Helene in the Novitiate? How she was about not having a wrinkle in her bib?

JOANNA: So what are you going to starch?

LESLIE: I don't know yet. Where is she anyway?

JOANNA: Putting on her designer mascara.

CAROL: [*Calls up steps.*] Helene!

HELENE: [*Upstairs.*] Be down in a minute!

CAROL: [*To others, mockingly.*] She'll be down in a minute. [*Calling up.*] Want a drink?

HELENE: [*Upstairs.*] Got any scotch?

CAROL: [*To* JOANNA.] Do we have any scotch?

[JOANNA *shakes head "No."*]

CAROL: [*Cont'd. Calling up.*] White wine or red?

HELENE: [*Upstairs.*] Are we having a party or a mass?

CAROL: [To JOANNA.] Is this a party or a mass?

JOANNA: Tell her it's a cheap party.

CAROL: [*Calling up.*] We're having a cheap party. Want to come?

LESLIE: [*Calling up.*] Helene—I got some cold beer if you'd rather have that.

HELENE: [*Upstairs.*] No thanks—I'll leave the beer bellies to you jocks.

LESLIE: [*Calling up.*] Stifle it!

JOANNA: Leslie, what's going on with you and Helene? She's been needling you all day.

LESLIE: Just teasing

ROSIE: [*Returning with chalks.*] OK, spring is about to arrive at the motherhouse. [*Starts putting apple blossoms on the trees.*]

LESLIE: And the tennis courts!

ROSIE: Yeah, yeah.

[HELENE *descends.* CAROL *sings: "Here she comes, Sister America" Others pick it up.* HELENE *plays to them, doing turns on the runway. Cheers, whistles. When noise subsides,* HELENE *notices drawing.*]

HELENE: Ah! How phallic.

ROSIE: What!

HELENE: The rising tower.

ROSIE: This is a *dome*, Dummy! Domes are *female* symbols. Don't you know anything about art?!

HELENE: I know a lot about rising towers.

JOANNA: This is better than a Rorschach test.

ROSIE: Then how come you're so horny?

HELENE: Me?—horny?

ROSIE: [*To others, but played to get a rise out of* HELENE.] You all thought we were late getting here this morning because of me. But for once I was on time. It was Helene's fault. When I stopped for her, she was upstairs pretending to be dressing. But really she was having one last screw with Neil.

HELENE: Rosalie! How can you say that!?

ROSIE: Because I *heard* you!

HELENE: You were supposed to be putting my stuff in the car.

ROSIE: [*Laughing.*] Shit, Helene—even a quickie takes longer than that.

HELENE: "And the two shall be one flesh." It says so in the Bible.

ROSIE: That's for *married* people, Helene. Not for you and Neil.

HELENE: Oh God—why did I say I would come to this reunion?

ROSIE: Because you wanted to *share*. Don't you remember? We talked about it in the car. How we really needed this long weekend of Deep Meaningful Sharing with people who really *cared* about us.

HELENE: You need it. I came for the suntan.

JOANNA: Since the sun has just set, would you settle for dinner. [*Hurls a string of spaghetti against the wall.*]

HELENE: What are you doing?!

JOANNA: It's not sticking yet. We'll have to have Chapter of Faults.

HELENE AND CAROL AND LESLIE: What?

JOANNA: Just like old times in the refectory.

HELENE: I couldn't possibly. I don't have any faults.

LESLIE: We'll help you remernher.

CAROL: This is sick. I mean this is really sick.

ROSIE: Come on, Carol—be a sport.

CAROL: God'll punish us for this.

JOANNA: All right, Sisters. [*Claps her hands softly.*] We'll line up here…hands in sleeves… [*They line up, facing audience.*] Eyes mortified. [*They cast their eyes down.*]

ROSIE: That's what took all the fun out of it!

JOANNA: Sister Rosalie! [*Puts a finger to her lips.*] Sister Leslie will go first.

LESLIE: She will?

[HELENE *pushes* LESLIE *onto her knees.*]

LESLIE: [*Cont'd.*] All right, all right.

[*Clears her throat, extends her arms out to the sides and starts to say something, but* ROSIE *gives a snort of laughter.* LESLIE *shoots her a dark look, composes herself again, and recites formally.*]

LESLIE: [*Cont'd.*] I, Sister Leslie, humbly acknowledge that I lost my temper.

CAROL: What she really means is that she threw a tantrum on the tennis court and smashed her racket.

JOANNA: *Whose* racket?

ALL: *Our* racket!

LESLIE: I, Sister Leslie, humbly acknowledge that I broke *our* racket when I lost *our* temper.

[LESLIE *gets up.* CAROL *kneels.*]

CAROL: I, Sister Carol, humbly acknowledge that I broke the Grand Silence… [*Everyone gasps.*]…by humming after night prayer.

JOANNA: What did you hum, Sister?

CAROL: "Wake up, Little Suzie."

[ALL *"tsk, tsk" as* CAROL *gets up and* HELENE *kneels.*]

HELENE: I, Sister Helene...humbly acknowledge...that I was vain about my appearance.

LESLIE: Is that the best you can do?

CAROL: Don't tell us you've lost your flair for the dramatic,

JOANNA: [*Acting it out.*] Who hid behind the statue of the Virgin and terrified Sister Pius with an apparition?

[HELENE *squeals with delight at the memory; others break up.*]

HELENE: I did!

JOANNA: Who put the rooster in the men's room when the Cardinal came to visit?

HELENE: That was Sister Prudence's idea!

JOANNA: Who did it?!

HELENE: [*Squeals.*] I did!

JOANNA: Who put old Sister Immaculata's mop in her coffin with her?.

ALL: What?

HELENE: How did you know that?

JOANNA: I was there.

HELENE: But I was last on wake duty the night before the funeral.

JOANNA: And I was next to last.

HELENE: You spied on me?

JOANNA: Mopping the corridor at midnight—I knew you were up to something!

HELENE: And you didn't tell?

JOANNA: She would have been eternally miserable without it.

HELENE: I humbly acknowledge that I underestimated Sister Joanna.

[*Resumes her place in line, as* ROSIE *kneels.*]

ROSIE: I Sister Rosalie humbly acknowledge that I ate between meals....I was late for choir....

CAROL: Very late.

ROSIE: I did not get up when the rising bell rang. I broke a dish. I used an object for a purpose other than that for which it was intended.

HELENE: What?

ROSIE: [*Breaking out of character.*] Don't you remember that one? It was my favorite. "I used an object for a purpose other than that for which it was intended."

JOANNA: What object was that, Sister?

ROSIE: My finger! [*Back in character, reciting.*] I humbly acknowledge that I used my finger for—

JOANNA: That will do, Sister. Too much contrition is a fault.

ROSIE: But didn't you just hate how superficial it was? We didn't dare tell our real sins.

JOANNA: It wasn't allowed. That would have given the rest of us ideas.

ROSIE: But weren't you all just dying for someone to admit something horrible and human?

JOANNA: Let's try it. [*Kneels and recites.*] I Sister Joanna humbly acknowledge that I nurtured lurid, lustful fantasies about fornicating with—

[*There is a knock at the door.* ALL *look towards it.*]

MARIA: [*From porch.*] Is this the Good Hope Retreat Center for the hopeless?

JOANNA: Maria!

[MARIA *enters.* OTHERS *run to her, squealing greetings and giving her hugs-except for* JOANNA *who sits back on her heels, smiling. The following are machine-gunned at* MARIA.]

CAROL: Where've you been?

LESLIE: We didn't know you were coming!

HELENE: You look terrific!

ROSIE: You didn't get lost, did you? Are you OK?

MARIA: [*Pointing to each as she answers their questions in reverse order.*] Yes, I'm OK. No, I didn't get lost. Thanks, you look terrific too. I didn't know I was coming. [*Finding the right questioner.*] I've been at the hospital all day. Whew!

CAROL: Are you sick?

MARIA: No, I'm a nurse.

[*They laugh.*]

HELENE: Come on in—you're just in time for Chapter of Faults.

[*The huddle around the door opens up;* MARIA *and* JOANNA *look at each other.*]

JOANNA: Hello, Ria.

MARIA: You haven't changed, Joanna.

JOANNA: Are you disappointed?

MARIA: No. I'm not disappointed.

[JOANNA *gets up and they embrace tentatively.*]

ROSIE: Joanna was just going to humbly acknowledge who she fantasized fornicating with back in the convent.

MARIA: Well! Don't let me interrupt.

JOANNA: I'll have to wait now. The readiness is all. How about a drink instead? [*Goes for wine.*]

HELENE: [*Raising her glass.*] Joanna is about to celebrate mass.

JOANNA: Oh—the spaghetti!

ROSIE: I'll get it.

LESLIE: So are we all here, Joanna? Or do you have more surprises in store?

JOANNA: This is it.

LESLIE: Why only six out of sixty?

HELENE: The top ten percent!

CAROL: Quality over quantity.

JOANNA: That's it, in fact. Big groups tend to be ... well, you know ... inhibiting. And I wanted ... I don't know really ...

HELENE AND ROSIE: Deep Meaningful Sharing!

LESLIE: But how did you pick us?

JOANNA: Maybe I liked you best.

LESLIE: Come on!

JOANNA: It's true. There was something special about each of you that I ... admired.

LESLIE: That might be true for the others. But why me? You were just being polite because I live with Carol.

JOANNA: I've always liked you, Leslie. I think it's because you were always so ... so clean.

[OTHERS *guffaw*.]

LESLIE: [*Embarrassed.*] If you'd been assigned to scrubbing showers instead of shelving books, you'd've been clean too.

JOANNA: That's not what I mean. You're ... wholesome—whole. There are no loose ends about you. You're a seamless garment. No frills. No secret compartments.

LESLIE: And you like that?

JOANNA: It's honest.

LESLIE: [*Touched.*] Gosh. I don't know what to say.

JOANNA: [*Approaching* MARIA *with wine glass*.] Anyway, of all the people in our class, you all mattered most to me.

MARIA: Not very charitable of you, Sister. You know what St. Paul says—no favorites. 'All to all.'

JOANNA: [*Touching* MARIA.] And a little more to some.

ROSIE: [*Pretending to be ringing a bell*.] Ding-a-ling-a-ling-a-ling.

JOANNA: [*Assuming a "Superior's" tone*.] Sisters—since our reunion is a major feast, I am suspending the rule of silence for this meal.

[OTHERS *respond with mock excitement, and, during the following dialogue, serve themselves and eat*.]

MARIA: Rosie—Joanna told me on the phone you had a little boy. [*Gesturing to drawing*.] Is he an artistic prodigy?

ROSIE: Impressionistic finger painting at three.

JOANNA: Imagine the mess!

ROSIE: And now Stephen wants another one—at my age!

CAROL: What do you mean? We're not forty yet?

ROSIE: Easy for you to say, Carol. You don't have kids.

CAROL: [*Wishing she did.*] Right. [*Crosses to table.*]

ROSIE: Shit. I'm running off at the mouth already.

HELENE: Who's dating anybody? Let's get all the good dirt.

JOANNA: Helene, ever think of taking sensitivity training?

HELENE: Come on—raise hands, everybody who did the singles-bar scene after you left?

[ALL *but* JOANNA *raise hands. They laugh.*]

HELENE: [*Cont'd. Pointing to* JOANNA.] Joanna—you don't know how lucky you are!

JOANNA: So tell me!

ROSIE: It sort of made you feel like you were in an "X" movie.

CAROL: Is that where you met your husband, Rosie?

ROSIE: Are you kidding? I met Stephen in church—he's an ex-priest.

HELENE: Everybody says they make the worst husbands.

CAROL: Helene, you're obnoxious.

HELENE: Ah-ha! Got your eye on the local curate, do you, Carol? Does she, Leslie?

LESLIE: Not that I know of.

MARIA: Where are you working now, Carol?

CAROL: I'm a music therapist for retarded children.

ROSIE: Isn't that *perfect*?

LESLIE: The kids are crazy about her. [*Looks teasingly at* CAROL.] The staff too—eh, Carol?

CAROL: [*Shyly.*] I dated my supervisor for a while.

HELENE: What happened?

CAROL: Well, I liked him . . . but . . .

HELENE: But what?

CAROL: Well, he liked me more than I liked him.

HELENE: You mean you wouldn't put out.

JOANNA: Helene.

CAROL: Maybe I'm just old-fashioned.

LESLIE: I don't see anything wrong with that. You're your own person with your own standards.

MARIA: Do you still teach Phys Ed. at Marian High, Leslie?

[LESLIE *nods.*]

CAROL: She's chairman of the department now.

ROSIE: Please! "Chairperson."

CAROL: Rosie—don't tell me you're a women's libber?

ROSIE: Well, of course I'm a feminist. Aren't we all?

HELENE AND CAROL AND LESLIE: No!

HELENE: [*Raising her glass in a toast.*] "Let wives be subject to their husbands."

ROSIE: You can tell she doesn't have a husband.

JOANNA: [*To* ROSIE.] I warned you there'd be a Total Woman in the crowd. [*To* HELENE.] Where did you meet Neil, Helene?

HELENE: He was my editor at *The Saturday Review.* What a hunk!

JOANNA: Do you still work for *The Review?*

HELENE: After we started living together, Neil became a foreign correspondent for AP. I'm sure you've read some of his stuff. He's won awards. We travel a lot.

JOANNA: So you've become a camp follower.

HELENE: [*Archly.*] I'm a free-lance writer.

JOANNA: [*Roasting.*] And the two shall become one career.

MARIA: How about you, Rosie?

ROSIE: I thought I'd never get my turn!

CAROL: Now we're in for it.

ROSIE: I'm into life-study photography. And I'm in a *very* productive cycle. It's *so* exciting. I just had a showing in the Village.

LESLIE: The village.

ROSIE: You know—Greenwich Village. I have a friend with a gallery there. And I've changed my name. To "Vita." Isn't it wonderful? It means "Life."

HELENE: Isn't that a scream?!

CAROL: Vita what?

ROSIE: Just "Vita."

MARIA: Officially? I mean legally?

ROSIE: Of course.

JOANNA: So what do you take pictures of?

ROSIE: Mostly I've done spiderwebs.

CAROL: Spiderwebs? Is that it? Anything else in the pictures?

ROSIE: Sometimes a spider. [*Beat.*] But this last show was different. Really very exciting. I feel I've come into my own. It's what I was *called* to photograph.

CAROL: What?

ROSIE: Old women.

CAROL: Well, that's really a sweet i—

ROSIE: Naked old women.

CAROL: —dea.

ROSIE: They're beautiful. Lovely, sagging breasts and drooping buttocks. Protruding veins. So many lines and wrinkles—gorgeous textures.

JOANNA: [*Genuinely appreciative.*] Nice.

ROSIE: But the best is yet to come.

LESLIE: [*Sarcastic.*] I'll bet.

ROSIE: I'm working on a way to superimpose the spiderwebs on the naked old women.

LESLIE: [*Sarcastic.*] Dynamite.

ROSIE: It means developing new techniques. I'm stretching and growing. It feels so good.

HELENE: When are you going to do dirty old men.

ROSIE: Helene—you're disgusting!

JOANNA: You should let us know when you have another show, Rosie. I'd love to see your work.

MARIA: What about you, Joanna? You're the only one of us who hasn't left.

HELENE: Still teaching new-wave psychology?

JOANNA: No, I'm not teaching anymore.

LESLIE: Why not? You're a born teacher. Got me through philosophy.

MARIA: And me through French.

CAROL: And me through math.

HELENE: Has the community tutor retired?

JOANNA: I do social justice work now.

CAROL: You mean like protesting nuclear missiles or picketing for migrant workers.

JOANNA: Well, I do work with minorities . . . sexual minorities. [*Beat.*] I'm in gay and lesbian ministry. [*Pause.*]

HELENE: You mean you counsel queers? What are you doing—bucking for canonization along with Damien the Leper?

JOANNA: No, I don't counsel queers. I listen to people whose problems are caused by other people calling them queer.

ROSIE: My God, Joanna, that's wonderful! I can't believe it!

HELENE: Admit it, Joanna—you're a closet case yourself; aren't you?

MARIA: Helene—it's none of your business!

HELENE: [*Pressing* JOANNA.] Aren't you?

CAROL: A person doesn't have to be—

HELENE: [*Cont'd. Pressing harder.*] Aren't you?

JOANNA: [*Beat.*] Yes, I am a lesbian. [*Pause.*] What does it matter so long as I'm celibate. [*Pause.*]

HELENE: Think of it—we spent our most impressionable years kneeling in the same pew with Sister Dyke! O, Sweet Jesus, please don't let it be contagious!

ROSIE: Helene—stop it!

MARIA: Is that how you got into the work, Joanna?

JOANNA: So many gays and lesbians are leaving the Church because they feel . . . rejected . . . because it's not a place where they can be themselves. I want to help.

CAROL: But isn't there a reason for the Church's teaching? I mean doesn't the Bible say—

JOANNA: The Church's teaching could change.

LESLIE: But doesn't it seem . . . well, unnatural? I mean what about those men you read about in the paper—the ones that go after little boys?

JOANNA: Thy're not homosexuals—they're pederasts.

HELENE: I thought a pederast was somebody with a foot fetish.

ROSIE: Joanna, this is so exciting! I mean it's so *good* that you're doing this. You're such a good person! It's too good to be true! I mean I just can't believe they're letting you *do* this. What does the order say?

JOANNA: Mostly they try not to notice me except when they have to.

MARIA: When's that?

JOANNA: When the paper does a story.

[JOANNA *crosses to another part of stage. Crossfade with her.*]

SCENE 3

Motherhouse. JOANNA *crosses to Motherhouse. Lights come up on* NAOMI, *waving a newspaper.*

NAOMI: How could you say this about the bishop?

JOANNA: How could I not?

NAOMI: By considering the consequences.

JOANNA: If this bill doesn't pass, the consequences for gays and lesbians will be—

NAOMI: You know that's not what I'm talking about.

JOANNA: But that's what needs talking about.

NAOMI: What did you think would happen when you said this?

JOANNA: Everybody would know.

NAOMI: What everybody knows is that an upstart nun is trying to shame her bishop.

JOANNA: It didn't work. He's shameless.

NAOMI: The man is head of the Church in this diocese and as such commands our respect.

JOANNA: "Commanding" respect is not the best way to get it.

NAOMI: And what about your methods? Testifying publicly before the City Council—

JOANNA: I'm a citizen and a voter, and have a right to—

NAOMI: —on the very day the bishop's letter of opposition is read.

JOANNA: I didn't know I was scheduled for—

NAOMI: You even wore your veil! Just to get more attention!

JOANNA: Isn't that what it's for?

NAOMI: You *use* the Church.

JOANNA: The bishop's using it too.

NAOMI: But you also need the Church—and the convent. Without them you'd be just plain Joanna Jordan. No one would care what you said. Remember that!

[NAOMI *exits*. JOANNA *returns to beach house. Crossfade with her.*]

SCENE 4

Beachhouse. As in Scene 2.

LESLIE: What did you say about the bishop?

JOANNA: That he was an irresponsibly myopic heterosexist.

ROSIE: [*Laughing.*] Oh my God! Joanna, you didn't! You're too much! You'll end up excommunicated!

HELENE: Excommunicated, hell! She'll end up exterminated! Barbecued for the pleasure of ecclesiastical cannibals. Like Joan of Arc—going up in a blaze of . . . faggots!

MARIA: Helene, your sense of humor is perverted.

HELENE: Well see who's perverted! This is no laughing matter! Remember Peter Abelard!

JOANNA: I do!

HELENE: Remember Galileo!

JOANNA: I do!

HELENE: Remember What's-his-face the Vatican just put the screws on.

JOANNA: Hans Kung!

HELENE: The Inquisition lives! [*Threatening* JOANNA.] And you've got to be ready for it, Sister, for you know neither the day nor the hour . . . . Have your lamp burning.

JOANNA: I have!

HELENE: Be a wise and prudent virgin.

JOANNA: I am!

HELENE: [*Turning out the lights.*] For on just such a dark and moonlit night as this, the Grand Inquisitor will come for you— [*Picks up a dark beach towel from back of sofa and throws it around herself.*] cloaked in clerical righteousness— [*Grabs a broom from the corner, turns it bristles up.*] armed with the crosier of oppressive authority, and accompanied by the mournful, foreboding strains of the *Dies Irae*. [*To* CAROL.] Accompaniment, please!

CAROL: It's sacrilegious!

JOANNA: Oh, go ahead—humor her. I may need the rehearsal. [CAROL *starts to chant the* Dies Irae.]

HELENE: [*Banging "crosier" on floor.*] Sister Joanna Jordan, you are summoned before this Court of Inquisition to render an account of your ... fairy heresies. Kneel in the presence of the Big Stick! [*She pounds the floor.* JOANNA *kneels.*] Did you or did you not defame the duly anointed, newly appointed shepherd of your flock—

JOANNA: [*Bleating.*] Baaaa!

HELENE: —by making crass allusion to His Excellency's sacerdotal short-sightedness? Wicked, articulate Woman, are you guilty?

JOANNA: Of truth-telling, Your Lordship.

HELENE: Did you or did you not refer to His Reverence's visionary deficiencies?

JOANNA: I did.

HELENE: [*Calling off stage.*] Light the fire! [*Warming up to it.*] Now we must tenderize the meat. Tell me true, my Daughter, have you fallen among the perverts? Do you socialize with sodomites?

JOANNA: Yes, Your Lordship, but most of them are straight.

HELENE: Liar! Who in this Holy Court has committed sodomy?

[ROSIE *raises her hand sheepishly.* HELENE *calls off stage.*]

HELENE: [*Cont'd.*] Put this Vita woman on the docket next! [*To* JOANNA.] Enough equivocating. You stand accused of fraternizing with fags, hanging out with hand-holding, hairdressing homos. How do you plead?

JOANNA: Guilty of brotherly love. I can't help myself, Your Lordship. I'm a closet Christian.

HELENE: Ah-ha! I see the flames mounting! But now we must bind you to the stake. Confess, O fallen female, have you ever had dinner with a dyke? Breakfast with a butch? Ever take a lezzie out to lunch? Do you cavort with camp counselors, lady wrestlers, racket-wielding, roller-skating, leather-jacketed jockettes?! Speak up!

JOANNA: They are my sisters.

HELENE: Heretic! You are a charred stick, a heap of ashes! [*Pounds stick.*]

JOANNA: Wait! Before you pass sentence in the name of the Holy Inquisition, maybe there are witnesses for my defense.

HELENE: [*Walks among others, poking each with her stick.*] Well? Any more...confessions of sisterly love?

[CAROL *stops humming.*]

HELENE: [*Cont'd.*] Are you all cowards then? Is there none will come forward and acknowledge this woman? [*Bends down to* LESLIE.] Listen, my Sweet—do you hear a cock crowing?

[LESLIE *tenses, looks uncomfortably at* CAROL.]

HELENE: [*Cont'd.*] Is there not another half-witted masochist among you who longs for the singeing of her flesh? Come on, Girls! [*Going limp-wristed and singing.*] 'Tis the season to be fairy, fa,la,la,la,la,la,la,la,la. Don we now our gay apparel, fa,la,la,la,la,la— [*Breaking off, to* CAROL.] What's become of the accompaniment?

CAROL: [*Uncomfortable.*] I only do plainchant.

HELENE: How monotonous. Nothing *gayer* than that? Where's your spirit of adventure?

LESLIE: [*Standing.*] Leave her alone.

HELENE: [*Turning on* LESLIE.] And how about you, Olympian of Old? Are you secretly the amazing Amazon of all our dreams?

LESLIE: That's enough-stop it.

HELENE: Do you ever flex your flabby muscles at your adoring tennis partner?

LESLIE: Shut up, Helene—the play's over!

HELENE: [*Caressing* LESLIE's *hair.*] Ever fantasize pulling her sweet, sweating body over yours?

[LESLIE, *lunging at* HELENE *to put a hand over her mouth, knocks her onto the sofa.* CAROL *and* JOANNA *try to restrain her.*]

CAROL: Leslie—no! Leave her alone!

MARIA: She's just goading you, Leslie—she doesn't mean it.

[*But* LESLIE *is stronger. She pins* HELENE *down and wrestles to grab both wrists.*]

HELENE: Don't touch me! Don't touch me!

[LESLIE *suddenly disarmed by* HELENE's *urgency and embarrassed by her own recourse to violence, gets off, and crosses to turn the lights up.* ROSIE *and* MARIA *help* HELENE *into a sitting position.* HELENE *cries onto* MARIA *who rocks her gently.*]

MARIA: What is it, Helene?

[*No response.*]

MARIA: [*Cont'd.*] Let it out.

JOANNA: Maybe we can help.

HELENE: [*Sobbing.*] I . . . it's not . . . I . . . I'm pregnant.

[*Pause.*]

CAROL: Do you want the baby?

HELENE: Yes. But Neil doesn't. [*Beat.*] And I want Neil.

ROSIE: Oh, Helene—how awful!

JOANNA: You must feel miserable. I'm sorry—

[*Pause.*]

HELENE: *I'm* sorry. [*Beat.*] Leslie, I'm sorry.

LESLIE: Why me, Helene?

HELENE: Because you . . . for a moment you minded me of somebody . . . .

LESLIE: Who?

[HELENE *shakes her head.*]

JOANNA: It might help to tell it, Helene.

HELENE: [*Takes a deep breath.*] When I first left the convent, I met a woman at grad school. Dana. She was an athelete—strong . . . stunning. People would stare at her on the street. We both loved being crazy. She got me to do . . . wild things— sky diving, mountain climbing . . . We talked for hours, drinking beer, laughing, singing . . . dancing. [*Beat.*] Finally we became lovers. But I think always knew it would be temporary. I couldn't have told my parents, other friends, people at work. I couldn't live like that—afraid of being discovered . . . . disapproved of. So I dated men all the while. She didn't. It was very painful for her. We argued.

[*Pause.*]

LESLIE: What happened?

HELENE: She died in a car crash. [*Pause.*] I met Neil and we lived happily ever after. [*Beat.*] Till Baby makes three.

ROSIE: Helene, what are you going to do?

HELENE: [*Getting up.*] I'm going to retire the Grand Inquisitor. [*Puts broom back in corner and fold beach towel.*] I only hope, Sister Joanna, that he did you some good.

JOANNA: Helene—would you like to . . . talk?

ROSIE: Why don't you? It might help. We all want to help.

HELENE: I know that. I do know that. [*Starts collecting empty paper plates.*]

JOANNA: Then let us.

HELENE: I'm so tired. So very tired. I want to sleep.

JOANNA: Go ahead, then. I'll clean up.

MARIA: I'll help.

JOANNA: You must be tired too, after a full day's work.

MARIA: A little.

JOANNA: I'm afraid you're stuck sharing the sofa bed with me.

MARIA: Is that my penance for being late?

CAROL: Tomorrow night you two can take the front bedroom and Leslie and I'll sleep down here,

MARIA: I was only teasing.

JOANNA: Would anyone like some tea or anything?

HELENE: I'd like something.

JOANNA: What?

HELENE: I'd like to sing. The *Salve Regina* like we always used to at the end of night prayer.

JOANNA: Carol, do you remember the little speech you used to give us about singing the chant?

CAROL: You still remember that?

JOANNA: It always touched me. Tell us again.

CAROL: We must all try to sing as one voice. The beauty of the chant is the unity of many voices in the single melody.

[CAROL *intones the* Salve Regina. *The others join in. When the singing ends,* CAROL, LESLIE, HELENE *and* ROSIE *exit upstairs, turning off some lights.* CAROL *can still be heard humming the hymn.* MARIA *gathers up glasses and puts away food.* JOANNA *unfolds sofa bed, gets sheets. They make up bed.*]

JOANNA: I was afraid you wouldn't come.

MARIA: So was I.

JOANNA: You seemed... reluctant when I called.

MARIA: I wasn't... expecting it. [*Beat.*] I had stopped expecting it.

JOANNA: What?

MARIA: Your call. About ten years ago, I stopped expecting you to call.

JOANNA: And before that?

MARIA: I kept hoping you would.

JOANNA: Why didn't you call me?

MARIA: I couldn't... I didn't know what to say.

[*They finish making the bed in silence. Both are reluctant to start undressing.* MARIA *crosses to suitcase still at the door, looks out at the moonlight, goes out onto the porch.* JOANNA *follows her. They look towards the beach. During the following exchange, both are awkward and tentative.*]

JOANNA: Are you observing the Grand Silence, Sister?

MARIA: I'm remembering all the nights we did observe it.

JOANNA: At least in the letter, if not in the spirit.

MARIA: [*Teasing.*] What could you mean by that?

JOANNA: Sneaking down into the novices' garden in our bathrobes—

MARIA: —to look at the full moon.

JOANNA: Until we were caught.

MARIA: And the apple orchard in spring—do you remember that?

JOANNA: Running off at noon recreation to lie on our backs in the tall grass under the apple blossoms . . . .

MARIA: And read poetry to each other.

JOANNA: Only the most spiritual poetry of course: Theresa of Avila . . . John Donne . . . Dante . . .

MARIA: Solomon.

JOANNA: Ah, yes—the Song of Songs.

MARIA: "Comfort me with apples, for I am faint with love . . . ."

JOANNA: "Under the apple tree I awakened you . . ."

MARIA: "You have ravished my heart, my sister, my bride . . . ."

JOANNA: "A garden enclosed, is my sister, my bride, a garden enclosed, a fountain sealed . . ."

MARIA: "Set me as a seal upon your heart..." [*Beat.*]

JOANNA: I loved you, Ria. I mean I was in love with you. I know that now.

MARIA: I was in love with you and I knew it then.

JOANNA: You were more perceptive.

MARIA: Or more realistic. [*Pause.*]

JOANNA: Why did you get married? And so soon after you left?

MARIA: I was lucky to meet Peter then. It would have been such a mistake to marry anyone else. And I think I would have.

JOANNA: Married anyone?

MARIA: After the Novitiate, when we were sent on our separate assignments, I grieved for you. I felt the loss of you so much more than you felt the loss of me.

JOANNA: It wasn't that I—

MARIA: [*Interrupting.*] You let go of me.

JOANNA: I wish we had been allowed to write or visit. But in those days the Rule was so strict. And no one thought of breaking it.

MARIA: I thought of it all the time.

JOANNA: But you didn't—break the Rule, I mean.

MARIA: Not that one.

JOANNA: Anyway, it probably would have made it just more frustrating.

MARIA: I mourned for you like you had died. For a year. Two years. When we all went back to the motherhouse for our renewal summer, you treated me like . . . like an old acquaintance that you had once been fond of. Told me all about your class-es and your students. And about Sister Sarah who had been so helpful to you.

JOANNA: I wanted us to be friends again.

MARIA: Again? Yes. And you worked so hard at it. That's what gave you away.

JOANNA: I wish you had been sent someplace else. St. Justin's wasn't good for you.

MARIA: That fall, one of the nuns in my convent became very solicitous. She came to my room after night prayer a few times—said she heard me crying and won-dered if I needed anything. One night she asked if she could stay ... and I let her.

[*Beat.*]

JOANNA: Did you ... did you feel guilty?

MARIA: Yes. But not about breaking the Rule.

JOANNA: What then?

MARIA: About being unfaithful to you. You see, I let myself pretend it was you.

[*Beat.*]

JOANNA: Is that what you do with Peter?

MARIA: No. Never.

JOANNA: Did you love her?

MARIA: You are the only woman I have ever loved. I've loved you for twenty years. It's been like an open sore that won't scab over because I can't stop picking at it.

[*Beat.* JOANNA *sits on steps.*]

JOANNA: Do you love Peter?

MARIA: I've come to love him very much. And I ... appreciate him. He's a good husband and father.

JOANNA: Did you ever tell him about ... the other?

MARIA: No. But I think he suspects there was ... something ....

JOANNA: What would happen if he knew?

MARIA: I don't think I want to find out.

JOANNA: Why did you marry him?

MARIA: We both wanted the same things out of life.

JOANNA: What did you want?

MARIA: [*Pause. Then sits next to* JOANNA.] I wanted to be respected for what I could give others. I wanted a home, and children, and—

JOANNA: [*Turns and looks at her.*] And me.

MARIA: [*Trying to tease her way out.*] Nobody gets everything they want.

JOANNA: Do you want me now?

MARIA: I've never been unfaithful to Peter.

JOANNA: Do you want me now?

MARIA: I'm not sure I could live with myself.

JOANNA: Do you want me now.

MARIA: Yes! [*Beat, then turning away.*] No! [*Jumping up.*] I'll tell you what I want—I want to wring your neck! Twenty years later—when it suits you—you come waltzing back into my life! Unleashing old feelings and... unfolding old memories as...as carelessly as you do a sofa bed! It's some kind of game for you, isn't it?—this reunion. Well, I've been thinking about it for years—wondering what I'd do if I ever saw you again.

JOANNA: I didn't mean to be careless.

MARIA: You have a special talent for it! [*Pause.*] Once when the kids were little and I was feeding them breakfast, the TV was on—some women's talk show. Suddenly—there you were, being interviewed. About some book you had written. I hurled the cereal bowl at the set and screamed till I cried. The children sat there stunned. And I thought: well, now I've finally got her out of my system. Then three years later, the *Post* carried that feature with your picture. When I saw you smiling distantly—carelessly—out at me, my heart sank, and I knew it wasn't over. I burned the paper. I wanted to see your face go up in flames.

[*Pause.*]

JOANNA: [*Gets up.*] Ria, I'm sorry...I'm so sorry.

MARIA: For what?

JOANNA: For letting go of you.

[JOANNA *extends her arms. After a beat,* MARIA *slides into her embrace.*]

MARIA: Why did you wait so long?

JOANNA: I don't know.

MARIA: And what do you want from me now?

JOANNA: I'm not sure. I...maybe I need your forgiveness.

[*Lights fade as ocean sounds come up.*]

ACT II
SCENE 1

Saturday afternoon. Beachhouse. JOANNA, MARIA, LESLIE, HELENE, CAROL, *and* ROSIE *in bathing suits and beach cover-ups, are energetically singing* Jubilate Deo. CAROL *playfully conducts. This time they do make it through, finishing with a flourish and applauding themselves.*

HELENE: The music, the ceremonies, the rituals—that's what I miss the most, I think.

JOANNA: I know what you mean, Helene. There was something special about doing everything exactly together. Having the same rhythms. Something almost... mystical.

HELENE: Magical.

CAROL: I never felt closer to all of you than when we were singing.

ROSIE: That's because you were most alive then, Carol. Really! I could see it in your eyes. Something inside you was...unleashed. I remember being in choir one day when it happened. It was scary kind of like an exorcism—only instead of devils, something good escaped. Some kind of power like...like a deep tone, all pure and holy...leaping out of you. I looked up, half expecting to see angels on the ceiling. But then all of a sudden, I felt the power in *me*—like a throbbing in my stomach.

CAROL: I felt it too—that power.

ROSIE: You were looking at me. We were somehow connected—singing in just the most absolute harmony. And the power was electricity between us. I felt like I was...Oh, God—like I was having a religious experience!

JOANNA: Maybe you were.

MARIA: Or maybe you were hungry from fasting.

CAROL: Gosh, I'm embarrased.

LESLIE: [*To* CAROL.] I've seen that look too. At home...when you play the piano after supper...sometimes I look up from the newspaper and... well... [*Matter-of-fact.*] it's just nice.

CAROL: What do you know? I'm always afraid I'm bothering you.

ROSIE: Well, you can bother me anytime, Sister!

LESLIE: Who's up for a swim? [*Crosses to door.*]

HELENE: I am. Let me get my towel. [*Runs upstairs.*]

CAROL: Sounds good to me. [*Gets up, crosses to door.*]

MARIA: Me too.

LESLIE: Rosie?

ROSIE: Well of course! You don't think I came all this way just for the Deep Meaningful Sharing!

LESLIE: How about you, Joanna?

JOANNA: I have to go into the city for a bit. I'll catch up with you later.

HELENE: [*Screams from upstairs.*] This is too much! [*Descends, holding by its edges her "Grand Inquisitor" towel which has been starched stiff.*] All right—who's the closet starch freak?

LESLIE: "Vanity of vanities and all is vanities." [*Bolts out the front door.*]

HELENE: [*Running after her.*] I'll drown you for this!

CAROL: Come on—I want to see this!

[CAROL, MARIA, *and* ROSIE *exit with towels, beach bags, etc., laughing.* JOANNA *looks after them for a moment, then picks up car keys and exits. Lights fade.*]

SCENE 2

An hour later. Beach area. Sounds of laughter in distance. CAROL *and* ROSIE, *in bathing suits, run on, drying themselves briskly.*

ROSIE: That was such fun! This reunion was a terrific idea! I feel so . . . vitalized—like a new woman,

CAROL: It has been some weekend. [*Looking down at her body.*] I've really got to lose some weight.

ROSIE: No you don't! It's unaesthetic to be skinny—ask any Renaissance model.

CAROL: They're all dead.

ROSIE: Well, they didn't die from anorexia!

CAROL: Neither will I.

ROSIE: You've got a great body, Carol.

CAROL: And it's getting "greater" every day. [*Spreads her towel.*]

ROSIE: Aw—come on!

CAROL: [*Picks up suntan lotion.*] I really can't figure it. I eat the same as I always did. Maybe it's just we're getting older. But you're still thin.

ROSIE: It's because you're not getting any.

CAROL: Any what?

ROSIE: *Sex!*

CAROL: [*Putting lotion on her arms.*] Come on—what does that have to do with it?!

ROSIE: Everything. You never saw a fat nymphomaniac, did you?

CAROL: I've seen plenty of skinny celibates.

ROSIE: Are you sure?

CAROL: [*Trying to put lotion on her back.*] Rosie! You're more outrageous than ever!

ROSIE: Here—let me do that. [*Takes lotion.*]

CAROL: Thanks. [*Lies on her stomach.*] I really don't know why I bother. I'll burn anyway.

[*Silence as* ROSIE *puts lotion on* CAROL'*s back.*]

ROSIE: You've got gorgeous skin, Carol. It's absolutely . . . translucent. I remember that from the old days.

CAROL: How could you? All we ever saw of each other was five pounds of serge and eight inches of face.

ROSIE: Once I saw you getting out of the tub in the Novitiate. I was waiting in line and the curtain wasn't pulled all the way. I remember it exactly: you put each leg on the side of the tub as you dried it. I remember thinking how nice the curve of your shoulder was. And that kind of scrubbed-pink flush of your skin—like now.

CAROL: [*A little embarrassed.*] It must be strange to be an artist. I mean things that embarrass other people are so ... clinical to you.

ROSIE: Clinical?

CAROL: You know—seeing everything like you were going to paint it—all curves and colors.

ROSIE: That's not the way I saw you.

CAROL: Oh?

ROSIE: What do *you* think was going on that day in choir?

CAROL: You said it was a religious experience.

ROSIE: Shit, Carol. With everybody there, what else *could* I say?

CAROL: [*Rolls over, facing ROSIE; a sincere question.*] I don't know. What else could you say?

ROSIE: I was having an *orgasm,* for Christ's sake!

CAROL: [*Sits up.*] An orgasm! In choir?!

ROSIE: What better place?

CAROL: Oh my God!

ROSIE: That's what I said. It was *won*derful!

CAROL: But how could you—? I mean ... without even touching!

ROSIE: It was a very spiritual orgasm.

[*Both burst into laughter. Then, an awkward silence.* CAROL *reaches for the cap to the lotion, screws it on nervously.* ROSIE *puts her hand on* CAROL'*s.*]

ROSIE: [*Cont'd.*] I'd like to make love with you.

CAROL: What!?

ROSIE: Well, not right this second. I mean we could go inside.

CAROL: [*Stares at her, dumbfounded.*] You too? [*Beat.*] I don't believe this is happening! What am I doing here?

ROSIE: Dammit, I've done it again. I'm sorry, Carol. I didn't mean to ... upset you.

[*No response.*]

ROSIE: [*Cont'd.*] Are you angry?

CAROL: Angry? [*Beat.*] No, I ... I don't know. I'm ... I guess I'm confused.

ROSIE: Yeah. Me too.

CAROL: I mean is this how it works?

ROSIE: How what works?

CAROL: You look across the room at somebody when you're singing. And you get sort of carried up in the music and you have these good feelings about each other and your eyes get all soft, and ... I mean is that how it works?

ROSIE: No, I don't think that's the way most people get their orgasms.

CAROL: I'm not talking about...that.

ROSIE: I know, I know.

CAROL: I mean, look—I'm a singer. I love to sing I sing at First Communions and weddings and parties. I get all emotional when I sing. It happens to me...a lot.

ROSIE: Do you ever act on it?

CAROL: On what?

ROSIE: Your feelings?

CAROL: What do you mean?

ROSIE: I mean when you have these feelings for somebody, just walk across the room and ask them to go to bed with you.

CAROL: Are you kidding?!

ROSIE: Why not?

CAROL: Why *not!!* This is unreal. I don't believe this is happening.

ROSIE: What?

CAROL: This conversation.

ROSIE: Carol, have you ever had sex with anyone? [*Beat.*] You don't have to answer.

CAROL: [*Beat.*] No.

ROSIE: Have you ever wanted to?

CAROL: [*Beat.*] I...I think so.

ROSIE: Well, why didn't you?

CAROL: Because the guy was always a priest. Or married.

ROSIE: Then maybe you didn't really want to. [*Beat.*] How about women.

CAROL: No!

ROSIE: You never loved a woman?

CAROL: No! [*Beat.*] I mean, yes, of course I've loved women. I love Leslie. I loved you. But not...not that way.

ROSIE: How do you know?

CAROL: I just know! [*An awkward silence.*] Look...please don't be...insulted, Rosie.

[ROSIE *shrugs.*]

CAROL: [*Cont'd.*] We're just...different.

[ROSIE *nods.* CAROL *softens.*]

CAROL: [*Cont'd.*] When did you find out about...I mean did you know in the convent?

ROSIE: [*Shaking her head "No."*] There was a woman in my support group two years ago—a writer. She was so good to me. And there was another artist who helped me with my superimposing techniques. We worked together a lot of nights, until...I mean when I like somebody and share and seem to be on the same wave length and all... it just seems natural for me to want to... I'm just such an *impulsive* person. You know what I mean? [*No response.*] I'm the demonstrative type. I mean I always want to show how I feel. Do you know what I'm talking about? [*No response.*] Carol?

CAROL: I remember your whole family was like that-always touching each other. I used to be a little jealous on visiting day. You all seemed to... to enjoy each other so much.

ROSIE: *Yes*, that's it! I *enjoy* people, I do! I mean I love Stephen... in a different sort of way. And I love my baby—I wouldn't give him up for the world. But I love other people too! Other women. And I want to know them—experience them. I mean isn't that what life's all about? Not making money or getting famous, but touching other people. I mean really touching.

CAROL: But what about... [*She trails off.*]

ROSIE: Go ahead—ask it.

CAROL: Don't you feel guilty?

ROSIE: Of course! I even thought that by coming here and being with you all again—I mean, you know, reliving all those days of innocence, that somehow I'd get the will power to... that I'd just hate myself so much that I'd stop being... the way I am.

CAROL: But you didn't.

ROSIE: Well, no! I can't tell you what I felt when Joanna said she was in gay ministry. I just wanted to cry. I mean somebody in the Church actually cared— one of my own sisters. I felt so... so relieved—like a human being again.

CAROL: But what about your baby, Rosie? What's going to become of him? Of your family?

ROSIE: I don't know.

CAROL: It seems so... unfair. I mean there's nothing I want more than children. And a husband, and a home of my own. And here you are—risking it all.

ROSIE: It's terrible, isn't it? [*Starting to cry.*] You probably hate me. You're such a *per*fect person—things like this don't happen to you. You probably think I'm... perverted or something.

CAROL: No, Rosie— [*Touches her hand.*] I don't think you're perverted.

ROSIE: Are you sure?

CAROL: [*Beat.*] I'm sure.

[*They look at each other for a moment. ROSIE leans over and kisses CAROL on the mouth, gently, their bodies not touching. CAROL after a second pulls back, surprised by her own response. ROSIE looks at her apprehensively. Beat. CAROL leans over and kisses ROSIE gently on the mouth. During this exchange, LESLIE enters, unseen by the others, in time to see both kisses. She stops and stands stunned, then starts to leave. CAROL notices her, jumps up.*]

CAROL: Leslie! Wait a minute!

[LESLIE *doesn't stop or answer.* CAROL *runs after her, reaches for her.*]

CAROL: [*Cont'd.*] Where are you going?

LESLIE: [*Pulling away from* CAROL.] Home.

CAROL: No—wait!

LESLIE: You can come with me if you want.

CAROL: But we can't...I mean, the others will—

LESLIE: I don't give a damn about the others!

ROSIE: Leslie, it's not what you think.

LESLIE: How do you know what I think?!

ROSIE: We were just trying to—

LESLIE: I saw what you were trying to do. I have eyes, goddammit

CAROL: Leslie, please don't leave.

LESLIE: Why not? You seem to be having a good enough time without me.

CAROL: Stop saying that!

LESLIE: Well, what do you want me to say?

CAROL: I don't want you to say anything! I want you to listen!

LESLIE: All right. I'm listening.

CAROL: Rosie was telling me about her...well some...problems she's having and...and I...I was just trying to...comfort her.

LESLIE: Is that what you call it?

CAROL: Isn't that true, Rosie?

ROSIE: Leslie, I know what you think—you think I was trying to seduce Carol. But I wasn't. What you saw...I mean it just...happened. I know you feel betrayed, but there's no reason to—

LESLIE: Betrayed? Why should I feel betrayed?

ROSIE: Because of...your relationship with Carol.

LESLIE: My relationship with Carol has nothing to do with...with that!

ROSIE: Then why are you so anxious to take her home?

LESLIE: Because I...I don't want her to get hurt.

ROSIE: Did she look like she was hurting?

[*Beat.*]

LESLIE: Are you coming, Carol?.

CAROL: I don't think it would be right to just...leave. I mean it would spoil the weekend for the others. What about Joanna and Maria and—

LESLIE: What about me!

ROSIE: What about you, Leslie? If you don't feel betrayed, what do you feel? Tell us.

LESLIE: It's none of *your* business, is it?

ROSIE: Then tell Carol. [*Picks up her towel.*] Tell her what you feel.

LESLIE: [*Looking at* CAROL.] Maybe she should tell me what she feels.

ROSIE: I'm going up to the house. I'll see you at dinner, Carol. I hope I'll see you too, Leslie.

LESLIE: [*After a pause.*] Well?

CAROL: Well what? Is this the Last Judgment or something?

LESLIE: I don't judge you.

CAROL: Could've fooled me.

LESLIE: What you do is . . . up to you.

CAROL: [*Gently.*] Do you feel betrayed?

LESLIE: I feel . . . scared. I don't understand . . . what's happening.

CAROL: Me either.

LESLIE: Did you . . . did you like it?

CAROL: I . . . I don't know. I was more surprised than anything.

LESLIE: At what?

CAROL: That it was . . . that I was letting myself do it. That it didn't seem so . . . I mean . . . when you're in it.

LESLIE: And now?

CAROL: Now what?

LESLIE: Now what do we do?

CAROL: We don't have to do anything. I mean what happened isn't a big deal.

LESLIE: What would've happened if I hadn't come when I did?

CAROL: Nothing . . . We would have been embarrassed and . . . and gone for another swim. [*Beat.*] I'm sorry . . . I'm sorry you came when you did.

LESLIE: I bet you are.

CAROL: Leslie, don't be like this.

LESLIE: Well, how do you want me to be?

CAROL: I want you to be what you've always been—my best friend.

LESLIE: Your best friend?

CAROL: Yes.

[*Pause.*]

LESLIE: Is that enough?

CAROL: There's nothing better, is there?

LESLIE: Not as long as you think so too.

[*Beat.*]

CAROL: I think so too.

[*Crossfade.*]

SCENE 3

Motherhouse. Lights up on NAOMI *and* JOANNA.

NAOMI: How's the reunion going?

JOANNA: [*Quoting.*] "I have heard the mermaids singing, each to each."

NAOMI: [*Quoting.*] "I do not think that they will sing to me."

JOANNA: [*Nostalgic.*] You should have come. You know you really should have come.

NAOMI: Why?

JOANNA: Because you were the most special of all.

NAOMI: Is that what it's about?

JOANNA: Do you remember my crisis of faith in the Novitiate?

NAOMI: [*Teasing.*] Which one?

JOANNA: I was having terrible cramps. I said that any God who created women to menstruate four hundred times just to produce a half dozen children was too inefficient to be believed in. And that in any case, nuns should be exempt.

NAOMI: I brought a hot toddy to your cell that night.

JOANNA: It restored my faith.

NAOMI: You were always too hard on yourself. Perfectionists are prone to cramps.

JOANNA: Is that how you rationalized it?

NAOMI: What?

JOANNA: Singling me out.

NAOMI: My darling Joanna, it was you who singled yourself out. All that burning intensity...When I explained the Rule, it was you who questioned every archaic phrase. When I quoted Eliot, it was your eyes that lit up. When the others came for counseling they talked of homesickness; you talked of St. Teresa's ecstasies. Your appetite for sanctity was insatiable. You devoured God like some possessed cannibal. And you devoured me.

JOANNA: Was I that bad?

NAOMI: You were the joy of my life. [*Beat.*] Joanna—the Council voted "no support" for your work in gay ministry.

JOANNA: You're the Provincial Superior. You could override the Council.

NAOMI: You know it doesn't work that way anymore.

JOANNA: I liked you better as God.

NAOMI: For the record, I voted against censuring you.

JOANNA: I'll bet! Written right into the minutes as the shining liberal since you knew the bigots would carry the vote anyway.

NAOMI: Give it up, Joanna.

JOANNA: I can't.

NAOMI: Think about it, please, before you say that, Sister. And pray. Because if you decide to continue in this work, you will not do so as a nun.

JOANNA: No! Mother—you can't do that. You wouldn't.

NAOMI: So long as you are vowed to Obedience, I can. And if it's necessary, I will. But believe me, Joanna, I don't want to. You were one of my own novices. I've watched you over the years hold steadfast as so many of the others left. I feel a special loyalty to you as a daughter. But I have other daughters—your sisters. I must think of them. And so must you.

JOANNA: But I do.

NAOMI: You care for the few at the expense of the many.

JOANNA: You told us on profession day: 'Those with the greatest need have the first right to help."

NAOMI: And they have help—God's help.

JOANNA: That's easy to say if you haven't been there.

NAOMI: No, Sister, it's only easy to say if you have been there.

[*Pause, as* JOANNA, *wondering if this is a confession, waits for* NAOMI *to say more. When she doesn't,* JOANNA *decides to risk a confession herself.*]

JOANNA: Mother, I'm a lesbian. I always have been. I know that now.

NAOMI: Do you mean you've felt...affection for other sisters?

JOANNA: More than affection for a few. [*Beat.*] Including you.

NAOMI: We're all drawn to some people more than others. It's only natural.

JOANNA: It's more than that.

NAOMI: Have your relationships...have they included...?

JOANNA: No. But I *have* felt sexual attraction...yearning that I...I couldn't quite identify. But you recognized them, didn't you?

NAOMI: I?

JOANNA: You came between Maria and me.

NAOMI: Particular friendships threaten community spirit. It was my responsibility to preserve it

JOANNA: You resented Maria.

NAOMI: For what?

JOANNA: She didn't idolize you the way I did. Besides, she was a mere human who sapped the energy I could have been giving to God...and to you. You were jealous.

NAOMI: It's God who's the jealous lover.

JOANNA: I was lonely.

NAOMI: The grace is given to those who ask.

JOANNA: You were jealous.

NAOMI: I was Mistress of Novices! [*Softening.*] You showed such promise, Love. Whatever insights I offered, the very energy in the air between us, you inhaled. You sucked at my spirit like some hungry babe at the breast . . . I had such hopes for you . . . such fond hopes that you would become all the things I—

JOANNA: All the things you were.

NAOMI: All the things I could never be.

JOANNA: And your desire for my spiritual growth—your . . . passion for me—was it entirely maternal?

NAOMI: What else?

JOANNA: Once I came to you and confessed that I . . . that I longed for the day when we might be equals—teaching together at some parish school, because then—when I was older—then we might be friends, and I could give you the understanding . . . the comfort that I couldn't give you as a novice.

NAOMI: I remember.

JOANNA: You took my hands in yours, and I knew . . . I knew from the look in your eyes that I had guessed your own yearnings. Then you laughed. You held my hands and said—

NAOMI: [*Taking* JOANNA's *hands.*] I held your hands and said: "It could happen, Love. Maybe twenty years from now I'll be out there with you."

JOANNA: Time's up, Love. Are you out here with me?

NAOMI: What do you want from me, Joanna?

JOANNA: Your blessing. I want your blessing—on me and my work.

NAOMI: I love you, Joanna.

JOANNA: I want your blessing.

[*They look at each other; then* NAOMI's *eyes drop. Lights fade.*]

SCENE 4

Beach house. Saturday evening. ROSIE, CAROL, LESLIE, HELENE, *and* MARIA *are gathered around* JOANNA.

HELENE: Shit, Joanna, why don't you just leave the convent? Hey—you can come and live with Neil and me!

ROSIE: Sure. And cook spaghetti dinners.

MARIA: And take care of the baby.

JOANNA: I don't think I'm cut out for the domestic scene.

HELENE: What *would* you do if you left?

JOANNA: I've never thought about leaving.

MARIA: Never?

JOANNA: From the time I was seven, I knew I had to be a nun.

HELENE: So did I. At seven we didn't know any better.

JOANNA: But I still feel called.

HELENE: You mean you're not fit for anything else.

JOANNA: It's where I can be most effective.

CAROL: Because people put more stock in what nuns say?

JOANNA: Because God wants me here.

MARIA: Then what *are* you going to do, Joanna? Give up your work?

JOANNA: I don't want to. But I . . . I can't imagine leaving the convent.

HELENE: Why not? We did.

JOANNA: [*With resignation-accusation.*] Yeah.

ROSIE: It doesn't seem fair. I mean if you believe this is what God wants you to do, they have no right to stop you.

LESLIE: Maybe they do have a right to be concerned. I mean as long as Joanna's in the order, what she does is a reflection on all of them.

JOANNA: But that's just it—they're afraid of their own reflection. Afraid to take a hard look at the reality.

CAROL: What reality?

JOANNA: The reality that there are lots of perfectly decent people who happen to be homosexual. Some of them nuns. Or ex-nuns. I mean look around the room!

[*Pause. They look at* HELENE.]

HELENE: Don't look at me!

ROSIE: I think we should come out to Mother Naomi. Maybe it would make a difference.

JOANNA: I did, and it didn't.

HELENE: [*To* ROSIE.] What do you mean, "we"?

ROSIE: Well, you. And . . . and me.

HELENE: You! Oh God, here come the sordid tales of geriatric orgies!

CAROL: Shut up, Helene.

JOANNA: How long have you known, Rosie?

ROSIE: A couple of years. [*Beat.*] It just feels right to me. So . . . natural and comfortable.

MARIA: Does Stephen know?

ROSIE: I wish I could be honest with him. But I'm afraid. Oh, it's all a big mess. And it must sound awful to you all. But maybe I wouldn't be in this mess if there had been somebody back then doing the work Joanna's doing now ... I mean maybe I never would've gotten married. That's why it's so important for you to go on, Joanna. Couldn't you talk to the Council?

JOANNA: I've tried.

CAROL: Maybe if you promised to keep it out of the newspapers.

JOANNA: But I want people to know there are nuns and priests who question the party line. It's the first step to change.

HELENE: They don't want change! And they certainly don't want that kind of publicity.

JOANNA: That's true enough. Every time I've been called to the motherhouse, it's been right after some article was published. They say people have called in and said they're scandalized.

MARIA: What people?

JOANNA: They won't tell me their names.

ROSIE: Maybe *we* should call in and say we're delighted.

CAROL: Oh sure.

JOANNA: That's not a bad idea.

LESLIE: What!?

HELENE: [*Miming phone call.*] "Hello, Mother Noami? This is Helene Burgess. I'm calling because I saw this article in the paper about Sister Joanna defending queers. And I just want to say I think it's wonderful 'cause I was queer myself once."

ROSIE: But seriously—what if we did speak up?

MARIA: You mean tell Mother Naomi to leave Joanna alone?

JOANNA: Well, it would have to be more than that. Some sort of public statement.

LESLIE: Public statement? Of what?

ROSIE: Of support! You know—like taking out an ad in *The New York Times*.

HELENE: Oh, right. "Attention world: we five nobodies think Sister Joanna is doing great work."

ROSIE: Shit! If we were still nuns, we'd be somebodies.

CAROL: Jo—you've been doing this work for years. Was there something that ... tipped the scales against you?

JOANNA: I organized a retreat for lesbian nuns.

ROSIE: Oh, my God!

[JOANNA *crosses. Crossfade with her.*]

SCENE 5

Motherhouse. NOAMI *and* JOANNA.

NAOMI: This is the last straw, Joanna.

JOANNA: Look, Mother—ten percent of the population is gay. You must know there are nuns who are lesbians.

NAOMI: Why should they be encouraged to acknowledge it publicly?

JOANNA: Because they have special problems living in a community of women.

NAOMI: The individual sister should discuss these problems with her superior.

JOANNA: But they feel so isolated, so different. It isn't celibacy that gives them the most trouble. It's fear—fear that they'll be dismissed if they confide in superiors, fear that other nuns—their own friends—would turn away in disgust if they knew. They need to hear other sisters say they share their feelings. Is that asking too much?

NAOMI: I understand their distress.

JOANNA: Do you?

NAOMI: But there is more than the welfare of these individuals to consider. There is the reputation of the entire community.

JOANNA: Reputation?

NAOMI: If we admit that there are . . . a few homosexually-orientated sisters, people will think . . . well, people will think that . . .

JOANNA: All nuns are lesbians?

NAOMI: Yes.

JOANNA: What does that matter if they think that—so long as we're celibate?

NAOMI: Don't be naive, Joanna.

JOANNA: We can't afford to worry so much about what people think!

NAOMI: We can't afford not to! How many Catholic families would encourage their daughters to become nuns if—

JOANNA: How many are doing it now? We had sixty novices in my class. This year there are two. What have we got to lose?

NAOMI: Our opportunity to do good as a religious community.

JOANNA: Then maybe we'll have to find some other way to do good.

NAOMI: Are you prepared to jeopardize a way of life that has worked for fifteen hundred years?

JOANNA: Yes, if it doesn't work any more!

NAOMI: Have you no loyalty to the community? To the Church?

JOANNA: My loyalty is to the Gospel.

NAOMI: Your loyalty is to the press.

JOANNA: Because I want the truth to be known?

NAOMI: Joanna, people don't always know what to do with the truth.

JOANNA: Does that mean they shouldn't hear it?

NAOMI: It means they don't *want* to hear it until—

JOANNA: You mean *you* don't want them to hear it. You don't want people to know there are nuns who are lesbians.

[JOANNA *returns to beach house. Crossfade with her.*]

SCENE 6

Beach house. As in Scene 4.

ROSIE: That's it then!

LESLIE: What?

ROSIE: We'll tell people.

CAROL: Tell people that there are lesbian nuns?

ROSIE: Tell people that *we* were lesbian nuns.

LESLIE: But we weren't! I mean some of us weren't. I wasn't. Carol wasn't. Maria wasn't.

JOANNA: [*To Maria.*] Ria?

MARIA: I...I did have...strong feelings for...I was in love with...another Sister...once. [*Pause. All wait for her to go on. She doesn't.*]

CAROL: We all had...feelings. It's not the same thing. I mean how can you be homosexual if you don't have sex with women?

ROSIE: How can you be heterosexual if you don't have sex with men? Anyway, maybe it doesn't have to include sex. Maybe it's just where a person's real emotional investment is.

JOANNA: Carol, apart from your family, who's your strongest bond with?

CAROL: Well, Leslie, of course. I mean we've been best friends for twenty-five years. But we're not...lovers.

ROSIE: That's a shame.

LESLIE: We don't need your goddamn sympathy!

JOANNA: All right, all right. We couldn't all say we were homosexually active in the convent. But couldn't we admit that attraction for women played some part in our choosing that life? I know I entered partly because I wanted to live with other women.

HELENE: But even that's not true for the rest of us.

JOANNA: Will you or Rosie or Maria deny your attraction to women?

HELENE: OK, I was attracted to Dana. But it takes more than one relationship to make a homosexual.

JOANNA: Does it take more than one to make a heterosexual? . . . Rosie, how many men have you slept with?

ROSIE: Well . . . only Stephen.

JOANNA: And how many women?

ROSIE: I guess . . . a few.

JOANNA: [*To* HELENE.] So what does that make her?.

HELENE: What about Maria? She's happily married. [*To* MARIA.] Aren't you?

MARIA: Yes.

HELENE: So maybe you were attracted to women just because there weren't any men around.

JOANNA: Maria, if you saw that Sister today—the one you were in love with— would you . . . would you still love her? . . . in the same way?

MARIA: [*Beat.*] Yes.

JOANNA: And what about you, Helene? If Dana were alive today, would you still love her?

HELENE: But she's not alive.

JOANNA: Would you?

HELENE: So what does that make me? Dana was the only . . . I'm not attracted to other women!

JOANNA: Not even to Leslie?

LESLIE: Leave me out of it!

JOANNA: Isn't that what last night's 'scene' was all about?

HELENE: You'd like to think so, wouldn't you?

JOANNA: Wasn't it?

HELENE: For a moment Leslie reminded me of Dana. That's all.

JOANNA: Maybe it was Dana that reminded you of Leslie.

LESLIE: That's not true!

HELENE: Stop distorting everybody's life to fit your own scenario, Joanna. You're not Mother Superior here!

JOANNA: Look—you're the people I'm trying to help! Don't you see—

LESLIE: Now wait a minute!

JOANNA: We belong to an oppressed group that—

LESLIE: [*Shouting.*] *I* do not belong to any oppressed group!

MARIA: Jo, I understand why you're doing this, but no one should have to say she's . . . something she . . . doesn't believe she is.

JOANNA: Even if she *is* what she doesn't believe she is?

LESLIE: Come off it, Joanna! Who do you think you are—God? I mean what the hell is this all about? Sure, I'd like to see you do whatever work you feel called to do. And if you have some personal stake in it, that's your business. But don't make me out to be some kind of traitor because I'm not what you are!

HELENE: OK, OK, look—we're just not going to find a label that we can all agree on. So why waste time trying?

ROSIE: But I wish there were *something* we could do.

HELENE: Our stories are different. That's all there is to it

[*Pause. They seem to be at an impasse.*]

JOANNA: Maybe that's it—we could just tell our different stories.

MARIA: What do you mean?

JOANNA: Well, I could say I've always been attracted to women. [*To* MARIA.] You could say you were in the convent. Helene could say she was once, but isn't now. Rosie could say she wasn't before, but is now. Carol could say—

LESLIE: Carol!

JOANNA: What could you say, Carol?

CAROL: Well, I . . . don't think I could say anything.

LESLIE: She couldn't say anything!

JOANNA: Could you say you've never been sexually attracted to men—even the ones you liked?.

[CAROL *starts to say something, but doesn't.*]

ROSIE: [*To* CAROL.] Couldn't you say that what you felt passing between us . . . that day in choir . . . might have been a sexual feeling?

LESLIE: Stop trying to put words in her mouth!

JOANNA: Could you say the feelings you have for Leslie may have just the slightest—

LESLIE: Listen, Sister, if you don't shut up, I'm going to—

JOANNA: And what about you, Leslie? What exactly is it you feel when you look up from your newspaper at Carol playing the piano?

LESLIE: [*Shouting.*] Nothing! I feel nothing! Don't you understand that? I have never in my life felt anything sexual for anybody! Not for anybody! And that's the truth. Now leave me alone! All of you!

[*Storms out front door.* CAROL *gets up to follow her, but is intercepted by* JOANNA.]

JOANNA: Don't Carol.

CAROL: That was brutal.

JOANNA: Somebody had to ask her the question she won't ask herself.

CAROL: Is that your version of charity?

JOANNA: She's not one of your retarded children, Carol. She's a grown woman.

CAROL: A woman in pain, thanks to you.

JOANNA: She asked to be left alone. [*Softening.*] Wait a little. You know she won't let you help her now.

[*Knowing this to be true,* CAROL *reluctantly sits back down. Pause.*]

HELENE: Well! Isn't it nice that small groups are so uninhibited?

CAROL: What do you want from us, Joanna? Why did you bring us here? Why the five of us—and not the other fifty-five?

ROSIE: You suspected we were the gay ten percent, didn't you?

JOANNA: Well, I mean, I never suspected you, Rosie.

CAROL: Then why?

JOANNA: I told you—you mattered most to me. It matters to me what you ... do.

HELENE: You mean it matters what we think of what *you* do.

JOANNA: Is that so different?

HELENE: Of course it's different! Can't we approve of you without being the same as you?

JOANNA: Then for God's sake *do* it! Approve of me! Stand up and be counted!

HELENE: By saying we're like you?

JOANNA: By telling your own story—including whatever small part of it makes you like me. By telling the *truth*! Is that too much to ask?!

HELENE: [*Shouting.*] *Yes!* Why is it so goddamn important to tell the truth?!

JOANNA: Because the truth will make us free.

HELENE: It'll make *you* free. The rest of us will be crucified! Can't you get that through your self-centered little skull?

JOANNA: Look—you owe me this! I loved you—I loved each of you and you abandoned me!

CAROL: What?

JOANNA: [*Desperate.*] We were sisters—a family, a community ... with ideals. We were going to do God's work ... together. What happened to that? All the wrongs we were going to right, all the needy we were going to serve—they're still there. But youre not! You left! And now you've got your husbands and lovers and children and your homes and your work. And I've got none of that. For twenty years I've kept my vows with no one but God to tell what I was feeling. And where were you?! Don't you see—I need you now. You're all I have! [*Pause.*]

MARIA: What can we do, Jo?

JOANNA: Tell your stories.

MARIA: I don't think I understand ... what good would they do ... these confessions?

JOANNA: If the five of us admit publicly to having homosexual feelings, people will know that ... some nuns are lesbians.

CAROL: Who would these stories be told to?

JOANNA: A reporter. Helene-how about you? You could send it to the *Saturday Review*. Do you still know anybody there?

HELENE: No. Write it yourself.

ROSIE: Yeah! You could send it to *Psychology Today*—a case studies thing.

HELENE: At least that way you could change the names.

JOANNA: But we'd have to identify the order or our purpose is defeated.

MARIA: I think I've lost track. What *is* our purpose?

ROSIE: To give them bad publicity.

MARIA: And how does that help Joanna?

HELENE: They kick her out—we make them squirm. "Vengeance is mine," says the Lord. But I thought we wanted to persuade them *not* to kick her out.

ROSIE: Good point.

JOANNA: What if I write the article . . . but don't publish it—

ROSIE: But what's the point

JOANNA: —yet. First I show it to Mother Naomi. [*Pause.*]

CAROL: That's blackmail.

JOANNA: You said it.

CAROL: That's pretty low.

ROSIE: Any lower than the ultimatum they've given her?

CAROL: But I thought it was the Council's decision.

JOANNA: She could get the Council to reverse its decision . . . if she tried.

MARIA: And if she doesn't? Will you publish it?

JOANNA: Yes.

MARIA: Jo—are you sure you can do that—to Mother Naomi?

JOANNA: No. But I'll try.

HELENE: You're really a dangerous animal, aren't you?

JOANNA: Only when wounded.

ROSIE: It would work, though, wouldn't it? We've got to go through with it!

CAROL: Joanna—are you sure this is what you want?

JOANNA: I know it's asking a lot of you. But we'd all be taking the risk together.

ROSIE: That's it! That's what sisterhood is all about. Joanna—you've got my story.

JOANNA: Maria? Are you with us? Can you do it . . . for the Sister you loved?

MARIA: [*After a beat.*] Yes. I'll do it.

JOANNA: Helene? How about it?

HELENE: Ask me in the morning.

JOANNA: Don't you owe it to Dana?

HELENE: I said I'd tell you in the morning! I won't be blackmailed into this, Joanna! Look, we've all had a long, stressful twenty-four hours—thanks to you. And I don't think it's fair to put this kind of pressure on us. You could at least give us time to sleep on it.

[*Pause.*]

JOANNA: Fair enough. [*Starts out door.*]

MARIA: Where are you going?

JOANNA: To find Leslie. And apologize.

[JOANNA *exits. Others freeze as lights crossfade to porch as* LESLIE *comes onto it. The two look at each other. Beat.*]

JOANNA: Full moon.

LESLIE: I told you to leave me alone.

JOANNA: I didn't come to . . . I came to apologize.

LESLIE: And that's supposed to make everything OK?

JOANNA: No. But maybe it'll make some things . . . better.

LESLIE: Like what?

JOANNA: Like our damaged friendship?

LESLIE: We're not friends. We were classmates twenty years ago. That doesn't make us friends.

JOANNA: All right. Then the good will between us.

LESLIE: I don't need your good will.

JOANNA: But I need yours. I'm sorry, Leslie. I really am sorry. I guess I . . . had you wrong.

LESLIE: Why do you have to do this?

JOANNA: I don't expect you to understand.

LESLIE: I'm sure I'm too stupid for that?

JOANNA: I don't understand it myself. [*Beat.*] I wish it were a simpler problem—with a simple solution. [*Beat.*] Remeber when old Sister Margaret had the stroke, and you built that contraption so she could feed herself.

LESLIE: Basic mechanics.

JOANNA: Compounded with imagination . . . and compassion.

LESLIE: It was no big deal.

JOANNA: Why do you always underestimate yourself?.

LESLIE: Don't start on me, Joanna!

JOANNA: I'm sorry. Again. Leslie, if I could just make the whole weekend go away for you, I would.

LESLIE: Why don't you just make yourself go away?

[*Beat.* JOANNA *walks off porch. Lights fade. Sounds of sea come up.*]

SCENE 7

Sunday morning. Beach area. Sounds of seagulls, ocean. Lights up on MARIA *sitting, looking out.* JOANNA *approaches her.*

JOANNA: Is this apple tree taken, Miss?

MARIA: I'm expecting the snake any minute.

JOANNA: And what will she do?

MARIA: Tempt me, of course.

JOANNA: Do you still need tempting?

MARIA: I'm afraid what I need is to resist.

JOANNA: Oh. [*Beat.*] Want some help?

MARIA: Won't that be out of character? Can the snake really change her skin?

JOANNA: Reverse psychology. Very serpentine. Temptation Number One: any decision that makes you feel rotten must be a bad one. Describe symptoms.

MARIA: No sleep. Sick stomach. Clammy palms. Dry mouth.

JOANNA: Classic. Temptation Number Two: consideration of potential losses. Enumerate.

MARIA: Husband. Children. Security.

JOANNA: Impressive list. Temptation Number Three: questioning of motives. Let's see . . . you've doing this because . . . you want to be honest.

MARIA: I am honest. I honestly *am* happily married.

JOANNA: And honestly not a lesbian.

MARIA: I have passionately loved one woman in my life. This obsession had given me moments of pure joy followed by years of pain and anger.

JOANNA: Who needs it, eh?

MARIA: Joanna—last night you extorted my confession to pressure the others without knowing how I would feel about making it.

JOANNA: Why did you go along?

MARIA: Because you needed it so desperatly

JOANNA: Why did you care?

MARIA: I love you. Because you're passionate and uncompromising. Because you see things as you think they should be—as you want them to be—and are intolerant of anything less. Because you're specal. And for a moment—for as long as I was important in your life—I was special too . . . ordinary as I am. You had me believing I could write poetry and . . . modernize the whole Church. And last night you did it again. You had me—and the others too—believing we could change the world. Five of us were going to reverse centuries of discrimination. But we can't, Jo—any more than I can write like Dante.

JOANNA: Your terza rima was coming along nicely.

MARIA: The trouble is you challenge people to rise to dangerous heights. And then you're not there to catch them if they fall.

JOANNA: What do you mean?

MARIA: Where will *you* be when Carol and Leslie destroy a good friendship? When Neil walks out on Helene? When Stephen gets custody of Rosie's boy? If Peter puts me out, will you be there to take me in?

JOANNA: You're being melodramatic. Peter's not going to—

MARIA: Answer me! Are you ready to leave the convent and pick up where we left off? Would you have called me at all if I hadn't been safely married? Is that what you waited for?

JOANNA: No! I mean yes—I would have! Ria, I didn't know what I was. For years. But I knew I had failed you in some important way that wasn't clear and couldn't be talked about before. And I wanted to talk about it. I'm glad we did.

MARIA: Is it over then? Are we going to see each other any more?

JOANNA: Do you want to?

MARIA: I would like to be friends. Do you think we can be friends—without the romance?

JOANNA: Are you sure that's what you want?

MARIA: It's what I can afford.

JOANNA: But *can* we be friends without the romance? What if it's not something superimposed like Rosie's spiderwebs? What if it's in our chemistry? Or in our history?

MARIA: You never used to be such a determinist.

JOANNA: Before this reunion I wondered. Now I know.

MARIA: What?

JOANNA: That even if we meet in a restaurant instead of the apple orchard, I will be distracted by how wonderful you smell. That even if we talk of nothing but work and children and books, I will want, afterwards, to lay my head on your breast and be comforted . . . for all the things that are not as they should be.

MARIA: Perhaps in time that desire would pass.

JOANNA: I don't want it to! It's precious to me.

MARIA: But in the long run, wouldn't it be destructive?

JOANNA: Then there must be no long run. We won't see each other.

MARIA: There it is still—that same exasperating all-or-nothing attitude!

JOANNA: You used to find it charming.

MARIA: It is charming—in adolescents. But grown-up people learn to make compromises.

JOANNA: So now I'm Peter Pan.

MARIA: You always did want to fly.

JOANNA: Ria, I love you. I don't want to disrupt your marriage. I'm not asking you to be deceitful. But you mustn't ask it of me either. Don't ask me to subdue my feelings into something tamer and less true. I won't do it!

MARIA: What do you want, Joanna—perpetual tension and frustration?

JOANNA: I refuse to turn into a zombie just to spare myself the pain. I won't let go of you again.

MARIA: Not even if I . . . won't tell my story?

[JOANNA *looks away*.]

MARIA: [*Cont'd*.] I can't do it, Jo. I'm not a risk-taker like you. I don't want to fly. [*Beat*.] Are you surprised?

JOANNA: Disappointed, I guess.

MARIA: Maybe you wouldn't be if you didn't have unrealistic expectations.

JOANNA: I can't change that.

MARIA: Can't or won't?

JOANNA: I feel so . . . alone.

MARIA: Then stop making that choice.

JOANNA: What do you mean?

MARIA: You still imagine there's some ideal state of what "should be." As though perfection were possible.

JOANNA: Yes, I long for it.

MARIA: Jo, listen to me. There is no Garden of Eden. The world's a messy place. People eat their apples and throw away the cores, and other people trip over them. Innocence is a dangerous illusion.

JOANNA: We had it once.

MARIA: Give it up, Jo . . . before it's too late.

JOANNA: I tell you we had it! All of us. We were sisters. A bonding as simple and pure as . . . chanting.

MARIA: The music of real life is not Gregorian chant. Open your ears, Jo. People don't sing in unison.

JOANNA: Not even you and I?

MARIA: Not even you and I.

JOANNA: Why not, Ria? Why can't we?

MARIA: Because I'd always be disappointing you.

[*Pause*. JOANNA *gets up*.]

JOANNA: You're not ordinary, you know. [*Beat*.] And you really could write poetry if you put your mind to it.

[JOANNA *crosses to beach house. Crossfade with her*.]

SCENE 8

Beach house. CAROL *is folding the sheets from the sofa bed. Her suitcase and beach bag are packed.* JOANNA *enters from the porch, sees the packed bags.*

JOANNA: Up so early.

CAROL: I didn't sleep much anyway.

JOANNA: How's Leslie?

CAROL: She's . . . stil! upset.

JOANNA: Want some juice?

CAROL: No thanks. [*Folding up sofa bed.*] Truth is, we'd like to get an early start back. Leslie's packing the car now.

JOANNA: Oh.

CAROL: Joanna, listen . . . I know this is going to upset you, but . . . I've thought about it all night, and . . . I don't think I can . . . go through with it.

JOANNA: Because of Leslie?

CAROL: I don't see how I can do it—talk about my feelings for women—without having people assume that I'm . . . that we're . . . I mean if the order is identified . . . well, even if the details are changed, some people might recognise us. And I . . . I just don't think I have the right to make the decision for both of us.

JOANNA: Couldn't you talk to Leslie about it? I know I was kind of rough on her last night. Maybe coming from you it would seem . . . somehow less threatening.

CAROL: I know her. [*Shaking her head.*] There's a lot to Leslie that most people . . . never get a chance to see. She's a good person. [ROSIE *comes running frantically down the stairs in her nightgown.*]

ROSIE: My car! My car's gone!

JOANNA: What?

ROSIE: I looked out the window while I was sitting on the john—and it's not *there* anymore.

CAROL: Are you sure that's where you left it?

ROSIE: Well sure I'm sure! I was right out back next to yours and Maria's. And now it's not *there* anymore!

CAROL: Where did you leave the keys?

ROSIE: The keys?

CAROL: The car keys.

ROSIE: Well, on the dresser in the bedroom, I guess. Or maybe in my purse. Or the beach bag. Oh, God, I don't remember!

CAROL: Come on, Rosie, try to think. Let's all be calm a minute and maybe you'll be able to—

ROSIE: Be calm! Are you kidding? Stephen's gonna kill me when he finds out I did this again.

CAROL AND JOANNA: Again?

ROSIE: Aw ... [*Miserable.*] Once before I left the keys in the car and some kid took it for a joy ride and wrecked the transmission. Stephen was *so* pissed.

JOANNA: Maybe we ought to call the police.

ROSIE: [*Going to phone.*] Oh God, if it's wrecked, I can't go home. [*Dials 911. Beat.*] Yes, I'd like to report a stolen car—I mean a missing car. [*Beat.*] Danger? No. [*Beat.*] Because I want the police, and 911 is the number to c— [*Beat.*] Well, this is an emergency! [*Beat. Then to others.*] I'm on hold.

JOANNA: How about some coffee?

ROSIE: Oh God, do I need it. [*Picks up phone, carries it to door, and sticks her head out looking for car.*]

CAROL: Joanna—I hope you understand ...

JOANNA: [*Pouring coffee.*] That your first commitment is to Leslie?

CAROL: I'm frightened for myself too. I mean if anyone at work read about it, I'd probably lose my job.

JOANNA: You too?

CAROL: And my family couldn't handle it, I know that. And to tell the truth, I can't handle it myself.

[ROSIE *who has been vaguely aware of this conversation, now realizes what* CAROL *is doing.*]

ROSIE: Can't handle what, Carol?

CAROL: I can't go through with it.

ROSIE: Why *not?*

CAROL: Because even thinking about the possibility makes me feel ... well, you know, guilty.

ROSIE: You could get over that.

CAROL: I just don't want to risk messing up my life.

ROSIE: Is it so wonderful the way it is?

CAROL: At least I'm not cheating on my husband!

[ROSIE *hangs up the phone.*]

CAROL: [*Cont'd.*] I'm sorry, Rosie, I didn't mean to sound ... I'm sorry. I'm probably just jealous. I mean I guess *I'd* like to meet somebody I could love and share with and settle down with.

ROSIE: But you already *have.*

LESLIE: [*Offstage.*] Carol!

CAROL: Look ... Joanna. Yesterday I sort of ... got carried along. I mean I don't really think my feelings for women are ... sexual. I don't really believe I'm gay. And ... and I don't want to be!

ROSIE: Nobody *wants* to be gay! Not in *this* world!

CAROL: [*To* ROSIE.] This is between Joanna and me. It doesn't have anything to do with you.

ROSIE: [*Miserable.*] Oh God, I wish it didn't.

JOANNA: What do you mean?

ROSIE: Well ... I figured if just one person said no, it probably wouldn't make that much difference. But ...

JOANNA: But what?

ROSIE: Dammit, I wish I weren't so impulsive! I promised my therapist I wouldn't make any impulsive decisions all week. You see the truth is that I don't consider all the pros and cons when I make a decision. I mean I don't weigh all the consequences. Know what I mean?

JOANNA: What consequences?

ROSIE: Well, like I love my work, but face it, the money I make from my photography wouldn't keep me in dog food.

JOANNA: What makes you think Stephen won't find out anyway?

ROSIE: It's true—he might.

JOANNA: You said yourself you wished you could be honest with him.

ROSIE: I *do*. But I can't—not yet. And anyway, do you know what he'd *do*?

CAROL: Divorce you if he has any sense.

ROSIE: I just can't bear the thought of losing my little boy. He'd feel deserted. I can't take that chance. I just can't.

JOANNA: But aren't you already taking chances?

ROSIE: Well, yes, but I try to be discreet.

CAROL: *You*—discreet?!

ROSIE: [*Ignoring this.*] Joanna, if I were single and self-supporting—like *Carol*—you know I'd be there for you. Don't you?

[*Pause.* JOANNA *crosses to table, puts mug down, notices an envelope addressed to her. She picks it up, studies the handwriting.* ROSIE *crosses to her.*]

ROSIE: [*Cont'd.*] It's Helene's handwriting.

CAROL: What does it say?

JOANNA: [*Opens envelope, reads aloud.*] "I Sister Helene humbly acknowledge that I am a coward."

ROSIE: Oh no.

JOANNA: [*Continuing.*] "I want my baby. I want Neil to want it. And spilling my guts about Dana is not the way to persuade him. I know you will forgive me—that's what sisterhood is all about. And in time, I may be able to forgive myself. Thanks for the weekend of deep meaningful sharing. Joanna, you will do whatever you must, and we will be the richer for it. Your Sister, Helene." [*Beat.*] "P.S.: I've taken Rosie's car to the bus station. Key is under seat. I need the long ride home alone. It'll be my penance."

[JOANNA *slides onto a chair.* ROSIE *moves behind her, puts her arms around her.* CAROL *moves closer too.*]

ROSIE: I'm sorry, Joanna... about all of us. Oh, why does everything have to be so... complicated? If people could just be free to love each other... it could all be so simple.

JOANNA: Amen.

LESLIE: [*Offstage.*] Carol! Are you coming?

[*Sound of car engine starting.*]

JOANNA: [*Jumping up and calling offstage.*] She's being held captive—someone will have to come rescue her!

CAROL: Please don't start anything, Jo.

JOANNA: Me? Start something?

[LESLIE *bursts in, then is somewhat embarrassed by her own urgency.*]

JOANNA: [*Cont'd.*] Behold your knight in shining... polyester!

LESLIE: Shut up.

CAROL: Joanna, I hope... I hope you'll be all right.

[*Picks up bags and exits.*]

LESLIE: [*Crossing to* JOANNA.] You know what your trouble is? Everybody's always told you you were special. And you believed it.

ROSIE: Leslie—can you give me a ride to the bus station?

LESLIE: Like that?

ROSIE: [*Pulling* LESLIE *out the door and onto the porch.*] Come on.

LESLIE: Where are you going in your nightgown?

ROSIE: No place.

LESLIE: Then why do you want a ride to the bus station?

ROSIE: A lot of old ladies ride buses. I thought I might pick up a few models.

[*They exit. Sounds of car doors slamming and car taking off.* JOANNA *crosses to drawing, takes it off the wall and tears it up. The pieces trail behind her as she crosses to another part of the stage. Crossfade with her.*]

SCENE 9

Motherhouse. Lights up on NAOMI *and* JOANNA.

JOANNA: I wanted it so badly. I had to do it.

[NAOMI *nods.*]

JOANNA: [*Cont'd.*] It was all such a surprise—the weekend.

NAOMI: Not what you expected.

JOANNA: I don't know what I expected. But I always seem to expect too much. And everybody else pays.

NAOMI: Don't be so hard on yourself, Love.

JOANNA: Why not? Maybe if I were harder on myself, I could be easier on the rest of the world.

NAOMI: And maybe if you were easier on yourself, you could be easier on the rest of the world.

JOANNA: What kind of marshmallow philosophy is that from a novice mistress? Where's all the Spartan training of my youth?

NAOMI: In your own selective memory.

JOANNA: [*Beat.*] Why are you still so important to me? [*Beat.*] Why am I still asking for your blessing . . . and the others for their approval. Why? Shouldn't it be . . . isn't it enough . . . to bless myself?

NAOMI: Can you?

JOANNA: I want to. Do you think I'll ever come to it?

NAOMI: Why is it so hard?

JOANNA: I don't know . . . I guess I resist blessing what isn't . . .

NAOMI: Perfect?

JOANNA: Yes.

NAOMI: Even the Church canonizes imperfect people.

JOANNA: That doesn't mean I have to! [*Beat.*] The trouble is everywhere you look . . . even inside . . . people are only . . . human.

NAOMI: What more do you want?

JOANNA: God!

NAOMI: Maybe God is only human.

JOANNA: That's not what you told us, dammit! Why? Why did you seduce us with the dream of perfection? I don't know if I can ever forgive you for that?

NAOMI: Can you forgive yourself?

JOANNA: I need that dream, Mother.

NAOMI: Having a dream is one thing. Expecting it to come true is another.

JOANNA: But the possibility has to be there. What's the point without it?

NAOMI: Maybe the point is striving.

JOANNA: Are you content with that?

NAOMI: Maybe that's all there is.

JOANNA: Doesn't that make you angry? I mean all this "striving" with no chance of success.

NAOMI: But there is success—in striving well.

JOANNA: But never to reach the goal, never to . . . arrive.

NAOMI: Oh, I don't know . . . . Arriving might turn out to be a real bore. [*Beat.*] Like heaven.

[JOANNA *smiles in spite of herself. Beat.*]

NAOMI: [*Cont'd.*] What are you going to do, Love?

JOANNA: I don't know. I just don't know.

NAOMI: How do you feel?

JOANNA: Afraid.

NAOMI: Of what?

JOANNA: That maybe I'm . . . maybe I'm not fit for anything but the convent.

NAOMI: What do you mean?

JOANNA: That I'm no good at . . . other things.

NAOMI: At what other things?

JOANNA: At being really close to another human being. I mean, when you think about it, God isn't half as demanding as most people.

NAOMI: "He has placed his seal upon you that you may admit no other lover."

JOANNA: Yes . . . [*Beat.*] Convenient, isn't it?

[*They look at each other. Fade.*]

© Bob Hsiang, 1991

Canyon Sam

INTRODUCTION TO *THE DISSIDENT* BY CANYON SAM IN THREE PARTS

CANYON SAM, SOLO PERFORMANCE ARTIST

Toni Press

Canyon Sam, an oft-published writer of fiction and non-fiction, has taught, lectured, and conducted workshops about writing, spiritual practice, human rights, and cultural and sexual identity at colleges, conferences, and writer's programs across the United States. Her work as a Tibetan activist was preceded by a decade of gay and women's rights activism.

Perhaps it is inevitable then that her first dramatic work would grow out of the burgeoning solo performance movement in American theater. In *The Dissident*, the solo form allows artistic imagination, spirituality, and social activism to perfectly coalesce.

It is not accidental that many solo writer/performers are artists of color, lesbians, and gay men. Because much solo work concerns the search for identity in a society that marginalizes non-white, non-heterosexual people, many dramatists who grew up outside mainstream society have turned to this unique form.

In *The Dissident*, the Narrator's urge to return to the country of her ancestors is just such an identity quest; she seeks to find not just a geographic place, but a psychological, emotional, psychic, and spiritual place where she feels a deep sense of belonging. In China, she hopes to find the key to unlock some vital part of herself, rendered silent by a society that sees her as "other." The psychic whom she consults about the trip she is planning says, "I see an explosion. What is exploding . . . is YOU." The solo performance form itself is such an explosion: the writer does not create an elaborate plot and invent characters to explicate meaning; the writer tells her story.

Despite its apparent shift of focus from the Narrator to Tashi, the Tibetan nun who challenges the Chinese occupation of Tibet, *The Dissident* remains the

Narrator's story. She travels to China, not exactly knowing what she hopes to find. "Some kinda roots thing," her father says. Quickly, she encounters a people stripped of affect; she is told that friendliness is not permitted and sees for herself, when she witnesses the accidental death of a construction worker, that compassion is not permitted either. The [other construction workers] "saw nothing, knew nothing, cared nothing." As shaken as she is, the Narrator realizes that this horror is indeed a part of her identity. "I shuddered when I thought about the fact that had my grandfather's dreams of opening a candy store in Shanghai come true, I would have been born *here*, not in California."

The theme of the complexity of identity and the necessity to embrace and understand various parts of oneself is doubled by Canyon Sam's speaking in many voices in *The Dissident*. Using the solo form in a complex way that provides the audience with a cacophony of voices, she tells her own story through them—including the voices of people with whom she does not sympathize, but nevertheless listens closely to, allowing them also to inform her self-understanding.

After her encounter with the Chinese workers, the Narrator decides to travel to Lhasa, Tibet, which has serendipitously been moved to the open list of tourist destinations just prior to her leaving the United States. Here she finds the welcoming people she had imagined populated the "land of [her] ancestors," including Tashi, from whose transcendent story of resistance, she learns the relationship between spiritual practice and working for social change. This realization transforms the Narrator's life.

Ingeniously, Canyon Sam relates Tashi's story, at first exclusively through the Narrator's voice, then in little spurts through Tashi's voice. Finally, Tashi tells the story of her incarceration and torture, Tibetan resistance, and the inspiration afforded her people by the Dalai Lama, in a beautiful, simple, climactic monologue.

The Narrator's journey comes full circle when she meets the Dalai Lama in San Francisco. She talks about her life's transformation: "I keep a picture of his mother right next to a picture of my own grandmother, my mother's mother, who came over at sixteen from Guangzhou, Canton, with bound feet...I started out in China, looking for wisdom. I ended up in Tibet, working for justice."

Canyon Sam tells her story by telling the story of Tibetan resistance to the repressive regime in the People's Republic of China. In so doing, she employs in *The Dissident* one of solo performance's most crucial characteristics—storytelling. Storytelling is a dramatic technique used in cultures throughout the world, but virtually absent from mainstream American theater. Solo performance has reclaimed this technique, drawing in audiences just as deeply by the straightforward telling of a story as by the creation of conflict among several characters. Using storytelling gives artists of color whose experiences have not been reflected in society a way to say, "Listen to my story. *This* is who I am." Canyon Sam's elaboration of the technique has the Narrator's voice giving way to Tashi's voice, and thus addresses the idea that Tashi's struggle and hers are the same; in fact, that Tashi's struggle is all of our struggle.

The play asserts that to be fully alive, we must be fully awake, as the Chinese workers the Narrator encounters are not. *The Dissident* is an eloquent plea for self-awareness and conscious participation in life's struggle. Toward the end of the piece, the Narrator is surprised to hear from a friend that Tashi is "...fine! Laughing, joking, she's in high spirits...the usual." It is only by leading a conscious life that one can lead a full and happy life, and it is only by embracing one's spiritual life that one can lead a fully conscious life.

In her complex, dense and beautiful drama, Canyon Sam suggests that a successful search for self-knowledge leads to the understanding that we are all one. But for her it is not enough to awaken, to discover your spirit. The true spiritual life must include working for social change; it is not until we acknowledge our connection to one another's suffering that we can understand ourselves more deeply. It is not until we act to change that suffering that we can truly lead full lives.

CANYON SAM, SOCIAL ACTIVIST
Victoria Rue

People come to theatre for various reasons. A few come because they see it as a crucible, a vortex for social change. Having created theatre pieces about lesbian lives and struggles, the lives of women with cancer, women with AIDS and Palestinian women, I turn with hope and appreciation to the social activist artistry of Canyon Sam. Canyon Sam's work is both the story of Tibetan resistance and her own journey as a lesbian activist. Ironically, she went to China in search of her ancestry. "But it was the cousin country of Tibet that took me in. Little girls would take my hand as I walked down the street, women would hail me over from two fields away to invite me to their picnic."

Illustrating feminist belief that our personal stories/lives create political history, *The Dissident* enacts an interplay of the personal and historical, the micro and the macro, building bridges to the existence of marginalized peoples everywhere. The dramatic presence of Sam's voice calls us to build these sorely needed bridges among our own communities of resistance. In describing how a lesbian actress might approach interpreting the role of the tortured Tibetan nun Tashi, she said to me, "It is courage in the face of terror. A young lesbian might know this courage in her own coming out—how to stand up to a homophobe or a bully."

Canyon Sam's work weaves a tapestry of human rights—the right each woman has to decide that her own journey is linked inextricably to the human right of religious freedom. Through Canyon's socially committed artistry, we are again reminded of the powerful work that can be accomplished when activism is fueled by spirituality, story rooted in personal experience, and a cry for justice is blessed by relationship.

CANYON SAM, BUDDHIST
Judy Schavrien

I first met Canyon Sam in 1984 through her photo: we had both contributed to *New Lesbian Writing*. In 1986 I recognized her in the airport—both on our way to the Himalayas. "Maybe we'll trek together." But it never happened. When we met again in 1994, we had something else in common: Buddhist practice.

The Dissident, especially as Canyon Sam performs it, links wisdom with compassion. This is the Tibetan Buddhist moral and spiritual attitude: wise compassion, compassionate wisdom. Canyon does more than awaken compassion, draw attention to it; she becomes the thing *itself* as she enacts one moment the shy, modest, yet fiercely determined nun and just as quickly becomes a brute Chinese soldier. While the nun folds inward, pained and hesitant, but unbreakable through her dedication to a higher cause, the soldier yanks and kicks the nun, dislocates her shoulder, drags her off. Canyon's ability to portray them both—and a wide array of characters—in quick succession suggests a new definition for compassion: it is the unobstructed imagination moving fluidly into action. As a Buddhist, one *becomes* the All, recollects one's own self as the wide Self. With no creature separate from you, what creature can be your enemy?

In a discussion of the Holocaust as it related to her play and to the Chinese genocide of Tibetans, I asked Canyon about the following: Saul Bellow deeply objected to Hannah Arendt's characterization of the Nazis in *Eichmann in Jerusalem*, where she coined the phrase "banality of evil." Arendt considered the Nazis ordinary people too devoted to their careers—banal careerism enmeshed them in evil. Canyon said: "Yes, the Chinese of the mainland *are* people buckling to the pressures of the system, not monsters. They are so bullied by the system that they themselves, many of them, become bullies and petty despots." Is the Chinese soldier a victim of the political system? "Yes and no," she replied, "it's a complex matter; yet even under oppressive conditions, people must and do make their choices."

Who is the enemy? It's a complex matter. In one scene, Canyon wants to interview Tashi, the nun who has escaped from prison in Tibet, so that she can make Chinese atrocities in Tibet known and further the Tibetan cause. She fears, however, that Tashi has demurred from the interview, having glimpsed Canyon's Chinese face. She had, after all, begun this journey fueled by a romantic yearning to explore her Chinese self, ancient and modern, her living relatives and her roots. Instead she finds that she hates the callousness of the Han Chinese of the mainland: there is the incident in which a tribal woman lies trapped beneath a boulder while her Han fellow workers, "see nothing, know nothing, care nothing." When, by contrast, Canyon meets the Tibetans she finds them warm, open, awake; she is taken in by a Tibetan family, falls in love with the landscape, studies the spirituality; she becomes a friend of the oppressed while wearing the face of the oppressor.

This seeming paradox reaches its culmination when Canyon meets the Dalai Lama, the buddha of compassion incarnate, for the second time. They had met previously, right after her journey through China and Tibet. In the brightest moment of the play, almost a turning about, he lets out a laugh so wholehearted and generous that it lights the theatre: "*You look Tibetan!*"

Only ignorance is the enemy. In *The Dissident* there is as much if not more tragedy for the Chinese soldier as for the Tibetan nun: those who govern China and their agents do violence to their own natural compassion, preferring to "see nothing, know nothing, care nothing." They are energetically engaged in killing off—more completely than they can slaughter anything or anyone else—their own best selves.

© Bob Hsiang

Canyon Sam in The Dissident

PLAYWRIGHT'S NOTES

The impetus for creating *The Dissident* sprung from my many years as a Tibet activist in the United States, beginning in the mid-eighties (before which I had been an activist in the feminist and gay/lesbian community in San Francisco for a decade), my personal affinity for the Tibetan people, and my admiration for the Dalai Lama's staunch belief in the importance of linking compassion, or a kind of spiritual underpining to political endeavor. Theatrically, *The Dissident* combines personal narrative and theater in what the Buddhists would call an awakening story. It also contains elements of performance art, travelogue, humor, and theater of conscience. The show, which has always been performed by myself, premiered in November 1991 in San Francisco in an independent production staged at the Phoenix Theater. It won arts grants on both coasts and went on to tour the United States and Canada to critical acclaim. My collaborator in the initial birthing of the piece was performance artist Nina Wise, after which director Christine McHugh patiently helped me craft its development to the stage. Wendy Gilmore's lighting design beautifully supplemented the play.

All characters in this piece are played by a female actor, the narrator—a late-twenties to early thirties Chinese-American woman, spirited, politically progressive, but naive to the real nature of the P.R.C. government—the psychic, a Russian, a Chinese co-worker, and the narrator's father in the US. In Asia, she plays the indifferent Chinese construction worker, her Tibetan friend in her early twenties, that friend's mother, and then the Tibetan nun, Tashi, twenty-three years old. She also portrays various Chinese officials and the Dalai Lama at the end. The piece spans several years, from 1984 to 1991, and takes place in San Francisco, the People's Republic of China, central Tibet, and Dharamsala, India.

Tashi's experiences are based on actual transcripts. Her experience is a common one for political activists in Tibet, many of whom are nuns. Nuns, being both women and religious figures, draw a special wrath from the Chinese. According to a 1988 *New York Times* article based on a survey of released political prisoners, among Tibetan prisoners, lay and cleric, male and female, it is Tibetan nuns who are treated the most severely of all in prisons, in terms of torture, beatings, and general living conditions.

The terms narrator and interviewer are used interchangeably, although Interviewer usually refer to the narrator present in the interview scene with Tashi in Dharamsala in 1990.

The voices of the Tibetan friend and Tibetan mother are unique. They have a softness, a joyful innocence and a serenity that would be hard to find in the Western world. The fact that their culture is a deeply spiritual one, which has been cut off from outside influence for centuries, may account for this. The Tibetans are renowned for hospitality and graciousness, and this also must be part of the rendering of these characters.

Tashi's demeanor is different, darker, more wary because she is not meeting the narrator as a friend, but as a reluctant interview subject, apprehensive about recounting her experiences to a stranger, and frightened that her public sharing of them may bring terrible consequences to her loved ones. Her two most important scenes are the demonstration scene, where she and her colleagues risk their lives to speak out for freedom and against repression ('quit' in this scene means get out) and her closing monologue.

In the demonstration scene the nuns are unarmed protesters, usually cloistered members of a convent, citizens of an occupied country without any rights facing the absolute power, the "merciless repression" as the Chinese boast, of the P.R.C. police state. It is a shining moment because though she and the others are terrified to near paralysis, Tashi is determined to speak out, and ultimately does so.

In her last monologue, delivered in a volume just above a loud whisper, we see to a greater extent the horrors of post-Tianamen Tibet—those incidents which do not reach Western newspapers, nor probably even human rights reports; we also see Tashi's humanness, her very real physical pain, her sorrow and anguish as a Tibetan, and at the same time, the gifts of her spiritual training which shelter her from despair.

The Dalai Lama's laugh is very distinct—a deep-tenored, profoundly joyous roar. A Tibetan pilgrim once exclaimed after surviving decades of travail and then meeting the spiritual leader: "The Dalai Lama cleaned my heart!" The Dalai Lama character's laughter and very presence should hint at this kind of power and grace. "Re-bay?" literally means "isn't it so?" He addresses here his aide-de-camp in Tibetan, asking the equivalent of "Don't you agree?"

NOTES ON STAGING

The play is most effective when staged in an intimate theater seating about 75 to 300 people. In the original production, set and props consist of five galvanized metal buckets of various sizes from half gallon to ten gallon; a metal folding chair, drab or metallic in color; and a small blanket of burgundy color. The actor wears dark pants and a goldenrod sleeveless blouse. Goldenrod and burgundy are the colors worn by monastics in the Tibetan Buddhist tradition, hence the colors are important. The set will represent at various times the monastery housing where Yangchen lives, the river valley where the plane lands, the Himalayan mountains during Tashi's escape, etc.

The chair is used as a chair, and also to represent the person of Tashi in the interview scene and Chinese prison scenes. It is the stack of lumber in the cold-water-in-the-cell scene and the police official's pedestal when he evicts the nuns. The buckets represent different cities in China; various single buckets become the hand drum, the tea cup at Yangchen's house, the camera in the prison scene, the bowl in her cell, etc. The blanket serves as the narrator's bed at Yangchen's house, the tarmac at the airport, Tashi's prison blanket, but most importantly, it is used as Tashi's nun's robe, worn like a shawl, during her escape and in her ending monologue.

Sound effects and sound design are created with the buckets and chair. When the large boulder crashes down on the woman worker below, it is a bucket that drops to the stage floor from the hand of the actor standing on the chair digging out dirt from the hillside. Later in that scene when the narrator realizes she escaped by an eyelash being born in China instead of America, she uses a bucket under her arm like a hand drum, tapping an insistent, chilling, driving rhythm. One bucket is beaten with both hands to a deafening pitch during the toilet bucket, interrogation room scene. And one of the smaller buckets is beaten against the chair, metal thrashing metal, in shrill, bone-chilling strikes, to represent the punishment that Tashi receives at the hands of prison interrogators.

Lights come up on actor center stage, standing in front of a metal folding chair, beside which on the floor, at a diagonal, is spread a small maroon blanket. Five shiny, metal galvanized buckets of various sizes are placed around the floor of the stage. The backdrop and floor are black, bare.

NARRATOR: [*1990.*] I've been living in Dharamsala several months now. Dharamsala is the capital of Tibet in exile in northern India, and I lived here four years ago too during my first trip to Asia. I'm from San Francisco, grew up by Golden Gate Park, but I've been involved with Tibet—strangely enough—ever since that trip to China four years ago.

[*Flashback.*]

"I'm thinking of going to China...for an extended time. A year. Do you see anything?" I asked my longtime psychic in my annual Christmas reading, 1984. "It'd be spring after next...'86...does it look good?"

I had a warmth in my heart for old country China. Grandparents on both sides came from villages in Guangzhou, old Canton, north of Hong Kong. And I grew up part of the year every year with my grandparents on my mom's side in Fresno, California.

PSYCHIC: [*Eyes closed as she observes the image, then open as she speaks.*] I see an explosion. A mass explosion. What's exploding...is you. This trip will not be an ordinary journey, it will be a spiritual odyssey. This trip is a major turning point in your life, a transformation like nothing you've experienced in this incarnation. You'll come to measure your life by it: you'll think of your life *before* your trip to Asia, and your life *after* your trip to Asia.

Oh...by the way...are you planning to go to Tibet?

Tibet is completely lit up for you...in brilliant letters. Blinding white light—the size of a city. There's a tremendous amount of energy there...for you. Be sure and go to Tibet.

NARRATOR: Neither my Chinese co-worker who'd spent seven years escaping from Shanghai in the People's Republic of China, nor my Russian co-worker who'd spent nine years escaping from Leningrad in the Soviet Union could understand why anyone in their right mind would *leave* a free country to move to a Communist country.

RUSSIAN CO-WORKER: "Itz kur-ra-tzy ideea, Canyon," Yakov said.

CHINESE CO-WORKER: "Aiya! Bai-la, Bai-la," Ed Chao said.

NARRATOR: My parents couldn't understand it either.

FATHER: Why do you have to go to China for a year? You can see China in three weeks.

NARRATOR: [*Passionate.*] No, Dad. I want to really see it, learn the language, live with the people, engage in...

FATHER: Awright, awright! I get it. Hmph! You kids. [*Beat.*] Some kinda *Roots* thing. Then you take the five-week tour.

NARRATOR: [*Moving among buckets.*] I traveled off the beaten track of showcase tourist spots, starting in the south to Guangzhou, old Canton, with tiny, half-deserted villages and vast tracts of ricefields; to Guangsi, where spectacular limestone peaks jutted straight out of the earth, inspiring centuries of Chinese poets and painters; to Yunnan Province in the southwest, bordering Burma and Laos, home of many of China's minorities: the Bai people, the Dai people, the Naxi, the Hmong. I met a woman who said to me: 'My husband is bi.'

I thought, 'Gee they're really open here.'

Hotel clerks would see through me as I stood in front of them waiting for service; when they thought I wasn't in my room, they barged in with passkeys looking for cameras and cash and valuables.

Friendly, English-speaking Chinese told me they were punished—pulled off the front desk, put down in the stock room for being too friendly with foreigners.

The way the Chinese carried their faces, they saw nothing, knew nothing, cared nothing. Saw nothing, knew nothing, cared nothing.

I watched a construction site in Yunnan where 75 workers were digging out a hillside, widening a road. When all of a sudden way up high, a ten foot round boulder broke loose, tumbled down, and crushed this minority worker with long braids in a long dress.

Her Chinese co-workers stood around, sucked on their cigarettes, picked at the dirt with their shovels, looked right through her beseeching friends pleading for help. They saw nothing, knew nothing, cared nothing, saw nothing, knew nothing, cared nothing.

Only after twenty minutes of cajoling did the Chinese workers saunter over to help push the room-size boulder off the woman's limp body.

[*Shaken and horrified.*] I shuddered when I thought about the fact that had my grandfather's dreams of opening a candy store in Shanghai come true, I would have been born here, not in California. I would be one of these Orwellian people!

[*Shift, crosses stage back to center.*] As per my itinerary, in my fifth week I flew from Chengdu to Lhasa, Tibet. Tibet had lived in isolation for hundreds of years, then been cut off by the Chinese government for the last thirty. The only Westerners allowed in Tibet were a handful of organized tour groups who paid fabulous sums of money to the Chinese government in the early 1980's to tour the country, their whereabouts strictly controlled.

But right before I left the States, Lhasa was moved from the closed list to the open list of tourist destinations by the Chinese government, so for the first time in history, Tibet was open to independent foreign travelers.

[*Bewildered.*] I landed in the middle of a broad, high desert valley. Not an airport building, a sign, an official authority in sight. We stood on the tarmac for 45 minutes, then some buses came and drove us away—down this long river valley where bright colored bits of cloth were stretched over the water, fluttering in the wind. After an hour, it was clear we weren't going to an airport terminal, but I didn't know where we were going. After two hours we drove into a city, and the driver dumped us in a depot. All the other passengers scattered; I was the only Westerner on the flight. I wandered around looking for my luggage: 'Deuimhji, wo shih . . .' until I saw a hand-lettered sign in English tacked to a tree: 'Disorganized Tourists Information. This Way.'

That afternoon I met a young Tibetan woman who spoke a little English.

The next afternoon she invited me to her family's house for tea; we climbed a steep, ancient, wooden staircase in an old monastery complex hidden off the street, crossed over huge stone thresholds, crouched under low doorways, groped around dark corners to her house—where I met her mother. "Hello..."

Somewhere between innumerable cups of sweet milk tea—I couldn't keep track of exactly how many because everytime I took two sips they refilled my teacup to the brim, so I could never finish drinking. Even if I insisted, they would start to pour the tea through my fingers! Yangchen, my new friend pointed to a thick, blue, Tibetan carpet covering a single bed.

YANGCHEN: [*Points to each of three single beds, in turn.*] I sehleeping here. Middle sister, Dolma, sehleeping here. Younger sister, Pema, sehleeping here. Dolma job, Nepal border; Dolma no sehleeping here. How long you stay Lhasa? You sehleep here. [*Pats the third bed.*] Dissa your bed.

NARRATOR: Being a middle child of three myself, I felt right in my element.

[*Blissful.*] I fell in love with the high desert land, the piercing sapphire blue skies—where I lay on my back and counted five, six, sometimes even seven distinct layers of cloud patterns piled one on top of another. I loved the vast tracts of mountains where I knew no one had ever walked. I baptized myself in the Yarlang Tsangpo River, in a scene of pure sunlight on water like something from the Bible.

I fell in love with the warm, laughing people, and their gentle acceptance of everything in life. Yangchen and I planned our old age together in Lhasa. I decided I wanted to die in Tibet.

[*Pause.*] But after two months, promising myself I'd return in the winter, I forced myself to go back to China: You're Chinese; you came here to go to China. Give it another chance. Chin up.

My Tibetan mother, Amala, offered me money out of her special hiding place. [*Takes bills from cleavage.*]

AMALA: Take...take. Need money traveling.

NARRATOR: No, Amala. No need.

AMALA: [*Aside to audience.*] Tibetans had no money.

NARRATOR: Thank you, Amala.

AMALA: I keep your winter coat, your books, your medicine, safe here. Come back. Come back live here, live Lhasa... You marry Tibetan boy?

NARRATOR: I floated down the Yangtze River in China in a third class, upper bunk wilting in the July heat, surrounded by Chinese cabinmates scarfing watermelon, spitting seeds. I read a book, *In Exile from the Land of Snows*, by John Avedon, about the Chinese occupation of Tibet the last thirty years.

I was outraged: over one million Tibetans had died, 99% of monasteries, the cultural equivalent of universities, libraries, and temples, were cannonballed to the ground. The national literature was torched. And we knew nothing about it in the West. We knew about Guatamala and El Salvador, about apartheid, the Holocaust, the Palestinians. We knew nothing about what had happened to this country: one of the most highly refined spiritual civilizations on earth. The International Commission of Jurists called Tibet the worse case of genocide since WWII.

[*Re-enters Dharamsala scene, 1990, from the top of the show: stands center stage in front of chair, same lighting.*]

So ever since that trip to China four years ago, I've been involved with Tibet.

Here, now in Dharamsala, on this second trip, I write on Tibetan issues for an international newswire service out of their New Delhi office. I do development work for Tibetan nuns to help them build a school, because they're not allowed into the schools for monks. I've started a book of oral histories of Tibetan women. And sometimes my American friend and I do research for colleagues in the States.

One day, I receive a letter from a colleague in Washington, D.C. John asks for my help with a report he's writing on religious conditions in Tibet. He has plenty of information on monks, nothing on nuns. Could I see if I could locate some women who have recently come out of Tibet and interview them?

I find out that two nuns from Lhasa escaped from Tibet and arrived in Dharamsala the day before yesterday, so I go looking for them in the Newcomers' Hall, a three-story, yellow-painted concrete building near the post office—without success.

The next day I return with my translator, Chimee, high school senior, top debator, pre-law, sharp; we search town all afternoon, till finally at nightfall we find the two women at their bunks in the Newcomers' Hall.

[*Shift to Newcomers' Hall.*]

[*Apprehensive.*] They are young, early twenties, with dark fear in their eyes. We introduce ourselves, we explain the project, but they seem to recoil from our mere presence. We set up a time to meet, but they don't show up.

Cultural Lesson Number One in Asian manners: They say yes, but they don't show up: that means no. Apparently they're reluctant to talk to us because they've been warned not to speak to anyone about their activity in Tibet. Security leaks recently have been devastating. In the back of my mind, I wonder if they look at my face and think, She's Chinese! So I go to my friends in the Office of Information and International Relations—it's like our State Department—and the two women get authorized government clearance to speak to me; we set a date, but again they don't show up.

This time, as Chimee and I climb the stairs to the Newcomers' Hall looking for them, an old Tibetan granny wringing her hand laundry at the water spigot stares at us as we enter the building. Chimee whispers to me, "She's a spy."

When I look back, the old woman's gold teeth glint in the sunlight. [*Shocked, sobered.*] Oh my God, it is dangerous here.

[*Shift.*]

Finally, they appear. We sit in Chimee's house in the afternoon. It's hot, in the 80's. Chimee's mother serves us cool orange drinks in plastic tumblers. They wear maroon, floor-length robes, mustard-colored, sleeveless blouses. They sit near the door, and won't look me in the eye. But Chimee says one of them has agreed to talk to me.

NARRATOR AS INTERVIEWER: [*Addressing* TASHI, *represented by chair.*] I know you have family inside Tibet and you're afraid for their safety if you talk. But I won't tape record your voice, I won't take your photograph. I don't even know your real name. I can just call you...um...Tashi. This information will go to groups around the world that can help Tibet. Will you answer my questions?

NARRATOR: [*Addressing audience.*] She was twenty-three years old, from Garu Nunnery, a nunnery a few kilometers outside Lhasa. I asked what her political involvement had been, and she said the nuns made demonstrations every week. Nine, ten, eleven women. Sometimes as few as three. Every week.

Tashi told me she'd been arrested for demonstrating.

She said the day of her arrest, six of them from Garu Nunnery walked to the Barkor, the center of town. She saw sharpshooters on the roof of the Jokhang Temple, the police station, and all the houses and shops around the Barkhor. She saw soldiers at their corner patrols, and plainclothes police in scruffy overcoats. All the shops in the market circle were closed.

INTERVIEWER: Why were they closed? They rarely ever close.

TASHI: Day before, we give shopkeepers small paper. "Tomorrow demonstration. Close shop." They read paper, eat paper, swallow. All shops closed.

NARRATOR: I knew every demonstration in Tibet was swiftly, brutally repressed by the Chinese; they like to boast of it. Every demonstration in Tibet was Tianamen Square without cameras. Wasn't she scared?

TASHI: Very scare, big scareful. No can go, no can go home, no can move.

But I think: We suffer much. I want suffer stop. I think [of] His Holiness. I see him [*She becomes serene.*], I no fear. I have small Tibetan flag, no legal. We walk to Barkor. [*She lifts the flag between her fingers, as the nuns lift their voices, timid at first, growing in boldness. They are utterly terrified but strongly determined.*]

FREE TIBET...FREE POLITICAL PRISONERS...CHINA QUIT TIBET...FREE TIBET!

NARRATOR: Fifty paramilitary police in full riot gear poured from the police station and pounced on the six women. [*Rapid stomps.*] Her shoulder was dislocated, and she was dragged to Drapchi Prison.

She was stripped naked, and beaten with electric cattle prods.

CHINESE PRISON INTERROGATOR: [*Full-out strikes of bucket against chair punctuate queries.*] Who are the leaders of the underground? Where is the center of counter-revolutionary activity in Lhasa? Is it Lhasa University? Is it Drepung Monastery? Who gives you money and arms? The Americans? The Japanese? Hostile foreign forces! We will smash this Dalai Lama clique that tries to split the motherland!

NARRATOR: They put her in a room where she was attacked by police dogs. Then they made her stand all day. If she sat down, she got beaten; if she fell down, she got beaten.

They manacled her arms and legs, and put her in solitary confinement.

The next day they photographed every part of her body: her calves, her back, her neck, each ear, each eye, her belly, her knees, her toes. They investigated her private parts.

[*Sobered.*] She didn't even know a word for rape in Tibetan. She just said they kept taking the cattle prod in and out, over and over, and that she couldn't control her bladder.

For breakfast, they gave her a thin rice porridge full of baking powder, so it gave her diarrhea; for lunch and dinner, she got one small steamed dumpling, which they always forced her to dip in her toilet bucket before eating. A cup of tea twice a day was laced with chili powder, so it burned her digestive tract.

They gave her one thin blanket—[*Rolls on floor in blanket, freezing.*]—which she always had to decide whether to lay on the cold concrete floor, but have nothing to cover her body, or cover her body, but have to lay on the cold concrete floor. They never let her out of her cell, except to dump her toilet bucket.

One day, she was following the guard, going off to dump the toilet bucket, when he led her instead in to the interrogation room, where they dumped the bucket on her head, made her wear it 'round her shoulders, and beat it with their batons...for hours...until she thought she'd go deaf.

NARRATOR: [*To audience.*] I almost couldn't go on. No one spoke. Chimee's mother stood in the doorway. Chimee, a good translator, waited for my cue. Tashi sat bent over. I saw only the crown of her shaved head. I hated to put her through anymore, but at the same time, my outrage was mounting.

INTERVIEWER: [*To* TASHI *(chair).*] How often were you beaten, Tashi? [*Listens to her answer.*]

NARRATOR: [*To audience.*] She couldn't remember. She remembered the first three days clearly, but then she was never quite in her right mind. All the time, she said. It was endless. If she lost consciousness, they threw cold water on her to wake her up.

In the winter, the Chinese poured cold water into her cell and made her lie down in it [*Lies flat on floor, pulling chair on top of her crushed, shivering body.*] while they stacked heavy lumber on top of her emaciated, black and blue body submerged in water in the middle of winter in the Himalayas. [*Pause.*]

Tashi was released from Drapchi Prison after seven months. She returned to Garu Nunnery, which was now occupied by Chinese authorities most of the year. They held political re-education sessions eight hours a day. When they weren't there, they dictated what subjects were taught, which teachers could teach, which women were allowed to join.

Five months after her release, Tashi and every single other woman at Garu Nunnery was expelled for celebrating the Nobel Peace Prize award to the leader of Tibet, the Dalai Lama.

CHINESE SECURITY POLICE OFFICIAL: Based on eyewitness reports of your activity in the Barkhor yesterday, and evidence found on this premises last night, the following Tibetans are herein notified:

The burning of incense in the public square is a counter-revolutionary crime, of which you are guilty.

The singing of the Tibetan National Anthem is a counter-revolutionary crime, of which you are guilty.

The possession of a Tibetan flag is a counter-revolutionary crime, of which you are guilty.

The throwing of barley flour is a counter-revolutionary crime, of which you are guilty.

According to the Central Committee of the Chinese Communist Party, active counter-revolutionary elements are the most dangerous type of criminal! You are therefore expelled from the religious order! You are forbidden to practice the Buddhist religion! And you are ordered to evacuate this premises permanently by noon tomorrow, or face life in prison!

Contribute to the Unity of the Motherland, and the Building of the Four Modernizations!

NARRATOR: Tashi had felt the spiritual calling since she was a teenager. When she became a nun, she took lifelong vows. Forbidden to pray, to study Buddhism, to honor her vows as a nun, she had nothing.

After three months in her home village, she and Joebar, another Garu nun decided to escape to India.

They walked by night, slept by day, stayed off main roads, for food they melted snow and mixed it with barley flour. Sometimes they didn't eat for two or three days, because they ran out of barley flour.

INTERVIEWER: Where'd you sleep?

TASHI: [At first puzzled by the question, then simply gestures to the ground.] No can walk more, so sleep.

INTERVIEWER: It was an escape story that I heard over and over again in Dharamsala. No map, no tent, no stove, no sleeping gear, nothing. Just fleeing on foot over the highest mountains in the world. [Beat.]

Villagers at the northwest border of Tibet near Mt. Kailash helped raise money to pay Nepali traders huge bribes—equal to two and a half times a person's yearly salary per nun—to lead the women in the hush of night over the ice blue Himalayan passes into India.

I asked her my own question, off the record: After everything she'd been through . . . Did you ever lose hope?

TASHI: I not despair. Even bad, bad times, because I know His Holiness work hard. Minnie people work hard for Tibet. [Pause. Quiet.]

The Chinese beat, torture, shoot, poison, starve us. [Beat. Quiet.]

Some monks and nuns now . . . they alive . . . but no can hold bodies. No minds. [Beat. Quiet.]

All anilas, all nuns in prison, dey . . . womantorture . . . with 'lectric sticks, cattle sticks. [Pause.]

One monk from Sera Monastery, Chinese say him, 'Stand on block of ice,' in winter. Next day, say him, 'Stand off ice.' Part him feet stay on ice. [Three beats.]

They have slow poison—dey put in food day before leave prison . . . [Looks to translator for English word.] . . . release. You eat food, you go home. Next day, bad sick. Next day . . . [Asks translator for English.] Katz zer ray? . . . Coma.

Next day, die. Three days after release: Die. [*Beat.*]

Chinese say: "We release political prisoners." [*Pause. Several beats.*]

Me health, no good. Every morning, big pain. Here…here…here. Dis my problem. [*Beat.*] But [in] Tibet, here India, I not feel despair. [*Two or three beats.*]

Dis our role in independence. We accept. We accept everything, what happens, okay….We do this till die. Or till Tibet independence.

NARRATOR: About a week after the interview, I ran into a mutual friend of Tashi and mine. She said she'd spent all day with Tashi and Joebar at Delek Hospital taking care of Tashi's health problems—the clinic, the pharmacy, the x-ray. "So how is Tashi?" I asked.

FRIEND: Tashi? She's fine! Laughing, joking, she's in high spirits…the usual.

NARRATOR: [*Incredulous.*] Tashi?! From Garu Nunnery?! [*Beat.*] It was such a different image of the woman than the woman I interviewed.

Cheerful, resilient, forebearing—that was the Tibetan temperment. But after everything she'd been through, I was amazed it was still there.

[*Moves downstage right, to scene in San Francisco, 1991. A hotel reception room.*]

Earlier this year, I met His Holiness the Dalai Lama in San Francisco. He clapped me on the shoulder after all the other Westerners had left the reception hall.

THE DALAI LAMA: Ha ha ha. You're looking just likka Tibetan. [*Full-bodied, joyous laugh.*] Hah, hah, hah! Just likka! Reh-bay? Just likka!

NARRATOR: I keep a picture of his mother on my altar, right next to a picture of my own grandmother, my mother's mother, who came over at sixteen from Guangzhou, old Canton, with bound feet.

I went to China looking for the truth of my ancestors, and I found it in Tibet. Found myself working to help free Tibet from the grip of these Orwellian people who rule my ancestors' land. [*Pause.*]

I started out in China, looking for wisdom. I ended up in Tibet, working for justice.

This is the story of my travels, between China and Tibet, between wisdom and justice.

[*Lights slowly dim out until the chair alone, center stage, is bathed in light, the blanket coiled on the seat; focus lingers there several long seconds, then slowly fades to black. Curtain.*]

Collection of Joan Schenkar

Joan Schenkar

AN AMAZON REVENGER'S COMEDY

Vivian Patraka and Annette Wannamaker

Patraka: Does your sexual orientation influence your playwriting?

Schenkar: I think it's the other way around. I think language influenced my sexual orientation. Like Emma Bovary, my imagination was seduced by what I read—and at a very early age, too. Not to mention the fact that my middle name is after Marlene Dietrich, a woman whose richly varied sexual life I was always aware of. The inclusiveness of my own sexuality has gone through my work, as Emily Brontë might say, like wine through water. Its suppleness allows me to stand in many places on the mental and emotional stage. And although I've never seen any reason to reduce something as spiritual and mysterious as sexual attraction to a politic, the tyranny of the times (but times are always tyrannous), compels my imagination towards transgression. [Patraka, 1995.]

Playwright Joan Schenkar has had over three hundred productions of her plays. Her theatre work has been shown throughout North America, England, and Western Europe at experimental theatres, universities, theatre festivals, and theatre conferences. She is the recipient of more than thirty-five grants, fellowships, and awards for playwriting (including seven National Endowment for the Arts grants), and has been reviewed in every major (and many minor) newspaper in the United States.

Schenkar's published plays include *Signs of Life* (recipient of a CAPS grant and an NEA Fellowship for Playwriting) and *Cabin Fever* (nominated for an OBIE AWARD), both published by Samuel French. *The Universal Wolf* is published both by *The Kenyon Review* and by Applause Books, *Family Pride in the 50's* is published by *The Kenyon Review*, and *Fulfilling Koch's Postulate* and *The Last of Hitler* have been excerpted by *The Drama Review*. Her plays produced on stage, radio, and video include *Signs of Life* (1979), *Cabin Fever* (1980), *Mr. Monster* (1981), *The Last of Hitler* (1982), *Bucks and Does* (1983), *Fulfilling Koch's Postulate* (1985), *Hunting Down the Sexes* (1986), *Family Pride in the 50's* (1987), *The Lodger* (1988), *Fire in the Future* (1988), *Between the Acts* (1989), *The Universal Wolf* (1991/3), *Murder in the Kitchen* (1993), and *Burning Desires* (1994). Current works in progress include *The Viennese Oyster*, *Big Bad Brain*, and *Truly Wilde*, a biography of Oscar Wilde's niece Dolly.

Joan Schenkar is best known for her "comedies of menace for the mental stage," and critics have frequently praised her "powerful, disturbing theatre," for its "unorthodox and bold experimental staging," "its echoing, austere, and dazzling language," and its "darkly hilarious and brilliantly creepy" comedy that challenges and provokes while giving no quarter to easy answers or mass popularity. Using an embroidered tapestry of the real and the invented and a lyrical, witty language that is skewed and repetitive, Schenkar's plays create disturbing, surreal landscapes of collective mind. The insistence in the plays on a community of obsessions, motives, and nightmares conveys the unconscious as a complex, entangling web among the characters created in collaboration with the culture they inhabit. Schenkar is fascinated by epistemology, by how people know what they know, and when they know it, and what they do with it. Tracking this knowledge by means of condensed, unusual theatrical metaphors drawn from cannibalism and cooking, from pathology and freakishness, from gardening and comic strips, and from performance and ritual, Schenkar's theatre creates a continuing exploration of gender politics and sexuality, fascism and violence, language and invention, and memory and history in relation to our psychic lives. The world of these plays is, as one critic described it, "the familiar haunted by the unknown," a world that elicits "a shudder of recognition" from audiences in the midst of their laughter.

In *The Lodger*, Schenkar creates what she calls "a revenger's comedy . . . a feminist revenge fantasy" set in a surreal, claustrophobic world infused with comic menace and the threat of physical violence. In short, episodic scenes punctuated by blackouts, two Amazon women, April and May, negotiate among conflicting memories in an attempt to recapture a lost sense of their Amazon history and mythic past. The play takes place in a suspended present, a kind of post apocalyptic afterwards to whatever has happened before it. In this sense *The Lodger* might be said metaphorically to mark a moment of diminishment in feminism's movement. But, as Schenkar told us, "just because the play ends at the moment where there are no possibilities of victories but only different ways of losing, doesn't mean that every bit of violence against the men isn't savored. I believe in revenge, at least in imaginative revenge."

As is often the case with revenge, pleasure comes from the fact that the victim of the revenge has committed a great atrocity (or is associated with those who have), a crime that warrants an excessively violent response. In the case of *The Lodger*, this atrocity is the murder of Amazon women, and, most particularly, the dismemberment and murder of Iris, their matriarchal leader, by a band of men. As with classic tragedy, the physical violence by both men *and* women mostly occurs off-stage. But while April and May's descriptions of what they physically enact upon their off stage prisoner are gory and specific, they are also, in the play's more comedic vein, quite playful, and, even casual.

The Lodger also ironically echoes certain feminisms, more particularly those based in matriarchal, Amazon goddess myths and revisionings. The women aggressively posture, sharpen weapons, and capture and torture men with a certain retaliatory relish. Moreover, the text, with its emphasis on story telling, ritual action, and war between the sexes satirically reverberates with Monique Wittig's novel *Les Guerillieres*. As Schenkar told us recently, "It is both a send-up and it's not. When you send anything up you have to have internalized it in a very large way. It's got to have meant something terribly important to you before you put a little helium in it and float it." This is the kind of critique that someone on the outside of feminism could not have written, even if Schenkar playfully allows her text to summon the opposition's fears about women, feminism, and anger.

If there is a serious satire of feminist utopias in *The Lodger*, it is rooted in the way metaphor is translated into action: the double ax is no longer only a symbol of women's power, it is an instrument to be taken off the wall and used. Thus *The Lodger* performs the slippery space between myth as informing world view and myth taken to its most literal, material and comically hyperbolic level. In doing so, the play implicitly raises several issues: Where should women's power come from and how should it function? If women's language, sexuality and history are repressed, then how do women recover them? Is it possible to recover them through myth, or even desirable? Do relationships between women deteriorate in "battle" situations, or are they sustained by an external enemy?

But like much else in *The Lodger*, the physical materiality, the "realness" of the violence, is ambiguous. We never know if the tortures inflicted upon the women's captive are "real" or fantasy. We never know if this play is set in a "real" war zone, if the war between men and women is still going on, if it has ended, or if it ever existed at all. In the world of this play it doesn't much matter. "And whether that war is taking place or not is irrelevant," Schenkar told us. "And anyway it is always taking place . . . as we know to our horror."

Indeed, there is no reason why the play can't be taking place in a mundane, rural present where the two women construct the war, Iris, and even the prisoner himself. The "reality" of this play *is* language itself. The play examines women's need for narrative to invent a ritual, collective memory. But language is treacherous. April and May crave stories and demand them from one another, but claim each other's stories are never performed quite right: "You never tell that story properly," they repeat. Perhaps this marks the violent loss of leaders— women, like Iris, who told the stories "right," or, at least, with authority. In itself this can be an oblique reference to the fate of many powerful, articulate women in any era. Or perhaps their disagreements mark the futility of the search for consuming narratives, the ones that "get it right" by explaining everything.

The male prisoner (or the series of them) tells April and May nothing they want to hear either; he only remembers his father. May's characterization of the connection between the prisoner's father, his language and his central forelimb refers back to the idea of a phallocentric process of naming: "[His father] taught him to put his name upon everything unresisting and deny everything that resisted him. [He] taught him to win by any means and always keep . . . his organ erect." May's irreverent conflation of the man's father, his organ, and his inability to tell stories could be viewed as undercutting the power of men over women in the world of this play. But it also points to a need to mark his maleness in order to define a superior femaleness. And in contrast to the invocations of women's names and naming in Wittig's novel, these two women seem once-removed from the source of this power, able only to carve their "name" upon their male prisoner's body. Thus Schenkar suggests the male's presence in actuality or in language is still what they define themselves against.

Schenkar says that she often hears language as music. "When I direct my plays, I conduct them more than direct them. I really hear them orchestrally and always know what they should sound like. And I use language like a composer. I frequently work in a kind of symphonic form" [Patraka 195]. In *The Lodger* this music-based narrative comes out through the repetitions of key phrases and through repeated patterns of conversation. This repetition also recalls other literary texts and a distant, archaic language. "In *The Lodger* I tried to use a very ironic imitation of translations from Greek tragedies—Euripidean language, very simple. I used stichomythia and deliberately set the tone as a kind of mock attic" [Patraka 191]. Taking this language, mocking and repeating it, ironically exposes the "phallacy" of monumental scale and portent. Perhaps Schenkar would endorse Peggy Phelan's idea that, at least in language, there is "productive power" in "facing the inevitability of annihilation, castration, misrecognition" [25] and that no one mythology can contain or obliterate this.

When interviewed by Elin Diamond in *The Drama Review*, Schenkar said she never wrote "herstory.... But I make a sexuality. I think my plays are really bisexual. They're also bicameral, bicoastal, often bilingual... [a bisexual play is] a play that can imagine congress anywhere. And even those plays of mine that completely lack erotics, still there's always an erotic connection with food, or an erotic aperture...so that the congress, the act of sexuality—which is not necessarily limited to human bodies laying upon each other—can occur between anything and anything" [117–119].

The Lodger is not overtly erotic. As Schenkar told us "The eroticism [between the two women], like everything else, is over. The strong suggestion is, of course, that they had once been lovers." There is, certainly, eroticism in the gestures of the women, the way they sit, and the way they use props and furniture. The very first stage directions of the play, for example, read "APRIL seated, in yearning profile. MAY seated, sharpening a knife." The eroticism between the two women also takes the form of desire in narrative: longing descriptions of their lost leader Iris, memories of the two characters meeting in a bar, at a wedding, and vivid descriptions of perpetrated violence. It is a cerebral, almost sadistic eroticism played out in terse dialogue, gestures, and song.

Finally, the erotics of *The Lodger* are indistinguishable from its aesthetics: the short, sharp undercutting exchanges, the ways in which the women annul each other's narratives, produces a post-apocalyptic quality of desire—fragmented, ambivalent, cruel, but always willing to re-kindle.

WORKS CITED

Diamond, Elin. "Crossing the Corpus Callosum: An Interview with Joan Schenkar." In *TDR*. 35:2 (Summer 1991) 99-128.

Patraka, Vicki. "An Interview with Joan Schenkar." In *Studies in American Drama, 1945 to Present* (Vol. 4, 1989) 187-202.

____. A 1994 version of "An Interview with Joan Schenkar." In *Speaking on Stage: Interviews with Contemporary American Playwrights*. Eds. Philip Kolin and Colby Kulman. U Alabama: forthcoming 1995, 21 ms. pages. [Epigraph to this essay is taken from here.]

Phelan, Peggy. *Unmarked: The Politics of Performance*. New York: Routledge, 1993.

Wittig, Monique. *Les Guerilleres*. Trans. David Le Vay. New York: Viking Press, 1971.

The Lodger

Two women, APRIL *and* MAY, *dressed in the uniforms of some outmoded Amazon army, move around the cramped room of a cabin. A table and two chairs are center stage; on a side wall is* MAY's *collection of war instruments—knives, hatchets, axes, darts, tridents, a labyris, and a net—and* APRIL's *lyre. A window is upstage left, a door upstage right. On the upstage wall is an enormous dart board, as large as the women's bodies, which lights up when a symbolic score is made.* APRIL's *area is stage left,* MAY's *area is stage right, all stage directions are given from the audience's vantage.*

MAY *begins provocatively to hum the "J'ai perdu mon Eurydice" aria from Gluck's* Orphée et Eurydice *in* APRIL's *ear as* APRIL *vainly tries to recall the words. When* APRIL *finally produces a triumphant "J'ai perdu!"* MAY *turns and scores an immediate bullseye on the dart board. Blackout.*

Lights up. APRIL *seated, in yearning profile.* MAY *seated, sharpening a knife.*

APRIL: What *was* that song you used to sing? In the old days?

MAY: You mean . . . [*Begins to sing the Gluck aria as though it were a war song.*]

APRIL: Yes, yes that one.

MAY: Wasn't *that* a war song. [*With satisfaction.*]

APRIL: I thought it was a *love* song. A *longing* song.

[*Pause.*]

APRIL: What *was* that song?

[*Blackout.*

Lights up. APRIL *standing at window, back to audience.* MAY *standing by chair, dart aimed at the board.*]

MAY: Did you hear?

APRIL: *What.* Did I hear *what.*

MAY: They're bringing Iris down this afternoon.

APRIL: [*Gently.*] Ahhh . . . So soon.

MAY: Yes. They're bringing her down in white.

APRIL: She . . . *loved* white.

MAY: [*Musing.*] The color for ritual, she always said.

    [*Pause.*]

APRIL: I hope they . . . did a good job on her.

MAY: I don't see how they could fix *that* up.

APRIL: The women are . . . uh . . . clever with their hands.

    [*Slight pause.*]

MAY: [*Definitively.*] It doesn't seem likely they could fix *that.*

APRIL: [*Irritated.*] Well, it won't *show*, you know. No one's going to be *looking* for it.

MAY: *Still.* I'd hate to be buried without it.

APRIL: A *terrible* thing. She was a *real warrior.*

    [*Pause.*]

MAY: Do you . . . know how it happened?

APRIL: In the *usual* way. She was the last one in line and they...came up behind her . . . and did their business. And then they . . . *cut* her . . . according to their custom.

MAY: [*Slowly and with malicious glee.*] Love the enemy . . . and *seek vengeance.* [*She scores a bullseye on the board.*]

    [*Blackout.*
      Lights up. APRIL *seated on chair.* MAY *seated on table, back to audience.*]

APRIL: And where is *he*?

MAY: I've got him locked in the guest room now.

APRIL: Is he still doing *that*?

MAY: Doing what.

APRIL: That incessant *tapping.*

MAY: Oh yes, certainly. To be sure. His feet move, his fingers move, his eyes roll in concert. He tells me he's measuring his last moments. Doesn't want to let them go unacknowledged.

APRIL: He needn't worry.

MAY: [*Ingenuously.*] Really? Why not?

MAY: They're *acknow*ledged.

    [*Blackout.*
      Lights up. APRIL *seated on chair facing* MAY *across table.* MAY *seated on chair facing* APRIL *across table.*]

MAY: And of course he's *hungry* all the time.

APRIL: [*Surprised.*] You're *feeding* him?

MAY: I'm doing what I can. But I have...*trouble*...being near him...there's something *disgusting*...His *flesh*...

APRIL: *Such* a strong odor...

MAY: His *speech*...

APRIL: Inexact and unpoetic.

MAY: The way he *moves*...

APRIL: Mechanical, without grace.

MAY: Even his clothing...

APRIL: Axiomatically without beauty.

MAY: [*The final judgment.*] And he has *no stories*.

APRIL: None?

MAY: So far as I can tell.

[*They pause and marvel.*]

MAY: He might as *well* be dead.

APRIL: Not yet. Not quite yet.

MAY: I know, I know.

[*Pause.*]

APRIL: But he has memories?

MAY: Oh yes, certainly. To be sure. He remembers [*With infinite malice.*] his...*father.*

APRIL: Oh no.

MAY: [*Lyrically mocking.*] He remembers his father who taught him to kill small animals and regard all women with suspicion. Who taught him to put his name upon everything unresisting and deny everything that resisted him. Who taught him to win by any means and always keep...his organ erect.

APRIL: And I suppose he misses this monster?

MAY: With tears in his eyes.

APRIL: [*Shaking her head.*] It dies hard with them, it dies hard.

MAY: [*Solidly.*] But it *dies*.

APRIL: Finally. Finally. In the end...when *they* do.

[*Blackout.*
  Lights up. APRIL *standing at window, back to audience.* MAY *seated on floor, down front.*]

MAY: Tell the story of your first public appearance.

APRIL: As a...singer?

MAY: Of *course* not. As a *woman*.

APRIL: [*Immediately.*] It was shortly before the...uh...hostilities began, before the first *real* blooding. One could still go outside then and I was walking the pasture behind the barn...*Looking*...just looking. *Marvelling* at the season. [*A reverie.*] He was following me, of course. I could hear his big feet crushing things behind me. At first I wanted to run—and pretended I didn't. Then I didn't want to run, and started to, anyway...[*Pause.*] He caught me quickly and put his thick arms around my body. The sharp stone at my feet... seemed to...*spring up* into my open hand...

[*Slight pause.*]

MAY: Every time you tell that story, I'm less...*certain* of it.

[*Blackout.*
    Lights up. APRIL *seated on floor, leaning on* MAY'S *legs.* MAY *seated on chair.*]

APRIL: ...the mountain camps...

MAY: What did you say?

APRIL: I was just remembering how we used to be in the mountains.

MAY: Ah yes. Oh those mountains. How we sang in those mountains.

APRIL: We did? We *sang*?

MAY: [*Rapturous.*] Every morning. First thing every morning. Our voices rose with the sun. And Iris conducting...Oh how we sang in those mountains.

APRIL: I believe you're right. I believe we *did* sing in those mountains.

MAY: [*Terribly pleased.*] Why, thank you.

APRIL: Oh, it was nothing.

MAY: No, no. It was *something*.

[*Blackout.*
    Lights up. APRIL *seated and calm.* MAY *up and excited.*]

MAY: It was *really something*!

APRIL: Tell another story. It will calm you.

MAY: The story of the Old Religion?

APRIL: *Good.*

MAY: [*Immediately.*] The women were in the nurseries. It was only the middle of the night shift and they were already as tired as they were used to being when the shift was over. From time to time a child would awaken and one woman or another would stop her spinning and nurse the child or rock it, each according to her function. Once, a woman in a green shawl leaned back her head to yawn and a scream like a bird flew from her throat. She saw that the ceiling was covered with grape vines that were growing down to her. And the fat purple grapes hung like promises of pleasure. Then all the women rose as one woman and they broke their distaffs and smashed their spindles and they lifted their children from their cradles and dashed them to the ground. For they knew the sign of the Great Mother and they knew she had come to lead them. And so they ran from the nurseries to the groves and the high places outside the city. And they ate of the grape until they were intoxicated and they danced all the night and took much pleasure in each other's bodies. [*Solemnly.*] And...since...that... time, the old order is ignored...and nothing...has...ever been the SAME.

[*Appreciative pause.*]

APRIL: I *love* that story.

MAY: You didn't...interrupt me.

APRIL: No.

MAY: You...*agree* then?

APRIL: No. You *never* tell that story properly. But...I love it.

[*Blackout.*
Lights up. APRIL *seated, elbows on table, looking at* MAY. MAY *seated, elbows on table, looking at* APRIL.]

MAY: No difference between us.

APRIL: Not yet.

[*Blackout.*
Lights up. APRIL *standing down center in front of table.* MAY *curled around* APRIL, *humming the Gluck aria.*]

MAY: Do you remember...in the old days...that song we used to sing?

APRIL: You mean the duet.

MAY: I couldn't exactly put a finger on the form.

APRIL: [*Firmly.*] It was a duet.

MAY: Well. Do you remember it?

APRIL: Certainly not.

[*Blackout.*
Lights up. APRIL, *same position.* MAY, *drawn back a bit.*]

MAY: *I* remember it.

[*Blackout.*
Lights up. APRIL, *classic opera duet position.* MAY, *classic opera duet position. both singing the Gluck aria.*]

MAY: C'est ton épouse, ton épouse fidéle.

APRIL: J'entends ta voix, ta voix qui m'appelle.

APRIL AND MAY: [*Together.*] Ta voix qui m'appelle.

[*Blackout.*
Lights up. APRIL *upstage of table near door.* MAY *upstage of table, closer to door than* APRIL.]

MAY: Isn't it time *he* did something for us.

APRIL: I can't bear the sight of him.

MAY: It's a problem.

APRIL: You can't have a prisoner who keeps you prisoner.

MAY: It's a problem.

APRIL: You'd better get him.

> [MAY *leaves and returns through the door with a long thin cord attached to a speaking tube.*]

MAY: [*Brightly.*] Here we are. [*Thinks better of it.*] That is, here *I* am and here [*Points to tube.*] *he* is.

APRIL: [*Not a question.*] He refuses to come out.

MAY: As always.

APRIL: No sense trying to force him.

MAY: You can't have a prisoner who keeps you prisoner.

APRIL: You *know* I can't bear the sight of him.

MAY: [*Agreeing.*] His wounds *are* disgusting . . .

APRIL: I'll try him. [*Puts speaking tube to her mouth.*] WELL?!!!

> [APRIL *puts tube to her ear, shakes her head,* MAY *takes tube, puts it to* <u>*her*</u> *ear.*]

APRIL: What's he *saying.*

> [MAY *motions for quiet.*]

MAY: He wants to know what's expected.

APRIL: [*Thinks.*] He can . . . *amuse* us.

MAY: [*Puts tube to her mouth.*] YOU CAN AMUSE US! [*Puts tube to her ear.*]

APRIL: What's he *saying?*

> [MAY *motions for quiet.*]

MAY: He says he has no sense of humor. [*Puts tube down in disgust.*]

APRIL: That's obvious.

> [*Pause.*]

MAY: Oh, let him alone, it's hopeless.

APRIL: Let's have a *story.*

MAY: The story of your birth day? Tell the story of your birth day.

APRIL: [*Immediately.*] On the day I was born, or so the women told me, a dragon with seven jeweled heads appeared in the sky. It was the first time, or so they said, that the dragon had revealed more than five of her heads at once . . . [*An afterthought.*] *No* one seemed to think that was important.

MAY: [*Brightly.*] No answers there.

APRIL: [*Darkly.*] None.

> [*Blackout.*
>> *Lights up.* APRIL *seated on chair.* MAY *seated on table.*]

APRIL: *You* tell the story of *your* birth.

MAY: [*Very slowly, as though remembering.*] If I told you...what I saw...you'd think I was *crazy*.

> [*Blackout.*
>> *Lights up.* APRIL *seated on table.* MAY *seated on table.*]

MAY: Uh...[*Indicating tube.*] what about *him*?

APRIL: He'll have his day.

MAY: He's *had* it.

APRIL: *Not quite.*

> [*Tube squeaks and* MAY *picks it up and puts it to her ear.*]

APRIL: What's he *saying*?

> [MAY *motions for quiet.*]

MAY: He says he thinks he's *had* it.

APRIL: *Not quite.*

APRIL: Well...he's not *going* anywhere. [*An explanation.*]

MAY: But he's *here*.

APRIL: That's *enough*.

MAY: *More* than enough.

> [*Blackout.*
>> *Lights up.* APRIL *standing down front, locked in mortal arm wrestle with* MAY. MAY *standing down front, locked in mortal arm wrestle with* APRIL. MAY *wins as scene ends.*]

MAY: No difference between us?

APRIL: None!

> [*Blackout.*
>> *Lights up.* APRIL *upstage of table, tight against* MAY, *looking at tube.* MAY *upstage of table, tight against* APRIL, *looking at tube.*]

APRIL: [*Picks up tube, puts it to her mouth.*] WELL?!! [*Puts tube to her ear, waits, shakes head, hands tube to* MAY *who puts it to her ear.*]

APRIL: What's he *saying*?

> [MAY *motions for quiet. Grim pausĕ.*]

MAY: *Nothing*. He says nothing.

> [*Slight pause.*]

APRIL: [*Brightly.*] Let's have a story. Tell the story of our first meeting.

MAY: [*Immediately.*] The bar was both dark and light, the drinks were expensive. It was a slow night and only two or three women were balanced on the high stools watching the bartender as she . . . hummed an aria.

APRIL: [*Clenched teeth.*] We did not meet in that kind of a bar.

MAY: [*Ignoring her.*] As she salted the last rim of the last glass, the bartender's glance happened to fall on m . . .

APRIL: Can't you tell a story *straight?* What's the matter with you?

MAY: *You* tell the story.

APRIL: It was at your wedding, of course. Your *second* wedding. I saw you, dressed for the sacrifice in a quiet suit . . .

MAY: My father's.

APRIL: . . . in a quiet suit, mocking them all with your eyes. I couldn't . . . *distinguish* the bridegroom from the rest of them . . .

MAY: He was indistinguishable . . .

APRIL: . . . and so finally I gave up trying. I wanted only to look at you. At the right moment, before you mounted the altar, you turned toward me, murder on your mouth . . .

[*Tube squeaks,* APRIL *picks it up, glares at it, then automatically hands it to* MAY.]

MAY: He says he's been thinking.

APRIL: Unbelievable.

MAY: He says he used to sing, on occasion.

APRIL: This is an occasion.

MAY: He says he's shy.

APRIL: Tell him I'll harmonize.

MAY: He says he only knows . . . songs of war.

APRIL: *What* war? *Which* war?! [*Waits*] What's he *saying?!*

MAY: He says . . . the *current* war.

APRIL: *Enough!* That's *enough!* [*Grabs tube and shouts into it.*] MONSTER!

[*Blackout.*
Lights up. APRIL *straddles chair, dejected.* MAY *massages her.*]

MAY: Would you like to sing?

APRIL: [*Depressed silence.*]

MAY: Now, I mean.

APRIL: I can't. I can't.

MAY: [*Watchful silence.*]

APRIL: How can I sing? There's nothing to celebrate.

MAY: [*Wicked grin, hand tightening on the throat of the speaking tube.*] I think perhaps there *might* be.

APRIL: But you asked for *now*.

MAY: [*Haughtily.*] I believe I was speaking of a *continuous* present.

APRIL: [*Offended.*] I cannot sing *continuously*.

[*Blackout.*
   Lights up. APRIL *straddles chair, head on table.* MAY *straddles chair, head on table.*]

MAY: Perhaps he is our punishment.

APRIL: For what?

[*Blackout.*
   Lights up. APRIL *on knees on chair.* MAY *sitting, facing away from table, polishing knife.*]

APRIL: [*Agitated.*] Tell the . . .

MAY: It's *your* turn. *You* tell it. Tell the story of how men were created.

APRIL: [*Immediately.*] From the wrist-bones of women . . .

MAY: No, no. The *other* one. From *camel* droppings . . .

APRIL: *Toe*nail clippings

MAY: *Fuse*lage oil . . .

APRIL: *Rock* salt . . .

MAY: *I*-beams . . .

APRIL: *Used* blades . . .

MAY: Everything ex*tra*neous . . .

APRIL: Re*main*dered . . .

MAY: Left*over* . . .

APRIL: *Hard*-edged . . .

APRIL: *Fi*nal . . .

APRIL: No! That's not the story I want. Tell a . . . a *woman's* story. Tell the story of your first day at school.

MAY: [*Immediately.*] The teacher was of the *other* order—she had kept *both* her breasts. They interfered *terribly* with her archery. I could not stop myself from staring at them. They were *so round* . . . *two* of them . . . *such* an invitation. For my insolence, I was made to sit in the corner, where I could watch the other girls crying for their mothers. [*Proudly.*] I . . . did . . . not . . . utter a sound . . . all afternoon.

[*Blackout.*
   Lights up. APRIL *back to audience, throwing darts.* MAY *back to audience, throwing darts.*]

APRIL: I suppose we should warm up a bit. It's *my* turn.

MAY: We're out of practice. You have to do the exercises every day.

APRIL: Do you *remember* the exercises?

MAY: Iris is the one who remembers those things.

APRIL: [*Tartly.*] We've lost the benefit of her counsel. How many?

MAY: One. [*Slowly.*] If I could just put my mind where her mind is, I could remember for us.

APRIL: Wasn't it fifths, and then thirds? And then . . . half steps?

MAY: I don't think so. Oh if only I could put my mind where Iris' mind is.

APRIL: Iris' mind is *dead. Bullseye.*

> [*Blackout.*
> Lights up. APRIL *in profile at window.* MAY *downstage looking out.*]

APRIL: I wonder how it's *really* going.

MAY: Out there?

APRIL: Out there.

MAY: We're lucky enough to know what we know.

APRIL: I wonder . . . if it's over.

MAY: The battle?

APRIL: The *struggle.*

MAY: Never.

APRIL: Well, the *battle*, then.

MAY: No one knows.

> [*Pause.*]

APRIL: And today they bury Iris.

MAY: Not . . . exactly.

APRIL: What do you mean, not exactly?

MAY: Well, not *precisely.*

APRIL: You told me *distinctly* they were bringing her down in white.

MAY: And so they are . . . but not to bury. The women don't bury each other any more. There are too many bodies . . .

APRIL: [*Slowly.*] So it's come to that.

MAY: [*Nods.*]

APRIL: And are we . . . *winning*?

MAY: No one knows that . . . either.

APRIL: And their *spirits*, do the women keep their spirits up?

MAY: As in the old world, they chant in battle and sing in council. But I am told that the rituals are performed without love and each woman in her heart wishes herself dead.

APRIL: The Adversary? What about the Adversary?

MAY: They...He...they do not communicate with any forms we can recognize. They betray each other at every opportunity. They bind their minds with supremacy. They...lose to win.

[*Pause.*]

APRIL: They are as we are, then.

MAY: If you like.

[*Pause.*]

APRIL: [*Bitterly.*] But we are trapped here with this... [*Indicates tube.*]

MAY: He's the last one in captivity, you know. The last one *alive*.

APRIL: [*Slowly.*] How...do...you...know?

MAY: By all accounts...

APRIL: Informed sources?

MAY: Insist that he is...

APRIL: For the moment.

MAY: For the moment.

[*Blackout.*
  Lights up. APRIL *kneeling on chair, facing* MAY. MAY *kneeling on chair, facing* APRIL.]

MAY: No difference between us.

APRIL: If you like.

[*Blackout.*
  Lights up. APRIL *seated, playing the lyre.* MAY *at doorway with tube behind her back, suppressing a laugh.*]

MAY: There's something I'd like us to sing. Something from the old repertoire.

APRIL: Really.

MAY: Something...*moving*, something *beautiful*.

APRIL: [*Engaged.*] Really?

MAY: But we can't now. No no of course we can't.

APRIL: What do you mean? We can sing anything we like. Really, I think you're getting stranger.

MAY: But this piece requires more than two voices.

APRIL: How many more?

MAY: Uh...one more. One more than two.

APRIL: We might manage that. I could double. You could double. What's the range? Mezzo? Dramatic soprano?

MAY: [*Moving in for the kill.*] It's...uh...*baritone.* [*Pulls out the tube.*]

APRIL: You were right the first time. We can't do it. Take him back.

[*Blackout.*
  Lights up. APRIL *standing.* MAY *sitting.*]

APRIL: Take him back. It's gone on...too long.

MAY: The interview?

APRIL: *Everything.* Everything too long.

MAY: [*To tube.*] Back you go.

[*Tube squeaks.*]

MAY: [*Holds tube to her ear.*] He says he'd like to ask a favor.

APRIL: A favor? For *him*?!

MAY: He says his room is so empty. He says...

APRIL: Take him AWAY!!

[MAY *turns to go.*]

[*Blackout.*
  Lights up. APRIL *where she was.* MAY *emerging from doorway.*]

MAY: What about a little victory song.

APRIL: You think this was a victory?

MAY: If we sing a song about it, it will *be* a victory. People will *say* it was a victory.

APRIL: [*Excited.*] You really think this was a victory?!

[MAY *grabs* APRIL'*s arm and raises it in a victory gesture.*]

[*Blackout.*
  Lights up. APRIL *stands behind* MAY, *fixing her hair.* MAY *sits, face out.*]

MAY: You're getting careless.

APRIL: [*Looks at* MAY.]

MAY: You showed a feeling.

APRIL: I surprised myself.

MAY: It's Iris.

APRIL: It's all of us.

[*Blackout.*
  Lights up. APRIL *on chair, rubbing a foot against* MAY'*s foot.* MAY *on floor in front of table, rubbing a foot against* APRIL'*s foot.*]

APRIL: We had been...lovers...for some time, Iris and I, and our concentration was intense. There were...almost no differences between us. *She* wore white, *I* adored it, *I* inhaled, *she* exhaled, *her* heart pumped, my blood went round and round. We were together. *Together*. The night she met you—at some *bar* I think she said it was—she began to recede from me . . . a tide burning unexpectedly . . . and not turning back again. Suicide, always a sweet thought, was out of the question: my pain was too de*vel*oped; I knew it would outlive my body . . .

MAY: I think perhaps . . .

APRIL: BACK!! You invited this! . . . We went on for awhile, of course, mending and patching, but the tide had turned and I lost her. [*A reverie.*] And to this moment, each part of her body is impressed upon every part of mine—smells, feels, tastes, and touches. And I shall never know a woman in that way again.

[*Pause.*]

MAY: Every time you tell that story, I am less . . . *certain* of it.

APRIL: [*Agreeing.*] As am I . . .

[*Blackout.*
    Lights up. APRIL *sits with lyre.* MAY *sits with hatchet.*]

MAY: [*Hums from Gluck's aria, clearly the only music she knows.*]

APRIL: I was just going through my old concert programs.

MAY: Hmm hmm hmm hmm hum.

APRIL: From concerts I used to give when the war was just beginning.

MAY: La la la la la hmm hmm.

APRIL: I'd like to give a concert now.

MAY: [*Stops humming abruptly.*] Right here? Right away?

APRIL: Soon. I'd like to give a concert soon.

MAY: All by yourself? No . . . [*Disappointed.*] . . . partner?

APRIL: A real concert. Just as I did in the old days. How the women used to applaud me. [*Sighs.*] How I miss that applause.

MAY: [*Thinks a little, then begins to applaud ritualistically.*]

APRIL: [*Blossoms.*] Why, thank you.

MAY: Oh it was nothing.

APRIL: No, no it was *something*.

[*Blackout.*
    Lights up. APRIL *at table with lyre, sitting.* MAY: *DL with huge axe.*]

MAY: [*Out of nowhere.*] *Imagine* the obsequies.

APRIL: [*Starts.*] WHAT.

MAY: *Think* of the ceremonies.

APRIL: *Which* ones.

MAY: *Iris'* of course. Her *rites*, her *services*, I can just see them. [*A grand tone.*] All the warriors who can be summoned on such short notice will be invited. And they will honor her each according to the customs of their countries.

APRIL: I thought you said they weren't *burying* anymore.

MAY: I changed my mind. This will be the largest gathering of the women since the first blooding. All the old rituals will be performed—the dance of the seven maidens, the flaunting of torches and crescents—*all* the rituals. A general amnesty will be declared. Even the collaborators will be freed to do her honor. Only you and I will be absent because of our...*special duties*...and we shall spend the day in constant sacraments of praise for her.

[*Pause.*]

APRIL: You've begun to get on my nerves.

MAY: Not possible.

APRIL: You and that...*straight* man of yours.

MAY: He's an accident.

APRIL: You brought him here.

MAY: *Captured.* I *cap*tured him and brought him here.

APRIL: [*Scornfully.*] The *last one in captivity.*

MAY: First and last.

APRIL: And your *stories*, your *stories* are degenerating. They lack color. *And* fire. *And* imagination. They've become...almost...oh...impersonal.

MAY: You criticize?

APRIL: I correct. You're getting on my nerves.

MAY: [*Looks carefully at* APRIL.]

APRIL: And your person, your *self*. The care you used to take with your clothing, your *consciousness*. Why the first time I met you...

MAY: At the wedding...

APRIL: No, no at *Iris'* house. Surely you remember *that*, you were dressed in your father's suit. *And* tie. *So* elegant.

MAY: And now?

APRIL: You have renounced.

MAY: Only you.

APRIL: Ah. A difference.

MAY: The first.

[*Blackout.*
Lights up. APRIL *standing, looking at* MAY. MAY *standing, looking at* APRIL.]

APRIL: Where did you *really* find him?

MAY: What is *actually* going on out there?

[*Blackout.*

Lights up. APRIL *downstage, facing front.* MAY *downstage, facing front.*]

APRIL: [*Ascending scale.*] La la la la la la la la la.

MAY: [*Descending scale.*] La la la la la la la la la.

APRIL: [*Aggressively.*] La!

MAY: [*Retaliatorily.*] La la!

APRIL: [*Moving in for the kill with an appogiatura.*] La la la la aaa aaaa ah ah ah!

MAY: Oh cut that out!

[*Blackout.*

Lights up. APRIL *sitting at table.* MAY *standing behind table.*]

MAY: [*Immediately.*] Just after the...uh...*hostilitie*s began, oh years ago it was, with the blood still fresh on the ground, all the women assembled to decide who had made the first kill. Each woman wanted the honor for herself; each woman produced evidence to show she was responsible...Well, the proofs were so convincing and the witnesses so determined, that there was nothing to do but announce that the first kill belonged to everyone, that all women shared the honors. Naturally, no one was satisfied with this decision, but their dissatisfaction united them...and they were happy once again.

APRIL: Your worst story yet. I could scarcely keep my eyes open.

MAY: [*Sullen.*] I can't help it. It's the *confinement*, I'm losing touch with my material. *You* tell the story.

APRIL: [*Immediately.*] It was Iris who called the women together. She invented everything in those days. She sent her messengers to the corners of the continent and when they returned and the women had assembled in the appointed place, you could not see a patch of ground for the bodies. So...many...bodies. [Pause.] As usual Iris declined to speak, but she was prevailed upon at last and I shall remember her words until my bones bleed. "Women", she said,—she always only called us women— "It does not matter what we lose so long as the battle is fought and not lost. In concealment or in clarity we must do our work. And at the end of it, there shall be *none* of them, *no one* of them, *not one* of them left alive..." She was implacable. And then the cheering began. And it grew and swelled and grew again until each woman was howling from her heart. And the light struck the breastplate that Iris wore, and the red of her lips looked like blood in the sun. And since that time...*nothing* has ever been the same.

MAY: I *love* that story.

APRIL: You agree then?

MAY: No. You never tell that story properly. But I love it.

[*Blackout.*

Lights up. APRIL *seated, with lyre.* MAY *starting at door with net and hatchet, trapping and hacking imaginary males.*]

MAY: I always wanted to be a singer.

APRIL: [*Not paying attention.*] Is that so.

MAY: Since I was a child. The talent is in my throat you know.

APRIL: Is that so.

MAY: But my other abilities began to appear and that was the end of my singing.

APRIL: Is that so.

MAY: Yes. My skills with the knife and the net, my prowess in archery and the darts...All these took precedence over my singing.

APRIL: Is that so.

MAY: As the muscles of my arms and legs increased in girth, the muscle of my throat, the *music*-making muscle, fell into a terrible flaccidity.

APRIL: Is that so.

MAY: And so, although I still wanted to be a singer, I had to admit...that I no longer had...the raw material of song.

[*Pause.*]

APRIL: [*Very interested.*] *Is that so.*

[*Blackout.*
Lights up. APRIL *throwing darts.* MAY *at door.*]

APRIL: It's almost time to trot *him* out again.

MAY: You're awfully *fixed* in your intentions.

APRIL: It's a problem.

MAY: He makes us ill.

APRIL: It's a problem.

MAY: He gives no pleasure.

APRIL: It's a problem.

MAY: He's hard to feed.

APRIL: It's a problem.

MAY: [*Experimentally.*] He killed Iris.

[*Pause.*]

APRIL: The problem is *solved*.

MAY: [*Hastily.*] Per*haps*. Per*haps* he killed Iris. I didn't mean to be so defini...

APRIL: THE PROBLEM IS SOLVED. Bring him out.

[MAY *leaves and returns with the speaking tube.*]

APRIL: We invited you to amuse us.

MAY: You failed.

APRIL: We beguiled you with our stories.

MAY: You interrupted.

APRIL: We requested a song.

MAY: You declined.

APRIL: We *fed* you...

MAY: *Housed* you...

APRIL: *Not*iced you...

MAY: Im*pris*oned you...

APRIL: Only to discover...

MAY: Your crime.

> [*Pause. Tube squeaks in* MAY'S *hand.*]

MAY: He says he thinks he'd like to be buried.

APRIL: No time for that.

MAY: Too many bodies.

> [*Tube squeaks again.*]

MAY: He says he wants a quick death.

APRIL: That should be easy.

MAY: A pleasure.

APRIL: Ask him does he want to know why he's accused.

MAY: He wants to know does it matter.

APRIL: Yes.

MAY: No.

> [*Tube squeaks again.*]

MAY: He says he doesn't want to know.

> [*Pause.*]

MAY: I'd like to kick him a bit...before the end.

APRIL: You brought him here.

MAY: Nevertheless I'd like to kick him and...oh...I think...hurt his face. [*Looks carefully at tube.*] The *right* side.

APRIL: [*Encouraging.*] *How? How* would you do it?

MAY: Oh...I dunno, a razor blade to the tongue, I guess, and...uh...maybe I'll slit the corners of his eyes—*right there*. They're too small anyway.

APRIL: That's not the custom, you know.

MAY: [*Shrugs.*]

APRIL: Well go on. Tell the *story* of it.

MAY: [*Immediately.*] Well, after that, of course, I couldn't control myself. After I slit his eye, I mean. There was so little blood, it was almost an . . . abstraction. And it was *real blood* I wanted to see.

APRIL: Yes? And then . . . ?

MAY: When I went for it . . . his *organ* . . . it was limp as an angleworm. *Hardly* a challenge, but I cut it according to our custom. [*Pause.*] There was real blood then, *lots* of it. After that, not much left but a few fingers to bruise, a metatarsal to break . . . no blood at all. Were it not for his constant crying, I would have been . . . oh . . . actually *bored* before it was over.

[*Tube squeaks.* MAY *picks it up.*]

APRIL: What's he saying?

MAY: [*Motions for silence.*]

MAY: He says I'm lying. He says . . . [*Listens again.*] he didn't make a sound all afternoon.

APRIL: [*Pressing.*] But the rest is *true?* The rest *happened?*

[*Tube is silent.*]

APRIL: [*Yells into tube.*] Show me your wounds!

[*Tube squeaks.*]

MAY: He wants to know what is required.

APRIL: [*Rising voice.*] Show me what she *did.* Show me the *gash,* the *gouge,* the *cicatrix,* the *bruise,* the *break,* the *WOUNDS!* YOUR BANDAGES WOULD BE ENOUGH!!

[*Tube squeaks.*]

MAY: [*Listens, then smiles.*] He says he's shy.

APRIL: You go too far.

[*Blackout.*
   Lights up. APRIL *seated, crossed legs, facing out.* MAY *seated, crossed legs, facing out.*]

MAY: Well, perhaps he didn't cry *constantly.* Perhaps it was . . . an *intermittent* crying.

[*Slight pause.*]

APRIL: Let's have another story.

MAY: The story of the public sacrifice?

APRIL: *Ex*cellent. I'll tell the story. [*She begins immediately.*] It must have been shortly after the first meeting that we caught him. He was trying to hide himself in a woodchuck hole. We were . . . young enough to laugh at that. He was awful, even in that sea of awfulness, he was awful. A great, fat, stinking body: awkward, irritating, entirely without talent. He made me think constantly of his destruction. But he was our first prisoner and we locked him away.

MAY: But we couldn't *keep* him very long, he was *so* dull. And he had no stories. *None at all.*

APRIL: He was *so large* too.

MAY: He took up all our room.

APRIL: Finally, of course, we did what had to be done...

MAY: But we did it publicly...

APRIL: An unusual act...

MAY: For unusual circumstances...

APRIL: Heavy with meaning...

MAY: Fat with imputation...

APRIL: *Perfectly final.*

MAY: We took him to town...

APRIL: And in the presence of many...

MAY: We ended his life.

APRIL: Painfully.

MAY: Painfully.

APRIL: And when we reassembled the parts of his body...

MAY: Which had been somewhat...uh...scattered...

APRIL: We sent them back to the Adversary...

MAY: In a plain box, nothing fancy...

APRIL: With suitable inscriptions...

MAY: *So they would learn.*

    [*Pause. Tube squeaks.*]

MAY: [*Listens to tube.*] He says it was his brother.

APRIL: Ahhhh.

    [*Tube squeaks again.*]

MAY: He says it was his eldest brother. He says he opened the box.

    [*More squeaking.*]

MAY: He says the next day they beat us in battle.

APRIL: I don't recall that.

MAY: It never happened.

    [*Tube squeaks again.*]

APRIL: What's he *saying*?

MAY: He...uh...seems to be...it's a *narrative* of some kind. Wait...I'll...

    [MAY *begins to speak in a baritone as though imitating what is being said to her.*]

MAY: We hid in the trees on the mountain. We watched the women coming closer. They were making small sounds. I could not take my eyes off the last one in line. She was all in white. I *knew* she was the one I was waiting for. When she came up to the tree, my knife was already in my hand...

[*PAUSE.*]

APRIL: [*Flatly.*] The wrong story.

MAY: His first.

APRIL: And last. Take that thing away.

MAY: Nothing...else?

APRIL: Take it away.

[MAY *coils the cord, puts tube under her arm and exits.* APRIL *begins to throw darts.*]

APRIL: She'll say he got away. [*Bullseye.*] Or she'll say she let him go. [*Bullseye.*] Either way it'll be over. [*A miss.*] For a while.

[MAY *appears in doorway.*]

MAY: [*Unemotionally.*] He got away.

APRIL: [*Unemotionally.*] What? How did that happen?

MAY: He's running toward the meeting place. He said he would kill himself. He said that would be the best revenge.

APRIL: I suppose we'll have to start over.

MAY: I have another one picked out already.

APRIL: Can he sing?

MAY: I've been watching him for a week.

APRIL: You haven't left this room in a week.

MAY: He's...uh...medium size, I never could stand the thin ones, and he passes through the back meadow going to and from.

APRIL: To and from what?

MAY: Yesterday I watched him walking the woodline for mushrooms.

APRIL: How do you know it was mushrooms he was after?

MAY: That's how I'll catch him. Not like the other one. Not by accident. I'll creep up behind him with my net while he's bent over looking for mushrooms and sssssssst he's mine!

APRIL: *Ours*, my love, *ours*.

MAY: You never use...endearments.

APRIL: Blandishments, that was a blandishment.

MAY: You *never* use them.

APRIL: This is a peculiar...time.

MAY: Well, we'll soon be back to normal again.

[*Blackout.*

Lights up. APRIL *in* MAY's *chair, holding knife and hatchet.* MAY *standing behind* APRIL's *chair, playing lyre.*]

MAY: [*Trying out a phrase.*] All art aspires to the condition of music.

APRIL: Where did you get that?

MAY: [*A little louder.*] All art aspires to the condition of music.

APRIL: No really where did you get that. It's rather . . . good.

MAY: You don't remember?

APRIL: Would I be asking you if I remembered?

MAY: It's what Iris used to say after the competitions.

APRIL: *What* competitions?

MAY: The singing competitions. That was always her last sentence before she placed the laurel wreath on the winner's head and moved to the lyre.

APRIL: *Singing* competitions!

MAY: You weren't there?

APRIL: *Singing* competitions!

MAY: [*Slyly.*] You have no wreath?

APRIL: SINGING COMPETITIONS!

MAY: And after the wreath was placed on the winner's brow, Iris would always play the lyre and recite for us a little poem about feeling. About *music* and feeling. What *was* that poem?

APRIL: Just as my fingers on these strings make music
So the selfsame sounds on my spirit make a music too.

MAY: Music is feeling, then, not sound
And thus it is that what I feel here in this room

APRIL: Desiring you

MAY: Is music . . . You *do* remember the competitions. [*Pause, slyly.*] Where is your wreath?

APRIL: I have no wreath.

MAY: You didn't win a wreath? [*Sweetly.*]

APRIL: You go too far.

MAY: [*Big smile.*] Too far is my favorite direction.

[*Blackout.*

Lights up. APRIL *sitting on table.* MAY *sitting in* APRIL's *chair, head in* APRIL's *lap.*]

APRIL: [*Almost a child's tone.*] Let's have a story. It's your turn after all.

MAY: I . . . don't . . . know. It's hard to start without . . . without, oh *you know* without . . .

APRIL: You don't . . . feel like trying?

MAY: The conditions are . . . un*com*fortable. Wait 'til I catch another one.

   [*Pause.*]

APRIL: Perhaps if we *begin* again . . . ?

MAY: Without one of *them*? I don't think I can.

APRIL: Who knows if he'll pass through the meadow tomorrow?

MAY: I hadn't thought of that.

   [*Blackout.*
      Lights up. APRIL *throwing darts in* MAY'*s position at the beginning of the play.* MAY *at window, back to audience, in* APRIL'*s position at beginning of play.*]

APRIL: Have you *heard*?

MAY: *What.* Have I heard *what.*

APRIL: They caught a man in the back meadow yesterday.

MAY: [*Gently.*] Ahh . . . so soon.

APRIL: Yes. They caught him trying to . . . violate . . . Iris.

MAY: He's the *first one*, isn't he?

APRIL: The *first.*

   [*Slight pause.*]

MAY: I wonder . . . what did they do to him?

APRIL: *I'll* tell you the story.

MAY: Why a story? Why not a song? What about a little victory song.

APRIL: You think this was a victory?

MAY: If we sing a song about it, it will *be* a victory. People will *say* it was a victory.

APRIL: [*Horrified.*] *You really think this was a victory?!*

   [*Blackout.*]

FINIS

Willa-Willie-Bill's Dope Garden was first produced in Griffith Park, Los Angeles, 1975, directed by Hedy Sontag. It was filmed for video by Max Almy with Cynthia MacAddams, Teda Bracci, Sylvia White, Linda Van Winkle.

Megan Terry

WILLA CATHER'S PICNIC

Nancy Hellner

Megan Terry, whom Helen Keyssar hails as "the mother of American feminist drama," began to write in the 1950s in Seattle and then moved to New York to help found the famed Open Theater in the 1960s. Her innovative style and attempts to break down sexual stereotypes immediately established her as a writer of substance, and her Off-Broadway plays experimented with a number of avant-garde techniques which resulted in, among other types, transformation plays and rock musicals. Author of more than fifty plays, Terry developed the first rock musical, *Viet Rock*, in 1966. Later, the musical *Hair* was a product of one of her workshops. Critics and audiences alike embraced her, and in 1970 she won an Obie Award for Best Play for the sophisticated docudrama *Approaching Simone*, which traced the life of Simone Weil from childhood to sainthood.

Terry's plays reflect and critique contemporary culture in a variety of styles in order to "develop and produce the most vital and innovative new performance style for the American theatre that will speak directly to contemporary audiences." As such, many of the plays are political public service pieces which focus on and question views about personal and community identity, family, liberty, responsibility, and language, all of which engage audiences on a number of different levels. Whether commenting on self-censorship in *Body Leaks* or examining the dilemma of women in prison in *Babes in the Bighouse*, her plays are performed by feminist theatres all over the country.

It is curious that a playwright of such stature, steeped in the avant-garde and worldliness of the Big Apple, would move to Omaha. Terry's primary reason for making the move to the Midwest seems to be a pursuit of personal and artistic freedom. In Omaha in 1974, Terry felt a sense of community. Since she moved to Nebraska, where she has the support and encouragement of people whose opinions she values, especially those of Jo Ann Schmidman, the founder of the Omaha Magic Theatre, she has written more.

It is also curious that one of her first Midwest plays would be a traditionally structured, realistic play entitled *Willa-Willie-Bill's Dope Garden*, focusing on a female Nebraska writer whose main audience consisted of "librarians and third grade teachers" [Terry 18]. In a telephone interview, Terry said that she wrote the play as "a honeymoon gift to the feminist movement." Later, she added, "I wrote the play when everyone was all together, and straight women were standing up and saying, 'I'm a lesbian' if people complained about gay women being in NOW. Those were the halcyon days, and I wanted to catch the moment." The play was videotaped in 1975 and was first published by Ragnorok Press in 1977.

Willa-Willie-Bill's Dope Garden recovers a bit of lesbian history, something that is rarely easy to do because biographers, willingly and unwittingly, eradicate lesbian history through silence, distortion, suppression, and erasure. For example, Mildred R. Bennett, the author of *The World of Willa Cather* [1951], delivered a lecture on Cather at Kearney State College, Kearney, Nebraska, in the early 1970s. Asked if Cather had been a lesbian, Bennett quipped, "Who cares?" thereby trivializing a portion of Cather's life and discarding an opportunity to further explore the literary ramifications of the question.

Megan Terry, long familiar with the problem of decoding literature, states, "Before everything was out in the open, one spent one's life in the library looking for clues. I keep re-reading Collette. It is wonderful." She said of reading Mildred Bennett's palimpsestic *World of Willa Cather*, "One had to sort of read between the lines, and what struck me was the year that she [Cather] died from that stupid gall bladder operation, she sat in front of the incinerator of her apartment house and burned all the letters to and from Nelly, [Isabelle McClung] and I thought 'Oh, what did those letters contain? What could that have been that she who loved her so much burned those specific letters?' I thought it was a great loss not to have her letters. It was very sad."

Some lesbian-feminist critics have proposed that Cather's internalized homophobia had a negative effect on her. Terry responded to that idea. "She [Cather] was very, very smart. She knew people, after all, coming from the plains. People are conservative. You're up against the elements; you protect yourself...as best you can. And growing up in a small town, she knew about people who pry. I think it was all a part of that." Contrary to the assumption that Cather was homophobic, Terry suggests that Cather was a selfless woman who put others, especially friends, before herself. At the play's end, Jessica's volunteering to keep guard for the others is reminiscent of Willa Cather burning the correspondence between herself and Isabelle McClung as a last, loving, protective act concerning Isabelle and the McClung family.

Like many of Terry's works which exalt the necessity of personal freedom, *Willa* reflects the freedom which comes with self-disclosure instead of self-censorship. The play is one of " ...celebration. Of especially friendship. The incredible trusting friendships and taking each other into each other's home and sharing nature. No one was homeless." Hedy Sontag, the director of the video, feels that the expansiveness and freedom offered by nature plays an integral part in the bonding of the four women of the play.

Terry, who once said that her plays "explore rather than make a point," knows the power of humor. Humor is especially evident in this meditation on Cather.

In fact, one of the video actors fondly refers to the play as "Willa Cather's picnic," emphasizing playfulness in spite of the work's larger issues [MacAddams]. Terry's juxtaposition of lesbian dialogue and political absurdities produces subversive humor which calls attention to such taboo topics as masturbation, lesbianism, and group sex. The title itself is playfully alliterative, and the declension of Willa's "proper" name suggests Cather's youthful propensity to cross-dress and refer to herself as "William." *Willa* at once provokes thought and laughter about Cather as an historic figure and role model for feminists and lesbians.

The "Dope" of the title suggests several meanings. Marijuana or hemp, which grows wild in Nebraska and which the government asked farmers to cultivate during WWII because it made strong rope, was also the drug of choice of the Woodstock era. Then, smoking marijuana was seen as an innocuous experiment that "allowed people the freedom to get inside their heads" and to revert to the innocence of the "garden." But dope is also a metaphor for the physical, euphoric sensation of thinking, and it is comic slang for speculation or knowledge.

It is humorous that the four women want their love-making to occur on the exact spot where Cather wrote. The "Garden" obviously refers to the terrain the four characters are trying to find, and yet it connotes the garden imagery which permeates Cather's works, the importance of the land and nature in Cather's life, and the fecundity of Cather's wonderful imagination. The title is humorous yet underscores the fact that Cather successfully appropriated a male tradition and subject when she wrote about the Midwest. Terry reminds us that Cather's life and works transcend sexual roles, draw attention to female subjects, reclaim women's voices, and provide alternatives to conventional femininity.

The four characters mean to find the exact spot where Cather wrote in order to make love on that hallowed ground. The play's stage directions— "the going is a bit rough but not impossible... their progress is slow as though they are climbing" —reflect the struggles of the early feminist movement as the characters reflect the diversity of the women involved in the movement.

The characters are very different from each other in physique, interests, skills, and ambitions. Jessica, a literary procrastinator, angry that the "spare sentence is attributed to Hemingway" instead of Cather, has been contemplating a paper on Cather's garden imagery for fifteen years. She is a big woman who can recite the introduction to *My Antonia* while she holds back branches to make the others' passage less difficult. At the play's end, she volunteers to protect the other women from intruders while they make group love.

M.J., the photographer, is less philosophical than Jessica, and when she spies a spot where trees were uprooted during a lightning storm and hurricane of 1938, she exclaims, "What fucking sexy roots." M.J. points out that similar activities garner dissimilar social reactions, depending on whether the actions are performed by men or women. She conducts research by photographing her genitals and compares the importance of her lone "private" research to numerous studies done on male orgasms. She mocks and inverts the traditional "objective" male paradigm of perception because her perception is excessively subjective but honest.

Jeanne, the artist, admits "It took dope to get me to enjoy the inside of my head." She sketches the others while they walk; she is angry that she never heard about Cather before. Jeanne has a sculpture garden, and she vows to do a bust of Willa Cather. She is kind and fair and, although she is enamored of the women and wants to make group love, she firmly insists that Jessica be involved in the fun, that "they will take turns guarding."

Ava, a down-to-earth historian, knows Cather's life well enough to note that Cather was a cross-dressing tomboy with whom "Up to now, only librarians and third grade teachers were in love." Ava mocks Jeanne for getting grants to photograph her vulva, although she admits that she herself used to masturbate in the shower.

The play's genius lies in its economy. Cather herself once said that selection of detail is what matters. As ideology of feminism as theatrical experience, this ten-minute play at once recovers history, denounces Cather's confinement to the margins of canonical literature, redresses wrongs made to a major American writer, celebrates rather than trivializes women's contributions to art, acquaints audiences with Cather as a person, and comments on the importance of personal, political, and artistic freedom.

Terry believes that truth is far more important than form [Betsko 396]. "My basic concern is that people have the freedom to be what they are" [Sanchez]. She urges us to move away from self-censorship—-not saying something we want to say or should say or saying something in one context but refraining from saying it in a different context [Keating].

Cather affirmed, "That is happiness; to be dissolved in something really great." Megan Terry was indeed dissolved in something great, experiencing the impact of the women's movement as a playwright in the early 1970s. Of the movement she says, "I am sorry that the honeymoon was so short for the feminist movement. But it happened once; therefore, it can happen again." And like the women in the play, who are better for knowing the life and works of Willa Cather, "Now everyone is stronger and fairer minded."

Tillie Olsen's observation, that "a writer of wrongs is a righter of wrongs... that writing nurtures tradition as it fosters change and voices the unvoiced," applies to both Willa Cather and Megan Terry. Inasmuch as writing is an act of hope, of optimism, of celebration—inasmuch as writing about a lesbian in the USA today is to confront, to resist, to mock, or to expose—Willa is a liberating work which becomes more powerful as the community realizes its power. Because the personal is political, because writing a play is a social action, because theater is the most immediate and arguably the most political of the arts, Megan Terry's short play recovers history, reminds us of the extraordinary talent of Cather, and celebrates a brief but beautiful moment of a wonderful time.

WORKS CITED

Betsko, Kathleen and Rachel Koenig, eds. *Interviews with Contemporary Women Playwrights*. New York: Beech Tree Books, 1987.

Keating, Douglas J. "The Avant-Garde from Nebraska." *Philadelphia Inquirer*. 17 Oct. 1990: 21.

MacAddams, Cynthia. Telephone interview. 12 April 1995.

Olsen, Tillie. "What I Would Pass On: A Meditation On My Life as History/History as My Life." Arizona State University, Tempe, Arizona. 12 March 1991.
Sanchez, Lynn. "Omaha Magic Theatre." *High Performance*. Fall 1988: 50.
Sontag, Hedy. Telephone interview. 19 April 1995.
Terry, Megan. Telephone interview. 30 April 1995.

PLAYS BY MEGAN TERRY
BY DATE OF FIRST PRODUCTION

Beach Grass, 1955; *Go Out and Move the Car*, 1955; *Seascape*, 1955; *The Dirt Boat*, 1955; *New York Comedy: Two*, 1961; *When My Girlfriend Was Still All Flowers*, 1963; *Eat at Joe's*, 1963; *Ex-Miss Copper Queen on a Set of Pills*, 1963; *Calm Down Mother: A Transformation Play for Three Women*, 1965; *Keep Tightly Closed in a Cool Dry Place*, 1965; *The Gloaming, Oh My Darling: A Play in One Act*, 1965; *Comings and Goings: A Theatre Game*, 1966; *Viet Rock: A Folk War Movie*, 1966; *The Magic Realists*, 1966; *The People vs. Ranchman*, 1967; *The Key is on the Bottom*, 1968; *Jack-Jack*, 1968; *Changes*, with Tom O'Horgan, 1968; *Home: Or Future Soap*, 1968; *Sanibel and Captiva*, 1968; *Massachusetts Trust*, 1968; *One More Little Drinkie*, 1968; *The Tommy Allen Show*, 1969; *Approaching Simone: A Drama in Two Acts*, 1970; *American Wedding Ritual Monitored/Transmitted by the Planet Jupiter*, 1972; *Grooving*, 1972; *Choose a Spot on the Floor*, with Jo Ann Schmidman, 1972; *Susan Perutz at the Manhattan Theatre Club*, 1973; *St. Hydro Clemency; or, A Funhouse of the Lord: An Energizing Event*, 1973; *Thoughts*, with Lamar Alford and Joe Tapia, 1973; *Nightwalk*, with Sam Shepard and Jean-Claude van Itallie, 1973; *Couplings and Groupings*, 1974; *Babes in the Bighouse: A Documentary Fantasy Musical about Life inside a Women's Prison*, 1974; *Women's Prison*, 1974; *The Pioneer*, 1974; *Pro Game; The Pioneer: Two One-Act Plays*, 1974; *Fifteen Million Fifteen Year Olds*, 1974; *Henna for Endurance*, 1974; *Hospital Play*, 1974; *All Them Women*, 1974; *The Narco Linguini Bust*, 1974; *We Can Feed Everybody Here*, 1974; *Women and Law*, 1976; *100,001 Horror Stories of the Plains*, 1976; *Lady Rose's Brazil Hide Out*, 1977; *Brazil Fado: You're Always with Me*, 1977; *Sleazing toward Athens*, 1977; *American King's English for Queens*, 1978; *Attempted Rescue on Avenue B: A Beat Fifties Comic Opera*, 1979; *Goona Goona*, 1979; *Running Gag*, with Jo Ann Schmidman, 1979; *Fireworks*, 1980; *Advances*, 1980; *Reflected Light*, with Jo Ann Schmidman and Sora Kimberlain, 1980; *Yellow Strapping*, with Jo Ann Schmidman and Sora Kimberlain, 1980; *White Out*, with Jo Ann Schmidman and Sora Kimberlain, 1980; *Blue Tube*, with Jo Ann Schmidman and Sora Kimberlain, 1980; *The Trees Blew Down*, 1981; *Flat in Afghanistan*, 1981; *Katmandu*, 1981; *Performance Piece*, 1981; *Winners: The Lives of a Traveling Family Circus and Mother Jones*, 1981; *Aliens Under Glass*, with Jo Ann Schmidman, 1982; *Mollie Bailey's Traveling Circus: Featuring Scenes from the Life of Mother Jones*, with JoAnne Metcalf, 1983; *Kegger*, 1983; *X-Rayed-Iate: E-Motion in Acation*, with Jo Ann Schmidman, 1984; *Objective Love*, 1985; *Family Talk*, with Jo Ann Schmidman, 1986; *Sea of Forms*, with Jo Ann Schmidman, 1986; *Dinner's in the Blender*, 1988; *Amtrak*, 1988; *Babies Unchained*, with Jo Ann Schmidman, 1988; *Headlights*, 1988; *Retro*, 1988; *Breakfast Serial*, 198; *Cancel That Last Thought*, with Jo Ann Schmidman, 1989; *Snow Queen*, 1990; *Do You See What I'm Saying*, 1990; *Body Leaks*, with Jo Ann Schmidman and Sora Kimberlain, 1990; *Sound Fields Are We Hear*, with Jo Ann Schmidman and Sora Kimberlain, 1992; *Belches on Couches*, with Jo Ann Schmidman.

Omaha Magic Theatre Ensemble

CHARACTERS

JESSICA

M.J.

JEANNE

AVA

(Four women. They may be any age.)

Four women are walking in the woods. They carry knapsacks and sleeping bags on their backs. One has a collapsed fishing pole in a small case tied to the backpack. Another, JEANNE, walks with an open sketch pad behind the others, drawing them very fast as they walk before her. AVA laughs to herself from time to time as she walks. The largest woman, JESSICA, leads the way. She munches on blood sausage as she walks, a stick in a free hand to insure good footing or to hold branches out of the way for the others. M.J. has a camera with many different lenses in leather cases hanging about her neck as well as her pack on her back. The going is a bit rough, but not impossible. The progress is slow as they are climbing. For purposes of staging, they might walk in place, or they might use a zig zag pattern, as if they were climbing to the top of a small mountain, or they could continually walk around the room where the play is to be staged. It depends on how you seat the audience, and the physical conditions you have to work with.

JESSICA: [*Not looking back but gesturing with food to one behind her.*] Want a bite of blood sausage?

M.J.: What? [*She takes picture.*]

JESSICA: That's a damned expensive art form.

M.J.: Tell me about it.

JEANNE: Want some bread for your sausage?

JESSICA: Naw ... I always just munch it. There! See that cleared place? Natural flat there, in among the birches. That's another good place to build a cabin.

JEANNE: Perfect.

JESSICA: There was a terrible lightening storm here in 1938, and Willa never came back here again.

AVA: Lots of trees have grown back, but you can see where the earth was wrenched.

M.J.: [*Stooping and clicking.*] What fucking sexy roots.

JESSICA: Must a been about up yonder where Will used to walk every morning out from the inn, and work on her books. Set up a little camp stool so's every time she looked up, there was the valley stretching out, and the mountain at her back.

AVA: I used to see places like this while coming.

M.J.: In my first orgasms, I was a lotus blossom floating down the river.

JEANNE: You make me feel retarded. I was so scientific, but I did insist on *being* the doctor. I loved keeping my eyes open and looking ... It took dope to get me to enjoy the inside of my head.

JESSICA: My professor at NYU tried to get me to expand that paper on Willa.

AVA: You going to?

JESSICA: Been thinking about it.

M.J.: [*Clicking.*] How long?

JESSICA: Fifteen years.

M.J.: You don't look that old.

JESSICA: [*Winking at her.*] Don't feel it either.

JEANNE: We're going to make love where Willa used to write. The vibrations should be fantastic.

JESSICA: We can't get to the exact spot.

JEANNE: Why not?

JESSICA: It was blown away in the hurricane of '38. She came here to visit two women friends who lived on an estate called High Mowing.

JEANNE: Oh Wow! Oh Wow! [*She draws faster.*]

JESSICA: They pitched a tent for her if she wanted to get out of the sun.

M.J.: Was she always alone?

JESSICA: Except when she had proofs to correct, then Edith Lewis came with her, and they corrected proofs together.

JEANNE: [*Dreamy-excited.*] They must have lain in the wild flowers to work, and every so often, when they were overcome with tension, stretched out and gazed up into the pine needles.

AVA: Smells so good.

M.J.: I'm starving.

AVA: Jessica, check your compass. Is this as close as we can get to where she worked? [*They all sit, and stretch out, and remove shoes and packs.*]

JESSICA: You go to school in America. You major in English. You get a Ph.D. in English; all you ever hear about is that the spare sentence started with Hemingway. They act like Cather didn't exist. She did it long before.

AVA: I have a present for you.

JESSICA: The profile on Mary Baker Eddy?

AVA: A darling older woman in Syracuse found it for me. This friend of mine who's been in Christian Science all her life had never heard of it.

JESSICA: Didn't know it either till M.J. brought me the bio by Brown and Crone.

JEANNE: Think of them together. What an explosion in Boston.

AVA: She lived there nine months doing a long profile on Eddy for McClure's magazine.

M.J.: When?

AVA: 1906.

M.J.: Goddess! That's four years before my mother was even born!

JEANNE: I adore you, you take everything so personally.

M.J.: [*Turning and clicking her camera at* JEANNE.] They just found in the latest study that people who think they're the center of the Universe live longer than anyone else.

JESSICA: It'll take you that long to develop your pictures.

[M.J. *answers with a click of her camera at* JESSICA.]

AVA: [*Leans over and kisses* JEANNE *on her neck, then looks down at her drawing.*] I like it. I liked you the first day I met you.

JEANNE: I like you too.

AVA: [*Eyes dancing.*] M.J., how old were you when you discovered your clitoris?

M.J.: Too old.

JEANNE: She's making up for lost time. Photographs her vulva, clitoris and cervix in time lapse at random intervals twenty-four hours straight.

AVA: No wonder she gets so many grants.

M.J.: They found males can get erections every eighty minutes while in REM sleep. I wanted to see how many more women can get.

JESSICA: When do you release your findings?

M.J.: [*Teasing and clicking.*] Have to photograph more women. Can't prove *everything* by my own body.

[*They all laugh.*]

JEANNE: This looks like a perfect *troll garden*.

AVA: Jeanne—endlessly romantic.

JEANNE: Sagittarius rising.

JESSICA: She's just putting you on.

AVA: I've got a shot for you M.J. I used to have to masturbate upside down in the shower. You know those tin showers.

JEANNE: Like mine.

AVA: Can you imagine the noise, banging around trying to get the water in the right place. I was nine when I first discovered this terrific sensation on my clitoris. Then it took me a month to get into the right position. My mother couldn't figure out what had happened to me. I ran home from the school bus and right into the shower, screaming about the filthy kids at school always getting me messed up.

JESSICA: My paper for NYU was on the garden imagery in Cather's work. It's in all her books, in the title of her first story collection. The garden figures in...

JEANNE: I thought her books were built on rocks.

JESSICA: The garden grew on top of the rock.

[JEANNE *nods and sketches furiously.*]

M.J.: [*To* JESSICA.] You have such a powerful torso Jessica. *I want to see your upper arms.*

JESSICA: They used to put Willa down for being sentimental...they called her conservative, and thought she was turning her back on a new age.

JEANNE: Right on! Look at this honky tonk culture we have to live in.

M.J.: I love it. I love to photograph it at night. I love to drive ninety-wild down the strip and...JESSICA, would you please take off your shirt?

[AVA *and* JEANNE *exchange a kiss and a caress and look out over the valley.* JEANNE *rolls some joints and they pass them around.* JESSICA *declines with a wave of her hand, opens a bottle of Reisling, and takes a long drink, then hands that around.*]

JESSICA: Sure. [*She looks at* M.J. *for a beat, then takes off her shirt.*] Willa was into the garden even in the introductions to her books....

JEANNE: Gets me pissed to think I never learned anything about her before.

AVA: Up to now, only librarians and third grade teachers were in love with her.

JEANNE: Right on! They kept the faith.

JESSICA: That's how they were able to discredit her, but Mencken always put her up there...the machos tried to bring her down associating her with grade school and romance, and reaction, but she kept the garden growing even though she saw like Simone did, that when the oil drippings of the tractors began to replace the horsedroppings it was the beginning of the end for a healthy Mother Earth... [*Trance state quoting.*] "We were talking about what it is like to spend one's childhood... buried in wheat and corn, under stimulating extremes of climate: burning summers when the world lies green and billowy beneath a brilliant sky, when one is fairly stifled in vegetation, in the color and smell of strong weeds and heavy harvest..."

AVA: Are we on the path to the cemetery?

JESSICA: ... She didn't come back here after the hurricane of '38... tore up all her favorite views... but she's buried at the foot of Mt. Monadnock...

JEANNE: Willa, Willie... we want you to join us.

AVA: When she was in her early teens she cut off all her hair and put on her brother's clothes and walked all over town.

JEANNE: O Wow, just like Casse Culver*!

AVA: And just like Casse Culver's groupies...

JEANNE: And just like you...

AVA: [*Squeezing her hand.*] You're so beautiful...

JEANNE: I love to be with you all. I'm going to carve a bust of Willa for my sculpture garden, and I'm going to carve all of us making love, floating in Willa's eternal garden... and I'm...

M.J.: Oh Jeanne, you're so romantic.

JEANNE: Let me tell you it's a pleasure... men have rubbed my nose in shit... Being with you makes me feel like dancing... and I believe in romance again... come here into my arms, I want to *feel* you all. I've looked at you long enough...

[M.J. *and* AVA *crawl close to* JEANNE, *and they begin to fondle and softly kiss one another.*]

JEANNE: [*Lights candles and places them around the edges of a blanket, puts oil on the forehead of each of the women... Lights incense and passes around one more joint...*] This loving is for Willa Cather...

AVA: Come join us Jessica?

JESSICA: Thanks, but I think somebody better stand guard...

M.J.: [*Taking one last shot of* JESSICA.] Oh Goddess, the light on you is fantastic! [*She puts down her camera and turns to embrace the other two...*]

JEANNE: [*While kissing* M.J. *and* AVA.] We'll take turns guarding...

[*The lights blaze up, then down and out.*]

---

*Casse Culver, according to Megan Terry, was one of the first musicians on the women's music circuit who played in the midwest in overalls and cut all her hair off.

Paula Vogel

PAULA VOGEL'S *DESDEMONA*
(*A PLAY ABOUT A HANDKERCHIEF*)

Jill Dolan

Desdemona (a play about a handkerchief) continues in playwright Paula Vogel's tradition of resisting theatrical and social pieties. She turns conventions upside down and on their heads to see what falls out of their pockets, pushing them aside, offstage, before she'll ever allow them to resume what others have considered their "rightful" place in an ideological or literary hierarchy. There's always something askew in a Vogel play, something deliciously not quite right, which requires a spectator or reader to change her perspective, to give up any assumption of comfortable viewing or reading ground, and to go along for a refreshing change of performance pace, style, and scenery.

For example, *Baltimore Waltz* (1992), Vogel's most frequently produced play, both addresses and skirts commonly held assumptions about emotional and social responses to AIDS by writing a fantasy travelogue in which the heroine, suffering from the dreadful ATDS (Acquired Toilet-Seat Disease Syndrome), tours Europe with her brother, indulging in non-stop, flamboyant promiscuity. Their roles finally reverse, and the text admits it's the brother who is dying of AIDS. Vogel, in fact, wrote the play as a journey with her brother, Carl, to a "Europe that exists only in the imagination"; Carl died of AIDS in 1988.

But Vogel manages to wrest her text from the presumptions of "AIDS plays." *Baltimore Waltz* encourages spectators to look carefully at the resonances between the repressed status of women's sexuality and that of People With AIDS; at ill-founded public fears of contracting AIDS by contact with toilet seats; and at homophobic ragings against homosexual teachers (and the teaching of homosexuality). In Vogel's wildly theatrical imagination, politics are omnipresent and wickedly funny, as humor replaces didacticism with sharp social insight and critique.

Baltimore Waltz was widely well-received, accumulating over sixty productions in three years, yet Vogel has described the subcultural grumblings that responded to the play's success in New York and in regional theatres. Some gay men resented that the woman suffered the ravages of disease in the play, rather than accurately portraying the more widespread afflictions of gay men; some lesbians critiqued Vogel for not writing about lesbians and AIDS, or for not writing about lesbians at all. These complaints miss the power and poignancy of Vogel's writing: through her command of theatricality and her nuanced critique of social systems, each of her plays writes a solid, wry, biting satire of the ideologies that deny full sexual, emotional, and political expression for women, lesbians, and gay men. Vogel's plays inevitably begin with sex, as the foundational (if sometimes foolish) interaction of social and political life.

Desdemona (1993) is no exception. In her deconstruction of the dubious heroine's role in Shakespeare's *Othello*, Vogel once again changes the lens, refocusing the spectator's view toward the backside of the play's action. Shakespeare's character is excessively, self-destructively chaste, virtuous, and faithful; in Vogel's play, she participates enthusiastically in the world's oldest profession. Where Shakespeare's Desdemona, Emilia, and Bianca are one-dimensional in their expressions of piety, honesty, and fidelity, Vogel imagines them as the prostitutes Othello fears them to be, at Iago's evil prompting. Vogel's play neatly overturns Shakespeare's moral universe, building a more complicated, autonomous, and satisfying experience (if secretive and, finally, doomed) for *Othello*'s women.

Desdemona rewrites discussions in *Othello* between Emilia and her lady, in which the horrifically proper, pure, chaste women can't imagine "abusing" their husbands by being unfaithful to them, except, as Emilia says, for a very high price. Vogel chews through the subtext of Shakespeare's play, impugning Emilia's motives for stealing the handkerchief for Iago in the first place, and imbuing her with her own lust for power. *Desdemona* opens with Emilia's theft and Desdemona's frantic, frustrated search for her daintily embroidered handkerchief. But while Shakespeare's character fears the loss, Vogel's Desdemona is not at all sentimental about the misplaced linen, shouting crossly, "Oh, piss and vinegar!! Where is the crappy little snot rag!" [7].

In Shakespeare's play, character after character insists on his or her honesty; in Vogel's play, no one is particularly honest, as most are out for their own gain, typically at each other's expense. Bianca, perhaps most vilely abused in the original, is most honorable in Vogel's version, as she's very open and matter-of-fact about the brothel business in which she engages. As Desdemona's friend and abettor (maybe even her suitor), Bianca teaches her lady sexual practices such as the notorious "l 'n' b" ("lam and brim," the play's "Elizabethan" version of s/m) that increase her pleasure and that of her potential customers. Emilia is jealous of their relationship, for reasons not entirely selfless, since, in Vogel's view, sexual attraction floats freely among all three women.

While the women remain deluded about their ability to control their destinies (after the 100th brushstroke, even in Vogel's play, Desdemona's fate is sealed), they escape the deprecations flung by Shakespeare's men. Cassio's laughter at Bianca's expense in the original is turned here against the men, as their sexual prowess, in particular, becomes the object of derision among the women. Desdemona is obsessed with the size of men's members, which apparently none of them are very good at using. Men are absent in Vogel's play, except as objects of the women's ridicule, identified by their sexual habits or anatomical attributes (all compared to the size and heft of a hoof-pick, the play's reigning phallic symbol) or by their proximity to power that's carefully defined as male.

Othello's offstage jealousy boils fast as Vogel's short scenes progress. The Moor never appears in Vogel's play, although his power, and his temper, and his desires haunt the edges of the scenes among Desdemona, Emilia, and Bianca. Male desire sets off the play's action, as Emilia steals for Iago the handkerchief that dooms Desdemona, but the dialogue among the three women courts a deeper understanding of their desires, for sexuality, for money, for power. Their men become means to what the three women willingly clarify as mercenary ends.

Vogel's dialogue only occasionally lapses into emulated Shakespearian verse. She peppers her characters' speech with anachronisms, references to *Othello* (Desdemona: "Don't be silly, nothing will happen to me. I'm the sort that will die in bed" [12]), and modern colloquialisms. Desdemona, Emilia, and Bianca are distinguished by their accents, which loudly announce their class differences and influence their dreams and desires. Emilia tries to be respectable but mispronounces French; Bianca speaks with an almost impenetrable Cockney.

The stately Desdemona throws off the restraints of her class position and fulfills her "desire to know the world" [20] by substituting occasionally in Bianca's brothel, where she enjoys claiming her own body, if only to sell it to others. Through her assignations with strange men, Desdemona throws off the "purdah" of her situation: "And they spill their seed into me, Emilia—seed from a thousand lands, passed down through generations of ancestors, with genealogies that cover the surface of the globe. And I simply lie still there in the darkness, taking them all into me; I close my eyes and in the dark of my mind—oh, how I travel!" [20]

Formally, Vogel's plays follow an absurdist pattern rather than a realist one. Her stage directions here indicate that each scene or "cinematic 'take'" should "simulate the process of filming: change invisible camera angles, do jump cuts and repetitions, etc." [4]. Perspective is all, as the relationships between the bodies on stage represent the ideological work the biting humor of the play accomplishes. Vogel's *ouevre* indicates profound disinterest in truthfully representing the "real"; each of her plays offer an outrageous, imaginative situation, original or quoted from another source, which through its twisted perspective, manages to make more sense of the workings of ideology than most more linear, expository, realist efforts.

And Baby Makes Seven (1987), for instance, in which a lesbian couple and a gay man create an imaginary family of small but intellectually precocious children whom they finally must murder, quotes George and Martha's imaginary child in *Who's Afraid of Virginia Woolf*. Vogel's play entangles its characters in reimagined family structures and reenvisioned sexual desires, in a manner that requires refreshing leaps of imaginative faith. *The Mineola Twins* (1995) wreaks the same havoc with the complacencies of suburban Long Island life, disrupting its facades with wild sexual practices performed in unlikely places.

With six plays produced and several published, a 1992 Obie Award for *Baltimore Waltz*, Pulitzer Prize and Susan Smith Blackburn Award nominations, as well as numerous fellowships and residencies, Paula Vogel is a major lesbian playwright. She teaches in the Creative Writing Program at Brown University, where she fosters the talents of younger lesbian playwrights. One student, Madeline Olnek, for example, recently produced her play *Spookyworld* at the WOW Cafe in New York; its quirky setting (in a floundering horror-amusement park) and its non-linear, non-sequitor style clearly show the influence of Vogel's teaching.

Yet for lesbian critics and spectators, one can't help but be frustrated that Vogel's work hasn't moved to Broadway alongside Terrence McNally's plays or Tony Kushner's. While McNally's writing is conventional, Kushner's shares the depth of Vogel's political vision, and its hugely theatrical, non-realist imagination. While some commentators trumpet the glorious age of gay theatre, gender politics leave lesbians lingering behind in reputable regional theatres, when they need to be seen and heard by national audiences.

Cherry Jones, the first openly lesbian actor to win a Tony Award, for her magnificent performance in *The Heiress* in the 1994 New York theatre season, has performed in many of Vogel's productions. She played Bianca in both the Bay Street Theatre Festival and the Circle Repertory Company productions of *Desdemona* in 1993. Jones' recent success, in addition to that of openly gay male American playwrights, signals that Paula Vogel's turn for national awards and attention is well past due.

© Gerry Goodstein

Cherry Jones as "Bianca" and J. Smith-Cameron
as "Desdemona"

"*Desdemona* was originally produced in association with CIRCLE REPERTORY COMPANY by BAYSTREET THEATRE FESTIVAL. Sag Harbor, Long Island, New York, July, 1993."

NOTE TO DIRECTOR:

Desdemona was written in thirty cinematic "takes"; the director is encouraged to create different pictures to simulate the process of filming: change invisible camera angles, do jump cuts and repetitions, etc. There should be no black-outs between scenes.

Desdemona was written as a tribute (*i.e.*, "rip-off") to the infamous play, *Shakespeare the Sadist* by Wolfgang Bauer.

CHARACTERS

DESDEMONA: Upper-class, very

EMILIA:　　Broad Irish Brogue

BIANCA:　　Stage Cockney

SETTING: *A back room of the palace on Cyprus.*

TIME: *Ages ago. The prologue takes place one week before Desdemona's last day on Cyprus.*

PROLOGUE

A spotlight in the dark, pin-pointing a white handkerchief flying on the ground. A second spotlight comes up on EMILIA, *who sees the handkerchief. She pauses, and then cautiously looks about to see if she is observed. Then, quickly,* EMILIA *goes to the handkerchief, picks it up, stuffs the linen in her ample bodice, and exits. Blackout.*

SCENE 1

A mean, sparsely furnished back room with rough, whitewashed walls. Upstage left there is a small heavy wooden back entrance. Another door, stage right, leads to the main rooms of the palace. There are a few benches lining the walls, littered with tools, baskets, leather bits, dirty laundry, etc. The walls bear dark wooden racks which neatly display farm and work equipment made of rough woods, leathers and chain.

　　In the center of the room, there is a crude work table with short benches. As the play begins, DESDEMONA *is scattering items and clothing in the air, barely controlling a mounting hysteria.* EMILIA, *dark, plump and plain, with a thick Irish brogue, watches, amused and disgusted at the mess her lady is making.*

DESDEMONA: Are you sure you didn't see it? The last time I remember holding it in my hand was last week in the arbor—you're sure you didn't see it?

EMILIA: Aye—

DESDEMONA: It looks like—

EMILIA: —Like any body's handkerchief, savin' it has those dainty little strawberries on it. I never could be after embroiderin' a piece of linen with fancy work to wipe up the nose—

DESDEMONA: —It's got to be here somewhere—

EMILIA: —After you blow your nose in it, an' it's all heavy and wet, who's going to open the damn thing and look at the pretty stitches?

DESDEMONA: Emilia—are you sure it didn't get "mixed up" somehow with your... your things?

EMILIA: And why should I be needin' your handkerchief when I'm wearing a plain, soft shift which works just as well? And failing that, the good Lord gave me sleeves...

DESDEMONA: It's got to be here! [DESDEMONA returns to her rampage of the room.] Oh—skunk water! [A man's undergarment is tossed into the air behind DESDEMONA's shoulder.] Dog piddle!!

EMILIA: I'm after telling you m'lady—

DESDEMONA: Nonsense! It's got to be here! [There is a crash of overturned chain. DESDEMONA's shifts are thrown into the air.] God damn horse urine!!!

EMILIA: It was dear, once upon the time, when m'lady was toddling about the palace, and all of us servants would be follerin' after, stooping to pick up all the pretty toys you'd be scatterin'—

DESDEMONA: Emilia, please—I can not bear a sermon.

EMILIA: There was the day the Senator your father gave you your first strand of pearls from the Indies—you were all of five—and your hand just plucked it from your neck how you laughed to see us, Teresa, Maria and me, scrabbling on all fours like dogs after truffles, scooping up the rollin' pearls— [There is a ripping noise.]

DESDEMONA: Oh, shit. [Two halves of a sheet are pitched into the air.]

EMILIA: But you're a married lady now; and when m'lord Othello gives you a thing, and tells you to be mindin' it, it's no longer dear to drop it willy nilly and expect me to be findin' it—

DESDEMONA: Oh, piss and vinegar!! Where is the crappy little snot rag! [DESDEMONA turns and sees EMILIA sitting.] You're not even helping! You're not looking!!

EMILIA: Madam can be sure I've overturned the whole lot, two or three times... It's a sight easier hunting for it when the place is tidy; when all is topsy-turvy, you can't tell a mouse dropping from a cow pie—

[DESDEMONA returns to the hunt: EMILIA picks up the torn sheet.]

EMILIA: [Cont'd.] —Now see, this sheet here was washed this morning. Your husband, as you know, is fussy about his sheets; and while it was no problem to have them fresh each night in Venice—I could open the window and dunk them in the canal—here on Cyprus it takes two drooling orderlies to march six times down to the cistern and back again. [EMILIA regards the sheet carefully.] It's beyond repair. And now that your husband commands fresh sheets, my Iago has got it in his head to be the lord as well; he's got to have fresh sheets each night for his unwashed feet.

DESDEMONA: Emilia, please—I may puke. [DESDEMONA, in frustration, stamps on the clothes she's strewn from the basket.] It's got to be here, it's got to be here, it's got to be here Emilia—Help me find it!

EMILIA: You're wasting your time, m'lady. I know it's not here.

DESDEMONA: [*Straightening herself.*] Right. And you knew this morning that my husband wasn't mad at me. Just a passing whim, you said.

EMILIA: Ah, Miss Desdemona . . . not even a midwife can foretell the perfidiosity of men.

DESDEMONA: Give me strength. Perfidy.

EMILIA: That, too.

DESDEMONA: It can't have walked off on two feet!

EMILIA: Mayhap m'lady dropped it.

DESDEMONA: Oh, you're hopeless. No help at all. I'll find it by myself. Go back to your washing and put your hands to use.

EMILIA: Yes, m'lady.

SCENE 2

EMILIA *and* DESDEMONA. EMILIA *scrubs sheets.*

DESDEMONA: Will it come out?

EMILIA: I've scrubbed many a sheet, but this is the worst in my career . . . It's all that Bianca's fault. I paid her well for the blood, too. "And be sure," I says, "it's an old hen—one on its last gasp—young chick blood's no good for bridal sheets, it's the devil to come out. Madam's sheets," I says, "are the finest to be had in Venice, and we don't want them ruined and rotted from the stain." And Bianca swore, "I've an old hen on crutches that will wash out clear as a maidenhead or a baby's dropping." Ah, but that chick wasn't a week old. And what with it bakin' in the sun for a month now—but if anyone can, Mealy will scrub it virgin white again.

DESDEMONA: Oh, hush about it. I can't stand to think on it . . . barbaric custom. And my best sheets. Nobody displays bridal sheets on Cyprus.

EMILIA: There aren't any virgins to be had on Cyprus.

DESDEMONA: Half the garrison came to see those sheets flapping in the breeze.

EMILIA: Why did the other half come?

DESDEMONA: To pay their last respects to the chicken! [*They laugh.*]

SCENE 3

We hear EMILIA, *in a good humor, humming a tune such as "When Irish Eyes Are Smiling." Another clatter of heavy metal things being tossed onto the floor.*

DESDEMONA: JESUS! WHAT IS THIS?!

EMILIA: [*In disbelief.*] You didn't find it!

[DESDEMONA *crosses to* EMILIA, *holding a long, crooked bit of iron with a wicked point.*]

DESDEMONA: No—this!!

EMILIA: 'Tis a hoof-pick.

DESDEMONA: A hoof-pick? What is it used for?

EMILIA: After all your years of trotting m'lady's bum over field and farrow, and you've never laid your eyes on the like? When your mount picks up a stone in its foot, and it's deep, you take the pick and hold on tight to the hoof—and then you dig it in and down to the quick and pry it out—

DESDEMONA: You dig this in? Good lord—

EMILIA: Aye, takes a goodly amount of sweat and grease—it's work for a proper man, it is.

[DESDEMONA, *absorbed in fondling the hoof-pick, stretches out on the table.*]

DESDEMONA: Oh me, oh my—if I could find a man with just such a hoof-pick—he could pluck out my stone—eh, Emilia?

[*They laugh.*]

DESDEMONA: [*Cont'd.*] Emilia—does your husband Iago have a hoof-pick to match?

[EMILIA *turns and looks, then snorts.*]

EMILIA: What, Iago?

[DESDEMONA *puts her hand on the base and covers it.*]

DESDEMONA: Well, then—this much?

EMILIA: Please, mum! It's a matter o' faith between man and wife t—

DESDEMONA: —Ahh—not that much, eh? [DESDEMONA *covers more of the pick.*] Like this?

EMILIA: Miss Desdemona!

DESDEMONA: Come now, Emilia—it's just us—

EMILIA: Some things are private!!

DESDEMONA: It's only fair—I'm sure you know every detail about my lord—

EMILIA: [*Shrugging.*] When the Master Piddles, a Servant holds the Pot—

DESDEMONA: [*Persisting.*] This much 'hoof?'

EMILIA: Not near as much as that!

DESDEMONA: This much? [*Pause.*]

EMILIA: [*Sour.*] Nay.

DESDEMONA: Good God, Emilia, I'm running out of—

EMILIA: —The wee-est pup of th' litter comes a'bornin' in the world with as much—

[DESDEMONA *laughs.*]

EMILIA: [*Cont'd.*] There. Is m'lady satisfied?

DESDEMONA: Your secret's safe with me.

SCENE 4

EMILIA, *scrubbing.* DESDEMONA *lies on her back on the table, feet propped up, absent-mindedly fondling the pick, and staring into space.*

SCENE 5

We hear the sound of EMILIA, *puffing and blowing. Lights up on* DESDEMONA *getting a pedicure.*

DESDEMONA: Where is she? It's getting late. He'll be back soon, and clamoring for me. He's been in a rotten mood lately . . . Headaches, handkerchiefs, accusations—and of all people to accuse—Michael Cassio!

EMILIA: The only one you haven't had—

DESDEMONA: —And I don't want him, either. A prissy Florentine, that one is. Leave it to a cuckold to be jealous of a eunuch—

EMILIA: [*Crowing.*] —Bianca would die!

DESDEMONA: Then we won't tell her what I said, will we?

[EMILIA *becomes quiet.*]

DESDEMONA: [*Cont'd.*] What Bianca does in her spare time is her business.

[EMILIA'*s face clearly indicates that what Bianca does in her spare time is* EMILIA'*s business, too.* DESDEMONA *watches* EMILIA *closely.*]

DESDEMONA: [*Cont'd.*] You don't much like Bianca, do you, Mealy?

[*No response.* EMILIA *blows on* DESDEMONA'*s toes.*]

DESDEMONA: [*Cont'd.*] Come on, now, tell me frankly—why don't you like her?

EMILIA: It's not for me to say . . .

DESDEMONA: Emilia!

EMILIA: It's just that—no disrespect intented, m'lady, but you shouldn't go a'rubbin' elbows with one o' her class . . . Lie down with hussies, get up with crabs . . .

DESDEMONA: Her sheets are clean. [*Pause.*] You've been simmering over Bianca for some time, Mealy, haven't you?

EMILIA: [*Rancorously.*] I don't much like to see m'lady, in whose employ I am, traipsing about in flopdens, doin' favors for common sloppots—Bianca! Ha! She's so loose, so low, that she's got to advertise Wednesday Night Specials, halfprice for anything in uniform!

DESDEMONA: Well, purge it out of your blood; Bianca will soon be here—

EMILIA: —Here! Why here? What if someone sees her sneaking up to the back door? What will the women in town say? A tart on a house call! How can I keep my head up hanging out the wash and feedin' the pigs when her sort comes sniffin' around—

DESDEMONA: —She's coming to pay me for last Tuesday's customers who paid on credit. And to arrange for next Tuesday—

EMILIA: [*Horrified.*] Not again! Once was enough—you're not going there again! I thought to myself, she's a young unbridled colt, is Miss Desdemona—let her cool down her blood—but to make it a custom!—I couldn't let you go back again—risking disease and putting us all in danger—

DESDEMONA: —Oh, tush, Mealy—

EMILIA: —You listen to me, Miss Desdemona: Othello will sooner or later find out that you're laying for Bianca, and his black skin is goin' to blister off with rage!! Holy Jesus Lord, why tempt a Venetian male by waving red capes? My Iago would beat me for lookin' at the wrong end of an ass! [*Very worked up.*] Your husband will find out and when he does! When he does!! [EMILIA *makes the noise and gesture of throat cutting.*]And then! And then!! AIAIaiaiaiahhh!! My lady!! What's to become of me! Your fateful hand-maid! Where will I find another position in this pisshole harbour!

DESDEMONA: Stop it, Mealy! Don't be . . . silly, nothing will happen to me. I'm the sort that will die in bed.

EMILIA: [*Beseechingly.*] You won't leave your poor Mealy stranded?

DESDEMONA: You'll always have a position in this household . . . Of some sort.

[EMILIA's *face turns to stone.*]

DESDEMONA: [*Cont'd.*] Oh, come now, Mealy, haven't I just promoted you?

EMILIA: Oh, m'lady, I haven't forgot; not only your scullery maid, but now your laundress as well! I am quite sensible of the honor and the increase in pay— of two pence a week . . . [EMILIA *suddenly turns bright and cheery.*] —and whiles we are on the subject—

DESDEMONA: —Oh, Christ, here it comes.

EMILIA: But m'lady, last time an opening came up, you promised to speak to your husband about it in Venice; I suppose poor old Iago just slipped your mind—

DESDEMONA: —Look, I did forget. Anyway, I recommended Cassio for my husband's lieutenant. An unfortunate choice. But that subject is closed.

EMILIA: Yes, mum.

[EMILIA *starts to return to her laundry. There is a knock at the door, and* DESDEMONA *brightens.*]

DESDEMONA: There she is! Emilia, let Bianca in—No, no wait—

[*To* EMILIA's *annoyance,* DESDEMONA *arranges herself in a casual tableau. The knock repeats.* DESDEMONA *signals* EMILIA *to go answer the door.* EMILIA *exits through the door to the palace, and then quickly returns.*]

EMILIA: M'lady, it's your husband. He's waiting for you outside.

DESDEMONA: [*Frightened.*] Husband? . . . Shhhittt . . . [DESDEMONA *pauses, arranges her face into an insipid, fluttering innocence, then girlishly runs to the door. She flings it open, and disappears through the door. We hear a breathless* DESDEMONA, *off.*] Otello!

[*And then, we hear the distinct sound of a very loud slap. A pause, and* DESDE-MONA *returns, closes the door behind her, holding her cheek. She is on the brink of tears. She and* EMILIA *look at each other, and then* EMILIA *looks away.*]

SCENE 6

DESDEMONA *and* EMILIA. DESDEMONA *frantically searches.*

DESDEMONA: It's got to be somewhere!!—Are you quite sure—

EMILIA: —Madam can be sure I overlooked the whole lot several times.

DESDEMONA: Um, Emilia—should, should you have "accidentally" taken it—not that I'm suggesting theft in the slightest—but should it have by mistake slipped in with some of your things—your return of it will merit a reward, and all of my gratitude. [DESDEMONA *tries to appear casual.*] Not that the thing itself is worth anything—it's a pittance of musty linen—but still . . .

EMILIA: [*With dignity.*] I've never taken a thing, accidently or not. I don't make no "accidents." Mum, I've looked everywhere. Everywhere. [*Quietly.*] Is m'lord clamoring about it much?

[*They eye each other. Pause.*]

DESDEMONA: Which position, Mealy?

EMILIA: [*Puzzled.*] Which position?

DESDEMONA: For your husband.

EMILIA: Oh, Miss Desdemona! I won't forget all your—

DESDEMONA: —Yes, yes, I'm sure. What opening?

EMILIA: It's ever so small a promotion, and so quite equal to his merits. He's ensign third-class, but the budget's ensign second-class.

DESDEMONA: Very well, the budget office. Can he write and account and do—whatever it is that they do with the budget?

EMILIA: Oh, yes—he's clever enough at that.

DESDEMONA: I really don't understand your mentality. Emilia. You're forever harping on how much you detest the man. Why do you beg for scraps of promotion for him? Don't you hate him?

EMILIA: I—I—[*With relish.*] I *despise* him.

DESDEMONA: Then?

EMILIA: You see, miss, for us in the bottom ranks, when man and wife hate each other, what is left in a lifetime of marriage but to save and scrimp, plot and plan? The more I'd like to put some nasty rat-ridder in his stew, the more I think of money—and he thinks the same. One of us will drop first, and then, what's left, saved and earned, under the mattress for th' other one? I'd like to rise a bit in the world, and women can only do that through their mates—no matter what class buggers they all are. I says to him each night—I long for the day you make me a lieutenant's widow!

SCENE 7

EMILIA *and* DESDEMONA. *We hear the sounds of scrubbing between the scenes.*

DESDEMONA: Please, my dear Emilia—I can count on you, can't I? As one closest to my confidence?

EMILIA: Oh, m'lady—I ask no greater joy than to be close to your ladyship—

DESDEMONA: Then tell me—have you heard anything about me? Why does Othello suspect Cassio?

EMILIA: Oh, no, m'lady, he surely no longer suspects Cassio; I instructed Iago to talk him out of that bit of fancy, which he did, risking my lord's anger at no little cost to his own career; but all for you, you know!

DESDEMONA: You haven't heard of anything else?

EMILIA: No Ma'am. [*But as* DESDEMONA *is to* EMILIA's *back,* EMILIA *drops a secret smile into the wash bucket.* EMILIA *raises her head again, though, with a sincere, servile face, and turns to* DESDEMONA.] But if I did know anything, you can be sure that you're the first to see the parting of my lips about it—

DESDEMONA: Yes, I know. You've been an extremely faithful, hard-working servant to me, Emilia, if not a confidante. I've noticed your merits, and when we return to Venice well—you may live to be my *fille de chambre* yet.

EMILIA: [*Not quite sure what a* fille de chambre *is.*] I'm very grateful, I'm sure.

DESDEMONA: Yes—you deserve a little reward, I think [EMILIA's *face brightens in expectancy.*] —I'll see if I can wheedle another tuppence out of my husband each week... [EMILIA *droops.*]

EMILIA: [*Listlessly.*] Every little tiny bit under the mattress helps, I always says to myself.

[*A pause.* DESDEMONA *paces, comes to a decision.*]

DESDEMONA: —Mealy—do you like the dressing gown you've been mending?

EMILIA: It's a lovely piece of work, that is, Miss. I've always admired your dresses...

DESDEMONA: Yesss...yes, but isn't it getting a bit dingy? Tattered around the hem?

EMILIA: Not that anyone would notice; it's a beautiful gown, m'lady...

DESDEMONA: Yes, you're right. I was going to give it to you, but maybe I'll hang on to it a bit longer...

[EMILIA, *realizing her stupidity, casts an avaricious, yet mournful look at the gown that was almost hers.*]

EMILIA: Oh, m'lady...It's—it's certainly a lovely cloth, and there's a cut to it that would make one of them boy actors shapely...

DESDEMONA: [*Peeved at the analogy.*] Hmmmm—tho', come to think of it, it would fit Bianca much neater, I think...

EMILIA: Bianca! Bianca! She's got the thighs of a milch cow, m'lady!

DESDEMONA: [*Amused.*] I've never noticed.

[EMILIA, *sulking again, vigorously scrubs.*]

DESDEMONA: [*In conciliation.*] No, come to think of it, I believe you are right—it's not really Bianca's fashion. It's all yours. After tonight.

EMILIA: Oh, Miss Desdemona!!

SCENE 8

The same. In the darkness we hear EMILIA *singing a hymn: "la la la la—Jesus; la-la-la-la—sword; la-la-la-la—crucifix; la-la-la-la—word." Lights come up on* DES-DEMONA *lying stretched out on the table, her throat and head arched over its edge, upside down. A pause.*

DESDEMONA: You really think his temper today was only some peeve?

EMILIA: I'm sure of it; men get itchy heat rash in th' crotch, now and then; they get all snappish, but once they beat us, it's all kisses and presents the next morning—well, for the first year or so.

DESDEMONA: My dear mate is much too miserly to give me anything but his manhood. The only gift he's given me was a meager handkerchief with pid-dling strawberries stitched on it, and look how he's carrying on because I've lost it! He guards his purse strings much dearer than his wife.

EMILIA: I'm sure my Lord will be waitin' up for you to come to bed. Full o' passion, and embracin' and makin' a fool o' himself—You just see if your Mealy isn't right.

DESDEMONA: Yes, of course you're right. Good old Mealy, I don't know what I'd do without your good common sense. Oh, it's the curse of aristocratic blood— I feel full of whims and premonitions—

EMILIA: Perhaps it was something m'lady et?

DESDEMONA: [*First she smiles—then she laughs.*] Yes—that must be it!

[DESDEMONA *laughs again.* EMILIA *can't understand what is so funny.*]

SCENE 9

EMILIA *and* DESDEMONA.

EMILIA: Ambassador Ludovico gave me a message and is wantin' a response.

DESDEMONA: What does my cousin want?

EMILIA: [EMILIA *digs into her bodice.*] It's somewhere in here . . . wait— [EMILIA *searches.*]

DESDEMONA: Oh, good Lord, Mealy, you could lose it in there! [DESDEMONA *runs to* EMILIA, *peers in her bosom, and starts to tickle her.*]

EMILIA: Miss Desde—! Wait, now—no, STOP!! Here it is now—[EMILIA *finds a fold-ed paper. She hands it to* DESDEMONA, *and then peers over* DESDEMONA'S *shoulder.*]

DESDEMONA: [*Sighing.*] Oh, Ludovico, Ludovico. "Deeply desiring the favor, etceteras." " . . . Impatient until I can at last see you in private, throwing off the Robes of State to appear as your humble friend." He's just too tiresome.

EMILIA: What response are you wanting me to give?

DESDEMONA: Oh, I don't know. Let the old lecher wait. I told him it was entirely past between us, and then he bribes his way into being appointed Ambassador!

[DESDEMONA *in a loquacious mood.* EMILIA *gives her a rub-down.*]

DESDEMONA: [*Cont'd.*] Ah, Emilia, I should have married Ludovico after all. There's a man who's always known the worth of ladies of good blood! A pearl for a pinch, a broach for a breast, and for a maiden-head... [DESDEMONA *breaks into laughter.*] Ah, that was a lover!

EMILIA: I don't know how those sainted sisters could let such is-sagnations go on in their convent—

DESDEMONA: —assignations. Really, Emilia, you're quite hopeless. However can I, the daughter of a senator, live with a washerwoman as *fille de chambre?* All fashionable Venice will howl. You must shrink your vowels and enlarge your vocabulary.

EMILIA: Yes, mum. As-signations, as it were. [*Muttering.*] If it were one o' my class, I could call it by some names I could pronounce. I've put many a copper in their poor box, in times past, thinkin' them sisters of charity in a godly house. Not no more. They won't get the parings of my potatoes from me, runnin' a society house of ass-ignations!

DESDEMONA: Oh, those poor, dear sisters. I really don't think they knew anything about the informal education their convent girls receive; for one thing, I believe myopia is a prerequisite for Holy Orders. Have you ever noticed how nuns squint? [*Beat.*] Each Sunday in convent we were allowed to take visitors to chapel; under their pious gaze Ludovic and I would kneel and there I could devote myself to doing him *à la main*— [DESDEMONA *gestures.*] —right in the pew! They never noticed! Sister Theresa did once remark that he was a man excessively fond of prayer.

SCENE 10

EMILIA*'s credo.*

EMILIA: It's not right of you, Miss Desdemona, to be forever cutting up on the matter of my beliefs. I believe in the Blessed Virgin, I do, and the Holy Fathers and the Sacraments of the Church, and I'm not one to be ashamed of admittin' it. It goes against my marrow, it does, to hear of you, a comely lass from a decent home, giving hand jobs in the pew; but I says to myself, Emilia, I says, you just pay it no mind, and I go about my business. And if I take a break on the Sabbath each week, to light a candle and say a bead or two for my employers, who have given me and my husband so much, and who need the Virgin's love and protection, then where's the harm, say I? [*Breath.* EMILIA *gets carried away*] Our Lady has seen me through four and ten years of matreemony, with my bugger o' a mate, and that's no mean feat. Four and ten years, she's heard poor Mealy's cries, and stopped me from rising from my bed with my pillow in my hand to end his ugly snores 'til Gabriel— [EMILIA *stops and composes herself.*] —

Ah, Miss Desdemona, if you only knew the peace and love Our Lady brings! She'd help you, mum, if you only kneeled real nice and said to her—and said—

[EMILIA *can't find the words that such a sinner as* DESDEMONA *should say as polite salutation to Our Lady.* DESDEMONA, *erupts into laughter.*]

SCENE 11

EMILIA *eats her lunch.* DESDEMONA *plays in a desultory fashion with a toy. Then, frightened.*

DESDEMONA: Emilia—have you ever deceived your husband Iago?

EMILIA: [*With a derisive snort.*] That's a good one. Of course not, miss—I'm an honest woman.

DESDEMONA: What does honesty have to do with adultery? Every honest man I know is an adulterer... [*Pause.*] Have you ever thought about it?

EMILIA: What is there to be thinkin' about? It's enough trouble once each Saturday night, than to be lookin' for it. I'd never cheat, never, not for all the world I wouldn't.

DESDEMONA: The world's a huge thing for so small a vice.

EMILIA: Not my world, thank you—mine's tidy and neat and I aim to keep it that way.

DESDEMONA: Oh, the world! Our world's narrow and small, I'll grant you—but there are other worlds—worlds that we married women never get to see.

EMILIA: Amen—and don't need to see, I should add.

DESDEMONA: If you've never seen the world, how would you know? Women are clad in purdah, we decent, respectable matrons, from the cradle to the altar to the shroud... bridled with linen, blinded with lace... These very walls are purdah.

EMILIA: I don't know what this thing called "purr-dah" means, but if it stands for dressing up nice, I'm all for it...

DESDEMONA: I remember the first time I saw my husband and I caught a glimpse of his skin, and oh, how I thrilled. I thought—aha—a man of a different color. From another world and planet. I thought—if I marry this strange dark man, I can leave this narrow little Venice with its whispering piazzas behind—I can escape and see other worlds. [*Pause.*] But under that exotic facade was a porcelain white Venetian.

EMILIA: There's nothing wrong with Venice; I don't understand why Madam's all fired up to catch Cyprus Syph and exotic claps.

DESDEMONA: Of course you don't understand. But I think Bianca does. She's a free woman—a new woman, who can make her own living in the world—who scorns marriage for the lie that it is.

EMILIA: I don't know where Madam's getting this new woman hog-wash, but no matter how you dress up a cow, she's still got udders. Bianca's the eldest one of six girls, with teeth so horsy she could clean 'em with a hoof pick, and so simple she has to ply the trade she does! That's what your Miss Bianca is!

DESDEMONA: Bianca is nothing of the sort. She and I share something common in our blood—that desire to know the world. I lie in the blackness of the room at her establishment ... on sheets that are stained and torn by countless nights. And the men come into that pitch-black room—men of different sizes and smells and shapes, with smooth skin, with rough skin, with scarred skin. And they spill their seed into me, Emilia—seed from a thousand lands, passed down through generations of ancestors, with genealogies that cover the surface of the globe. And I simply lie still there in the darkness, taking them all into me; I close my eyes and in the dark of my mind—oh, how I travel!

SCENE 12

EMILIA *and* DESDEMONA. DESDEMONA *is recklessly excited.*

EMILIA: You're leaving?!! Your husband?!!

DESDEMONA: It's a possibility!

EMILIA: Miss Desdemona, you've been taking terrible chances before but now—if my Lord catches you giving him th' back wind, he'll be after murdering both of us for sure

DESDEMONA: Where's my cousin Ludovico? Is he in his room?

EMILIA: He said he was turnin' in early to get some rest before th' morning—

DESDEMONA: Yes—he'll catch the first tide back. Well, there's no harm in trying.

EMILIA: Trying what!

DESDEMONA: Trying on the robes of the penitent daughter. Ludovico can surely see how detestable this island, this marriage, this life is for me. [DESDEMONA *has worked herself to the point of tears. Then she smiles.*] Perhaps a few tears would move him to intercede with my father on my behalf. If the disgrace of eloping with a Moor is too great for Venetian society, a small annual allowance from Papa and I promise never to show my face in town; and then ... who knows ... Paris! Yes, I'll go write Ludovico a note right away, asking to see him tonight.—Mealy—just in case—could you pack a few things for me?

EMILIA: And what if your husband discovers—

DESDEMONA: I'll leave first thing in the morning.

EMILIA: If I may make so bold to suggest—

DESDEMONA: What, what—

EMILIA: That you by all means sleep with your husband tonight. So's he won't suspect anything. While you and he lie together, and if your cousin agrees, Mealy could pack up your things quiet-like in your chamber.

DESDEMONA: Yes, that's good. My life rests on your absolute discretion, Emilia.

EMILIA: No one will hear a peep out o' me. But my lady—

DESDEMONA: Now what is it?

EMILIA: What becomes of me?

DESDEMONA: Oh, good heavens, Mealy—I can't think of trivia at a time like this. [*Smoothly.*] I tell you what. Be a good girl, pack my things—and of course, should I leave tomorrow, I can't very well smuggle you on board, too—but I will send for you within the week. And your services will be remembered in Venice; with freer purse strings—who knows? Eh, my *fille de chambre*?

EMILIA: [*At this sop to her feelings,* EMILIA *becomes fierce.*] That won't do, m'lady. If you leave me behind, I'll not see you again, as your laundress, much less as your "fee der schomer"—

[DESDEMONA, *realizing the power that* EMILIA *now has, kneels beside* EMILIA.]

DESDEMONA: All right. I'll intercede with my cousin on your behalf. I'll plead with him to take you, too. But I can't promise anything. Are you sure it's what you want?

[EMILIA *nods.*]

DESDEMONA: [*Cont'd.*] You'd leave your husband behind?

[EMILIA *nods vigorously.*]

DESDEMONA: [*Cont'd.*] Then—not a word. [DESDEMONA *rises, and in turning to go.*] Oh, Emilia—since you're just dawdling over that laundry—why not stop and peel some potatoes for Cook. When my husband comes in, he'll want his usual snack of chips before he turns in—just the way he likes them—[DESDEMONA *shudders.*]—greasy.

EMILIA: But Miss, it's not my place no more to peel potatoes! I'm promoted now! I'm no mere [*With disgust.*]—SCULLERY MAID.

DESDEMONA: Now, Mealy, just this once—

EMILIA: —You said I wouldn't have to do potatoes anymore!

DESDEMONA: [*Harshly.*]—I can leave you rotting on Cyprus all together, you know. Do as you're told. Peel the potatoes, and then look sharp and have that wash on the line by the time I return. Do I make myself clear?

EMILIA: Yes, m'lady.

DESDEMONA: [*Sweetly.*] And Emilia, dear—if Bianca comes when I'm gone, let me know immediately—I'll be in my chamber.

EMILIA: Very good, Miss Desdemona.

[DESDEMONA *exits.* EMILIA *grudgingly gets up, and finds the barrel of potatoes. On the bench there is a paring knife.* EMILIA *brings everything back to the table, sits, and begins paring potatoes—venting her resentment on gouging out eyes, and stripping the skin from a potato as if flaying a certain mistress alive. Then, she snorts out in contempt.*]

EMILIA: [*Cont'd.*] Fee der shomber! [*Then* EMILIA *pauses and wonders if* DESDEMONA *might not be for real in her offer—and questions the empty room with.*] Feeyah der schomber? [*Before* EMILIA's *eyes, she visualizes splendid dresses, the command of a household of subservient maids, a husbandless existence—all the trappings that go with the title.* EMILIA *begins energetically, resolutely and obediently to slice the potatoes.*]

SCENE 13

EMILIA *is hanging up the wash.* BIANCA *knocks several times. Then enters.*

BIANCA: Gaw Blimey!

EMILIA: And where is' you've lost your manners? Lettin' the door ajar and leavin' in drafts and the pigs—

BIANCA: Aw'm sorry, Aw'm sure... [BIANCA *closes the door. Hesitates, and then with friendly strides, goes towards the clothesline.*] 'Ow do, Emilia!

EMILIA: I'd be doin' a lot better if ye'd stop your gaddin'and lend a hand with these things.

BIANCA: Oh. Right you are, then.

[BIANCA *goes briskly to the clothesline, and works. Silence as the women empty the basket.* EMILIA *leaves* BIANCA *to finish and starts in on her sewing. Pause.*]

BIANCA: [*Cont'd.*] Well, it's—it ain't 'arf swank 'ere, eh? [BIANCA *indicates the room.*]

EMILIA: [*Snorts.*] Swank? What, this? This is only the back room. The palace is through those doors—

BIANCA: Oh. Well, it's swank for a back room wotever it 'tis. Aw niver got to see it much; the Guv'nor in the owld days didn't let me near, said Aw made the men tomdoodle on their shifts; like as they'd be distracted by me atomy. Aw think it's sweet o' him to gi' me such credit; me atomy ain't that bleedin' jammy— but then, the owld Guv was the first to gi' me the sheeps' eye 'imself—very sweet on me, 'e was. So you see, Aw'd niver got close to the place before. Aw fink it's swank!

EMILIA: [*Icily.*] I'm sure you do.

BIANCA: Yes, it's quite—wot do ye call it—lux-i-o-rious.

EMILIA: Lux-i-o-ri-us!! If I was you, I'd large my voc-abulary, an' shrink me vowels.

BIANCA: [*Offended.*] 'Ere now! Wot bus'ness is me vowels to you?! Leave me vowels alone—

EMILIA: —I'm after talking about your voc-abulary—your patter—not your regularity.

BIANCA: Oh. [*Keeping up a friendly front with difficulty.*] Right. Well, then, is Desdemona 'ere?

EMILIA: [*Sharply.*] Who?

BIANCA: Uh—Des-de-mona...

EMILIA: Is it m'lady you're referrin' to as if she were your mess mate?

BIANCA: Look 'ere—Aw'm only doin' as Aw was towld. She tells me to call her Desdemona, and she says Aw was to call and settle up accounts for last Tuesday night for those johns who paid on tick—oh, you know, who paid on credit, as yew la-de-da Venetians would say.

EMILIA: [*Softly hissed.*] You listen to me, lassie: you're riding for a fall the likes of which you never got paid for by your fancy men. The mistress of this house is not at home, nor will be to the likes of you. What m'lady does in the gutter is her own business, same as yours, but what happens here is the common buzz of all.

BIANCA: [*Stunned.*] Wot! Miss Desdemona herself is callin' us mates; Aw niver—

EMILIA: —then she's gullin' you, as sure as 'tis she's gullin' that ass of a husband who's so taken with her; but let me tell you, you'll go the way like all the other fancies she's had in Venice...I should know. We all of us servants in her father's house talked on end about Miss Desdemona.—For a time, she wanted to be a saint, yes! A nun with the sisters of mercy. At age twelve she was washin' the courtyard stones for penance, with us wiping up behind her. Then she was taken with horses, thank Jesus, and left sainthood behind—and then in turn again, she thought she was dyin'—stopped eating, and moped, and talked all dreamy and a little balmy-like—until her father finally saw sense and sent her to the convent to be bred out of her boredom. You're nothin' but the latest whim, a small town floozy with small town slang, and if she's lucky, she'll tire of you before the master finds out. [*Significantly.*] If she's lucky.

BIANCA: [*Somewhat subdued.*] So wot am Aw t'do, Emilia? Aw arsks you—

EMILIA: —Then ask me by "Miss Emilia" to you—[*With great dignity.*] I'll have you know, I've hereby been promoted to "fee der shimber" and if I was you, I'd keep on my right side.

BIANCA: [*Impressed, scared.*] Oh—"fee dar shimber"—Aw niver met one o' those before—Aw arsks yer pardon, Miss Emilia, Aw'm sure.

EMILIA: That's a bit of all right. You just listen to me: I know what side of me bread is buttered; behind this whimsycal missus is a power of a master—so you mind yourself; the smell of your sin's goin' to catch m'lord's whiffin' about, and he's as jealous as he's black. If m'lord Othello had a mind to it, he could have that little lollin' tongue of yours cut clean out of your head, with none of the citizens of Cyprus to say him nay. And then what would you do for your customers! If he catched you degineratin' his wife—

BIANCA: [*Starting to cry with fear.*] Aw swear, Miss Emilia, Aw'm not degineratin' m'lady; we was just mates, that's wot; if Missus Desdemona wants to lark and gull her smug of a husband, that's her business, then, ain't it? Aw done as she towld me, an' that's all—she's a good lady, an' all, and Aw've just been friendly-like to her—

EMILIA: —Don't be a little fool hussy. There's no such creature, two, three, or four-legged, as "friend" betwixt ladies of leisure and ladies of the night. And as long as there be men with one member but two minds, there's no such thing as friendship between women. An' that's that. So turn yourself around, go out and close the door behind you, and take all traces of the flophouse with you—includin' your tall tales about your "friendships" with ladies—

BIANCA: [*Anger finally conquering fear.*] You can call me wot you like, but Aw'm no liar! Aw'm as 'onest a woman as yerself. And wot's more, mebbe you can wipe yer trotters on women who have to crack their crusts by rolling blokes in Venice, but 'ere it's differnt.—Aw have a place 'ere and Aw'm not ashamed t'own it—Aw'm nice to the wives in town, and the wives in town are rather nice to me. Aw'm doin' them favors by puttin' up wif their screwy owld men, and Aw like me job! The only ponk Aw has to clean up is me own. [*Starts to leave but.*] —And wot's more, Aw likes yer lady, whefer you think so or not. She can see me as Aw am, and not arsk for bowin' and scrapin'—she don't have to be nobby, 'cause she's got breedin', and she don't mind liking me for me own self—wifout th' nobby airs of yer Venetian washerwomen! Aw'm at home 'ere in my place—you, you Venetian washerdonna—you're the one out o' yer element! [BIANCA *stalks to the door, but before she can reach it,* DESDEMONA *enters.*]

DESDEMONA: Emilia.

SCENE 14

The same. DESDEMONA, EMILIA *and Bianca.*

DESDEMONA: Emilia. I thought I told you to tell me the instant Miss Bianca arrived. Well?

EMILIA: I didn't want to be botherin' m'lady with the ambassador—

DESDEMONA: —I want none of your excuses for your rudeness to our guest. My dear Bianca! I've been waiting impatiently—I could have just died of boredom. [DESDEMONA *bestows a warm hug on* BIANCA.]—May I kiss you? [DESDEMONA *"kisses"* BIANCA *by pressing both sides of their cheeks together.*]

BIANCA: [*Stammering.*] Aw'm not worthy of it, m'lady—

DESDEMONA: Oh, Bianca, so stiff and formal!—What have I done that you should be so angry with me?

BIANCA: [*Quickly.*] Nofing! Your lady's been all kindness to me . . . but mayhap . . . Aw'm not the sort o' mate for one o' your company!

DESDEMONA: Nonsense! I'll decide my own friendships . . . [DESDEMONA *looks meaningfully at* EMILIA. *To* BIANCA.] You must excuse my entertaining you in such a crude barn of a room; my room's much cozier, but I don't know when my . . . my . . . "smug"—is that right? [BIANCA *nods.*] —when he'll return. [DESDEMONA *laughs.*] Right now Othello's out in the night somewhere playing Roman Orator to his troops.

[DESDEMONA *guides* BIANCA *to the table: they sit side by side.*]

DESDEMONA: [*Cont'd.*] Emilia . . . Ask Miss Bianca if she'd like some wine. [*To* BIANCA.] It's really quite good, my dear. [EMILIA *glumly approaches* BIANCA.]

EMILIA: Well, are you wantin' any?

DESDEMONA: Emilia! "Would you care for some wine, Miss Bianca?"

EMILIA: [*Deep breath, red.*] "Would you care for some wine, Miss Bianca?"

BIANCA: Why thank you—D-desdemona, Aw could do w' a sneaker—

DESDEMONA: [*Laughs.*] How I love the way you talk! . . . Emilia, fetch the wine and two goblets. That will be all.

EMILIA: Yes, mum. [EMILIA *exits and* BIANCA *relaxes.*]

DESDEMONA: My poor Bianca; has Emilia been berating you?

BIANCA: Well, Aw don't know about that, but she's been takin' me down a bit. Aw don't thinks she likes me very much.

DESDEMONA: Oh, what does that matter! Why should you want her friendship—you don't have to care what anyone thinks about you—you're a totally free woman, able to snap your fingers in any one's face!

BIANCA: Yea, that's wot all right—but still, Aw likes people to like me.

DESDEMONA: Oh, well, you mustn't mind Emilia. She's got a rotten temper because her husband—her "smug"—is such a rotter. Oh, Iago! [DESDEMONA *shudders.*] Do you know him?

BIANCA: [*Smiling, looking away.*] Aw know 'im by sight

DESDEMONA: You know the one, then—the greasy little man. He's been spilling his vinegar into her for fourteen years of marriage, until he's corroded her womb from the inside out—and every day she becomes more and more hallowed out, just—just a vessel of vinegar herself.

BIANCA: [*Disturbed.*] Wot a funny way of lookin' at it [BIANCA *is bewildered.*]

SCENE 15

BIANCA *and* DESDEMONA.

BIANCA: So you don't fancy Iago, then, do you?

DESDEMONA: Detest him. But of course, I don't have anything to do with him—I only need suffer his wife's company. Poor old Mealy—

BIANCA: —"Mealy?" [BIANCA *laughs, her fear of* EMILIA *diminishing.*]

DESDEMONA: Yes, I've nicknamed her that, because I suspect it annoys her. Still, it fits.

[DESDEMONA *and* BIANCA *giggle.*]

DESDEMONA: [*Cont'd.*] Alas, when Othello and I eloped it was on such short notice and my husband's so stingy with salary that the only maid I could bring was my father's scullery maid.

BIANCA: Yer scullery maid! Not—not yer—wot-de-ye-call it—"Fee dah—Feyah der—"

DESDEMONA: *"Fille de Chambre!"* Heavens, no! I keep her in line with the prospect of eventual advancement, but she's much too unsuitable for that—why she doesn't speak a word of French, and she's crabby to boot. Still, she's devoted and that makes up for all the rest.

BIANCA: Wot makes you fink she's devoted?

DESDEMONA: Ah, a good mistress knows the secret thoughts of her maids. She's devoted.

BIANCA: Well, it's a cooshy enough way to crack a crust . . .

DESDEMONA: Crack a crust?

BIANCA: Oh—beg yer pardon; Aw mean t'earn a livin'—

DESDEMONA: [*Enthralled.*] "Crack a crust!" How clever you are, Bianca!

SCENE 16

DESDEMONA, BIANCA *and* EMILIA. EMILIA *stands before* DESDEMONA, *bearing a pitcher and two mugs on a tray.*

EMILIA: Wine, m'lady . . .

DESDEMONA: Ah, excellent.

[EMILIA *serves* DESDEMONA *first with all the grace she can muster; then she negligently pushes the wine in the direction of* BIANCA.]

BIANCA: Thank you, Mealy.

DESDEMONA: [*Toasting* BIANCA.] Now, then: to our friendship!

BIANCA: T' yer 'ealth—

[DESDEMONA *delicately sips her wine, as* BIANCA *belts it down so that the wine trickles from the corner of her mouth.* EMILIA *is aghast. As* BIANCA *wipes her mouth with her hand, she notices* EMILIA's *shock and blurts.*]

BIANCA: [*Cont'd.*] 'Scuse me guttlin' it down me gob—

DESDEMONA: Oh, tush, Bianca. Mealy, haven't you mending to carry on with?

[EMILIA *silently seats herself apart and picks up the drawers.*]

DESDEMONA: [*Cont'd.*] I tell you, Bianca, it's a disgrace. My husband refuses to buy new linen for his drawers, so Emilia must constantly mend the old. [*Confidentially.*] He's constantly tearing his crotch-hole somehow.

BIANCA: [*Amused.*] And how does that happen?

DESDEMONA: [*Demurely.*] I have no idea.—More wine, dear?

SCENE 17

The same. BIANCA *and* DESDEMONA, *drinking.* EMILIA *sews.*

DESDEMONA: How about another . . . round?

BIANCA: All right, then.

[DESDESMONA *pours generously.*]

BIANCA: [*Cont'd.*] —But not so much! Aw could get lushy easy.

[BIANCA *sips her wine:* DESDEMONA *knocks it back, and wipes her mouth with her hand. They laugh.*]

SCENE 18

DESDEMONA *and* BIANCA, *drinking. They are giggling helplessly, spluttering.* EMILIA *sews.* DESDEMONA *starts to choke on her wine from laughing.*

SCENE 19

The same. DESDEMONA *and* BIANCA *try to control themselves. Then* DESDEMONA *holds up the hoof pick, and* BIANCA *and* DESDEMONA *explode in raucous laughter.* EMILIA *is furious.*

SCENE 20

The same.

BIANCA: Listen, luvs, where's yer five-minute lodging?

DESDEMONA: My...what?

BIANCA: Yer Drury Lane? Yer—where's yer bleedin' crapper! Yew know—where do yew make water?

EMILIA: M'lady makes her water in a hand-painted Limoge pot, a holy sight with angels havin' a grand time—it's not for the like of you!

DESDEMONA: There's an outhouse in the back by the shed...careful of the muck and the pigs.

BIANCA: 'Ta. Be back in a few...Aw've got t' go see a bloke about a horse. [*Bianca exits.*]

EMILIA: And you're after havin' yourself a proper time.

DESDEMONA: Oh, Mealy, I'm sorry—we were just having fun—

EMILIA: At my husband's expense. You finagled that out o' me, and then you went and told it to My Lady of the Public Square...

DESDEMONA: It...It just...slipped out. [DESDEMONA *goes into another gale of laughter. Then.*]—Mealy—I'm going to ask her about Cassio!

EMILIA: Why must you be knowin' every man's size?! [DESDEMONA *laughs again.*]

DESDEMONA: —No, I mean I'm going to tell her that Othello suspects him.

EMILIA: Are you daft from the wine?

DESDEMONA: Why not? Maybe we can get to the bottom of this...

EMILIA: Why is it mattering? Tomorrow morning we're leaving with the ambassador—

DESDEMONA: —Yes, yes, but I can find out why—

EMILIA: —I don't understand why m'lady is in such a rush to havin' her throat slashed our last night on Cyprus—

DESDEMONA: —Look, I'll just tell her that my husband is under some false impression, and ask her for—

EMILIA: —And why should she be believin' you?

DESDEMONA: She'll believe me! She'll believe me because...I'll give her...I'll give her...my word of honor.

EMILIA: And just how much goat cheese does that buy at market?—I know the world! I've seen flesh buckets fightin' for their fancy men in the streets in Venice, and a pretty sight it was!

DESDEMONA: Oh, Mealy—

EMILIA: —You'll be bleedin' on the wrong time of the month! Those trullies, all of them, carry slashers down in their boots—

[BIANCA *throws open the door and sticks her head in;* EMILIA *and* DESDEMONA *are startled.*]

BIANCA: Did-jew miss me?

SCENE 21

BIANCA, DESDEMONA, *and* EMILIA.

BIANCA: 'Ere now—let me settle w' you fer Tuesday night—let's see... [BIANCA *rummages in a pocket of her dress.*] It were six pence a john, at ten johns makes fer...five bob, an' tuppence fer tips. [EMILIA *gasps.*]

DESDEMONA: I can hear what you're thinking Mealy—Holy Mother, I made more in twenty minutes than you do in a week of washing!

EMILIA: Five bob...

DESDEMONA: How large now the world for so small a vice, eh, Mealy?

EMILIA: I'm—I'm not to be tempted, Miss Desdemona.

DESDEMONA: Brave girl!

BIANCA: 'Ere's the brass ready. Tuppence for tips is bleedin'-well for a Tuesday.

DESDEMONA: Really?

BIANCA: It so be as how Wednesday is pay-day 'ere; Tuesday nights are the cooshiest layin', but the stingiest payin'—

EMILIA: Aye, "Men earns their money like Horses and spends it like Asses"...

DESDEMONA: Never mind Mealy, Bianca; she's over there calculating what price fidelity. Now about next week—

EMILIA: —You two can cackle with laughter at me if you like, but it's a duty for me to stop your ladyship from gettin' into danger—

BIANCA: [*Offended.*] Danger! Wot danger! She helped me out on me Adam an' Eve Night—there's no danger; Aw gave her me lambs; the feisty, firkin' lads come on th' other nights, not on Tuesday. It don't take no elbow grease; Tuesday's just lying back and Adam an' Evein' it—

EMILIA: I don't understand your "Adam and Eve" and I don't think I want to...

DESDEMONA: Oh yes you do, Mealy; "Adam and Eve" is what you and Iago did on your wedding night...

BIANCA: She just might fink it means fallin' asleep—

[EMILIA *vigorously stitches the linen.*]

DESDEMONA: She's right, tho', Bianca, she's only trying to protect me; how about if we leave next Tuesday night open. If I can sneak away into the darkness of your boudoir, then I'll send word by Emilia—

BIANCA: Right, then, but you understand me, Miss Desdemona there'll be no firsky johns when you comes clandecently; just the meek ones who are low on pocket-brass, or the stingy-mingy-gits who don't want to pay for nothin' wild; an' there'll be a fresh bed, an' the room so dark that your own husband wouldn't know you—

DESDEMONA: —Oh, Bianca—what a thought—do you think he'd come? I'd die for sure— [DESDEMONA *laughs.*] —And wouldn't he be mad if he'd paid for what he got for free at home!!

BIANCA: Well, the room's bleedin' black—blacker than he is.

[BIANCA *and* EMILIA *laugh together;* DESDEMONA *is affronted.*]

DESDEMONA: I beg your pardon?

BIANCA: No, no—all my Tuesday johns are reg'lars—Aw know 'em all. So if you want, let me know—it'll be treacle next to wot Aw had today—

DESDEMONA: —Do tell, Bianca—

EMILIA: —Hasn't m'lady had enough—

DESDEMONA: —Oh, hush, Mealy—just mend your crotches, and don't listen.

BIANCA: All right, then. Aw have this one john who comes once a week for an L & B—

DESDEMONA: "L & B?"

BIANCA: In th' Life, it's known as a lam an' brim—first they lam you, an' mayhap you lam them, then you brim 'em— [DESDEMONA *looks blank.*] You know—first they beat you, an' then you beat them, and then you give 'em wotever—an Adam an' Eve, or a Sunnyside Over—

DESDEMONA: [*Dawning.*] You mean men actually pay to beat you? And to be beaten?

BIANCA: Oh, well, it costs 'em a pretty penny, Aw can tell you; there's nothin' doin' for less than two bob.

DESDEMONA: [*Eyes wide.*] My. Well, carry on.

BIANCA: Well, there's this one john, an owld mate, who's been on tick for some weeks, an' 'e's got quite a bill. But Aw feels sorry for 'im' 'is wife really lams 'im at 'ome, an' Aw figure 'e needs t' get it off 'is chest—So 'e comes in, an' Aw says: "Tom—you owe me over two quid, now; when's it comin'?" "Gaw, Bianca," 'e says, "Aw just been out o' Collar, an'—"

DESDEMONA: —"Out of Collar?"

BIANCA: Wot yew call un-deployed... "Bianca," 'e says, "Gawd luv yew, me owld woman an' Aw've had a row an' Aw'm all done in. Aw'll pay th' soddin' bill, some'ow; but fer now, fer owld times," 'e says—well Gawd's Wounds, wot was

Aw t'do? "Right, then, Tom," Aw said, an' Aw lays down on the bed—'cause 'e liked me to go first an' 'e puts the straps on me—"Tom," Aw says, "listen, luv, th' straps are bleedin' tight—" An' before Aw knew wot, 'e was lammin' me fer real!! 'E did me fer a jacketin' such as Aw thought would be me last L 'n' B!! Aw bite me teeth not to scream, 'cause the bobbies won't put up with no row, no matter how many quid Aw pay 'em ... Well, Tom finally gets it over wif, an' it's my turn. "Aw'm sorry, Bianca," 'e says, "if Aw got a bit rough." "Oh, it's nofin', Tom," Aw says—'cause Aw'm determined t' get me own back ... So Aw tie 'im down on th' bed—'e's a big strapper o' a bloke—An' then Aw lam th' pudding out o' 'im—!! An' 'e's 'ollerin' like it's th' Second Coming. Then after Aw gi' 'im a royal pasting, Aw go through 'is togs, an' in the back pocket—Aw find a sod-din' crown! "You been 'olding out on me, Tom! Aw've had it wi' yer dodges an' flams—wot kind o' a soup kitchen do yew fink me?"—An' Aw let into 'im again!!—"Bianca—let me go, an' Aw'll niver flam to ye again!" "BLEEDIN'-RIGHT!" Aw says. So Aw copped 'is brass, takes up the belt, an' let 'im loose—straight into the street 'e runs, naked as a blue-jay—Aw had to throw 'is togs after 'im. "Yew Owld Stringer!" Aw yelled:—"'Ere's yer togs, an' fer yer change, take this!" [BIANCA *raises her fist and slaps her elbow,—excited, she catches her breath.*]

DESDEMONA: Jesus. Weren't you scared?

BIANCA: Aw'd be lyin' if Aw said nay. Aw thought it was me last trick. You can't be too careful, there's a lot of maggotbrained doodles in me bus'ness. But Aw can take care o' meself.

DESDEMONA: Doesn't—doesn't it hurt?

BIANCA: Naw—not usual. It's stingy-like, but it's all fakement. [BIANCA, *looking into* DESDEMONA's *eyes, gets an idea.*] ... Aw c'n show you if you likes ... C'mon, it won't hurt you none—

DESDEMONA: Well ... yes, all right, Bianca, show me.

SCENE 22

The beating scene. EMILIA, BIANCA, *and* DESDEMONA.

EMILIA: Are you out o' your mind? Lettin' a strumpet strap you in your own house like a monk in Holy Week?

DESDEMONA: Turn around, Emilia, and mind your own business. Go on, turn around, and say your beads. Pay no attention. [*To* BIANCA.] Sorry—please continue. [EMILIA *says her beads through the following.*]

EMILIA: Hail Mary Full of Grace the Lord is with Thee—

BIANCA: Get up on the table wi' yer tail end up—

EMILIA: Holy Mary, Mother of—[EMILIA *turns and sees* DESDEMONA *spread-eagled.*] —GOD!!!

BIANCA: Right now. Aw'll just take a strap 'ere—an' Aw'll just brush you wi' it— but when Aw let's go, you move yer tail up—all right?

DESDEMONA: I—I think so; it's rather like rising to the trot on a horse—

BIANCA: Right then. One—up, Two—down; all right, now, One: [DESDEMONA *moves up.*] Two—: [BIANCA *lightly straps* DESDEMONA *as she moves down.*] One—: [DESDEMONA *moves up.*] An' Two—: [DESDEMONA *moves down; a strap.*] —Does it hurt?

DESDEMONA: No—no, it doesn't, really.

BIANCA: Right then. Let's have some sound e-ffecks. One; Two—

[DESDEMONA *screams,* EMILIA *clutches her rosary.*]

BIANCA: [*Cont'd.*] —NO!!—not that loud! The bobbies would be in on yew so fast yew wouldn't get yer panties up—just a moan enow to get 'im excited... Right, then? Now: One—Two; One—Two; One—Two; One—Two; One—Two; One—Two!!

[DESDEMONA *perfects her synchronized moans, building to a crescendo, at which point she breaks into peals of laughter.*]

DESDEMONA: It's smashing!—Mealy—you really must try it!

SCENE 23

As before.

BIANCA: Aw want you t'take this in th' right way, now; but if you weren't born a lady, you'd a been a bleedin'-good blowzabella. One o' the best. An'—well, no matter what fate holds, there's always room fer you in me shop. [*Bashful.*] Aw means it, too—

EMILIA: —Holy Mother, if anyone had so much as whispered in Venice that you'd be makin' a bonnie whore, there'd be a blood duel to settle in the streets!

BIANCA: Aw'm payin' yer lady me respecks as one professional t'anofer. You—you got as much notion of me craft as a donkey has of Sunday.

EMILIA: Why, thank you—at least someone has noted me merit.

DESDEMONA: [*Gently.*] I'm very complimented, Bianca...and I really did enjoy Tuesday night—but I don't think I'd better risk covering for you again.

BIANCA: —You're—you're not brimmin' fer me anymore?

DESDEMONA: No—I don't think I'd better.

EMILIA: [*To herself.*] Heigh-ho! On to the next—

BIANCA: [*Trembling.*] But—but we c'n still be mates, wot?

DESDEMONA: Of course we can! I want that very much. I never tire of hearing your stories. They're so lively, so very funny. What else have I got for amusement's sake.

[BIANCA *is disturbed.* EMILIA *smiles.*]

DESDEMONA: [*Cont'd.*] —but you haven't told me yet about your evening off with Cassio last Tuesday...did you enjoy yourself?

BIANCA: You don't want to 'ear about it none, it's not anyfing amusing—

DESDEMONA: Now, just tell me all about it, Bianca; you can tell me your secrets, too. Woman to woman. What did you two do?

BIANCA: [*Shy.*] We just talked.

EMILIA: [*Snorting.*] All night?

BIANCA: Yes! 'E's differnt, you know. 'E's a gen'l'man, 'e is—an' 'e makes the rest o' the blokes round 'ere look like the ninny-hammers they are—

EMILIA: Oh, he's diffrent, all right. You'd think after all week of tom-foolin' with the like of hicks, you'd have more sense than to go prancin' about with some nancy town stallion.

BIANCA: Wot! Nancy! Nancy, is it? Who're you callin' "Nancy?"

DESDEMONA: Now, Mealy, don't tease her—

EMILIA: —the way I see it, it's no acc-i-dent for himself to be an army man—

BIANCA: —Aw tell you wot, M'lord Cassio 'twill make a smug more obligin' in bed than the one you've got—

DESDEMONA: [*Warningly*] —Ladies, ladies—

EMILIA: —Well, you'll never find out what it is to be havin' the like of a proper husband in the bed.

BIANCA: Mayhap Aw will, too. Aw'm ready to let my way of life go fer wash the second 'e arsks me.

DESDEMONA: What!

BIANCA: Aw'm giving 'alfe me brass each week to the priest, Father Donahue, so's 'e c'n pray fer me sins an' t'gi' me apsolution—Aw'm ready t' say yes whenever 'e arsks me 'and—an' Aw c'n go to th' altar as unstained as you were on yer weddin' night.

EMILIA: [*Seeing* BIANCA *in a new light.*] So—you're after goin' to the priest regular? [*Impressed.*] That's a lot of money.

BIANCA: Bleedin'-right.

DESDEMONA: [*Crestfallen.*] Oh, Bianca—oh, surely you're—you're not the type that wants to get married? [*Depressed,* DESDEMONA *goes and pours herself another mug of wine.*]

BIANCA: Wot's wrong wif that? Aw'm still young, an' Aw've got a tidy sum all saved up fer a dowry. An' m'lord Cassio's only got t'arsk fer a transfer to th' garrison 'ere; we'd make a bleedin'-jolly life of it, Aw c'n tell you. Aw'd get us a cottage by th' sea, wif winder-boxes an' all them kinds of fings, an' 'e could go to th' tipple'ouse as much as 'e likes, wifout me sayin' nay. An' then—then Aw'd be bearin' 'im sons so's to make 'im proud—

EMILIA: [*Triumphantly.*] There! There's your new woman, m'lady! Free! Does for herself!

BIANCA: Why, that "new woman" kind o' fing's all hog-wash

[EMILIA *nods her head in agreement.*]

BIANCA: [*Cont'd.*] All women want t'get a smug, it's wot we're made for, ain't it? We may pretend differnt, but inside every born one o' us want smugs an' babies, smugs wot are man enow t' keep us in our place.

DESDEMONA: [*Quietly into her wine.*] I don't think I can stand it...

BIANCA: 'Scusin' my cheek, but you're a lucky lady, an' you don't even know it. Your 'ubby might be wot you call a bit doo-lolly-tap-tap up 'ere—[*Bianca taps her head.*]—but th' maritle knot's tied good 'n' strong. Every time Aw 'ear—[*Dreamily.*] " Til deaf do us part"—Aw starts t, snurfle. Aw can't 'elp it. If only Cassio would say them words an' make me th' 'appiest o'—

EMILIA: —And what makes you think m'lord Cassio—who's Venetian born, an' wears silk next to his skin, not none of your Cyprus scum, is goin' to be marryin' a tried-on strumpet?

BIANCA: 'Coz a gen'l' men don't lie to a bird—Aw should soddin'-well know where ofs Aw speak. Besides, m'lord Cassio gi' me a "token o' 'is es-teem"—

EMILIA: Hmmpf! And I'm after supposin' you gave him the same, as you've given tokens of esteem to all your customers—a scurvy clap—that's your token.

[DESDEMONA *becomes curious.*]

DESDEMONA: —Hush, Mealy. [*To* BIANCA.] Never mind her, Bianca—I believe you. What type of token did Cassio give?

BIANCA: [*As enthused as a teenage girl.*] It's a real flashy bit o' goods. It's a muckenger so swank Aw don't dare blow me beak in it. [*Confidentially.*] So Aw carry it down in me knockers an' next to me 'eart.

DESDEMONA: [*Lost.*]—A swank...muck...

BIANCA: —Wot Aw mean is, it ain't yer typic sneezer. [BIANCA *gropes into her bodice, and tenderly takes out an embroidered handkerchief, proudly.*] 'Ere it is, now.

DESDEMONA: [*Starting.*]—Why— [DESDEMONA *looks carefully, then in relief.*] Oh, thank God, Bianca, you've found it. I'm saved. [DESDEMONA *stops.*] But what—whatever are you doing with my handkerchief

EMILIA: [*To herself.*] Oh, Jesus, he gave it to Cassio!

BIANCA: [*Blank.*] Your handkerchief? Yours?! [*Dangerously.*] What's Cassio doin' wi' your hand-ker-chief?

DESDEMONA: That's precisely what I want to find out—Emilia—

BIANCA: [*Fierce.*]—Aw bet. So—you was goin' t' 'elp me out once a week fer Cassio? [*Advancing.*] You cheatin' hussy—Aw'll pop yer peepers out—

[BIANCA *lunges for* DESDEMONA; EMILIA *runs.*]

EMILIA: —She's got a knife!—

DESDEMONA: —Listen, Bianca—

BIANCA: When Aw'm gulled by a woman, she don't live to do it twice—

DESDEMONA: —Bianca, I swear!—

[BIANCA *sees the hoof-pick and picks it up, slowly advancing on* DESDEMONA *who backs away towards the clothesline.*]

BIANCA: —Aw'll carve you up into cag-meat an' feed you to the pigs—Aw'll gag yer puddings out yer gob, you'll choke so hard—

DESDEMONA: —I never!—

[BIANCA *swipes at* DESDEMONA *with the pick; the two clench each other; breaking away,* DESDEMONA *falls, and picks up a wine bottle in defense.*]

BIANCA: Yer gonna snuff it, m'lady—so say yer prayers, yew goggle-eyed scab o' a WHORE.

[DESDEMONA *ducks behind the hanging clothes, with* BIANCA *following. We hear a scuffle, grunts and screams.* EMILIA *runs for the palace door, calling.*]

EMILIA: —GUARD!—GUARD—!! [EMILIA *flings the door open. Then she realizes she can't call the guard, and quickly closes the door behind her, turning to face the room with grim desperation, Softly.*] Jesus.

BIANCA: [*Off.*] —BLOODY!—

DESDEMONA: [*Off.*] —MEALY!!

EMILIA: [EMILIA *runs away from the door, taking out her crucifix.*] Oh, Jesus. Oh, Jesus.

[*And then, we hear a scream, a splash—and the sound of a bottle breaking. Slowly a dark, wet stain spreads on a cloth drying on the clothes-line. For a moment, there is silence.* BIANCA, *looking grim and fierce, strides out from behind the clothes, holding the hoof-pick. She looks at* EMILIA, *who backs away. There is a pause. Then,* DESDEMONA *steps from behind the hanging clothes, holding a broken wine bottle. The torso of her gown is splashed with dark, indelible burgundy. Softly.*]

EMILIA: [*Cont'd.*] O, thank Jesus—

DESDEMONA: Bianca!... Bianca, I never did.

BIANCA: Leave me alone...Aw've lost me chance of a smug! [BIANCA *erupts into weeping, starts to wipe her nose with the handkerchief.*] —There! Take yer filthy linen! Aw wouldn't blow me nose in it—

DESDEMONA: Bianca—I never did. I never did.

BIANCA: Aw loved 'im—

DESDEMONA: —Bianca—

BIANCA: —An' Aw lost 'im—

DESDEMONA: —Bianca—

BIANCA: —An' oh, oh, the cottage by the sea...

DESDEMONA: If it makes a difference, I didn't.

BIANCA: —You gulled yer 'usband an' you gulled me! An' Aw thought we was mates!

[BIANCA *starts to leave;* EMILIA *calls after her.*]

EMILIA: I told you there's no such thing as friendship with ladies—

BIANCA: —You!! Washerdonna!! Shut yer potato-trap! Don't you be so 'igh an' mighty smart!! [*Reaching the door,* BIANCA *opens it, and turns.*] And just where was your Iago last Tuesday night!

[*Triumphantly,* BIANCA *slams the door behind her. A very long pause. Then,* DESDEMONA *tries to sound casual.*]

DESDEMONA: Um, Emilia, dear, just—just where was Iago last Tuesday night?

EMILIA: [*Distressed.*] He ... he said ... he said he was on guard duty ...

[EMILIA *begins to cry.* DESDEMONA *sits beside her, and tentatively puts her arms about* EMILIA. *Then,* DESDEMONA *rocks her maid.*]

SCENE 24

Lights up on DESDEMONA *and* EMILIA, *seated at the table, drinking wine, saying nothing.*

SCENE 25

DESDEMONA *and* EMILIA, *at table, staring ahead into air.* DESDEMONA *wearily looks into her cup, and pours herself and* EMILIA *another cup of wine. They look at each other, nod to each other, and drink together.*

SCENE 26

DESDEMONA *is drinking.* EMILIA *grasps her own mug. Then, in a low voice.*

EMILIA: Do you know which one he was?

DESDEMONA: No ... I don't think so. There were so many that night.

EMILIA: Aye, you were having a proper time at it. Travellin' around the world!! [*Pause.*]

DESDEMONA: There was one man ... [*Hesitating.*] It might have been him.

EMILIA: [*Laughs harshly.*] My husband's a lover of garlic. Was that the man you're remembering?

DESDEMONA: No—it's not that—although ...

EMILIA: Well, what is it you remember!

DESDEMONA: There was one man who ... didn't last very long.

EMILIA: Aye. That's the one.

SCENE 27

The same.

EMILIA: When I was married in the Church, the knot tied beneath the Virgin's nose, I looked forward to the bed with as much joy as any girl after a hard day. And then Iago—well, he was still a lad, with the softness of a boy, and who could tell he'd turn into the man? [EMILIA *pauses to drink.*] But all that girl-nonsense was knocked out of me by the nights. Night followin' night, as sure as the day's work came after. I'd stretch myself out on the bed, you see, waitin' for my good man to come to me and be my mate—as the Priest said he could—but then. But then I saw it didn't matter what had gone on between us—the fights, my crying, a good meal or a cold one. Days could pass without a word between us—and he'd take his fill of me the same. I could have been the bed itself. And so, you see, I vowed not to be there for him. As he'd be lying on me in the dark, I'd picture up my rosary, so real I could kiss the silver. And I'd start at the Blessed Cross itself, while he was somewhere doin' his business above, and I'd say the first wooden bead, and then I'd finger the next bead in my mind, and then onto the next— [EMILIA *stops.*] But I never did make it to the medallion. He'd be all through with me by the time of the third "Hail Mary." [*Pause.*] Does my lady know what I'm saying?

DESDEMONA: I'm not sure. I . . . I don't think it's . . . happened to me like that.

EMILIA: Ah, well, men are making fools of themselves over you. The Ambassador is traipsing from the mainland just to hold onto your skirt; and your husband— [EMILIA *stops herself.*] —Well, maybe it's all different for the likes of you.

[DESDEMONA *says nothing.*]

EMILIA: [*Cont'd.*] And then, maybe not. It's hard to be seeing, when you're young and men watch you when you pass them by, and the talkin' stops between them. But all in all, in time you'll know. Women just don't figure in their heads—not the one who hangs the wash, not Bianca—and not even you, m'lady. That's the hard truth. Men only see each other in their eyes. Only each other. [*Beat.*] And that's why I'm ready to leave the whole pack of them behind and go with you and the Ambassador. Oh, to see my husband's face tomorrow morning! When he finds out that I can get along by myself, with no thanks to his plotting and hatching!—But it's leave him now or be countin' my beads through the years, waitin' for his last breath!

DESDEMONA: [*Quietly.*] Emilia—I'll be honest with you, even if it puts me in risk to do so . . . You're to stay behind tomorrow. I've asked my cousin for my own safe passage. I wish to go alone with Ludovico.

[EMILIA *stands very still.*]

DESDEMONA: [*Cont'd.*] I am in your hands. You can run and tell my husband all— but I don't want to trifle with your feelings and desert you with the first tide. This way, you see, I'm only temporarily leaving you behind. But I promise I'll need your service in Venice as much as tonight. So, you're to follow me when all household matters are in hand, taking with you whatever my husband permits. As a token of my esteem—here— [DESDEMONA *takes off a ring, and gazes at it wistfully.*] I want you to have this. It's a momento given me by Ludovico for—well, never you mind what for. Little did he think it would wind up 'round the finger of an honest woman. [DESDEMONA *gives the ring to* EMILIA.]

EMILIA: This ring is for me? but it's of value, m'lady—

[EMILIA *tries to return it;* DESDEMONA *insists.* EMILIA *makes a decision.*]

EMILIA: [*Cont'd.*] Listen, Miss, you've gone and leveled with me, and I'm after doing the same with you— [EMILIA *blurts.*]—M'lady, don't go to your husband's bed tonight. Lie apart—stay in my chamber.

DESDEMONA: Why? Whatever for? It would raise suspicion.

EMILIA: I'll say you're ill—with woman sickness.

DESDEMONA: But why?

EMILIA: Because ... because ... oh, m'lady, you know how easy it is to be seduced by a husband's soft word, when it's the like of angry words he pours down upon your head—

DESDEMONA: [*Very still.*] Emilia—what have you done?

EMILIA: I took the handkerchief.

DESDEMONA: You took the handkerchief ... I thought you did.

EMILIA: It was to be a joke, you see; my husband put me up to it, as a lark, he said, just to see—

DESDEMONA: [*Very softly*] —Iago—Oh, my sweet Jesus—

EMILIA: And he was laughing about it, ye see, and he was as gay as a boy; he said he'd just ... hide it for a while, all in jest—

DESDEMONA: Oh, no—he ... he must have ... planted it on Cassio—that's why ...

EMILIA: It was just for a lark!

DESDEMONA: Emilia—what has your husband been thinking!

EMILIA: I don't know what he thinks.

DESDEMONA: [DESDEMONA *twists the handkerchief.*] What use is this to me now! If I return it, my husband will say that my lover gave it back to me!!

EMILIA: Miss Desdemona—oh my lady, I'm sure your husband loves you!

DESDEMONA: How do you know that my husband—!

EMILIA: More than the world! He won't harm you none, m'lady.—I've often seen him—

DESDEMONA: —What have you seen?!

EMILIA: I've seen him, sometimes when you walk in the garden, slip behind the arbor just to watch you, unawares ... and at night ... in the corridor ... outside your room—sometimes he just stands there, Miss, when you're asleep—he just stands there—

DESDEMONA: [*Frightened.*] Oh, Jesus—

EMILIA: And once ... I saw ... I came upon him unbeknowin', and he didn't see me, I'm sure—he was in your chamber room—and he gathered up the sheets from your bed, like a body, and ... and he held it to his face, like, like a bouquet, all breathin' it in— [*The two women pause: they both realize Othello's been smelling the sheets for traces of a lover.*]

DESDEMONA: That isn't love. It isn't love. [*Beat.*] Why didn't you tell me this before?

EMILIA: [*Carefully.*] I always thought it was not my place.

[*The two women do not speak for a moment.* EMILIA *looks towards the palace door.*]

EMILIA: [*Cont'd.*] Well, what are we to be doin' now?

DESDEMONA: We have to make it to the morning. You'd better come with me—it's not safe for you, either.

[EMILIA *says nothing.*]

DESDEMONA: [*Cont'd.*] We'll have to leave all behind. It's not safe to pack. [DESDEMONA *thinks, carefully.*] Now listen, carefully, Emilia. I'll go to my own chamber tonight. You're to wait up for my husband's return—tell him I'm ill and I've taken to my own bed. He's not to disturb me, I'm not well. I'll turn in before he comes, and I'll...pretend to sleep if he should come to me. [*Pause.*] Surely he'll not...harm a sleeping woman.

EMILIA: I'll do it.

DESDEMONA: Good. I'd better go to bed. [DESDEMONA *starts towards the palace door and stops.*]

EMILIA: Would you like me to brush your hair tonight? A hundred strokes?

DESDEMONA: Oh, yes, please, Emilia...

SCENE 28

EMILIA *brushes* DESDEMONA's *hair.* DESDEMONA *leans back, tense, listening to the off-stage palace.*

EMILIA: Now, then— [EMILIA *starts.*] One, two, three, four, five, six—

SCENE 29

The same.

EMILIA: Forty-five, forty-six, forty-seven—

SCENE 30

Desdesmona and EMILIA. EMILIA *reaches the hundredth stroke.*

EMILIA: Ninety-seven...ninety-eight...ninety-nine... [*They freeze. Blackout.*]

END

BIOGRAPHICAL INFORMATION ON PLAYWRIGHTS AND SCHOLARS

BOBBI AUSUBEL (essay on Gloria Joyce Dickler) teaches acting at the Boston Conservatory, where she was formerly Chair of the Theatre Department. In the late 1960s, she was co-founder and co-director of Caravan Theatre in Cambridge, Massachusetts, one of the first feminist theatres in the USA. In 1968 she co-authored the play *How to Make a Woman*; post-performance discussions during its four-year run led to the formation of consciousness raising groups. Caravan produced new plays for thirteen years. With Union Sister, Ms. Ausubel directed *Silkwood*, a drama about unions which toured two hundred cities. In the 1990s, she has been founding artistic director of Ark Theatre's Up From Silence. This non-profit educational theatre presents performances, workshops, and training seminars for health professionals, students, parents, teachers, therapists, recovery groups, children, and the general public on topics such as sexual abuse of children. Ms. Ausubel also teaches inner child classes.

JANE CHAMBERS (*The Quintessential Image*) paved the way for lesbian playwrights in the USA. Her plays, which have been produced Off-Broadway, in regional and community theatres in the USA and abroad, and on television, include *A Late Snow*, *The Common Garden Variety*, *Last Summer at Bluefish Cove*, *My Blue Heaven*, *Kudzu*, and *The Eye of the Gull*. She has published two novels, *Burning* (Jove Press, 1978, JH Press, 1983, TNT Classics, 1995) and *Chasing Jason* (JH Press, 1987), and a book of poetry, *Warrior at Rest* (JH Press). She has been the recipient of the Connecticut Educational Television Award (1971, *Christ in a Treehouse*), a Eugene O'Neill fellowship (1972, *Tales of the Revolution and other American Fables*), a National Writers Guild Award (1973, "Search for Tomorrow," CBS), the New York Dramalogue Critics Circle Award, the Villager Theatre Award, the Alliance for Lesbian and Gay Artists Media Award, the Robby Award, the Oscar Wilde Award, the Los Angeles Drama Critic's Circle Award and a Proclamation from Los Angeles for Outstanding Theater (1980–83, *Last Summer at Bluefish Cove*), Dramalogue Award, Betty Award, (1987, *Kudzu*, and 1985, *The Quintessential Image*), and the Fund for Human Dignity Award (1982). She died of a brain tumor in 1983. The Women in Theatre Program created the Jane Chambers Playwriting Award to encourage women writing plays that present women's experience and offer a majority of principal roles for women.

ROSEMARY KEEFE CURB (editor) is professor and head of English at Southwest Missouri State University and was founding director of women's studies at Rollins College. She has beem awarded an NDEA fellowship for graduate study, three NEH grants, and a Fulbright senior lectureship in American studies at Canterbury University, New Zealand. Dr. Curb has served as co-chair of the Lesbian/Gay Caucus of the Modern Language Association, chair of the Lesbian Caucus of the National Women's Studies Association, and coordinator of the Southeast Women's Studies Association. She is on the editorial boards for *Belles Lettres* and *The Lesbian Review of Books*. She has published biographical essays in reference books on Alice Childress, Clare Coss, and Adrienne Kennedy. She has published articles in books: *Intersecting Boundaries: The Theatre of Adrienne Kennedy*; *Radical Revisions: Lesbian Texts and Contexts*; *Making a Spectacle: Feminist Essays on Contemporary Women's Theatre*; *Women in American Theatre*; and in journals: *Hypatia: A Journal of Feminist Philosophy*; *Theatre Journal*; *MELUS*; *Chrysalis*; etc. With Nancy Manahan she co-edited *Lesbian Nuns: Breaking Silence* (1985).

TISH DACE (essay on Susan Miller) is professor of English at the University of Massachusetts at Dartmouth and the New York critic for *Plays International*. Dr. Dace has published extensively on such playwrights as Marsha Norman, Paula Vogel, Beth Henley, Harvey Fierstein, Lanford Wilson, Martin Sherman, Amiri Baraka, Wendy Kesselman, Charles Ludlam, John Arden, Margaretta D'Arcy, Arnold Wesker, and Bernard Kops. Cambridge University Press has just published her latest book, *Langston Hughes: The Contemporary Reviews*. Her work also has appeared in scholarly volumes from such publishers as St. Martin's Press, St. James Press, Gale Research, and Garland, as well as in the *Village Voice*, *London Times*, *New York Times*, *American Theatre*, *Back Stage*, *Playbill*, *Ms.*, etc. A New York theatre critic for over twenty years, she serves as chair of the American Theatre Wing Design Awards, on the Executive Committee of the American Theatre Critics Association, and as Vice President of the ATCA Foundation.

NANCY DEAN (essay on Jane Chambers) is former professor of English at Hunter College where she specialized in Chaucer and medieval literature and taught creative writing and women's studies. Dr. Dean has published articles in medieval studies and a book on writing, *In the Mind of the Writer*, and co-edited and introduced with Myra Stark a collection of feminist short stories, *In the Looking Glass*. In 1983 she began to write plays. Her first play, *Larks and Owls*, was a finalist in Theatre Rhinoceros national contest. She became a playwright in residence for Actors Alliance, directed by Melanie Sutherland, who presented readings of *Gloria's Visit* and *Wrath and Avocadoes* and produced *Which Marriage?* as well as her translation and update of Moliere's *Misanthrope*. *Blood and Water* and *Burning Bridges* were produced in New York City at the Madison Avenue Theatre. In 1995, her comedy *Upstairs? In the Afternoon?* was produced at Play Quest Company in New York City. She is a member of the Women Playwrights Collective and the Dramatists Guild and was the first recipient of the Nancy Dean Award, created in her honor by a lesbian playwrights' collective, Sisters on Stage.

JANIS ASTOR DEL VALLE (*I'll Be Home Para La Navidad*), Bronx-born, Puerto-Rican lesbian actor, writer, producer, is co-founder of Sisters on Stage and works as an actor/teacher for the NYU Creative Arts Team. She is a member of Actors Equity Association. She was a member of the Joseph Papp Public Theatre's Latino Writers Lab and a Van Lier Playwriting Fellow. Her plays have been produced in New York at Primary Stages, the Nuyorican Poets' Cafe, Perry Street Theatre, 42nd Street Collective, Hamlet of Bank Street, and Theatre on 3, as well as in Washington, DC, at the University of DC. In 1994, her play *Where the Senoritas Are* was co-winner in the Mixed Blood

Theatre's National Playwriting Contest. Her work appears in *Torch to the Heart: Anthology of Lesbian Art and Drama* (Lavender Crystal Press). Her other works include: *The Androgynous Zone, Mother to Daughter, Sisters, Gyn, El bloque de la escritora, Trans Plantations: Straight and Other Jackets Para Mi, Fuschia*, and *Mi Casa Es Tu Casa*.

GLORIA JOYCE DICKLER (*The Postcard*) was the founder and Artistic Director of Common Stage Theatre in Woodstock, New York, a theatre collective founded to produce plays by and about women, and the Director of Acting Out Repertory, Kingston, New York. Her plays include *Psyche's Waltz, Moonflowers, No Roses*, and *Community*. She was chosen playwright and director in residence for the Pima Arts Council in Tucson, Arizona. She currently lives in Los Angeles and writes screenplays.

JILL DOLAN (essay on Paula Vogel) is an executive officer of the Ph.D. Program in Theatre at the City University of New York Graduate Center. She is the author of *The Feminist Spectator as Critic* and *Presence and Desire: Essays on Gender, Sexuality, Performance* (both University of Michigan Press). Dr. Dolan has published numerous articles on feminist theatre theory and gay and lesbian performance in *The Politics of Theatre and Drama, Performing Feminisms, Making a Spectacle: Feminist Essays on Contemporary Women's Theatre, Critical Theory and Performance*, and in *Women and Performance Journal, Modern Drama, Theatre Journal, Theatre Topics, Kenyon Review*, and elsewhere. A past-president of the Women and Theatre Program, she is currently President of the Association for Theatre in Higher Education.

MARIA IRENE FORNES (*Springtime*) is recipient of seven Obie awards, an NEA Distinguished Arts Award, a Rockefeller Grant, a Guggenheim Fellowship, a Lila Wallace Readers Digest Literary Award, and the Lifetime Achievement Award from the Association for Theatre in Higher Education. She has produced dozens of plays off-Broadway, including *Promenade, The Successful Life of 3, Fefu and Her Friends, Eyes on the Harem, The Conduct of Life, Abingdon Square*, and others. Ms. Fornes conducts playwriting workshops in theatres and universities throughout the USA and abroad and has directed plays by Calderon, Ibsen, Chekhov, and other contemporary playwrights.

CAROLYN GAGE (Book and Lyrics for *The Amazon All-Stars*) is a lesbian-feminist playwright and activist. Her plays include *The Second Coming of Joan of Arc, The Roar of Silence, Battered on Broadway, The Anastasia Trials in the Court of Women, Sappho in Love, Ugly Ducklings, Artemesia and Hildegarde, The Last Reading of Charlotte Cushman*, etc. Her awards and honors include the Oregon Playwrights Award, the Walden Writer's Fellowship from Lewis and Clark College, and the Individual Artist Grant from the Oregon Arts Commission. A member of the Dramatists Guild, Gage has toured nationally in her one-woman show. She is the author of *Take Stage!*, the first manual for lesbian theatre production (Scarecrow Press, 1996). Her collection of plays, *The Second Coming of Joan of Arc and Other Plays*, was a national finalist for the 1995 Lambda Literary Award in drama.

NANCY HELLNER (essay on Megan Terry) teaches English and Women and Film at Mesa Community College, Mesa, Arizona. She has a B.A. and an M.S. from Kearney State College in Nebraska and a Ph.D. from Arizona State University, where she wrote a doctoral thesis on lesbian comedy. Dr. Hellner is co-editor of *Gay and Lesbian American Plays: An Annotated Bibliography*. Currently she is reviewing books for various publications and working on a book about American lesbian playwrights.

SHIRLENE HOLMES (*A Lady and a Woman*), playwright and actor, is associate professor of communication at Georgia State University. She holds an M.F.A. and a Ph.D. from Southern Illinois University. In 1991, *Onstage Atlanta* nominated her best actress for her portrayal of Lena Younger in *A Raisin in the Sun*. In addition to numerous appreciation awards at Georgia State, Southern Illinois, and City University of New York, in 1992, Dr. Holmes was given the Barbara Jordan/W.E.B. DuBois Faculty Award by African-American Student Services and Programs at Georgia State. In 1992, *A Lady and a Woman* was a finalist for the Jane Chambers Award. In 1994, her play *ELLE* was given the Spyglass Award for Best Staged reading and nominated for Best New Play by Theatre Conspiracy in Washington, DC. Her other plays include *Walking Out, Living in the Shadow, 5th Floor, Cousins, In Women's Rooms, Family Tree, Current Events, Peaches, Lesbian Quarrel, Silences, No Detour Ahead, Brown in Black and White*, and *Oh Slavery Days*.

ASSUNTA KENT (essay on Maria Irene Fornes) teaches theatre at the University of Southern Maine, edits the Book Review section of *New England Theatre Journal*, and has forthcoming *Maria Irene Fornes and Her Critics*. Dr. Kent has published reviews and articles in *Theatre Topics, Theatre Studies, Theatre Insight, Theatre Journal*, and *Journal of Dramatic Theory and Criticism*. She also has an essay in *Teaching Theatre As If Our Future Depended On It*. Dr. Kent's production work includes direction, dramaturgy, script adaptation, oral interpretation, creative drama, and advocacy theatre. She regularly appears on "Power and Steele on Theatre," a criticism program televised in the Southern Maine region.

JOAN LIPKIN (*Small Domestic Acts*) is artistic director of That Uppity Theatre Company in St. Louis, where she founded the Alternate Currents/Direct Currents Series, Women Centerstage!, and After Rodney, a poetry performance group of white women and women of color. A lecturer in the Performing Arts Department at Washington University, Lipkin was an official delegate from the United States at the Third International Women Playwrights Conference in and serves on the Theatre Review Panel for the Missouri Arts Council. Her plays include *Some of My Best Friends Are, He's Having Her Baby* (with Tom Clear), *Love & Work Other Four-Letter Words, Will the Real Foster Parent Please Stand Up?, One Sunday Morning*, and *Stories from Generation X (Y, Z...)*. Her work is also included in *Upstaging Big Daddy: Directing Theater as if Race and Gender Matter, Mythic Women/Real Women: Plays and Performance Pieces by Women, Monologues for Women by Women*, and *Nice Jewish Girls: Growing Up in America* and the forthcoming *Sexuality in Performance, Literature, and Gender* and *Interviews with International Women Playwrights*.

SUSAN MILLER (*Nasty Rumors and Final Remarks*), playwright, is the recipient of two Obie Awards, the Susan Smith Blackburn Prize, two NEA awards, and a Rockefeller grant. Her plays include *My Left Breast; It's Our Town, Too; Cross Country; Flux; Confessions of a Female Disorder; For Dear Life;* and *Arts and Leisure.* Her work appears in Applause Books' *The Best American Short Plays 1992–1993* and *The Best American Short Plays 1993–94*, and Penguin's *Actors Book of Lesbian and Gay Plays*, among others. Her plays have been produced by Actor's Theatre of Louisville, the New York Shakespeare Festival, the Mark Taper Forum, Second Stage, Naked Angels, Home, and Watermark. A member of PEN and the Dramatists Guild and a Yaddo Fellow, she is a part time faculty member of NYU's Dramatic Writing Program and serves as a Director of the Legacy Project, a writing workshop at The Public Theatre for people with life-threatening illness.

MADONNE M. MINER (essay on Patricia Montley) is associate professor of English and Women's Studies at the University of Wyoming. She is the author of *Unsatiable Appetites: Twentieth-Century American Women's Bestsellers* and of various articles on women as writers and readers. Recent articles have focused on the childbirth episode of "Murphy Brown," and on feminist reactions to contemporary fiction by men.

PATRICIA MONTLEY (*Sisters*), a Dramatists Guild member and Director of Theatre at Chatham College, Pittsburgh, has had over eighty productions of her works. She has received grants from the Pennsylvania Council on the Arts and the Shubert Foundation and was an invited participant in a Warner Brothers Writers Workshop. Her earliest plays—feminist satires *Bible Herstory* and *Not So Grim Fairy Tales*—are published by Samuel French. *Sisters* was given a professional reading at Center Stage, Baltimore, and subsequently won or placed in several contests and received six full productions. Dr. Montley's other works include adaptations of classics—*The Trojan Women, Lysistrata, Sotoba Komachi*—and of Julia O'Faolain's novel *Women in the Wall*, as well as an original musical, *Rosvitha's Review*, and an epic-theatre piece, *Mother Jones.* Her most recent work, *Dancing the God*, was produced at the Nebraska Repertory Theatre in 1994.

BONNIE J. MORRIS (essay on Carolyn Gage) teaches in the women's studies program at George Washington University and has also taught at Harvard Divinity School, St. Lawrence University, and on a 100-day global voyage for the University of Pittsburgh's "Semester At Sea" program. Dr. Morris is a senior associate at the Center for Women and Policy Studies and a five-year staff member of the Michigan Womyn's Music Festival. Her original one-woman plays include *Passing* and *Revenge of the Women's Studies Professor*. Performances include main stages at the National Women's Music Festival, the Gulf Coast Women's Festival, the East Coast Lesbian Festival, the Gay, Lesbian and Straight Teachers' Network Conference [GLSTN], and universities throughout the United States. Dr. Morris has contributed essays to more than thirty anthologies, journals, and feminist periodicals, most recently serving as staff writer for *HOT WIRE: The Journal of Women's Music and Culture.*

VIVIAN PATRAKA (essay on Joan Schenkar) is professor of English at Bowling Green State University. Dr. Patraka has published in journals such as *Theatre Journal, Modern Drama, Discourse, The Drama Review, Women & Performance, The Michigan Quarterly Review*, and *The Kenyon Review*. Her feminist work has been included in the books *Making a Spectacle: Feminist Essays on Contemporary Women's Theatre* (Michigan), *Performing Feminisms: The Critical Act* (Johns Hopkins), and *Acting Oct: Feminist Performances* (Michigan). Her book, entitled *Spectacular Suffering: Theatrical Representations of the Holocaust and Fascism*, will be published by Indiana University Press.

TONI PRESS (essay on Canyon Sam) was one of twelve playwrights from a field of fourteen hundred selected to participate in the 1995 Eugene O'Neill National Playwrights Conference, which presented her play, *Stand*. A recipient of a California Arts Council Playwright's Fellowships in 1991, she has written ten full-length and four one-act plays which have been produced throughout the United States. Ms. Press is a member of ThroughLine, a playwrights group in San Francisco. She received a B.A. in Playwrighting from UCLA in 1974 and an M.A. in Theatre and Film from the University of Connecticut in 1976.

DOLORES PRIDA (essay on Janis Astor del Valle) is a Cuban-American playwright, author of *Beautiful Señoritas & Other Plays*, published by Arte Publico Press-University of Houston. She was a Distinguished Visiting Professor of Latino Literature at Dartmouth College in the Spring and Fall of 1995. She taught playwriting as part of the Latino Writers Lab at the Joseph Papp Public Theatre and also teaches playwriting techniques elsewhere.

VICTORIA RUE (essay on Canyon Sam) feminist theologian, theatre director, and teacher, holds a Ph.D. from the graduate Theological Union, Berkeley, California, in theology and the arts. Her recently performed plays include *Ruffled Irises: Women Struggling with Cancer* (formerly known as *Cancerbodies*), *The Landscape of My Body*, and *Ecstasy in the Every Day*. Dr. Rue is Director for the Institute for Religion and the Arts in Berkeley.

CANYON SAM (*The Dissident*) is a writer, performance artist, and activist based in San Francisco. Her one-woman show, *The Dissident*, toured the US and Canada, including engagements at the Walker Art Center, Cleveland Performance Art Festival, Women in View, Vancouver, National Women's Theater Festival, Solo Mio Festival, and the National Gay/Lesbian March on Washington, 1993. Her fiction appears in *New Lesbian Writing*, the bestseller *Lesbian Love Stories*, *The Seattle Review*, and elsewhere. Since the mid-1980s, she has lived, traveled, and worked extensively in Central Asia, where she gained inspiration for her current book of creative non-fiction entitled, *One Hundred Voices of Tara: Tibetan Women Speak*. Her plays include *Taxi Karma* (Callboard, September 1992), which won the HBO New Writers Project, Honorable Mention, 1994; and *All That Shattered* (Lesbian Word: State of the Art, 1995). She has won numerous arts grants, including a National Endowment for the Arts scholarship at the age of eighteen.

JUDY SCHAVRIEN (essay on Canyon Sam) is core faculty in Women's Spirituality at California Institute of Integral Studies, where she teaches such courses as Women and Buddhism, Writing Lesbian Poetry, and Gay and Lesbian Spirituality: the Erotic and the Mystical. She holds the M.F.C.C. and Ph.D. degrees. Her translations and poetry are published by New Rivers Press in *What Rhymes with Cancer?* and in the prize-winning anthology *New Lesbian Writing*. Dr. Schavrien recently won the international *Abiko Quarterly* prize for her essay on James Joyce's *Finnegan's Wake*: "All Moodmoulded Marryvoising History—A New and Perennial Reality." She has won national and international prizes for her poems, which are collected in the manuscript *Ho, Big Mama Artemis with your 10,000 Breasts!* As a psychotherapist, she serves on the National Board of the Association for Humanistic Psychology.

JOAN SCHENKAR (*The Lodger*) is the recipient of more than thirty-five grants, fellowships, and awards for playwrighting, including seven NEA grants. She has worked as playwright-in-residence with such experimental companies as Chaikin's Winter Project, the Polish Laboratory Theatre, and the Minnesota Opera New Music Ensemble. Her plays include *Signs of Life, Cabin Fever* (nominated for an Obie in 1980), *The Last of Hitler, Fulfilling Koch's Postulate, Fire in the Future, Family Pride in the 50's, Between the Acts, Bucks and Does, Mr. Monster, The Universal Wolf, Big Bad Brain,* and *the Viennese Oyster*. Her plays have been produced at such places as American Place Theatre, Public Theatre, Theatre of the Open Eye, WPA Theatre, St. Clement's, La Mama Hollywood, Studio 17, HOME, New Dramatists, Theatre for the New City, Horizons Theatre; in London at King's Head and the Gate; and at colleges, universities, and theatre festivals in North America and Western Europe. Ms. Schenkar is an alumna of New Dramatists and a current member of PEN, Societe des auteurs et compositeurs dramatiques, the Dramatists Guild, and The Women's Project.

WILLA J. TAYLOR (essay on Shirlene Holmes), Education Director at Lincoln Center since 1992, sits on the Lincoln Center Education Council and the New York Art-in-Education Roundtable. She established the Allan Lee Hughes Fellows Program for Arena Stage in Washington, DC; designed the arts education program for the New Victory Theater in New York City; and is designing curriculum-based programs for grades 5 through 12. Ms. Taylor began her career as an actor at sixteen, and freelanced as production coordinator, stage manager, and sound designer for theatre, opera, radio, and TV. She holds an M.F.A. in film from American University. She taught literature at Harvey Milk School and has given guest lectures at many colleges and universities. For twelve years she served as Russian-Arabic linguist in the Navy. She produced USO shows in Greece and ran a radio station in Turkey. She produced the "Profiles in Black" series for radio; "DARK EYES: Visions of Black Women" series for a film festival; and "A Woman's Place" series for cable. She was associate producer for "Sleeping Beauty." On Broadway she produced Ian McKellen's one-man show *A Knight Out* and Anna Deveare Smith's one woman show *Twilight L.A.* She is on the Board of the National Black Lesbian and Gay Leadership Forum and facilitates the People of Color Institute for the National Gay and Lesbian Task Force.

MEGAN TERRY (*Willa Willie Bill's Dope Garden*) has received world wide production of her more than sixty published plays, which are available from the Omaha Magic Theatre, Samuel French, and Broadway Play Publishing. She has won major playwrighting grants and served on public and private granting committees. Her documentary play *Approaching Simone* won the Obie Award for Best Play, 1970. Her book of theatre photographs, *Right Brain Vacation Photos*, for which she wrote the text with Jo Ann Schmidman and Sora Kimberlain, was nominated for the Bernard Hewitt Theatre Research Award. A member of PEN, Ms. Terry was recently elected to lifetime membership in the College of Fellows of the American Theatre. At present she is Literary Manager and tours internationally with the Omaha Magic Theatre as a musician and performer. Her plays include *Babes in the Bighouse*, *Viet Rock*, *Breakfast Serial*, *Objective Love*, *Calm Down Mother*, *Ex-Miss Copper Queen on a Set of Pills*, *Sanibel and Captiva*, *Mollie Bailey's Traveling Family Circus: Featuring Scenes from the Life of Mother Jones*, *American King's English for Queens*, *Body Leaks* (written with Schmidman and Kimberlain), *Hothouse*, and many others.

PAULA VOGEL (*Desdemona*), playwright, teaches playwriting in the M.F.A. creative writing program at Brown University. In 1992, her play *The Baltimore Waltz*, which has had more than sixty productions, won the Obie for Best Play. It and *Hot 'N' Throbbing*, produced in 1994 at the American Repertory Theatre in New York and Harrogate Theatre in London, were nominated for the Pulitzer Prize. She has been awarded NEA Fellowships, a Bunting Fellowship, a PEW/TCG Senior Artist Fellowship, a Guggenheim Fellowship, and a nomination for the Susan Smith Blackburn Award. Her other plays include *The Oldest Profession*, *And Baby Makes Seven*, and *The Mineola Twins*. A collection of five of her plays is being published by TCG simultaneously with this collection.

ANNETTE WANNAMAKER (essay on Joan Schenkar) is a doctoral candidate in the Bowling Green State University English Department. She currently is completing her dissertation titled "Twentieth Century Revisions of *Antigone*: Searches for Postmodern Justice."

STACY WOLF (essay on Joan Lipkin) is assistant professor in the School of Theatre at Florida State University. She has published articles on theatre audiences in *The Journal of Dramatic Theory and Criticism*, *New Theatre Quarterly*, and *Theatre Research International*, and is working on a book about lesbians and musical theatre. She served on the board of the Women and Theatre Program of ATHE and is also a member of the Mickee Faust Club.

SELECTED RECENT ANTHOLOGIES OF WOMEN'S AND LESBIAN/GAY PLAYS (MOSTLY FROM USA)

Allen, Claudia. 1993. *She's Always Liked the Girls the Best* (includes *Roomers, Rain check, Hannah Free,* and *Movie Queens*). Chicago: Third Side Press.

Barlow, Judith E., ed. 1994. *Plays by American Women 1930–1960. (The Women* by Clare Boothe, *The Little Foxes* by Lillian Hellman, *It's Morning* by Shirley Graham, *The Mother of Us All* by Gertrude Stein, *Goodbye, My Fancy* by Fay Kanin, *In the Summer House* by Jane Bowles, *Trouble in Mind* by Alice Childress, *Can You Hear Their Voices?* by Hallie Flanagan & Margaret Ellen Clifford.) New York: Applause Books.

Barnes, Noreen C. and Nichola Deutsch, eds. 1992. *Tough Acts to Follow: One-Act Plays on the Gay/Lesbian Experience* (includes *One Fool* by Terry Baum, *Bert & Jessie* by Robyn Barr Gorman, *The Scent of Tulips* by Marty Kingsbury, *Love Slapped Me Boom Upside My Head* by Claire Olivia Moed, and *What Do You See?* by Ana Maria Simo). San Francisco: Alamo Square Press.

Butler, Audrey. 1990. *Radical Perversions: Two Dyke Plays.* Toronto: Women's Press.

Chavez, Denise, ed. 1992. *Shattering the Myth: Plays by Hispanic Women. (Shadow of a Man* by Cherrie Moraga, *Miriam's Flowers* by Migdalia Cruz, *Gleaning/Rebusca* by Caridad Svich, *Simply Maria or The American Dream* by Josefina Lopez, *My Visits with MGA* by Edit Villarreal, and *A Dream of Canaries* by Diana Saenz.) Houston: Arte Publico Press.

Davis, Jill, ed. 1987. *Lesbian Plays. (Any Woman Can* by Jill Posener, *Chiaroscuro* by Jackie Kay, *The Rug of Identity* by Jill W. Fleming, and *Double Vision* by The Women's Theatre Group.) London: Methuen.

_____. 1989. *Lesbian Plays II. (Coming Soon* by Debby Klein, *Julie* by Catherine Kilcoyne, *Supporting Roles* by Sandra Freeman, *The Housetrample* by Sue Frumin, *Cinderella, The Real True Story* by Cheryl Moch.) London: Methuen.

Dreher, Sarah. 1988. *Lesbian Stages* (includes *Alumnae News: The Doris Day Years; Base Camp; Backward, Turn Backward; The Brooding Sky; Hollandia '45*). Norwich VT: New Victoria Publications.

Gage, Carolyn. 1994. *The Second Coming of Joan of Arc and Other Plays. (The Roar of Silence Trilogy, Calamity Jane Sends a Message to Her Daughter, Cookin' with Typhoid Mary.)* Santa Cruz: Herbooks.

Helbing, Terry, ed. 1993. *Gay and Lesbian Plays Today* (includes *Belle Reprieve* by Bette Bourne, Peggy Shaw, Paul Shaw, and Lois Weaver, *Eye of the Gull* by Jane Chambers; and *One Tit, a Dyke, & Gin!* by Pennell Somsen). Portsmouth, NH: Heinemann Educational Books.

Lamont, Rosette C., ed. 1993. *Women on the Verge: Seven Avant Garde Plays. (Occupational Hazard* by Rosalyn Drexler, *Us* by Karen Malpede, *What of the Nights?* by Maria Irene Fornes, *Birth and After Birth* by Tina Howe, *Letters to a Student Revolutionary* by Elizabeth Wong, *The Death of the Last Black Man in the Whole Entire World* by Suzan-Lori Parks, and *The Universal Wolf* by Joan Schenkar.) New York: Applause Books.

Mahone, Sydne, ed. 1994. *Moon Marked and Touched by the Sun: Plays by African-American Women*. (*White Chocolate for my Father* by Laurie Carlos, *Cage Rhythm* by Kia Corthron, *X* by Thulani Davis, *WOMBmanWARs* by Judith Alexa Jackson, *The Dramatic Circle* by Adrienne Kennedy, *Sally's Rape* by Robbie McCauley, *The Death of the Last Black Man in the Whole Entire World* by Suzan-Lori Parks, *The Mojo and the Sayso* by Aishah Rahman, from *The Resurrection of the Daughter: Liliane* by Ntosake Shange, from *Fires in the Mirror* by Anna Deveare Smith, *Live and in Color!* by Danitra Vance.) New York: Theatre Communications Group.

McDermott, Kate, ed. 1985. *Places, Please! The First Anthology of Lesbian Plays*. (*Dos Lesbos* by Terry Baum and Carolyn Myers, *Immediate Family* by Terry Baum, *8x10 Glossy* and *Ruby Christmas* by Sarah Dreher, *Going Up* by Julia Willis, *Out of Bounds* by Mariah Burton Nelson, and *Soup* by Ellen Gruber Garvey.) Iowa City: Aunt Lute Book Company.

Miles, Julia, ed. 1980. *The Women's Project: The American Place Theatre*. (*Acrobatics* by Joyce Aaron & Luna Tarlo, *In the Midnight Hour* by Kathleen Collins, *Property* by Penelope Gilliat, *Letters Home* by Rose Leiman Goldemberg, *Killings on the Last Line* by Lavonne Mueller, *Separate Ceremonies* by Phyllis Purscell, and *Signs of Life* by Joan Schenkar.) New York: Performing Arts Journal Publications.

_____. 1982. *The Women's Project 2: The American Place Theatre*. (*The Brothers* by Kathleen Collins, *Little Victories* by Lavonne Mueller, *Territorial Rites* by Carol K. Mack, *Heart of a Dog* by Terry Galloway, and *Candy & Shelley Go to the Desert* by Paula Cizmar.) New York: Performing Arts Journal Publications.

_____. 1989. *WOMENSWORK: 5 Plays from the Women's Project*. (*Ma Rose* by Cassandra Medley, *Five in the Killing Zone* by Lavonne Mueller, *Etta Jenks* by Marlane Meyer, *Abigdon Square* by Maria Irene Fornes, and *Mill Fire* by Sally Nemeth.) New York: Applause Books.

Perkins, Kathy A. 1989. *Black Female Playwrights: An Anthology of Plays before 1950* (many short plays by Georgia Douglas Johnson, Mary P. Burrill, Zora Neale Hurston, Eulalie Spence, May Miller, Marita Bonner, Shirley Graham). Bloomington: University of Indiana Press.

Smith, Marisa, ed. 1994. *Women Playwrights: The Best Plays of 1993*. (*Arthur and Leila* by Cherylene Lee, *Christchild* by J. e. Franklin, *Cross-Dressing in the Depression* by Erin Cressida Wilson, *Floating Rhoda and the Glue Man* by Eve Ensler, *My Son Susie* by Cheryl Royce, *Why We Have a Body* by Claire Chafee.) Newbury, VT: A Smith and Kraus Book.

Uno, Roberta, ed. 1993. *Unbroken Thread: An Anthology of Plays by Asian American Women*. (*Paper Angels* by Genny Lim, *The Music Lessons* by Wakako Yamauchi, *Gold Watch* by Momoko Iko, *Tea* by Velina Hasu Houston, *Walls* by Jeannnie Barroga, *Letters to a Student Revolutionary* by Elizabeth Wong.) Amherst: Univ. of Massachusetts Press.

Wilkerson, Margaret, ed. 1986. *9 Plays by Black Women*. (*A Black Woman Speaks* by Beah Richards, excerpt from *Toussaint* by Lorraine Hansberry, *Wedding Band* by Alice Childress, *The Tapestry* by Alexis DeVeaux, *The Brothers* by Kathleen

Collins, *Brown Silk and Magenta Sunsets* by P. J. Gibson, *spell #7* by Ntosake Shange, *Unfinished Women Cry in No Man's Land While a Bird Dies in Gilded Cage* by Aishah Rahman, *Paper Dolls* by Elaine Jackson.) New York: New American Library.

Willis, Julia. 1993. *We Oughta Be in Pictures*... San Francisco: Alamo Square Press.

SELECTED BOOKS IN FEMINIST DRAMA AND PERFORMANCE AND LESBIAN THEORY

Allen, Jeffner. 1986. *Lesbian Philosophy: Explorations*. Palo Alto, CA: Institute for Lesbian Studies.

_____, ed. 1990. *Lesbian Philosophies and Cultures*. Albany: SUNY Press.

Austin, Gayle. 1990. *Feminist Theories for Dramatic Criticism*. Ann Arbor: University of Michigan Press.

Brown-Guillory, Elizabeth, ed. 1988. *Their Place on the Stage: Black Women Playwrights in America*. Westport, CT: Greenwood Press.

Card, Claudia. 1995. *Lesbian Choices*. New York: Columbia University Press.

_____, ed. 1994. *Adventures in Lesbian Philosophy*. Bloomington: Indiana Univ. Press.

Case, Sue-Ellen, ed. 1990. *Performing Feminisms: Feminist Critical Theory and Theatre*. Baltimore: Johns Hopkins University Press.

Chinoy, Helen Crich and Linda Walsh Jenkins, eds. 1987. *Women in American Theatre* (Revised and expanded edition). New York: Theatre Communications Group.

Creekmur, Corey K. and Alexander Doty, eds. 1995. *Out in Culture: Gay, Lesbian, and Queer Essays on Popular Culture*. Durham, NC: Duke University Press.

Cruikshank, Margaret, ed. 1982. *Lesbian Studies: Present and Future*. Old Westbury, NY: The Feminist Press.

Cruikshank, Margaret. 1992. *The Gay and Lesbian Liberation Movement*. New York: Routledge.

de Lauretis, Teresa. 1994. *The Practice of Love: Lesbian Sexuality and Perverse Desire*. Bloomington: Indiana University Press.

Dolan, Jill. 1988. *The Feminist Spectator as Critic*. Ann Arbor: UMI Research Press.

_____. 1993. *Presence and Desire: Essays on Gender, Sexuality, Performance*. Ann Arbor: University of Michigan Press.

Frye, Marilyn. 1983. *The Politics of Reality: Essays in Feminist Theory*. Trumansburg, NY: Crossing Press.

_____. 1992. *Willful Virgin: Essays in Feminism*. Freedom, CA: Crossing Press.

Furtado, Ken and Nancy Hellner. 1993. *Gay and Lesbian American Plays: An Annotated Bibliography*. Metuchen, NJ: Scarecrow Press.

Fuss, Diana, ed. 1991. *Inside/Out: Lesbian Theories, Gay Theories*. New York: Routledge.

Garber, Linda. 1994. *Tilting the Tower: Lesbians Teaching Queer Subjects*. New York: Routledge.

Grosz, Elizabeth and Elspeth Probyn, eds. 1995. *Sexy Bodies: The Strange Carnalities of Feminism*. London: Routledge.

Haggerty, George E. and Bonnie Zimmerman, eds. 1995. *Professions of Desire: Lesbian and Gay Studies in Literature*. New York: Modern Language Assocation.

Hamer, Diane and Belinda Budge, eds. 1994. *The Good, the Bad and the Gorgeous: Popular Culture's Romance with Lesbianism*. London: Pandora.

Hart, Lynda, ed. 1989. *Making a Spectacle: Feminist Essays on Contemporary Women's Theatre*. Ann Arbor: Univ. of Michigan Press.

Hart, Lynda and Peggy Phelan, eds. 1993. *Acting Out: Feminist Performances*. Ann Arbor: University of Michigan Press.

Hoaglund, Sarah Lucia. 1988. *Lesbian Ethics: Toward New Value*. Palo Alto, CA: Institute for Lesbian Studies.

Jay, Karla, & Joanne Glasgow, eds. 1990. *Lesbian Texts and Contexts: Radical Revisions*. New York University Press.

Jay, Karla, ed. 1995. *Lesbian Erotics*. New York: New York University Press.

Keyssar, Helene. 1985. *Feminist Theatre*. New York: Grove Press.

Laughlin, Karen and Catherine Schuler, eds. 1995. *Theatre and Feminist Aesthetics*. Cranbury, NJ: Associated University Presses.

Malinowitz, Harriet. 1995. *Textual Orientations: Lesbian and Gay Students and the Making of Discourse Communities*. Portsmouth, NH: Heineman.

Munt, Sally. 1992. *New Lesbian Criticism: Literary and Cultural Readings*. New York: Columbia University Press.

Penelope, Julia and Susan Wolfe, eds. 1993. *Lesbian Culture: The Lives, Work, Ideas, Art and Visions of Lesbians Past and Present*. Freedom, CA: Crossing Press.

Phelan, Peggy. 1993. *Unmarked: The Politics of Performance*. New York: Routledge.

Steadman, Susan M. 1991. *Dramatic Re-visions: An Annotated Bibliography of Feminism and Theatre 1972–1988*. Chicago: American Library Association.

Zimmerman, Bonnie. 1990. *The Safe Sea of Women: Lesbian Fiction 1969–1989*. Boston: Beacon.